W9-CIP-985

For Reference

Not to be taken from this room

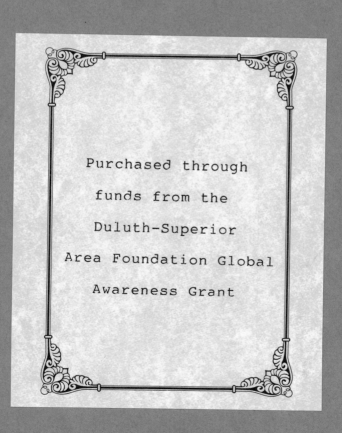

Purchased through
funds from the
Duluth-Superior
Area Foundation Global
Awareness Grant

WORLD ENCYCLOPEDIA OF

POLITICAL SYSTEMS
AND PARTIES

SUPERIOR WIS.
PUBLIC LIBRARY

WORLD ENCYCLOPEDIA OF

POLITICAL SYSTEMS AND PARTIES

THIRD EDITION

EDITED BY George E. Delury

THIRD EDITION EDITED BY
Deborah A. Kaple

VOLUME I

AFGHANISTAN– FRANCE

Facts On File, Inc.

Cop. 1

WORLD ENCYCLOPEDIA OF POLITICAL SYSTEMS AND PARTIES

R
324.2
W893d
v. 1

Copyright © 1983, 1987, 1999 by George E. Delury

All rights reserved. No part of this book may be reproduced or utilized in any form or by any means, electronic or mechanical, including photocopying, recording, or by any information storage or retrieval systems, without permission in writing from the publisher. For information contact:

Facts On File, Inc.
11 Penn Plaza
New York NY 10001

Library of Congress Cataloging-in-Publication Data

World encyclopedia of political systems & parties / edited by George
    E. Delury. —3rd ed. / supervised by Deborah A. Kaple.
       p. cm.
    Includes bibliographical references and index.
    ISBN 0-8160-2874-5 (set) (alk. paper)
        0-8160-4162-8 (vol. I)
        0-8160-4163-6 (vol. II)
        0-8160-4164-4 (vol. III)
    1. Political parties—Handbooks, manuals, etc.   2. Comparative
government—Handbooks, manuals, etc.   I. Delury, George E.
II. Facts on File, Inc.   III. Title: World encyclopedia of political
systems and parties.
JF2011.W67   1999
324.2′03—dc21   99-17256

Facts On File books are available at special discounts when purchased in bulk quantities for businesses, associations, institutions or sales promotions. Please call our Special Sales Department in New York at 212/967-8800 or 800/322-8755.

You can find Facts On File on the World Wide Web at
http://www.factsonfile.com.

Text design by A Good Thing, Inc.

Printed in the United States of America

VB AGT 10 9 8 7 6 5 4 3 2 1

This book is printed on acid-free paper.

TABLE OF CONTENTS

authored or edited and coauthored 10 books, with 3 more scheduled for 1998 publication: *Latin America: Its Problems and Its Promise* (3d ed.), *Recycled Rhetoric and Disposable People*, and *Development in Theory and Practice: Bridging the Gap* (2d ed.). She has also published more than 100 chapters and articles in reference books and anthologies, journals, magazines, and newspapers.

Carlo J. Bonura, Jr., is a doctoral student of political theory in the Department of Political Science, University of Washington. His research focuses on ethnic minorities and questions of nationalism along the Malaysian-Thai border. He is currently pursuing research in these areas in Thailand.

John A. Booth is Regents' Professor of Political Science at the University of North Texas. He is the author of *Costa Rica: Quest for Democracy* (1998) and *The End and the Beginning: The Nicaraguan Revolution* (1985), coauthor of *Understanding Central America* (3d ed.,1999), and coeditor of *Elections and Democracy in Central America, Revisited* (1995). He has published articles and anthology chapters on the political systems of and political participation, culture, violence, elections, and democratization within Central America, Mexico, and Colombia.

Vince Boudreau is assistant professor of political science at the City College of New York and directs its M.A. Program in International Relations. His research interests include Southeast Asian social movements and Philippine politics and culture. He is working on a comparative study of state repression and protest forms in the Philippines, Indonesia, and Burma (now Myanmar).

Kirk Scott Bowman, Ph.D., is assistant professor at the Sam Nunn School of International Affairs, Georgia Institute of Technology. He lived and conducted fieldwork for four years in Belize, Costa Rica, and Honduras. His research has been published in various books and journals, including the *Journal of Peace Research* and *World Development*. Two of the focuses of his present research are the relationship between militarization and development and the political economy of tourism in developing countries.

Mary P. Callahan is assistant professor, Naval Postgraduate School, Monterey, California.

William Crowther is associate professor of political science at the University of North Carolina at Greensboro and codirector of the Parliamentary Documents Center for Central Europe. His research centers on issues of democratization and interethnic relations. He is the author of numerous works on various aspects of Moldovan and Romanian politics.

Richard Dale, who earned his Ph.D. in political science

at Princeton University, was present in Botswana for its independence celebration in 1966. He visited the country in 1967, 1970, 1976, 1985, and 1987, and he has published a book, monographs, and articles about Botswana. He taught at the University of New Hampshire, Northern Illinois University, Southern Illinois University at Carbondale, and the U.S. Army School of International Studies at Fort Bragg, N.C. He retired from Southern Illinois University at Carbondale in 1997 and is working on a book dealing with the Namibian war of independence.

Jacob A. Darling is a 1998 honors graduate of Davidson College, receiving a B.A. in political science with an economics minor. He is employed as a financial analyst by First Union Real Estate Capital Markets. He aspires to a career in international development or trade relations.

Robert Dayley is assistant professor at Oglethorpe University in Atlanta. Previously he was visiting assistant professor of government at St. Lawrence University in Canton, N.Y. He holds a Ph.D. in political science from Northern Illinois University. In addition to five years of formal language training in Thai, he lived in Thailand for three years. His doctoral dissertation, "Modeling Chaos: Alternative Explanations of Policy Formulation in Thailand," was based on research conducted as a Fulbright Research Fellow at the National Institute of Development Administration (NIDA) in Bangkok.

Juan del Aguila, who received his doctorate from the University of North Carolina, is associate professor of political science at Emory University. He is the author of *Cuba: Dilemmas of a Revolution* (3d ed., 1994) and of many journal articles, book chapters, and scholarly book reviews focusing on Cuba's government and domestic and foreign policies.

Mark DeLancey is professor of African politics in the Department of Government and International Studies at the University of South Carolina. A former Peace Corps volunteer (Nigeria, 1962–64), he has taught at the University of Nigeria, the University of Yaoundé, Somali National University, and the University of Western Cape. He has published several books and articles on African comparative and international politics.

Edward Dew is professor of politics at Fairfield University, Fairfield, Connecticut. He teaches courses in the politics of Latin America and the Caribbean and is interested in the dynamics of ethnic conflict. He has authored two volumes on Surinamese political history and another on ethnic conflict in the high Andes of Peru.

Yomi Durotoye is visiting associate professor of politics at Wake Forest University in North Carolina. He taught for several years at the Obafemi Awolowo University in Nigeria, where he also served as the chair of the Department of Political Science. He obtained his Ph.D. from Duke University. He writes and works on African politics and policy analysis.

Christine Ehrick is assistant professor of history at the University of Northern Iowa. She received her Ph.D. from the University of California at Los Angeles in 1997. Her dissertation, "*Obrera, Dama, Feminista*: Women's Associations and the Welfare State in Uruguay, 1900–1930, "compares a number of women's political organizations and studies the relationship between Uruguayan feminism and the emerging welfare state. Her publications include "*Madrinas* and Missionaries: Uruguay and the Pan-American Women's Movement," published in *Gender and History* in November 1998.

Neil C. M. Elder is reader emeritus in politics at the University of Hull, UK. He is the author of *Government in Sweden* (1970) and of numerous articles on Swedish and Scandinavian government and politics and coauthor of *The Consensual Democracies* (revised 1988). He is coauthoring a book on government-agency relations in the UK, Sweden, and Germany with Edward Page of the University of Hull history department.

Sheila Elliott is associate professor at Columbia College, Columbia, South Carolina. Her areas of research are women, women's religious association, and social change in Africa. She has traveled extensively in southern Africa and Asia.

Mahmud A. Faksh is professor of political science at the University of Southern Maine. Previously he taught at the University of Connecticut, King Saud University, and Duke University. He has published extensively on Middle Eastern and Islamic affairs. He is the author of *The Future of Islam in the Middle East: Fundamentalism in Egypt, Algeria, and Saudi Arabia* (1997).

Martin F. Farrell is professor of politics and government and director of global studies at Ripon College, Ripon, Wisconsin. He has a doctorate in political science from the University of Chicago.

Karl J. Fields is director of Asian studies and associate professor of politics and government at the University of Puget Sound in Tacoma, Washington. He has published on various topics of East Asian political economy including government-business relations, economic reform, and regional integration. His first book, *Enterprise and the State in Korea and Taiwan* (1995), examines the roles of government and big business in the economic miracles of Taiwan and South Korea. His forthcoming book, *KMT,*

Inc., discusses the stable of enterprises owned and operated by Taiwan's ruling political party.

T. Bruce Fryer (Ph.D., University of Texas–Austin) is professor of Spanish in the Department of Spanish, Italian, and Portuguese at the University of South Carolina. He is editor of Spanish and Portuguese for *Business and the Professions*, published by NTC Contemporary Publishing and the American Association of Teachers of Spanish and Portuguese and is author of numerous books, articles, and reviews on the use of the Spanish language for professional purposes in international cross-cultural contexts. He has conducted research and workshops in Spain, Trinidad and Tobago, Colombia, Mexico, Puerto Rico, and Costa Rica and recently completed a Fulbright project in Cameroon and Equatorial Guinea.

Joel Gordon, assistant professor of history at the University of Nebraska at Omaha, is a specialist in modern Egyptian politics, film, mass media, and popular culture. The author of *Nasser's Blessed Movement: Egypt's Free Officers and the July Revolution* (1992), he is writing a book on popular civic culture in Nasser's Egypt.

Sergei Gretsky is adjunct professor of political science at the Catholic University of America and the Washington editor of *Tsentral'naya Aziya I Kavkaz* (Central Asia and the Caucasus), a journal of social and political studies published in Sweden. He is the author of *Russia's Policy toward Central Asia* (1997) and of a number of book chapters and articles in English, Russian, and Tajik on Islam and various aspects of domestic and foreign policy issues of Central Asian states.

Robert Griffiths is associate professor of political science and director of the International Studies Program at the University of North Carolina at Greensboro. He teaches courses in African politics, politics of development, international law and organization, and international political economy.

Rima Habasch is a doctoral candidate at Boston University. She has several years of work experience with the European Union in Brussels and United Nations agencies in Lebanon.

Olafur Th. Hardarson is associate professor of political science at the University of Iceland and director of the Icelandic Election Studies. He obtained his doctorate from the London School of Economics and Political Science. His publications include *Parties and Voters in Iceland* (1995).

Jeffrey K. Hass earned a Ph.D. from Princeton University. He is studying economic change and market transitions in Eastern Europe (especially Russia) and Latin America and

the *Journal of African History* and the *Canadian Journal of African Studies*.

Ken Menkhaus is associate professor of political science at Davidson College in Davidson, North Carolina. He specializes in African and Middle East politics.

B. David Meyers is associate professor of political science at the University of North Carolina at Greensboro. He is the author of numerous articles concerning African politics. In the early 1980s he served as a policy assistant on southern Africa and the southwest Indian Ocean islands in the Office of the Secretary of Defense.

Siamak Namazi is director of Future Alliances International, a private consulting group that concentrates on Iran and the Caspian region. He is also managing editor of *Iran Quarterly Report* and a frequent contributor to *Iran Focus*. He has an M.S. from the School of Planning and Public Policy, Rutgers University.

Richard S. Newell is emeritus professor of history, University of Northern Iowa. He received his Ph.D. from the University of Pennsylvania in South Asia regional studies. He is the author of *The Struggle for Afghanistan* (1981).

Elizabeth Normandy received her Ph.D. from the University of South Carolina. She teaches international relations, comparative politics, and African politics at the University of North Carolina at Pembroke. She has published works on African politics and international relations in *International Studies Notes*, *Liberian Studies Journal*, and *Journal of Political Science*. She has traveled in Senegal, Mali, Ivory Coast, and Cameroon.

Eugene Ogan is professor emeritus of anthropology, University of Minnesota. He received his Ph.D. from Harvard University and has published widely on the ethnology and history of the Pacific Islands.

Valerie O'Regan, Ph.D., is assistant professor of political science at North Dakota State University. Her main research interests are in European studies and gender politics.

Thomas O'Toole is professor of anthropology at St. Cloud State University, where he is active in the African Studies Program. He remains very interested in Africa and has written extensively about the continent. He is also the author of three editions of the *Historical Dictionary of Guinea* and *The Central African Republic: The Continent's Hidden Heart*. He is the translator of the *Historical Dictionary of the Central African Republic*.

Hun Joo Park is assistant professor of international relations at the Korea Development Institute (KDI) School of International Policy and Management. Among other pursuits, he is the author of *Triumph and Crisis of Dirigisme: The Political Origins of Financial Policy towards Small Business* (forthcoming). His present research project focuses on the impact of globalization on state politics and national identity, especially in the wake of the Asian crisis.

Andrew Parkin is professor of political and international studies at Flinders University in Adelaide, Australia, and a past president of the Australasian Political Studies Association. A graduate of Adelaide and Harvard Universities, he has published extensively on Australian government and politics, immigration and ethnic policy in the Asia-Pacific region, federalism and intergovernmental relations, criminal justice policy, housing policy, urban policy, and liberal-democratic theory.

William D. Pederson is professor of political science at Louisiana State University in Shreveport. Research for his entries (Czech Republic, Slovakia) was done under a grant from the Summer Research Lab of the Russian and East European Center, University of Illinois at Champaign.

Michele Penner is an advanced graduate student in the Department of Politics at Princeton University. She is completing a dissertation entitled "The Differential Evolution of Single-Party Systems in the Middle East: Turkish Democratization and Authoritarian Continuity in Tunisia."

Orlando J. Peréz received his Ph.D. from the University of Pittsburgh in 1996 and is assistant professor in the Department of Political Science at Central Michigan University. He has written chapters on Panamanian politics and voting behavior in Central America for edited volumes. He has completed a book-length manuscript on elite political culture in 20th-century Panama, along with an edited volume on Panamanian politics after the U.S. invasion.

Kenneth J. Perkins is professor of Middle Eastern and North African history at the University of South Carolina in Columbia. His research focuses on the 19th and 20th centuries and particularly on the interactions between the indigenous North African population and the European colonizers. He has traveled to and lived in the region extensively over the past 25 years.

Lawrence G. Potter is deputy director of the Gulf/2000 Project and adjunct assistant professor of international affairs at Columbia University. He holds a Ph.D. in history from Columbia University and is coeditor with Gary Sick of *The Persian Gulf at the Millenium: Essays in Politics, Economy, Security and Religion* (1997).

Bernard Reich is professor of political science and international relations at George Washington University. He received his Ph.D. in foreign affairs from the University of Virginia. A specialist in Middle East politics and foreign relations, he has written or edited many books and articles on those subjects, U.S. Middle East policy, and the Arab-Israeli conflict. With Gershon Kieval, he is the author of *Israel: Land of Tradition and Conflict* (2d ed., 1993).

Jeffrey Rinne is a 1999 Ph.D. candidate at Princeton University. His dissertation is entitled "Redesigning the State in Latin America: Pundits, Policy Makers, and Organized Labor in Argentina and Brazil."

K. Roberts is at present completing a Ph.D. in politics at an Australian university. The thesis deals with political and economic development in Singapore with a special emphasis on the colonial period.

Leo Rose is professor emeritus of political science, University of California at Berkeley. He has conducted research programs in the Himalayan states of Nepal, Sikkim, Bhutan, Arunachal (North East Frontier Area), and Ladakh in India since the mid-1950s. He has published or edited 19 books and innumerable articles on this area.

Curtis R. Ryan, Ph.D., is assistant professor of political science and international affairs at Mary Washington College in Fredericksburg, Virginia. As a Fulbright Scholar (1992–93) to the Hashimite Kingdom of Jordan, he served as guest researcher at the Center for Strategic Studies at the University of Jordan in Amman. His articles on Jordanian and Middle East politics have appeared in the journals *Democratization*, *Middle East Journal*, *Middle East Policy*, and the *Southeastern Political Review*.

Gamini Samaranayake is senior lecturer in the Department of Political Science at the University of Peradeniya, Sri Lanka. He obtained his Ph.D. from the University of St. Andrews, Scotland.

Gregory D. Schmidt, who received his Ph.D. from Cornell, is associate professor of political science at Northern Illinois University in DeKalb. He has published two books and over a dozen journal articles, book chapters, and monographs on political institutions in Peru. He has held fellowships from the Social Science Research Council and the Fulbright Program, served as a consultant to the United States Agency for International Development, and taught at several Peruvian universities.

Robert O. Schneider, Ph.D., is associate professor and chair of the Department of Political Science at the University of North Carolina at Pembroke. He is an expert on the American political process and public policy, and his recent research and publication include work on emergency management policy and implementation at the local level. He has also written on American national politics.

David W. Schodt received his Ph.D. in economics from the University of Wisconsin–Madison. He teaches in the Department of Economics at St. Olaf College, where he is also director of the Hispanic Studies Program. He is the author of two books as well as numerous articles on Ecuadorian political economy. He editor for the Ecuador: Economics section of the *Handbook of Latin American Studies*, published by the Library of Congress.

Reeva S. Simon is assistant director of the Middle East Institute at Columbia University. She is the author of *Iraq between the Two World Wars* (1986) and coeditor of the *Encyclopedia of the Modern Middle East* (1996).

Gordon Smith is emeritus professor of government at the London School of Economics. He specializes in German and European politics and has written extensively on both. He is coeditor of the journal *German Politics* and also of *West European Politics*.

Dale Story is professor and chair in the Department of Political Science at the University of Texas at Arlington. He has written extensively on the political economy of modern Mexico. Among his major works are *Industry, the State, and Public Policy in Mexico* (1986) and *The Mexican Ruling Party* (1986).

Martin Stuart-Fox is professor and head of history at the University of Queensland, Brisbane, Australia. He was previously a correspondent for United Press International for three years in Indochina during the Vietnam War. He has written six books and more than 50 articles and book chapters on Laos. His latest publication is *The Lao Kingdom of lan Xang: Rise and Decline* (1998).

Alastair H. Thomas is professor of Nordic politics in the Department of Social Studies at the University of Central Lancashire, Preston, England. His publications include *Social Democratic Parties in Western Europe* (1977), *The Future of Social Democracy* (1986), *The Consensual Democracies?* (1988), and *The Historical Dictionary of Denmark* (1998). His *Nordic Democracy in the New Europe* is to be published in 2000.

Cris Toffolo, assistant professor in the Department of Political Science at the University of St. Thomas, St. Paul, Minnesota, is also the Pakistan expert of the South Asia Coordination Group of Amnesty International (U.S.A.). Her areas of specialization include South Asian politics (Pakistan, human rights, women's issues, development and democracy) and early liberal and contemporary political theory. She earned her Ph.D. at the University of Notre Dame.

been torn by war and civil strife, the existence of such long-term, peaceful competitive political rule is nothing short of miraculous. During the last decade, politics in the United States continued to center on single-issue movements or weak coalitions around a group of leaders, instead of strict reliance on one or another political party, although the two-party system is as entrenched as ever. Obviously the most dramatic turn of events occurred in Eastern Europe and the former Soviet Union (FSU). Poland and the Czech Republic are the most hopeful areas, since the shift to the market was accompanied by the successful holding of elections and several peaceful transfers of power. Even if Romania and Bulgaria remain social and economic disasters, opposition parties were able to defeat previously entrenched regimes. In the former Yugoslavia, at least Slovenia achieved what could be called a democratic regime without modifiers, while the situation in Croatia is more ambiguous and that of the rump state of Yugoslavia looks more like its predecessors. In the old Baltic republics of the USSR, debates about citizenship and economic policy made transition to democracy more difficult, but once again, one could argue that democratic regimes were at least developing if not fully achieving consolidation. Ukraine and Belarus faced such difficult economic problems that democracy still remains more of a hope than a reality. In the Central Asian republics, the old apparats and nomenklatura largely replaced the Communist Party with new dictatorships in slightly different clothing. Nevertheless, even these authoritarian regimes now have to step more carefully than their Soviet predecessors. Finally, in Russia, democracy did not bring about a solution to the economic social and political problems associated with the collapse of communism. But a semblance of free press and some islands of democratic competition have made a return to the status quo ante highly improbable.

Even if democracy has not represented the cure-all that many had expected, one has to look at the last decade as an optimistic sign for the development of political rights. If many countries failed to meet the established criteria for democratic regimes, at least those criteria were remotely relevant for many more of them. If one did not particularly like the winners, if the process was often less than clean, nevertheless, the arena of political competition had become more institutionalized and more peaceful. With few exceptions, it has become impossible to deny (at least officially) citizens a role in the definition of who rules them. If democracy is at least a government that recognizes its temporary claim to authority, then the world has become a much more democratic one.

Problems obviously remain. For parts of the world, including Africa and parts of the former Soviet Union, the decision about who will rule the state is almost irrelevant in the absence of a central authority. Increasing inequality, degrading poverty, gender biases, and ethnic hatreds make it unlikely that Westminster democracy will be universal in the 21st century. However, democracy has become the only recognized legitimate system for rule for perhaps the first time in the 20th century, and there are no other important ideological competitors. Of course, issues of defining individual liberty as opposed to collective rights remain, as do managerial problems of how to conduct competitive elections, how to organize transitions, how to respect the rights of those who lose, and how to assure the rule of law definitely remain. But it is not impossible to imagine that the 21st century will see a resolution of these problems and that most citizens of the world can participate in the often-frustrating, yet exhilarating, exercise of democratic rights.

This encyclopedia serves as a guide to the world's countries and where they stand in the spectrum of democracy and party politics. Where relevant we concentrate on the relative power of political parties. In other cases, we attempt to look inside the black box of authoritarian regimes. In all of them we try to always answer a basic question of political studies: Who rules? Our answers are as accurate as possible; we hope you find them useful.

Deborah A. Kaple
Princeton, N.J.
February 11, 1999

The study of politics is a study of conflict. Whenever a few people gather to decide on common aims and means, some degree of conflict appears. Individual ambitions, more or less incompatible social and economic interests, and ideals that are often mutually exclusive compete for the resources of the group. When confined to a small institution—a church, a fraternal order, a business—the means by which such conflict can be pursued are limited and the potential gains and losses are relatively small. When the conduct of a sovereign state is at issue, however, the potential gains in wealth, prestige, and economic and physical power can be immense and the potential losses proportionately severe. Furthermore, the full resources of the state and society can be brought to bear on the conflict—money, people, institutions, and if necessary, weapons. National politics is a serious business, often deadly serious.

The business of politics is conducted within a system of interacting elements that include the state and its government with executive, legislative, and judicial functions and customary and/or written rules of procedure; a variety of social and economic interests that may or may not express themselves through political parties; and processes through which political parties or interests bring their influence to bear on the government. This encyclopedia describes these elements of the political systems of 170 sovereign nations and eight dependent territories in a relatively narrow cross section of time, roughly the summer and fall of 1985.

The standard format of an article begins with an introductory section that provides a basic description of the institutions of government along with the historical background necessary to understand the present political arrangement in the country. This section looks first at the executive functions, the formal locus of policy- and decision-making power in the country. It then outlines the structure and powers of the legislature or any similar body that purports to represent at least some of the population and that discusses, debates, and approves new laws. The judiciary is examined with particular concern for its independence from political pressures or control and its relative power vis-`a-vis the other branches of government. Finally, this section briefly describes regional and local structures of government and tries to assess the degree of local autonomy and political-party activity.

The next section takes up the electoral system. It notes the extent of suffrage, registration and balloting procedures, whether voting is compulsory, and the level of voter turnout for elections. It describes how the country is geographically organized for elections and usually assesses the relative fairness and honesty of elections. Most importantly, this section describes the way in which election winners are determined in the state under consideration; this is important, for there are several systems, which differ markedly from one another. Proportional representation systems, which are used in many countries, require a special explanation.

The simple plurality system now used in most English-speaking countries met with serious objections on the European continent when the suffrage was expanded to include the vast mass of working people who tended to vote socialist. The traditional parties were faced with the possibility that socialist parties could consistently win large parliamentary majorities, even if they did not win a majority of the votes nationwide. It was also noted that a small party that represented an important but scattered minority in the country could be closed out of the legislative process altogether.

To overcome these objections, proportional representation (PR) systems were introduced, beginning with Denmark in 1855. After considerable debate over what constituted a fair system, Victor d'Hondt in 1878 devised a method that is still in common use, although with many variations. At its simplest, the d'Hondt method works as follows. Assume that three parties are competing for nine legislative seats in a multimember district. Voters, who in PR systems usually vote for party lists of candidates rather than for individuals, give Party A 10,000 votes; Party B, 7,000; and Party C, 3,000. The first seat goes to Party A, and its vote is divided by 2. Each time Party A wins another seat, its total vote is divided by the next-highest number—2, 3, 4, and so on. In some countries the process ends there, but in others leftover votes (1,750 for Party B, for example) are pooled at the national level and additional seats are distributed by the same process.

ment to the ideal of knowledge for its own sake. All showed a deep concern to make clear to the general reader the essential political elements operating in each country. Many submitted far more information and expended much greater time and energy on the project than the editor asked for. The editor thanks them heartily for their support, understanding, and patience.

Carol Simon, Muriel Bennet, Tina and A. La Russo,

and the editorial staff of Facts On File, Inc., have also contributed to the success of this project. Most particularly, the encouragement and unrelenting demands of Ed Knappman have given this encyclopedia its extra measure of thoroughness.

George E. Delury
January 1983

WORLD ENCYCLOPEDIA OF

POLITICAL SYSTEMS
AND PARTIES

AFGHANISTAN

By Richard S. Newell, Ph.D.

THE SYSTEM OF GOVERNMENT

Afghanistan is a country of 647,500 square kilometers in southern Asia, bordering Iran, China, Pakistan, Tajikistan, Turkmenistan, and Uzbekistan. Its ethnic groups include Pashtun, Tajik, Uzbek, Hazara, and a number of others.

Afghanistan is a putative Islamic Republic convulsed by a civil war between factions of the resistance movement that took power upon the collapse of the Marxist government in 1992. Until the Taliban movement took control of Kabul, the capital, in 1996, the central government was nominally recognized as legitimate, but its writ was limited by disagreement over leadership, ethnic rivalries, and foreign interference. Regional and local government had been controlled by varied combinations of resistance commanders, councils of local notables, and militant religious leaders. At the end of 1998 the Taliban had consolidated control over 90% of the country, but it still faces resistance from factions holding ethnic enclaves in the north.

The consequences of the seizure of power by Afghan Marxists in 1978 followed by the Soviet invasion to maintain them in power have been devastating. More than 10% of the population have been killed or maimed and more than half have been uprooted as internal or external refugees in the 14 years of liberation war and civil war that ensued. The small modern industrial and commercial sectors have been decimated and agricultural output has been cut to less than half through depopulation of the countryside and destruction of irrigation systems. The ruling elite and the monarchical institutions it created to govern have disappeared. Afghanistan confronts the task of building a new political order out of the ruins of war, disillusioned with its past and the active interference of the Muslim nations that surround it.

The Marxist regime managed to fend off the opposition of the *mujahidin* (Islamic warriors) for three years after Soviet troops were withdrawn in 1989. The collapse of the Soviet system in 1991 doomed the Kabul Marxists. When Mohammad Najibullah, the president of the Kabul government, announced on March 18, 1992, that he was willing to resign to facilitate a political settlement, his government lost civil and military control. No defense of the capital was attempted. The *mujahidin* won the civil war by default, and a peaceful transfer of power was carried out on April 28. Three days earlier, fighting began between the victorious factions.

THE INTERIM GOVERNMENT OF THE ISLAMIC REPUBLIC

After taking power, the leaders of the former resistance movement attempted to govern Afghanistan on the basis of legitimacy earned by its victory. They failed to establish a constitutional basis for governing. Government at all levels functioned by ad hoc political arrangements. The search for consensus was gravely complicated by combat for control of Kabul. For the first time since the mid-19th century, all regions were independent of the capital city.

The *mujahidin* factions created an interim presidency that was to govern an Islamic Republic through a Cabinet of ministries retained from former governments. The president was to be answerable to a separate leadership council. It had some 50 members, most of whom represented the seven *mujahidin* parties. Many were relatives of the party leaders. The council was an institutional extension of the contest for power between the parties that had developed during their 13 years of expatriate politics in Pakistan. The council was thus an attempt by the parties to continue to control the government they had created.

Lacking effective procedures and coherent organization or a set of precedents to guide it, the council immediately became dysfunctional, subject to the shifting alliances between the parties. Its confusion quickly made it irrelevant. The interim presidency was denied a means of maintaining a consensus between the *mujahidin* parties. Instead it soon became subject to threats from the most powerful of the military commanders who emerged from the struggle for power.

THE POLITICAL PARTIES

All seven of the parties formerly based in Pakistan had been led by religious figures committed to establishing a government that would enforce Islamic principles and teachings. Early in the struggle against the Soviet Union, dominance among the parties came to be shared by two archrivals, the *Hizb-e-Islami* (Islamic Party), led by Gulbuddin Hekmatyar, and the *Jamiat-e-Islami* (Islamic Society) of Burhanuddin Rabbani. Both came to be characterized as "fundamentalist" due to their doctrinaire approaches to the role of religion in government and insistence upon control of political power by religious, not secular, leaders. Otherwise, there were great differences in the organization and style of leadership between these two parties and the tactics adopted by their leaders. Rabbani sought a religious revolution based on military victory and social transformation brought about by the generation of mass support. Hekmatyar called for a total Islamic revolution to be carried out by a disciplined vanguard of Muslim warriors. Support for these two parties came from different ethnic sources—Hekmatyar from the Pashtuns, Rabbani from Tajiks and also from different types of foreign assistance.

Two other Peshawar-based parties were also lumped as fundamentalist: the *Hezb-e-Islami*, led by Yunis Khalis, who broke away from Hekmatyar's *Hezb* but kept the same label; and the *Ittehad-e-Islami* (Islamic Union Party) of Rasul Sayyaf. An established Islamic scholar, Khalis had concentrated support among Pashtuns in the three eastern provinces of Nangrahar, Kunar, and Paktia. Sayyaf's religious status was based upon his Arabian education and political connections. Like Hekmatyar, he came from a small Pashtun tribe. Lacking a large traditional political base, Sayyaf's political importance stemmed mostly from the generous political and economic support provided in return for his championing of Wahhabism, the puritanical sect dominant in Saudi Arabia.

The other three Peshawar parties were considered to be moderately Islamist. They would allow considerable secular leeway within government even to the extent of reestablishing the monarchy. These were the *Jabha-ye-Milli-ye-Afghanistan* (Afghan National Liberation Front), led by Sibghatullah Mojaddedi, the *Mahaz-e-Milli-ye-Islami-ye-Afghanistan* (National Islamic Front of Afghanistan), led by Sayyid Ahmad Gailani, and the *Harakat-e-Engelab-e-Islami*, led by Mohammad Nabi Mohammadi. Their moderate stances notwithstanding, each of these leaders was closely identified with religious charisma and Islamic institutions.

All of these Peshawar-based parties represented Afghanistan's Sunni communities, which account for approximately 80% of the population. When the Islamic Republic of Afghanistan was established in 1992, two significant Shia parties participated: the *Harakat Islami* (Islamic Party) of Assef Mohsini and the *Hezb-e-Wahdat-e-Islami* (Unified Islamic Party), led by Abdul Ali Mazari. Mohsini's small party had cooperated with the Sunnis throughout the war against the Soviet forces. Many of his followers had urban and educated backgrounds. Mazari presided over a composite party of Hazaras brought together with Iranian pressure and support at the time of the *mujahidin* victory. He controlled its military wing based primarily on the large Hazara population in the eastern suburbs of Kabul. In the Hazarajat region a Shia *shura*, or council of leaders representing at least eight parties, exercised virtual control.

The Attempt to Form a Government

Sibghatullah Mojaddedi was selected as first interim president in an accord reached in Peshawar by the parties with Pakistani urging on April 25, 1992. His successor, Burhanuddin Rabbani, was then to serve for six months. After some protest by Mojaddedi the transfer was made. The accord charged Rabbani with preparing a draft constitution subject to popular ratification in some form of referendum at the end of his term. Following its approval, an election was to produce the first fully established government under the Islamic Republic.

Instead, Rabbani opted to hold a conclave (*Shura-ye-Ahl-e-Hal - u-Aqd*, or Council of Resolution and Settlement) of some 1,400 dignitaries from all regions and communities, which elected him interim president for another two years. It also elected a parliament of approximately 250 members to draft a constitution. These results were immediately challenged by most *mujahidin* parties. The constitutional process was further disrupted by the resumption of civil war.

A temporary agreement between the conflicting parties in Pakistan's capital, Islamabad, on March 7, 1993, created new arrangements. Rabbani was permitted to remain president, but only for a period of 18 months ending in late June 1994. The Leadership Council, which was supposed to be guiding him, was abolished at Rabbani's insistence. He was to share power with his longtime rival, Gulbuddin Hekmatyar, who was to serve as prime minister. A commission was to be formed to conduct the election of members of a constituent assembly by November 1993. Elections for the presidency and a parliament were then to be carried out in June 1994.

The Islamabad arrangements were modified in another meeting at Jalalabad after Hekmatyar and his allies launched a fierce assault on Kabul in late April. Under increasing pressure from most of the parties, Rabbani made concessions, including the dismissal of his powerful defense minister, Ahmad Shah Mausood. Procedures for Hekmatyar's choosing and Tabbani's accepting appointments to the Cabinet were also clarified. The Jalalabad agreement brought relative peace to the capital throughout the rest of 1993.

The struggle for control of Kabul escalated in 1994 when Hekmatyar was joined by Abdul Rashid Dostam, a well-armed former ally of the Marxist regime who controlled much of northern Afghanistan. They put aside their own enmity and launched the most furious assault on Kabul to date, on January 1, 1994. Rabbani then disowned the Islamabad agreement, apparently resuming his commitment to the arrangements made by his *Shura* in December 1992.

As long as armed camps, with massive weapon stockpiles, foreign assistance, and large numbers of rootless *mujahidin* eager for combat and spoils, remained free to operate on their own terms, no political formula offered peace. Past Afghan experience suggested that the likelihood of peace lay in the ability of one force overawing and subduing the rest. Such a protagonist would not emerge until late in 1994.

FEATURES OF GOVERNMENT

As suggested above, the most prominent features of the Afghan state are the weakness of its authority throughout the countryside and the fluidity of its politics in the midst of a civil war. All the powerful groups agreed that an Islamic Republic should be established, but no consensus on a constitution existed. Numerous declarations during their 13 years of *jihad* strongly suggested that the intent was to create a government based on Islamic law (*Sharia*) with differences of opinion on the degree of puritanism in its interpretation. Traditionally among Afghanistan's large Sunni majority, the cosmopolitan Hanafi legal system has prevailed. How it would be defined and implemented appeared to be determined by the strongly held views of the religious figures who had dominated the *mujahidin*. The Shias were also a serious factor. In addition to the two Hazara parties, the Ismailis, who dominate the northern province of Baghlan, were prepared to fight for their own interpretations of Islam and for some form of social and political autonomy.

In accepting the concept of a republic, all sides frequently invoked and proclaimed their commitment to a democratic, popular government. This derives from the overwhelmingly popular character of their *jihad*. It was also consistent with the Afghan tradition of regional and community autonomy. The minority Tajiks, Uzbeqs, Shias, and others made clear their desire for a formalized federalism. The success of such a demand depended heavily on the acquiescence of the formerly dominant Pashtun tribes and the defeat of Sunni advocates of an authoritarian centralized state. A consensus among Afghans on questions concerning the status of women, the role of education, and economic principles (to name a few) required remarkable statesmanship. Despite constant debate and much rhetoric, political distractions kept Afghan leaders from thoroughly confronting the constitutional challenge.

Executive Authority

Interim arrangements and political conditions required a powerful presidency that could establish policy and control resources. Following prior Afghan experience, attempts to create an effective Cabinet brought limited results. It functioned virtually without a prime minister. Funding was too meager for more than nominal activity except in defense and foreign affairs. The *mujahidin* parties were essentially its constituents; it did not answer to a parliament. Its limited ministerial activities were administrative, not policy-generating. There was a high retention rate of middle-level and sub-Cabinet officials from the previous Marxist regime, largely because of the limited pool of experienced and educated *mujahidin* personnel. The table on the next page shows the composition of the Cabinet as of July 1993.

Judiciary

Like the Marxists before it, the Islamic Republic has inherited a nominally independent judiciary. Determination of its powers and roles awaits the promulgation of a new constitution. Islamic law, or the *Sharia*, was certain to guide judicial procedure and content. Without clear indications establishing which interpretations of the *Sharia* would apply, both senior government–appointed judges and locally recognized *qazis* have been free to make independent decisions. One instance of political action, if not judicial independence, was the ruling by the Supreme Court that President Rabbani should continue in office until the end of 1994.

Regional and Local Government

Despite the posturing of Afghanistan's past central governments, much autonomy has always been maintained by local communities, often at the provincial level. This has been especially true of the Pashtun tribes clustered in southern and eastern Afghanistan. To a lesser degree it has also applied to the "minority" communities of Tajiks, Uzbeqs, Turkmen, Hazaras, Nuristanis, Baluch, and others. Local notables—who are often religious figures in the minority regions—have traditionally mediated between their followers and government officials. Significant growth of central involvement at the village and the tribal levels had only begun with education, improved roads, and the beginnings of a national economy in the 1960s.

The legacy of the Marxist and Soviet era has been the near collapse of central government authority in nearly all of rural Afghanistan. In the course of 13 years of guerrilla war, *mujahidin* commanders, both of secular and religious origins, came to dominate local and provincial arenas. Local and regional autonomy has grown stronger within the Islamic Republic, whose emergence was made possible by the collapse of Kabul's authority. With the

provinces that were associated with the Durrani confederacy. The region was identified with Afghanistan's monarchy during the previous two centuries.

The *mujahidin* failure to unite and their descent into banditry, corruption, and brutality brought general disgust. They had created a vacuum into which the sudden emergence of a religious movement offering a pure form of Islam was welcome among most Afghans. This appeal was reinforced by the disciplined and pious impression the Taliban projected.

The movement's reputation began with its removal of roadblocks in the southern provinces, especially the highway between the Pakistan border and Kandahar city. *Mujahidin* and local highway gangs had smothered legitimate trade and kidnapped travelers for ransom. In its early stage, the Taliban fought for control of the roads in Helmand, Zabul, and Uruzghan provinces. Their popularity suddenly grew when they rescued a trade caravan that had been organized by Naziruddin Babur, Pakistan's minister of interior. He was attempting to demonstrate the feasibility of shipping goods over Afghan roads between Pakistan and Turkmenistan and other Central Asian republics. Three local gangs stopped the caravan, seized the cargo, and took prisoners. The Taliban broke up the gangs and chased them into their strongholds in Kandahar city, where they were killed or scattered. Overnight a religious community emerged as a potentially powerful political movement.

The rise of the Taliban was made possible by the presence of a community of religious students disillusioned at the behavior of the *mujahidin* and by the palpable support of the Pakistan government. The Taliban swarmed from a network of *madrasas* (religious schools) that had spread rapidly throughout southern Afghanistan and the adjoining provinces of Pakistan in the course of the Soviet-Afghan war. Most of the students were destitute youths who had grown up in Afghan refugee camps inside Pakistan. Many others were Pakistani and eventually Arab and other Muslims who had joined up in the *jihad* against the Soviet Union. The *madrasas* not only provided education and religious guidance, they attracted students by offering food and shelter.

The discipline and piety displayed by these students appeared to offer a means for ending Afghanistan's chaos. After a tentative start, the movement became increasingly politicized. The capture of Qandahar demonstrated its political potential. In addition to disarming the *mujahidin* they had captured, the Taliban seized weapons throughout the Pashtun region under their control. No Afghan government had achieved such physical control over the traditionally well-armed Pashtuns.

Political success quickly became closely related to the religious vision taught and then imposed by the Taliban's elders. They identified Afghanistan's troubles with religious failure. Their movement offered a mullah's cure: strict puritanism mixed with authoritarian control. The roots of this version of Islam lay in the hard and pious life of village mullahs in the bleak countryside of southern Afghanistan. Peace and order were to be achieved by a literal application of Islamic law, the *Sharia*, which was to govern all aspects of Muslim life.

Criminal punishment required amputation for theft, stoning for adultery, and beheading or hanging for murder. Interpretation of the role of women meant total covering of the body when in public, virtually no contact with men who were not relatives, and, consequently, no work or education outside the home. Men were to be punished for not growing full beards and for failing to attend Friday services in the mosque or not completing the required five daily prayers. This strict code extended to literal elimination of music and art and abolishing modern forms of imagery such as photographs, videotapes, and motion pictures.

Conviction and commitment were to be total. Enforcement was inflicted by the Taliban students organized into a religious police force with the authority to make arrests and administer beatings. The most active public agency created by the Taliban—other than its army— was its Department of the Propagation of Virtue and the Suppression of Vice. The full range of doctrinal applications developed progressively. The remarkable rise to power came to be seen as validating a rural mullah's view of Islamic life.

Early statements by the movement's leaders suggested humility concerning their political role. Expanding power quickly changed this attitude. They had been concerned about their ability to rule. Senior Taliban mullahs discussed calling upon pious secular leaders to take political leadership. Consideration was given to asking the former Durrani king Zahir Shah to return and establish a new government. During this short period of uncertainty, their mission was described as the sweeping out of tyrants and then perhaps returning to the mosque and the *madrasa*.

Further combat settled the issue. In the course of routing an archenemy, Gulbuddin Hekmatyar, they overran the city of Ghazni, whose governor was renowned for political and religious virtue. The pressure of war compelled the Taliban to remove a legitimate ruler from power. After the Ghazni episode the Taliban asserted their moral right to defeat all opponents in order to unite the country under their rule.

In late 1996 the Taliban appeared to be close to their goal of military victory. After two failed attempts they seized Kabul and had brought two-thirds of Afghanistan under their control. Taliban victories had mostly occurred in the Pashtun regions with little or no resistance. In most cases victory, including the fall of Kabul, resulted from the bloodless surrenders of Gulbuddin Hekmatyar's Pashtun commanders.

In May 1997, these victories appeared to be repeated when most of Dostam's large Uzbek army was split by a dispute with his senior commander, Abdul Malik. Malik took a large share of the army over to the Taliban. This enabled them to take over Mazar-i-Sharif, the last remaining major city. Four days later Malik's forces turned on the Taliban troops who had rushed into the city. The Uzbeks and their Shia allies refused to obey Taliban religious demands or to turn over their weapons. Trapped and outnumbered, many of the best Taliban officers and troops were killed or captured and the rest of the army was demoralized. The opportunity to seize the north and eliminate all serious opposition seemed lost.

Malik joined with Massoud, who had reorganized his army after its retreat from Kabul. The various Shia forces in central and northern Afghanistan also joined the alliance. It took the title of United National Islamic Salvation Front, or the Northern Alliance.

The Alliance pushed the reeling and isolated Taliban troops out of most of the north. Mausood reached the outskirts of Kabul and then dug in, expecting the Taliban to crumble from internal dissent or a Pashtun revolt.

Instead, the Taliban launched a counterattack in September 1997 based on troops who had held out in northeastern Afghanistan with the support of local Pashtun commanders in Kunduz and Baghlan provinces. Their assault on Mazar-i-Sharif was thrown back in early October.

With heavy reinforcements including Pakistani and other Muslim recruits, the Taliban finally launched a successful assault on Mazar-i-Sharif in August 1998. More than 90% of Afghanistan had been brought under their control.

NATIONAL PROSPECTS

Afghans continue to face tragedy and disaster. In addition to the enormous human cost, the economy is devastated. Virtually all their former export commodities—fruit, fur, cotton, carpets, and even the natural gas they sold to the Soviets—were seriously disrupted. Subsistence crops yielded perhaps one-half their prewar level. Until the Taliban seized Kabul there was no central authority to initiate a national economic recovery or to draw the foreign support it would require. The Taliban government itself has neither the resources nor the foreign support to start significant rebuilding. Instead, rogue activities dominate the economy: theft, smuggling, extortion, and dependence on opium cultivation have distracted Afghanistan from genuine recovery.

Political chaos has aggravated Afghanistan's predicament. In those areas where a semblance of stability had been achieved there were signs of improvement: mine clearing, road and irrigation reconstruction, refugee re-

settlement, resumed farming, and the beginnings of regional commerce. These improvements have been stunted by the waste and fragmentation of scarce resources caused by civil war.

Even though the Taliban have brought nearly all of Afghanistan under one government, ethnic enmity between the major communities and the Sunnis and Shias continues to threaten the stability needed for national reconstruction. While constant warfare brought economic and social ruin to much of Afghanistan, the minorities at the same time experienced a high degree of self-rule. Taliban dominance based upon a rigid doctrine that provides little room for cultural expression or differing religious interpretations suggests an eventual backlash of resentment.

The possibilities of resentment are aggravated by opportunities for meddling by neighboring states into the ethnicity of Afghanistan's politics. Pakistan has historical reasons to worry about the Pashtun factor in its future relations with Afghanistan. It is deeply involved in the provinces adjacent to its border. Iran's links to the Shia communities in Afghanistan threatens the stability of Herat and the Hazarajat. Uzbekistan's newly independent government has offered political and material help to its Afghan counterparts. Afghan Tajiks in the far northeast have been drawn into the civil war that spilled over from the new Tajikistan republic.

Moreover, there are dangerous connections in men, money, and ideas within the international Islamic revolutionary movements. Gulbuddin Hekmatyar's *Hezb* was their greatest Afghan beneficiary. His links with terrorist groups were publicly proclaimed in 1993 when he offered asylum to Sheikh Omar Rehman after the latter was indicted in the World Trade Center bombing in the United States. Training of radical Muslims from the Middle East and beyond had become a major function of Hekmatyar's party.

To some extent his activities have been continued in association with the terrorist allegations of Osama bin Ladin, who has developed amicable relations with the Taliban. Radical terrorism and illicit drug connections portend continued tragedy for Afghanistan's long-suffering people.

Further Reading

Barnett, R. Rubin. *Mirror of the World: Afghanistan's State and Society in the International System.* New Haven, Conn.: Yale University Press, 1994.

Bradsher, Henry S. *Afghanistan and the Soviet Union.* Durham, N.C.: Duke University Press, 1983.

Cordovez, Diego, and Selig S. Harrison. *The Inside Story of the Soviet Withdrawal.* New York: Oxford University Press, 1995.

Dupree, Louis. *Afghanistan.* Princeton, N.J.: Princeton University Press, 1973.

Gregorian, Vartan. *The Emergence of Modern Afghanistan.* Stanford, Calif.: Stanford University Press, 1969.

Maley, William, and Fazel Saikal. *Political Order in Post-Communist Afghanistan.* Boulder, Colo.: Lynne Rienner, 1992.

Newell, Richard S., and Nancy P. Newell. *The Struggle for Afghanistan.* Ithaca, N.Y.: Cornell University Press, 1990.

Rais, Rasul. *War without Winners.* New York; Oxford University Press, 194.

Roy, Oliver. *Islam and Resistance in Afghanistan.* Cambridge: Cambridge University Press, 1990.

Rubin, Barnett R. *The Fragmentation of Afghanistan.* New Haven Conn.: Yale University Press, 1995.

———. *The Search for Peace in Afghanistan.* New Haven, Conn.: Yale University Press, 1995.

Yousuf, Muhammad. *The Bear Trap: Afghanistan's Untold Story.* London: Leo Cooper, 1992.

REPUBLIC OF ALBANIA

(Republika e Shqiperise)

By Stephen C. Markovich, Ph.D

THE SYSTEM OF GOVERNMENT

The Republic of Albania is a small country located in southeastern Europe. Bordered by the Adriatic and Ionian Seas on the west, Greece on the south, and Yugoslavia on the east and north, it is inhabited by 3.2 million people (1996 estimate). Over 95% them are Albanian, less than 3% are Greek, and the remaining 2% include several nationalities. While the number of Greeks is only about 70,000, they are concentrated in the south and their presence does create some difficulties in the country and in Albania's relations with Greece. The overwhelming number of Albanians suggests a highly homogenous nation, but this apparent homogeneity is qualified by the fact that the Albanians themselves are divided into two subgroups, the Gegs and Toske

1944, he governed with an iron hand until his death in 1985. His successor, Ramiz Alia, tried to ease this rule and introduce some political-economic reforms; while his reforms were limited in scope and modest in achievement, they did set the stage for a gradual collapse of communism. Compared with the violence and war that accompanied the demise of communism in neighboring Yugoslavia, communism in Albania fell with a relative whimper over a year or two. Student riots started the fall in December 1990, and a defeat at the polls ended it in March 1992. Between these dates the communists had conceded the registration of opposition parties and the establishment of a presidential-parliamentary system. What they or the opposition could not establish was a constitution.

agenda and presides over Cabinet meetings, convenes and dissolves parliament, requires parliament to reconsider bills it has passed, appoints and receives ambassadors, and acts as commander in chief.

These powers made Sali Berisha, the first postcommunist president, elected to the office in 1992, a formidable leader in the country. Early in his term he began governing democratically but then became increasingly authoritarian in his rule. By 1996 he could orchestrate an overwhelming parliamentary victory for his Democratic Party and a year later, in March 1997, have a controlled parliament elect him to a second term by a vote of 113 to 1. Four months later, however, beset by domestic problems and foreign pressures, Berisha resigned from the presidency. Internally, riots throughout the country, precipitated by a pyramid investment scam that bilked thousands of Albanians of their savings, resulted in Berisha's losing physical control over much of the land. Externally, there was constant criticism from foreign leaders of Berisha's manipulation of the 1996 parliamentary elections. As a result, Berisha called for new parliamentary elections in the summer of 1997, which his party lost; when this loss was overlapped by riots, Berisha decided to resign. His successor, Rexhep Mejdani, elected in July 1997, has been less aggressive in governing style and appears inclined to share the executive role with the premier.

Constitutionally the premier and the Cabinet, formally responsible for implementing

both times. But the 1996 elections were judged as seriously flawed by the Socialist Party, which boycotted the elections, and by international observers, who monitored the voting, and consequently new elections were held in 1997 in which Berisha's Democrats were defeated by Nano's Socialists.

The constitution states that the People's Assembly exercises sovereignty on behalf of the people and is the highest organ of state power. As the highest organ, it has the power to enact laws, amend the constitution, adopt public budgets and economic programs, ratify treaties and agreements, elect the president, confirm and discharge the premier and other ministers, appoint judges to the Supreme Court, and generally oversee the government and hold it responsible. As soon as the communists were removed from power, the People's Assembly became an active legislature in wielding these powers in the political system. Usually the ruling government could get its way, but the opposition could at times block bills that did not appeal to them; thus, the opposition played an important part in defeating the government's constitutional draft in 1994 and persevered against Berisha's authoritarianism long enough to oust him from office.

Judiciary

Albania uses a system of code law that is applied by a judicial branch consisting of a Constitutional Court, a appellate court, and courts on the

host of judges, all Berisha appointments, on the grounds that they were unqualified.

Regional and Local Government

There are 27 districts, 43 municipalities, and 310 communes that have mayors and councils directly elected by the people for four-year terms. In the local elections of October 1996, which international monitors judged were fair, the Democratic Party outpolled the Socialists and gained control of a majority of the local governments. These governments are responsible for raising their own finances and drafting their own budgets in order to cover matters relating to housing, utilities, education, culture, and other community needs.

THE ELECTORAL SYSTEM

The 1991 parliamentary elections gave Albanian citizens 18 years of age and older their first opportunity to cast their ballots in a competitive campaign. Though the ruling Communist party won that election, the fact that the first-time opposition won nearly 40% of the popular vote and 75 of the 250 legislative seats did not bode well for the Communists. The next year Communist rule did indeed come to an end when the opposition Democrats won 62% of the vote and 92 of 140 seats in defeating the Socialists or ex-Communists, who won 26% of the vote and 38 seats. The Democrats won a second term in 1996, but that election, as noted earlier, was seriously flawed and had to be rerun in 1997. This time the Socialists regained power by gaining 53% of the popular vote and 99 of 155 seats; the Democrats managed only 26% of the vote and 29 seats, and several minor parties got the remaining votes and seats.

In each of the above elections, the system underwent some changes from one election to the next, either in number of seats or electoral rules. The system finally adopted for the 1997 election was a combination of the two-ballot principle and proportional representation. Of the 155 members elected to the People's Assembly—the only national officials directly elected by the people—115 are elected in single-member constituencies through the two-ballot system and 40 are elected through proportional representation. Under the two-ballot system, a candidate needs a majority of the votes in order to claim the seat; if no candidate wins a majority on the first ballot, then the top two candidates vie for the seat in a second election held one week later. Under proportional representation, the percentage of seats that each party earns is a direct reflection of the percentage of the total vote the party received. Since the major parties seem to have accepted this system, it most likely will remain in place for future elections.

THE PARTY SYSTEM

Toward the end of 1990, riots by university students mushroomed into a broader revolt that ultimately forced the Communist government to make some concessions to the people, one of which was the legalization of opposition parties. Within a short time there were over 20 parties that registered and began to compete with the ruling Communists. However, due to the advantages the Communists had in organization and financing, all but one of these parties had a difficult time mounting effective challenges. The one exception, the Democratic Party, rapidly made inroads on Communist support and made a respectable showing in the 1991 elections. A year later, in the 1992 elections, it was more than respectable as the Democrats defeated the Communists, now called the Socialists, and formed the government. However, after five years in power, the Democrats in turn were defeated by the Socialists and once again forced into opposition. By this time, despite the fact that a dozen or so parties were competing in the various elections, it was clear that there were only two major parties in Albania—the leftist Socialist Party and the rightist Democratic Party. Essentially Albania began to operate as a two-party system from the outset, an unusual phenomenon in aspiring democracies.

THE SOCIALIST PARTY OF ALBANIA
(Partia Socialiste e Shqiperise; PSSH)

The Socialist Party is the successor to the Communist party that was actually called the Albanian Party of Labor. At the 10th congress of the Party of Labor, held in June 1991, the party changed its name to the Socialist Party, replaced its leadership, restructured its organization, and passed a reform program. The man placed in charge was Fatos Nano, a former premier and minister for economic relations, who had a reputation as a reformer within the old party. He immediately created an executive committee and a steering committee to supplant the politburo and central committee and promoted democratic principles and market economics to move the party toward a social democratic philosophy. As premier following the March 1991 elections, he had actually initiated some political and economic changes before the June party congress but these neither quelled the unrest that was rising among the people nor slowed the deterioration of the economy. In June, no longer able to govern effectively, Nano resigned from office in order to allow his party to form a coalition "Government of National Stability" with four other parties, one of which was the rival Democratic Party.

While this coalition had some success in improving in-

DEMOCRATIC AND POPULAR REPUBLIC OF ALGERIA

(Al-Jumhuriya al-Jaza'iriya al-Dimuqratiya al-Sha'biya)

By Kenneth J. Perkins, Ph.D.

THE SYSTEM OF GOVERNMENT

Algeria, a nation of some 28 million 'people, has been an independent republic since July 5, 1962, following a violent and protracted war of independence with France. In 1965, after a bloodless coup d'état by Colonel Houari Boumédienne, Algeria's fledgling constitution was suspended and its National Assembly dissolved. A National Charter was approved by 91% of the nation's resident voters in 1976. It affirmed "Islamic Socialism" as the guiding principle of the state and paved the way for a referendum on a new constitution, which 99.2% of the electorate (93% of registered voters) approved later in the same year.

This constitution, which remained in force for the next 13 years, provided for a single-party socialist state with Islam as the state religion and Arabic as the official language. Political ideology was the province of the National Liberation Front (FLN), which the constitution called "a vanguard force, guiding and organizing the people for the building of socialism." The fundamental law also outlined the organization and responsibilities of the National People's Assembly, the executive branch of government, and the judiciary. In reality, however, the 1976 constitution simply legitimized the military government that had been ruling Algeria by decree since the 1965 coup. Under the constitution, Boumédienne became secretary general of the FLN and the head of a powerful executive branch that dominated the National People's Assembly.

In late 1985, the FLN proposed a revised National Charter more in line with the thinking of Chadli Benjedid, who had become Algeria's head of state on Boumédienne's death in 1978. The new document moved the country away from the dogmatic and austere socialism of the Boumédienne era, while keeping intact such long-standing national policies as state control of key sectors of the economy and the one-party system. Almost 96% of all eligible voters participated in a referendum on the charter in January 1986, with just over 98% casting affirmative votes.

When deteriorating social and economic conditions sparked riots throughout the country in October 1988,

FLN reformers drafted constitutional amendments that represented an extraordinary break with the past. For the first time in independent Algeria's history, the state and the FLN were separated; the formation of other political organizations was authorized; the commitment to socialism was abandoned; the role of the army was circumscribed; and individual rights were emphasized. Just under three-quarters of the 79% of the electorate who participated in the referendum on the new document in February 1989 approved it.

The initial round of the country's first multiparty legislative elections, held in December 1991, threatened to break the monopoly of political power the FLN had enjoyed for almost three decades. Faced with this challenge, a coalition of high-ranking military officers forced Benjedid to resign, halted the electoral process, and suspended the National People's Assembly, initiating a period of intense political unrest. In 1996, with an eye toward ending what had degenerated into civil war, the newly elected president, Lamine Zeroual, convened a conference attended by the leaders of some, although not all, of Algeria's legal political parties and the representatives of trade unions, civil associations, and similar national organizations.

The "Declaration of National Understanding" produced at this meeting identified Islam, Arabic, and Tamazight (the Berber language) as the three pillars of Algerian identity and forbade their exploitation for political purposes. A national referendum held in November 1996 sought approval for the inclusion of this conviction in the preamble of the constitution and for significant amendments in other facets of the fundamental law pertaining to all three branches of the government. Some 85% of the approximately 13 million voters who took part in the referendum endorsed the changes, although several important opposition groups accused the authorities of manipulation and fraud in the balloting. Similar accusations followed the June 1997 multiparty legislative elections, in which 66% of all eligible voters participated. In September 1998, amid continuing political violence, President Zeroual announced his intention to resign from office in February 1999, a year and a half prior to the end of his term.

Executive

The constitution, as amended in 1996, mandates the election of the president by universal, secret, direct suffrage every five years. The chief executive may serve no more than two consecutive terms, must be at least 40 years of age, Algerian by birth, and Muslim. If born prior to 1942, he or she must have participated in the revolution against the French, but if born since that year, his immediate family must not have engaged in antirevolutionary activity. He is the head of state and the head of the armed forces and is also responsible for national defense. He presides over the Council of Ministers, appoints the prime minister, conducts foreign policy, and may, under certain circumstances, dissolve the parliament and call early elections. While the legislature is not in session, the president may rule by decree, although laws issued under such circumstances must subsequently receive parliamentary confirmation.

In January 1992, President Benjedid resigned under pressure from high-ranking military officers who opposed his acceptance of the victory of the Islamic Salvation Front (FIS) in a first round of elections to the National People's Assembly that had been held in the previous month. The High Security Council (*Haut Conseil de Sécurité*), consisting of the prime minister, the ministers of justice and foreign affairs, and three generals, named a five-member High Committee of State (*Haut Comité d'Etat*) to fill the remainder of Benjedid's term, which expired in December 1993. Its chairman (Muhammad Boudiaf until his assassination in June 1992 and Ali Kafi thereafter) was Algeria's de facto president. In January 1994, the High Security Council disbanded the High Committee of State and appointed Brigadier General Lamine Zeroual, then minister of defense, as the new president. Zeroual faced the electorate for the first time in November 1995. In winning some 60% of the vote, he defeated three other candidates in an election that the largest and most important opposition parties urged their members to boycott. Less than three years into his term and facing escalating civil strife, Zeroual announced in September 1998 that he would resign from the presidency in the following February.

Legislature

Until the constitutional reforms introduced in 1989, the National People's Assembly, whose members were elected every five years from a list of exclusively FLN candidates, exercised very little power. In the opening round of the country's first national multiparty elections for the legislature, held in December 1991, 49 political parties fielded 5,712 candidates, while another 1,000 independent candidates also contested the elections. The FIS won 188 seats; the Socialist Forces Front (FFS) 25 seats; independents 3 seats; and the FLN only 15 seats.

The second round of polling, which was almost certain to give the FIS a clear majority, was canceled, and the National People's Assembly suspended, by the High Security Council after President Benjedid's ouster in January 1992. In April, the High Committee of State appointed a National Consultative Council (*Conseil Consultatif National*), which met monthly in the building of the National People's Assembly but had no legislative powers. Soon after assuming the role of head of state in 1994, President Zeroual established a National Transition Council (*Conseil National de Transition*), composed of 175 appointed members, to serve as an interim forum for the discussion of national issues pending new elections.

The 1996 constitution restructured the legislature. It consists of two chambers, the directly elected 380-seat National People's Assembly (*Assemblée Populaire Nationale*) and the Council of the Nation (*Conseil de la Nation*), which is half the size of the Assembly. Two-thirds of the Council's members are chosen by local government assemblies from among their own numbers, while one-third are appointed by the president. Members of the National People's Assembly serve five-year terms; members of the Council of the Nation serve terms of six years. The legislature meets in three-month sessions no more than twice a year. To carry out its prerogative to initiate legislation, which it shares with the head of government, the Assembly convenes permanent committees dealing with various affairs of state. Thirty-nine parties contested the first parliamentary elections held under the modified constitution in June 1997. The National Democratic Rally (RND), a progovernment party, won 155 seats; the Movement for a Peaceful Society (MSP) 69 seats; the FLN 64 seats; the Renaissance Party 34 seats; and the Rally for Culture and Democracy (RCD) and the FFS 19 seats each. Several small parties accounted for the remaining 20 seats.

Judiciary

At the apex of Algeria's judicial system are the Supreme Court (*Cour Suprême*) and the Council of State (*Conseil d'État*). The latter was created by an amendment to the constitution in 1996 and is charged with protecting citizens from abuses of public power and offering advice to the government on legislation it plans to introduce. The amended constitution also established a Tribunal of Conflicts (*Tribunal des Conflits*) to determine which of these two bodies has competence in specific cases. The 1996 amendments also inaugurated a State High Court (*Haute Cour de l'Etat*) empowered to try the president and the head of state in cases of treason or other high crimes. A Supreme Council of the Magistrature (*Conseil Suprême de la Magistrature*), whose president is the president of the republic and whose vice president is the minister of justice, appoints all judges.

Under the Supreme Court are district courts in each of

the country's *wilayas* and more than 180 courts of first instance. Special courts, created by the Ministry of Justice in 1966, hear cases involving economic crimes against the state. Defendants in these courts have no right of appeal. The Court of State Security (*Cour de Sûreté de l'État*), made up of judicial and military figures, tries cases related to state security. In response to the escalation of political violence, special courts to try suspected terrorists were established in 1993 but were abolished two years later.

Regional and Local Government

Algeria is divided into 48 administrative districts (*wilayas*), which are further divided into subdistricts (*da'iras*) and more than 1,500 communes. Communal popular assemblies (with 10 to 80 members) and *wilaya* assemblies (with around 30 members each) have functioned since the 1960s. Until the constitutional reforms of 1989, however, electors' choices were limited to slates of FLN candidates. The minister of the interior appoints local administrators, but the president names the governor (*wali*) of each administrative district.

THE ELECTORAL SYSTEM

Prior to the promulgation of the 1989 constitution, the selection of candidates to run for the National People's Assembly fell completely within the purview of the FLN. To accommodate the political pluralism guaranteed in 1989, a new electoral law was adopted in April 1991 and amended in October 1991. It retained both the practice of electing members of the Assembly by a direct, secret vote of all Algerians 18 years of age and over and the five-year terms of office for Assembly members, but it lowered the minimum age for candidates from 35 to 28 and facilitated independent candidates' access to the ballot. At the same time, the number of seats in the assembly was increased from 295 to 430. In another new provision, the law also mandated a second round of voting in constituencies in which no candidate received more than 50% of the first-round votes. Turnout for the opening round in the 1991 elections was 59%.

The only elections held since 1991—the presidential elections of 1995, the referendum to amend the constitution in 1996, the parliamentary elections in 1997, and communal and departmental elections held later in the same year—took place amid severe political unrest, with some government critics openly threatening voters and others urging their followers to ignore the balloting. Official statistics placed the turnout in the presidential election at 75% and in the constitutional amendment referendum at just over 70%, but opposition figures cited levels as low as 33% on both occasions. Turnout for the 1997 national legislative elections was officially placed at 66%.

THE PARTY SYSTEM

For more than a quarter of a century after independence in 1962, the FLN enjoyed constitutional status as Algeria's sole legal political organization. Only in 1989 did a new constitution sanction the "creation of associations of a political nature." In the course of the next two years, some 50 parties came into existence. Multiparty elections for communal popular assemblies and *wilaya* assemblies were held in June 1990 and for the National People's Assembly in December 1991, but the experiment in pluralism was short-lived. Following the victory of the FIS in the first round of the parliamentary elections, hard-line military officers seized control of the government in January 1992 and thwarted the second round of voting. Both the High Committee of State, which acted as a collective presidency for the next two years, and Lamine Zeroual, the army officer whom the High Security Council named as president of the republic in January 1994, held out the prospect of new parliamentary elections. The government's focus on quelling the violence that had erupted in the wake of the aborted elections polarized the political culture, but Zeroual interpreted his 1995 election to the presidency in a multicandidate race as a mandate to hold parliamentary elections in 1997, albeit under an amended constitution that outlawed parties based on religion, language, ethnicity, gender, or region.

Since a multiparty political culture has existed for less than a decade of Algeria's 36 years of independence, and has failed to function effectively even during much of that time, few parties have had the opportunity to articulate detailed campaign procedures or develop sophisticated institutions. Party financing has, for the most part, come from individual members, although the government did provide financial assistance to fledgling parties in 1989 to enable them to organize themselves and prepare for the first elections. During each day of the 1991 campaign, the government made limited broadcast time on state-run radio and television available to candidates. The larger parties publicized their platforms through partisan newspapers established when press restrictions were relaxed in 1989. Political rallies also served to draw attention to party policies.

NATIONAL LIBERATION FRONT
(Front de Libération Nationale; FLN)

HISTORY

Ahmed Messali Hadj headed a succession of political parties (the *Etoile Nord-Africain*, the *Parti du Peuple Algérien*, and the *Mouvement pour le Triomphe des Libertés Démocratiques*) in Algeria between 1926 and 1962, all of which demanded the country's independence. At the same time, French-educated Algerian moderates such as Farhat Abbas organized parties (the *Amis du Mani-feste et de la Liberté* and the *Union Démocratique du Manifeste Algérien*) that sought guarantees of Algerian rights but not necessarily a complete break with France.

By the post–World War II years, the lack of success of these older, established Algerian political leaders prompted younger men to press for more militant solutions to Algerian grievances against France. In 1954, a breakaway group of Messalists formed the FLN. The front assumed responsibility for the political direction of a revolution, which was carried out by guerrilla forces inside Algeria and by the *Armée de Libération Nationale* (ALN), an FLN component based on territory adjacent to Algeria. Within a few years of the opening of the liberation struggle, competing organizations were either coopted by the FLN or had ceased to be significant factors. In 1958, FLN leaders formed a provisional government—the *Gouvernement Provisoire de la République Algérienne* (GPRA). Farhat Abbas was appointed the first premier of the GPRA, which based its government-in-exile in Tunis.

Under pressure from the United Nations General Assembly and the North Atlantic Treaty Organization, French President de Gaulle accepted the principle of national self-determination for Algeria in September 1959. In March 1962, the French and the FLN finally agreed to an immediate cease-fire, and France recognized the FLN as the sole legal representative of the Algerian people.

When independence formally came, in July 1962, a power struggle within the FLN pitted Ben Youssef Ben Khedda, who had succeeded Abbas as head of the GPRA in the previous year, against Ahmed Ben Bella, a more radical leader recently released from a French prison. To avert civil war, Ben Khedda struck a deal acknowledging Ben Bella's primacy, only to find himself, along with other FLN figures who differed with the new leader, excluded from the party's list of candidates for the Constituent Assembly. Algeria's first constitution, passed by the National Assembly in September 1963, enshrined the FLN as the nation's sole political party.

In June 1965, Colonel Houari Boumédienne, whose ALN forces had supported Ben Bella in his struggle with Ben Khedda, deposed his former ally in a military coup. Boumédienne then proceeded to consolidate power in his own hands and those of a few close associates, essentially eclipsing the FLN. Although it remained the only legal party during the 13 years of Boumédienne's rule, it became a tool of the government rather than its guiding force.

Under the leadership of President Benjedid, the party experienced a revival, although during the 1980s a serious split developed between the FLN's old guard and its reformist wing. The former clung to the authoritarian and socialist principles that had characterized the party from the outset, despite their increasingly apparent ineffectiveness in addressing Algeria's socioeconomic woes. The latter viewed liberalization and democratization as

essential to the future well-being of the country. In a series of measures taken at party congresses in 1988 and 1989, and then embodied in the 1989 constitution, the reformers, with Benjedid's support, appeared to have achieved their goal of moving Algeria toward political pluralism and a liberal economy. But the poor showing of the FLN in Algeria's first multiparty elections—for the communal and *wilaya* assemblies in 1990 and the first round of voting for the National People's Assembly in 1991—revealed the magnitude of popular discontent with its 30 years of unchallenged rule. Their political and economic interests threatened by the impending cessation of the party's dominance, hard-liners, especially within the military, pressured Benjedid to resign and canceled the second stage of the National People's Assembly elections in January 1992.

ORGANIZATION

From independence until the outbreak of political strife in the 1990s, the chief executive and the military dominated the FLN. The principal party organs are a Congress, which convenes every five years; a Central Committee of 272 members; and a 14-member Political Bureau, whose importance was greatly reduced during Benjedid's presidency. At the local level, party federations operate in the *wilayas*, *da'iras*, and communes.

During its years of uncontested power, the FLN established or took over already existing mass associations, including the General Union of Algerian Workers (*Union Générale des Travailleurs Algériens*; UGTA), the General Union of Algerian Muslim Students (*Union Générale des Etudiants Musulmans Algériens*; UGEMA), the National Union of Algerian Women (*Union Nationale des Femmes Algériennes*; UNFA), the National Union of Algerian Peasants (*Union Nationale des Paysans Algériens*; UNPA), and the National Organization of Veterans (*Organisation Nationale des Mujahidin*; ONM). The organizations increased token popular participation in FLN policymaking. More importantly, they provided the party with mechanisms for reducing and managing domestic discontent, although their ability to do so declined as Algeria's socioeconomic situation deteriorated in the 1980s.

POLICY

From its founding until the late 1980s, the central ideology of the FLN was Islamic socialism. Under Boumédienne especially, this translated into state capitalism, with most Algerian industries owned and managed by appropriate ministries. By the Benjedid era, however, the deficiencies in this system were looming large. Party congresses criticized previous economic policy for creating trade deficits, shortages, and corruption. In 1985, the FLN began distancing itself from exclusively socialist policies and opening the door for increased private investment and development. The 1989 constitution, which reflected the outlook of party reformers, dropped its predecessors' explicit commitment to the socialist path.

Arabization, especially of the education system, was also a persistently stated goal of the FLN. The imposition of Arabic as the language of instruction in state-run schools was not, however, without controversy. Berbers, who make up at least one-sixth of the population and have a language of their own, expressed strong reservations about Arabization. Even Arabic-speaking students felt disadvantaged, since high-level business and government affairs, including those of the FLN, generally continued to be conducted in French, giving the former colonial language an aura of elitism and privilege. Islamist parties appearing on the political scene in the late 1980s and demanding greater respect for Algeria's Arabo-Islamic heritage were especially critical of the FLN's ambivalence and apparent hypocrisy on the Arabization issue. Similar concerns were voiced by parties such as the FFS and the *Rassemblement pour la Culture et la Démocratie* (RCD), which had primarily Berber constituencies.

In foreign policy, the FLN took an active role in the Third World nonaligned movement. With its own roots deeply embedded in an anticolonial struggle, the FLN supported such "national liberation movements" as the Palestine Liberation Organization and the Polisario, although it distanced itself from the Polisario in order to forge a regional North African organization, the Union of the Arab Maghrib (*Union du Maghreb Arabe*; UMA), in 1989. The party advocated a massive redistribution of wealth in the world economic order and championed higher prices for developing countries' exhaustible resources. But at the same time, Algeria's close economic relationship with the United States and Western Europe gave FLN leaders an interest in working with the West on crucial issues of mutual importance. They sometimes acted very successfully as mediators between Western and Middle Eastern nations as, for example, in the case of the American hostages held in Iran from 1979 to 1981.

MEMBERSHIP AND CONSTITUENCY

Following independence, full membership in the FLN was restricted to those over the age of 18 who had fought in the war (a requirement necessarily dropped with the passage of time), adhered to the socialist ideology of the party, worked actively to spread party programs, paid regular dues, and were considered to be of good moral character. Such members were called "militants" and were grouped into cells at the commune level. "Adherents" were associate members of the party not subject to any entrance requirements. They had their own cells under the tutelage of militants but could not vote or serve on party committees.

Despite public proclamations by Boumédienne that only party members would hold positions of political leadership, top-level industrial managers and administrators did not always belong to the party. An increase in party membership and a greater role for the FLN in the implementation, if not the formulation, of policy marked the early years of Benjedid's leadership. Amid the growing economic disorder of the 1980s, however, disillusionment with the party set in and membership stagnated.

LEADERSHIP

With each change in regime, the type of leaders who filled elite positions within the FLN changed. During the Ben Bella government, intellectuals and revolutionaries made up the core of the FLN elite. Boumédienne's tenure saw many positions filled by members of the military. Benjedid was selected as secretary-general of the FLN in a political compromise between a pragmatic faction of the party that wished to liberalize Algeria's politics and economy and more radical hard-liners, many of them military officers, who supported an unaltered continuation of the policies of the Boumédienne government. Benjedid engineered dramatic political and economic reforms, including the formal separation of the party and the government through his resignation as FLN secretary-general (an office previously coterminous with the presidency of the republic) in 1988. He was succeeded in that post by Abdelhamid Mehri, a party militant since the revolution.

Following Benjedid's ouster and the suspension of the National People's Assembly in 1992, Mehri, like the leaders of other parties, unsuccessfully demanded the restoration of a pluralist political system. Although the FLN engaged in periodic episodes of dialogue with the government and joined with other major opposition groups meeting in Italy in 1995 to issue a program aimed at ending the violence and restoring a genuinely plural political culture (the Sant' Egidio Pact), it refused to participate in the 1995 presidential elections unless the FIS was also permitted to do so. The FLN was virtually alone among the major political parties in endorsing the amendments to the constitution presented in the November 1996 referendum. Shortly before the 1997 legislative elections, the FLN split into two camps, the mainstream of the party aligning itself with the policies of President Zeroual but a splinter group remaining critical of the government. Holding 64 parliamentary seats after the 1997 elections, the FLN joined the RND and the MSP in forming a coalition government.

CHALLENGE
(al-Tahaddi)

The Socialist Vanguard Party (*Parti de l'Avant-Garde Socialist*; PAGS) took the name *al-Tahaddi* in 1993. Since its own creation in 1966 as the heir of the banned Algerian Communist Party, the PAGS had been the only political organization tolerated by the FLN, albeit without official sanction. The PAGS had generally supported the state socialism of the Boumédienne years but had disapproved of Benjedid's reforms. Led by Cherif al-Hashimi, the PAGS formally registered as a political party in 1989. It failed, however, to mount an organized campaign for the 1990 municipal and regional assembly elections and boycotted the 1991 parliamentary elections entirely. After 1993, the newly named party was contemptuous of both the Islamists, whom it regarded as fanatics, and the government, which it considered repressive. The party generally avoided dialogue with the government, did not field a candidate for the presidential elections of 1995, and boycotted the referendum on amending the constitution in the following year.

ISLAMIC SALVATION FRONT
(Front Islamique du Salut; FIS)

The FIS was founded in Algiers in February 1989. Its most prominent leaders were Abbasi Madani, an education professor at the University of Algiers who became the party president, and Ali Ben Hadj (Belhadj), one of the most charismatic preachers in the city. Both had participated in a wave of Islamist activity that had met with vigorous government repression in the early 1980s, although Madani had once been an FLN member of the Algiers regional assembly and had studied for his doctorate in London under government auspices. The party was managed by an executive bureau and a consultative council of some 40 members.

The political program of the FIS attacked the inefficient state-run economy with its bloated bureaucracy and advocated an emphasis on private-sector development. It demanded that all laws conform to the precepts of the shari'a (Islamic law) and specifically called for the segregation of the sexes in public life, a ban on the consumption of alcohol, and the promotion of Arabic as the national language. Acknowledging the current pluralist environment, the program envisaged FIS cooperation with other reformist forces. Support for the party came from small businesspeople (who supplied considerable financial aid); from university students, especially in scientific and technical fields; and, most extensively, from the heavily unemployed and increasingly marginalized and frustrated population of young people born since independence.

After the FIS secured 55% of all votes cast in the communal and regional assembly elections of 1990 and won majorities in 31 of the wilaya assemblies and in 856 communal popular assemblies, it pressed for elections to the National People's Assembly, in which it hoped to repeat its triumph. In April 1991, the government introduced changes in the electoral law that the FIS regarded as inimicable to its interests. The party reacted by organizing mass antigovernment protests that resulted in the cancellation of the elections and the arrests of Madani, Ben Hadj, and hundreds of FIS members. Leadership of the party devolved on Abdelkader Hachani, a moderate figure who accepted the terms of a revised electoral law and led the FIS into the December 1991 parliamentary elections, in which it ran candidates in every constituency.

The results of the first round of balloting made a FIS-controlled parliament a virtual certainty, prompting the Algerian army to seize power and cancel the remainder of the electoral process. Many of the thousands of FIS members who were arrested along with Hachani were sent to detention centers in the Sahara. In March 1992, the government dissolved the party and many of the local assemblies that the FIS had run since 1990. Attempts by FIS leaders in exile in Europe, headed by Rabah Kabir, to reconstruct the shattered party began in 1993. By then, however, a spiral of violence pitted FIS supporters, some of whom had taken up arms as the Islamic Salvation Army (Armée Islamique du Salut; AIS), against the government forces. The ensuing violence spawned extremist groups over which the essentially leaderless FIS had no real control.

The most prominent of these radical organizations was the Armed Islamic Group (Groupe Islamique Armée; GIA), which carried out acts of terrorism directed against the security forces, secular Algerians who opposed its objectives, and foreigners resident in the country. Such attacks, along with reprisals carried out by extremist supporters of the government, full-scale battles between Islamist militants and government forces, and others between factions within the Islamist camp itself, have taken an estimated 80,000 lives and dragged Algeria into civil war.

FIS representatives joined the FLN and other Algerian opposition parties in proposing a program early in 1995 that was intended to serve as a point of departure for a negotiated settlement of the conflict and a restoration of political pluralism, but President Zeroual steadfastly refused to engage the FIS in dialogue. Thus, the party was banned from presenting a candidate in the 1995 presidential elections and encouraged its supporters to boycott the 1996 constitutional amendment referendum. The ongoing inability of the FIS to find a political solution to Algeria's problems incited increased activity on the part of the GIA and other extremists from whom the party's leadership sought to distance itself. Following the 1997 parliamentary elections, both Madani and Hachani were released from prison, although Madani remained free for only a short time before being placed under house arrest. The AIS declared a cease-fire in October 1997, but the GIA and other extremist factions refused to participate and the violence went on unabated.

Further Reading

Ageron, Charles-Robert. *Modern Algeria: A History from 1830 to the Present*. London: Hurst, 1989.

Annuaire de l'Afrique du Nord. Paris: Editions CNRS, annually.

Baduel, Pierre Robert, ed. *L'Algérie incertaine*. Aix-en-Provence: Edisud, 1994.

Entelis, John P., and Philipp Chiviges Naylor. *State and Society in Algeria*. Boulder, Colo.: Westview Press, 1992.

Leveau, Rémy. *L'Algérie dans la guerre*. Paris: Complexe, 1995.

Malley, Robert. *The Call from Algeria: Third Worldism, Revolution, and the Turn to Islam*. Berkeley: University of California Press, 1996.

Pierre, Andrew J., and William Quandt. *The Algerian Crisis: Policy Options for the West*. Washington, D.C.: Brookings Institution, 1996.

Rouadjia, Ahmed. *Grandeur et décadence de l'état algérien*. Paris: Karthala, 1994

Ruedy, John. *Modern Algeria: The Origins and Development of a Nation*. Bloomington: Indiana University Press, 1992.

Stora, Benjamin. *L'Algérie en 1995: La guerre, l'histoire, la politique*. Paris: Michalon, 1995.

PRINCIPALITY OF ANDORRA

(Principat d'Andorra)

By Robert S. Kadel

Andorra, a nation of just 450 square kilometers (174 square miles), lies in a pocket of the Pyrenees Mountains between France and Spain. The government is a coprincipality, with the president of the French Republic and the bishop of Seu d'Urgell in Spain as the two heads of state. This form of government dates back to 1278. Andorra's official language is Catalan.

Prior to 1993, no written constitution existed for Andorra. The nation was formed in 1278 under an agreement known as *Pariatjes*, an act in which the bishop of Urgel and the French count of Foix sanctioned the territory. Various administrative statutes were written in 1748 and 1763. In 1793, France's claim to the coprincipality was interrupted when its revolutionary government renounced its position as coprince. Napoleon reinstated the coprincipality rule in the early 1800s. A Plan of Reform was passed in 1866, and a Political Reform Law was passed in 1981. Political parties were prohibited throughout these periods; however, the Democratic Association of Andorra, a "quasi-party," continued to call for democratic constitutional reforms.

On March 14, 1993, Andorra voted to become a sovereign nation and adopt its own constitution. This constitution reestablishes the coprincipality as a single constitutional monarch and as part of the executive branch of government. The coprinces are responsible for calling general elections for the *Consell General*, sanctioning bills passed by the *Consell General* into laws, and dissolving the *Consell General* for new elections.

The new constitution also establishes a head of government (also referred to as the president of government) to act as an executive. The head of government is appointed by the coprinces but must first be elected by the people to the *Consell General* and then elected by the *Consell General* to this office. The president's Cabinet is also elected by the *Consell General* and consists of the ministers of agriculture, education, finance, foreign affairs, management of the territory, and social issues and culture. The president countersigns any act sanctioned by the coprinces. The power of veto lies in the presidential office, though prior to the constitution the coprinces held such power.

Legislative power rests with the *Consell General* (General Council), a body elected every four years. Andorra is separated into seven parishes. Each parish elects 2 members to the *Consell General,* while another 14 are elected at large for a total of 28. However, the constitution allows for a maximum of 42 members to be elected to the *Consell*. The *Consell* is responsible for budgetary activities, international treaties, and constitutional amendments.

Once the constitution established sovereignty for Andorra, elections were held, in 1993, to establish the first *Consell General*. In the most recent elections, in 1997, Andorran voters distributed the 28 seats as follows:

Party	Seats
Liberal Union (UL)	16
National Democratic Group (AND)	6
New Democracy (ND)	2
National Democratic Initiative (IDN)	2
Union of the People of Ordino (UPO)	2

The judicial system in Andorra consists of five separate groups. Magistrates and *batlles* hear civil cases as a part of the *Tribunal de Batlles*. Criminal matters are decided by the *Tribunal de Corts*. Appeals are heard by the *Tribunal Superior de Justícia d'Andorra* (High Court of Justice). The Higher Council of Justice, whose five members serve six-year terms, is responsible for the general administration of the courts. Finally, the *Tribunal Constitucional* (Constitutional Court), whose four members are appointed to eight-year terms, is responsible for interpreting constitutional matters.

Andorra's prospects as a nation are quite broad. As a sovereign nation, Andorra is only a few years old; thus the new government system has opened the door to increased nationalism and opportunities. While Andorra's economy rests mainly on tourism and agriculture, its relations to Spain, France, and the European Community are increasing opportunities for trade and commerce. Andorra became the 184th member of the United Nations in July of 1993.

party's presidency at the 1998 party congress, prompting speculation on his future.

Executive

The president is directly elected by a secret ballot for a term of five years and may be reelected for two consecutive or nonconsecutive terms. The president is the head of state, head of government, and commander in chief of the armed forces. He or she also has the power to appoint and dismiss the prime minister, the Cabinet ministers, and other government officials, appoint the Supreme Court judges, preside over the Council of Ministers, declare war and make peace with the authorization of the National Assembly, preside over the National Defense Council, declare a state of siege or emergency, announce the holding of general elections, issue pardons and commute sentences, and perform all other duties specified by the constitution.

Legislature

The National Assembly is made up of 223 deputies elected for a term of three years. The government is responsible to the National Assembly. The National Assembly meets twice a year and in special sessions when convened by the president or on the initiative of the Standing Commission of the National Assembly or of no less than one-third of the deputies. The Standing Commission represents the National Assembly and exercises legislative powers between sessions. Angola's first multiparty democratic elections in 1992 produced the following distribution of seats:

MPLA-PT–129

UNITA–70

Social Renewal Party–6

National Front for the Liberation of Angola–5

Liberal Democratic Party–3

Angolan Democratic Forum, Angolan National Democratic Party, Democratic Alliance of Angola, Democratic Party for Progress–Angolan National Alliance, Democratic Renewal Party, Party of the Alliance of Youths, Workers, and Farmers, and the Social Democratic Party—1 seat each (3 seats set aside for overseas Angolans were not filled)

Judiciary

According to the constitution, the organization, composition, and competence of the courts shall be established by law. Judges are to be independent in their duties. There is a Constitutional Court that can rule on legal and constitutional matters and consists of seven judges, three of whom are nominated by the president, three elected by the National Assembly, and one elected by a full session of the Supreme Court. In addition to the Supreme Court, there are also provincial courts and municipal courts. Supreme Court judges are appointed by the president.

Regional and Local Government

Angola is divided into 18 provinces, each headed by a provincial assembly that consists of 55 to 85 deputies. The executive bodies of the provincial assemblies are the provincial governments, led by provincial governors who are answerable to the provincial assemblies, the Council of Ministers, and the president. The provinces are further subdivided into councils, communes, circles, neighborhoods, and villages.

THE ELECTORAL SYSTEM

Prior to the 1992 elections the MPLA and UNITA agreed to a proportional representation system. Under this system, each province is represented by 5 members. The remaining 130 deputies are elected at the national level according to proportional representation.

THE PARTY SYSTEM

Popular Liberation Movement of Angola–Labor Party (MPLA–PT).

The MPLA was established in 1956, and was one of the original three groups that took up arms against the Portuguese. The MPLA was backed by the former USSR and proclaimed the People's Republic of Angola after independence in 1975. The MPLA became a Marxist-Leninist party after its first party congress in 1977. Locked in a bitter civil war with UNITA, the MPLA gradually introduced reforms in the last few years, and at its 1990 party congress the party abandoned its Marxist-Leninist tenants and endorsed multiparty elections. The party leader is José Eduardo dos Santos.

National Union for the Total Independence of Angola (UNITA)

UNITA was founded in 1966 and took part, along with the MPLA and FNLA, in the struggle against Portuguese colonialism. UNITA proclaimed a rival Democratic People's Republic of Angola in conjunction with the FNLA at independence in 1975. UNITA became the sole opposition to the MPLA after the demise of the FNLA in the late 1970s and waged a 20-year civil war with the MPLA for control of the country. Although its early ideological roots were influenced by Maoism, UNITA was subsequently backed by the United States and South Africa. The only real constant in its stance has been the desire of

UNITA's leader, Jonas Savimbi, to wield power. Aid from the United States and South Africa enabled UNITA to continue its effort to unseat the MPLA, but Savimbi's decision to reject the 1992 election results and return to war brought domestic and international criticism. Nevertheless, UNITA's access to diamond-mining revenues has allowed it to pursue a two-track strategy of negotiation combined with military action. Savimbi continues to head the party and has been designated head of the opposition in the unity government.

National Front for the Liberation of Angola (FNLA)

Organized in 1962, the FNLA was also one of the original resistance groups to Portuguese colonialism. The FNLA collapsed in the late 1970s and remained inactive throughout the 1980s. The FNLA leader, Holden Roberto, returned to Angola in 1991 after a long exile and announced his intention to run for president. The FNLA fared poorly in the 1992 elections, however, as Roberto received just over 2% of the presidential vote and the party managed to secure only five seats in the National Assembly.

Social Renewal Party (PRS)

The PRS came in third in the 1992 elections, gaining six seats in the National Assembly.

Democratic Renewal Party (PRD)

The PRD started as a faction of the MPLA when an abortive coup in 1977 led to a purge of the MPLA leadership. The PRD was the first party to receive the Supreme Court's permission to gather signatures in order to gain legal status. The party's president, Luis da Silva dos Passos, received less than 2% of the presidential vote in 1992 and the party secured only one seat in the National Assembly.

Liberal Democratic Party (PCD)

The PCD won three seats in the National Assembly in the 1992 elections, but its leader, Amalia de Vitoria Pereira, finished 10th among the candidates for president.

Other Parties

Several other parties won a seat each in the 1992 elections. They include: the Angolan Democratic Forum (FDA), founded by UNITA dissident George Chicoti, which also holds the justice minister's portfolio in the current government; the Angolan National Democratic Party (PNDA); the Democratic Alliance of Angola (ADA); the Democratic Party for Progress–Angolan Na-

tional Alliance (PDP–ANA); the Party of the Alliance of Youth, Workers, and Farmers of Angola (PAJOCA); and the Social Democratic Party (PSD).

Several other parties did not win any seats in the 1992 elections or have formed since then. They include: the Angolan Democratic Party (PDA), whose leader, Antonio Alberto Neto, finished a distant third in the presidential election; the Angolan Democratic Liberal Party (PDLA); the Angolan Labor Party (PTA); the Social Democratic Center (CDS); the United Front for the Salvation of Angola (FUSA); the Angolan Party of African Identity Conservative (PACIA); the Angolan Democratic Party for Peace (PDPA); the Angolan Democratic Unity Movement for Reconstruction (MAUDR); the Angolan Liberal Party (PAL); the Angolan Independent Party (PAI), the Angolan National Ecological Party (PNEA), the Angolan Social Democratic Party (PSDA); the Front for Democracy (FPD); and the National Union for the Light of Democracy and Development in Angola (UNLDDA).

FUTURE PROSPECTS

Angola's peace has been tenuous, and the country seems to be heading for renewed war. As many as 30,000 UNITA troops deserted the UN demobilization camps, and there is speculation that UNITA may have up to 25,000 troops under arms. Amid numerous reports of UNITA attacks, fighting between government and the rebels has repeatedly flared. Fighting in neighboring Democratic Republic of Congo (DRC) has provided a further provocation to the conflict in Angola. The Angolan government intervened on behalf of DRC President Laurent Kabila in his battle with rebels opposed to his regime. The MPLA government sought to solidify relations with Kabila and thereby deny UNITA access to DRC territory as a safe haven. UNITA announced that it too had interests at stake in the DRC conflict, including a corridor through which to sell its diamonds in contravention of the UN sanctions imposed on UNITA for its failure to comply with the Lusaka Accords. It also wanted to continue to use DRC territory as a staging area for its troops. With Angolan government troops deployed in the DRC, UNITA has been able to continue its armed struggle. The death of the longtime UN special envoy to Angola, Alioune Blondin Beye, in a plane crash in June 1998 also dealt a further setback to the peace process.

A recent split in UNITA resulted in a breakaway faction that the government quickly recognized as its negotiating partner. The splinter group is headed by Eugenio Manuvakola, who signed the Lusaka Accords on behalf of UNITA, and Jorge Valentim, a UNITA member and minister of hotels and tourism in the Government of Unity and National Reconciliation. Observers believe that government recognition of this group is designed to pave the way for an offensive to deafeat UNITA's military

REPUBLIC OF ARGENTINA

(República de Argentina)

By Roberto Patricio Korzeniewicz, Ph.D., and Aldo Vacs, Ph.D.

THE SYSTEM OF GOVERNMENT

Argentina encompasses about 2,791,810 square kilometers (1,077,921 square miles), making it the fourth-largest country in the Americas (after Canada, the United States, and Brazil). Extending 3,650 kilometers (2,268 miles) from north to south and 1,430 kilometers (889 miles) east to west, the country is about four times the size of Texas, or one-third the size of Europe. Argentine governments have also claimed sovereignty over additional territories in Antarctica (477,000 square miles, overlapping with territories claimed by other nations such as Chile or Britain) and several islands controlled by Great Britain in the South Atlantic (the Falkland/Malvinas Islands, the South Georgia/Georgia del Sur Island, the South Orkney/Orcadas del Sur Islands, the South Sandwich/Sandwich del Sur Islands, and the South Shetland/Shetland del Sur Islands). The country is politically divided into 23 provinces and a Federal Capital (*Capital Federal*).

The country is shaped roughly like an inverted triangle. The southernmost point of Argentina is Tierra del Fuego, above Cape Horn. In the south and west, Argentina shares a long border with Chile along the Andean Mountains. Much of the country's east runs along the Atlantic Ocean, in a coastline measuring 2,850 kilometers. Above the Rio de la Plata, the eastern border of Argentina meets with Uruguay and Brazil. In the north, Argentina shares borders with Bolivia (in the high plateau of the Andes Mountains) and Paraguay (across the Pilcomayo, Paraguay and Alto Paraná Rivers). At the present time, the only territorial dispute affecting the country is a minor one with Chile over a small, glacier-covered portion of their border.

Argentina's population grew from 500,000 in the 1810s to 4 million by the 1890s, 8 million immediately before World War I, 16 million in the aftermath of World War II, an estimated 34,665,000 in 1995, and a projected 36,238,000 by the year 2000. Much of this growth, particularly in the late 19th and early 20th centuries, was accounted for by large waves of immigration from Europe and neighboring countries. Spanish is the official language of the country, although many also speak English, French, German, and Italian, and the country is heavily urbanized.

The country has a republican and representative political system with moderate federal features. The constitution, originally written in 1853 but amended five times thereafter (most recently in 1994), provides for a division of powers among the executive, a bicameral Congress, and a judicial branch. Much of the 20th century, however, has been characterized by considerable political instability and long periods of authoritarian rule.

Executive

The executive branch consists of the president, the vice president, and the Cabinet. Executive power is vested in the president. The 1853 constitution introduced a presidentialist system that has been retained through subsequent amendments. As "supreme chief of the nation," the president has extensive powers over domestic and foreign policy, including the general administration of the country, the appointment of administration officials, the implementation of the laws, the right to introduce laws before Congress and to veto or approve legislation in part or as a whole, the nomination of justices for the Supreme Court of Justice (*Corte Suprema de Justicia*), and the conduct of foreign relations. As commander in chief of the armed forces, the president appoints and promotes (with the approval of the Senate) senior military officers. The president may declare, in case of external attack or domestic disturbances, and with the approval of the Senate, a state of siege, temporarily suspending some civil liberties.

Historically, the executive branch has dominated the legislature and the judiciary, which often have been unable to provide an effective counterweight to the power of the president. The 1853 constitution invested a large amount of power in the presidency. The importance of parliamentary and judicial institutions was further reduced throughout the 19th and 20th centuries. Authoritarian regimes periodically closed Congress and removed distrusted judges at will, and even elected charismatic presidents often limited debate and dissent within Congress and used a variety of mechanisms to shape the judiciary to their needs. This weakness of parliament and the judiciary relative to the executive has persisted in recent decades despite the return to democracy in 1983.

Until 1994, the president and vice presidents were elected for six-year terms—with no possibility of immediate reelection—by an electoral college whose members were elected by popular vote. With the constitutional reforms of 1994, the president and vice president are now directly elected by popular vote for four-year terms, with the possibility of immediate reelection for one term only. Elections are held under a *balotaje* system, with runoffs between the two most popular tickets held if in the first round the leading ticket (1) has less than 40% of the vote or (2) has between 40% and 45% of the vote but less than a 10% advantage over the second-most-popular ticket. The president and vice president are elected together, and must be at least 30 years old.

In case of death, illness, absence from the country, resignation, or removal from office, the president is succeeded by the vice president. Next in the succession line are the president of the Senate, the president of the Chamber of Deputies, and the president of the Supreme Court, although new elections must be called within three months if one of these three positions is forced to assume the presidency.

President Carlos Saúl Menem, of the Justicialist Party, first served during the 1989–95 period. The constitutional reforms introduced in 1994 allowed President Menem to run in the 1995 national elections. In that year, current President Menem and Vice President Carlos Ruckauf were elected with 49.8% of the vote. The next presidential elections are scheduled for 1999.

The president can appoint and remove ministers at will. Ministers must countersign all presidential decrees referred to their respective areas to validate them, and are considered individually and collectively responsible for the acts of the administration that they legalize. Ministers may be called to testify before Congress and may participate without vote in its deliberations. Constitutional amendments in 1994 created the position of chief of Cabinet, who is answerable to the president but politically responsible to Congress and can be removed through a vote of no confidence. The chief of Cabinet undertakes the general administration of the country; appoints administrative employees; convenes, coordinates, and chairs Cabinet meetings in the absence of the president; sends bills to Congress; and responds to congressional inquiries. The chief of Cabinet must appear at least once a month before Congress, alternating between the two chambers.

Legislature

The legislative branch consists of a National Congress (*Congreso Nacional*) divided into two houses: the Chamber of Deputies (*Cámara de Diputados*) and the Senate

(*Senado*). According to the constitution, the deputies represent the nation as a whole and the senators represent the provinces and the Federal Capital. The chambers meet simultaneously in regular session between May 1 and September 30 but can be recalled by the president for a special session.

Deputies are elected by popular vote through a system of proportional representation, with each of the 23 provinces and the Federal Capital considered a separate electoral district. The total number of deputies serving in 1997 was 257. Congress periodically determines the number of inhabitants required to elect 1 deputy as well as the total number of representatives assigned to each district. As of 1994, 1 representative was elected for each 161,000 inhabitants or remaining fraction no smaller than 80,500, with each province electing a minimum of 5 deputies. The constitution requires that deputies be at least 25 years old, that they have been citizens for at least four years, and that they be natives of the province in which they seek election, or have resided there for at least the two previous years. Deputies serve four-year terms and may be reelected. One-half of the seats in the Chamber go up for election every two years.

In the last congressional elections, held in 1997, the Justicialist Party received 36.2% of the national vote; the main opposition force, an alliance composed of the UCR and the Frepaso, jointly received 45.7% of the votes (including ballots going individually to the two main members of the alliance). After these elections, deputies from the Justicialist Party accounted for 46.3% of the Chamber of Deputies, those of the Alianza for 43.2%, and the rest were divided among small political parties with fewer than three deputies each.

Until 1994, the Senate consisted of 48 members: 2 for the provinces (appointed by their respective legislatures) and 2 for the Federal Capital (chosen by an electoral college selected for that purpose). The 1994 constitutional reforms established the direct election of senators in each province and the federal capital, and the number of senators was increased from 2 to 3 per district (with 2 senators representing the majority party and 1 elected by the first minority). Upon full implementation of the 1994 reforms, the total number of senators will be 72. The 1994 reforms also reduced the term of office from nine to six years (with the possibility of reelection). One-third of the seats in the Senate are up for election every two years. Senators must be at least 30 years old, citizens for at least six years, and natives of the province in which they seek election, or must have resided there for at least the two previous years.

After the 1997 congressional elections, the Justicialist Party retained a majority in the Senate (with 40 seats out of 72), with the main opposition alliance (UCR and Frepaso) holding 26 seats and the remaining 6 positions going to assorted small (and primarily provincial) political parties.

commanded strong electoral majorities at some point in their history.

Radical Civic Union
(Unión Cívica Radical; UCR)

The UCR, founded by Leandro Alem, emerged in the 1890s as the first modern political party in Argentina, demanding political and administrative reform. Focusing on efforts to attain greater electoral transparency, demands by this party were instrumental in promoting the important electoral reforms of 1912 (*Ley Saenz Peña*), introducing universal, secret, and obligatory suffrage for adult males; providing for minority representation in Congress; and introducing a cleaner system of electoral registries. Following the adoption of these reforms, the UCR actively participated in elections with a vague but moderately nationalistic and redistributionist platform, upon which leader Hipólito Yrigoyen was twice elected president (his first term lasted between 1916 and 1922; his second term began in 1928 but was brought to an end by the conservative military coup of 1930). Support for the party was particularly strong among university students, middle- and low-income groups in both urban and rural areas, and marginalized sectors of the elite (such as landlords from the provinces).

After World War II, the UCR defined itself in opposition to Peronist rule. In 1955, the party supported the military coup that overthrew the Perón government, but thereafter it became divided between those who advocated reconciliation with Peronism (eventually splitting into the Intransigent UCR, or *Unión Cívica Radical Intransigente*, led by Arturo Frondizi, elected president in 1958 and overthrown by the military in 1962) and those remaining in strong opposition to any alliance with the Peronists (eventually becoming the People's UCR, or *Unión Cívica Radical del Pueblo*, led by Ricardo Balbín and including Arturo Illía, elected president in 1963 and overthrown by the military in 1966). The political activities of the UCR, as those of most parties, were officially banned during the subsequent military dictatorships (1966–73, 1976–83), and the party remained in the opposition during the brief return of Peronism to power (1973–76).

Raúl Alfonsín played a crucial role in promoting the UCR's return to power in the 1983 elections. However, the Alfonsín administration (1983–89) was beset by political and economic problems. Politically, the administration had to deal with the legacy of authoritarian rule and faced frequent conflicts with the military and organized labor. Most crucial was an endemic economic crisis, with economic recessions followed by periods of runaway inflation. In the 1989 elections, the UCR candidate, Córdoba's governor Eduardo Angeloz, was defeated by Carlos Saúl Menem, the Peronist candidate.

Electoral support for the UCR fell dramatically for the 1994 constitutional elections, when leaders of the party were perceived as too willing to enter into political compromises with the Menem administration. In the 1995 presidential elections, the candidate of the UCR, Rio Negro's governor Horacio Massaccesi, came in third, receiving 17.1% of the vote. In the last congressional elections, in 1997, the UCR formed an alliance with the Front of a Country in Solidarity (*Frente del País Solidario*, or Frepaso). Together, these parties gathered 45.7% of the vote and won several electoral districts throughout the country, including most notably in Buenos Aires. The current president of the UCR is Rodolfo Terragno. Former president Raúl Alfonsín remains an important force within the party. Other important leaders include Fernando de la Rúa (current mayor of Buenos Aires).

Justicialist or Peronist Party
(Partido Justicialista o Peronista)

The Justicialist or Peronist Party was created to advocate support for Juan Domingo Perón. Shortly after a military coup in 1943, Colonel Perón was appointed to head the national labor agency (*Secretaría del Trabajo*). In the next two years, Perón used his new position to rapidly develop a strong following among the ranks of labor. At the same time, Perón began to advocate the need for countries to pursue a third position between capitalism and communism and for the state to take an active role in promoting cooperation between workers and capitalists so as to achieve national grandeur. In a famous synthesis of his position, Perón called for Argentina to become "economically independent, socially just, and politically sovereign."

As a strong charismatic leader and upon being elected president (1946–52, 1952–55), Perón developed a strong hold over the Peronist Party and was able unilaterally to appoint or remove party authorities. The influence of organized labor grew considerably during Perón's first term in office. His second term was characterized by growing political conflicts and deepening economic problems. President Perón was overthrown in 1955 and spent the next two decades in exile.

In the physical absence of Perón, the Peronist Party experienced a growing division into factions. Organized labor became one of the strongest forces within the party, but trade unions were themselves divided along the ideological spectrum, over the degree to which economic aims should be subordinated to political goals, and over the role of Perón leadership within the party. The more traditional political leaders within the party not only contended with the challenges of organized labor but were themselves split along ideological and regional lines. And throughout the 1960s and early 1970s, the party experienced the growth of leftist tendencies that strengthened the bargaining power of the Peronists but further intensified the basis for political segmentation.

In 1973, as the military experienced a rapid erosion of their hold on power, Perón returned to Argentina. Around the same time, the Peronist Party was reorganized as the Justicialist Party. Elected president for the third time in history, Perón sought to restore tight controls over the party structure. These efforts were not very successful: old and new factions within the party intensified their efforts to gain political control, and Perón's old age and expectations of his demise only served to intensify these conflicts. Upon Perón's death in 1974, María Estela (Isabel) Martínez de Perón succeeded him as president of the country and as leader of the party. The Isabel Perón administration (1974–76) was characterized by a growing disarray and ultimately the virtual collapse of the Justicialist Party. After the coup of 1976, the party was banned, and many of its leaders were jailed or persecuted by the new military authorities.

In the return to democracy in 1983, the candidate of the Justicialist Party, Italo Luder, lost the presidential elections to Raúl Alfonsín. This loss was widely blamed on the appearance that the party remained too closely tied to its personalist and rather authoritarian forms of organization. During the next years, the party experienced intense conflicts between traditional and reform-minded leaders. Carlos Menem, at the time governor of La Rioja, was tied primarily to the more traditional forces within the party and was able to defeat more reformist leaders for the candidacy to the presidency in 1988. Upon winning the national elections with 51.7% of the vote and coming to office in 1989, the Menem administration moved toward adopting free-market policies, favoring fiscal and monetary austerity, and seeking to limit state regulation of the economy.

The shift of the Menem administration toward free-market policies generated strong opposition within his own party, as some argued that the new economic policies would increase unemployment and raise poverty rates. Within the mainstream of the party, former vice president (and current governor of the province of Buenos Aires) Eduardo Duhalde, a presidential hopeful for the 1999 elections, has often voiced criticism of the social impact of the free-market policies instituted by the Menem administration. There was also a split within the Justicialist Party when the Peronist national senator (for the province of Mendoza), José Octavio Bordon, created the Open Politics for the Social Country (*Política Abierta para el País Social*, or PAIS) in 1994. PAIS merged with other left-of-center forces to challenge President Menem in the 1995 elections, and presidential candidate Bordon received 29.2% of the vote, coming in second. In subsequent elections Bordon lost his initial popularity, and at times has expressed his intention to withdraw from electoral politics.

ALLIANCES AND MINOR PARTIES

An important political alliance in recent years has been the Front for a Country in Solidarity (*Frente del País Solidario*, or Frepaso), created in 1995. The alliance advances a center-left political platform to oppose the free-market policies of the Menem administration; the alliance advocates clean government and more equitable economic policies. The Frepaso originally brought together several forces: PAIS (the dissident Peronist organization led by José Octavio Bordon, which eventually abandoned the alliance), a coalition of parties of the left previously known as the Big Front (*Frente Grande*), a second coalition known as Socialist Unity (*Unidad Socialista*), the Christian Democrat Party (*Partido Democráta Cristiano*, or PDC), and some smaller, left-of-center political parties. Current important leaders within the Frepaso include Carlos Alvarez (a dissident Peronist) and Graciela Fernandez Meijide (a human rights activist).

In the early 1990s, the Big Front agglomerated various parties of the left, including remnants of the Communist Party (*Partido Comunista*), the Intransigent Party (*Partido Intransigente*), the Movement of the Left (*Movimiento de Izquierda*), and a dissident Peronist faction called the Front for Democracy and Social Justice (*Frente por la Democracia y la Justicia Social*, or Fredejuso). Electoral support for the Big Front in the early 1990s was limited to the traditionally small leftist constituencies (in this case, ranging between 2% and 4% of the vote in national elections), but grew in 1994 as the leftist alliance broadened its platform to attack corruption and the concentration of power in the Menem administration. To further broaden its appeal, in 1995 the Big Front joined other political currents in creating the Frepaso. In the 1995 presidential elections, the candidate of the Frepaso, José Octavio Bordon, came in second, receiving 29.2% of the vote. In its more current version, the Frepaso joined the UCR to oppose the Menem administration in the 1997 congressional elections.

Several other parties and political alliances have played important roles at the national and/or provincial levels. Over the last decade, the most important conservative force has been the Union of the Democratic Center (*Unión del Centro Democrático*, or Ucede). The organization was formed in 1983 by a convergence of small conservative forces led by Alvaro Alsogaray, one of Argentina's best-known advocates of free-market policies. The popularity of the Ucede increased significantly in the 1980s, when support among the middle class allowed it to increase its share of the vote from 3% in 1985 to 10% in 1989 (when the party claimed nine deputies in the new Congress). As the Menem administration began to introduce its own free-market policies, it found a willing ally in the Ucede, and important party figures were appointed to government positions. At the same time, however, the electoral influence of the Ucede began to decline, drop-

policies corresponding to a conservative interpretation of Roman Catholic teachings, regardless of the authoritarian or democratic origin of these administrations. Throughout the 1976–83 period, a majority of the bishops and cardinals of the Argentine Episcopal Conference (*Conferencia Episcopal Argentina*, or CEA) supported the military regime or adopted neutral positions, while only a few openly opposed the authoritarian government's policies. The CEA did engage in some significant conflicts with the Alfonsín administration (particularly over legislative bills affecting paternal authority, the legalization of divorce, and educational reforms).

During the Menem administrations, conservative sectors of the church have criticized the introduction of programs dealing with acquired immune deficiency syndrome (AIDS) and have called for harsher policies to repress pornography, drug addiction, homosexuality, abortion, corruption, and other activities they deem sinful. More progressive sectors of the church have criticized the Menem administrations' application of market policies, claiming that such reforms tend to undermine welfare conditions for the poor.

National Prospects

The persistence of democracy since 1983, the commitment of most forces in the opposition to channel their demands through their participation in electoral politics, and the gradual loss of importance of corporate mechanisms of political representation (particularly among the military but also within organized labor and the business sector) are all indicative of the gradual consolidation of democracy in Argentina in a century previously marked by the prevalence of political instability and dictatorship. In the mid-1990s, the prospects for the continuation of democracy in Argentina are probably brighter than ever before.

Probably contributing to the consolidation of democracy, the 1990s have been characterized by high rates of economic growth. Economic expansion has been widely attributed to major reforms engaged by the Menem administration. Indeed, this administration would claim that thanks to its policies, economic growth and democratic consolidation in Argentina are now engaged in a virtuous cycle in which each is destined to become further strengthened over time.

While acknowledging the political and economic accomplishments of the 1990s, the opposition claims that the reforms of the Menem administration have been accompanied by a reassertion of personalistic leadership and a concentration of power in the executive branch. Furthermore, this concentration of power, according to the opposition, has allowed for niches of corruption to entrench themselves within the current administration.

Finally, according to these arguments, the economic reforms of the 1990s have been accompanied by considerable exclusion, leading to unprecedented levels of unemployment and a growing vulnerability of much of the population to poverty.

Recent elections in Argentina suggest that each line of interpretation carries considerable weight, creating a virtual stalemate among the forces of support and opposition for the Menem administration. Undoubtedly, economic trends, particularly as they pertain to employment and income, will be of crucial importance in shaping the outcome of the 1999 elections. Despite their actual outcome, however, future elections are unlikely to cast doubt on the legitimacy of democracy itself.

Further Reading

Brysk, Alison. *The Politics of Human Rights in Argentina: Protest, Change, and Democratization*. Stanford, Calif.: Stanford University Press.

Epstein, Edward. *The New Argentina Democracy: The Search for a Successful Formula*. Westport, Conn.: Praeger, 1992.

McGuire, James H. *Peronism without Perón: Unions, Parties, and Democracy in Argentina*. Stanford, Calif.: Stanford University Press, 1997.

O'Donnell, Guillermo. *Bureaucratic-Authoritarianism: Argentina 1966–1973, in Comparative Perspective*. Berkeley: University of California Press, 1988.

Potash, Robert A. *The Army and Politics in Argentina, 1945–62*. (3 volumes). Stanford, Calif.: Stanford University Press, 1980.

Rock, David. *Argentina: 1516-1982, From Spanish Colonization to the Falklands War*. Berkeley: University of California Press, 1985.

Smith, William C. *Authoritarianism and the Crisis of the Argentine Political Economy*. Stanford, Calif.: Stanford University Press, 1989.

Snow, Peter and Luigi Manzetti. *Political Forces in Argentina*. Westport, Conn.: Praeger, 1993.

Tulchin, Joseph. *Argentina and the United States: A Conflicted Relationship*. Boston: Twayne, 1990.

Web Sites

University of Texas: lanic.utexas.edu/la/argentina

Gardel: vishnu.nirvana.phys.psu.edu/argentina/argbody.html

Presidency of the Argentine Republic: www.presidencia.ar

Ministry of Justice: www.jus.gov.ar

Departamento de Información Legislativa: platon.mecon.ar/infoleg.htm

Buenos Aires Herald: www.buenosairesherald.com

Clarín: www.clarin.com.ar

La Nación: www.lanacion.com

Página 12: www.pagina12.com

Frente del País Solidario: www.geocities.com/capitolhill/8343/

Unión Cívica Radical: www.geocities.com/capitolhill/1220

REPUBLIC OF ARMENIA

By Robinder S. Bhatty

THE SYSTEM OF GOVERNMENT

Armenia is located in the South Caucasus region. It is bordered to the north by the Republic of Georgia; to the south by the Republic of Iran and the Azerbaijani territory of Nakhichevan; to the west by Turkey; and to the east by the Republic of Azerbaijan. Armenia is a parliamentary republic. The current Armenian population is uncertain because of a fluctuating refugee population and massive emigration. In 1991, it was estimated at close to 700,000, but it is now thought to be between 2.8 and 3.2 million people.

The territories that make up the present-day Republic of Armenia were under Persian control for centuries before being absorbed into the Russian Empire in 1828. Following the collapse of the czarist regime, an independent Armenian republic was in existence from May 1918 until December 1920. Armenia was at the forefront of the nationalist tide that swept the Soviet Union in the late 1980s and was one of the first of the Soviet republics to declare independence, in September 1991.

Since independence, Armenia has experienced substantial economic hardship due to the end of Soviet subsidies and the collapse of interrepublic trade. In particular, Armenian support for ethnic Armenian insurgents in the territory of Nagorno-Karabakh, a region of Azerbaijan, led Azerbaijan to blockade deliveries of petroleum and natural gas to Armenia.

As late as 1990, Armenia had a substantial population of as many as 200,000 ethnic Azerbaijanis, living primarily in small rural communities. Virtually all of these people were driven or fled from Armenia in 1990 after clashes with Armenian nationalist activists, and they became refugees in Iran and Azerbaijan. A small Kurdish population remains in western Armenia, along the Turkish border, and a small Russian population resides primarily in the cities. Today Armenia is essentially a monoethnic state.

Executive

The president is the head of state and is directly elected. The prime minister is head of the government and is appointed by the president. The prime minister and his Cabinet do not hold seats in the parliament. The current president is Robert Kocharian. The prime minister is Armen Darbinian. President Levon Ter-Petrossian resigned in February 1998 under pressure from the ministers of defense and internal affairs/national security and then Prime Minister Kocharian.

Presidential elections last took place on March 16, 1998, with a second, runoff election being held on March 30, 1998. President Kocharian won with 60% of the vote. Both elections were criticized by OSCE observers for a veriety of fraudulent praticices.

On July 5, 1995, Armenia adopted a new constitution that shifted a great deal of power to the executive from the legislature. The president serves a five-year term and may not serve more than two consecutive terms. He may dissolve parliament; appoint or remove the prime minister; appoint four of the nine members and the president of the Constitutional Court and the Court of Appeals; appoint or remove any judge serving in any court other than the Constitutional Court; and appoint or remove the prosecutor general and any other prosecutor. The president may also declare martial law and rule by decree.

In early February 1998, the Armenian National Movement's parliamentary bloc collapsed when President Levon Ter-Petrossian was forced to resign. Many fromer ANM members of parliament moved quickly to join other parties. Many of the defectors joined Yerkrapah, a party representing veterans of the Karabakh War. It was begun as a veterans' union in late 1994 under the auspices of the Ministry of Defense, with perhaps 3,500 members across Armenia. Yerkrapah members had been accused of involvement in a series of attacks on foreign religious groups in the summer of 1995. Yerkrapah had registered as a parliamentary party in October 1997 with 17 seats, all sitting independents who agreed to join the new party. Following Ter-Petrossian's resignation, Yerkrapah became the largest party in parliament.

Also following Ter-Petrossian's resignation, the acting president, Kocharian, relegalized the Dashnaktsutyun party. This is a hard-line nationalist group with strong links to the Armenian diaspora in North America and Europe; it was banned by the Ter-Petrossian regime in 1995 following allegations of involvement in terrorism, murder, and drug trafficking. While the party currently holds no seats in parliament, it is expected to do well in future parliamentary elections and, along with Yerkrapah, will form the core of the post-Hanrapetutyun government bloc.

Presidential elections were held on March 16, 1998. The front runners were acting president Kocharian, running as the incumbent with the support of the security ministries, and Karen Demirchyan, the Soviet-era chief of Armenia who had been running a factory since his retirement in 1990. Kocharian scored highest with 38.76% of the vote, followed by Demirchian, who won 30.67%. As neither contender received a majority, a runoff election was scheduled for March 30, when Kocharian won with 59.48% of the vote while Demirchian recieved 40.52%.

Legislature

The Armenian parliament is the National Assembly, a single-chamber body with 190 seats, 140 of which are single-member districts and 50 of which are allocated on the basis of proportional representation. The number of seats will decrease to 131 in the next round of parliamentary voting, which is scheduled to be held in 1999.

Over 40 political parties contested the 1995 parliamentary elections, and 52 were registered by the middle of 1996. The largest party in parliament is Yerkrapah, the political wing of a union of veterans of the Karabakh War. The bulk of Yerkrapah's parliamentary representives are made up of former supporters of the Armenian National Movement.

Parliamentary elections last occurred in July 1995. OSCE observers characterized them as "free but unfair." Nine opposition parties were refused certification by the Central Election Commission, and the single largest opposition party, the Armenian Revolutionary Federation, or *Dashnaktsutyun*, was banned in January 1995 after members were charged with involvement in drug trafficking and murder. The ARF was legalized by President Kocharian shortly after the forced resignation of President Ter-Petrossian.

The 1995 constitution engineered a massive shift of power from the legislature to the presidency, and the parliament has few options when dealing with the chief executive.

Judiciary

The 1995 constitution ordered extensive judicial reforms, which have not yet been completed. A three-tiered system is to be introduced consisting of Courts of First Instance, Review Courts, and a Court of Appeals. Two other new judicial institutions are already functioning: the Council of Justice and the Constitutional Court.

The Council of Justice is an administrative body chaired by the president. It reviews the performance of judges and prepares lists for promotion of judges and prosecutors; nominates judges and prosecutors for positions; and prepares disciplinary proceedings against judges.

The Constitutional Court is a nine-member body, four of whom are appointed by the president and five by the National Assembly. The court reviews the constitutionality of laws, parliamentary decisions, and presidential decrees.

At present, Soviet-era judicial institutions still function at the local level in Armenia. District courts handle all civil and criminal matters within a given province. Armenia's Soviet-era Supreme Court has been superseded by the Constitutional Court.

Judges are often neither impartial nor honest. Stories of corruption in the judicial system are widespread, and most Armenians prefer to avoid resorting to the courts. Judges rarely rule against the state in politically sensitive matters.

Regional and Local Government

Armenia is divided into 10 administrative districts plus the city of Yerevan. The provincial governors and the mayor of Yerevan are accountable only to the president, who appoints them, rather than to the local populace or the parliament. The governors, in turn, have the authority to remove local elected officials and exercise substantial control over the administration of each province. The governors do not control local police forces, which remain under the control of regional offices of the Ministry of Internal Affairs.

Elections to local bodies known as village councils were held in November 1996. These were boycotted by the opposition to protest fraud and vote tampering by the government in the 1996 presidential elections.

THE ELECTORAL SYSTEM

The parliament is a 190-member body; 140 seats are winner-take-all, single-member ridings, while 50 are allocated on the basis of proportional representation. Under the terms of the 1995 constitution, the number of seats in parliament will drop to 131 during the next round of parliamentary voting, in 1999.

THE PARTY SYSTEM

Armenian political parties are in general weak and poorly institutionalized, with small memberships. Most of the parties in the governing Republic bloc are backed by powerful individuals within the government or the economy. In fact, Armenian politics is more a case of rule by a shifting set of powerful individuals heading up networks of supporters held together by patronage links.

ARMENIAN NATIONAL MOVEMENT (ANM)
(Hayots Hamazgayin Sharzhum)

The Armenian National Movement, the ANM, is the largest party in parliament and forms the core of the Republic bloc, which controls the parliament. It began as an umbrella group of a variety of informal organizations in the summer of 1988, which in turn had emerged to take advantage of the new rules of glasnost and perestroika. Led by a group of young, non-Communist intellectuals known as the Karabakh Committee (due to their central cause, the gaining of Armenian sovereignty over the Azerbaijani territory of Nagorno-Karabakh), the group solidified into a political party by 1989, when it fielded candidates in runoff elections to the Armenian parliament. A number of the original members of the Karabakh Committee remain in the ANM, including the president, Levon Ter-Petrossian.

The ANM disintegrated in the weeks leading up to the February 1998 resignation of President Ter-Petrossian. Most members defected to Yerkrapah, a party representing veterans of the Karabakh War that is closely linked with the Ministry of Defense. Yerkrapah is currently the largest party in parliament. The ANM has increasingly come to represent the interests of powerful economic "mafias" to the exclusion of almost all other groups in society, and in fact President Ter-Petrossian and several powerful ministers have said exactly this on a number of occasions, referring to the party as the vehicle of "entrepreneurs and businessmen" rather than of the nation as a whole.

ARMENIAN REVOLUTIONARY FEDERATION (ARF)
(Dashnaktsutyun)

The Armenian Revolutionary Federation, the ARF, is the oldest political party active in Armenia. Founded in 1890 by members of the Armenian population of the Ottoman Empire, the ARF was the ruling party of the first Armenian Republic, from 1918 to 1920. Driven from Armenia by the Bolsheviks, the party transferred its base to the Armenian diaspora communities in Lebanon, France, the United States, and elsewhere, where it remains a powerful force. Its platform at the time stood on the twin pillars of socialism and uncompromising Armenian nationalism, both of which it retains today.

The ARF became a legal party in Armenia in 1991. Relations with President Ter-Petrossian rapidly became adversarial. The ARF campaigned for a strong parliament (at the expense of the executive), large-scale public spending, and the formal annexation of Nagorno-Karabakh to Armenia, and won 18 seats in the 1992 parliamentary elections, making it the largest opposition party in the National Assembly.

In December 1994 the mayor of Yerevan, Humbartsum Galstian, was murdered, and President Ter-Petrossyan accused the Dashnaktsutyun of the murder. Several members of the party were put on trial for belonging to an alleged secret organization within the party that was engaged in murder, drug trafficking, and extortion. The Dashnaktsutyun were legalized by President Kocharian in 1998 and enjoy great popularity with the public.

THE NATIONAL DEMOCRATIC UNION (NDU)
(Zgayin Zhoghovurtakan Mioutyun)

The NDU was founded in 1992 and is led by Vazgen Manukian, a former member of the Karabakh Committee and the ANM who held a number of senior positions under President Ter-Petrossyan in 1991 and 1992. Like most Armenian political parties, the NDU is small, with a membership estimated at about 100.

On September 10, 1996, during the presidential election campaign, the NDU created a coalition with several other parties and put forward Manukian as the presidential candidate of the unified opposition. The move caught the Ter-Petrossian government completely by surprise and revived the opposition campaign. When the election was finally held, on September 21, Manukian and Ter-Petrossyan finished neck and neck, with the incumbent being declared the winner with 51.75% of the vote, a razor-thin margin just large enough to prevent a runoff election between the two men. International observers cited numerous irregularities in the vote-counting procedures and expressed a lack of confidence in the overall process and the announced results. Opposition supporters rioted in the capital and the government responded by deploying troops and armored vehicles. A number of opposition leaders were arrested, and Manukyan went into hiding for some time.

The opposition alliance has since disintegrated, but Manukyan remains the best-known opposition politician. It is widely believed in some quarters that he in fact won the election.

OTHER POLITICAL FORCES

The Nagorno-Karabakh War

The Azerbaijani territory of Karabakh is a region of predominantly Armenian population lying within Azerbaijan. In 1979 (the last year for which reliable figures are available) the population totaled 160,000, 37,000 of whom were Azerbaijani and 123,000 of whom were Armenian. Armenians refer to the territory as "Artsakh" and Azerbaijanis as "Yuxari Karabagh." In recognition of the concentrated nature of Armenian settlement in the region, it was given the status of an autonomous *oblast* by the Soviet government in 1924—a status that conferred a substantial degree of self-governing authority upon the *oblast* government while maintaining Azerbaijani sovereignty.

Gaining jurisdiction over Karabakh has long been a goal of Armenia and of the population of Karabakhs. Demonstrations demanding the transfer occurred in the mid-1960s and recurred periodically thereafter in Yerevan and Stepanakaert. In January 1988 demonstrations began again and quickly spread throughout Armenia and Karabakh. Unrest escalated rapidly, with clashes between the local population and Soviet internal affairs troops and between local Azerbaijanis and Armenians becoming a daily event.

The Azerbaijani Supreme Soviet abolished Nagorno-Karabakh in November 1991; the Karabakh authorities responded by holding a referendum on independence. On January 6, 1992, Karabakh formally declared its independence from Azerbaijan.

The war for Karabakh led to approximately 50,000 deaths and the creation of about 740,000 Azerbaijani refugees and 40,000 Armenian refugees. The war was a military disaster for Azerbaijan, which lost control of almost all of Karabakh and a substantial amount of undisputed Azerbaijani territory bordering on Karabakh as well. Fighting halted in May 1994 when the two sides signed a Russian-mediated cease-fire, but a comprehensive settlement has thus far proved elusive. Although Armenia has denied direct involvement in the war, Armenian regular forces played an active role between 1992 and 1994, and Armenia continues to serve as a source of finance, supplies, and manpower for the Karabakh government.

The war has been a major factor influencing Armenian and Azeri political development. Two Azerbaijani presidents were overthrown following military defeats in Karabakh: Ayaz Mutalibov in March 1992 and Abulfaz Elcibey in June 1993. Both the Azerbaijani Popular Front and the Karabakh Committee, which led the independence movements in their respective countries, derived much of their popularity from their hard-line positions on the dispute. Parties and politicians on both sides remain highly sensitive to the need to appear tough on Karabakh.

NATIONAL PROSPECTS

Lacking any resources that could attract international investment, crippled by massive emigration, and with what remains of the national economy strangling under the weight of government corruption, Armenia's prospects are grim. Furthermore, as the legitimacy of the government comes under increasing attack due to the clumsy theft of elections and heavy-handed repression of the opposition, it is forced to rely ever more heavily on its only real achievement, its record of success in the Karabakh War against Azerbaijan.

This in turn makes it unlikely that the Armenian side will be able to make any real compromises in peace negotiations with Azerbaijan for fear of weakening its remaining supporters, the hard-liners in Armenia and the diaspora who oppose any concessions to Azerbaijan, and would seem to ensure that Armenia will be frozen out of the oil boom that is beginning to transform the Georgian and Azeri economies.

Further Reading

Bremmer, I., and C. Welt. "Armenia's New Autocrats." *Journal of Democracy* 8, no. 3 (July 1997).

Dudwick, N. "Political Structures in Post-Communist Armenia: Images and Realities." In *Conflict, Cleavage and Change in Central Asia and the Caucasus*. Ed. Karen Dawisha and Bruce Parrott. New York: Cambridge University Press, 1997.

Libaridian, G. *The Question of Karabakh: An Overview*. Cambridge, Mass.: Zoryan Institute, 1988.

Suny, Ronald Grigor. *Looking towards Ararat: Armenia in Modern History*. Bloomington: Indiana University Press, 1993.

THE COMMONWEALTH OF AUSTRALIA

By Andrew Parkin

THE SYSTEM OF GOVERNMENT

Australia is one of the world's relatively advanced, industrialized, urbanized, and increasingly multicultural nations, with a population in 1998 of around 18.8 million people. Its liberal-democratic system of government has both a federal and a parliamentary structure.

Federalism reflects the circumstances of Australia's colonial origins. On January 1, 1901, six self-governing British colonies—New South Wales, Victoria, Queensland, South Australia, Western Australia, and Tasmania—federated to form the Commonwealth of Australia. The six colonies remained as component States of the new federal system. There are also two Territories—the Northern Territory and the Australian Capital Territory—directly administered for most of their history by the Commonwealth (national) government but that now enjoy a degree of self-government comparable with that of the States. The legislative, judicial, and central executive institutions of Commonwealth government are geographically located in the national capital, Canberra.

The act of the British Parliament that established federation did so by providing Australia with a written constitution. This constitution specifies the allocation of powers between the Commonwealth and the States. The specified Commonwealth powers are mainly the obvious "national" ones: defense, foreign affairs, immigration, international trade, currency, and postal service. Few of these powers are exclusive, most being formally "concurrent" with continuing State powers, though Commonwealth law prevails in any case of inconsistent concurrent legislation. The States retain all powers not exclusively transferred to the Commonwealth.

Since federation, there has been a steady expansion of the significance of the Commonwealth government. This has been partly achieved by constitutional amendment, though such amendments, requiring approval in a referendum by a majority of voters in at least four of the six States as well as by a majority of voters nationwide, are difficult to achieve. Only eight out of 42 proposed amendments submitted to referendum have been approved. Some of these, however, have increased Commonwealth power,

such as the 1946 expansion of its authority to provide welfare benefits and the 1967 amendment providing power to assist Aboriginal Australians.

Rulings by the High Court, which exercises judicial review over constitutional matters, have also served to promote the prominence of the Commonwealth government. For example, the High Court has sanctioned the effective monopolization of income taxes by the Commonwealth since the 1940s; this, in turn, makes the States dependent on the disbursement by the Commonwealth of financial grants. Another important High Court ruling allows the Commonwealth, which under the constitution may "grant financial assistance to any State on such terms and conditions as the Parliament thinks fit," to specify such "terms and conditions" for financial grants in terms that involve powers otherwise "reserved" to the States. The High Court has also sanctioned application by the Commonwealth of its constitutional "external affairs" power even where the terms of international treaties encompass domestic policy areas otherwise regarded as under State jurisdiction.

The intergovernmental balance is to a very significant degree affected by political as well as by legal-constitutional factors. Politically, the States are much stronger than their weakened constitutional status would suggest. A perception that a Commonwealth government is attempting to impose its will on an unwilling State tends to be unpopular with voters, and this acts politically as a deterrence to Commonwealth politicians and as a potential bargaining resource to State politicians.

The federal system coexists with parliamentary institutions. The British Westminster parliamentary model was adopted in the 19th-century colonies and has persisted after their redesignation in the 20th century as States. The melding at the national level of parliamentarism with federalism required use of North American as well as British precedents and nomenclature. The national legislature (the Parliament) consists of two chambers: a House of Representatives in which the majority party (following Westminster conventions) forms the government, and a Senate in which there is (following the Washington model) an equal allocation of seats to each State.

Executive

The Australian head of state is technically the British monarch, whose powers are formally vested in a governor-general appointed by the monarch on the advice of the Australian government and who is thus, in practice, a government appointee. It is the firm convention of the parliamentary system that this head of state should act only on the advice of the government and, in particular, of the prime minister.

The prime minister is, by convention, the leader of the majority party or coalition in the House of Representatives. Other ministers are drawn from either house of Parliament, with most coming from the House of Representatives. The maximum number of ministers is fixed by legislation. As of late 1998, the coalition government under Prime Minister John Howard featured the maximum number (30) currently permitted. It has become a bipartisan convention that the prime minister and most senior ministers (numbering 16 in the current Howard government) form the Cabinet, with the remainder in the "outer ministry" only participating in Cabinet discussions when necessary to deal with matters specific to their portfolios.

The Cabinet, chaired by the prime minister, is the central engine room of government. It determines the government's strategic, policy, and legislative program, within the political constraints imposed by broad party expectations, by any necessary deals with the Senate, by advice received from public-service officials, and by public opinion as shaped and reflected in the mass media.

The major parties vary in how they, in government, choose their ministers. In the Liberal Party and the National Party, the party leader, elected by a meeting of parliamentary members of the party, is empowered to nominate his or her ministerial team. With the Liberal and National Parties normally allied in a formal coalition, the relative allocation of portfolios between them is determined by negotiation and is normally reasonably proportionate to their relative parliamentary strengths. In the Labor Party, the ministry is determined in a ballot of all parliamentary caucus members, though the party leader (especially if the party is in government) can exercise a considerable personal influence on the outcome of this ballot.

Ministers are nearly always given policy and management responsibility for a particular portfolio of departments and agencies within the Commonwealth bureaucracy, though in some cases "senior" and "junior" ministers share responsibility for the same portfolio.

Departments and agencies are staffed by a nonpartisan public service. The 1980s and 1990s have been notable for the introduction of significant structural and managerialist reforms intended to improve the effectiveness, efficiency, and accountability of the public-sector bureaucracy.

Some departments, because of their key coordinating role and traditional prestige, are regarded as more significant. The Department of Prime Minister and Cabinet is centrally involved in policy coordination through its advice to the prime minister and its administrative support for Cabinet. The Treasury is responsible for the formulation of economic policy and advice. The Department of Finance oversees the expenditure of all other departments and coordinates the construction of the annual budget.

There are some important statutory authorities that formally operate outside the public-service structure, with varying degrees of financial and policy independence. Among the more significant are Australia Post (which runs the postal service), Telstra (the telecommunications authority whose former monopoly has been diluted and which the Howard government has partially privatized), and the Australian Broadcasting Commission (which provides a national public television and radio service in competition with private networks).

Legislature

The House of Representatives is the forum that, by convention of Westminster origins, determines the composition of the elected government. Under the constitution, the House of Representatives must have "as nearly as practicable" double the number of members as the Senate, and each of the six States must have at least five members. Apart from the latter provision, which gives Tasmania an overrepresentation, single-member electoral districts are allocated between States and Territories as nearly as possible in proportion to population.

Members of the House of Representatives are elected for terms that may, at a maximum, extend to three years and three months. An election may be held sooner if the government loses its parliamentary majority and no alternative party or coalition can build an alternative majority or, more commonly, if the government perceives some electoral advantage in going to the polls early.

Table 1 displays the results of the October 1998 elections for the House of Representatives, showing the distribution of seats in each State and Territory and the number won by each political party. In this election, the coalition government (comprising the Liberal Party and the National Party), which had been elected to office in March 1996 after defeating the incumbent Labor Party government, was returned to office. John Howard, the Liberal Party leader, thus continued in his position as prime minister while Tim Fischer, leader of the National Party, continued as deputy prime minister.

Each State has 12 senators, elected at large for six-year terms, half of them retiring every three years. Senate elections are customarily arranged to coincide with House of Representatives elections, but this is not always possible when the House is dissolved early. Even when the election dates coincide, the terms of office may not. For example, the senators elected at the general election in October 1998 take office at the beginning of July 1999, leaving the Senate with something of a "lame duck"

TABLE 1
Results of the 1998 House of Representatives Election

Liberal State/Territory	Distribution of Seats by Party				
	National Party	Labor Party	Party	Independent	Total
New South Wales	18	9	22	1	50
Victoria	16	2	19	—	37
Queensland	14	5	8	—	27
Western Australia	7	—	7	—	14
South Australia	9	—	3	—	12
Tasmania	—	—	5	—	5
Australian Capital Territory	—	—	2	—	2
Northern Territory	—	—	1	—	1
Total	64	16	67	1	148

character in the meantime. There have been several attempts to tidy up this matter through a constitutional amendment equating a Senatorial term precisely with two House terms, but the necessary referenda have been defeated. Since 1975, the two Territories have each had two senators who, unlike their Senatorial colleagues, must all seek reelection with every House of Representatives election.

Although the Senate generally reviews legislation originating in the House of Representatives, the constitution provides that the two houses "shall have equal power" except in a few specific instances; the Senate, for example, cannot originate money bills. For a bill to become law, it must be passed in identical terms by both Houses. There are cumbersome mechanisms provided in the case of a prolonged disagreement. Within certain time constraints, if the Senate twice fails to pass a bill and if the government is prepared to fight an election on the issue, there can be a so-called double dissolution. This means that the entire membership of both houses must face simultaneous reelection. If there is still a deadlock after a double-dissolution election, there can be a joint sitting of both houses (in which senators are outnumbered two to one) to consider the disputed bill(s). Double dissolutions have occurred six times, most recently in 1987. The only joint sitting took place after the 1974 double dissolution

TABLE 2
Results of the 1998 Senate Election

State/Territory	Distribution of Senators by Party					
	Liberal Party	National Party	Labor Party	Australian Democrats	Others	Total
New South Wales	2	—	3	1	—	6
Victoria	2	1	3	—	—	6
Queensland	2	—	2	1	1[b]	6
Western Australia	3	—	2	1	—	6
South Australia	3	—	2	1	—	6
Tasmania	2	—	3	—	1[c]	6
Australian Capital Territory	1	—	1	—	—	2
Northern Territory	—	1[a]	1	—	—	2
Total	15	2	17	4	2	40

[a] Country-Liberal Party.

[b] One Nation party

[c] Independent senator.

opposition or minor-party amendments that do not significantly subvert the essence of its proposed legislation.

A sensitive aspect of government-Senate relations concerns the Senate's power with respect to the government's budget, without whose legislative authorization a government cannot operate. Under the constitution, the Senate is prohibited from amending bills dealing with taxation or financial appropriations, though it is assumed that it can defeat such bills and thereby effectively pressure the House of Representatives to make amendments.

Until 1975, the Senate had never voted to defeat a government's budgetary legislation. In that year, however, the Liberal-National opposition in control of the Senate attempted to force what it perceived as an unpopular Labor government to resign and contest a new election. It therefore did not allow the Senate to pass the budget legislation. The government, however, refused to resign, citing the Westminster convention that a government that retains the confidence of the House of Representatives stays in office. A stalemate—a "constitutional crisis"—developed.

The most appropriate solution would probably have been a political one, with the stalemate persisting until public funds started to run out and the pressure of the crisis or public opinion or perceived political advantage produced a compromise on one or both sides. Instead, the situation was "resolved," dramatically and controversially, by the unprecedented intervention of the head of state. The governor-general, contrary to the tradition that he act only on the advice of ministers but consistent with a literal reading of the constitution, dismissed Prime Minister Whitlam and his Labor government. He installed the leader of the opposition as prime minister of a caretaker government, even though this new government had only minority support in the House of Representatives, and called a double-dissolution election. This election endorsed the new government with an overwhelming majority in both houses.

Debate still continues over the propriety of various actions in the constitutional crisis, particularly those of the governor-general. Another "constitutional crisis" resulting from a threat to the government's budget is unlikely in the foreseeable future because of a pervasive sentiment that the events of 1975 should be avoided if possible.

Judiciary

The High Court exercises judicial review over matters relating to the constitution as well as being the final court of appeal within the Australian system of justice. In many respects, the High Court was modeled on the United States Supreme Court and exercises a similar capacity to invalidate legislation it has deemed unconstitutional. The other courts created at the national level include the Family Court (established in 1975 to handle matrimonial, divorce, and associated custody and prop-

erty matters), the Federal Court (established in 1976 with responsibility for a range of matters such as bankruptcy and administrative appeals), and the Industrial Relations Court (established in its current form in 1993 to exercise judicial power over industrial relations matters). Beyond these specialized courts, no further system of national-level courts has been established. Instead, the court systems of the States have been vested with jurisdiction over Commonwealth law.

High Court interpretations have been a factor in the increasing prominence of the Commonwealth government. It is common to demarcate four phases in the history of the Court, two of them (1900–1920, 1942–71) being periods in which a Court majority exercised restraint on Commonwealth powers and the other two (1920–42, 1971 to the 1990s) revealing a Court majority more inclined to loosen those restraints. The character of the Court in the late 1990s is unclear, following several retirements and new appointments.

The High Court's varying interpretations of Section 92 of the constitution illustrate the political impact of its decisions. Section 92 declares that "trade, commerce and intercourse among the States . . . shall be absolutely free" and was presumably intended to prevent the reemergence of barriers to inter-State trade such as the tariffs that had existed during the colonial period. High Court interpretations in the first half of the century gradually made Section 92 a significant restraint on any form of economic regulation, culminating in 1945 and 1948 in the annulment of attempts by the Chifley Labor government to nationalize the private airlines and the private banks. Such a broad-brushed interpretation of Section 92 was overturned, however, by a later High Court in 1988 so that the original apparent intent of the section—to create an Australian "common market"—now seems to prevail.

In recent times, the Court, besides revising its approach to Section 92, has also been innovative in other important areas. A Court majority in the early 1990s "discovered" several hitherto-unrecognized citizen rights guaranteed under a constitution that, in formal terms, features (in contrast to the U.S. Constitution) only a few explicit rights-type provisions. For example, the Court ruled in 1992 (in overturning legislation that attempted to prohibit, on cost and equity grounds, paid political advertising in the electronic media) that the constitution guaranteed freedom of speech in relation to political matters. The Court has also overturned long-standing common-law interpretations to rule that some Aboriginal Australians hold, under certain conditions, "native title" to land hitherto thought to have been totally usurped by the British crown at the time of colonization. The Keating Labor government took advantage of this ruling (known as the *Mabo* decision) to institute a formal procedure for the resolution of "native title" claims. A later High Court ruling (in the *Wik* case) that "native title" could coexist with pastoral leases presented the Howard coalition with a difficult political problem, requiring it to find some legislative resolution that appeased its supporters in the pastoral and related rural industries without negating the native-title rights the Court had discovered. The government legislation on this matter finally passed through the Parliament, after tortuous Senate negotiations, in July 1998.

Through its judicial review of legislation and role as ultimate arbiter on legal cases brought before it, the High Court is a significant political actor. The justices of the High Court—the chief justice and six associate justices—are directly appointed by the government of the day. Appointed justices occasionally have had party and/or parliamentary associations (both coalition and Labor governments having at various times appointed their own former attorneys general), and the appointment process probably precludes potential appointees regarded as antithetical to government perceptions of the Court's role. However, the notion of judicial independence also remains as a strong value, and most appointees have had extensive experience in lower courts or in a State court system. Under a 1977 constitutional amendment, all justices must retire at the age of 70. Otherwise, they can be removed only by a resolution of both Houses of Parliament on the grounds of "proved misbehaviour or incapacity," something which has never happened.

Regional and Local Government

In terms of providing direct public services to citizens, the States are a very prominent level of government. State-level identification remains fairly strong among Australians, reinforced by a social geography that sees 60% of the population residing in five major metropolitan areas that also happen to be the seats of State governments and by the focus of the State-based mass media (though national networking is weakening this factor).

Services that in many Western countries would be provided by national or local authorities are in Australia firmly entrenched at the State level. State governments provide and manage public school systems, public hospitals, personal welfare services, police services, regional economic development, urban planning, public housing, regulation of industry and labor, highways, ports, various agricultural services, subsidies to industrial development, electricity and gas networks (in most States), and other property services. While States differ a little in the style, quality, and range of public services, standards and policy styles are fairly uniform by comparison with other federations. The modesty of the inter-State variation is assisted by an equalization component in the formula by which untied Commonwealth grants are distributed to the States and by regular national meetings of ministers responsible for specific portfolios.

It is common at any particular time for different States to be governed by different political parties, with inter-State variation in party fortunes partly explained by moderate social and demographic differences between States and partly by particular State-level histories and political circumstances. As of late 1998, for example, the Liberal Party forms the dominant partner in the national coalition government and is also involved in governing three States. Meanwhile, the Labor Party, in opposition at the national level, also governs in three States.

TABLE 4
State Parliaments: Lower House

State (Year of Most Recent Election)	Distribution of Parliamentary Seats by Party				Governing Party or Coalition
	Liberal Party	National Party	Labor Party	Other	
New South Wales (1995)	29	16	51	3	Labor
Victoria (1996)	49	9	29	1	Liberal/National
Queensland (1998)	9	23	44	13[a]	Labor[b]
Western Australia (1996)	29	6	19	3	Liberal/National
South Australia (1997)	23	1	21	2	Liberal[b]
Tasmania (1998)	10	—	14	1	Labor
Australian Capital Territory(1998)	7	—	6	4	Liberal[b]
Northern Territory (1997)	—	18[c]	7	—	Country-Liberal

[a] 11 One Nation party, 2 independent.

[b] Minority government.

[c] Country-Liberal Party.

Each State has its own constitution, most dating from the mid-19th century, and each State operates under a parliamentary system, with parliaments normally having a maximum three-year or four-year term in office. In five of the States, the parliament is bicameral, with the composition of the government being determined in the lower house. The other State, Queensland, abolished its upper house in 1922. Both Territories are unicameral.

Table 4 reports the parliamentary situation as of late 1998 in the lower houses in the six States and two Territories. In some cases, the numbers differ slightly, due to later by-elections, from the result obtained at the most recent general election.

Much of what has been noted above, with respect to the Commonwealth level, about the dominance of the executive, the importance of the bureaucracy, the weakness of the lower house of Parliament, and the possible significance of the upper house (depending on party balance) applies also to the States. The premier (the State-level equivalent of the prime minister) and the cabinet are the most visible focus of government, with the governor as the formal representative of the monarch.

The two Territories, which were administered directly by the Commonwealth for most of their history, have over the past few decades been granted a large degree of self-government by the Commonwealth to the point where they now have (with a few interesting exceptions) virtually the same effective powers as States. However, the degree of autonomy was tested in 1997 when controversial legislation passed by the Northern Territory legislature that had permitted voluntary euthanasia was overturned by a bipartisan majority in both houses of the Commonwealth Parliament. The Northern Territory government has for many years been controlled by the Territory's unique Country Liberal Party, whose campaign to win full Statehood for the Territory suffered a setback when narrowly defeated in an indicative Territory referendum in October 1998. In the Australian Capital Territory, where self-government is complicated by the colocation of the central organs of the Commonwealth government and where a proportional representation system produces a diverse and sometimes strange membership in the Territory assembly, a minority Liberal Party administration is currently in office with the support of independent members of the assembly.

Except for some sparsely populated areas that remain unincorporated, Australia is divided into a patchwork of local government jurisdictions. These local governments possess many of the superficial characteristics of sovereign political systems, with an elected legislature (the council) whose members then elect one of their number as mayor (though in some jurisdictions the mayor is elected directly by the voters). Local government as a whole, however, only accounts for about 5% of total public-sector expenditure and is of less significance than in most other Western democracies. Local authorities principally are involved with property services—garbage, nonarterial roads, parking, street lighting, sanitation, development control, and so on—though in some States there is also involvement in water, sewage, energy reticulation, recreation facilities, and some welfare services.

A long history of property qualifications in most States for the local voting franchise has given way over the past few decades to full adult franchise, usually with provision for nonresident ratepayers. Nonpartisanship is the norm in local elections in South Australia, Western Australia, and Tasmania, and party involvement is not a common feature in the other States, though there are no legal prohibitions on party involvement. The Labor Party contests inner-city and industrial municipalities in Sydney and Melbourne and has also for long periods governed the City of Brisbane, which is Australia's only consolidated metropolitan local authority.

THE ELECTORAL SYSTEM

Australians directly elect representatives to two houses of Parliament at the Commonwealth level, to two at the State/Territory level (except for unicameral Queensland and the two Territories), and to their local council. Different electoral systems may be in operation for each arena.

There has been a long history of universal adult suffrage, of which Australian colonies were 19th-century pioneers (though relatively inclusive property qualifications applied until the 1970s in some State upper houses and until the 1980s for some local government systems). The Australian colonies also pioneered such devices as the preprinted secret ballot, still sometimes termed "the Australian ballot" in American political science textbooks. For voting purposes, adulthood is now defined as beginning at the age of 18 years. Except for most (though not all) local council elections, registration and voting are compulsory. Noncompliance without sufficient reason (such as illness) attracts a small fine. Turnouts of above 95% of eligible voters at Commonwealth and State elections are common.

Electoral boundaries generally are drawn up by independent commissioners, so that blatant gerrymandering is virtually unknown. Malapportionment, however, in the sense of an overrepresentation of rural voters, used to be quite common. Reforms over the past several decades now mean that only in Western Australia is there still an explicit system favoring rural representation over urban representation. In the Commonwealth House of Representatives, rural overrepresentation was completely eliminated in 1984.

The most common electoral system—used for elections for the House of Representatives and for all State lower houses except in Tasmania—is based on preferential voting and single-member districts. Under preferential voting, voters rank candidates on the ballot in numerical order. If no candidate wins an absolute majority of first-preference votes, then the lowest-scoring candidate is eliminated and his or her votes are redistributed at their full value according to the second preference indicated on those ballot papers. The process of elimination and redistribution continues until a candidate wins by acquiring an absolute majority of votes. The necessity for voters to write down a ranked preference for all candidates means that parties distribute "how to vote" instruction cards with a recommended order of preference.

Although only major parties can usually hope to win a seat, the single-member preferential system allows some role for minor parties. In exchange for recommending to their supporters a particular ranking of major party candidates, minor parties sometimes hope to win policy concessions from major parties. The 1990 national election provides a good example. The Labor Party was returned to government despite winning just over 39% of all first-preference votes. This was sufficient to account for a majority of seats largely because the preference distribution from the unusually large number of first-preference votes for minor party candidates (especially those espousing environmental causes) strongly tended to favor Labor. Labor had attempted (successfully, as it turned out) to ensure such a flow of preferences by making a number of explicit environmental policy concessions.

The preferential system allows allied parties to endorse separate candidates for the same district without necessarily harming the alliance. For example, both the Liberal Party and the National Party may offer candidates for the same district. These candidates "exchange preferences," i.e., each candidate recommends that his or her supporters give their second preference to the other candidate. This helps the higher vote winner of the two effectively to benefit from their combined vote if neither of them wins an absolute majority of first preferences.

Though a similar preferential method of voting is employed, the election system for the Australian Senate is more complicated because 6 members (12 in a double dissolution) are elected at large from each State. Candidates are elected if they receive a quota of votes calculated as one-seventh (one-thirteenth in a double dissolution) plus one of the total valid votes. Candidates who win more than the requisite quota have "surplus" votes distributed to other candidates at their full value according to the second or subsequent preferences recorded by the voter. In this way, and with the progressive elimination if necessary of the lowest-scoring candidates and the distribution of their votes to other candidates according to the voters' recorded preferences, the requisite number of winning candidates is identified. Because candidates are listed on the ballot paper in party groupings and because most voters follow party recommendations in recording preferences (a practice now institutionalized by the introduction of an option for voters simply to indicate an endorsement of a particular party's registered preference ordering), the effect is very similar in practice to proportional representation. The system, however, is best described as multimember preferential.

Casual vacancies, caused by the death or resignation of an elected member during a term, are handled differently for each Commonwealth house. In the House of Representatives, a by-election is conducted for the vacated seat. In the Senate, a replacement senator is chosen at a joint sitting of the relevant State houses of parliament. The requirement under a 1977 amendment to the constitution that the replacement senator be from the same party prevents any alteration to the party balance in the Senate. This requirement is the constitutional entrenchment of a previous convention to the same effect, a convention which was nonetheless broken twice in 1975 by non-Labor State governments intent on curtailing the then national Labor government and creating the basis for the "constitutional crisis" that followed.

THE PARTY SYSTEM

Origins

Australia waited some 40 years after the expansion of the franchise in the 1850s for its first modern parties. The emergence and almost immediate success of the Australian Labor Party (ALP) in the 1890s served to solidify conservative interests. By the time of federation in 1901, the ALP was opposed by two relatively coherent groups, the Free Traders and the Protectionists, which fused in 1910 to form the Liberal Party. Thereafter, the major party on the right underwent several changes in structure and name, absorbing various breakaways from the ALP, until in 1945 the modern Liberal Party was established. The Liberal Party generally operates in coalition with the rural-based National Party. No other parties have won seats in the House of Representatives since the Second World War, though there have been several independent members including 1 out of the 148 elected to the House in 1998. In the Senate, multimember elections facilitate minor-party representation.

Legal Status

Political parties are the key organizing devices that structure Australian political life and the character of elected governments. A party affiliation is not a legal requirement for becoming a candidate for Parliament—any person paying a nominal fee, which is refundable if he or she wins a specified proportion of the vote, is placed on the ballot—but usually only party candidates have viable prospects of success, and certainly the formation of governments seems inconceivable except through parties.

In 1977, the constitution, which had hitherto not mentioned parties, was amended as already noted to provide that casual Senate vacancies should be filled by a member of the "same political party," but this provision fails to define what a party is. More recently, public financing of party election expenses has been introduced for national and some State elections, and this has led to parties being officially registered and distinctively recognized in law. Otherwise, however, parties are simply voluntary associations with a legal status and obligations similar to those of any other voluntary associations. Thus their internal rules and procedures are largely self-regulated.

Party Organization

The major parties are primarily federal or confederal in nature, and most organizational activity takes place within State-level branches. This has important ramifications for national politics, for it means that national politicians have their political origins and prime organizational bases within State or local branches.

Within the States, the basic unit is the local suburban or district branch to which fee-paying members belong. Delegates from local branches meet, typically annually, in State conferences, at which platforms for the State parties are debated. Delegates from the States then attend periodic national conferences responsible for national party platforms. The extent to which national-level party organizations can or should intervene in the affairs of a State branch is a matter of occasional debate and controversy, with such interventions becoming more frequent when national election prospects appear to justify it.

The major parties differ in the formal status accorded to parliamentary representatives vis-à-vis the party organization, though in practice the difference is not as acute as formal status suggests. While the Liberal Party formally affirms the autonomy of its parliamentary representatives, there is occasional pressure to the contrary from the party organization. In the Labor Party, the policies and platform endorsed by the organization are formally supreme and binding on parliamentary representatives; in practice, elected politicians and governments are accorded substantial autonomy.

Election Campaigns

Compulsory voting means that election campaigns in Australia differ slightly from those in most other Western democracies. Parties need not be concerned with "getting out the vote"; what matters is influencing the actual vote itself.

Increasingly, election campaigns are centered on the media image of the parties and particularly of the party leaders. The major parties direct a large proportion of their campaign expenditure into media advertising, especially on television, and have begun to develop sophisticated marketing techniques to target specific subgroups through direct mailing or niche advertising.

Local campaigning by candidates in their districts is usually of less significance than the national campaign and judgments made by voters about the performance of political parties in government and the regional economy in their own particular State. Some politicians may attract a personal following worth a few percentage points that may be crucial in a close contest; recently a few disendorsed members of Parliament have managed to be reelected in opposition to the newly endorsed candidate from their own former party. Generally, however, variations in electoral support can be explained by national or State factors rather than local ones. Most House of Representatives seats are reasonably safe for one or another of the major parties: only about 25% of seats could conceivably change hands in any one election, and intensive campaigning by the parties, involving visits by national leaders and targeted advertising in the local media, is largely restricted to these marginal seats.

Voters

Table 5 provides an indication of patterns of party support since the Second World War in national House of Representatives elections. The relative stability of the basic two-party system, which pitches Labor against a Liberal-National coalition, is quite apparent. While a majority of voters consistently vote for the same party, there are enough crossovers between elections to ensure a very competitive party system even though the net nationwide swing from election to election is rarely more than about 5%. The 1990 election was notable for the greater support given to minor parties and independents, and the advent of the new One Nation party saw an even greater shift away from the traditional parties in 1998.

Political science research suggests that about 85% of adult Australians identify with a political party and that this identification is a reasonably accurate, though certainly not perfect, predictor of voting support. In the past, the best predictor of party identification was occupational class, with blue-collar voters tending to support the Labor Party and those with a white-collar background tending to support the Liberal Party. However, this relationship is weakening in what is, for most people, a socially mobile, suburban, relatively affluent, and increasingly multicultural society. For example, the Labor Party has increased its support base among middle-class professionals, particularly those with occupational links to the public sector.

TABLE 5
Party Voting for the House of Representatives: 1946–98

	% of First-Preference Vote by Party						
Year	Liberal Party	National Party	Labor Party	Australian Democrats	One Nation	Other	Election Winner
1946	33	11	50	—	—	6	Labor
1949	39	11	46	—	—	4	Lib/Nat
1951	41	10	48	—	—	2	Lib/Nat
1954	39	9	50	—	—	3	Lib/Nat
1955	40	8	45	—	—	8	Lib/Nat
1958	37	9	43	—	—	11	Lib/Nat
1961	34	9	48	—	—	10	Lib/Nat
1963	37	9	46	—	—	9	Lib/Nat
1966	40	10	40	—	—	10	Lib/Nat
1969	35	9	47	—	—	10	Lib/Nat
1972	32	9	50	—	—	9	Labor
1974	35	11	49	—	—	5	Labor
1975	42	11	43	—	—	4	Lib/Nat
1977	38	10	40	9	—	3	Lib/Nat
1980	37	9	45	7	—	2	Lib/Nat
1983	34	9	49	5	—	2	Labor
1984	34	11	48	5	—	2	Labor
1987	34	12	46	6	—	2	Labor
1990	35	8	39	11	—	6	Labor
1993	37	7	45	4	—	7	Labor
1996	39	8	39	7	—	7	Lib/Nat[a]
1998	34	5	40	5	8	8	Lib/Nat[a]

[a] Lib/Nat = Liberal Party/National Party coalition.

LIBERAL PARTY

History

The Liberal Party was founded in 1944, but it is the fourth in a continuous succession of anti-Labor parties. Its 1944 materialization brought together the non-Labor members of Parliament, under the leadership of Robert Menzies, and fashioned a mass organization to sustain these parliamentarians. The success of the product was manifested in an unbroken 23 years in office that the Liberal Party enjoyed in coalition with the National Party (then known as the Country Party) from 1949 until 1972, the first 17 of these years with Menzies as prime minister.

Some leadership instability developed after Menzies' retirement, and the coalition lost office in 1972. It was returned to government under the leadership of Malcolm Fraser in 1975, was reelected in 1977 and 1980, and was then defeated, still under Fraser, in 1983. The Liberal Party then had to endure a prolonged unaccustomed and uncomfortable opposition role, losing another four suc-cessive national elections under various leaders until led to victory by John Howard in the election of March 1996 and reelection in October 1998. The party has been quite successful in the 1990s at the State level.

Organization, Membership, and Financing

The Liberal Party has managed to graft a cadrelike parliamentary party onto a mass-party base. This has allowed a relatively autonomous parliamentary leadership largely to develop its own policies and strategies while receiving organizational support for election campaigns.

The Liberal Party has around 70,000 members, disproportionately middle-class and Protestant. In comparison with their long-standing minority position within the ALP, women have long constituted about half of the Liberal Party membership. An important function of the membership is to provide financial and election assistance, with local branches engaging in various fund-raising social activities. The Liberal Party also benefits from substantial business donations.

Far more than for the ALP, the members of Parliament are central to the Liberal Party ethos. The party organization is strongly federalist, with each State division enjoying a large measure of autonomy. Some variation exists in organizational structure, but generally local branches within the States, combined where necessary to cover each parliamentary electorate, have a primary role in selecting candidates and running local election campaigns. At the State level, central councils representing local branches, members of Parliament, women's organizations (a feature of the party), and Young Liberal Associations consider matters of general party business and policy, though their decisions characteristically do not bind the members of Parliament.

National business and policy are considered by the Liberal Party federal council, which has equal representation from each State (including delegates from the women's and young Liberal organizations), and by the federal executive. Sometimes, such extraparliamentary bodies attempt to influence the members of Parliament, but generally the parliamentary party sustains its autonomy.

Among the parliamentary members, the elected leader assumes great significance. He or she chooses members of a Cabinet or Shadow Cabinet, in contrast to the ALP, where those positions are elective. In theory, Liberal Party members are free to vote as they choose in Parliament, but apart from some rare cases of nonconformity (usually in the Senate), party discipline is in practice generally as firm as in the ALP.

Though factionalism is far less entrenched in the Liberal Party than in the ALP, there are groupings among parliamentary members based loosely on differences in policy or strategic orientation. These divisions sometimes manifest themselves in support for rival leadership contenders. In the 1980s, the main line of policy division was between the market-oriented "dries" and the more pragmatic and socially oriented "wets." There has been something of a reconfiguration in the 1990s, partly because the "dries" seemed to have triumphed in intellectual and policy terms and partly because leading "wet" figures of the 1980s are no longer in Parliament. The current situation may be better expressed as a spectrum stretching from "moderates" who are more pragmatically oriented toward an electorally successful formula to "hard-liners" with a paramount interest in pursuing market-oriented principles. A spectrum based on orientation toward economic policy, however, would not necessarily be consistent with a spectrum based on social policy: some market "ideologues" are libertarian with respect to social policies, while others are explicitly conservative.

The national headquarters are located at Blackall and Macquarie Streets, Barton, Australian Capital Territory.

Policy

As the discussion of the internal spectrum of opinion suggests, the Liberal Party features a mixture of classical liberalism, social liberalism, conservatism, and pragmatism. Its parliamentary members range from enthusiastic free-market advocates to supporters of a relatively generous welfare state, from social libertarians to conservative defenders of the traditional family, from moderate protectionists to evangelical free traders.

A brief listing of the important common elements of the Liberal Party platform would begin with individualism. There is a pervasive attachment to the sanctity and rights of individuals, who are regarded as responsive to incentives, such as profits, which lead to greater effort and productivity. Although the party in the past promoted a significant degree of public intervention and regulation, its long-standing strong support for private enterprise has become even more pronounced over the past decade. Whereas nearly all ALP members and politicians would, at least in principle, regard significant social and economic inequality as a matter for prima facie concern, Liberals would tend to accept some inequality as inevitable and perhaps socially necessary. Stability and order are also recurring themes. Liberal Party foreign policy was strongly anticommunist during the cold war period and strongly in favor of traditional alliances, such as with the United States.

In 1992, facing an electorally successful Labor government that had adopted a number of market-oriented policies, the Liberal Party constructed a detailed and more radical promarket policy package entitled "*Fightback!*" The electoral defeat of 1993, widely attributed to the perceived radicalism of "*Fightback!*," led to a more low-key approach to the successful 1996 election. The Howard government in office has vigorously pursued a number of proposals anticipated in the "*Fightback!*" agenda, including industrial relations reform, an attempt to weaken the influence of organized labor on the waterfront, and a proposal for a new broad-based Goods and Services Tax. The government claims that its reelection in October 1998 gives it a popular mandate for further progress in such matters, especially with respect to reforming the tax system.

Voting Support

Electoral support for the Liberals has been socially more widespread than for the ALP, though it is strongest among those with a professional or managerial (about 65%) or lower-white-collar background (about 55%) than among blue-collar occupations (about 40%). The safest Liberal seats are in more affluent residential suburbs. Women, members of Eastern European ethnic groups, and older-age cohorts tend to support the party in disproportionate numbers. Liberal members of Parliament are overwhelmingly from a professional, managerial, or business background.

Leadership

The parliamentary leader holds the preeminent party position. Current prominent figures include the following:

- **John Howard** (born 1939), from New South Wales, is the prime minister. Howard is an experienced and astute politician who served as treasurer in the Fraser coalition government in the late 1980s and early 1990s and was an electorally unsuccessful leader of the opposition at the 1987 election. Howard's return to the leadership in the mid-1990s was widely interpreted as indicating a dearth of alternative leadership talent in the Liberal Party, but this move justified itself with the party's triumph in the 1996 and 1998 elections. Identified as having a strongly promarket orientation that is proving to be tempered by pragmatism in government, Howard is more socially conservative than many of his parliamentary colleagues.
- **Peter Costello** (born 1957), the national deputy leader of the Liberal Party and the treasurer within John Howard's Cabinet, comes from Victoria. Still relatively young, Costello has moderated his initial profile as a hard-line right-wing ideologue but still projects a blunt and aggressive political style. He would be Howard's most likely successor.
- **Jeff Kennett** (born 1948) is the premier of the State of Victoria. Kennett is also noted for an aggressive political style and has successfully made a public virtue out of austere policy commitments (such as downsizing of the public sector, the closure of public schools with small enrollments, and opposition to trade union demands), whose necessity he has blamed on the alleged excesses of the previous Labor government in Victoria. Kennett is also an unashamed practitioner of competitive federalism and promoter of business investment in Victoria.

Prospects

In the 1950s and 1960s, the Liberal Party was Australia's dominant governing party. After some rotation in office in the 1970s, the Labor Party usurped that position in the 1983–96 period, leading to some uncertainty within the Liberal Party about its strategic and policy orientation. The national electoral victories of March 1996 and October 1998 and the more consistent successes at the State level suggest that the party can approach the next century with considerable confidence.

AUSTRALIAN LABOR PARTY (ALP)

History

The Australian Labor Party emerged in the early 1890s when the failure of maritime and shearers' strikes persuaded trade unions to seek parliamentary representation. By 1899, a minority Labor government—the first Labor government in the world—held office in the Queensland colony, albeit for only five days before being defeated in Parliament. The ALP held the balance of power in the first Commonwealth Parliament from 1901, formed a minority national government for four months in 1904, and then won clear control of both houses in 1910. Since those early decades, the ALP's history has been varied and volatile. At the national level, its relatively long recent period in office from 1983 until 1996 contrasts with an earlier history when it enjoyed only a few short periods in office, primarily because of three devastating internal splits.

The first split came in 1916 over opposition within the party (particularly among Irish Catholic elements) to military conscription for service in Europe in the world war. This opposition caused Labor's prime minister (W. M. Hughes) to leave the party with many of his ministerial and parliamentary colleagues. These defectors joined the then opposition to form a new National Party, which kept the ALP out of office until 1929. The Labor government that acceded in that year ruptured over the appropriate policy response to the Depression, losing office in 1932. Again, some ALP parliamentarians formed a new anti-Labor grouping (the United Australia Party) in combination with the conservatives. After another decade in the wilderness, the ALP in the 1941–49 period enjoyed a sustained period of national government under Prime Ministers Curtin and Chifley, producing innovative policies in social welfare, national development, economic management, public enterprise, and immigration. The third major fissure took place from 1955 to 1957 when a strongly anticommunist and predominantly Catholic group broke away to form the Democratic Labor Party, which again helped to keep the ALP in opposition for many years. In the 1972–75 period, Labor finally assumed national office again, under Prime Minister Gough Whitlam, for another brief period of government terminating with the "constitutional crisis." Its subsequent spell in opposition this time was comparatively brief, and Labor won back control of the national government in 1983 and was reelected three times under Prime Minister Bob Hawke and once under his successor, Paul Keating, until the Keating government lost office in the 1996 election.

This national history is interwoven with varied experiences in the States, where generally the ALP has enjoyed greater success. As of late 1998, Labor governs in three States (New South Wales, Queensland, and Tasmania) but remains electorally less popular in the other three States (Victoria, South Australia, and Western Australia) where it has been tainted by allegations of financial mismanagement in the 1980s. Labor's 33 years in national government this century contrast with 55 years in Tasmania, 51 years in New South Wales, 47 years in Queensland, 45 years in Western Australia, and 33 years in South Australia. Victoria (19 years) has been Labor's conspicuous problem State, even allowing for the party's 10-year stretch in government there from 1982 to 1992.

Organization, Membership, and Financing

The ALP is a federal party with its historical origins in the trade unions. Both aspects are essential for understanding its organization.

The key organizational components of the ALP are the State branches. The national components are largely umbrella bodies made up of delegates from the States, and most of the real life of the party remains at the State level. The trade union connection manifests itself in the formal affiliation of unions with the party in the States. Thus there is a basic dualism in party membership, with about 50,000 dues-paying voluntary members of local branches and well over 1 million members of trade unions affiliated with the party. Branch members are typically from a more middle-class background than are the unionists passively affiliated through their union. The proportion of women members, which used to be quite low, has risen substantially in the past decade and now averages around 40%.

State conferences, usually annual, are the supreme policymaking bodies in each State, with 60% of voting power typically wielded by union delegates and 40% by delegates from local branches. State branches differ in their procedures for selecting parliamentary candidates: in some States such selection is conducted at State conferences, while in others there are selection panels consisting of conference delegates and local members or, as in New South Wales, a plebiscite of local members.

The annual national conference and the more regular national executive meetings accord representation to the State branches roughly in proportion to population. The national bodies are the supreme organs of the party, able in principle to impose their authority on State branches. In recent decades, the State branches in Victoria, Queensland, and Tasmania, regarded at the time as electoral liabilities, have been forcibly reconstructed. Mostly, however, the national bodies are reluctant to intervene. There is a small national secretariat that is most conspicuous in organizing national election campaign strategies, but the party's most visible national presence is its representation in the national Parliament.

In the ethos and formal rules of the ALP, parliamentarians are subordinate to the organization, and all party candidates are pledged to uphold the party platform. In practice, the parliamentary caucus and especially a Labor government enjoy a greater degree of policy and strategic autonomy than this formal pledge might suggest. Potential conflict between politicians and the organization is also attenuated by the influence of some members of Parliament in the party organization and, conversely, by the granting of endorsement for parliamentary seats to influential figures in the organization.

Some awkward conflicts have occurred, most recently with the Hawke and Keating governments in the 1980s and 1990s taking some positions (such as on privatization of public enterprises) that appeared to be in tension with official party policy and with the sentiments of many local branch members. But it is revealing that the party organization now typically defers to a Labor government's expressed position in such cases.

The ALP cannot be understood only in terms of its formal organizational structure. Semiformalized "factions" have become increasingly prominent at the national level, both within the parliamentary caucus and in national organizational bodies, and now provide the strongest trans-State linkages within the party. These factions represent loose alliances based on ideological affinities, power groupings, personalities, and, occasionally, patronage. Each faction tends to have its own caucus meetings, publications, and voting tickets for party ballots. The factions are self-described on a left-right (or radical-pragmatic) spectrum, and this does give an approximate indication of ideological predisposition while sometimes exaggerating the degree of ideological coherence.

The Right faction, which in some States bears a distinctive local name such as Labor Unity, is the largest grouping, strongest in New South Wales, and has been the main party base of both recent Prime Ministers Bob Hawke and Paul Keating and of the current leader of the opposition, Kim Beazley. The Left faction has been strongest in Victoria and now features some internal friction between traditional Left loyalists and pragmatic Left elements who are more prepared to accept the compromises and disciplines of governmental office. A Center faction, the smallest of the three with the self-appellation of "the Centre Left," developed in the 1980s as an explicit broker between the Right and the Left but has weakened considerably since the mid-1990s.

The main sources of finance for the ALP are membership dues, periodic fund-raising events organized by branches, affiliation fees paid by unions, and donations, usually by unions, though support from business sources has increased substantially in recent decades.

The ALP national headquarters are located at Centenary House, 19 National Circuit, Barton, Australian Capital Territory.

Policy

The ALP always has purported to be a reformist party, though its ideological and policy positions have sometimes been complex and sometimes volatile. As an organizational coalition of reformers, ideologues, and pragmatists that seeks electoral majorities, the ALP is best described as a social democratic party. Its platform has long declared somewhat radically that it favors the "democratic socialization of industry, distribution, production and exchange," but this is immediately qualified by the rider "to the extent necessary to eliminate exploitation and other anti-social features in these fields."

The essential elements guiding ALP policy can be briefly, though simplistically, summarized. The ALP has traditionally been critical of inequality and injustice arising from capitalist economies, though it has accepted private enterprise within a mixed economy and its critical stance has probably owed more to Christian and humanist sources than to Marxism. In any case, this critical stance has been considerably tempered in recent decades. The Hawke and Keating Labor governments in the 1980s and 1990s were favorably disposed toward promarket policies and implemented important measures promoting business deregulation, privatization, competition, international trade, and reduced tariff protection.

The party generally stands for redistributive policies to promote a greater degree of social and economic equality. Today, this is likely to be expressed in terms of equality of opportunity and nondiscrimination in education, ethnic, urban, and social policy, as well as in industrial and welfare policy. Labor governments have twice put in place compulsory and inclusive national health insurance schemes, the first in the 1970s known as Medibank (effectively abolished by a later Liberal government) and a still-functioning successor instituted in the 1980s known as Medicare. In industrial matters, the ALP lends general support to the trade unions, with whom the Hawke and Keating Labor governments negotiated a formal "Accord" in the 1983–96 period representing an agreed position on wages, economic policy, and industrial restructuring. This Accord produced a gradual evolution away from Australia's traditional centralized national wage-fixing system toward a moderate degree of enterprise-level bargaining, though still within a framework of strong union involvement and not a radical enough change for the new coalition government that won office in 1996.

The ALP tends to promote a rationalistic and benevolent view of government as an instrument for reform. The party also tends to promote Australian nationalism, which makes it prorepublican in the current debate about the monarchy. Many party members are skeptical of traditional international military alliances, though the Hawke and Keating governments were careful to endorse the alliance with the United States. At the national level, the party has in the past tended to regard federalism as an undesirable impediment to the power of the national government, but its recent prime ministers have been prepared to sponsor a more pragmatic approach to cooperative intergovernmental relations, in recognition of the entrenched power of the States and of the reality of prominent State-level Labor governments that share the traditional State-level skepticism of Canberra.

Voting Support

The ALP's voting support has traditionally been strongest in urban, industrial, working-class districts, with about 60% of blue-collar Australians voting ALP compared with around 40% of lower-white-collar and about 30% of middle-class professionals. These numbers appear, however, to becoming more volatile, and there is some concern in the party that some of its traditional blue-collar base has become disillusioned with the party's style of politics in the 1980s and 1990s or has become attracted to the social conservatism of the Liberal Party. Rural support for the ALP is generally low, though the party does attract some support in provincial cities with an industrial base and in mining towns. Support for the ALP among women has been lower than among men, with this "gender gap" narrowing briefly in the early 1990s before reasserting itself. Among non-English-language-background ethnic groups, the ALP receives disproportionately good support from Southern European–origin voters but performs relatively poorly among Eastern European–origin voters.

Leadership

While some prominent Labor Party figures in the past were powerful "machine" figures in the State branch organizations, increasingly the parliamentary leaders have monopolized public attention. Parliamentary leadership in the ALP has gradually shifted since the mid-1960s from union-background working-class men to educated professionals. This was typified by the accession in 1967 to national parliamentary leadership of Gough Whitlam, a lawyer, later to become prime minister. Notable contemporary ALP leaders include the following:

- **Kim Beazley** (born 1948) was elected unopposed by the national Labor caucus as its parliamentary leader, and hence leader of the opposition, in March 1996 following the electoral defeat of the 13-year Labor government. He has retained the position after leading the party to a creditable, though still losing, outcome in the October 1998 election. Beazley is identified with the Right faction and is from Western Australia. A former minister of defense and minister of finance, he is regarded as a pragmatic leader with an avuncular image in contrast to the more abrasive style of his predecessor, Paul Keating.

- **Cheryl Kernot** (born 1948) was the parliamentary leader of the Australian Democrats until she defected to Labor in a stunning maneuver in October 1997. Party strategists counted on her apparent national popularity, gender appeal, and "yuppie" image winning votes for Labor in the 1998 election. As it happened, Kernot barely won her own House of Representatives seat. Immediately installed into the shadow Cabinet despite having no factional alignment, she is regarded in some quarters as a potential future party leader.
- **Bob Carr** (born 1947) is the premier of the most populous State, New South Wales. He is identified with the Right faction. As a State premier, Carr necessarily experiences some of the tensions between the ALP's national reformist impulses and the political necessities of strong State governmental systems.

Prospects

From March 1983 until March 1996, the ALP enjoyed an unprecedented interval of national electoral dominance. Labor was also relatively successful at the State level in the 1980s, led by several premiers with a professional background and managerial style typical of the party's continuing transition away from its older blue-collar, union-based image. The mid- and late 1990s have provided mixed fortunes for the party. It now governs in three States and is competitively placed to make further gains in future elections elsewhere.

NATIONAL PARTY

History

The National Party can be understood as the political representative of Australia's rural sector. It was instigated by farmer and grazier organizations in the 1914–22 period and was known, until the early 1980s, as the Country Party. Despite consistently winning only about 10% of the national vote, the National Party has been able to maintain a continual parliamentary presence since 1919 because of the geographical concentration of its voting strength.

In 1922, the party agreed to form a coalition with the larger anti-Labor party. This arrangement has continued ever since, so that the viable alternative to Labor governments at the national level and in most of the States is a Liberal-National coalition. The National Party is particularly strong in Queensland, where it is the main non-Labor party, and to a lesser extent in New South Wales and Western Australia. It has always been very weak in South Australia and Tasmania.

Organization, Membership, and Financing

The National Party is estimated to have over 120,000 members, making it the largest party organization in Australia and giving it a particularly high ratio of membership to voting strength, a good subscription income, and less dependence than other parties on outside funding. The majority of members, and all the party's national parliamentary seats, are located outside of the major metropolitan areas. The party remains closely associated with the national farmer and grazier organizations.

Considerable autonomy, even over candidate endorsement, is delegated to local branches. Within the States, the hierarchy is fairly simple. Local branches send delegates to electorate councils, while chairs of electorate councils form most of the State executive. As in the Liberal Party, National Party members of Parliament enjoy considerable autonomy in pursuing policies and electoral strategies.

The National Party headquarters are located at McEwen House, National Circuit, Barton, Australian Capital Territory.

Policy

As a representative of rural interests, the National Party has long supported public intervention to provide services to rural areas, to coordinate the marketing of agricultural products, and to guarantee incomes in the rural sector. This orientation sometimes creates friction with the deregulatory approach that increasingly characterizes its coalition partner, the Liberal Party. Because it is usually crucial to the survival of the coalition, the National Party has been able to secure policy concessions from the Liberal Party, but it also faces criticisms from its rural constituency when it makes concessions to its coalition partner. Policy tests under the Howard government have included the decision to pursue a national uniform system of stringent gun regulations, angering the mainly rural-based gun lobby and some National Party backbenchers, and the attempt to find a resolution to the apparent conflict between "native title" and the interests of pastoral leaseholders. On matters of economic, social, and foreign policy, the National Party tends to take a conservative position.

Leadership

- **Tim Fischer** (born 1946) became the national parliamentary leader in 1990, after his predecessor lost his seat in the election of that year, and is now deputy prime minister and minister for trade in the Howard government. A somewhat quirky character who has both admirers and skeptics, Fischer has embarked on a "back to the bush" strategy to return the National Party to its rural heartland.

Prospects

For years, commentators have been predicting the demise of the National Party in the face of steady urbanization and rural decline. However, the party has generally maintained its share of the vote and, notwithstanding the current situation in the House of Representatives, is likely to remain indispensable to the Liberal Party's long-term electoral success. The party successfully fought off a major challenge in its rural heartland from the new One Nation party in the October 1998 election. The National Party is unlikely to weaken significantly in the near future.

AUSTRALIAN DEMOCRATS

Geographical concentration translates the National Party's relatively modest share of the vote into a solid parliamentary presence. The Australian Democrats are a party that usually achieves a comparable level of national support but that cannot win House of Representatives seats because this support is dispersed. It has achieved consistent success, however, in the Senate and currently has seven senators and holds the balance of power in that chamber. As Table 5 demonstrated, the national vote for the Australian Democrats in the House of Representatives peaked in 1990, collapsed somewhat in 1993, and has partially repaired itself since then. The Democrats win a higher share of the vote in the Senate than in the House of Representatives.

The Australian Democrats were formed in 1977 around Don Chipp, a former Liberal Party minister who resigned from that party after a public disagreement with the Fraser government. The Democrats have sought to occupy the "middle ground" between the major party groupings but have in recent years also increasingly assumed a moderate-Left image on social and economic issues as the Labor Party has moved somewhat to the pro-market Right. The Democrats can be seen as supporting individualism within the context of a welfare state and have demonstrated a particular interest in such policy areas as education and the environment. They have held a balance of power in the Senate since 1984 and thus have been able to exert some influence on government legislation. Voting support is found mainly among educated middle-class professionals. The party has about 2,000 members.

- **Meg Lees** (born 1948), a senator from South Australia, became party leader after the defection of Cheryl Kernot to Labor in October 1997. She

had enjoyed only a low public profile up to that time. Lees led the Australian Democrats to its best-ever Senate result in the election of October 1998, ensuring that from July 1999 she will head a parliamentary grouping of nine senators holding the balance of power and become a major factor in the Howard government's legislative strategy.

The Democrats' national headquarters are located at 108 Brisbane Avenue, Barton, Australian Capital Territory.

ONE NATION

The One Nation party has emerged as a novel factor in Australian political life in the past few years. At the March 1996 election, Pauline Hanson was elected from Queensland to a House of Representatives seat despite being disendorsed by the Liberal Party for remarks about Aboriginal Australians. In Parliament, she attracted media attention and, in due course, a popular following for her controversial criticisms of Aboriginal land rights, multicultural social policies, high levels of immigration especially from nontraditional sources, and cuts in tariff protection.

Her movement institutionalized itself as "Pauline Hanson's One Nation" party, and it won unexpected support (23% of the vote and 11 parliamentary seats) at the Queensland State election of June 1998. However, its claim to be a new national force was dealt a harsh blow at the October 1998 national election: it won no House of Representatives seats (with Hanson herself not re-elected to the House) and just one Senate seat. Still, the party attracted 8% of the national vote, suggesting that a constituency remains for its populist policies and anti-establishment style.

The address for One Nation is 15 The Corso, Manly, New South Wales.

NATIONAL PROSPECTS

Australians belong to an English-speaking democracy more culturally akin to Britain, Europe, and North America than to its Asian neighbors, and they expect the Australian government to maintain the country's advanced standard of living. Australia's mineral resources and its efficient unprotected agricultural producers have long been its economic strength and, in the past, were able to shield a protected manufacturing sector. Increasing pressure from international competition, the vagaries of world markets, and the economic crisis in nearby Asian economies present Australia with problems and with new opportunities. The Australian economy is adjusting, with a steady decline in manufacturing protection, though at some cost in terms of historically high rates of unemployment and with uncertain political ramifications.

The principal tasks of the Australian government in the foreseeable future are, first, the continuing management and restructuring of the national economy to take account of the new international economic order and, second, the maintenance of a degree of social consensus about the immigration-driven ethnic diversification of the population and the need for reconciliation with Aboriginal Australians. Australia is likely to remain a politically stable, relatively affluent, and increasingly multicultural Western nation linked, with increasing self-assuredness, to its Asia-Pacific region.

Further Reading

Bean, Clive, et al., eds. *The Politics of Retribution: The 1996 Australian Federal Election.* St Leonards: Allen & Unwin, 1997.

Galligan, Brian. *A Federal Republic: Australia's Constitutional System of Government.* Cambridge: Cambridge University Press, 1995.

Galligan, Brian, Ian McAllister, and John Ravenhill, eds. *New Developments in Australian Politics.* South Melbourne: Macmillan, 1997.

Hughes, Owen. *Australian Politics*, 3d ed. South Melbourne: Macmillan, 1998.

Jaensch, Dean. *The Politics of Australia.* South Melbourne: Macmillan, 1997.

Maddox, Graham. *Australian Democracy in Theory and Practice*, 3d ed. Melbourne: Longman, 1996.

Parkin, Andrew, ed. *South Australia, Federalism and Public Policy.* Canberra: Federalism Research Centre, 1996.

Sawer, Marian, and Marian Simms. *A Woman's Place: Women and Politics in Australia*, 2d ed. St Leonards: Allen & Unwin, 1993.

Simms, Marian, ed. *The Paradox of Parties: Australian Political Parties in the 1990s.* St Leonards: Allen & Unwin, 1996.

Winterton, George. *Monarchy to Republic: Australian Republican Government.* Melbourne: Oxford University Press, 1994.

Woodward, Dennis, John Summers, and Andrew Parkin, eds. *Government, Politics, Power and Policy in Australia*, 6th ed. Melbourne: Longman, 1997.

REPUBLIC OF AUSTRIA

(Republik Österreich)

By Valerie O'Regan

THE SYSTEM OF GOVERNMENT

The Republic of Austria is a federal republic composed of nine provinces (*Bundesländer*), each with its own government and assembly. The Austrian system of government is a mixture of the presidential and parliamentary systems; this includes a directly elected president, as in the United States, and a chancellor who is chosen by the political party with the strongest support in the legislature.

The Austrian Republic was established following the dissolution of the Austro-Hungarian Empire in November 1918. At that time, a Council of Ministers was formed, led by Karl Renner. In 1920, a new constitution was adopted introducing the federal form of government. Due to economic and political instability in the nation, the short-lived dictatorship of Engelbert Dollfuss was imposed in 1933. Dollfuss was assassinated by the National Socialists during the civil war of 1934, and national instability and political repression culminated in the 1938 Nazi occupation and incorporation of Austria.

Following the Second World War, a provisional government was established under Renner. In July 1945, Austria was divided into four zones, occupied by the Allied forces. The first post-war elections were held in November 1945, resulting in a coalition government (known as the Great Coalition) of the conservative Austrian People's Party (ÖVP) and the Social Democratic Party (SPÖ); in December, Renner became the first president of the republic. Austria regained its full independence and neutrality with the signing of the Austrian State Treaty on May 15, 1955.

The Great Coalition endured for more than 20 years under a succession of chancellors. However, in April 1966 the ÖVP won a legislative majority and formed a single-party Council of Ministers. The majority shifted to the SPÖ in 1970; this one-party government lasted until the general elections of 1983 when the SPÖ lost its absolute majority in the legislature and formed a coalition government with the right-wing Freedom Party (FPÖ), led by Fred Sinowatz.

In September 1986, the ruling coalition collapsed, prompting the rescheduling of the April 1987 elections for November 1986. Although no party received an absolute majority, a coalition was formed in January 1987 between the SPÖ and the ÖVP. This coalition has continued to the present day.

Despite the nation's commitment to neutrality following the signing of the Austrian State Treaty, Austria has maintained a strong economic relationship with its Western neighbors. Acknowledging the importance of this connection with the West, both coalition partners have supported Austrian participation in an integrated Europe. Consequently, a key governmental goal was achieved in the national referendum of June 1994; with 81.3% of the electorate turning out for the elections, 66.4% of the voters supported Austria's admittance into the European Union (EU). As a result, Austria became a full member of the EU on January 1, 1995, while maintaining its brand of active neutrality.

In the Austrian system, the established division of powers between the federal government and the individual provincial governments is rather complicated; however, most important political matters are delegated to the federal government. Legislative and executive powers regarding major policy areas are the responsibility of the federal government. These include issues relating to foreign policy, the military, immigration, the constitution, judiciary, criminal and civil law, and law enforcement. For other policy issues such as housing, education, social welfare, land reform, population policy, and matters concerning electrical power, the federal government formulates the policies, but it is the responsibility of the provinces to execute the laws. The individual provinces possess legislative and executive jurisdiction over zoning and regional planning, hunting, land transfers, conservation and local law enforcement issues.

The individual rights of Austrian citizens are detailed in the Basic Law of 1867, the 1929 Constitutional Act, and the 1950 European Convention for the Protection of Human Rights and Fundamental Freedoms. These fundamental rights include equality before the law, individual privacy in the home and in communication, and freedom of association, movement, expression, conscience, religion, and property.

to allow open advertisement and acceptance of applications from interested individuals.

The Constitutional Court (*Verfassungsgerichtshof*) was also established by the constitution act of 1929. This court determines the constitutionality of government statutes, as well as officiating over cases that involve monetary claims against the government, cases involving conflicts between the administration and the courts, conflicts between the different courts, and conflicts between the different levels of government. The constitutional courts can also arbitrate cases involving statutes, elections, human rights violations, treaties, regulations, and impeachment of public officials. As with the administrative court justices, up to 1995, the 14 regular members and 6 substitutes were selected by presidential appointment from candidates who were proposed by the federal government and the parliament. Since 1995, judicial vacancies must be publicly advertised and open to individual applications.

Besides the three higher courts, the Austrian judicial system also includes 4 higher provincial courts (*Oberlandesgerichte*), 17 provincial and district courts (*Landes- und Kreisgerichte*), and various local-level courts (*Bezirksgerichte*).

Provincial and Local Governments

Although the Austrian constitution places most of the governmental power at the federal level, the provinces are given a considerable amount of responsibility for local government administration. Austria is composed of nine provinces (*Länder*); each province has its own provincial assembly (*Landtag*), directly elected by the citizens of the province by a proportional technique, and an administration supervised by a governor chosen by the assembly. The provincial assemblies function in the same way as the *Nationalrat* when governing the provinces; they are responsible for the implementation and execution of basic laws that have been formulated in the *Nationalrat*, such as those embodying education, fiscal, and social policies. The assemblies are also responsible for the legislation and execution of local policies such as zoning, regional planning, and local law enforcement. In addition to these duties, the provincial assemblies elect the members of the *Bundesrat*.

Since 1984, the smaller political parties, such as the Green parties, have prevailed in winning seats in the provincial assemblies. During the 1990s, Green parties have acquired as few as two and as many as seven seats in five of the nine provinces; the Greens have been the most successful in Vienna.

Besides the provincial government, each community has a council. One member of the council is chosen by the other members to act as the head of the community (*Burgermeister*). The members also choose a committee to execute and administer the council resolutions.

THE ELECTORAL SYSTEM

A system of proportional representation is used in Austrian parliamentary elections. Seat allocation is accomplished in two stages. During the first stage, the total vote in each electoral district (*Wahlkreis*) is divided by the number of seats apportioned to that district. The resulting number is referred to as the electoral quota: the number of votes needed to win a seat in that district.

To be eligible to get additional seats in the second stage, a party must win at least one seat in the first stage. Votes and seats that are not allocated in the first stage are proportionately appropriated in the second stage between two larger provincial units (*Wahlkreisverbande*); the first of these larger units is made up of the three eastern provinces (Vienna, Lower Austria, and Burgenland) and the second is composed of the other six provinces. The purpose of the second stage is to benefit smaller parties by gathering votes that may be scattered across the provinces.

In 1970, an electoral law was instituted to increase the number of *Nationalrat* deputies from 165 to 183; the law also decreased the number of electoral districts from 25 to 9. Once again, the purpose of this law was to help small parties by making the number of votes necessary to win a seat more equal. Following the establishment of this law, each of the provinces became an individual electoral district.

At present, all Austrian citizens over the age of 19 are eligible to vote. Citizens vote by means of an equal, direct, and secret ballot that lists party names in their order of electoral strength from the last election. To indicate the voter's choice, the voter places a mark next to the preferred party list. Only three of the provinces have compulsory voting in the parliamentary elections; however, voting turnout is high in all provinces despite the lack of a compulsory requirement in six of the provinces. Voting in presidential elections was compulsory for the entire country until 1982 when a constitutional amendment gave the provinces the authority to impose such voting requirements.

THE PARTY SYSTEM

Origins of the Parties

Traditionally the Austrian party system has been dominated by three *Lager*, or encampments: the Social Democratic-Marxist; the Catholic-conservative; and, the weakest of the three, the pan-German nationalist. These *Lager* originated in the 19th century and have been powerful forces in shaping political structures. After both world wars, the parties stepped into the political vacuum to revive political life. In the second republic, the *Lager* have managed to coexist in contrast to their battles of the interwar period. Although instances of single-party and all-party government have taken place (ÖVP government from 1966 to 1970 and SPÖ government from 1971 to 1983; all-party government from 1945 to 1947), coalition governments between the ÖVP and SPÖ (grand coalition) have spanned the years from 1945 to 1966 and after 1987 to the present.

The same cooperation between the two parties can be found in other areas of government. In the postwar period, a system was established to distribute appointive offices according to partisan affiliation and support. The *Proporzsystem* (the Austrian version of the spoils system) is used to determine employment and other benefits in various Austrian institutions such as state-owned industries and businesses; hence, the system offers the two principal parties the opportunity to reward party loyalty as well as maintain their influence over the bureaucracy. Up to 1966, the ÖVP and SPÖ applied this system in determining Cabinet appointments and other government jobs.

There are two ways to get a new party on the ballot. The first way is for the party's application to be supported by three parliamentary deputies. If the party lacks the necessary support, the new party must obtain between 200 and 500 signatures from voters in each of the provinces within the 30-day period prior to the election for the party to be included on the ballot. This task is not as simple as it appears since many voters are unwilling to identify with a nonestablished party.

Currently, there are two dominant political parties in Austria: the liberal Social Democrats (SPÖ) and the conservative People's Party (ÖVP). However, the populist, right-wing Freedomites (FPÖ) party has gained support in recent years. Besides these three parties, only the Communist Party (KPÖ), the Liberal Forum (LF), and the ecology-minded Greens have been represented in parliament.

Party Organization

There are two distinct types of party organization in Austria: direct membership and indirect membership. The SPÖ and Freedomites use direct membership, whereby partisan support is established by locality and province; this method of organization centralizes party power and contributes to higher partisan discipline. On the other hand, the ÖVP uses an indirect method of membership through various associations.

Party leader selection is based on seniority and party loyalty. Due to strong party discipline, incumbents in the *Nationalrat* and other elective offices tend not to be challenged from within the party. Party discipline among the electorate contributes to the stability of the political parties and the assurance that most elected officeholders will be reelected. The role of the average party member is usually a passive one; most members claim to have joined the party for political reasons or for materialistic gain. However, within the parties, a substantial group of activists can be found. For party activists, special services are pro-vided; these services include public-financed party academies and research centers that offer educational activities, facilities, and material relating to party activity.

Campaigning

The early stages of campaigning begin approximately one year before a scheduled election, with campaign activity suspended during the summer months. The onset of serious campaigning starts a few months prior to the election. However, over the years, the intensity of political campaigns has decreased because races have become less ideological. Rather than attempting to raise specific issues or ideologies, campaigns strive to appeal to the positive emotions of the electorate.

Recently, the style of campaigns has become more "Americanized." Parties use the mass media to communicate to the voting public. Party leaders meet on television to discuss the election and provide information that may influence the voters' decisions. Campaigning and the marketing of candidates have become the responsibility of experts; as a result, the process has become more expensive. The use of survey techniques and information to test the appeal of possible campaign issues has also increased the expense of the campaign.

During the 1995 campaign, televised debates were conducted to inform the voters about party agendas. Representatives from all of the parties debated the issues in 10 two-party confrontations; 2 five-party debates were also held. According to the polls, 71% of the electorate watched more than one of these debates. When questioned about the importance of the debates, 45% of the viewers said they have gained important information about the campaign from the debates and 32% said the debates had influenced their voting decisions.

Financing

Changes in the financing of campaigns occurred in July 1975 when the Party Law of 1970 was first applied. This electoral law provides federal monetary support to political parties for publicity and campaigning purposes. All parties with at least five members in the *Nationalrat* are entitled to a specific amount of funding with additional funds distributed on the basis of the amount of votes obtained in the previous election. Smaller parties that have remained unrepresented in the *Nationalrat* but have captured 1% of the vote are also granted monetary support based on the proportion of votes received. All parties that are eligible for funds must be registered with the Ministry of the Interior; the parties must also have established measures defining membership rights and duties. Because the Party Law lessens the financial advantage held by the big parties, smaller parties like the Freedomites that acquire less financial support from membership and association contributions have benefited from this electoral reform.

Independent Voters

Although party identification has been traditionally strong in Austria, it has decreased over the years and voters are more inclined to shift party loyalties from one election to another. Since the 1960s, the number of "floating" or independent voters has increased, ranging from an estimated 5% in the early years to over 10% of the electorate in the 1990s.

Despite the increase of "floating" voters, party membership still remains high compared with other European countries; the majority of voters still associate with one of the two dominant parties, the SPÖ or the ÖVP, or the smaller Freedomites. The high level of party attachment is attributed to the belief that party affiliation can result in personal benefits such as employment and advancement opportunities.

AUSTRIAN SOCIAL DEMOCRATIC PARTY
(Sozialdemokratische Partei Österreichs; SPÖ)

HISTORY

The Social Democratic Party was originally formed in 1889 and was subsequently redesignated the Austrian Socialist Party (*Sozialistische Partei Österreichs*) before it returned to its original name in 1991. The party successfully united the previously separate factions of the Social Democrats and the radical Socialists without adopting extreme socialist radicalism. The SPÖ of the First Republic identified with orthodox Marxism; in the Second Republic the party took a less ideological stand. From 1947 to 1966, the SPÖ served as the junior coalition partner with the ÖVP. In 1970, the party returned to office as a minority party under the chancellorship of Bruno Kreisky before winning a majority in 1971; the majority was maintained in the 1975 and 1979 elections. Due to increasing domestic problems, in 1983 the SPÖ lost its majority in parliament. Rather than form a minority government as they did in 1970, the SPÖ formed a coalition with the FPÖ that lasted until 1986, as a result of the FPÖ's swing to the right. Realizing the need for support to rule the nation, the SPÖ as the senior member and the ÖVP re-formed a coalition, which continues to exist at present.

ORGANIZATION

Organizationally, the SPÖ is more centralized than either the Freedomites or the ÖVP. Party leadership decisions are almost always accepted by the party congress. Although the same can be said about the other parties given the high level of party discipline in Austria, the need for compromise is less necessary in the SPÖ because of the party's ideological, policy interest and regional uniformity.

The party is supported by approximately as many regional groups as the ÖVP. These groups include local, district, and provincial party organizations. The SPÖ also has strong ties with corporate organizations such as the Austrian Trade Union, the Federal Chamber of Workers and Employees, and the Austrian Labor Farmers' Association; however, these organizations are not components of the SPÖ like the ÖVP suborganizations. Membership in the SPÖ is done on a personal level. Rather than establishing party affiliation through membership in associations as is the case in the ÖVP, citizens who subscribe to the ideals of the party personally choose to join the SPÖ.

In the local groups, a special party official known as the "confidant" provides the connection between the party members and the party leaders. There are approximately 70,000 confidants making up about 10% of the total SPÖ membership. Confidants are trained at the party headquarters. Most of the top officials of the SPÖ are chosen on the basis of seniority, achievement, and adaptability from this group of confidants; other top officials have been recruited from qualified technocrats.

Delegates to the party conferences are chosen by provincial and local party organizations, the Austrian Trade Union, the youth organization, and other auxiliary organizations. Additional delegates include the party members of the *Nationalrat*. A special party council assembled by the party leader is responsible for candidate ranking and selection, although the council does consult with other party organizations.

Up to 1991, the party published a daily newspaper, *AZ*; financial problems then forced the newspaper to stop publication. The SPÖ continues to print a monthly theoretical journal, *Die Zukunft* (The Future).

POLICY

Up to the 1950s, the party's platform was aligned with orthodox Marxism. In 1958, the party's orientation changed to a more humanistic socialism. The new approach concentrated on the economic, political, and social development of each citizen through reform. In addition, the new SPÖ program declared that socialism and Christianity were compatible. By 1966, the party had become less of an ideological party and more of a pragmatic left-wing liberal party.

The SPÖ advocates a progressive taxation approach with high social expenditures and economic planning. Along with this approach, the party has worked to maintain a low level of unemployment while keeping inflation under control. The electorate regards the SPÖ as providing political stability; in 1995, the SPÖ was elected on the basis of its apparent commitment to securing jobs and pensions and because of its opposition to an ÖVP–FPÖ coalition. In addition, the SPÖ supports Austria's permanent neutrality.

MEMBERSHIP AND CONSTITUENCY

In comparison with the ÖVP, the SPÖ is a mass-membership party; SPÖ membership is direct and individual rather than based on indirect membership through organizations that are associated with the party. The party represents a majority of the workers and a substantial portion of the lower middle class. SPÖ supporters mainly come from in and around the larger cities; members also tend to oppose or be indifferent to the Catholic Church. Most of the electorate who vote for the SPÖ are members of the party. As of 1995, the membership of the SPÖ was approximately 700,000.

Because the party's platform is popular with female voters, women constitute over a third of the party membership. This can be viewed as significant since women make up over 54% of the electorate. The party also relies on young voters who support the party's liberal policies. Besides maintaining its support in the urban communities, the SPÖ has increased its support in rural and Catholic areas.

Reflecting some of the antinuclear and ecological concerns of portions of the urban electorate, some prominent members of the SPÖ have transferred their support to the Green parties. Beginning in 1983 and up to the current time, the effects of the shift in party support to the Greens can be seen in the *Nationalrat*. In 1983, the Green parties (ALO and VGÖ) won 3.3% of the vote; during the most recent election, the Greens won 4.8% of the vote. Support for the SPÖ decreased through the 1980s and early 1990s with a slight increase in the 1995 election.

FINANCING

Financial support for the SPÖ comes from membership dues, the party tax on functionaries, and federal subsidies.

LEADERSHIP

From 1967 to 1983, Bruno Kreisky led the SPÖ. Kreisky was viewed as a father figure to many Austrians during a time of international insecurity. When the SPÖ lost its parliamentary majority in 1983, Kreisky resigned as party leader and Fred Sinowatz, the former vice chancellor, became party leader. In protest over the Waldheim presidency, Sinowatz resigned as chancellor and party leader. In June 1986, a former finance minister, Dr. Franz Vranitsky, became the new federal chancellor and party leader and continues to hold the position today. Since 1986, Vranitsky has lost much of the popularity he once had, but he is still considered the most popular of all the party leaders.

AUSTRIAN PEOPLE'S PARTY
(Österreichische Volkspartei; ÖVP)

HISTORY

Founded in April 1945, the ÖVP evolved from the prewar Christian Social Party (1918–38). The party is regarded as an antiliberal, nonsocialist collective party basing its ideology on Christian Democratic political thinking. Furthermore, the ÖVP supports the independent and democratic rule of the Austrian nation. The Christian Social Party was part of an antisocialist alliance with other Christian, fascist, and authoritarian groups during the 1920s and 1930s; however, despite the common antisocialist bond, these groups rarely agreed on other issues such as economic policies or the nation's position on Mussolini's Italy and Hitler's Germany.

Originally, the fundamental doctrine of the party was that religion (Catholicism) is essential for the education and coexistence of the people. However, since 1965, the ÖVP portrays itself as a party of the political center; the religious view has been replaced by a nonideological perspective. Although many of the members of the ÖVP were affiliated with the Christian Social Party, most do not consider the ÖVP to be the actual successor to the Christian Social Party since the ÖVP has avoided establishing a link with the church. One of the reasons for the avoidance of party-church ties may be the decree issued by the Austrian bishops prohibiting the church's political activity.

Following the war, the ÖVP was considered the dominant party from 1946 to 1970. Since then, the ÖVP has lost political ground to the SPÖ, becoming the loyal opposition.

ORGANIZATION

The party was formed by the union of three influential vocational associations: the Austrian Farmers' Association (OBB), the Austrian Economic Association (OWB), and the Austrian Association of Workers and Employees (OAAB). There are three other less-influential groups that are included in the composition of party organization: women, youth, and retirees. Each group is financially and economically independent, issuing its own programs. All six of the separate groups are organized at the provincial level. Besides the individual provincial groups, the ÖVP has an organization in each province and each local district. The combination of separate interests must be defined and integrated to determine the objectives for the party as a whole, making the party's organization a modern "mass" party. The efforts of the party continue to be maintaining contact with party supporters and recruiting new voters.

The ÖVP is considered a member party rather than a voter party; member:vote ratio is approximately 1:2.3. Intraparty democracy is a priority of the party. Each unit is entitled to send 25 delegates to the national party conference; these delegates are joined by at least 10 delegates from the provincial organizations of the party, the party's members of the provincial governments, and the ÖVP's *Nationalrat* deputies.

ÖVP candidate selection and party list ranking are a complex process. First, the candidates are proposed at the district level; the candidates are then discussed by the party leaders in each province and their proposals are submitted to the national directorate. The candidate proposals can be vetoed by the national party leaders, but the provincial organizations retain the right to choose at least 5% of the nominations. Although candidate rankings are also the prerogative of the provinces, the provincial suborganizations have a major role in determining the ranking of the candidates' names on the ballot. Ultimately, the national leadership can reject rankings made by the provincial suborganizations; however, most disputes are resolved by negotiation.

POLICY

During the postwar period, the ÖVP has distanced itself from the fascist-authoritarian faction it was associated with and has emphasized its commitment to democracy. Due to the influence of the farmers and business personnel who make up the ÖVP constituency, the party advocates a strong conservative economic and social policy and staunchly supports EU membership. The 1972 Salzburg Program characterized the ÖVP as a progressive center party and adopted a social market economy policy.

The party must consider the interests of the different groups that form the party constituency. The farmers want the party to maintain the conservative, Christian ideology of the past; they request state subsidies to sustain their farming lifestyles through difficult weather and land conditions and to halt the flow of labor and resources to the urban areas. Constituents associated with the business groups want the ÖVP to uphold the nonsocialist agenda by challenging socialist-endorsed welfare and education policies. In addition, employment issues are important to many of the groups that compose ÖVP membership. According to an exit poll, members of the electorate voted for the ÖVP in the 1995 election because of the party's commitment to reducing expenditures and preventing tax increases.

MEMBERSHIP AND CONSTITUENCY

Although direct membership in the ÖVP does occur, most members join the party indirectly through the previously mentioned suborganizations. As of 1995, party membership totaled 760,000; although membership figures have been disputed due to the indirect method of party recruitment and the chance of members belonging to more than one of the suborganizations, election results appear to indicate that the ÖVP has a solid membership. During the 1990s, the ÖVP has been the dominant party in five of the provincial governments; in the 1995 general election, the

party won 53 seats with 28.3% of the vote. Most members and ÖVP elected officials are practicing Catholics.

FINANCING

Approximately 30% of the federal party's income comes from membership dues to the suborganizations. Other party funds come from party taxes gathered from functionaries who acquired their positions due to party influence, business donations, and the federal government.

LEADERSHIP

The current chair of the ÖVP is Dr. Wolfgang Schüssel. Recently, Schüssel replaced former party chairman Erhard Busek because Busek had made too many enemies within the party. Besides taking over the chairmanship, Schüssel was moved within the Cabinet from the Economic Affairs Department, where he was not extremely effective, to the Foreign Affairs Department. This decision is viewed as an opportunity for Schüssel to compete with the federal chancellor on international matters.

PROSPECTS

Although the ÖVP continually lost parliamentary seats during the 1986, 1990, and 1994 elections, the party gained one seat in the 1995 contest. The ÖVP was unable to fulfill its ambition of replacing the SPÖ as the leading party; however, the ÖVP maintains its status as the second-strongest party and retains its position for coalition formation. In addition, the office of federal president is once again held by a member of the ÖVP, Thomas Klestil.

FREEDOMITES OR THE FREEDOM PARTY
(Die Freiheitlichen)

HISTORY

In January 1995, the Freedom Party of Austria (FPÖ) officially changed its name to the Freedomites. The party was founded in 1956 by a former Nazi, Anton Feinthaller, and drew a considerable amount of its support from former National Socialists. The party is considered the successor to the right-wing League of Independents; in the 1970s, the party shifted away from its extreme right-wing tendencies to a more liberal perspective. However, the party does not consider itself a liberal party. Due to this shift in political ideology, the party suffers from factional disputes between the right-wing nationalists and moderate liberals.

After the 1983 election, the party formed a coalition with the SPÖ; this was the first time that the party had participated in a federal government. The coalition collapsed in 1986 with the election of a right-wing party chairman, Jörg Haider. However, during the 1986, 1990, and 1994 elections, the party made substantial gains in

Nationalrat balloting at the expense of the ÖVP and, to a lesser extent, the SPÖ. Over this period, the Freedomites also gained electoral strength in provincial elections, especially in Vienna. In 1980, the party contested the presidential election, winning 17% of the vote; party support was also evident in the 1992 presidential election when Heide Schmidt won 16% of the first-round votes.

ORGANIZATION

Delegates to the national conference are elected by provincial congresses; the delegates select the party leader and chief deputies. Senior party appointments and party activities are the responsibility of the party leader. Despite the centralized nature of the leader's authority, the party is plagued by factional disputes that influence the decision making of the leader; furthermore, the party discourages excessive centralization and encourages a considerable level of local independent activity.

The party publishes a weekly newspaper, *Neue Freie Zeitung* (New Free News), and a theoretical journal, *Freie Argumente* (Free Debate).

POLICY

The Freedomites are considered a populist, right-wing party advocating moderate social reform, worker participation in management, and more stringent immigration controls. The party has also maintained an anti-EU membership position although the party's position did not halt Austrian EU membership. Recently, the party has tilted away from an extreme nationalist character and has liberalized its perspective on important issues; its adoption of the name Freedomites was intended to show the party's rejection of "old-style party politics." This change is viewed as resulting from generational changes in the party's top ranks; however, the Freedomites continue to advocate "Austria First" interests. The party's platform stressing opposition to the immigration of Eastern Europeans almost doubled the party's *Nationalrat* representation in 1990.

Because of its belief in individuality and achievement, the party platform is antisocialist and anti-Catholic, perceiving both convictions as constraints on individual freedom and liberty. The party disapproves of excessive government regulation and the established Proporzsystem that distributes jobs and benefits according to party affiliation and support; as a result, the two major parties have monopolized the distribution of significant government jobs.

MEMBERSHIP AND CONSTITUENCY

Party membership is approximately 35,000; 10% of the voters who vote for the Freedomites are also members of the party. Most of the party supporters are civil servants, white-collar workers, or self-employed; many come from small towns. The provinces that show the strongest support for the party in provincial elections of the 1990s are Vienna, Carinthia, and Vorarlberg where the party won the second-most votes.

FINANCING

Since the party receives less money from membership donations (due to a smaller membership) and external economic help, it depends more on government subsidies to finance party campaigns and programs than the SPÖ and ÖVP.

LEADERSHIP

Over the years, the leadership of the old FPÖ party and the current Freedomites has fluctuated from a right-wing orientation to a more liberal attitude. The current leader of the Freedomites, Dr. Jörg Haider, is considered a right-wing nationalist. This perception of his conservative leadership has caused Haider to be blamed for the collapse of the party's coalition with the SPÖ that was formed following the 1983 election.

PROSPECTS

In 1986, the FPÖ began to show gains in electoral support. Support continued to increase in the 1990 and 1994 elections, to the detriment of the two major parties. With its 22.6% share of the vote, confidence in the party's support was high enough to elicit Jörg Haider's claim that he was working toward winning the chancellorship in 1998. However, in the 1995 election, the party suffered a small setback slipping to 22% of the vote and losing two *Nationalrat* seats.

MINOR POLITICAL PARTIES

Austrian Communist Party (Kommunistische Partei Österreichs; KPÖ)

The KPÖ was formed in 1918 in Vienna. Under the Dollfuss dictatorship (1933–34), the party was banned and forced to go underground until 1945. After the Second World War, the KPÖ gained some importance because of the support it received from the Soviet occupying force; consequently, the party was given positions in the government. Following the signing of the Austrian State Treaty in 1955 and the withdrawal of the Soviets, the party was unable to win a seat in the *Nationalrat* (the party had one seat in the *Bundesrat* from 1945 to 1954). Other events, such as the invasion of Czechoslovakia, so increased the Austrian people's fear of a Soviet threat to their own homeland that the party lost more support. The party lost the few provincial-level seats it held by 1970. Currently, the party remains a weak political force and is considered inconsequential in the electoral arena; the KPÖ won 0.3% of the vote in the elections of 1994 and 1995.

The KPÖ organization is based on the principle of democratic centralism. The party advocates land reform, nationalization, and a policy of strict foreign neutrality; it

The first non-Communist president of independent Azerbaijan was Abulfaz Elcibey of the Popular Front, who took office in June 1992 after elections that were considered free and fair by international observers. President Elcibey was overthrown in a coup d'état and replaced by the current president, Heydar Aliyev, in June 1993. President Aliyev was directly elected on October 3, 1993, allegedly winning 98% of the vote. Two other candidates received less than 1% of the vote each. The Azerbaijan Popular Front boycotted the vote, which was declared undemocratic by international observers.

Legislature

The Azerbaijani parliament is the *Milli Mejlis*, which has a single chamber with 125 seats, 100 of them single-member ridings and 25 divided on the basis of proportional representation. Elections to the parliament were last held in November 1995 and February 1996. Eight parties contested the race. President Aliyev's New Azerbaijan Party won 78% of the vote to take 18 of the 25 proportional representation seats.

International observers criticized the elections as neither free nor fair. Voting was accompanied by blatant fraud, ballot box stuffing, and some violence. Several major opposition parties—the Musavat Party, the Communist Party, and the People's Democratic Party—were barred from participating in the election by the State Election Commission, as were approximately 600 of the 1,000 independent candidates who contested the 100 open seats. The major opposition party, the Popular Front, was allowed to field candidates, but the Election Commission ultimately disqualified 87 of its 111 candidates.

Follow-up elections to 15 vacant seats were held on February 4, 1997. At present, observers believe that the opposition holds eight seats in parliament. Since there were no international observers for this last round of elections, it appears that there is no definitive count of parliament.

The Nakhichevan Autonomous State (under the terms of the 1995 constitution, it is no longer referred to as an "autonomous republic"), a region under Azeri jurisdiction but physically separated from Azerbaijan by territory of the Republic of Armenia, has its own parliament, its own cabinet, and its own constitution. It does not have a president or prime minister. The Nakhichevani parliament has jurisdiction over social and economic matters and can impose taxes. It has no formal armed forces and no independent foreign policy; however, relations between the Nakhichevani government and Iran are much warmer than are Iran's relations with the Azeri central government in Baku. This is a reflection of Nakhichevan's geographic situation, sandwiched between Iran and Armenia; in particular, it is heavily dependent on Iran for food and energy supplies.

Both the Nakhichevani and the national parliaments are controlled by President Aliyev's New Azerbaijan Party.

Judiciary

The Azeri legal system has undergone some reform since the end of the Soviet era. In particular, the 1995 constitution set up a system of district courts around the country and a Supreme Court in Baku that also serves as a court of appeals. The Supreme Court also has exclusive jurisdiction over cases involving national security. Much of the legal code remains unchanged from the Soviet era, however. The Popular Front government (1992–93) did revise some of the criminal statutes, introducing new classifications of crimes and setting out minimum and maximum sentences in each category.

Judges are appointed and removed by the president, and in general the judiciary is heavily politicized and favors the state. Trials are generally public and defendants are entitled to court-appointed attorneys. However, defense lawyers in political cases have often been subject to harassment by police or thugs.

Regional and Local Government

Azerbaijan is divided into 59 *raions*, or provinces. Each province is administered by a governor, called the head of the executive power, appointed directly by the president, who may also remove them at his discretion. They serve until relieved. There are also 11 major cities that have their own mayors, also appointed by the president. Some of these *raions* and cities are currently under Armenian occupation. There is no elected government at the regional or local level, although the 1995 constitution calls for the creation of such bodies and some preparations were being made for local elections that are to be held in 1997–98.

Provincial and municipal civil servants are employees of the central government in Baku. Subnational governments have no authority to levy taxes and depend completely on disbursements from the national government.

ELECTORAL SYSTEM

Azerbaijan's national parliament, the *Milli Mejlis*, employs a mixed system of proportional representation/winner-take-all. Of the 125 seats in the parliament, 100 are single-candidate, winner-take-all ridings; 25 are reserved for proportional representation and are divided among competing parties on the basis of their percentage of the national vote. A party must achieve at least 8% support in order to qualify for proportional representation seats.

THE PARTY SYSTEM

Prior to independence in December 1991, the only legal party in Azerbaijan was the Azerbaijan Communist Party. The Popular Front, founded in the fall of 1989 as a coalition of liberal Baku intellectuals, hard-line nationalists, and a broad assortment of other political factions, did not function as a political party until 1992. The Musavat Party, which governed the first Azerbaijani Republic between 1918 and 1920, was able to remain active in Turkey during the Soviet era and became active again in Azerbaijan in 1992, first as part of the Popular Front government and subsequently as an independent party. All other Azerbaijani political parties were created during or after 1992.

Excepting the Communist Party, the ruling New Azerbaijan Party, the Popular Front, and the Musavat Party, Azeri political parties tend to have small memberships and are weakly institutionalized. In general, they serve as platforms for the ambitions of individual leaders. More than 45 parties applied for official status in the run-up to the 1995 parliamentary elections. Of these, 32 were recognized by the Ministry of Justice, meaning they were able to submit lists of 50,000 signatures to the Ministry, the minimum required for official status. The Election Commission barred the majority of these from participating in the election, provoking a round of mergers between them. Some of these mergers dissolved after the elections; others remain.

Parties do campaign, but financial constraints limit all but a few to the cities of Baku and Ganje. Most voters are independent, if not apathetic. Party leaders tend to claim large memberships, but this appears to be based on the signature lists required for registration rather than on actual, card-carrying memberships.

Azerbaijani politics is dominated less by political parties than by clans, based on kinship, patronage, and personal ties. These in turn frequently have a strongly regional character. Beginning in the Brezhnev era, Azeri politics was strongly shaped by rivalries between clans based in the autonomous republic of Nakhichevan, the home of then Chairman Heydar Aliyev, the city of Baku and the regions surrounding it, and the city of Agdam. The Nakhichevani clans became dominant in politics and the state, a position they have regained since Aliyev's return to power. The Agdam clans, traditionally well entrenched in the Azeri agricultural regions around Nagorno-Karabakh, were able to make strong political inroads during the 1980s, after Mikhail Gorbachev forced Aliyev's removal from the Soviet Politburo and appointed a former diplomat and ethnic Azerbaijani, Abdulrahman Vezirov, as chairman of the Azeri Communist Party. Vezirov appointed a number of individuals from the Agdam and Baku clans to responsible positions in an effort to break the power of the pro-Aliyev Nakhichevanis.

Following Vezirov's ouster, President Ayaz Mutalibov continued to try to break the power of the Nakhichevanis but relied heavily on backing from Soviet troops and central government support, leaving him vulnerable to nationalist attacks from the Popular Front. Mutalibov was driven from office following the Khodjaly massacre, the slaughter of between 200 and 600 Azeri civilians by Armenian irregulars at the village of Khodjaly, in Nagorno-Karabakh.

Azerbaijan's political elite, whether government or opposition, retains a strongly Nakhichevani flavor. Almost all political parties are headed by individuals born in the cities and villages of Nakhichevan. Since the creation of the New Azerbaijan Party, Nakhichevanis have become steadily more entrenched in the state bureaucracy in Baku. This development has caused a good deal of resentment among the non-Nakhichevani population of the country.

NEW AZERBAIJAN PARTY
(Yeni Azerbaijan Partisi)

The New Azerbaijan Party was founded following the ascension to power of President Heydar Aliyev. It is heavily populated by members of his immediate and extended family and supporters from the autonomous state of Nakhichevan and is strongly entrenched in the upper and middle reaches of the state bureaucracy. The party's policy is essentially pro-Western; it seeks to maximize the involvement of Western companies in the Azerbaijani economy and in seeking a resolution to the Karabakh conflict. It opposes a political role for religious institutions and has thus been quite hostile to Iranian interests.

The party structure consists of a series of riding organizations, consisting of the local ruling party boss and his associates in the towns and villages in a given *raion*, who answer to party bosses in the *raions*, who in turn report to the national party headquarters in Baku. Party bosses not infrequently hold government positions, and state assets have been used for party functions.

Party financing, as is the case with most Azeri parties, is extremely opaque. The party is one of the primary vehicles through which patronage is distributed from the center to the periphery; most local chapters receive funds from the national party headquarters. Where the national party raises its funds is unclear. Large contributions by prominent business interests are known to occur but are not widely publicized.

The New Azerbaijan Party is headed by President Aliyev, although day-to-day matters are handled by vice chairmen. The party's prospects are very positive as long as the current president is able to remain in power. Should he be removed from the scene by illness or malfeasance, a prolonged period of confusion is likely, as no obvious successors within or without the party appear to exist.

THE POPULAR FRONT
(Xalk Cephesi)

The oldest and still the largest opposition political party in Azerbaijan, the Popular Front began as a group of liberal intellectuals based in Baku in 1988–89 who attempted to press the then Communist government to make greater reforms in keeping with the spirit of Gorbachev's glasnost and perestroika. The movement grew rapidly to encompass almost every non-Communist political faction in the country, and in the process lost what little coherence it had, save for the goal of achieving independence from the USSR. Although the front formed the first non-Communist government in 1992, it is a considerable misstatement to describe it as a political party at that time. The party in Baku had little effective control over those claiming to be Popular Front members in the regions. Only with the overthrow of the Popular Front government in 1993 by a rebellious warlord, Suret Huseynov, did a period of consolidation occur.

Today, the front is much reduced in size and moral authority, a result of the rampant corruption of front government officials in 1992–93. Nonetheless, it retains much of its nationwide presence and is the dominant partner in the Democratic Congress, the alliance of opposition parties created in 1997.

Party financing is less opaque than that of the government, although it is still unclear in many respects. The front has received financial support from German foundations seeking to encourage democracy in Azerbaijan and from Azerbaijani supporters within and outside the country, especially in Turkey and Germany.

Former president Elcibey has remained the de jure head of the party since his overthrow, but in fact it has been administered by the first vice chairman, Ali Kerimov. However, Elcibey has been elected head of the Democratic Congress and is expected to return to Baku in the near future, where he will once again become active in political life.

OTHER POLITICAL FORCES

Islam

Azerbaijanis are predominantly Shiite Muslims. Soviet suppression of religion was quite effective, on the whole; Azerbaijan possessed few mosques upon independence and few Azerbaijanis worshiped regularly. Religious education experienced a sudden rise in popularity following independence, and there are many religious schools in Azerbaijan, funded primarily by Turkish interests. The popularity of religious schools, however, appears to be in large part a response by parents to the perceived material shortcomings of public education—unmotivated teachers, poor facilities, low budgets, and a lack of discipline—rather than an expression of interest in religion per se. In general, religion is more popular among the rural population.

Since independence, there has been an explosion of mosque building in Azerbaijan, funded by Turkish, Iranian, and Saudi foundations and individuals. Azerbaijani religious institutions are supervised by a state-supported Religious Practices Board, which controls the appointments of *imams*, or religious leaders, to mosques and the administration of mosque finances. The government is extremely sensitive to attempts to politicize religion and has moved aggressively against the Islamic Party of Azerbaijan, which has sought to challenge the board's control of the mosques. In 1997 the leaders of the party were arrested, charged, and convicted of espionage and subversion of the government of Iran.

The Nagorno-Karabakh War

The Azerbaijani territory of Karabakh is a region of predominantly Armenian population lying within Azerbaijan. In 1979 (the last year for which reliable figures are available) the population totaled 160,000, 37,000 of whom were Azerbaijani and 123,000 Armenian. Armenians refer to the territory as "Artsakh" and Azerbaijanis as "Yuxari Karabagh." In recognition of the concentrated nature of Armenian settlement in the region, it was given the status of an autonomous *oblast* by the Soviet government in 1924—a status that conferred a substantial degree of self-governing authority upon the *oblast* government while maintaining Azerbaijani sovereignty.

Gaining jurisdiction over Karabakh has long been a goal of Armenia and of the population of Karabakhs. Demonstrations demanding the transfer occurred in the mid-1960s and recurred periodically thereafter in Yerevan and Stepanakaert. In January 1988, demonstrations began again and quickly spread throughout Armenia and Karabakh. Unrest escalated rapidly, with clashes between the local population and Soviet internal affairs troops and between local Azerbaijanis and Armenians becoming a daily event.

The Azerbaijani Supreme Soviet abolished Nagorno-Karabakh in November 1991; the Karabakh authorities responded by holding a referendum on independence. On January 6, 1992, Karabakh formally declared its independence from Azerbaijan.

The war for Karabakh led to approximately 50,000 deaths and the creation of about 740,000 Azerbaijani refugees and 40,000 Armenian refugees. The war was a military disaster for Azerbaijan, which lost control of almost all of Karabakh and a substantial amount of undisputed Azerbaijani territory bordering on Karabakh as well. Fighting halted in May 1994 when the two sides signed a Russian-mediated cease-fire, but a comprehensive settlement has thus far proved elusive. Although Armenia has denied direct involvement in the war, Armenian regular forces played an active role between 1992 and 1994, and Armenia continues to serve as a source of finance, supplies, and manpower for the Karabakh government.

The war has been a major factor influencing Armenian and Azeri political development. Two Azerbaijani presidents were overthrown following military defeats in Karabakh: Ayaz Mutalibov in March 1992 and Abulfaz Elcibey in June 1993. Both the Azerbaijani Popular Front and the Karabakh Committee, which led the independence movements in their respective countries, derived much of their popularity from their hard-line positions on the dispute. Parties and politicians on both sides remain highly sensitive to the need to appear tough on Karabakh.

NATIONAL PROSPECTS

Azerbaijan is potentially the richest of the Soviet successor states, thanks to its enormous oil reserves. Since 1991, Western oil companies have competed fiercely for contracts to explore for and extract oil and natural gas. As of 1997, the value of these contracts stands at over $20 billion. Western direct investment in the Azerbaijani oil and gas sector now exceeds investment in the Russian oil and gas sector. While poverty remains endemic in Azerbaijan, as it does across the former Soviet Union, the massive injections of Western capital offer the possibility, if they are wisely invested, of revitalizing the national economy.

Nonetheless, the country faces some serious problems. Strong Armenian forces remain in control of a substantial portion of Azerbaijani territory, and there is little sign that Armenian leaders are willing to compromise on their demands for complete sovereignty.

Additionally, President Aliyev is now 74 years old. Although he is in robust health, Azerbaijani political stability is heavily dependent upon his continued presence. No obvious successors exist, either in the New Azerbaijan Party or among the opposition political parties.

Further Reading

Alstadt, Audrey. *The Azerbaijani Turks*. Stanford, Calif.: Hoover Institution Press, 1992.

Goltz, Thomas. *Azerbaijan Diary*. New York: M.E. Sharpe, 1997.

Hunter, Shireen T. "Azerbaijan: Searching for New Neighbors." In *New States, New Politics: Building the Post-Soviet Nations*. Ed. I. Bremmer and R. Taras. New York: Cambridge University Press, 1997.

Web Sites

OMRI Daily Digest: http://www.frerl.org/realaudio/index.html

Radio Free Europe/Radio Liberty Newsline: http://www.rferl.org/newsline/search/

COMMONWEALTH OF THE BAHAMAS

By Thomas D. Anderson, Ph.D.

THE SYSTEM OF GOVERNMENT

The Commonwealth of The Bahamas consists of over 700 islands and even more cays that lie about 80 kilometers east of south Florida and extend southeastward to the British Turks and Caicos Islands. Only about half of its roughly 10,000 square kilometers of area is occupied by its population of about 274,000. Some 85% of this total are black, including an indeterminate number of Haitian refugees; the remaining white proportion includes a growing number of affluent retirees. The language is English, with some Haitian Creole. It is a parliamentary democracy that was granted independence from Britain in 1973. The economy is relatively prosperous and based mainly upon tourism and financial services. Agriculture is insignificant with only 1% of the area planted.

Executive

The head of state is the British monarch, who is represented there by an appointed governor-general. Actual executive power is exercised by the prime minister and Cabinet. Although officially appointed by the governor-general, the prime minister is the leader of the elected majority party in the House of Assembly. The Cabinet, which is also appointed by the governor-general upon recommendation of the prime minister, oversees the affairs of state and originates nearly all legislation. The prime minister may at any time request the governor-general to dissolve the Parliament.

Legislature

The Parliament is bicameral, with a Senate and a House of Assembly. Of the 16 members of the Senate, 9 are appointed by the governor-general on the advice of the prime minister, 4 on the advice of the leader of the opposition, and 3 on the advice of the prime minister after consultation with the leader of the opposition. Appointments are for five years and may be renewed. The Senate serves primarily as a consultative body with the limited power to delay legislation proposed by the House of Assembly.

The House of Assembly consists of 43 members (an increase of 5 since 1982) elected to five-year terms. Bills may be introduced either in the House or the Senate, but the power of the purse is confined to the House. Should a bill be rejected twice by the Senate after having been passed twice by the House, it may still be formally approved by the governor-general. Proposed constitutional amendments must pass by a three-fourths majority in each chamber and then be submitted to a national referendum.

Judiciary

The justice system is based on English common law and is administered by the Supreme Court and the Court of Appeal. The Supreme Court consists of a chief justice, who is appointed by the governor-general on the advice of the prime minister in consultation with the leader of the opposition, and of two additional justices. Supreme Court decisions can be appealed to the Court of Appeal, which consists of a president and two judges, who also are appointed by the governor-general on the advice of the prime minister. The ultimate appeal is to the Judicial Committee of the Privy Council in London.

Regional and Local Government

Local divisions are based on 18 accepted island groupings and are, with two exceptions, administered by centrally appointed district commissioners. The islands of New Providence (site of the capital of Nassau) and Grand Bahama have locally elected governing bodies.

THE ELECTORAL SYSTEM

Elections must be held at least every five years, although early elections may be called by the prime minister. Such must be held within 90 days following dissolution of the Parliament. All citizens 18 years or older are eligible to vote. Each of the 43 constituencies returns one representative elected by a simple plurality. Turnout commonly exceeds 90% of a consituency that is over 90% literate in a society that has a free press. Elections in general have been regarded as fair, although in 1982 both main parties raised challenges on allegations of fraud. Neither was sustained. There are few barriers to the formation of a political party, and a number have competed at various times but have had little success. The two major parties are well organized with active local members in every constituency and frequent national conventions. Campaigns are spirited but focus mainly on personalities since ideological differences are minor.

THE PARTY SYSTEM

The main parties are the Free National Movement (FNM) and the Progressive Liberal Party (PLP). These two have alternatively held power since independence. Historically, the PLP has had the image of serving the needs of the oppressed blacks, whereas the FNM was viewed as favoring outside investment interests over the needs of the poor. The fact that both have won elections in a country that is 85% black suggests that a majority of voters do not always share these perceptions.

The Progressive Liberal Party was formed in 1953 by Lynden O. Pindling (born 1930), a black attorney who in 1997 was still the party's leader. Other than a leadership dispute in 1967 between Pindling and Cecil Whitfield, who briefly formed an offshoot body called the Free PLP, the party has demonstrated excellent unity and organization. Except for a short period in the mid-1970s, it has enjoyed firm support from the Trade Union Congress (TUC), the labor organization that originally spawned the PLP.

In the political spectrum, the party is slightly left-of-center but is basically a moderate, pro-American party with a free-enterprise perspective. Nonetheless, Pindling has at times argued that in periods of economic stress The Bahamas should strive to be less dependent on foreign investment.

In October 1984, a crisis erupted in the ruling PLP government over allegations of ministerial involvement in drug trafficking, an outcome of an investigation by a royal commission. Two PLP ministers resigned after being named in the probe by the commission. Demands for Pindling's resignation grew, both from the opposition FNM and from PLP officials when the commission reported that he had failed to disclose millions of dollars in loans and gifts from foreign businesses. Deputy Prime Minister Arthur Hanna, a loyal Pindling follower, resigned and many wanted him to assume party leadership. Pindling refused to step down, however, and then dismissed two Cabinet ministers who had urged him to do so. The effect was to erode the credibility of the party among the voters.

The Free National Movement was formed late in 1971 as a merger between the onetime United Bahamas Party and dissidents from the PLP who called them-

selves the Free PLP. In the 1972 elections, the FNM won 9 seats to the PLP's 29. In December 1976, the party suffered a split, with most of the old UBP forming a new party called the Bahamian Democratic Party (BDP). In the election of 1977 the BDP won five seats to only two for the FNM. In 1979, four BDP members of Parliament left to form the Social Democratic Party (SDP), which briefly became the offical opposition. The remaining BDP member of Parliament and, later, one of the SDP men rejoined the FNM. Going into the 1982 elections, the FNM held four House seats and the SDP three. The SDP then disbanded prior to the elections, from which the FNM emerged with 11 seats and 44% of the vote. A key factor in the reunification of the opposition forces was the return to politics in 1981 of Kendall Isaacs, who had retired for reasons of health in the early 1970s. As a former attorney general and senator, he resolved the personality conflicts and brought the FNM renewed respect.

OTHER POLITICAL FORCES

The Trade Union Congress (TUC) was firmly associated with the PLP until 1975, after which its leadership moved toward the FNM. That party's dissention late in 1976 caused the TUC to negotiate an agreement with the PLP under which the party promised to give the TUC greater weight in forming party policy. Although the 1977 elections failed to demostrate the relative political clout of the TUC, the experiment did demonstrate a degree of independence of the TUC from the PLP.

Recent Political Changes

In 1992 Lynden O. Pindling suffered his first electoral defeat in 25 years. The FNM won control under the leadership of Hubert Ingraham, who had replaced Hubert Alexander as party head. Once in power, Ingraham instituted some major revisions of Pindling's policies. These changes included the privatization of most of the economically unsuccessful state-owned hotels and the establishment of a minimum wage of $4.15 an hour. An associated surge in the economy caused the unemployment rate to fall from 14% to 10%.

These circumstances induced Ingraham in February 1997 to call for early elections, the first such in 30 years. Standing and ringing a school bell 34 times, Ingraham predicted his party would win 34 seats. The results on March 4 vindicated his confidence (and obvious political astuteness) when his supporters did indeed win 34 of 40 seats in the House. All FNM candidates were reelected, the first such triumph in 20 years, and the party's share of the popular vote rose by 2.6% to 57.6%. At the same time, however, Ingraham stated that he would not seek another term.

NATIONAL PROSPECTS

This recent demonstration of democratic vitality in The Bahamas, along with the probable replacement of Pindling (now in his late 60s) as head of the PLP, suggests that the relative prosperity of the past decade is likely to continue. Because the major sectors of the economy are tourism and financial services, an image of political stability is a major factor. Both activities are extremely sensitive to social and political unrest, and financial flight could occur with little advance notice.

Current concerns are much the same as those of the past. The Bahamas continue to be one of the major conduits for the drug trade, both to Anglo-America and to Europe. Greater official cooperation with foreign enforcement agencies certainly is desirable, but few are so naive as to believe that the flow actually can be stopped. The Bahamas are geographically too fragmented and too close to the United States. Governmental measures to protect the oceanside environments that attract tourists, however, can do much to maintain or to increase the returns from this activity.

Further Reading

Caribbean Week: The Regional Newspaper of the Caribbean. St. Michael, Barbados.
CIA World Factbook. Washington, D.C.: Government Printing Office, various years.

STATE OF BAHRAIN

(Dawlah al-Bahrain)

By Fred H. Lawson, Ph.D.

THE SYSTEM OF GOVERNMENT

Bahrain, an island nation in the Persian Gulf, is a non-party autocracy whose ruler governs the country's 400,000 citizens in consultation with a small group of advisers that includes members of the ruling family and professional administrators. The ruling family is descended from a branch of the Bani 'Utub tribal confederacy that arrived in the islands around 1780 and set up a commercial, estate-holding aristocracy over the local inhabitants. Class distinctions were reinforced by religious ones, as the new rulers were Sunni Muslims and the indigenous farmers, pearl divers, and fisherfolk were Shi'i Muslims.

Serious outbreaks of political violence have occurred repeatedly in the country from at least 1911 to the present. These protests can be grouped into four distinct waves on the basis of the political forces that have been most actively involved in them. During the 1910s and 1920s, local merchants and tradespeople joined together in opposition to economic regulations proposed by British colonial officials. From the 1930s through the 1950s, a similarly broad coalition of social forces demonstrated against continued British domination, against the presence of large numbers of foreign workers on the islands, and in favor of allowing local labor to unionize. From the 1950s to the 1970s, riots and strikes pitted Bahrain's working class against the ruling family and state officials. Some protests took on sectarian overtones, appearing as conflicts between Sunnis and Shi'a; however, these incidents were for the most part characterized as well by persistent demands for changes in the country's economy to benefit poorer workers. Partly as a result of a general strike by construction, shipyard, and aluminum-plant workers in March 1972 that threatened the regime's industrialization program, Bahrain's emir (ruler) authorized the establishment of the country's first, but short-lived, electoral system, in which he assumed the role of constitutional monarch and his closest advisers acted as an appointed Cabinet.

Beginning in 1991, popular unrest reemerged both among educated Bahrainis demanding the reinstatement of the elected parliament and among poorer Shi'is agitat-ing for a more equitable social order. This fourth wave of protest assumed a more violent form in 1994, after security forces arrested key Shi'i leaders and steadily escalated confrontations with demonstrators.

Executive

Shaikh 'Isa bin Salman Al Khalifah (born 1933) became ruler of Bahrain in 1961 upon the death of his father. According to the constitution adopted in 1973, the office of emir passes from father to eldest son unless the ruler chooses someone else to succeed him. This section of Bahrain's constitution is not subject to amendment. Other parts of this document authorize the emir to act as head of state, to serve as commander in chief of the armed forces, and to "conclude treaties by decree." Such legal prerogatives are buttressed by tribal authority within the Khalifah clan.

Close relatives of the emir fill the most important posts in the country's Cabinet. Ministers who are not members of the Al Khalifah have largely been drawn from sons of the country's established rich merchant community who received specialized training in Western universities. A major reshuffle in July 1995 brought younger faces into the government but also replaced the long-time minister of development and industry, Yusif Ahmad al-Shirawi, with a member of the ruling family. Bahrain's largest industrial concerns are managed by this same collection of ruling family members and influential civil servants.

Legislature

Bahrain's first national elections were held in December 1972. Chosen were 22 representatives to a constitutional assembly by the country's native-born male citizens 20 years of age and older, grouped into 19 electoral districts centered on the cities and towns. Several candidates ran for office in each district, with the winner in single-member districts being the one who received a plurality of the votes cast. In each of the three two-member districts in Manama and Muharraq, the two candidates getting the most votes were the winners. Candidates ran as individuals or as part of informal, personalist slates headed by such prominent local businesspeople as 'Abd al-'Aziz Shamlan and Hisham al-Shahabi. These same procedures were followed in December 1973, when Bahrain's first National Assembly was elected.

College-educated professionals, shopkeepers, middle-income merchants, and the owners of the country's newspapers were the strongest supporters of the new electoral system. The merchant elite remained noncommital on the issue of a popularly elected parliament and did not participate in the elections either as candidates or as voters. Employees of the state bureaucracy also avoided becoming involved with the assemblies, since they would have had to resign their government posts in order to run for seats.

Radical organizations, such as the local branch of the Popular Front for the Liberation of Oman and the Arab Gulf (PFLOAG), actively tried to convince potential voters not to go to the polls on the grounds that the new assemblies represented only a facade for the continuation of autocratic rule. These organizations—whose members were largely workers and students, both indigenous and expatriate—demanded more comprehensive freedoms of press and assembly, the release of those they claimed were political prisoners, and the adoption of laws permitting trade unionization as first steps toward a democratic order.

Purely by chance, radical demands coincided with the last-minute withdrawal of the al-Shahabi slate from the 1972 constitutional assembly elections. This coincidence led the Cabinet to suspect collusion between the radicals and this slate of candidates, generating a measure of opposition inside the ruling family to the election process in general. As a result, when a group of younger representatives led by Dr. 'Abd al-Hadi Khalaf of the banned National Liberation Front–Bahrain and Yusif Hasan al-Ajaji emerged as winners in the 1973 balloting, the government prevented many of them from taking their seats in the Assembly on the basis of technicalities in the election law.

Despite the fact that the National Assembly was authorized only to give advice and consent to laws initiated in the Cabinet, and was thus not a true legislature, its members began seriously to debate two volatile issues during 1974. One issue was the formulation of a general labor law that would have permitted trade union organization and restricted the importation of foreign workers. The other major issue was the continuation of a strict Public Security Law that had been used to suppress the PFLOAG, Ba'this, and local communists. It became clear by mid-1975 that the two largest informal blocs of delegates within the Assembly, the People's and the Religious blocs, acting together could not force the government to cancel the Public Security Law. At the same time, the Cabinet and the Religious bloc could find no grounds for collaboration. Consequently, the National Assembly became hopelessly deadlocked. In August 1975, the prime mininister submitted the Cabinet's resignation to the

emir, who dissolved the Assembly but reinstated the government, giving the Cabinet "full legislative powers."

In January 1993, the ruler issued a decree creating an appointed Consultative Council (*majlis al-shura*) to replace the National Assembly. Members of the reconstituted body were granted the right to discuss laws proposed by the Cabinet as well as—under strictly limited conditions—to offer legislative proposals of their own. The 30 individuals named to the Consultative Council later that month included 22 prominent businesspeople, 3 members of the religious establishment, the president of the Bahrain Medical Society, a lawyer, a university professor, the editor of the newspaper *Akhbar al-Khalij*, and the vice chair of the General Committee of Bahraini Workers. Ten of these delegates had held seats in earlier assemblies, although none of them represented a formal party organization.

At the end of September 1996, the ruler replaced the existing Consultative Council with a new 40-member Council: 22 members retained their seats in the enlarged body, joined for the first time by a number of state officials. The reconfigured Council was authorized to raise issues for discussion regarding social, educational, health, and cultural affairs in addition to advising the Cabinet on policy.

In addition to the Consultative Council, the emir holds an open public meeting (*majlis*) each Friday to hear requests from individual citizens. These requests are referred directly to state agencies for appropriate action.

Judiciary

Bahrain's system of autonomous religious courts has gradually been incorporated into a centralized judiciary closely linked to the state bureaucracy. Sunni courts have a history of subservience to tribal custom and thus to the interests of the ruling family. Shi'i courts have resisted integration into a central structure but have been forced to accept a secondary role by their need for government subsidies to fund religious schools and other institutions. Following the dissolution of the National Assembly, the ruler set up a State Security Court to hear the cases of those charged with political crimes.

THE PARTY SYSTEM

Political parties, like trade unions, are prohibited by law. What little party system there is in Bahrain only began to emerge during the brief life of the National Assembly.

Three informal blocs appeared in the Assembly in the early part of 1974. The first, the People's bloc, advocated traditional labor demands for unionization, worker participation in economic policymaking, and higher wages. Its members came from poorer families of Manama and Muharraq (Bahrain's largest urban centers) and included

Ba'th Party, communist, and PFLOAG sympathizers. The Religious bloc also supported a wide range of labor reforms but tied these to demands for puritanical restrictions on the licensing of youth clubs, the sale of alcoholic beverages, and various aspects of relations between men and women in public places. Its members came from rural and suburban districts in which the Shi'a was predominant; they were supported—directly and indirectly—by the country's Shi'i religious authorities. Finally, the Independents advocated a number of diverse programs that were largely in line with the maintenance of an unregulated market economy on the islands, as well as the delegates' individual vested interests. These representatives were almost all middle-ranking merchants, contractors, and employers who had the support of their respective business associations, families, and social clubs.

OTHER POLITICAL FORCES

Radical Organizations

Since 1974, when the local section of the Popular Front for the Liberation of Oman and the Arab Gulf (PFLOAG) split with the more active parts of the movement based in southern Oman, there has been little overt political activity by the resultant Popular Front in Bahrain (PFB). Regionally oriented movements, such as the Palestine Liberation Organization, are tolerated by the authorities; predominantly local organizations have been systematically harassed and suppressed. When 'Abdullah Madani, the owner-editor of Manama's conservative newspaper *al-Mawaqif*, was found murdered in November 1976, the government accused those responsible of being PFB members. This connection was never proved. Both the PFB and the more radical National Liberation Front–Bahrain went underground following the dissolution of the National Assembly.

Student and Youth Associations

Youth and athletic-social clubs continue to provide forums for political discussion and mobilization. In March 1977, Bahrain's interior minister announced the closing of two youth clubs allegedly "infiltrated" by "some destructive elements." Members of two student organizations, the National Bahraini Club and the Bahraini Students' Club, clashed at Kuwait University in January 1978, apparently as a result of political disagreements. The clash precipitated arrests of students and other young people inside Bahrain the following month.

Religious Organizations

Antigovernment agitation by Shi'i religious leaders sympathetic to the Islamic Republic of Iran finds fertile ground among poorer Bahraini workers. Attempts to detain and deport militant preachers resulted in widespread demonstrations in the fall of 1979. At least one Shi'i secret society, al-Sanduq al-Husaini, was raided and several of its members were arrested by the police during the summer of 1980. But political demonstrations again erupted in Jidd Hafs—a working-class, Shi'i suburb of Manama—in early December of that same year. Quick action by state security forces appears to have been necessary to prevent the rioting from spreading to Zarariah, a poor district of Manama populated by unskilled foreign laborers.

In December 1981, government officials announced the arrest of more than 70 members of the Islamic Front for the Liberation of Bahrain (IFLB) for conspiring to overthrow the regime. This organization, led by the Hojateslam Hadi al-Mudarrisi, called for the overthrow of the Al Khalifah and the creation of an Islamic republic on the islands. The conviction and imprisonment of IFLB activists the following spring severely weakened the local Islamist movement but left a number of smaller, more militant groups largely intact. The authorities tried to undercut the appeal of such organizations by authorizing the establishment of joint worker-management councils in the country's larger factories. Joint councils already existed at Bahrain Petroleum Company and Aluminum Bahrain; in mid-1980 they were extended to plants operated by Gulf Air, the Arab Shipbuilding and Repair Yards, and other larger enterprises.

Bahrain's Shi'i movement revived after the 1990–91 Gulf War, when the government refused to recognize a string of petitions demanding the immediate reinstatement of the National Assembly. A leading Shi'i preacher, Shaikh 'Ali Salman, used his Friday sermons to appeal to the population to support the drive to recall parliament. In addition, his sermons criticized the government for failing to take steps to combat rising unemloyment among Bahraini citizens and commented on trends in regional affairs. Other prominent Shi'i religious figures joined Salman in demanding political reforms. Their efforts mobilized not only the general public but also such previously apolitical forces as the members of local religious societies (*husainiyyahs*) and women in outlying villages. Growing activism among the Shi'a led to a series of clashes between protesters and the police throughout 1994 that culminated in Salman's arrest and deportation in January 1995.

In the wake of Salman's forcible exile, popular protests broke out across the country. Security forces suppressed the demonstrations by force, detaining suspected activists and subjecting them to unsupervised interrogation and corporal punishment. Officials immediately accused foreign operatives of fomenting the violence and even produced a group of young Shi'is who confessed on local television to belonging to a Bahraini branch of Iranian-sponsored Hizbullah. By the last months of 1995, political agitation had turned into outbursts of arson and sabotage. Luxury hotels, state-affiliated commercial and industrial establishments, and cafes catering to foreign laborers were all attacked during the course of 1996. Meanwhile, the authorities began negotiating with the Shi'i religious leadership. These talks resulted in the release of several imprisoned preachers in September 1995, but crowds took to the streets once again when it became clear that others remained under arrest. An October 1995 rally outside the residence of Shaikh 'Abd al-Amir al-Jamri, who had started a hunger strike to protest the continued detentions, attracted some 75,000 protesters, making the event by far the largest political demonstration in the country's history.

NATIONAL PROSPECTS

As of late 1998 it remained an open question whether popular violence would succeed in convincing the Al Khalifah and its political allies to reinstitute an elected National Assembly. A Cabinet reshuffle in July 1995, the first since the mid-1970s, put one of the country's senior military officers in charge of the Ministry of Education. The new minister quickly appointed one of his fellow commanders as president of the University of Bahrain. In April 1996, the ruler created a Higher Islamic Affairs Council charged with approving the credentials of all preachers and religious scholars. Such measures complemented the government's evident proclivity to clamp down on proponents of political liberalization, rather than engaging advocates of reform in a dialogue.

At the same time, the persistent lack of secure and well-paying employment for Bahraini citizens represented a source of growing disaffection. State officials moved to deflect criticism of the regime's handling of this matter at the beginning of 1992 by soliciting new investment in local manufacturing and requiring all enterprises operating on the islands to raise the proportion of nationals they employed. But in the lean times of the mid-1990s, such regulations did little more than provide firms with an additional incentive to join the steady exodus of foreign capital out of the country, thereby threatening to reduce rather than increase the number of jobs available to Bahraini nationals. Tensions generated by the country's persistent economic problems, as well as friction arising from class and religious divisions, provide a number of issues around which organized political parties might coalesce.

Further Reading

Bahry, Louay. "The Opposition in Bahrain: A Bellwether for the Gulf?" *Middle East Policy* 5 (May 1997).

Gause, F. Gregory. *Oil Monarchies*. New York: Council on Foreign Relations Press, 1994.

Khuri, Fuad I. *Tribe and State in Bahrain*. Chicago: University of Chicago Press, 1980.

Lawson, Fred H. *Bahrain: The Modernization of Autocracy*. Boulder, Colo.: Westview Press, 1989.

Nakhleh, Emile A. *Bahrain*. Lexington, Mass.: D. C. Heath, 1976.

PEOPLE'S REPUBLIC OF BANGLADESH

(Gana Prajatantri Bangladesh)

By Craig Baxter, Ph.D.

THE SYSTEM OF GOVERNMENT

Bangladesh is a unitary state comprising the former East Pakistan province of Pakistan. With a population of about 120 million it is one of the most densely populated countries in the world. Since Bangladesh won its independence from Pakistan in a civil war in 1971, continuing political strife has allowed neither government selection and policymaking processes nor norms of office to become established. In December 1990, the president, General Hossain Muhammad Ershad, was forced from office. Elections were held in February 1991 for a new Parliament under a neutral caretaker government. The new government fell in 1995 under pressure from the opposition that all future elections be held under a neutral caretaker government. Following an election in February 1996, which was boycotted by the opposition, this demand was conceded through a constitutional amendment, and new elections were held in June 1996. The acceptance by all parties of the concept that elections will be held under neutral caretaker governments raises hope that the parliamentary form of government will continue.

Prior to the present government system, Bangladesh had experienced three different governmental periods and styles:

(1) A parliamentary system from 1972 to 1975, under the strong leadership of Sheikh Mujibur Rahman (Mujib),[1] the father of independence and leader of the Awami League[2]

(2) A presidential system (already established under Mujib just before his assassination) from 1975 to 1982, under General Ziaur Rahman

(3) A military-dominated presidential system with aspects of one-party rule under General Ershad from 1982 through 1990

The transitions between these periods, including the one leading to the present parliamentary system, all involved assassinations, coups, or other extraconstitutional actions. Throughout, the constitution was not abrogated, although it was often suspended or amended, usually by decree, to authorize whatever changes the leader desired.

Executive

Executive power is wielded by the prime minister, who is the head of government. She is the leader of the parliamentary majority, which includes members of parties other than her AL. The current prime minister is Sheikh Hasina Wajid, daughter of Mujib. The head of state or president (a largely ceremonial position) is elected by the Parliament; the post is occupied by Shahabuddin Ahmed. The powers of the prime minister, assisted by her Cabinet, are those expected in a Westminster form of government.

Legislature

The parliamentary election on June 10, 1996, was only the third that could be (and was, by outside observers) judged as "free and fair." Campaigning was open to all contestants. The principal contestants were the Bangladesh Nationalist Party (BNP) of Khaleda Zia, the outgoing prime minister; the AL led by Sheikh Hasina Wajid; the Jatiya Party led by former president Ershad (who was in prison); and the Islamic revivalist Jama'at-i-Islam. The results of the 1991 and June 1996 elections

TABLE 1
Seats Won in 1991 and June 1996 Elections

	Feb. 1991	June 1996
Bangladesh Nationalist Party	168	116
Awami League	88	173
Jatiya Party	5	35
Jama'at-i-Islam	20	3
Independents and Others	19	3

Source: Bangladesh Election Commission.
Note: These include the 30 indirectly elected seats for women. In 1991, the BNP won 28 and the JI 2. In June 1996, the AL won 27 and the JP 3.

---

[1]Following Bangladshi usage, hereafter Sheikh Mujibur Rahman will be referred to as "Mujib." Similarly, Ziaur Rahman will be referred to as "Zia," except in the first usage.

[2]Except in their first use, the principal parties will be abbreviated as follows: Awami League, AL; Bangladesh Nationalist Party, BNP; Jatiya Party, JP; and Jama'at-i-Islam, JI.

are given in Table 1 (there was also an election in February 1996 that was boycotted by the non-BNP parties).

In the 1991 election the BNP fell short of a majority but allied with the JI in the indirect polling for the women's seats. The constitution provides that there are to be 30 seats reserved for women elected by members of Parliament in addition to the 300 directly elected seats (for which women may also contest as did both prime ministers since 1991). This indirect polling gave the BNP a majority. With the support of the AL and other parties, the Parliament passed a constitutional amendment changing the system of government from a presidential form to a parliamentary form.

The AL, which fell short of a majority of seats in the direct election in June 1996, formed an alliance with the JP to form a majority in Parliament. The BNP is now the major party in the opposition.

Judiciary

The Supreme Court headed by the chief justice is the highest judicial body in the country and comprises an appellate division (the court of last appeal) and a high court division. The high court is an intermediate court of appeals between the appellate division and the district courts. The president appoints the chief justice and all other judges, including those in the appellate division and the high court division of the Supreme Court, in consultation with the chief justice. This convention was upheld in 1994 when the chief justice protested that he had not been consulted on appointments. The government backed down, and some of the appointments were withdrawn.

Regional and Local Government

Each of the governments in Bangladesh has made modifications in the local government system that were intended to bring government closer to the people. In the present system there are five levels of local government: division, region, district, *upazila* (literally, subdistrict), and local councils. There are six divisions covering different areas of the country: Dhaka (central), Chittagong (southeast), Sylhet (northeast), Barisal (south), Khulna (southwest), and Rajshahi (northwest). There are 19 regions, 64 districts, 486 *upazillas*, and 4,405 local councils. Urban areas have municipal committees that combine individual local councils. Four cities are municipal corporations that have a consolidated local government. These are Dhaka, Chittagong, Khulna, and Rajshahi. The members of the corporation (city council) are directly elected, as are the mayors. A city administrator (roughly equivalent to a city manager) is appointed by the central government.

Powers are unevenly divided among the various levels. The divisions are coordinating bodies concerned principally with development issues. They are headed by a civil servant designated a commissioner. The regions were formally called districts. In the 1982 reorganization of local government no specific powers were assigned to the regions and they exist in name only. The current districts are headed by a deputy commissioner and have elected councils. Their powers are limited but again center on development issues.

The key level of local government is the *upazilla*. The administration is headed by an *upazilla* officer and has an elected body, the *upazilla parishad*. It is here also that the court system begins. The *upazilla* council can consider all local issues, including such matters as health, family planning, education, agricultural development, and small industry. The *upazillas* receive development grants from the central government. These must be spent in specified areas for which maximum and minimum percentages are prescribed (e.g., for agriculture the range is 30% to 40% of the grant). The decisions within the ranges are made by the *upazilla parishad*.

Below the *upazillas* are the union councils. These have directly elected members and also some appointed members to represent underrepresented segments of the population. The councils have limited legislative powers because most of those have been transferred to the *upazillas*. They are concerned with such quite local issues as roads, veterinary clinics, elementary education, and health. The average population covered by a union is about 26,000.

THE ELECTORAL SYSTEM

The Parliament is elected by universal suffrage by all citizens over the age of 18, with the exception of the reserved women's seats mentioned earlier. The election is held from single-member constituencies, which are reapportioned following each decennial census, the last in 1991. Elections are on a first-past-the-post (plurality) system. Candidates, both men and women over the age of 21, of all political parties are eligible to contest as well as independents. The government takes responsibility for the registration of voters. The rules for local body elections are the same.

THE PARTY SYSTEM

Origins of the Parties

Political parties in Bangladesh originated during the struggle against British colonial rule that culminated in the independence of Pakistan in 1947 and its separation from India. Prior to independence the two major parties were the Muslim League, a party limited in membership to Muslims but not a party that could be described as "fundamentalist," and the Krishak Praja Party (Farmer's

People's Party), which represented the rural small land-holders and was, in form at least, open to both Muslims and Hindus.

After independence, the AL was founded specifically to be open to both Muslims and Hindus. An alliance of the refounded Krishak Sramik Party (KSP; Farmer's and Worker's Party) and the Awami League—the United Front—trounced the then governing Muslim League in the East Pakistan provincial assembly election in 1954. After martial law was imposed in 1958, the KSP gradually disappeared, leaving the Muslim League and the AL the major contestants in the 1970 election, in which the AL won an enormous victory and led Bangladesh to independence. Since the independence of Bangladesh the Muslim League has all but disappeared, although a small party operates under that name. The AL is a centrist party and has disclaimed the socialism espoused by Mujib. It and the other major parties, the BNP and the JP, are not communally (religiously) or regionally based, although the BNP and the JP are often described as center-right parties. The exception is the JI, which is an Islamic revivalist party.

The Parties in Law

There are at present no restrictions on political party activity although there have been in the past. Following the coup against Mujib in 1975 and the imposition of martial law by Ziaur Rahman in the same year and by Ershad in 1982, political activity including activity by parties was banned. As martial law was relaxed in each case, political party activity was allowed.

Party Organization

In general, Bangladeshi parties are hybrids combining mass- and cadre-party characteristics. In large part, party adherence reflects traditional patron-client relationships, particularly in the rural countryside (where more than 80% of the population lives). Kinship groups such as *gushti* (patrilineage) and *poribar* (family of procreation) and their residential distribution in the *bari* (cluster of households with a common courtyard) play a central role in local political alignments. Typically, political parties mobilize support from dominant and well-connected lineages, and much local political activity centers on recruiting locally powerful persons who head economically (ownership of land being an important indicator) or demographically dominant lineages that can activate a host of kin-group ties in their political support. The various small Marxist and left-wing parties also use kinship ties to mobilize support, often by capitalizing on tensions between rich and poor *baris* and on intralineage conflicts over landownership. The loyalty of influentials cannot be ensured by political parties as other parties try to win them over and are often successful

Policy or ideological issues have generally played little part in campaigns except in the urban areas, although issue-based politics is increasing in the rural areas. Of greater importance is the role played by personalities and their manipulation of traditional patron-client structures. Violence has been a common feature in campaigning, although much less was reported in the 1991 and June 1996 campaign and balloting.

Bangladesh has over 50 parties of varying size and strength, most of them little more than projections of personalities. The following are the most important.

AWAMI LEAGUE (AL)

HISTORY

The AL was founded as the Awami Muslim League in 1949 by Husain Shaheed Suhrawardy and Abdul Hamid Khan Bhashani (who subsequently broke away to form another party, the National Awami Party). The word "Muslim" was soon dropped in order to open the party to all communities, most notably the Hindus, who formed nearly one-fifth of the population of East Pakistan in the 1950s. The AL headed several coalition governments in East Pakistan from 1956 to 1958 and was represented in several coalitions in the Pakistan central government in 1956, 1957, and 1958. Suhrawardy was Pakistan's prime minister, 1956–57.

In the elections held in 1970, the AL won 160 or the 162 East Pakistan seats in the Pakistan National Assembly and 288 of the 300 seats in the East Pakistan Assembly. Subsequently, under Mujib's leadership, it led the movement for independence and was the ruling party in Bangladesh from 1971 to 1975.

After Mujib's assassination in August 1975, the party was temporarily banned along with all other parties and the leader, Abdul Malek Ukil, was jailed. In the 1978 presidential election, it supported the unsuccessful campaign of General Muhammad Ataul Ghani Osmany against the BNP's General Ziaur Rahman. The same year the party split when a small group led by Mizanur Rahman Choudhury formed its own AL; Mizan later joined the JP and was briefly prime minister. In February 1981, Mujib's daughter, Sheikh Hasina Wajid, was recalled from India, where she had been in exile, and assumed the leadership. She is the present prime minister.

ORGANIZATION

The personalized nature of the party and the severity of factional conflict weaken the party's organizational structure. Factionalism was to some extent inherent in the "umbrella" nature of the AL: as the party of independence, it was composed of divergent interests. Factionalism can also be attributed to what is often characterized as a Bengali propensity for political schism. With Mujib's death and the party's loss of power, factional conflict erupted and led to the 1978 split. Factionalism has also been rampant in the various fronts organized by the party among students (Bangladesh Students League), labor (Jatiyo Sramik League), peasants (Jatiyo Krishak League), and youth (Awami Jubo League). However, it can be said that the assumption of the leadership by Sheikh Hasina has moderated the degree of factionalism, as has the party's success in the June 1996 election.

The party's central office is located at 23 Bangabandhu Avenue, Dhaka.

POLICY

Early on, the party was an advocate of a socialist economy. The four principles of Mujib's program were democracy, socialism, secularism, and nationalist. Of the four, socialism has been abandoned, and the party now stands for a market economy, although in office it has been slow to move in this direction. Nonetheless, many of the more senior leaders appear reluctant to abandon socialism and state-owned enterprises completely. The major campaign issue for the AL in the 1991 election was the restoration of a parliamentary system of government. In the eyes of many voters in that election, the demand for democracy was tempered by the recollection that it was Mujib who first ended democracy. Another key demand was the punishment of the assassins of Mujib, who, although known, have not yet been tried.

MEMBERSHIP AND CONSTITUENCY

Initially emerging as a middle-class body representing urban professionals (lawyers, businesspeople, teachers, doctors) and students, its support base expanded during the Bangladeshi independence movement to incorporate a wide variety of interests. Popular support for the party (strongest in 1971) diminished rapidly in the face of its poor record in office and the growth of corruption in its ranks. While the elections of 1979 and 1981 demonstrated the reemergence of considerable support for the AL, its defeat indicated that the majority of people still recalled its record in office uneasily. The same concerns seemed to be a primary factor in limiting the appeal of the AL in 1991, but it was able to gain a plurality in both the popular vote and in seats in Parliament in June 1996. As a party advocating secularism, it appeals strongly to the Hindu minority (now approximately 12% of the population). No membership figures are available.

FINANCING

No information is available on party financing.

LEADERSHIP

Party leadership is now dominated by persons in their mid- and late 40s. Among the important leaders now are Sheikh Hasina Wajid (born 1947, Gopalganj district),

chairperson and prime minister, who has a power base in her home district and also draws strength from being the daughter of Mujib; Abdur Razzak (born 1942, Shariatpur district), former general secretary and minister of water resources, whose power base is in the Faridpur region; and Tofail Ahmed (born 1943, Bhola district), minister of industries and commerce and earlier an important student leader, whose power base is in the southern areas of the country.

PROSPECTS

The party banked on what it described as the failures of the BNP government of Khaleda Zia and was successful in gaining the leadership of the government following the June 1996 election. It also won in 1994 the mayoral elections in Dhaka and Chittagong, urban areas where the BNP had previously been the stronger party. It is too early to tell how the present government will fare, but the party clearly hopes that its record will earn it reelection in 2001.

BANGLADESH NATIONALIST PARTY (BNP)
(Bangladesh Jatiyabadi Dal)

HISTORY

The BNP was formed in September 1978 by President (General) Ziaur Rahman from sections of the parties that had supported his successful candidacy in the 1978 presidential election: the National Democratic Party (launched in February 1978 under the leadership of Vice President Abdus Sattar with Zia's blessing), the pro-Beijing National Awami Party (NAP), the leftist United People's Party, a portion of the Muslim League, and an organization representing Hindu scheduled castes ("untouchables"). After Zia's assassination in May 1981, power struggles in the BNP, particularly over the selection of its presidential candidate in 1981, seriously threatened its unity. An open split was averted by the timely intervention of the army chief, General Ershad, who persuaded Acting President Abdul Sattar to stand for election as a compromise candidate. Despite his election victory, Sattar was unable to control intraparty factionalism, thus provoking the military to depose him. Other causes of Ershad's coup included allegations of corruption and Sattar's refusal to agree to Ershad's demand for a constitutional role for the military in the governance of the country.

The party strongly opposed Ershad's regime, although some dissidents deserted and joined Ershad. Zia's widow, Khaleda Zia, became chairperson in May 1984; being consistent in her opposition, she stemmed the outflow of members. The BNP refused to contest the 1986 and 1988 elections under Ershad's government and worked with the AL to cause Ershad's fall in December 1990. In the 1991 election for Parliament, the BNP won a plurality of seats and was able to form a government with Khaleda Zia as prime minister. She is now the leader of the opposition.

ORGANIZATION

The BNP began as a hastily assembled, loosely structured party formed to support Zia's political ambitions. It comprised four distinct and seemingly incongruent strands: (1) Zia's own factional followers, many of whom formerly belonged to the military and the bureaucracy; (2) much of the leadership and party cadres of the Muslim League; (3) many from Bhashani's faction of the leftist NAP; and (4) a number of prominent people who had not previously been active in party politics. Fissures in the BNP were thus inherent in its heterogeneous composition and focused on divisions such as retired military and civilian bureaucrats versus politicians; socialists versus nonsocialists, Islamists versus secularists, freedom fighters versus "collaborators." It was Zia's personality and official patronage that held this uneasy coalition together. The party suffered a number of defections to Ershad's JP after the 1982 coup and the partial civilianization of that government (for example, a former minister, Moudud Ahmed, who rose to become prime minister and vice president under Ershad but who has now rejoined the BNP, an example of the limited loyalty to parties in Bangladesh).

Khaleda Zia as leader must put forward considerable effort to retain a workable balance in a party that still has sharp differences, some personal and some ideological. These were evident even when she was prime minister and are likely to continue with the party in opposition.

The party has a student wing (*Jatiyotabadi Chhatra Dal*), which is also factionalized. It played a major role, as did the AL's student front, in the overthrow of the Ershad regime.

The party's central office is located at 28/1 Nayapaltan, Dhaka.

POLICY

The platform of the party is based on the 19-point program announced by Zia prior to his election to the presidency. It is a general program of development for Bangladesh that includes improvements in agriculture, education, health services, and population planning. Nationalism is stressed, but this does not mean self-reliance; it is understood that foreign assistance is required to reach the development goals. In general the party displays some distrust of India and is not fully supportive of the 1996 agreement with India, negotiated by the AL government, that governs the division of the waters of the Ganges River between the two countries. The BNP supports free-market economics and the continuance of the privatization program of Ershad. Secularism is not as strongly advocated as in the AL program, but modifications of secularism have been limited; an Islamic state is not a goal.

In the 1991 election, the BNP favored a presidential system of government. However, after the election, it reversed its position and joined with the AL in supporting a return to a parliamentary system. Among the reasons for the change was the recognition that with only 31% of the popular vote in the parliamentary election, a BNP victory in a directly elected presidential poll was anything but assured.

MEMBERSHIP AND CONSTITUENCY

The BNP draws support from a broad cross section of society. Like the AL and the JP, it is not regionally centered. It perhaps draws less support from the Hindu minority than the AL. No membership figures are available.

FINANCING

No information is available on party financing.

LEADERSHIP

Current leaders are Khaleda Zia (born 1945), party chairperson and leader of the opposition in Parliament; and Abdul Mannan Bhuiyan, general secretary.

PROSPECTS

Having lost the June 1996 election, the BNP must be seen to be acting as a responsible opposition, both in the sense of cooperating with the government in passing legislation and working to modify bills. The BNP is surely to remain as one of the key parties in Bangladesh.

JATIYA PARTY (JP)

HISTORY

The JP was formed in 1985 as a vehicle for the political ambitions of Ershad. It included a number of defectors from the BNP and the AL, along with some who entered politics from business and the bureaucracy (many of the latter did not remain in politics). Among those brought into the party from the BNP were former ministers Moudud Ahmed and Kazi Zafar Ahmad and from the AL, Mizanur Rahman Choudhury, all of whom became prime ministers under Ershad.

ORGANIZATION

Ershad was jailed following his fall from power and was not released on bail until January 1997. During the time he was in jail, Mizanur Rahman Choudhury was acting chairperson. Ershad remains the key leader of the party and with his freedom the party organization may be strengthened. Anwar Hossain Manju, minister of communications, represents the party in the Sheikh Hasina Cabinet and is general secretary of the party. Moudud Ahmed who had been parliamentary leader in the Parliament elected in 1991 has since left the JP and rejoined the BNP.

The party office is at 85 Elephant Road, Magh Bazar, Dhaka.

POLICY

It is difficult to find significant differences between the policies of the JP and the BNP other than the treatment of Ershad. Although Ershad made major changes in policy on local government, his changes in the 19-point program of Ziaur Rahman were slight. An early attempt by Ershad to move toward Islamization was abandoned, although his party's commitment to secularism, like that of the BNP, is not as firmly rooted as that of the AL. Ershad hastened the divestment of state-owner properties. The party remains favorable toward the presidential system, although its members are working within the parliamentary system.

MEMBERSHIP AND CONSTITUENCY

The JP, like the BNP, tries to draw support from a wide range of society. It undoubtedly had hoped to find additional support from the leadership of the union councils and the *upazilla parishads*; the additional powers gained by these groups have come through changes initiated by Ershad. This hope has not materialized.

FINANCING

No information is available on the financing of the party.

LEADERSHIP

As mentioned above, the leadership of the party is vested in Ershad. Others key to the party are Anwar Hossain Manju, general secretary and a minister, Mizanur Rahman Choudhury, who was acting leader while Ershad was in jail, and Kazi Zafar Ahmad.

PROSPECTS

The prospects for the JP are not bright. As a party it will probably remain a third force in Bangladeshi politics with some leaders continuing to be elected to Parliament on the basis of their personal local following. These include Ershad in his home district of Rajshahi. Defections have already hurt the party. The strong personal dislike between Khaleda Zia of the BNP and Ershad appears to preclude a merger. The alliance the JP has now with the AL is not likely to lead to a merger.

JAMA'AT-I-ISLAM (JI)
(Islamic Assembly)

HISTORY

The JI is the Bangladeshi manifestation of an Islamic revivalist party founded by Maulana Syed Abu Ala Maududi in 1940 in India. After independence in 1947, it became an important, but generally unsuccessful, party in Pakistan. The present party in Bangladesh is the successor to the party's branch in East Pakistan.

ORGANIZATION

The JI is a tightly organized, cadre-based party, whose head is the *amir* (leader). Below the central body of the party are district and lower-level organizations that owe allegiance to the central body and take direction from it. It is not fully organized in all areas of the country. It appears to be strongest in membership (not in voting strength) in urban areas. On the other hand, 11 of the 18 seats it won in the 1991 parliamentary election were in districts bordering India. This number was greatly reduced (to 3) in the June 1996 election, only 1 in a district bordering India.

Its central office is located at 505 Wareless Railgate, Elephant Road, Magh Bazar, Dhaka.

POLICY

The JI advocates the establishment of an Islamic state in which law would be based on and in agreement with Islamic law, the *sharia*. A precise definition of what this would mean in the context of Bangladesh has not been given, but it is generally assumed that among other things it would mean the restriction of rights for women and minority groups.

FINANCING

Although no information on financing is available, it is believed that a major source of funding is contributions from middle-class businesspeople to whom the program of the JI has the greatest appeal.

LEADERSHIP

Golam Azam, a longtime member of the JI who spent many years in Pakistan after Bangladeshi independence, is the present *amir*.

PROSPECTS

With its 6% of the popular vote and 18 directly elected seats (increased to 20 by the indirect election for women's seats) in 1991, the JI seems to have reached its peak. As noted, the party's share of the seats dropped to 3 in the June 1996 election. The policy of striving for an Islamic state is not widely accepted in Bangladesh, where Islam tends to be a personal matter not to be subjected to state policy.

MINOR POLITICAL PARTIES

There are a host of other so-called parties in Bangladesh, a few of whom might send representatives to Parliament. These representatives are usually local notables who could probably run on any party's ticket and win election. In the 1991 Parliament only two parties had as many as five members: the Communist Party of Bangladesh and BAK-SAL (Bangladesh Krishak Sramik Awami League), a remnant of the party formed by Mujib in 1975 when he decreed a one-party state. In the June 1996 poll, only three persons were elected from groups other than the four principal parties, and one of those described himself as an independent. However, one member from the tiny Jatiyo Samajtantrik Dal, a leftist group, was included in the Sheikh Hasina Cabinet.

OTHER POLITICAL FORCES

The military has twice declared martial law, in 1975 and 1982, under the leadership of Zia and Ershad, respectively. However, the role of the military in politics has decreased. When Ershad was forced to resign in 1990, the military reportedly refused to come to his assistance. Reported political actions by military officers in 1996 resulted in the dismissal of those accused. This met with no active response from other military officers. It is far too early to aver that the military will not play a role in politics in the future, but its participation seems far less likely than in the past.

The bureaucracy has also played a role at times. Most recently, during the 1995 agitation by the AL, JP, JI, and others against the BNP government's refusal to accept the demand for the holding of elections under neutral caretaker governments, several civil servants clearly stated their support of the demand. This, however, is rare. Another example came in 1971 when some civil servants left the Pakistan government positions they held, while others remained at their posts. Senior civil servants do exercise much power in decision and policymaking.

Students can be and have been mobilized for political activity. Each major party has a student wing. In the 1990 agitation against Ershad, the agreement between the BNP and AL student wings forced the parent bodies and their leaders, Khaleda Zia and Sheikh Hasina, to work together on a single-point program: the ouster of Ershad followed by free and fair elections.

Parties also have associated labor and farmers' groups. With a low level of industrialization, labor groups are not large, but they are mainly concentrated in urban areas and can at times, such as during the demonstrations against Ershad, add numbers to the demonstrators. Farmers' groups are less active if for no other reason than the lack of easy means to communicate in rural areas. In rural (as well as urban) areas, a more recent phenomenon is nongovernmental organizations. Many of these are centered on the "uplift" of women and therefore draw the wrath of the JI.

NATIONAL PROSPECTS

At its independence, Bangladesh was described as an "international basketcase." In the 25 years of independence,

it has clearly graduated from that category. It has made impressive strides in agricultural development and in population planning. Nonetheless, the country's economy remains subject to the pressure of population and the vagaries of climate that produce floods and cyclones. Bangladesh is short of three required resources for development: (1) financial resources for savings and investment; (2) human resources in the sense of a trained, well-fed, and healthy population; and (3) natural resources, other than a fertile soil and natural gas, that could lead to a greater share of industry in the gross domestic product. It has found some niches in industry, especially the highly successful garment industry, which has surpassed jute as the principal export. Bangladesh, however, will remain for many years to come a major recipient of international development assistance.

The political institutions are also weak. The parliamentary system would work more successfully if the role of the opposition were a constructive one and if the government would accord the opposition respect. This was not done in the 1991 Parliament and the beginning of the Parliament, elected in June 1996 does not auger well for this Parliament. The present BNP opposition has boycotted Parliament as did the AL, JP, and JI opposition toward the end of the 1991 Parliament. Interest groups are all but nonexistent, and the media are only now beginning to develop. However, the depoliticization of the military, if it continues, makes the continuation of the parliamentary system more likely.

Further Reading

Ahmed, Moudud. *Bangladesh: Era of Mujibur Rahman*. Dhaka: University Press, 1983.

———. *Democracy and the Challenge of Democracy*. Dhaka: University Press, 1995.

Banu, U.A.B. Razia Akter. *Islam in Bangladesh*. Leiden, Holland: Brill, 1992.

Baxter, Craig. "Bangladesh: Can Democracy Survive?" *Current History* 95, no. 600 (April 1996), 182–86.

———. *Bangladesh: From a Nation to a State*. Boulder, Colo.: Westview Press, 1997.

Baxter, Craig, and Syedur Rahman. *Historical Dictionary of Bangladesh*, 2d ed. Lanham, Md: Scarecrow Press, 1996.

Choudhury, Dilara. *Constitutional Development in Bangladesh*. New York: Oxford University Press, 1994.

Heitzman, James, and Robert L. Worden, eds. *Bangladesh: A Country Study*. Washington, D.C.: Library of Congress, 1989.

Hossain, Golam. *General Ziaur Rahman and the BNP*. Dhaka: University Press, 1988.

Maniruzzaman, Talukder. *The Bangladesh Revolution and Its Aftermath*. Dhaka: Bangladesh Books International, 1980.

Novak, James. *Bangladesh: Reflections on the Water*. Bloomington: Indiana University Press, 1993.

BARBADOS

By Thomas D. Anderson, Ph.D.

Barbados is a parliamentary democracy that gained independence from Britain in 1966. It is a small island (430 square kilometers) that lies in the Atlantic Ocean about 150 kilometers east of the Windward Islands. The population of about 257,000 is 80% black, 16% mixed, and perhaps 4% white. It is a largely Protestant, English-speaking populace with a literacy rate of 99% (age 15 and over). With an urban proportion of only 38%, the rural population density is one of the highest in the world. The inhabitants of Barbados call themselves "Bajans."

The formal head of state is the British monarch represented by a governor-general. The governor-general appoints as prime minister the leader of the political party that holds the most seats in the National Assembly. In practice, the prime minister exercises the executive power in the government.

The bicameral legislature consists of the Senate and the House of Assembly. The Senate has 21 members appointed by the governor-general: 12 on the advice of the prime minister; 2 on the advice of the leader of the opposition; and 7 on the advice of religious, economic, cultural, and community organizations. The House of Assembly consists of 28 members, who serve five years upon winning a plurality in direct elections.

The Barbadian judicial system is based on English common law, which is administered by a system of courts of summary jurisdiction and the Supreme Court of the Judicature. The latter consists of the High Court and the Court of Appeal.

Barbados is divided into 11 parishes and the municipality of Bridgetown, the capital. All local government units are under central government control. All Bajans 18 years of age or older are eligible to vote. Parliamentary candidates are elected by simple plurality in single-member districts. Voter turnout traditionally is approximately 70%.

General literacy on a small island with a free press provides a well-informed and politically conscious electorate. Campaigns usually are marked by spirited competition between well-organized constituency groups. Party loyalty notwithstanding, elections can be decided on the basis of personality. National elections are scheduled at five-year intervals.

Although at least five other parties regularly vie for Assembly seats, party identification is strongest with the Barbados Labour Party (BLP) and the Democratic Labour Party (DLP). The BLP, which developed out of the trade union movement, was founded by Grantley Adams in 1946 to work for economic improvement and the extension of political rights. Under the leadership of Grantley Adams's son, John Michael Geoffrey "Tom" Adams, the BLP has pursued a cautious domestic and foreign policy that supported free enterprise and encouraged foreign investment. It is an essentially social democratic party that has actively opposed Marxist political activities in the region. In the last general election, held in September 1994 following a no-confidence vote that went against the incumbent prime minister, Erskine Sandiford, the DLP was defeated and a BLP government headed by Owen Arthur (the current prime minister) came to power. Although the BLP has lost some support in recent times because of its stance on taxes, it still has a strong parliamentary majority.

The Democratic Labour Party was founded in 1955 under the chairmanship of F. G. Smith and consisted primarily of dissidents from the BLP. Once regarded as to the right of the BLP, the DLP has in recent years shifted to a social democratic position more similar to that of the BLP on many issues.

Since independence, Barbados has been one of the best-governed countries in the world, and there are no reasons to believe that this status will not continue. Like most small former colonial entities, it did not begin self-rule in a prosperous condition, yet it has emerged as one of the most economically successful of the new countries. Aside from some (currently) minor deposits of offshore natural gas, it has no mineral base and a very crowded rural sector. Nonetheless, in 1997 its GDP per capita was estimated to be $6,560 (US). Unlike most of its Caribbean neighbors, this stems from an economy that blends productive agriculture with light manufacturing and tourism. The latter is likely to continue to be the most important, but increasingly wedging into the economic triad is an electronic dimension that includes software and computer services. Internationally Barbados has cooperated with its neighbors and with the United States, although a traditional cautionary stance is maintained with respect to the latter. Prime Minister Owen Arthur in 1997 instituted a program of instruction in conversational Spanish in primary schools, an action that appears to be an increased recognition of the need for closer interaction with its Continental neighbors.

BELARUS

(Republika Bielorus')

By Jeffrey K. Hass, Ph.D.

A landlocked nation, Belarus is located in central-eastern Europe, with Poland and Russia on the western and eastern borders, Ukraine to the south, and Latvia and Lithuania to the north. The climate is between continental and maritime; the winters are cold and summers are cool. Much of the terrain is flat, and there are several square kilometers of marshland. Much of southern Belarus was contaminated by the Chernobyl accident; while Ukraine was host to the disaster, the radioactive fallout harmed Belarusian territory worse than Ukrainian land, contaminating more than 20% of Belarusian land and leading to, at one count, approximately 400,000 cancer deaths.

Belarus had, as of July 1996, a population of roughly 10.4 million, with 47% male and 53% female. While the death rate was higher than the birth rate, a slight immigration wave left population growth at 0.2%. The life expectancy for males was 63.2 years and for females 74.2 years; however, such statistics might not take into account deaths resulting from Chernobyl radiation. Belarusians make up 77.9% of the population, followed by Russians (13.2%), Poles (4.1%), Ukrainians (2.9%), and various others. Eastern Orthodoxy reigns as the religion of the majority, while Roman Catholics and Muslims make up minorities. Belarusian and Russian are the dominant languages, but the extent of a "pure" Belarusian language is not entirely clear.

THE SYSTEM OF GOVERNMENT

The Belarusian political system is, in theory, democratic and following a federal structure. Belarus is divided into six *voblasti* and one municipality (Minsk, the national capital). According to the Belarusian constitution, which was adopted on March 15, 1994, the legal system is one of civil law (rather than Anglo-American common law) and comprises three branches, the executive (president and prime minister), the legislature (Supreme Soviet), and the judiciary (Supreme and Constitutional Courts). In practice, however, Belarus is a dictatorship under the command of Aleksandr Lukashenko, who has used executive power to undermine the constitution, the legislature, local power, the judiciary, the media, and basic freedoms such as freedom of association and speech.

Executive

The executive branch is headed by the president, who serves as a national leader, and the prime minister, who acts as the head of government. The prime minister's duties are straightforward: He suggests and implements policies, leads the state bureaucracy, and coordinates the activities of the numerous ministries. However, the actual powers and duties of the president have been in flux.

Initially, Belarus did not have a presidency. In 1991, in the wake of a failed August coup, the Supreme Soviet named its deputy speaker, Stanislav Shushkevich, to be the "president of the [Belarusian] parliament" and carry out the duties of a weak president; that is, Belarus did not have a formal, Western-style presidency but had instead a temporary presidential position. Additionally, Vyacheslav Kebich served as prime minister for the now-independent republic, carrying out such duties as running the state bureaucracy and promoting and implementing domestic policies. Shushkevich's duties included meeting with foreign dignitaries and serving as a central figurehead for suggesting policies and legislation. However, in reality, Shushkevich had even fewer powers than the emasculated presidents of Eastern European nations or pre-Kuchma Ukraine.

Following labor protests in the autumn of 1993 and a signature campaign by the Belarusian Popular Front (BPF) to move parliamentary elections from 1995 to March 1994, the parliament, in January 1994, removed Shushkevich as parliamentary president, leaving executive functions with the prime minister. On March 15, 1994, the parliament added an article to the draft constitution (passed March 15, 1994) creating a presidency and called for elections to be held on June 26, 1994. Aleksandr Lukashenko won the first and second rounds of voting and became the first Belarusian president, and he then proceeded to consolidate power in the presidency.

According to the 1994 constitution, the president was

a weak figurehead whose basic function was to nominate the heads of the Constitution Court and the Electoral Commission, represent Belarus on the international stage, take part in the work of the Supreme Soviet (including suggesting legislation), and, in general, head the executive branch. In November 1994, in a move to enhance his own powers, Lukashenko created the "presidential vertical line," sending presidentially appointed representatives to regions and districts to abrogate local political power and to answer directly to the president, rather than the regional and district electorate. Then in April 1995, Lukashenko called for a referendum in which Belarusians expressed 75% support for returning Soviet-era political symbols to prominence, 77.6% support for presidential powers to dissolve parliament (if it violates the constitution), 82.4% support for economic integration with Russia, and 83.1% support for making Russian a second official language.

In another move to enhance his power, Belarus held a national referendum in November 1996 to replace the 1994 constitution with a new version drafted by Lukashenko. Originally planned for November 7 (in honor of the Bolshevik Revolution), the referendum was moved by Lukashenko to November 24. While the Constitutional Court and the Election Commission ruled that the referendum was illegal—the 1994 constitution gave this right to call one only to the Supreme Soviet—Lukashenko ignored the parliament and the Court and dismissed the head of the Electoral Commission. The newly passed constitution strengthened the powers of the president vis-à-vis the legislature—for example, the Senate was to be appointed by the president rather than directly elected (see below). Additionally, the new constitution lengthened the term of office.

In the referendum, 70.5% of Belarusians voted in support of Lukashenko's draft constitution while 7.9% supported the parliamentary draft of the constitution. Accusations of vote tampering followed the referendum but to little effect.

Legislature

Lukashenko's 1996 constitution altered the legislature. It renamed the Supreme Soviet the "National Assembly," which henceforth was to be bicameral. It was now composed of the Chamber of Representatives (the lower house), whose 110 members were to be elected directly through single-mandate elections, and the Senate (upper house), appointed directly by the president and by regional authorities (those elected and those executive representatives appointed by the president). The first members of the lower house were those delegates of the old Supreme Soviet who had remained loyal to Lukashenko during the political confrontations of 1996.

The Senate was now composed of 9 members from each *oblast* and Minsk, for a total of 63. Of the 9, 6 are elected at meetings of deputies of local- and *oblast*-level soviets; the other three in each *oblast* are appointed by the president. Further, the president, after his term, was to become a senator for life. The National Assembly comes up for election and appointment every five years.

According to the constitution, the National Assembly has the power to legislate. The Chamber of Representatives is authorized to "consider" legislation proposed by the president or by 150,000 or more citizens; further, the Chamber has the right to consider questions of no confidence and impeachment proceedings (at the risk of provoking dissolution). The Senate has the power to adopt or reject those laws passed by the Chamber and to elect six judges of the Constitutional Court. Bills that receive a majority vote in the Chamber (where legislation is initiated) must receive majority support in the Senate. If the president signs the bill or lets it sit for two weeks, the bill becomes law; if the president vetoes the bill, it returns to the National Assembly for reconsideration and possible alteration. A two-thirds majority in both houses can override the presidential veto.

In practice, however, Belarus's legislature has been more of a rubber stamp for Lukashenko. Not only is the legislature weak institutionally, but the Chamber delegates are those who were loyal to Lukashenko in 1996 and the senators are appointed by Lukashenko or his subordinates. In Stalinist fashion, Lukashenko has made the National Assembly "his" body through law and through the power of appointment. In the practice of power, the parliament has lost and remains today in the shadow of the president.

Judiciary

It may as yet be too early to speak about an effective, independent judiciary. In theory the judicial branch is autonomous from other branches and answerable only to the law. The job of lower courts, at the local and district levels, is to adjudicate disputes and rule on criminal cases. Belarusian law follows the continental system, where courts apply laws rather than rule on them or use precedent to establish legal interpretations. Cases coming before the court are argued de novo each time.

However, the courts do not appear to have autonomy, which may be in part because of pressure from above. Lukashenko repeatedly disavowed the rulings and legitimacy of the pre-1997 Constitutional Court, and so the present Court, being appointed by the president and aware of the history of interbranch relations, may be playing a game of political safety.

The highest judicial organ is the Supreme Court, which has the right and obligation to rule on the constitutionality of presidential decrees and parliamentary legislation and has the duty to rule on the grounds of poten-

tance on the world stage may have helped Lukashenko avoid the scrutiny that Boris Yeltsin constantly feels. Finally, the bulk of the Belarusian population does not seem actively opposed to Lukashenko's actions; in fact, Lukashenko appears to have some (tacit) support among the population, which desires a strong leader to guide Belarus out of political and economic problems.

For political stability to be achieved, either a compromise between Lukashenko and his opposition must be reached or one side must win the political battle. At present Lukashenko shows no signs of suggesting a compromise on any terms but his own. As long as he continues his dictatorial behavior, opposition will continue. A democratic outcome for Belarus appears dim at present; and some degree of political calm will only be achieved by repression.

The second issue that must be addressed is one of solving the problem of national identity. While Belarus does enjoy an historical heritage, stretching back to ties with the Grand Duchy of Lithuania and the Commonwealth of Poland in the 13th and 16th centuries, it lacks a widespread sense of contemporary unique identity as is the case in Ukraine or the Baltic states. Can local dialects, which differ from Russian, be considered Belarusian? How many Belarusians speak a "native tongue" fluently and as a first language? When we consider that until Soviet leader Mikhail Gorbachev undertook repressive measures in 1991, the Belarusian population at large did not support independence (as did the populations of Ukraine or the Baltic countries), this problem stands out.

The third issue is a need to clarify relations with Russia. On the one hand, the increasing integration of Belarus's economy into Russia's could result in important improvements. While adopting Russia's tariff and tax structures may bring initial pain, obtaining resources will be easier and cheaper, and being under Russia's "economic wing" may force additional economic reforms. However, integration could threaten both a political and nationalist backlash. On the one hand, Lukashenko has been supportive of integration; he even voted against the Belarusian Supreme Soviet's resolution to leave the Soviet Union. However, Lukashenko also wants Belarus to be admitted to Russia as an "equal partner," and it is not at all obvious that Russian leaders have such plans.

Were Belarus to be swallowed bit by bit into Russia, it might have at best a status as some sort of "special *oblast*," but this would not shore up Lukashenko's power, especially as regions in Russia have gained more autonomy and democratic procedures for choosing leaders; this cannot appeal to Lukashenko's drive for power. On the other hand, nationalism and national identity in Belarus have been weak, far weaker than in the Baltic states, Ukraine, or Eastern Europe; a unique, independent Belarusian identity does not seem so widespread beyond the elite as is the case in (western) Ukraine. Integration into Russia could cut out such an embryonic identity and could lead nationalist-inclined elites to grow even more vocal.

Further Reading

CIA Factbook, 1996. Washington, D.C.: Government Printing Office, 1996.

Eggleston, Roland. "Belarus: Country Headed toward Totalitarianism." RFERL, June 3, 1997 (www.rferl.org).

Fedor, Helen, ed. *Belarus and Moldova Country Studies.* Washington, D.C.: Federal Research Division, Library of Congress, 1995.

Mihalisko, Kathleen. "Belarus." *RFERL Research Report,* February 14, 1992, 6–10.

———. "Belorussia: Setting Sail without a Compass." *RFERL Research Report,* January 3, 1992, 39–41.

Open Research Media Institute (OMRI).

Radio Free Europe/Radio Liberty (RFERL). RFERL can be accessed on the Internet at www.rferl.org.

Report on the Belarusian Presidential Elections. Washington, D.C.: Commission on Security and Cooperation in Europe, 1994.

KINGDOM OF BELGIUM

(Koninkrijk Belgi; Royaume de Belgique)
By William G. Andrews, Ph.D.

THE SYSTEM OF GOVERNMENT

Belgium, with a population of 10.1 million, is a constitutional, federal, parliamentary monarchy. It formed when the Catholic southern provinces of the Netherlands, including part of present-day Luxembourg, seceded after the 1830 revolution. The 1831 Belgian constitution was more liberal and democratic than the authoritarian Dutch monarchy.

The unitary State that the constitution prescribed was reinforced by the dominant Roman Catholic Church. However, a sharp linguistic cleavage divided the French-speaking population of Wallonia from the Dutch-speakers of Flanders. That division was masked by the predominance of French-speaking elites in all walks of life and in the capital, Brussels, which became a French-speaking enclave within Flanders. In the 1960s, the Flemish began to reject Walloon dominance and to demand a decentralized State, leading to a series of sweeping constitutional reforms making Belgium "a federal State composed of communities and regions."

Executive

The king governs through a prime minister and Cabinet ministers recruited from and responsible to the lower house of Parliament, the Chamber of Representatives. Until 1950, kings participated actively in governmental matters, virtually daily. King Baudouin (1950–93) and Albert II (1993–), though influential behind the scenes, have usually played public roles only during ministerial crises. An exception was Baudouin's 1990 refusal, on moral grounds, to sign a bill legalizing abortion. This precipitated a constitutional crisis that was resolved by the king's stepping aside temporarily on the grounds of "incapacity," permitting the bill to become law. Amendments of 1993 restrict narrowly the king's authority to pick prime ministers and to dissolve Parliament. The constitution requires that each government include the prime minister, seven French-speaking ministers, seven Flemish-speaking ministers, and an indeterminate number of secretaries of state. Members of Parliament appointed to a government lose their parliamentary seats immediately and cannot return until reelected.

Governments have maximum lives of four years, corresponding to the four-year term of the Chamber of Representatives. Until the 1960s, a stable three-party system (Christian Socials, Liberals, and Socialists) produced an equally stable pattern of government. Since the party system fragmented in the 1960s, governments have been short-lived, collapsing by the breakup of coalitions, not through adverse votes in Parliament. In this situation, the king is a unifying factor encouraging the formation of broad coalitions. Governmental stability has been further undermined in recent decades by preoccupation with two basic problems: reform of the State and the severe, perennial budget deficit.

Legislature

The constitution distributes legislative authority among federal, regional, community, local, and provincial bodies. At the national level, the 150-member Chamber of Representatives, elected by proportional representation, is dominant. The Senate, which was reduced from parity to a secondary chamber in 1993, has a complex electoral system. Flemish voters elect 25 senators and Walloons 15 by proportional representation. The Flemish Council and the French Community Council each designate 10 senators from among their members, and the German Community Council names 1. The Flemish senators thus chosen co-opt 6 more members and the Walloons 4 more. At least 1 Fleming and 6 Walloons must be Brussels residents. The total includes 41 Flemings, 29 Walloons, and 1 German—reflecting the distribution of the population (1991 census: 58% in Flanders, 33% in Wallonia, 9% in Brussels). In addition, the king's heirs are senators by right. Senatorial seats are distributed among the political parties within each linguistic group proportionately to the share of the votes won by their lists for the directly elective senators. Both chambers serve four-year terms.

The 1993 amendments define the legislative competence of the federal government as "only the matters formally attributed to it by the Constitution and laws passed in conformity with it" and confer "the other matters" on

tronage system. Moreover, since the bulk of social security schemes are administered by party-affiliated organizations, the parties have a highly privileged position at both local and national levels.

Party Organization

The structure of Belgian parties has been largely determined by the strong "associational" features of the society. Party membership is important and there is a fairly high ratio of members to voters. Also, the parties' links with organized interest groups have considerable importance. Of particular interest in this respect are the three labor unions—Christian, socialist, and liberal—each linked to the respective party. The Christian Socials benefit most from "association," with numerous ties to Catholic organizations and to the Flemish *Boerenbond* (Farmers' League). The organizational strength of the parties depends on their linguistic homogeneity, which resulted from the breakup of the traditional parties.

The larger parties have similar national structures: a supreme congress of delegates from the districts that meets yearly and a small executive national committee or bureau that manages party affairs. Between the congress and the national committee is a general council, consisting of members of both bodies, that has a watchdog function. A marked "separation of powers" exists between the national party organization and the parliamentary bloc. Party presidents are not usually government officeholders (elected or appointed) but nevertheless rank somewhat above a Cabinet minister. The party leaders' status is based largely on their role as chief negotiators in intra-party disputes over linguistic issues. Once such a dispute is resolved, the party's ministers in government have little or no freedom of action. Failure to resolve such disputes has regularly caused governing coalitions to collapse. The linguistic splits in the older parties mean that the Flemish and Walloon communities retain only tenuous links with each other and cooperate only on policy questions not related to the linguistic issue. Candidate selection is local, but the central organizations have vetoes. Something like party primaries have been used for candidate selection, but that practice has declined in recent years.

The smaller community parties lack the powerful organizational base of the larger ones, largely because all major organized economic and cultural activities are pre-empted by the major parties. The smaller parties do benefit from high local concentrations of support.

Campaigning

Elections to the Chamber of Representatives take place every four years, at least. In fact, seven of the eight elections before 1991 were called before time. However, three of the four most recent parliaments have run nearly full term. Despite the apparent intensity and intractability of the linguistic issue, survey data suggest that most Belgians place its resolution lower on the list of priorities than, say, the economic situation of the country. Nonetheless, the average voter has great difficulty ignoring the linguistic appeal, and the ramifications spill over to the economic sector because of the varying economic fortunes of the two regions.

Much of the campaign momentum is preserved by party activists and elites rather than the mass of the electorate. Voters are well aware that a forthcoming election will not be decisive, and campaigning centers on mobilizing existing support to increase a party's representation and thus enhance its bargaining power. Parties can enter the government without great difficulty, if they so wish, because prime ministers strive to gain broad interparty support with an "excess majority."

Campaigns are media-dominated, each region in its own language. The powerful regional press is largely formally independent of the parties but committed to definite political directions. The role of personalities is important, because of the "personalized" vote. Although voting is compulsory, interest is high and voters are made to feel they should not "let down" their language communities.

Independent Voters

Traditionally, party identification was strong in Belgium and cut across linguistic boundaries. Thus, the Social Christians could rely on the Catholic vote throughout the nation, particularly in rural Flanders. The stability of party identification weakened in the 1960s: thus the Socialist, Christian Democratic, and Liberal Parties' 95% share of the vote in 1958 fell to between 70% and 73, from 1981 to 1995.

To some extent, the initial growth of support for the new community parties was a protest vote that weakened as the major parties divided into linguistic wings. The new parties have not built up stable identification with substantial parts of the electorate. Their radicalism is a partial antidote to immobility in the political system, on economic as well as linguistic matters. But the efforts of successive governments to resolve some of the outstanding problems seem to have induced a good share of their voters to return to their former voting loyalties.

SOCIALIST PARTIES

(Parti Socialiste, PS; Socialistische Partij, SP)

HISTORY

These two parties had a common origin and history until their linguistic division in October 1978. The party was founded in 1885 as the Belgian Workers' Party and soon became a political force by winning manhood suffrage through the pressure of a general strike. During the interwar years, the party participated in government both with the Catholic Party and in "tripartite" governments that included the Liberals. In 1944, the party sought wider appeal by changing its name to Socialist but still found it difficult to compete successfully against the Christian Socials, with their close connections to the Catholic Church. Nonetheless, the two parties were highly compatible and regularly joined in coalition governments after 1945.

ORGANIZATION

Even before the final break in 1978, the two wings of the party had developed separately. From 1971, two party presidents were elected, one Walloon and one Flemish, and the two sections of the party entered elections in Brussels on competing lists. The structures of the two parties are similar: each has an annual congress as the authoritative decision maker, an executive that manages the organization, and a general council to make decisions between congresses and coordinate the different elements of the party. They form a joint coordinating committee on national-level policies. The regional federations of the parties are relatively independent, especially in the selection of parliamentary candidates, where primary elections are still important.

PS and SP headquarters are in the same building, denominated Boulevard de L'Empereur 13 in French and Keizerslaan 13 in Flemish, B-1000 Brussels.

POLICY

The PS is traditionally socialist and anticapitalist, while the SP tends to be moderate and reformist. During the early constitutional disputes, the PS favored more autonomy for Brussels than did the SP. Both parties support European Union and NATO membership. The PS favored the installation of Cruise missiles during the 1984 controversy, while the SP opposed it. The two parties have worked with recent governments to moderate the austerity policies adopted to deal with the budget problems, especially the limits on wage increases and the social security cuts. The PS is the most outspoken major party advocate of economic equity for Wallonia.

MEMBERSHIP AND CONSTITUENCY

The PS is strongest in the old centers of coal mining and the steel industry of Wallonia and consistently records a much higher share of the regional vote than does the SP in Flanders. The PS draws support much more from the manual occupations than does the SP and has a more uniformly anticlerical tradition. The SP lacks a solid base of industrial support and competes with the well-organized Christian Socials. The combined parties claim a membership of about 135,000, divided roughly evenly between them; the ratio to votes in 1995 was 1:13.

FINANCING

Both parties rely heavily on government subsidies, high membership dues, and trade union sources. Mutual-aid societies associated with the parties also contribute to their support.

LEADERSHIP

PS leaders include the president, Philippe Busquin, born 1941, the national secretary, Jean-Pol Baras, and Deputy Prime Minister Elio di Rupo. SP leaders are the president, Louis Tobback, the national secretary, Linda Blomme, and Deputy Prime Minister Johan Vande Lanotte.

PROSPECTS

Recent political scandals have hit the PS especially hard, and its Marxist-flavored doctrine is a liability. However, it seems likely to maintain its hold on the Walloon electorate, because of its militant advocacy of federal support for the lagging Walloon economy. If the constitutional question has finally been resolved, the moderation of the SP is likely to be rewarded. If not, it will continue to lose support to its more nationalist competitors.

CHRISTIAN DEMOCRATIC PARTIES
(Christelijke Volkspartij, CVP;
Parti Social Chrétien, PSC)

HISTORY

Catholic political organizations developed between 1846 and 1884, coalescing in that year to form the Catholic Party, which then became the dominant force in Belgium for the next 30 years. When the party was reconstituted in 1945 as the Christian Social Party, an attempt was made to move away from a strict confessional appeal. Since then, the Christian Socials have participated in almost all coalition governments, with either or both of the Liberals and Socialists. Though the party was made up of the two distinctive linguistic elements, it maintained a unitary structure until 1968, when the two "wings" held separate party congresses; the common presidency fell into disuse from 1972 onward. Since 1993, they have moved back together somewhat.

ORGANIZATION

The formal structures of the PSC and CVP are similar, each having a national congress as the supreme policy-making organ, a president, and an executive bureau. Each also has a national council, consisting of members elected from the congress and selected members, that oversees party policy between congresses. Although the PSC and CVP are now separate parties, there is fairly close liaison between them, and they share the same

PEOPLE'S UNION
(Volksunie, VU)

Volksunie is a moderate Flemish nationalist party in a tradition that began primarily as a cultural movement in the 19th century. Several specifically Flemish parties emerged in the interwar years. During the German occupation in World War II, the movement became an active, separatist political force. Volksunie was formed in 1954 by a number of smaller parties and reached a high point in 1974 with 22 seats. It declined somewhat after 1974 and lost its more nationalist supporters to VB in 1991. Volksunie draws support from all social classes. Its success precipitated the restructuring of the Belgian party system. Volksunie's demands for constitutional changes have been largely met, though it opposed the creation of a Brussels region, which effectively ensures the predominance of French-speakers in two of three regions. Moreover, it objects to Flemish subsidies for the ailing Wallonian economy. It is antiabortion and anti-immigrant. Volksunie has a relatively high membership of about 60,000, giving it a 1:6 member-voter ratio in 1995. It has 400 local branches, a national council of 100, and a national executive committee of 15 members. Its president is Bert Anciaux and its director is Nico Moyaert. Its headquarters are at Barrikadenplein 12, B-1000 Brussels.

MINOR POLITICAL PARTIES

Communist Party (Parti Communiste; PCB)

The Belgian Communist Party was formed in 1921 as a breakaway from the Workers' Party. It never succeeded in becoming a mass party, though it served in government in 1946–47. Thereafter, it declined. The party dropped its hard-line Communist strategy in 1954, but its decline continued. In 1990, it dropped its Flemish section and by 1991 polled less than 1% of the vote. It has won no parliamentary seat since 1981. Membership is 5,000. The party has a national central committee and political bureau and three regional councils. It advocates a parliamentary road to communism.

The party president is Pierre Beauvois, born 1927. Party headquarters are at 4 rue Rouppe, B-1000 Brussels.

French-Speaking Democratic Front
(Front Democratique des Francophones; FDF)

The FDF, founded in 1964, is the party of French speakers in the Brussels area. It opposed the 1993 reforms, though it strongly supports autonomy for Brussels with its French character protected. The FDF is closely allied with the Walloon Party and claims about 18,000 members. Its electoral strength peaked in 1978, when it won 11 seats, but declined to 3 in 1985–91 and 2 (on joint tickets with the PRL) in 1995. Recently, it has been moving toward merger with the PRL. Its president is Olivier Maingain, born 1958, member of the federal parliament (1991–) and the Brussels Regional Council and the French Community Council (1991–95). George Clerfayt, born 1935, is its other federal MP, and Serge de Patoul is its general secretary.

Its headquarters are at Chaussée de Charleroi 127, B-1060 Brussels.

Walloon Party
(Parti Wallon; PW)

The Walloon Party was formed in 1985 by a merger of the Walloon Rally, the Popular Walloon Rally, and the Walloon Independence Front. The first and largest of them had been formed in 1968 by a number of smaller French-speaking groupings as a direct reaction to the success of the Flemish Volksunie. The PW is much more regional than linguistic, as demonstrated by its primary concern with Wallonian economic problems. The party is more left-leaning than the other community parties, drawing some support from previous adherents to the Socialist Party but differing from the Socialists in its greater appeal to practicing Wallonian Catholics. The party is linked with the Brussels FDF through their joint advocacy of a "special relationship" between Brussels and Wallonia. The party has declined steadily since the early 1970s, especially as a result of splits, one faction leaving for the PVV in 1976 and another for the PS in 1981. It has won no seats in Parliament since 1981. It claims 9,500 members. Its president is Jean-Claude Piccin, and its headquarters are at 14 rue du Faubourg, B-1430 Quenast.

National Front
(Front National; FN)

A radical right, anti-immigrant French-speaking party founded in 1988 in imitation of Jean-Marie Le Pen's party in France. The leader is Daniel Feret. It won one seat with 1.1% of the vote in 1991 and two seats with 2.3% of the vote in 1995. Its headquarters are at Clos du Parnasse 12, B-1040 Brussels.

ROSSEM

A protest party organized in 1991 by former a heroin addict and onetime millionaire, Jean-Pierre Van Rossem, who was jailed on fraud charges at election time. He advocated privatizing social security and abolishing the monarchy and marriage and won 3.2% of the vote and three seats in 1991 but no seats in 1995.

Party of German-Speaking Belgians
(Partei der deutschsprachigen Belgier; PDB)

A German-speaking minority of about 60,000 people in Belgium is concentrated in the eastern border area. Although the PDB has never won representation nationally, it has 7 of the 21 seats on the German cultural council. Its president is Martin Schroeder.

Party of Labor
(Partij van de Arbeid; PdvA)

The PdvA is a Marxist-Leninist party that opposes the orthodox Communist Party. The PdvA called itself "All Power to the Workers" until 1979. It has never won as much as 1% of the vote or any seat in Parliament.

Humanist Feminist Party
(Humanistische Feministiche Partij/Parti
Féministe Humaniste; HFP/PFH)

A radical feminist, pacifist party, founded in 1972 as the United Feminist Party. It changed names in 1990. It has a nonhierarchical organization. It has never won a seat or polled as much as 1% of the vote. Recently, it has functioned as an interest group and information center.

NATIONAL PROSPECTS

The instability of Belgian coalition governments and the extreme multipartism that seemed endemic for decades have been ameliorated somewhat in recent years under the leadership of Jean-Luc Dehaene, prime minister since March 1992. Substantial progress has been made in meeting the linguistic demands of the Flemings and in decentralizing authority, although the status of Brussels remains a sore point.

Two underlying economic problems remain. One concerns the increasing economic imbalance between Wallonia and Flanders. The relative prosperity of Flanders and the structural problems of Wallonian industry exacerbate the linguistic rivalries. The other is the general economic weakness. The chronic State budget deficit runs 6% to 8%, and the public debt stands at 140% of GNP. This causes severe strain within the governments, as Walloons and Socialists lean toward tax rises and the Flemings and Christian Democrats tend to favor budget-cutting solutions. The unemployment rate has persistently been among the highest in Western Europe, and inflation tends to be worse and the currency weaker than in its neighbors. These problems have been aggravated by several serious political scandals in recent years that have further undermined public confidence in the government. Every time the constitutional crisis seems to be resolved, which should permit greater attention to the economic and budgetary crises, some new incident disproves the optimism. In short, the long struggle for community peace and prosperity in Belgium seems far from over and the breakup of the country remains a real, though probably distant, possibility.

Further Reading

Alen, André. *Federal Belgium after the Fourth State Reform of 1993*. Brussels: Ministry of Foreign Affairs, 1994.

Boudart, Marina, Michel Boudart, and Rene Bryssinck, eds. *Modern Belgium*. Palo Alto, Calif.: Society for the Promotion of Science and Scholarship, 1990.

Deprez, Kas, and Louis Vos, eds. *Nationalism in Belgium: Shifting Identities, 1780–1995*. New York: St. Martin's Press, 1998.

Fitzmaurice, John. *The Politics of Belgium: A Unique Federalism*. London: Hurst, 1996.

Fox, Renée C. *In the Belgian Chateau: The Spirit and Culture of a European Society in an Age of Change*. Chicago: I.R. Dee, 1994.

Hooghe, Liesbet. *A Leap in the Dark: Nationalist Conflict and Federal Reform in Belgium*, Ithaca, N.Y.: Cornell University Press, 1991.

Kitschelt, Herbert. *The Logics of Party Formation: Ecological Politics in Belgium and West Germany*. Ithaca, N.Y.: Cornell University Press, 1989.

Lijphart, Arend, ed. *Conflict and Coexistence in Belgium: The Dynamics of a Culturally Divided Society*. Berkeley: Institute of International Studies, University of California, 1981.

McRae, Kenneth D. *Conflict and Compromise in Multilingual Societies: Belgium*. Waterloo, Ont.: Wilfrid Laurier University Press, 1986.

Web Sites

Government: http://belgium.fgov.be
Parliament: http://www.lachambre.be
Agalev: http://www.agalev.be
PRL: http://www.prl.be
VLD: http://www.vld.be
CVP: http://www.cvp.be
FDF: http://www.synec-doc.be/fdf
Ecolo: http://www.ecolo.be
PSC: http://www.psc.be
PS: http://www.ps.be
Flemish Bloc: http://www.vlams-blok.be

which was expanded noticeably. Many observers and Esquivel himself suggested that the UDP was now the dominant party. However, the UDP lost to the PUP in 1989 in a very tight contest.

In September of 1991, with the PUP in control of the government, Belize and Guatemala formally established diplomatic relations, ending Guatemala's long territorial claim to Belize. In exchange for Guatemala's formal recognition of Belize, Belize agreed to give Guatemala favorable access to the Caribbean Sea. Esquivel, as leader of the UDP, in an act of bipartisanship, supported the agreement and toured the country in October 1991 to explain the terms and ramifications of the treaty. A nationalist faction within the UDP, led by a longtime political figure, Philip Goldson, split from the UDP over this support and launched the National Alliance for Belizean Rights (NABR).

Potentially disastrous consequences of this fissure in the UDP were averted when the NABR campaigned alongside the UDP in the 1993 national elections. After winning 16 of 29 seats in the parliament, the NABR was included in the Esquivel government. The NABR subsequently declined in influence and was not included in the 1998 party ticket. The disastrous results of the 1998 elections have led to soul-searching within the UDP and a call for new leadership.

NATIONAL ALLIANCE FOR BELIZEAN RIGHTS (NABR)

The party was organized in February 1992 by Philip Goldson. The NABR has been a vociferous opponent of concessions to Guatemala. Goldson, a longtime Guatemala critic, also decries the large influx of Spanish-speaking Mestizo refugees who have settled in Belize. This immigration coupled with emigration of Creole Belizeans to the United States has rapidly changed Belize from a majority Creole country to a majority Mestizo country, and the NABR treats this demographic shift as a threat.

NATIONAL PROSPECTS

With peace with Guatemala finally assured, Belize has undergone various changes. The 1,800-member British force that protected the country is gone. The Guatemala issue and Belize's relationship with the British are no longer the dominant political issues. The economy and living conditions for Belizeans will be key political issues in future elections. Belize's role in the transshipment of illegal drugs into the United States has created tensions that may spill over into politics.

While Belize's ethnic diversity has been as much a source of pride as its biological diversity, there are signs that ethnic divisions may play a larger role in politics in the future. Party leadership has been in the same hands for many years; new leadership is likely to emerge. A stable two-party parliamentary system appears firmly entrenched. One of the decisions awaiting future governments will be whether Belize remains a Caribbean country attached to the Central American isthmus or a more integrated member of Central American political and economic institutions.

Further Reading

Barry, Tom, and Dylan Vernon. *Inside Belize*, 2d ed. Albuquerque: Interhemispheric Resource Center, 1995.

Moberg, Mark. *Myths of Ethnicity and Nation: Immigration, Work, and Identity in theBelize Banana Industry.* Knoxville: University of Tennessee Press, 1997.

Phillips, Michael D., ed. *Belize: Selected Proceedings from the Second Interdisciplinary Conference.* Lanham, Md: University Press of America, 1997.

Shoman, Assad. *Party Politics in Belize: 1950–1986.* Belize City: Cubola, 1987.

———. *Thirteen Chapters of a History of Belize.* Belize City: Angelus Press, 1995.

SPEAR Studies on Belize Conference Reports. Society for the Promotion of Education and Research. Published annually in Belize since 1989.

Wright, Peggy, and Brian E. Coutts, eds. *Belize.* World Bibliographical Series, vol. 21. Santa Barbara, Calif.: ABC–Clio, 1993.

THE REPUBLIC OF BENIN

(République du Bénin)

By Michael Radu, Ph.D.
Revised by Peter Molotsi, Ph.D.
Revised by Benjamin N. Lawrance, B.A. (Hons.), M.A., A.M.

THE SYSTEM OF GOVERNMENT

Benin, a West African country of approximately 5,900,500 (1997), has a presidential, democratic, multiparty political system, in which the military plays a decreasing role.

The country was proclaimed independent from France on August 1, 1960, as the Republic of Dahomey, with a multiparty, presidential government structure. The three major political figures—Justin Ahomadegbe, Souro-Migan Apithy, and Hubert Maga—all of whom had served as president by 1972, were supported by the three most important ethnic groups in the country, the Fon, Yoruba, and Bariba, respectively. From October 28, 1963, when the first military coup occurred, until 1972, the country was known as the most unstable and coup-prone in Africa.

On October 26, 1972, a group of officers led by Major Mathieu Kerekou staged a coup. Kerekou installed a military Marxist-Leninist regime on November 30, 1974. One year later Dahomey became the People's Republic of Benin and came under the rule of the Popular Revolutionary Party of Benin (PRPB). The constitution of August 26, 1977, provided for all political activities to be centralized under the PRPB—the "leading nucleus" of the people. Kerekou reigned as president until a peaceful democatic revolution abandoned Marxism-Leninism in December 1989, in the wake of events in Eastern Europe. Political reforms were adopted in February 1990.

Nicephore Soglo was elected to the presidency with 68% of the vote between March 10 and 24, 1991. The full transition to a multiparty democractic constitution was completed on April 4, 1991. Soglo's election was followed with brutal economic measures. His popularity plummeted, and the opposition won control of the National Assembly (Assemblée Nationale) between March and May 28, 1995. On April 4, 1996, Kerekou was reelected.

Executive

The chief of state and head of government is the president. He or she is elected for a five-year term by popular vote of all Beninoise citizens and may be a member of a political party. The term may be repeated only once and the president should have been of Beninese nationality for at least 10 years. A presidential vacancy is filled by the Speaker of the National Assembly. A new head of state must be elected within 40 days. The president addresses the nation in a state of the nation address from the National Assembly once a year.

The current president, Mathieu Kerekou, was elected on March 18, 1996, by 52.49% of the voting electorate. He was inaugurated on April 4 of the same year. He is a member of the Action Front for Renewal and Development (FARD). His opponent, the incumbent, garnered 47.51% of the vote. The next election is scheduled for March 2001.

The Cabinet (Executive Council) is appointed by the president and approved by the Assemblée Nationale. The 1997 Cabinet consists of the president, the prime minister, and 17 ministries. The prime minister is Adrien Hougbedji. The ambassador to the United States and the permanent representative to the United Nations have de facto Cabinet presence but do not vote in Cabinet decisions.

Legislature

The democratic constitution of 1991 provides for one unicameral 83-seat National Assembly (Assemblée Nationale), elected every four years. Each member of Parliament (MP) represents approximately 70,000 inhabitants, and his or her position is renewable. The vacancy of the speakership is filled by a successor elected within 15 days when the Assembly is in full session or at an immediate meeting held in compliance with the rules of procedure. The vacancy of an MP is filled by his or her substitute, elected in the same manner.

There are two ordinary sessions starting within the first fortnight of April and the second fortnight of October, respectively. Each session cannot exceed three months. Decisions are taken by a simply majority. The current National Assembly is controlled by a coalition of parties loyal to President Kerekou and opposed to former President Soglo. MPs declaring their opposition to Soglo currently hold 49 seats. Seventeen political parties gained representation in parliament between March and May 28, 1995. The pro-Soglo Party of the Rebirth of Benin (PRB) holds the largest number of seats at 21. The pro-Kerekou Democratic Renewal Party (PRD) holds 18 seats. The six next-largest groupings are: FARD, Social Democratic Party (PSD), Our Common Cause (NCC), Rally of Liberal Democrats (RDL), Alliance for Democracy and Progress (ADP), and the Impulse to Progress and Democracy (IPD), with 14, 8, 4, 4, 3, and 2 seats, respectively.

Judiciary

The constitution provides for a Supreme Court (*Cour Supréme*). The judical system and law are based roughly on French civil and customary law. Judges are appointed by the executive and the appointments are ratified by the National Assembly.

Benin has not accepted compulsory International Court of Justice jurisdiction.

Regional and Local

Benin is divided into six administrative regions: Atakora, Atlantique, Borgou, Mono, Oueme, and Zou. There are direct local and regional elections every four years. The capital, Porto Novo, and the largest city, Cotonou, are mayoralties.

THE ELECTORAL SYSTEM

Suffrage extends to all citizens 18 years and over. The election of the president requires an absolute majority, and the constitution provides for a second, runoff election. The election for the National Assembly takes place over two consecutive months and is based on proportional representation. The constitution provides for an independent National Electoral Commission to govern and administer freedom and fairness in voter enrollment and election procedures.

THE PARTY SYSTEM

The multiparty constitution provides for freedom of political organization on every level of Benin society. Since the scrapping of the Marxist-Leninist system, dozens of parties have organized and registered. As of February 1996, more than 80 political parties were officially recognized; 72 of these stood for election in 1995. None of these parties officially existed prior to 1989. All of the parties have a broadly democratic party structure, with the exception of the Communist Party of Benin (PCB), which has a traditional communist power structure.

The following are the political parties currently represented in the National Assembly: coalition of the National Movement for Democracy and Development (*Mouvement nationale pour developpement et democratie*) and PRD (*Parti du renouveau démocratique*), party leader Pascal Chabi Kao; FARD (*Front d'action, pour le rénouveau et le développement*), Mathieu Kerekou; PSD (*Parti social démocrate*), and the National Union for Solidarity and Progress, Bruno Amoussou; Chameleon Alliance; ADP (*Alliance pour la démocratie et le progrés*), Adekpedjon Akindes; Alliance for Social Democracy, Robert Dossou; RDL (*Rassemblement des démocrates libéraux*), Severin Adjovi; PCB, first secretary, Pascal Fatondji; NCC (*Notre cause commune*), Albert Tevoedjre; Rally for Democracy and Progress; PRB (*Parti de la renaissance de Bénin*), Nicephore Soglo; National Union for Democracy and Progress; IPD (*Impulsion au progrés et la démocratie*); New Generation; African Rally for Progress and Democracy. The names of some party leaders are not available.

A comparative survey of the parties' standing in the first free election in 1991 with their standing in 1995 suggests considerable instability in the party system. At least four of the larger conglomerations of 1991 were refounded or no longer represented in the 1995 parliament. These include the Union for Liberty and Development, the Union for Solidarity and Progress, the Block for Social Democracy, and the Union for Social Democracy.

There is no state financing of political parties, and there are no restrictions on campaign fund-raising.

NATIONAL PROSPECTS

Inasmuch as Benin was a communist model in West Africa, many view it now as a model for post–cold war democratic transition. There is genuine political and press freedom, and Togolese and Nigerian opposition forces turn to the example of allies in Benin. Cotonou has hosted several West African conferences about related issues. Benin marches just behind Côte d'Ivoire toward the infrastructure and utilization of information technology. Kerekou's ironic reelection is softened somewhat by his clear commitment to neoliberal free-market economic policies. Recently, however, Kerekou has steered a path of rapprochement with his old rival, the president of Togo. Aligning himself too closely with the longest-ruling dictator of sub-Saharan Africa may yet prove his undoing.

Further Reading

"Corruption, Democracy and Human Rights in West Africa: Republic of Benin." Conferences of the Africa Leadership Forum, Abeokuta, Ogun State, Nigeria, September 19–21,

1994. New York: Africa Leadership Forum, 1994.

"On Sustainment of Democratization and Good Governance in Africa." Conferences of the Africa Leadership Forum, Cotonou, Benin Republic, October 5–6, 1992. Abeokuta, Nigeria: The Forum, 1993.

Young, Crawford. *Ideology and Development in Africa.* New Haven, Conn.: Yale University Press, 1982.

Internet Sources

Mathieu Kerekou, the president of Benin, may be contacted by electronic mail at mathieu.kerekou@planben.internet.bj.

Official government web site: http://planben.intnet.bj/index.htm

BHUTAN

(Druk Yul)

By Leo E. Rose, Ph.D.

The rule of the Wangchuk dynasty in Bhutan (*Druk Yul*—"Land of the Thunder Dragon") goes back only to the first decade of the 20th century when a hereditary monarchy replaced the theocratic Buddhist political system that had dominated most of Bhutan since the mid-17th century. The first two Wangchuk kings (Druk Gyalpos) held authoritarian powers until 1953 when the third Wangchuk ruler established a National Assembly (*Tshogdu*) that was granted some powers on legislative matters and in the selection of the Cabinet (*Lodoi Tsokde*) ministers. Over the years the Tshogdu has become increasingly assertive on important policy issues. While the final voice in decision making is still retained by the current ruler, Jigme Singye Wangchuk, he is usually very careful to ascertain the views of the Tshogdu in his decision-making process. Even more important, perhaps, is the substantial decentralization policies introduced by the king in the 1980s, under which elected district and local officials have been granted a major voice on a broad range of economic and social issues. The positive impact of the decentralization process is clearly evident in several key social and economic developments in the past decade. Enrollment in educational institutions increased from 42% (1985) to 72% (1997), while the literacy rate grew from 23% in 1980 to 54% in 1997. Basic health coverage rose from 50% in 1985 to 90% in 1997, and life expectancy grew from 40 years (1985) to 66 (1997). Per capita income has also more than tripled over the past decade, reaching $545 in 1997, while the average annual growth rate has been over 6% in the 1990s. These are all remarkable achievements, particularly when compared with the other states in the region.

What is even more amazing is that this has been accomplished in the context of serious ethnic conflicts in southern Bhutan where the migrant Nepali Bhutanese (*Lhotshampa*) community constitutes about 90% of the population. Several programs introduced by the royal government in 1988–89 to "preserve" the traditional Buddhist political and social culture (*Tsawa Sum*) met with strong resistance from some of the Hindu Nepali Bhutanese, resulting in the first serious conflict in modern Bhutan. About 20% of the Lhotshampa community in southern Bhutan were either forced out of their homes or fled the country, first to India and then most of them to refugee camps in southeastern Nepal. This led to a major crisis in Bhutan-Nepal relations that by mid-1997 was still unresolved. The two governments meet periodically to discuss this issue but have not yet made much progress in reaching an agreement.

The sentiment in Bhutan has turned increasingly hard-line toward the Lhotshampa dissidents—termed *ngolops* (traitors) by the Bhutanese. The *ngolop* "resistance" movements have established bases in the Indian-Bhutan border area from which raids are launched periodically into southern Bhutan, directed primarily at Lhotshampa families that have refused to leave Bhutan and join the resistance movement—or "terrorists" as the Bhutanese call them. In the 1997 Tshogdu session, some more hard-line Bhutanese members introduced a resolution stipulating that all relatives of *ngolops* should be excluded from the government service and security forces, and the demand was even made that they should be expelled from the country. What was even more disturbing was that a number of Cabinet ministers supported the resolution even though the king has stated repeatedly that no Bhutanese should be punished for acts committed by a relative. The debate on this issue may well be the most important and virulent in Bhutan's modern history with possible major consequences for the political system.

Bhutan's international relations with states other than Nepal remain very good. Several agreements reached with India on key developmental and economic issues in 1996 and 1997 should prove very beneficial for both countries. Three new major power projects and a cement plant have been approved, under which agreements India will finance most of the construction programs but on terms guaranteeing that much of the power produced will be sold to the power-short states in northeast India at a good price for Bhutan. Bhutan's relations with its other giant neighbor, China, remain good despite some minor disagreements on the border line in two small areas of the Himalayas.

REPUBLIC OF BOLIVIA

(República de Bolivia)

By José Antonio Lucero

THE SYSTEM OF GOVERNMENT

The political history of Bolivia is, like its Andean and lowland landscapes, full of dramatic peaks and valleys. Since independence, Bolivia has experienced overlapping periods of *caudillo* rule, oligarchy, social revolution, single-party rule, military regimes of left and right, and, most recently, multiparty electoral democracy. In economic terms, Bolivia has been both a classic example of economic disaster and, in the last five years, a paradigmatic case of successful structural adjustment. These and other contrasts make this multiethnic nation of over 7 million people—70% of whom self-identify as members of one of various indigenous communities—one of the more complex political environments in the region.

After independence from Spain in 1825, political factions formed largely around the personal struggles of competing strongmen, or *caudillos*. The first five decades of the republican period were characterized by fierce struggles among elites who often used state power to extract the nation's wealth, concentrated in silver and tin mines. It was not until the conclusion of the War of the Pacific (1870), during which Bolivia lost its coast, that political parties began to form. Between 1884 and 1899, Bolivia experienced its first period of long-term civilian rule.

A two-party political system ostensibly pitted Liberals against Conservatives. In actuality, political competition was less about ideology than about the personalistic struggles between a few powerful men. These elites were usually affiliated with tin or silver oligarchies and controlled most of the land. In this remarkably stratified society, indigenous peoples (*ind'genas*) and poor "mixed-race" Mestizos were often forced by landlords into highly exploitative land-tenure arrangements and personal labor service obligations. The small middle sectors of society depended on the political ruling class for the employment and wages that allowed them to maintain their social status.

Oligarchic rule, however, faced several challenges in the 20th century. Several catastrophic events—including the Great Depression and the devastating loss to Paraguay during the Chaco War (1932–35)—had profound effects on the Bolivian political system. Held responsible for much of the political and economic turmoil, ruling elites were greatly weakened. New actors entered the national stage and offered political alternatives that ranged from extreme right wing to Trotskyist. The most important of these new groups was the less extreme, but still revolutionary, multiclass Nationalist Revolutionary Movement (MNR).

In April 1952, after being denied the presidency it had won in the 1951 elections, the MNR led a social revolution that marked the beginning of a new chapter of Bolivian history. The tremendous inequality in land distribution (6% of landowners controlled 92% of cultivated lands) made the MNR's antifeudal, antioligarch platform extremely attractive to popular sectors. For 12 years (1952–64), the MNR ruled over a modernizing statist development project that in many ways took the Mexican PRI as its model in creating corporative, state structures to channel the politicized peasants and miners. The MNR created a Ministry of Peasant Affairs and peasant and labor unions, and thus forged a structure for an asymmetrical dependent alliance between the MNR-controlled state and rural sectors. After 1952, the MNR distributed land, installed universal suffrage, nationalized the tin mines, and inaugurated schools in its efforts to build a hegemonic party.

These efforts were shattered in 1964 when the vice president, General Rene Barrientos, put an end to MNR rule and inaugurated 18 years of military rule. One of the central pillars of the new regime was the so-called Military-Peasant Pact (PMC, *Pacto Militar Campesino*) that maintained the populist and clientelistic tenor of MNR rule. The PMC was based on clientelistic relations that the officer corps had built in the countryside. Like the MNR government, the military sought to maintain a monopoly on organizing labor and peasants. In 1969, Barrientos died in a helicopter crash. At the time of his death and during a rapid succession of unstable successor governments, opposition to the PMC on the part of peasants was growing on several fronts. A relatively rapid turnover of governments (three presidents in less than two years) and extreme dissatisfaction with state attempts to restructure agrarian life provided early opportunities for protests on the part of the masses, especially in the highlands of Bolivia.

General Hugo Bánzer Suárez (1971–78) finally ended the string of short-lived post-Barrientos governments. Less of a natural populist than Barrientos, Bánzer tried to maintain the PMC by making up with repression what he lacked in charisma. As with many authoritarian governments, Bánzer's rested upon a fragile and shifting foundation of support. Yet, through a mixture of military repression and institutional improvisation vis-à-vis the two major rival political parties, Bánzer's eight years of continuous rule made him the longest-serving president since 1871. In 1978, responding to international and internal pressure, Bánzer called for elections and Bolivia entered another transitional period. The transition was a rocky one for Bolivians. Between 1978 and 1982, seven military and two weak civilian governments tried to rule Bolivia.

In October 1982, military rule came to an end (again) as the military was forced by popular opposition, international isolation, and internal weakness to honor the results of the 1980 election. Hernán Siles Zuazo of the MNRI, the leftist splinter-party of the MNR, assumed the presidency with the support of a coalition of leftist parties and the help of the syndicalist movement. At that moment, Bolivia was experiencing the worst economic crisis in its history. In the years 1982–85, Bolivia under Siles Zuazo saw the failure of six successive stabilization plans. His leftist alliance did not make his job any easier as long-suppressed demands predictably increased from labor and peasant syndicalist groups. This was only made worse by the government's highly inflationary resort to printing more currency; each attempt at stabilization resulted in greater social protest. By 1985, hyperinflation reached more than 25,000%. The Siles government and the forces that had supported it were severely discredited. Siles was forced out a year early from his second term. The debacle that Siles presided over set the stage for the aggressive neoliberal reforms of MNR leader Jaime Paz Estenssoro.

Three days after Paz Estenssoro became president, he issued Decree Law 21060, the cornerstone of his New Economic Policy that managed to bring hyperinflation to an end. However, it was not without painful side effects. Massive layoffs (euphemistically dubbed "relocations") cut into the organizing and strategic strength of mineworkers and other labor groups. A majority of those poor continued to be *ind'genas*. Although an Emergency Social Fund did cushion some of the blow, the poor continued to bear a disproportionate share of the neoliberal burden.

Interestingly, the new economic policy of Bolivia was accompanied by some new political maneuverings. As is discussed below, Bolivia's electoral system is one where Congress often has the final say in electing the executive. Consequently, coalitions in Congress—more often than popular elections results—determine who will be president. In October 1985, Victor Paz Estenssoro struck a deal (*Pacto por La Democracia*) with the ex-general Bánzer, now president and head of the rightist Nationalist Democratic Action (ADN), whereby the ADN would provide legislative support for the MNR executive in return for a greater share of access to state patronage.

Coalitions would be important in other election years. In 1989, Jaime Paz Zamora, head of the leftist Revolutionary Leftist Movement (MIR) and third-runner-up in the elections, made a pact with the second runner-up, Bánzer, in order to become the next president. In 1993, the surprising alliance of MNR leader Gonzalo Sánchez de Lozada (Paz Estenssoro's neoliberal finance minister) and Victor Hugo Cárdenas, head of an Indian/syndicalist political party, the Tupak Katari Revolutionary Liberation Movement (MRTKL), won a plurality of the vote and had enough support in Congress to secure the executive.

Perhaps the most striking political twist of all is one that has occurred only recently. The June 1997 presidential elections were won by former dictator Hugo Bánzer with 22% of the vote. His ADN party entered into a "megacoalition" with several other right- and left-wing parties in the so-called *Compromiso Por Bolivia* (Commitment for Bolivia) Pact. This marks the first time in Latin America that a former military dictator has been democratically elected as president. While Bánzer has been able to secure the support of most members of congress, some fear that his megacoalition lacks ideological coherence. Neoliberal, antineoliberal, rightist, and leftist parties all negotiated the distribution of Cabinet positions and regional posts. Human rights activists have expressed alarm at the return of the former dictator, and the United States has publicly announced its unease over one of Bánzer's coalition partners, ex-president and MIR head Paz Zamora, for his alleged links to drug traffickers. Bánzer and his vice president, Jorge Quiroga, have reminded voters it was Bánzer who initiated the transition to democracy in 1978, and they assured the United States that they would "eradicate the drug problem" in five years.

Executive

Under the 1967 constitution (as amended in 1994), Bolivia is a unitary republic and a representative democracy. Article 2 stipulates that sovereignty resides in the people, and while it is inalienable, its exercise can be delegated to the legislative, executive, and judicial powers. The constitution gives substantial powers to the executive. It rests executive authority in the president, elected now to five-year terms (presidents before the 1997 elections served four-year terms), and his 12 ministers. If no candidate secures a simple majority—which no candidate has been able to do since democracy was restored—Congress selects the president from one of the top two candidates. The president makes ministerial appointments, has extensive powers in making foreign and economic policy, commands the armed forces, and in times of crisis can call a state of siege. The president's appointment powers allow him to distribute patronage to political allies, though since 1989 the public sector has diminished in size. The president can also use executive decrees to legislate important policy (e.g., the New Economic Policy) without congressional approval. The constitution bars consecutive reelection but allows presidents to run after sitting out at least one election.

In the July 1997 presidential election, the popular vote distribution was as follows: Hugo Bánzer Suárez (ADN), 22.3%; Juan Carlos Durán (MNR), 17.7%; Jaime Paz Zamora (MIR), 16.7%; Ivo Kuljis (UCS), 15.9%; Remedios Loza (CONDEPA), 15.8%; and five other candidates sharing 11.6%. Of the major parties, only the MNR is left out of the new ADN-led coalition. MIR, UCS, and CONDEPA were all assured representation in the new Council of Ministers, the president's cabinet, though CONDEPA left the coalition in August 1998 due in part to ideological differences over neoliberal reforms.

Legislature

The constitution provides for a bicameral legislative body. The *Congreso Nacional* (National Congress) is composed of two chambers: the *Cámera de Diputados* (Chamber of Deputies) with 130 members and the *Cámera de Senadores* (Chambers of Senators) with 27 members. The Congress meets for 90 sessions every year, unless the executive or a majority of Congress request more sessions. Members of both chambers serve five-year terms. Congress has the right to pass, abrogate, interpret, and modify all laws. While the president has veto power, Congress can override with a two-thirds majority.

The constitution grants the legislative branch 22 prerogatives that can be roughly divided into three categories: economic policy, foreign policy, and political powers. Congress's main economic power is approving the annual budget, though the executive has often bypassed Congress by approving the budget through decree. In foreign policy, Congress has the power to approve all treaties and international agreements. It also has the power to decide whether foreign troops may travel through Bolivia, though this too has not always been respected.

Congress's most important political power can be found in Article 90 of the constitution. The provision holds that if none of the candidates for the presidency or the vice presidency obtains the absolute majority of valid votes in the general election, the Congress will chose among the top two contenders. In Bolivia's multiparty system, a presidential contender has never passed this de-

manding electoral hurdle since democracy was reinstalled in the 1980s, so Congress is often put in the role of kingmaker. Beyond this electoral power, Congress has other significant oversight powers over the executive. For example, a single senator or deputy may call ministers to testify through a procedure known as *petición de informe oral* (request for an oral report). A request for a written report (*petición de informe escrito*) may also be used to request executive explanation of certain policies, events, and actions. The Congress may also use minutes of communication (*minutos de comunicación*) to call executive attention to particular issues.

This mixture of strong presidential authority and strong congressional checks on the executive makes Bolivia something of an institutional hybrid. Like many other countries in the Americas, it has features of a presidentialist system: presidents serve fixed terms, do not depend on votes of confidence, and can use executive decrees to bypass congressional checks. It also has some features of a parliamentary system: the legislature not only has important checks on the executive but actually selects who will fill the executive post. This combination has been labeled by some scholars as a case of "parliamentarized presidentialism." (See, e.g., Mayorga 1997.)

In the most recent congressional elections (June 1997), Bánzer's ADN party had the most success, winning 33 out of 130 seats. ADN's strong congressional performance helped assure Bánzer's selection as president. ADN was followed by MNR (26 seats), MIR (25), UCS (21), CONDEPA (17), Izquierda Unida (4), and Movimiento Bolivia Libre (4).

Judiciary

Judicial power is distributed in a rather complex manner. The Supreme Court of Justice, a Council of the Judiciary, and the Constitutional Tribunal are the most important upper bodies of the Bolivian judiciary. The Supreme Court of Justice (*Corte Suprema de Justicia*) is composed of a president and 11 ministers. Ministers are selected for 10-year terms by the Chamber of Deputies from a list proposed by the Council of the Judiciary (*Consejo de la Judicatura*). Ministers of the Supreme Court cannot be reelected. The constitution gives the Supreme Court power to appoint District Court judges, resolve appeals from lower courts, settle questions of jurisdiction among lower courts, and serve as the arena for the trial of presidents, vice presidents, ministers, and other officials for crimes committed while in office.

Nominees to the Superior District Courts are nominated by the Judicial Council. Once nominated by the Council, it is up to the Superior District Courts to actually fill lower judicial appointments. District Court judges serve six-year terms. Lower court judges (*Jueces de Partido*) serve four-year terms. Judicial appointments are often part of the political patronage that is a major part of Bolivian politics. While the judiciary is theoretically independent from the other branches of government, the patrimonial tenor of politics keep the courts politicized.

The Council of the Judiciary, the administrative and disciplinary body of the judicial branch, is presided over by the president of the Supreme Court and composed of four judicial counselors (*Consejeros de la Judicatura*). These counselors serve 10-year terms and are elected by the Congress. In addition to nominating Superior District Court judges, they also nominate lower court judges.

The constitution assigns constitutional interpretation, a task usually left to supreme courts, to another judicial body known as the Constitutional Tribunal (*Tribunal Constitucional*). Article 122 of the constitution gives the Tribunal various powers including the power to determine the constitutionality of the laws and decrees, resolve jurisdictional conflicts between public agencies, and arbitrate disputes between the other branches of government. The five magistrates of the Constitutional Tribunal are selected by Congress, and eligible candidates include judges, public officials, academics, or attorneys with over 10 years of experience. They serve 10-year terms.

Departmental and Local Government

While Bolivia is a unitary system, it has moved toward greater decentralization in recent years. Bolivia's administrative structure consists of 9 departments, 112 provinces, 311 sections, and 1,384 cantons. Until very recently, local officials were selected directly by the executive. Small rural communities were often out of the reach of the national state and national funds. In 1993, out of 311 municipalities, 181 received no federal money; the three major cities—La Paz, Cochabamba, and Santa Cruz—received 90% of federal funds. In 1994, the Law of Popular Participation (LPP) was passed in order to rectify the urban and central bias of Bolivian political organization. The LPP gives municipal councils (*Consejos Municipales*) and local mayors new powers and, more importantly, new funds. The LPP stipulates that 20% of the national budget should be redistributed to the 311 local section governments. To increase accountability, the law also creates Oversight Committees (*Comités de Vigilancia*) that ensure that new funds are being allocated properly. Significantly, the new law also gives juridical status to alternative forms of political organization—union, neighborhood association, or indigenous community—and gives these various base organizations (*Organizaciones de Base*, OTBs) representation in local governing bodies. The LPP is largely seen as the brainchild of former vice president Cárdenas. He calls it a "historic act of reparation" since it is the "first time [that] the indigenous population is being legally recog-

nized in this country." Internationally, sources as different as the United States Agency for International Development (US AID) and the Cuban Foreign Ministry have applauded the law.

THE ELECTORAL SYSTEM

The Bolivian electoral system is constituted by a National Electoral Court, electoral judges, electoral notaries, departmental notaries, and electoral justices. The National Electoral Court is the most important body in that it can recognize or deny the participation of any political party, front, or coalition. It approves ballots, tallies results, and investigates accusations of fraud. The Electoral Court is composed of six members elected by Congress, the Supreme Court of justice, the president of the republic, and the political parties with the highest number of votes in previous elections. Members serve for four years and are eligible for reelection. Voting is obligatory in Bolivia—only citizens over 70 may abstain from voting. Voters must show a birth certificate, national identification card, or a military service card in order to vote.

New electoral laws governed the most recent elections. While Bolivia has had universal adult suffrage since 1952, in 1997 the voting age was lowered from 21 to 18. Additionally, instead of serving four years, presidents and members of Congress will now serve five-year terms. Legislative elections are a now a mix of first-past-the-post and proportional representation systems. Half of the Chambers of Deputies are elected in single-member districts; the other half are allocated in terms of proportional representation (PR). The Senate is composed of three senators from each department, also according to a system of proportional representation. In an effort to reduce the number of small, weak parties that litter the Bolivian political landscape, Congress in 1986 reestablished the D'Hondt formula of PR and created a 9% threshold for seats in Congress. Another recent change to the constitution holds that if no presidential candidate wins an absolute majority, Congress will chose the president from between the top two candidates, rather than three.

THE PARTY SYSTEM

Origins of Party System

In the wake of the disastrous War of the Pacific (1870), the Bolivian political arena began to take shape as a new two-party system. The *Partido Liberal* (PL) was closely identified with the emergent tin-mining oligarchy. The declining silver oligarchy developed links with the *Partido Conservador* (PC). The Liberal Party soon dominated Bolivian politics, but lingering *caudillismo* and internal factional strife produced a political dynamic that continued to be extremely personalistic.

Politics was embedded in Bolivia's pattern of dependent, outwardly oriented economic development in which sources of wealth were largely limited to landholders and owners of export enterprises. Government service became a route to some of that wealth. Consequently, government posts became commodities that political factions struggled over and later distributed to their political clientele. The patrimonial dynamic of Bolivian politics is one of the more enduring legacies of the 19th century.

After the liberal elites were effectively eliminated by the aftermath of the Chaco War (1935), new parties of the right and the left filled the new political space. One of these parties to emerge during this period, the MNR, led a national revolution in 1952 and attempted to reshape the political arena. Attempting to recreate a Mexican-style single-party state proved unsuccessful, however, as the military intervened and Bolivian politics was for much of the century the story of military coups and weak civilian regimes.

The return of democracy in 1982 has seen the rebuilding of Bolivian parties. Initially, tiny parties with little followings proliferated throughout the country. They were dubbed "taxi parties" because it was said that the entire membership of any of these parties could hold a national convention in the confines of single taxicab. Over the years, electoral reforms have tried to reduce the number of parties, and a few parties have become dominant in Bolivian electoral campaigns.

Party Organization

By most accounts, political parties remain closed, hierarchical bodies. Decisions are made by a few individuals, and party members have little say in party operations. The MNR attempted to move away from this image of undemocratic internal party organization by using primaries and national conventions to increase participation. Despite these changes, most parties (including the MNR) are still characterized by a certain modern-day *caudillismo*.

Campaigning

Campaigning for the June 1997 elections began early. Already in February, parties were on the campaign trail. A common theme in many party platforms was criticism of the neoliberal reforms of the MNR. Bolivia, despite economic advances, remains a remarkably poor and unequal country. Some parties like La Paz–based CONDEPA were unapologetically antineoliberal. Others, like the victorious ADN of Bánzer, endorsed market reforms but pledged to "humanize" them.

An interesting aspect of the 1997 campaign was the use of the Internet as a medium for campaigning. ADN and MIR, among others, had sophisticated web sites that allowed on-line users to read party platforms, learn about the candidate, and even e-mail questions to the candidates. The Ministry of Communications and the Ministry of Popular Participation, among others, also have web sites highlighting the accomplishments of the past governments. The National Electoral Court has web sites providing detailed election data. While the relative number of Bolivians who can actually access the Internet is undoubtedly small, the sophisticated use of computer technology is doing much to change Bolivia's images as a "backward" political system.

The United States continues to exert a tremendous influence over Bolivian politics. The threat of decertification (i.e., not certifying Bolivia as a U.S. ally in the war on drugs) and the accompanying risk of losing U.S. aid has made electoral life almost impossible for any candidate the United States suspects of having possible drug-money connections. It has almost reached a point where one cannot run for office unless one has a U.S. visa. The denial of a U.S. visa to certain high-profile politicians, like the MIR leader, Jaime Paz Zamora, made major waves in the Bolivian political establishment.

THE MAJOR PARTIES

Bolivia has many parties, but three in particular have dominated the political scene is recent years: ADN, MNR, and MIR. Party formation in Bolivia continues to occur in one of two ways. Parties either splinter off from older, established parties, or new populist parties emerge as electoral vehicles used by political entrepreneurs. The three major parties and the more important minor parties are discussed here.

NATIONALIST DEMOCRATIC ACTION
(Acción Democrática Nacionalista; ADN)

The right-leaning ADN was formed by former dictator and current President Hugo Bánzer Suárez in April 1979. Bánzer skillfully used this new party as a vehicle to stay relevant in Bolivian politics after military rule ended. Over the years it has increased in popularity among the middle class and the industrial sector. It also had the support of unhappy members of the ultraright FSB (*Falange Socialista Boliviano*, Bolivian Socialist Falange) and MNR. Interestingly, one of the more important alliances in Bolivian politics is between Bánzer's rightist ADN and Paz Zamora's leftist MIR. This alliance allowed Paz Zamora the presidency in 1989, and it helped give Bánzer the presidency in 1997. Bánzer campaigned as a committed democrat and made fighting poverty a central pillar of his platform. He also pledged to eradicate the drug problem in the next five years. Such a promise was perhaps directed more at the United States than domestic audiences.

The ADN has splintered somewhat. One of the founders of the ADN and a vice presidential candidate, Eduardo Galindo, left the ADN and created a new party in 1985. Galindo's *Partido Democrático Boliviano* (PDB, Democratic Bolivian Party) made an alliance with the MNR, and Galindo himself was an MNR senator for the department of Cochabamba.

ADN holds 33 seats in the Chamber of Deputies and 13 seats in the Senate.

MOVEMENT OF THE REVOLUTIONARY LEFT
(Movimiento de Izquierda Revolucionaria; MIR)

Since the party's founding in 1971 by Jaime Paz Zamora, Oscar Eid Franco, and Antonio Araníbar (among others), MIR's platform has been moderately left-wing, though when occupying the executive, MIR continued the neoliberal reforms of Paz Estenssoro's New Economic Policy. While the MIR draws its support from the urban middle class, it has made some inroads into the peasant vote. The MIR joined the MNRI and the PCB (Bolivian Communist Party) in 1982 to form the Popular Unity Coalition, or UDP (*Unidad Democrática y Popular*). In 1985, MIR leader Paz Zamora campaigned on his own for the presidency. In 1989, a pact with ADN gave Paz Zamora the presidency.

MIR is a current member of President Bánzer's ruling coalition, though its prospects have been clouded somewhat by the accusation that the MIR leader, Paz Zamora, has drug-trafficking connections. The United States denied Paz Zamora a visa and publicly expressed its concern over his candidacy. Paz Zamora maintains that had it not been for U.S. opposition, he would again be president today.

MIR holds 25 seats in the Chamber of Deputies and 6 in the Senate.

NATIONALIST REVOLUTIONARY MOVEMENT
(Movimiento Nacionalista Revolucionario; MNR)

Founded in 1941 by Victor Paz Estenssoro, Hernán Siles Zuazo, and Walter Guevara (among others), the MNR has evolved from the statist party of the revolution to a party that champions the neoliberal economic reforms that have done away with much of the corporatist and populist features of the early MNR state. When it came to power in 1952, the MNR sought to integrate the masses—especially miners, peasants, and Indians—into a new hegemonic party. A military coup put an end to those plans. Infighting also changed the MNR's ideological composition. A split between two of the founders—Paz Estenssoro and Hernán Siles Zuazo—in 1978 resulted in the creation of the more left-leaning MNRI, headed by Siles Zuazo.

The MNR captured the presidency in 1985 amid conditions of economic crisis. Paz Estenssoro's stabilization plan managed to tame hyperinflation and inaugurated the economic orthodoxy that continues to guide economic policy. In 1993, the MNR again won the presidency as Gonzalo Sánchez de Lozada, Pas Estenssoro's finance minister, entered into an alliance with Katarista leader Victor Hugo Cárdenas. The alliance of a neoliberal technocrat and an Aymara Indian leader proved to be an effective electoral mix as Cárdenas helped take votes from more populist leaders that were targeting the urban indigenous, or *cholo*, vote in the La Paz department. Under the Sánchez de Lozada–Cárdenas administration, economic reforms in pensions and privatization were accompanied by political reforms in government decentralization and legal recognition of Bolivia's substantial indigenous population.

The MNR presidential candidate, Juan Carlos Durán, came in second behind Bánzer. While the MNR also came in second in the congressional elections of 1997, it is currently left out of the ruling ADN megacoalition.

MNR controls 26 seats in the Chamber of Deputies and 3 in the Senate.

MINOR POLITICAL PARTIES

Conscience of the Fatherland
(Consciencia de Patria; CONDEPA)

One of the more important new parties to emerge since 1985 is the populist CONDEPA. It was founded by television personality Carlos Palenque, known popularly as "el compadre." Palenque used a nightly television show in which he encouraged usually low-income indigenous and *cholo* La Paz residents to speak out about their problems. Palenque and his wife, Monica, were extremely popular, especially in La Paz, where Monica even served as mayor.

In what sounds like a soap opera, CONDEPA entered a crisis when Carlos and Monica had a public falling out and ultimately divorced. The crisis deepened when "el compadre" died unexpectedly in March 1997. While reports maintained that he had died of a heart attack, Monica left the country in part to get away from accusations that she had somehow contributed to Palenque's death. CONDEPA, however, remains an important player in Bolivian politics. It has a solid constituency in the La Paz department and among the urban poor in the city of La Paz. Remedios Loza, the first Aymara woman to run for president, currently heads the party and actively campaigned as an antineoliberal candidate. CONDEPA left the ADN coalition in August 1998 due to internal divisions and conflicts with the neoliberal elements of the ADN coalition.

CONDEPA controls 17 seats in the Chamber of Deputies and 3 in the Senate.

United Left
(Izquierda Unida; IU)

Founded in the mid-1980s by Isaac Sandoval to contest the 1985 election, IU achieved great success in attracting leftist parties to present a solid front in the legislature. For a short time, IU managed to bring in MBL, the Bolivian Communist Party, and other leftist groups. The broad alliance splintered after the 1989 election, and IU went out of existence for some time. It regrouped in 1997 and won representation in Congress. It has 4 seats in the Chamber of Deputies.

Movement for a Free Bolivia
(Movimiento Bolivia Libre; MBL)

Founded in 1985 by Antonio Aran'bar, the MBL splintered off from Jaime Paz Zamora's MIR. After a brief association with IU, MBL left the IU alliance in 1989 largely out of concern that continued association with such an explicitly leftist grouping would hurt its electoral chances. MBL actually did slightly worse than IU in the 1997 congressional elections. While both parties have 4 seats in the Chamber of Deputies, MBL won only 2.5% of the vote compared with IU's 3.7%.

Tupak Katari Revolutionary Liberation Movement
(Movimiento Revolucionario
Túpak Katar' de Liberación; MRTKL)

While the MRTKL has never been especially strong in electoral terms, it deserves special mention because it represents a wider political phenomenon in Bolivia and Latin America, the political relevance and resurgence of Indian identity. The MRTKL is one of many "Katarista" groups that take their name from an 18th-century Indian rebel leader and trace their political origins to the 1970s when Genaro Flores and other rural labor leaders founded the Katarista movement as an explicitly hybrid expression of class and ethnic consciousness. Using the structure of the syndicalist union that was a product of MNR and military populist rule, Flores and others organized indigenous peasants against the Bánzer dictatorship. They also advanced a critique of the colonial legacy

of racism that continues to exploit and degrade the substantial indigenous population of Bolivia.

Victor Hugo Cárdenas, head of the MRTKL, was more successful than most Katarista leaders in bringing *Katarismo* into the political mainstream. The peak of his political career, thus far, was his term as vice president under Sánchez de Lozada. His success was not celebrated by all, however. Branded by some as a "sellout," Cárdenas has had to endure criticism from within the Katarista movement and without. Katarista parties did miserably in the 1997 elections, but Cárdenas remains a national and international figure and seems to have benefited from a healthy relation with the powerful MNR.

Civic Solidarity Union
(Unión Cívica Solidaridad, UCS)

Founded in 1989 by Max Fernández, owner of Bolivia's largest brewery, UCS offered another populist alternative. Like CONDEPA, UCS has had to cope with the loss of its founder and leader, who died in a plane crash in 1996. Fernández enjoyed national support but had his strongest electoral base in the city of Santa Cruz. He was seen as a "cholo" success story and had a popular following among poor and indigenous voters. Fernández played the coalition-building game well. In 1993, UCS joined the MNR coalition and secured several posts in the Cabinet. In 1997, the party remains politically relevant under the leadership of Max Fernández's son, Johnny. UCS has also entered into an alliance with Bánzer's ADN. UCS presidential candidate Ivo Kuljis came in fourth in with 16% of the popular vote.

UCS controls 21 seats in the Chamber of Deputies and 2 in the Senate.

OTHER POLITICAL FORCES

Indigenous and Peasant Organizations

Among other political forces, Indian movements and organized rural labor movements are among the more important nonparty actors. While the Kataristas helped bring the "Indian" back to the attention of the La Paz elite, other groups on the other side of the republic had their own impact on national politics. The political energy of the "first nations" of Bolivia moved from Aymara-dominated Katarismo to a more plural assemblage of Indian movements that found their loci at the community level, no longer confined just to the altiplano. The most impressive organization of groups came from the eastern lowlands of Bolivia in the late 1980s and early 1990s. Various groups from throughout Bolivia came together under the *Confederación Indigena del Oriente, Chaco y Amazonia de Bolivia* (CIDOB; Indigenous Confederation of the East,

Chaco, and Amazonia of Bolivia). In 1991, one member group, the *Coordinadora de Pueblos Indígenas del Beni* (CPIB, Coordinator of the Indigenous Peoples of Beni) led a dramatic and well-publicized "March for Territory and Dignity," in which 12 different "first nations" walked over 700 kilometers until finally reaching La Paz. The march captured national and international attention for 40 days. In 1996, indigenous groups marched again in opposition to proposed agrarian reforms.

Organized Labor

Labor unions have historically been an important political force in Bolivian politics. The mineworkers' union in particular, the FSTMB (*Federación Sindical de Traba-jadores Mineros Bolivianos*, Bolivian Mineworkers Syndical Federation), has played a large role. FSTMB leader Juan Lechín was one of the founding members of the MNR-labor coalition. In the wake of the 1952 revolution, labor unions and peasant unions were organized into the Confederation of Bolivian Workers, the COB (*Confederación de Obreros Bolivianos*.) In the early years of MNR rule, the COB had significant influence over government appointments to ministries of mines, labor, and peasant affairs.

Lech'n and Paz Estenssoro parted company in the 1960s. The United States attempted to de-radicalize the Bolivian revolution by throwing its support behind the more conservative Paz. During the next two decades, military rule diminished the power of labor unions in government. However, the COB outside of government became an independent and active opposition political force. The COB joined forces with other syndicalist movements in opposition to military dictatorship. The most important peasant labor force was the Katarista-led CSUTCB (*Confederación Sindical Unica de Trabajadores Campesinos Bolivianos*, Unified Syndical Confederation of Bolivian Peasant Workers). These union organizations organized strikes and protests that constituted an important part of social opposition to the dictatorship of Bánzer.

The COB made clear its opposition to many of the privatization schemes of the Sánchez de Lozada government and continues to be an important protest voice in Bolivia. It is, however, less important today than in previous decades. Even the voice of the old left, Lech'n, has disappointed many leftists by publicly announcing that he was voting for the ex-general Bánzer. This announcement of the best-known labor leader in Bolivia, along with the strange coalitions of conservative ADN and leftist MIR, makes one wonder if the distinction between "left" and "right" means much these days in Bolivia.

Regional Civic Committees

Regional differences are also politically important in Bolivia. Since the 1960s, Bolivia has diversified economi-

cally with extensive lowland colonization and the development of the hydrocarbon industry, mainly in Santa Cruz. By 1978, Santa Cruz became the second most important city in the republic. Still, most decisions were made in La Paz. Growing frustration over centralized rule along with long-standing regional animosities led to the establishment of the Santa Cruz Civic Committee (*Comité Cívica Pro Santa Cruz*), which called for a greater role in national political life and administrative decentralization.

Civic committees have sprouted in other regions and seem to have supplanted political parties in the articulation of regional interests. In every election since 1985, parties have had to recruit regional committee members for their party lists. Moreover, when Congress members have to chose between party and regional loyalty, partisan considerations usually lose out.

NATIONAL PROSPECTS

Contradictions continue to characterize Bolivian economic and political life. Macroeconomically, Bolivia is in much better shape than in the lost decade of the 1980s. Still, neoliberal medicine had left many unemployed, and poverty remains the country's greatest problem. The election of Hugo Bánzer marks the fifth consecutive democratically elected president but also the return of a former dictator to power governing with an ideologically unstable coalition. Constitutional reforms have opened the doors to greater participation, but party organizations and regional bosses keep the tradition of patrimonial politics alive. Still, Bolivia has gone from being the "basket case" of Latin America to an impressive (if contradictory) "showcase."

Further Reading

Albó, Xavier. "And from Kataristas to MNRistas? The Surprising and Bold Alliance between Aymaras and Neoliberals in Bolivia." In *Indigenous Peoples and Democracy in Latin America*. Ed. Donna Lee Van Cott. New York: St. Martin's Press, 1994.

———. "From MNRistas to Kataristas to Katari." In *Resistance, Rebellion and Consciousness in the Andean Peasant World, 18th to 20th Centuries*. Ed. Steve J. Stern. Madison: University of Wisconsin Press, 1987.

Dunkerly, James. *Rebellion in the Veins: Political Struggle in Bolivia, 1952–1982*. London: Thetford Press, 1984.

———. "The Crisis of Bolivian Radicalism." In *The Latin America Left: From the Fall of Allende to Perestroika*. Ed. Barry Carr and Steve Ellner. San Francisco: Westview Press, 1993.

Gamarra, Eduardo A., and James M. Malloy. "The Patrimonial Dynamics of Party Politics in Bolivia." In *Building Democratic Institutions: Party Systems in Latin America*. Ed. Scott Mainwaring and Timothy R. Scully. Stanford, Calif.: Stanford University Press, 1995.

Klein, Herbert S. *Bolivia: Evolution of a Multi-Ethnic*

Society. Oxford: Oxford University Press, 1992.

Malloy, James. *Bolivia: The Uncompleted Revolution.* Pittsburgh: University of Pittsburgh Press, 1970.

Mayorga, Rene Antonio. "Bolivia's Silent Revolution." *Journal of Democracy* 8, no. 1, January 1997.

Rojas Ortuste, Gonzalo. *Democracia en Bolivia Hoy y Mañana: Enraizando La Democracia con las Experiencias*

de los Pueblos Ind'genas. La Paz: CIPCA, 1994.

Secretaria Nacional de Participación Popular. *Apre(he)ndiendo La Participación Popular*. La Paz: Ministerio de Desarrollo Humano and SNPP, 1996.

Ticona, Esteban, Gonzalo Rojas, and Xavier Albó. *Votos y Wiphalas: Campesinos y Pueblos Originarios en la Democracia*. La Paz: CIPCA, 1995.

BOSNIA AND HERCEGOVINA

(Bosna i Hercegovina)

By Stephen C. Markovich, Ph.D.

THE SYSTEM OF GOVERNMENT

Before the former Yugoslavia fell apart and war broke out, Bosnia and Hercegovina was often seen as a microcosm of the country. Geographically situated in the middle, its population was comprised mainly of three nationalities—Muslim, Serb, and Croat—who essentially spoke the same language and who generally got along well and made little issue of ethnic/religious background. According to official 1996 estimates, there were 4.1 million inhabitants in the country. Of these, 48% were Muslim, 39% Serb, 12% Croat, and 1% others. As a result of the civil war, especially due to the ethnic cleansing and population shifts, these demographic data may now be inaccurate. Some unofficial data suggest the current number of inhabitants is 3.7 million rather than 4.1 million and that Muslims make up 52% rather than 48% of this number.

The Republic of Bosnia and Hercegovina affirmed its independence as a nation-state following a popular referendum held on March 1, 1992. Though the Serbs boycotted the referendum, Muslims and Croats—over 63% of the eligible voters—came out strongly and overwhelmingly supported independence. Despite the success of the referendum and despite the fact that most of the international community officially recognized the Republic of Bosnia and Hercegovina, the new country got off to a rocky start. Ethnic differences and civil war marred its beginning and have since undermined its very existence as a state. So Bosnia and Hercegovina may exist de jure, but de facto its status is questionable.

Today its de jure status rests primarily on the Dayton Accords, signed in December 1995. What the Accords did, among other things, was bring the war to an end, impose a peace with NATO troops, and draft a constitution that frames a complicated government. On paper the constitution establishes a loose confederation that includes a central government for the country as a whole, now officially called Bosnia and Hercegovina rather than the Republic of Bosnia and Hercegovina, and recognizes two regional governments, officially referred to as entities rather than regions. One entity, the Federation of

Bosnia and Hercegovina, hereafter referred to as the Bosnian Federation, represents the union of Muslims and Croats and controls 51% of the territory. The other, the Bosnian Serb Republic, still referred to as the *Srpska Republika*, is dominated by Serbs and controls 49% of the territory. (Though the Accords refer to the Muslims as Bosniacs, the name has not caught on and Muslims seems to remain the more common appellation.)

Though the Dayton Accords have established a constitutional government for Bosnia and Hercegovina, this government has not yet transformed itself into an institutionalized system with accepted authority and powers. Rather, there are several centers of power, governmental and nongovernmental, civil and military, that cooperate on some occasions and compete on others. What this de facto division of powers does is qualify any descriptions of the existing governmental system, and this de facto division of powers has to be kept in mind when examining the de jure government—or governments, to be precise—that emerged from the Dayton Accords.

Executive

At present in Bosnia and Hercegovina there is an executive for the central government and executives for the entity governments. The executive for the central government includes a tripartite presidency, copremiers, and a council of ministers. The tripartite presidency includes one Moslem, one Croat, and one Serb, each of them directly elected by their own people; the copremiers are appointed by the presidency and confirmed by the House of Representatives and must be ethnically balanced in composition; and the ministers are appointed by the premiers and appointed by the House of Representatives. Within this executive group the tripartite presidency is the strongest, but that does not mean much since the powers of the central government collectively and its branches individually are limited.

Constitutionally the presidency can propose an annual budget and determine revenues, expenditures, and the printing of money; it has authority over foreign policy including the appointment of ambassadors, the making of treaties, and relations with international organizations; and it is supposed to resolve controversies between the entity governments. These presidential powers are limited not only by the fact that they cover so few jurisdictional areas but also by their being shared with the premiers and ministers, who may be slow in implementing them, and with the central legislative houses, which may reject presidential proposals. Even more restrictive than the checks within the central government are the checks available to the three ethnic groups in the entity governments. For example, if the dissenting member in a two-to-one vote in the tripartite presidency feels the decision or proposal is detrimental to his ethnic group, he may refer the action to his ethnic delegation in the respective entity legislature and this delegation—Muslim, Croat, or Serb—may veto the presidential action. This ethnic-entity veto over actions by the central government tilts political power toward the entity governments.

On the entity level the executive of the Bosnian federation consists of a president and vice president elected by the federation legislature and of a premier and ministers appointed by the president and confirmed by the legislature. The executive of the *Srpska Republika* consists of a president and vice president elected directly by the people and a premier and ministers appointed by the president and approved by the legislature. In both entity governments the executives share powers with their respective legislatures—and these powers are considerable inasmuch as they cover all the jurisdictional areas that have not been constitutionally assigned to the federal government. Thus, the regional governments have powers over police and military forces, economics and finance, education and culture, and communications and media as well as additional powers that in total allow them to control their own affairs and encroach on central powers. All in all, as noted earlier, more power rests with the entity governments than with the central government.

Legislature

The legislatures for the central government and the two entity governments share powers with their respective executives. These legislatures, set in variations of the presidential-parliamentary model, are genuine legislatures since they can approve, amend, or reject executive proposals and can confirm and remove premiers and ministers in their executive branches—but not the presidents, who are directly elected by the people.

The legislature in the central government is called the Parliamentary Assembly and is composed of a lower house called the House of Representatives and an upper house called the House of Peoples. The lower house has 42 members, who are elected directly by the people, and the upper house has 15 members—5 Muslims, 5 Croats, 5 Serbs—who are chosen by the entity legislatures and hold their seats as long as they retain the confidence of the entity legislatures. The legislature for the Bosnian Federation, called the National Assembly, has a lower house, the House of Representatives, which is composed of 140 members elected directly by the people, and an upper house, the House of Peoples, which is composed of 120 members chosen by the governments of 10 cantons. The legislature for the *Srpska Republika* is a unicameral body called the National Assembly and composed of 83 members elected directly by the people.

Judiciary

The judicial system in Bosnia and Hercegovina is a complex arrangement of courts that are trying to dispense justice based on a code system in a wartime environment that has shown little respect for law. At the apex of this system is the Constitutional Court for Bosnia and Hercegovina, composed of nine judges. Four of them are appointed by the House of Representatives of the Bosnian Federation, two by the National Assembly of the *Srpska Republika*, and three by the president of the European Court of Human Rights in consultation with the tripartite presidency. Initially terms are for five years, but subsequently judges may serve to age 70. This court is supposed to ensure the conformity of laws for the country and to adjudicate disputes between the branches of the central government and between the three governments as well.

In the Bosnian Federation there is a constitutional court, a supreme court, 10 cantonal courts, and a series of municipal courts, and in the *Srpska Republika* there is also a constitutional court, a supreme court, and a series of inferior courts on various levels. Despite their constitutional standing and despite their attempts to handle everyday cases in civil and criminal law, these courts are not firmly established; they have not had the opportunity to play the significant role that courts usually play in stable political systems, nor are they likely to develop this role until the political situation in Bosnia and Hercegovina is normalized.

Regional and Local Government

Prior to the civil war there were 109 municipalities in Bosnia and Hercegovina, but demographic transfers and political redistricting have increased this number to over 140 and additional changes suggest the number may soon be 150 or so. Each of these municipalities has an elected council and mayor and most of them tend to be dominated by one of the ethnic groups. In the *Srpska Re-*

publika the municipalities are the only form of local government, but in the Bosnian Federation there are cantons as well as municipalities. Here the municipalities are grouped into 10 cantons, each of which has a president chosen by a cantonal council that has been directly elected by the people for a two-year term. Within their cantons, the councils are responsible for police and security, education and culture, radio and television, land and energy, and regulation of local governments; some of these powers are exercised jointly with the federation government and others are delegated to the municipal governments. The municipalities in both the Bosnian Federation and the *Srpska Republika* are responsible for such matters as housing and property, public utilities, licensing of radios and newspapers, reconstruction and development, citizenship, and local courts.

THE ELECTORAL SYSTEM

Following the Dayton Accords, elections were held in September of 1995 for the tripartite presidency and the lower house of Bosnia and Hercegovina, for the lower house in the Bosnian Federation, and for the legislature in the *Srpska Republika*. Terms for all of these offices, for these elections only, were for two years, but in the elections held in the fall of 1998 the victorious candidates won established terms of four years. For all elections, all citizens 18 years of age or older who are listed on the 1991 census are eligible to vote; those who are not listed can gain eligibility by providing proof of citizenship, and refugees, about 900,000 of them, can also gain eligibility through a special registration process.

Members of the tripartite presidency of Bosnia and Hercegovina are elected directly by the people for four-year terms in majoritarian, first-past-the-post systems. Each of them is essentially elected by his or her own people in the Bosnian Federation and the *Srpska Republika*. In the 1996 elections each of the winners easily won his respective ethnic race by gaining the required majority on the first ballot: Alija Izetbegovic won the Muslim seat, Kresimir Zubak the Croat seat, and Momcilo Krajisnik the Serb seat. For the first term Izetbegovic assumed the chair of the tripartite presidency by virtue of his gathering the most total votes in the election, but for subsequent terms, beginning with the 1998 elections, the legislature decided that the three members would rotate the chair every eight months. Not only did the term and chair change following the 1998 election, but two members of the presidency also changed; Izetbegovic kept the Muslim seat, but the Croat seat was won by Ante Jelavic, a Bosnian HDZ candidate, and the Serb seat was won by Zivko Radisic, a coalition candidate. The 42 members of the lower house in

Bosnia and Hercegovina, the House of Representatives, are elected directly by the people for terms to be decided—28 of them through proportional representation in the Bosnian Federation and 14 of them through proportional representation in the *Srpska Republika*. In the 1996 elections the Muslim Party of Democratic Action won 19 seats, the Serb Democratic Party 9 seats, the Croatian Democratic Union 8 seats, and three minor parties 6 seats. In the 1998 elections the results were even more diffuse; a coalition led by the Muslim Party of Democratic Action won 17 seats, the Croatian Democratic Union 6 seats, and the Serb Democratic Party 4 seats, while seven coalitions and minor parties shared the remaining 15 seats.

The 140 members of the House of Representatives, the lower house of the Bosnian Federation, are directly elected by the people for terms to be decided through a system of proportional representation; as a result of the 1996 elections, the Muslim Party of Democratic Action gained a majority of 78 seats and was followed by the Croatian Democratic Union with 36 seats; a coalition called the United List won 11 seats, the Party for Bosnia and Hercegovina won 10 seats, and two smaller parties won the remaining 5 seats. In the 1998 elections the major parties dropped in representation and minor parties increased their seats; the coalition led by Democratic Action won 68 seats, the Croatian Democratic Union 28 seats, and the Social Democrats 19 seats, while 11 minor parties split the other 25 seats. The 83 members of the unicameral National Assembly of the *Srpska Republika* are similarly elected directly by the people for four-year terms through a system of proportional representation; in the November 1997 elections for this body, the Serb Democratic Party won 24 seats, the Serb National Alliance won 15 seats, and several smaller parties shared 43 seats; in the September 1998 elections, the Serb Democratic Party won 19 seats, the Coalition for a Unified and Democratic B&H 15 seats, the Serbian People's Union 12 seats, the Serb Radical Party 11 seats, and the Socialist Party 10 seats, while seven minor parties shared 16 seats. The president and vice president of the *Srpska Republika* are directly elected by the people through a majoritarian, first-past-the-post system; in the 1996 elections Biljana Plavsic and Dragoljub Mirjanic, her running mate, easily won on the first ballot with 60% of the vote; however, in the 1998 elections, Plavsic garnered only 39% of the vote and surprisingly lost the presidency to Nikola Poplasen, the ultranationalist leader of the Serb Radical Party, who got 44% of the vote.

The loss by Plavsic was a setback to Western policies since Plavsic had become a moderate Serb who supported the Dayton Accords and was backed by the NATO countries. However, her loss and Poplasen's victory are tempered by the fact that Poplasen's Radical Party won only 11 seats in the legislature, which will likely prevent him from naming his own prime minister, and also by the fact that Zivko Radisic, the Serb member of the tripartite presidency of Bosnia and Hercegovina, is a moderate.

THE PARTY SYSTEM

Following the collapse of communism in 1990, the government of Bosnia and Hercegovina permitted the establishment of opposition political parties to challenge the faltering communist party. Within a few months there were over 40 parties in the republic, many of them very small and not competitive. Thus, despite the large number of parties, in the first competitive elections, held in November of 1990, only three of them, all ethnically based, gained more than 10 parliamentary seats on their own and established themselves as major parties. The three parties—the Party of Democratic Action, the Serb Democratic Party, and the Croatian Democratic Union—remain the major parties in the country today, though a split in the Serb Democratic Party led to the rise of a fourth major party, the Serb National Alliance. Splits and mergers prior to the 1998 elections also led to the formation of several coalitions, often headed by major parties, and contributed to increased success for a number of minor parties.

PARTY OF DEMOCRATIC ACTION
(Stranka Demokratske Akcije; SDA)

The Party of Democratic Action was founded in 1990 by a group of Muslim leaders headed by Alija Izetbegovic. The SDA bases its party principles on Islamic ideas and feels that the Muslims should have a significant role in Bosnia and Hercegovina, in an integrated Bosnia and Hercegovina. Though the party also professes support of democratic ideas and free enterprise and cooperation among all the ethnic groups, this support and cooperation are colored by the fact that the party remains strongly nationalistic; however, Izetbegovic has tried to temper this nationalism in order to reach a governing consensus with the Croats and the Serbs. Under the leadership of Izetbegovic the party has organized support of the Muslim people and has been successful at the polls. In the 1996 elections Izetbegovic himself was elected chair of the tripartite presidency and his SDA led all parties in the House of Representatives in Bosnia and Hercegovina by winning 19 of the 42 seats; and in the elections for the House of Representatives of the Bosnian Federation, it won a majority 78 of the 140 seats. In the 1998 elections

Izetbegovic again was elected as the Muslim member of the tripartite presidency and his SDA, now the senior partner of a four-party coalition called the Coalition for a Unified and Democratic B&H, won 17 of the 42 seats in the Bosnian House and 68 of the 140 seats in the Federation House.

SERB DEMOCRATIC PARTY
(Srpska Demokratska Stranka; SDS)

The Serb Democratic Party was founded in 1990 by Radovan Karadzic and a close group of followers. Karadzic and his party were intensely in favor of preserving the former Yugoslavia as a single state, and when that state could not be preserved, they supported Belgrade's Slobodan Milosevic in his efforts to unite all Serbs into a new Yugoslavia. Though the union of Serbs has not been achieved, either through war or diplomacy, Karadzic and the SDS remain nationalistic and still prefer secession from Bosnia and Hercegovina and union with Serbia and Montenegro (Yugoslavia). Hard-core Serb support for Karadzic enabled his candidate, Momcilo Krajisnik, to be elected a member of the tripartite presidency in 1996 and his SDS to come in second to the SDA in the House of Representatives of Bosnia and Hercegovina. It also enabled the party to win a majority 45 seats in the National Assembly of the *Srpska Republika* in 1996, but this majority dwindled to a plurality 24 seats in the 1997 elections and to 19 in the 1998 elections. The drop in support was due in part to foreign pressures that forced Karadzic to resign his governmental posts and in part to a split in the SDS between Karadzic and Biljana Plavsic, a split that diminished support for the SDS.

SERB NATIONAL ALLIANCE
(Srpski Narodni Savez; SNS)

When Radovan Karadzic was not allowed to run for the presidency of the *Srpska Republika* in 1996, Biljana Plavsic, a leading member of the SDS and a Karadzic supporter, ran under the SDS banner and won the presidency. Once in office she began to drift away from the ultranationalist positions of Karadzic and follow a more moderate political path. As a result of this shift, she was expelled from the SDS in the summer of 1997 and forced to form her own party, the Serb National Alliance. Her vice president and some other members of the SDS joined her in the new SNS. Plavsic and her party, like the SDS, still think it would be better for the *Srpska Republika* to split from Bosnia and Hercegovina and gain independence, but, unlike the SDS, they also think it is practical and beneficial to cooperate with international authorities. Thus, American and European leaders have decided to throw their support behind Plavsic and help her government succeed. In the first elections in which the SNS participated, in the November 1997 National Assembly elections called by Plavsic, the party won 16% of the vote and 15 of the 83 seats compared with 26% of the vote and 24 seats gained by the leading SDS.

Despite the lack of a majority on her own, Plavsic had been supported by other moderate parties and therefore had been able to overcome the obstructionist tactics of the SDS and attempt to govern the *Srpska Republika*. At that time it appeared that her political star was rising and Karadzic's was falling. However, Plavsic suffered a setback in 1998 when she lost the presidential election to Poplasen and her party's support dropped to 14% and 12 legislative seats.

CROATIAN DEMOCRATIC UNION
(Hrvatska Demokratska Zajednica; HDZ)

The Croatian Democratic Union was founded in 1990 under the leadership of Stjepan Kljuivc. In its party platform it has precisely followed the orientation and policies of its sister party in Croatia, the HDZ of Franjo Tudjman. Like the Croatian HDZ, the Bosnian HDZ is a nationalist party that sees itself as the defender of Croats and Croatian interests in Bosnia and Hercegovina. Though it has supported the independence of Bosnia and Hercegovina and worked with the Muslim SDA in a fragile government coalition, the ties to Tudjman and Croatia remain strong, and consequently there is a latent stream within the Bosnian HDZ that yearns to have the territories it controls break away from Bosnia and Hercegovina and join the Republic of Croatia. On this point of "splitting and joining," the position of the HDZ is similar to the Serb position of Karadzic's SDS and Plavsic's SNS, a mutual position which makes the Muslims uneasy. In elections to date, the HDZ has expectedly come in third, reflecting the fact that it is the third-largest ethnic group. In the elections of 1996 its member of the tripartite presidency came in third with 15% of the overall vote, and it also came in third in the legislative elections for Bosnia and Hercegovina with 8 of the 42 seats. In the Bosnian Federation the HDZ expectedly came in second to the SDA with 36 of the 140 seats. In the 1998 elections the party's presidential candidate, Ante Jelavic, won the Croatian seat with 12% of the overall vote and the party itself won 6 of the seats in the Bosnian legislature and 28 of the seats in the Federation legislature.

MINOR POLITICAL PARTIES

In 1996 there were a myriad of minor parties in Bosnia and Hercegovina, but their number seemed to be fading at that time. By 1998, however, minor parties made a comeback, and now there are actually more of them participating in governments at all levels, either as members of coalitions or on their own. One of the major coalitions is the Coalition for a Unified and Democratic B&H, which is led by the Party of Democratic Action and includes the Social Democrats of B&H, the Liberals of B&H, and the Civic Democratic Community; a second is the SDS-List, which is essentially the Serb Democratic Party supported by the regional Democratic Party of Banja Luka and Krajina; and a third is Sloga, a group of three parties that merge only on the national level and separate on the regional level and is made up of the Serb National Alliance, the Socialist Party of the *Srpska Republika*, and the Party of Independent Social Democrats. The latter two are viable parties on their own within the *Srpska Republika*. The minor party that has made the most progress in terms of support is the ultranationalist Serb Radical Party; it gained 11 seats in the National Assembly of the *Srpska Republika* in 1998, and, more significantly, its leader, Nikola Poplasen, won the presidency of the *Srpska Republika*.

While the Serb Radical Party has done especially well, there are a large number of minor parties—nearly 30 of them—that have been less successful yet have managed to gain a few seats, from one to four, in one or more of the legislative houses. As a result, a party system that seemed to be filtering down to three or four major parties in 1996 had by 1998 again become a multiparty system characterized by a plethora of minor parties.

NATIONAL PROSPECTS

After all that has happened in Bosnia and Hercegovina, it is hard to be optimistic about the future of the country. How do ethnic groups—who have committed the grossest of atrocities against one another, who have participated in the ethnic cleansing of villages and towns, and who have abetted the expulsion of former friends and neighbors from their ancestral homes—forget their mutual crimes and hatreds and reunite as an integrated nation-state? Few observers familiar with the situation believe the country can be united again. Unfortunately, even fewer of the ethnic leaders believe it can be done or, more significantly, want it done. Given the hatreds among peoples, the distrust between leaders, and the fragility of the governments, the future appears dark for Bosnia and Hercegovina.

Most observers are surprised that the Accords have

held up as well and as long as they have. Although NATO forces have had to stay longer than intended, they have kept the peace, and the arranged governmental frameworks remain fragile, but, so far, they have stayed intact. The chances of Bosnia and Hercegovina surviving as a country are still bleak, to be sure, but less bleak than they were in 1995. The longer the Accords hold, the better the chances are for the country's survival. If the Accords fail, violence and partition are sure to follow.

Further Reading

Ali, Rabia, and Lawrence Lifschultz, eds. *Why Bosnia? Writings on the Balkan War*. Stony Creek, Conn.: Pamphleteer's Press, 1993.

Banac, Ivo. *The National Question in Yugoslavia: Origins, History, Politics*. Ithaca, N.Y.: Cornell University Press, 1988.

Cohen, Lenard J. *Broken Bonds: Yugoslavia's Disintegration and Balkan Politics in Transition*, 2d ed. Boulder, Colo.: Westview Press, 1995.

Donia, Robert J., and John V.A. Fine, Jr. *Bosnia and Hercegovina: A Tradition Betrayed*. New York: Columbia University Press, 1994.

Lampe, John R. *Yugoslavia as History: Twice There Was a Country*. New York: Cambridge University Press, 1996.

Malcolm, Noel. *Bosnia: A Short History*. New York: New York University Press, 1994.

Ramet, Sabrina P. *Balkan Babel: The Disintegration of Yugoslavia from the Death of Tito to Ethnic War*, 2d ed. Boulder, Colo.: Westview Press, 1996.

Rusinow, Dennison. *The Yugoslav Experiment, 1948–1974*. Berkeley: University of California Press, 1977.

Woodward, Susan L. *Balkan Tragedy: Chaos and Dissolution after the Cold War*. Washington, D.C.: Brookings Institution, 1995.

REPUBLIC OF BOTSWANA

By Richard Dale, Ph.D.

THE SYSTEM OF GOVERNMENT

Botswana, which is often mentioned as one of the economic and political success stories in a continent that is usually excoriated for an unsatisfactory postcolonial democratic record, had an inauspicious beginning. It was part of a larger area in southern Africa known as Bechuanaland, which was divided in the colonial era into northern and southern parts, with the southern part becoming a portion of the Cape Colony in South Africa and the larger northern area a British protectorate. It was the Bechuanaland Protectorate that became Botswana on September 30, 1966.

Earlier, both South Africa and Southern Rhodesia (now Zimbabwe) had territorial designs on parts, if not all, of the Bechuanaland Protectorate, primarily an impoverished ranching area where the small white population raised cattle, engaged in small commercial activities, or belonged to either the civil service or the police force. The Africans (known as Batswana) supported themselves by cattle ranching or working as migrant laborers in neighboring South Africa, Namibia, or Zimbabwe. The colonial administrative network was neither particularly dense nor exceptionally demanding (except for taxes) by the standards of the time, and traditional systems of governance remained largely intact.

Executive

At the pinnacle of the executive structure is the president, who combines the roles of head of state and head of government. Like prime ministers in a parliamentary system, the president is elected by members of Parliament, not by the electorate at large, for a five-year term of office, corresponding to the terms of the National Assembly members. Until recently, there was no limit to the number of times the president could be reelected, but the limit has now been fixed at two terms, beginning in 1999. The official opposition, the Botswana National Front (BNF), has proposed that the president be popularly elected, but the governing Botswana Democratic Party (BDP) has yet to accept this suggestion.

In addition to the president, there is a vice president, who currently holds the exceptionally important portfolio of minister of finance and development planning. The constitution follows the British (Westminister) model of responsible government, so that the Cabinet is responsible to the elected chamber of Parliament, the National Assembly. Cabinet members also have Parliament membership. Legislation passing the National Assembly is submitted to the president, who has limited veto powers. The president also serves as commander in chief of the Botswana Defense Force (BDF), which was not created until 11 years after the nation became independent. Sir Seretse Khama served as the first president from 1966 until his death in 1980, and he was followed by his principal lieutenant, Quett K. Masire, who has served continuously since 1980.

Legislature

For most purposes, Botswana is a unicameral state, with a National Assembly chosen by the entire electorate. For matters that may be considered in the traditional and/or tribal realm, there is a second chamber, the House of Chiefs, representing the eight major tribal components of the nation (each of which has its own leadership and separate geographic location). Although it is neither directly elected nor as inclusive in its legislative domain as the National Assembly, the 15-member House of Chiefs serves to sustain traditional legitimacy for the postcolonial state. The National Assembly, with its 44 members (known as members of Parliament, or MPs), who have five-year terms, is the focal point for much of Botswana's politics. It functions along the lines of the British House of Commons, which it resembles in many ways. Recently, the National Assembly developed a functionally specific committee system, akin to the one used in the United States, yet the National Assembly still retains the quintessential British parliamentary question period. The BDP secured 27 seats in the last (October 15, 1994) general election, while the BNF won 13; in addition there are 4 presidentially nominated MPs, all of whom belong to the BDP. Interest groups, which are often an integral part of Western political systems, are not yet especially significant or effective national political forces in Botswana and have no major and continuous impact upon the legislature.

Judiciary

Botswana utilizes both traditional (African customary) and modern systems of law, with the latter drawing upon English law as well as the Roman-Dutch one prevalent in the Cape Province of South Africa. South African–based lawyers often have transnational private practices in Botswana. The highest echelons of the Botswana judiciary have included a judge from Zimbabwe, and the law curriculum at the University of Botswana entails study at the University of Edinburgh in Scotland. There is a Judicial Service Commission that is responsible for recommending suitable persons to the president for subsequent appointment to high judicial office, and the court system stretches from the district magistrate's court to the High Court and thence to the Court of Appeal. The government, in order to curb alleged corruption among some elements of the legal profession, may enact appropriate legislation because there is no Law Society in Botswana to discipline its members. In 1994 Botswana created a Directorate on Corruption and Economic Crime, and there is a Botswana Center on Human Rights. Over the years, the New York–based Freedom House has given Botswana high marks on the quality of its civic culture and human rights.

Regional and Local Government

Like most other African states, Botswana has a unitary, rather than a federal, system of government. During the colonial era, the country was geographically divided into eight very unequal tribal areas, crown (that is, state) land, and enclaves for white residents. The country was predominantly rural, and both the Africans and the whites had consultative councils to advise the British resident (later the queen's) commissioner. Until the British instituted self-government in 1965, the administrative headquarters of the protectorate were located in the Cape provincial town of Mafikeng, just over the South African border. Since then there has been considerable urban growth, especially in the new capital city, Gaborone, which replaced Mafikeng. The overwhelming bulk of the population is located in the eastern perimeter of Botswana, where the rail line connects Mafikeng with the Zimbabwean city of Bulawayo.

There are several ethnic groups in Botswana who have transnational ties with their kinsmen in Namibia, South Africa, and Zimbabwe, and for the moment those with the Bakalanga in Zimbabwe are the most vexing for the dominant Tswana cultural groups. Governance at the subnational level is undertaken by nine district councils,

along with four town councils (for Francistown, Jwaneng, Lobatse, Selebi-Phikwe) and the Gaborone city council, and elections at the subnational and national levels are held at the same time, with political parties active at both levels.

THE ELECTORAL SYSTEM

Botswana uses the system commonly known as "first past the post" that their colonial mentors, the British, still use in their own elections. The candidate with the highest number of votes (who is first to cross the finish line) is declared to be the winner, even though that candidate may not have won a majority of the votes cast. The winning candidate is the sole representative of a given district, because Botswana, like the United Kingdom, uses the single-member constituency system rather than the multiple-member one found in proportional representation systems. As a result of the recently passed Constitutional Amendment Act, the voting age has been lowered from 21 to 18. This change, which was principally due to the pressure of the opposition BNF, may possibly benefit the BNF, which has a fairly stable electoral clientele in the urban areas, provided there is a high turnout of the newly enfranchised young adults, many of whom are un- or underemployed.

In addition, Botswana is to have an Electoral Commission, composed of seven members, that is to function in an independent fashion. In the past there have been isolated instances of electoral misconduct, which has tended to detract from the legitimacy of the electoral process, but the establishment of the Commission bodes well for the integrity of the process and for public respect for the probity of the parliamentary system.

THE PARTY SYSTEM

Currently, Botswana has a multiparty system at the national level, although only two parties—the BDP (the government) and the BNF (the opposition)—were able to elect MPs to the National Assembly in the 1994 parliamentary general election. Political parties in Botswana are of relatively recent origin, reaching back only to about 1960, when the Bechuanaland People's Party (BPP) was created. The BPP took its cue, in large measure, from African nationalist politics and ideologies and slogans in South Africa, where a number of Africans from Botswana worked permanently or on a migratory basis. Prior to that time, independence for the Bechuanaland Protectorate was not a concrete aim, for much of the Batswana's political capital (and that of the Britons) was expended on thwarting South Africa's and (to a lesser extent) Southern Rhodesia's efforts to incorporate all or part of Botswana into their own domains.

As the prospects for self-government for the protectorate increased in the early 1960s, the BPP began to face competition from the Bechuanaland Democratic Party (BDP), which was constituted in 1962 by the tribal notables and well-heeled white ranchers to ensure a less radical path to independence. Seretse Khama, whom the British had deposed as the heir to the chieftainship of the Bamangwato (the largest tribe) owing to his marriage to a Briton, enjoyed considerable traditional legitimacy in the protectorate and had studied law in Great Britain. In the first self-government elections held in March 1965, Seretse Khama's BDP emerged victorious, and Seretse became the country's first (and only) prime minister. Once the United Kingdom granted his nation independence, on September 30, 1966, Seretse occupied the office of president under the new constitution, which combined the offices of head of state and head of government.

BOTSWANA DEMOCRATIC PARTY

This party has enjoyed remarkable success in general elections, having won every one since the 1965 legislative assembly elections on the eve of independence. It has acquired the prestige associated with the accession to independence at a time when white minority rule was the rule, rather than the exception, in the southern African region. Initially it used the symbol of a jack and the (Afrikaans) phrase *domkrag* for those Batswana who had difficulty pronouncing the English term "democracy"; the imagery suggested that the BDF would lift up (and thus improve) the nation, which started its independence with the most meager of resources.

An amalgam of traditional leaders and their followers as well as of the small but affluent white community, the BDP was the dominant force in the 1969, 1974, 1979, 1984, 1989, and 1994 parliamentary elections, although recently it has lost electoral ground to the BNF and has been riven by factionalism. Some of its MPs have been tainted by scandal, which was quite unknown in the earlier years of the party, when Seretse Khama served as president. Part of the explanation for such lapses in conduct can be traced to the growing wealth of the country—which has made Botswana one of the great success stories of sub-Saharan Africa—and the strategic ruling location of the BDP, which has enabled it to dispense a wide range of public goods.

MINOR POLITICAL PARTIES

The BNF is now the official opposition in the National Assembly, which includes only two parties. In the 1989 general election the BDP and BNF secured, between

them, 90% of the popular vote, a figure that increased to 91% in the 1994 general election. Other national political parties have been marginalized. Led by Dr. Kenneth Koma, the BNF dates back to 1966 and has competed in every general election since 1969. Its core clientele tend to be the less traditional and urbanized Batswana as well as those who, from time to time, defect from the BDP. Observers have usually placed it to the left of the BDP on the political spectrum, if only on the basis of its political rhetoric. It has functioned as a critic of the BDP, suggested reforms (some of which the BDP has adopted), and has an outside chance of displacing the BDP. Were it to do so, many students of African democracy would assert that Botswana has become a full-blown democracy in which there is a peaceful transition of political power, a more difficult standard to meet than the usual one of competitive elections (which Botswana has met time after time).

OTHER POLITICAL FORCES

Although most observers of Botswana's political system comment favorably upon the professional competence, probity, and loyalty of the national civil service, which was slowly localized to maintain high-quality performance, they have recently drawn attention to the BDF. This small armed force (primarily infantry and air force) was one of the very few in sub-Saharan Africa to postdate independence; it was formed in 1977 in response to the independence war in Zimbabwe, which spilled over into Botswana. The BDF, headed by the eldest son of the late President Seretse Khama, consumes too much of the gross domestic product in the opinion of some Botswana watchers anxious to see a reduced BDF establishment and budget as Botswana's contribution to balanced arms reduction in the southern African region. There is less concern about a possible BDF coup d'état, however.

In addition to the civil service and the BDF, multinational mining firms, especially the De Beers Consolidated Mines of South Africa, which oversees diamond mining in Botswana under the title of Debswana Diamond Company, have played a significant role in Botswana's remarkable economic growth and are significant stakeholders in the political stability of Botswana.

NATIONAL PROSPECTS

Botswana can look forward to further successes and acolytes provided that its mineral-driven economy does not falter, on the one hand, and that it affords deeper and greater protection to those disadvantaged in terms of cattle, education, and marketable skills, on the other. Although very affluent by African standards, its economic and political system skews the allocation of political goods in the direction of the more well-to-do. Many commentators who are quite impressed with Botswana's political record are nevertheless discomforted in terms of the maldistribution of income, property, and life chances. These shortcomings attract the attention of the opposition BNF, which may more fully capitalize on these deficiencies in later general elections; much depends on the skill of the BDF in addressing these problems, thus neutralizing the BNF's appeals.

Further Reading

Dale, Richard. *Botswana's Search for Autonomy in Southern Africa*. Westport, Conn.: Greenwood Press, 1995.

du Toit, Pierre. *State Building and Democracy in Southern Africa: Botswana, Zimbabwe and South Africa*. Washington, D.C.: United States Institute of Peace Press, 1995.

Holm, John D., and Patrick P. Molutsi, eds. *Democracy in Botswana: The Proceedings of a Symposium Held in Gaborone, 1–5 August 1988*. Athens: Ohio University Press, 1989.

Parson, Jack. *Botswana: Liberal Democracy and the Labor Reserve in Southern Africa*. Boulder, Colo.: Westview Press, 1984.

Picard, Louis A., ed. *The Evolution of Modern Botswana*. London: Rex Collings, 1985.

———. *The Politics of Development in Botswana: A Model for Success?* Boulder, Colo.: Lynne Rienner, 1988.

Stedman, Stephen J., ed. *Botswana: The Political Economy of Democratic Development*. Boulder, Colo.: Lynne Rienner, 1987.

Wiseman, John A. *Democracy in Black Africa: Survival and Revival*. New York: Paragon House, 1990.

FEDERATIVE REPUBLIC OF BRAZIL

(República Federativa do Brasil)

By Jeffrey J. Rinne, M.A.

Brazil is the world's fifth-largest country. Occupying almost half of South America, it shares a border with every other South American country except Chile and Ecuador. Brazil's economy is the world's ninth-largest. However, the distribution of wealth in Brazil is highly skewed. There are over 160 million Brazilians. Over 40% live in poverty.

Brazil's long history of slavery is a key determinant of the country's ethnic and cultural heritage. Approximately 45% of Brazilians identify themselves as black or mulatto. About 54% identify themselves as white. Most whites are descendants of Portuguese, German, Italian, or Spanish immigrants. A large number of Japanese also emigrated to Brazil during the late 19th century. Today, there are over 730,000 Brazilians of Asian descent. The surviving indigenous population in Brazil numbers less than 200,000.

Roman Catholicism is by far the most prominent religion in Brazil, but evangelical churches have grown rapidly during the past 20 years, and they continue to thrive.

THE SYSTEM OF GOVERNMENT

During the past century Brazil's military has been a central actor in politics. In 1889, 1930, 1937, 1945, and 1954 the military directly intervened to shape the outcome of political struggles. In 1964, the military seized power and began 21 years of authoritarian rule under a string of military presidents. The military gradually began to relinquish power during the late 1970s, and in 1985 a civilian president was indirectly elected. Since 1989, Brazilians have chosen their president, legislators, governors, and mayors through free and direct elections.

Brazil is a federal republic composed of 26 states and a Federal District. A former colony of Portugal, Brazil became an independent monarchy in 1822. Dom Pedro I, the first emperor of newly independent Brazil, issued Brazil's first constitution in 1824. The constitution established a bicameral legislature, but the emperor could dissolve the Congress whenever he wished. Brazil's second emperor, Dom Pedro II, was deposed by the military in

1889. The republic was declared on the following day, November 16, 1889.

The 1891 constitution established a decentralized, federal system of government with a directly elected president. During the Old Republic (1889–1930), the "official" candidate for the presidency invariably won. Elections were controlled by local political bosses, while national-level politics was settled through bargains between the oligarchs of Brazil's most powerful states. São Paulo and Minas Gerais were the preeminent states in this "politics of governors."

After the world economic crash in 1929, disgruntled politicians and high-ranking military officers organized a military uprising to transfer power to Getúlio Vargas, the loser of the 1930 presidential election. The "Revolution of 1930" suspended the 1891 constitution, and for the next four years Vargas ruled by decree. A Constituent Assembly completed a new constitution in 1934 and elected Vargas president for a four-year term. In November 1937, the military dissolved Congress and sponsored a Vargas dictatorship from 1937 to 1945.

At the end of World War II, dictators were widely discredited throughout the world. In October 1945 the military deposed Vargas, and the following year a new constitution was drafted by a newly elected Constituent Assembly. From 1946 to 1964, the principal route to political power in Brazil was through competitive, popular elections.

Three major parties vied for power during this period; all three were formed in 1945. Two of these parties were founded by Vargas in anticipation of the return to electoral politics. The Social Democratic Party (PSD) organized many of Brazil's rural political bosses, while the Brazilian Worker's Party (PTB) was an urban-based party designed to attract support from Brazil's emerging working class. The anti-Vargas forces formed a third party, the National Democratic Union (UDN).

Over the next 15 years, the PSD and PTB dominated electoral politics in Brazil. Enrico Dutra, Vargas, and Juscelino Kubitschek were the first three presidents elected after 1945. Each was supported by one or both of these parties. Finally, in 1960, the presidential candidate backed by the UDN, Jânio Quadros, won a landslide victory. Mysteriously, Quadros resigned after just seven months, most likely expecting the Congress to grant him near-dictatorial powers to convince him to remain president. Instead, the Congress accepted his resignation and the vice president, João Goulart, ascended to the presidency.

Goulart's leftist policies and populist style were anathema to many powerful groups in Brazil, including the conservative military. Goulart sought to mobilize militant labor support, and despite threats from the military, he refused to distance himself from Brazil's Communist Party. At the end of March 1964, the military seized power.

One of the first acts of the military was to purge Congress of its most left-leaning members. The Congress then quickly elected General Castelo Branco as the new president. From 1964 to 1985, Brazil was governed by a succession of military presidents. Castelo Branco (1964–67) was followed by Artur da Costa e Silva (1967–69), Emílio Garrastazú Médici (1969–74), Ernesto Geisel (1974–79), and João Figueiredo (1979–85).

There existed a consensus among leaders of the armed forces that the military was duty-bound to protect the nation from "irresponsible" politicians. Yet a majority of officers retained an ideological commitment to democracy. Severe constraints were imposed on the Congress, elections, and individual civil liberties; but under military rule, elections were held regularly, and with the exception of 10 months in 1968–69, the Congress continued to function.

Recurrent manipulations of the party system and electoral rules were necessary to construct election results that could meet with the military's approval. From 1964 to 1985, the president was indirectly elected. Beginning in 1964, the mayors of state capitals (along with other principal cities) were also indirectly elected. In 1966, direct elections were eliminated for governors. In 1977, one-third of the Senate was indirectly elected. Representatives to the Chamber of Deputies and state legislatures continued to be chosen through direct elections.

In the late 1970s, President Geisel began a process of *abertura* (opening) that continued under his successor, President Figueiredo. In 1982, Figueiredo reintroduced direct elections for state governors. That same year, voters also elected one-third of the Senate, the entire Chamber of Deputies, and new state legislatures. The results of these elections were clearly a victory for the opposition Party of the Brazilian Democratic Movement (PMDB). The PMDB won the governorships of Brazil's most developed states and a majority of the seats in the Chamber of Deputies. The government party, the Democratic Social Party (PDS), retained control of the Senate. More importantly, the PDS maintained control of the electoral college that would elect the next president in 1985. (The electoral college was composed of the entire Congress plus six representatives from each state legislature.)

In 1985, the opposition candidate for the presidency was the elder statesman Tancredo Neves. Although the PDS was the majority party in the electoral college, Tancredo skillfully allayed the apprehensions of the military and convinced a group of PDS delegates to defect and support his candidacy. Tancredo was elected president but tragically died after undergoing intestinal surgery on the eve of his inauguration. The vice president–elect, José Sarney, ascended to the presidency.

The grand hopes that Tancredo had inspired were disappointed, but the democratization process moved forward. In May 1985, the Congress reinstated direct elections for all mayors, abolished the electoral college, and legalized communist parties. A new constitution was approved on October 5, 1988, and the following year Brazilians elected a president by popular vote for the first time since 1960. In 1993, a national referendum was held to choose among a presidential, parliamentary, or monarchical form of government for Brazil. Presidentialism won soundly.

Executive

After the 1964 coup, presidents were indirectly elected (first by the Congress and later by an electoral college composed of the Congress and representatives from the state legislatures). A series of institutional acts decreed by the military government also expanded the president's powers. The first act (April 9, 1964) permitted the president to cancel the mandates of elected members of Congress, state legislatures, and municipal councils. A later act (October 2, 1965) allowed the president to suspend Congress and deprive a citizen of political rights for up to 10 years.

Although the institutional acts no longer exist, Brazil's presidents retain considerable power under the 1988 constitution. The president appoints a Cabinet of ministers, prepares and executes a national budget, proposes legislation to Congress, and is commander in chief of the armed forces. The president controls a large number of federal appointments and federal spending projects that can (and are) distributed to craft support for the executive's agenda. The president can also exercise legislative power by issuing decrees that have the force of law. These decree-laws are valid for only 30 days, but if the Congress does not vote to rescind a presidential decree-law, it can be perpetually reissued by the executive every 30 days.

The 1988 constitution established a five-year presidential term. However, in 1994, the Congress reduced the term to four years through a constitutional amendment. Direct elections for president historically were decided by a single round of voting: the candidate with a plurality of votes was elected. In the new constitution, a runoff election was created for occasions when no candidate receives an absolute majority in the first round. The practice of barring presidents from seeking immediate reelection began in Brazil in the 19th century, but in 1997 the Congress amended the constitution to allow immediate reelection to a second term.

Fernando Collor de Mello was the first president elected under the 1988 constitution and the first popularly elected president since the 1964 coup. Collor was formerly governor of Alagoas, a poor state in northeast Brazil. Though virtually unknown at the start of the presidential campaign, he projected a young, energetic image that successfully capitalized on the sense of malaise produced by years of stagnant growth and double-digit monthly inflation.

Collor invented a new party, the Party of National Reconstruction (PRN), as an electoral vehicle for his candidacy. In a field of more than 10 candidates, Collor won the first round with just over 30% of the vote, advancing to a runoff election against the second-place finisher, Luis Inácio Lula da Silva of the Workers' Party (PT). Collor won the runoff by a relatively narrow margin of 35 million votes to 31 million.

Once in office, Collor governed almost entirely by decree. His economic stabilization plans failed, and in 1992 the president's brother made startling revelations of graft and influence peddling by the president and his campaign fund-raiser, Paulo César Farias. In September 1992, the Chamber of Deputies initiated impeachment proceedings against the president. Collor resigned on the eve of his trial in the Senate, but the Senate nevertheless voted to strip Collor of the right to run for any elective office until the year 2000.

The vice president, Itamar Franco, ascended to the presidency. During the final year of his administration, the Real Plan successfully reduced inflation to under 2% per month from the nearly 40% monthly inflation rates of a few months before. Franco's finance minister during the Real Plan, Fernando Henrique Cardoso, received much of the credit for the Plan's success. Moreover, as inflation continued downward in the months prior to the election, Cardoso's popularity rose steadily. On October 3, 1994, Cardoso was elected president after only the first round of voting with 54.3% of the vote.

Cardoso is a member of the center-left Brazilian Social Democratic Party (PSDB). He was formerly an academic and later a senator. The PSDB holds only a minority of seats in the Congress, but Cardoso has fashioned a loose alliance with other parties of the center and right to support his administration. He is a more skilled negotiator than his most recent predecessors in the executive. However, despite his "parliamentary" style, Cardoso has also made frequent use of the decree power granted to the president.

During Cardoso's first term, inflation remained low and economic growth was moderate. In October 1998, Cardoso was elected to a second term.

Legislature

Brazil has a bicameral National Congress composed of a *Senado Federal* (Federal Senate) and *Câmara dos Dep-* *utados* (Chamber of Deputies). The Senate has 81 members; 3 senators are elected from each state, plus 3 from the Federal District. Elections for the Senate are held every four years, alternately for one-third and two-thirds of its members. Senators serve eight-year terms.

The Chamber of Deputies currently has 513 seats. Deputies are elected to four-year terms; elections are held once every four years to renew the entire Chamber. Each state elects a number of representatives in proportion to its population. However, the constitution guarantees each state at least 8 deputies, and no state is allowed more than 70. This means that Brazil's least-populated states are significantly overrepresented. At present, Brazil's most populous state, São Paulo, is allotted 60 representatives. Although São Paulo has 23% of Brazil's population, this state elects only 12% of the seats in the Chamber of Deputies.

Candidates for the Chamber of Deputies must be at least 21 years old. Candidates for the Senate must be at least 35. Both senators and deputies can be reelected repeatedly. The most recent election was October 3, 1994, when two-thirds of the Senate and the entire Chamber of Deputies were renewed.

In making laws, each chamber operates as a revision body for the other. If a bill or law originates in the Chamber of Deputies, it must subsequently be approved by the Senate, and vice versa. If a piece of legislation is passed by one chamber, then approved with changes by the other, it must go back to the chamber where it originated for new debate and voting.

After legislation is passed by both the Chamber of Deputies and the Senate it is sent to the president. The president may approve the legislation in whole or in part, or veto it. A majority vote of the full Congress sitting in a joint session is necessary to override a whole or partial presidential veto.

As part of its oversight authority, the Congress is empowered to call any minister or administrative officer of the president before Congress to answer questions on a specified subject. The president must have the authorization of Congress to declare war, and congressional approval is also necessary to declare a state of emergency. All international treaties must be approved by the Congress, and the president and vice president must have authorization from Congress to be absent from the country for more than 15 days.

The Senate has exclusive competence in several areas. The Senate must approve the president's nominees for justices of the high courts, foreign diplomats, the attorney general, and the president and directors of the Central Bank. Borrowing by the federal, state, and local governments also must be authorized by the Senate.

The Chamber of Deputies may initiate impeachment proceedings against a sitting president, vice president, or minister with a two-thirds vote. The charges are then judged by the Senate.

Judiciary

The highest court in Brazil is the *Supremo Tribunal Federal* (Supreme Court). The Court is empowered to review the constitutionality of legislation and executive actions, both at the state and the federal levels.

There are 11 justices on the Court. Each is appointed for life. When there is a vacancy on the Court the president nominates a new Supreme Court justice. Supreme Court nominees must be between the ages of 35 and 65. The president's choice must then receive the approval of the Senate. The removal or retirement of a judge can be made by a two-thirds vote of the Court's members.

Brazil's *Superior Tribunal de Justiça* (Superior Court of Justice) is an appellate court that also serves as the first court of action for certain crimes and *mandados de segurança* (injunctions against action or legislation of the government). The Superior Court of Justice is composed of a minimum of 33 judges. They are appointed in the same way as Supreme Court justices. One-third of the appointees must be former judges of the Regional Federal Courts.

Tribunais Regionais Federais (Regional Federal Courts) are located in each of the state capitals and the Federal District. They have at least seven judges. Brazil also has special military courts, labor courts, and electoral courts.

In every state and the Federal District there is a *Tribunal Regional do Trabalho* (Regional Labor Court). These courts adjudicate questions relating to collective bargaining agreements and individual work contracts between employers and employees. The court of appeal for the Regional Labor Courts is the *Tribunal Superior do Trabalho* (Superior Labor Court). The Superior Labor Court has 27 justices.

The *Tribunais Regionais Eleitorais* (Regional Electoral Courts) adjudicate cases concerning the eligibility of candidates for elected office and the legality of the election procedures. There are electoral courts in every state capital and the Federal District. Each has seven members.

The *Tribunal Superior Eleitoral* (Superior Electoral Court) is composed of three judges from the Supreme Court, two judges from the Superior Court of Justice, and two lawyers nominated by the president from a list of suggested candidates provided by the Supreme Court. Judges on the Superior Electoral Court are appointed for a two-year term and cannot serve more than four consecutive years.

Military crimes are judged by the *Superior Tribunal Militar* (Superior Military Court). The Superior Military Court is composed of 15 judges: 3 from the navy, four from the army, 3 from the air force, and 5 civilians. Members of the Court are nominated by the president and must be approved by the Senate.

Regional and Local Government

Brazil is a federal republic composed of 26 states and a Federal District. The states are Acre, Alagoas, Amapá, Amazonas, Bahia, Ceará, Espirito Santo, Goiás, Maranhão, Mato Grosso, Mato Grosso do Sul, Minas Gerais, Pará, Paraíba, Paraná, Pernambuco, Piauí, Rio de Janeiro, Rio Grande do Norte, Rio Grande do Sul, Rondônia, Roraima, Santa Catarina, São Paulo, Sergipe, and Tocantins. The federal capital is Brasília.

Each of the states has an assembly. The number of representatives in each state assembly is equal to three times the state's representation in the federal Chamber of Deputies, up to a total of 36. Then, if the state has more than 12 representatives in the Chamber of Deputies, another representative is added for every additional federal deputy.

Governors and state representatives are elected to four-year terms. At the municipal level, *prefeitos* (mayors) and *vereadores* (city council members) are also directly elected to four-year terms. The number of council members is determined by the city's population. Each city council has a minimum of 9 *vereadores* and a maximum of 55. In 1995, there were 4,974 registered municipalities

---

Results of the 1996 Mayoral Elections by Party

Party		Mayoral Victories	% of Nationwide Vote
PMDB	Partido do Movimento Democrático Brasileiro	1,287	24.05
PFL	Partido da Frente Liberal	928	17.34
PSDB	Partido da Social Democracia Brasileira	911	17.02
PPB	Partido Progressista Brasileiro	624	11.66
PDT	Partido DemocráticoTrabalhista	435	8.13
PTB	Partido Trabalhista Brasileira	381	7.12
PL	Partido Liberal	221	4.13
PT	Partido dos Trabalhadores	112	2.09

Source: *Tribunal Superior Eleitoral* (TSE).

Note: Smaller parties are excluded from the table.

in Brazil. The most recent election for mayors and city council members in Brazil was in October 1996.

Prior to 1997, immediate reelection to any executive office (e.g., governors, mayors) was forbidden. However, the 1997 constitutional amendment permitting the immediate reelection of the president enabled governors and mayors to seek immediate reelection, as well.

THE ELECTORAL SYSTEM

Elections for the president, vice president, governors, senators, federal deputies, and state legislators take place every four years on the first Sunday in October. All Brazilians over age 16 are eligible to vote. Voting is *compulsory* for literate citizens between the ages of 18 and 70. It is *optional* for illiterates and those between the ages of 16 and 18. Women won the right to vote in 1932, the same year that obligatory voting was introduced. In 1985, illiterates were granted the right to vote.

Elections for the Senate alternate every four years between choosing one or two senators per state. Each state constitutes either a one- or a two-member district, depending on the election year. Voters cast a single vote if the election is for one senator and two votes if the election is for two. In an election to fill one Senate seat, the candidate who receives a plurality of the vote wins. If the election is for two Senate seats, the two candidates with the highest number of votes win. There are no runoff elections for Senate seats.

For elections to the Chamber of Deputies each state (and the Federal District) constitutes a multimember electoral district. Seats are allotted through open-list proportional representation. Each voter may cast a single vote, either for a candidate appearing on the ballot or for a party only (i.e., without indicating a preference for a specific candidate). To determine the party's seats in the chamber, electoral officials must first determine the electoral quotient (i.e., the number of votes needed to elect a single representative). This is calculated by dividing the total number of valid votes by the number of seats to be filled. Then, the vote total received by a party and all candidates registered to that party is divided by the electoral quotient to determine the number of seats won by the party. After the vote totals of all parties are divided by the electoral quotient, remaining seats are allocated to the parties with the largest remainders.

The candidate(s) who will occupy the party's seat(s) is (are) determined by rank-ordering the vote tallies of the party's candidates. The candidate with the largest number of votes receives the first seat, the candidate with the second-largest the second seat, and so on until all the seats won by the party have been filled. This method of allocating party seats forces candidates to compete not only against other parties but against members of their own party as well.

THE PARTY SYSTEM

Origins of the Parties

The parties of the Old Republic (1889–1930) were groups of elites rather than mass parties. (The Communist Party, founded in 1922, is a partial exception.) Two movements committed to mass mobilization emerged in the 1930s. Integralism was a paramilitary-style movement on the right with strong affinities to European fascist parties. At the other end of the spectrum, the *Aliança Nacional Libertadora* (National Liberating Alliance; ANL) was a popular front movement led by the Brazilian Communist Party. In 1935, the Vargas government moved to repress the left, and two years later, when Brazil entered the period of the *Estado Nôvo* (1937–45), the state cracked down on the Integralists as well.

Under the *Estado Nôvo* ("New State") all political parties were eliminated, all elections suspended, and the Congress was shut down. The state established a set of corporatist institutions designed to circumvent the role of parties and parliament. Business and labor interests were to be directly represented in the state. With the end of the *Estado Nôvo*, Brazil entered a democratic period (1946–64) more representative and competitive than at any former time in the nation's history. The three nationally based parties that emerged in 1945 were without precedent in Brazil. These parties retained elements of elitism and clientelism, but they relied upon broad-based, popular support to compete for power through electoral politics.

From 1946 to 1964 the PSD was the largest party in Brazil. The organizational base of the party was primarily rural. Vargas's political genius (and that of his protégé, Kubitschek) was to combine successfully the power of this old-style, clientelist party with the more progressive PTB. The PTB was another Vargas creation. However, the PTB was an urban-based party that focused on mobilizing support from Brazil's growing working class. The Ministry of Labor was particularly important in the formation of the PTB.

Those who opposed Vargas and his brand of populism formed the UDN. For most of the period from 1945 to 1964 the UDN was the second-largest party in the Congress. Though more conservative than the PSD, the UDN did not rely as heavily on rural areas for support. Like the PSD, the UDN experienced a gradual decline in voter support over time. The PTB, however, retained its strength and surpassed the UDN congressional delegation in 1962. The decline in the combined strength of these three parties can be seen in the accompanying table. Ten smaller parties organized by disparate political groups at the regional and state levels gradually captured a larger and larger share of the national vote.

The *Partido Communista Brasileiro* (Brazilian Communist Party; PCB) would likely have been a formidable electoral force during this period. The party was outlawed in 1935 under Vargas but legalized again in 1945.

Percentage of Vote Won by Brazil's Three Largest Parties
in Elections for the Chamber of Deputies, 1945–62

Party	1945	1947	1950	1954	1958	1962
PSD	42.7	35.2	27.0	23.1	19.9	18.3
UDN	26.6	34.3	17.0	14.3	14.3	13.2
PTB	10.2	13.8	16.5	15.7	15.9	14.2
Total	79.5	83.3	60.5	53.1	50.1	45.7

Source: Assembled from Bolívar Lamounier and Judith Muszynski, "Brasil," in *Enciclopedia Elec-toral Latinoamericana y del Caribe*, ed. Dieter Nohlen (San Jose, Costa Rica: Instituto Interameri-cano de Derechos Humanos, 1993).

Participating in the December 1945 elections, the PCB won nearly 10% of the national vote, earning 15 seats in the Chamber of Deputies and 1 in the Senate. In 1947 the PCB was again outlawed by the state.

After the military coup in 1964, the military initially allowed the purged pre-1964 parties to function. But in October 1965 the military dissolved Brazil's 13 existing parties and created a new, two-party system to replace them. The *Aliança Renovadora Nacional* (National Renovating Alliance; ARENA) was created as the party of the military government, and the *Movimento Democrático Brasileiro* (Brazilian Democratic Movement; MDB) was invented as the party of the opposition.

For a time the electoral results obtained under this new party structure conferred legitimacy on Brazil's military leaders. However, in November 1974 the opposition MDB won a third of all seats in the Chamber of Deputies and 16 of the 20 Senate seats up for election. Four years later the MDB won a majority of the popular vote. Elections clearly were no longer serving to legitimate military rule.

The two-party system imposed by the military simplified voter choices: Brazilians voted either in favor or against the regime. In 1979 the military government changed the party system yet again in an effort to diminish the "plebiscitary" quality of the elections. ARENA and the MDB were dissolved, and the formation of additional parties was legalized. The military hoped these changes would divide the opposition into several parties while maintain-

ing ARENA's support under a new name. The Social Democratic Party (PDS) replaced ARENA as the party of the government, while the MDB placed the word "party" before its name to become the PMDB.

The military's strategy was partially successful. Apart from the PDS and PMDB, three additional parties were founded and participated in the 1982 elections: the Democratic Labor Party (PDT), the Brazilian Labor Party (PTB), and the Workers' Party (PT). However, all three of these parties combined received little more than 5% of the vote. The PMDB continued to attract the vast majority of votes among those opposed to the military regime.

President Figueiredo's manipulation of the electoral law in anticipation of the 1982 elections actually helped to preserve the dominant position of the PMDB within the opposition. In July 1981, Senator Tancredo Neves and the federal deputies Magalhães Pinto, Thales Ramalho, and Miro Teixeira founded the *Partido Popular* (Popular Party; PP). The party's banner attracted moderate and conservative politicians in the expectation that the PP could win enough support in the 1982 elections to divide power with the PDS. However, the government's "November package" required voters to select candidates for all offices from a single party in order for their ballot to be counted. Since the PDS was strongest in local, rural politics, the government expected that the strength of candidates for local office would also win a vote for the party's state and federal candidates. How-

Percentage of Seats Won in the Chamber of Deputies by Party, 1966–78
(% of valid popular vote in parentheses)

Party	1966	1970	1974	1978
ARENA	67.7 (64.0)	71.9 (69.5)	55.8 (52.0)	55.0 (50.4)
MDB	32.3 (36.0)	28.1 (30.5)	44.2 (48.0)	45.0 (49.6)

Source: Bolívar Lamounier and Judith Muszynski, "Brasil," in *Enciclopedia Electoral Latinoameri-cana y del Caribe*, ed. Dieter Nohlen (San Jose, Costa Rica: Instituto Interamericano de Derechos Humanos, 1993).

ever, the unintended consequence of this *voto vinculado* ("tied vote") was to force the PP into a hasty retreat to join the PMDB. On December 12, 1981, one month after the "November package," the PP ceased to exist.

In January 1985 a sizable faction of the PDS defected to create a new party, the *Partido da Frente Liberal* (Party of the Liberal Front; PFL). When the prohibition against communist parties was removed in 1985, the PCB and the *Partido Comunista do Brasil* (Communist Party of Brazil; PCdoB) legally formed again. The *Partido Socialista Brasileiro* (Brazilian Socialist Party; PSB) also reorganized in 1985. And on the right, the *Partido Liberal* (Liberal Party; PL) was formed in 1985 by dissidents from the PFL and PDS.

Brazil's party system was gradually changing from a dominant two-party system to a multiparty democracy. However, through the mid-1980s, Brazil's party system continued to be dominated by only two parties. The PFL joined the PMDB in support of the Sarney government, and both parties benefited when the Cruzado Plan successfully brought down Brazil's high inflation rate. By mid-1986, serious economic imbalances threatened the sustainability of the Cruzado Plan, but the PMDB and the PFL conspired to mask these weaknesses until after the November legislative elections. The PMDB won an absolute majority in both chambers of Congress, and the PFL also fared well. But just days after the election, inflation shot back up and both parties were enormously dis-

credited. The PMDB held 261 seats in the Chamber of Deputies after the 1986 elections, but only 109 four years later. The PFL won 116 seats in 1986 but held only 83 after the 1990 elections. Brazil's smaller parties began to draw a much larger share of the popular vote.

This splintering of parties has diminished since the 1990 congressional elections. The vote share of the larger parties has been less volatile, and the four biggest parties (the PFL, PSDB, PMDB, and PPB), all formerly allied with the current government, have drawn some representatives from smaller parties to their banners.

Party Organization

Brazil today has the most fragmented party system in Latin America. There are 16 parties currently represented in the Brazilian Congress, and none holds close to a majority of seats. Brazil's system of proportional representation fosters this proliferation of parties by facilitating representation by small parties. The states constitute electoral districts for federal deputies, and this yields an extremely large district magnitude (total number of seats divided by the number of electoral districts). Large district magnitudes combined with the method of largest-remainders to allocate seats is one of the most permissive forms of proportional representation imaginable for the representation of small parties.

Brazil's numerous political parties are typically weak

Seats in the Brazilian Congress by Party, 1990–97

Party	Chamber of Deputies			Senate		
	1990	1994	Sept. 1997	1990	1994	Sept. 1997
PMDB	108	107	93	23	22	22
PFL	83	89	109	16	17	23
PSDB	38	62	96	10	11	13
PDS[a]	42	—	—	3	—	—
PDC[a]	22	—	—	3	—	—
PPB[b]	—	88	79	—	12	6
PT	35	49	51	1	5	5
PDT	46	34	24	5	6	3
PTB	37	31	22	6	5	4
PL	16	13	9	0	1	0
PRN	41	1	0	5	0	0
Others	35	39	30	9	2	5
Total	503	513	513	81	81	81

Sources: Compiled from data in Luis Fernandes, "Muito Barulho por Nada? O Realinhamento Pol'tico-Ideológico nas Eleições de 1994," *Dados* 38, no. 1 (1995); data for 1997 provided by the *Senado Federal* and *Cámara dos Deputados*.

[a] The PDS and PDC merged in 1993 to form the PPR.

[b] The PPB was formed in 1995 through the merger of the PPR and PP. For 1994 the table shows the combined seats won by the PPR and PP.

and fluid organizations. The Brazilian newspaper *Correio Brasiliense* reported on September 15, 1997, that since January 1995 federal deputies had changed parties at least 174 times. Party changes also occur in the Senate, though at a lesser rate. There are no legal obstacles to prevent a politician from changing parties while in office, and there are few barriers to creating new parties. Most politicians owe little to their parties. To win elections, politicians rely more upon their personal electoral appeal and ability to raise funds than upon their party organizations. In part because of this, politicians generally feel free to vote as they wish, often "selling" their vote in return for patronage benefits from the executive.

While most of Brazil's parties have weak national structures and ill-defined ideological positions, there is a great difference between some parties and others in their organization, level of cohesion, and ideological content. The parties of the left (the PT, PPS, and the PCdoB) have strong ideological identities. They are comparatively more disciplined parties—their representatives usually vote together in the Congress—and they have strong links to the labor movement and other social movements. (On the right, the voting record of PFL representatives has been fairly uniform by Brazilian standards.) The PSDB and the PDT, roughly centrist parties, are less dogmatic and less reliable as a block of votes in the Congress. Yet they are still more cohesive than many other Brazilian parties.

Campaigning

The Brazilian Congress approved a new electoral law in September 1997. In an election year, elections for president, vice president, senator, federal deputy, state deputy, mayor, and city council member are all held simultaneously on the first Sunday in October. Candidates must register by the 5th of July. Disseminating electoral propaganda is permitted only after July 5.

Registered parties are allotted free radio and television time, divided equally among the candidates. Political parties may register a number of candidates equal to 150% of the positions to be filled in each electoral contest. Candidates may purchase advertising space in newspapers, but radio and television propaganda is limited to the free hour provided by the public.

PARTY OF THE BRAZILIAN DEMOCRATIC MOVEMENT
(Partido do Movimento Democrático Brasileiro, PMDB)

HISTORY

The PMDB was launched in 1979 as a successor to the MDB. In addition to former MDB politicians, the PMDB also welcomed into its ranks many former members of ARENA and the PSD. In 1981, the PMDB accepted a merger with the more conservative *Partido Popular* (Popular Party; PP). Thus, the PMDB has served as a catchall party for politicians from many ideological currents.

In 1986, the PMDB held 308 seats in the Congress—an absolute majority in both houses. By 1990, the PMDB had lost 173 of these seats to other parties. This dramatic change resulted, in part, from the collapse of the Cruzado Plan. However, politicians also left the PMDB as a result of sharp internal cleavages generated by the party's heterogeneous makeup. In June 1988, the more liberal faction of the party left to form the PSDB.

ORGANIZATION

The PMDB has a national convention and party committees at the national, regional, state, and municipal levels.

POLICY

The PMDB was founded as a center-left party. Now roughly centrist, the party has a very heterogeneous makeup. The broad spectrum of views included within the party has made it difficult for the PMDB to present clear, concrete proposals. The party has preached fuller democratization as the key to solving all the nation's problems.

The PMDB has joined the current administration's governing coalition, but it has been common for many PMDB legislators to vote against key elements of the government's reform program.

MEMBERSHIP AND CONSTITUENCY

The PMDB was formerly strongest in the cities and most-developed regions of the country. However, the party is now strongest in the interior and less-developed regions. Today, the PMDB is a mostly rural, clientelist party highly reliant on state patronage.

LEADERSHIP

José Sarney, Brazil's president from 1985 to 1990, is now a senator from the state of Amapá and a prominent congressional leader of the PMDB. Michel Temer is currently president of the Chamber of Deputies, and Geddel Viera Lima is the party's leader in the Chamber. The PMDB's national president is Paes de Andrade.

PROSPECTS

In 1994 the PMDB won a plurality of seats in both houses of Congress. Following the 1996 municipal elections, the PMDB continues to control the greatest number of state capitals in Brazil. Nevertheless, support for the PMDB has been slowly declining. In 1992 the party won 1,497 cities, whereas in 1997 the PMDB won only 1,288. People both within the party and without have frequently declared that the PMDB lacks a real identity and is undergoing an existential crisis. The PMDB's position is threatened on the right by the appeal of the PFL and PPB and on the left by the PSDB.

LIBERAL FRONT PARTY
(Partido da Frente Liberal; PFL)

HISTORY

The PFL was formed in 1985 by a faction within the PDS opposed to their party's presidential candidate, Paulo Maluf. The PFL defected to support the candidacy of Tancredo Neves, thus securing his election as president in the electoral college. After the 1986 elections, the PFL was the second-largest party in the Congress. Between 1986 and 1990 the party lost 31 of its 134 seats as politicians switched parties, but since 1994 the PFL has grown to be the country's largest party.

POLICY

The PFL defends a liberal, free-market economic model. The party is a staunch supporter of the administration's reform program to restore the fiscal solvency of the state. In fact, the PFL has been the most reliable member of President Cardoso's coalition, more reliable than the president's own party, the PSDB.

MEMBERSHIP AND CONSTITUENCY

The PFL is strongest in the northeast, particularly in Bahia and Pernambuco.

LEADERSHIP

The PFL's António Carlos Margalhães is one of Brazil's most recognized and polemical politicians. He is currently a senator from the state of Bahia and has been governor of the state three times. António Carlos Margalhães is a key regional leader in the northeast, and his son, Lu's Eduardo Margalhães, was a powerful federal deputy and an important ally of the government in the constitutional reform process until his sudden death in 1998.

Inocêncio Oliveira is a prominent PFL deputy. He is a party leader and a former president of the Chamber of Deputies. Paulo Bornhausen is vice leader of the party and a federal deputy. The PFL's Marco Maciel is vice president of the republic.

PROSPECTS

The PFL has attempted to craft itself into a "modern" party, with a clear program and disciplined voting by the party's representatives in the legislature. Much of the party's success has resulted from mixing this "modern" ideal with traditional, clientelist political structures in the northeast. These two sides of the PFL are personified by

Senator Margalhnes and his son, Luis Eduardo Margalhães.

The PFL is focused on advancing the president's reform agenda and positioning a strong candidate for the presidential elections in the year 2002.

BRAZILIAN SOCIAL DEMOCRATIC PARTY
(Partido da Social Democracia Brasileira; PSDB)

HISTORY

The PSDB was formed in June 1988 by center-left dissidents within the PMDB. A few members of the PFL, PDS, and PTB were also founding members of the party.

In 1994 the PSDB allied with the PFL and the PTB to elect Fernando Henrique Cardoso president of Brazil. In order to construct a legislative majority capable of passing constitutional amendments, the PSDB has also drawn the PMDB and PPB into the governing coalition. These alliances have required compromises, while at the same time the party has fought to distinguish itself from its coalition partners, particularly the PFL.

POLICY

Unlike the advocates of neoclassical economic policy, the PSDB platform supports an active state involvement to address issues of social inequality and the promotion of industrial competitiveness in the international economy. The PSDB platform also defends land reform and environmental protection.

MEMBERSHIP AND CONSTITUENCY

The PSDB is identified as a gathering place for left-leaning but nonradical intellectuals. Many of the party's leaders, like the president himself, are former academics of one sort or another. The party is essentially middle class. It appeals to a constituency favoring greater political and social equality, but without endangering financial stability.

LEADERSHIP

Brazil's president, Fernando Henrique Cardoso, is a member of the PSDB. José Aníbal is a prominent leader in the Chamber of Deputies and an ex-leader of the party. Mário Covas, the governor of São Paulo, is another prominent PSDB politician.

PROSPECTS

The results of the 1996 municipal elections were mixed for the PSDB. The party received more votes than any other and grew from 513 mayoralities to 910 mayoralities. However, the PSDB lost in the leading municipalities, like São Paulo and Rio de Janeiro.

President Cardoso's reelection favors the continued growth of the PSDB. Since access to the government's largesse is so important to the health of political parties in Brazil, the PSDB will likely recruit more politicians to the party banner.

BRAZILIAN PROGRESSIVE PARTY
(Partido Progressista Brasileiro; PPB)

HISTORY

The PPB was founded in 1995 through the merger of the Progressive Reform Party (PPB), the Progressive Party (PP), and the Progressive Republican Party (PPR). Previously, the PPR had been formed through the merger of Paulo Maluf's *Partido Democrático Social* (Social Democratic Party; PDS) and the small *Partido Democrata Cristão* (Christian Democratic Party; PDC). Many PPR politicians were former supporters of the military government.

POLICY

The PPB is a right-wing party. It supports free-market reforms and international investment in Brazil. The party forms part of the ruling coalition stitched together by President Cardoso, but the PPB is one of the government's most unpredictable coalition partners.

MEMBERSHIP AND CONSTITUENCY

The PPB is strongest in the more developed southern region of Brazil. Many of Brazil's industrialists support the party.

LEADERSHIP

The most important leader of the PPB is Paulo Maluf, former governor of São Paulo, former mayor of the city of São Paulo, and candidate of the PDS for the presidency in 1985 and 1989. The senator Espiridião Amin is the party's president and leads the party in the Senate. Delfim Neto is a federal deputy from São Paulo and served as minister of finance and planning during the "economic miracle" years of the military governments. Neto is now a prominent leader of the right in the Congress and exercises a strong influence in legislative debates with an obvious economic content. The minister of industry, Francisco Dornelles, is also a member of the PPB.

PROSPECTS

The PPB was perhaps the biggest winner in the 1996 municipal elections. The PPB doubled its mayorships in the 100 leading cities of Brazil from 7 to 14 and won the mayorship of São Paulo, Brazil's largest city.

WORKERS' PARTY
(Partido dos Trabalhadores; PT)

HISTORY

The PT was born out the "new unionism" movement of the late 1970s. A new generation of labor leaders challenged the rules and structures of state-controlled unionism in Brazil, and some quickly began to consider that workplace activism might not be enough. In October 1979, they founded the PT to represent the interests of workers in Brazil.

The PT has always been strongest in the industrial centers of the country, particularly in the region of greater São Paulo, the industrial hub of the nation where the new unionism movement was born. The PT is divided between radical leftists and more moderate members, but the party has tended to vote as a bloc in the Congress. The PT is among the most disciplined and programmatic parties in the Congress.

In 1989, Lula da Silva, a union leader and founder of the PT, lost the presidential election by a mere 4 million votes. In the 1990 congressional elections the PT doubled its representation but still finished with a disappointing number of seats given the hopes that were sparked by Lula's strong performance in the election just a year before.

In the 1994 presidential election Lula da Silva again placed second, this time to Fernando Henrique Cardoso.

POLICY

The PT advocates structural reforms—both rural and urban—to bring about a profound redistribution of wealth and income in Brazil. Economic policy should be aimed at achieving full employment. Quality public education and health care should be made available to everyone. All workers should enjoy job stability, and the length of the workweek should be reduced. The PT is opposed to increased integration with the international economy.

The ultimate goal of the PT is socialism, but the party proposes to reach this goal democratically, within the framework of the Brazilian constitution. The PT opposes the constitutional reforms that are at the heart of the current administration's legislative agenda. The PT views these reforms as the revocation of limited conquests enshrined in the 1988 constitution, achieved through the mobilization and struggle of Brazil's laboring classes.

MEMBERSHIP AND CONSTITUENCY

The PT has strong support among the most active unions, peasant movements, and grassroots organizations. The PT is also supported by Catholic and nonfundamentalist Protestant churches. Students, intellectuals, and white-collar employees constitute a significant portion of the leadership and membership of the party.

ORGANIZATION

Internal democracy is extremely important to the party. The PT is organized in a pyramid structure such that the party's base controls the decision making of the party leadership. Decisions are transmitted from the *núcleos de base* (basic units), to the *zones* (an intermediate level encompassing several basic units), to the state regional directories, and on to the national directory. The national directory is composed of 85 members elected at a biannual national meeting for a two-year term. The national meeting unites approximately 500 delegates elected by the party's members.

LEADERSHIP

Luis Inácio Lula da Silva is the most nationally recognized and charismatic leader of the party. José Genoíno is a leading figure in the Chamber of Deputies. He writes regularly for the op-ed columns of the Brazilian papers and is regularly sought out by the press. Jair Meneguelli was formerly president of the labor federation CUT and is now a PT deputy.

PROSPECTS

The PT has grown steadily since the party was formed in 1979. However, this growth has been slow, far below the expectations of the party's leaders and supporters. The party remains an articulate and important voice of opposition to the current government but has been unable to expand greatly its representation in state and national elections. The party's charismatic leader, Lula da Silva, placed second three times in presidential elections. The results of the 1996 municipal elections were also unfavorable for the PT. They served to rekindle internal debates between different wings of the party.

DEMOCRATIC WORKERS' PARTY
(Partido Democrático Trabalhista, PDT)

HISTORY

Leonel Brizola founded the PDT in 1980. Brizola was the pre-1964 leader of the PTB and the governor of Rio Grande do Sul at the time of the military coup. Brizola fled into exile after the coup and returned to Brazil in 1979. He hoped to form a new party under the old PTB label, but the electoral authorities awarded the right to use the name to Ivete Vargas, a grandniece of the former president. Brizola then founded the PDT.

POLICY

The PDT's program is populist and reformist. Generally, the PDT is somewhat more moderate than the PT. The PDT believes the state has a fundamental role as regulator and defender of the national economy. The party favors the nationalization of foreign firms in strategic sectors and would restrict foreign capital.

MEMBERSHIP AND CONSTITUENCY

The party is strongest in Rio Grande do Sul and Rio de Janeiro. A great limitation of the party is that it has never successfully penetrated the state of São Paulo, the country's most populous state and the state with the largest number of industrial workers.

LEADERSHIP

Leonel Brizola is the honorary president of the PDT. He was elected governor of Rio de Janeiro in 1982 and 1990, and ran for president in 1989 and 1994. Miro Teixeira is the PDT's most prominent member of Congress. He is a federal deputy from the state of Rio de Janeiro.

PROSPECTS

The success of the party is tied to the political influence of Brizola. It seems unlikely that the PDT will be able to expand from the current geographic areas in which it is well established. The party has been slowly losing force in recent years. The PDT's limited influence in the Congress is possible only by acting in alliance with the other parties of the left.

MINOR POLITICAL PARTIES

On the left side of the political spectrum, Brazil's smaller parties include the *Partido Socialista Brasileiro* (Brazilian Socialist Party; PSB), the *Partido Comunista do Brasil* (Communist Party of Brazil; PCdoB), and the *Partido Popular Populista* (Popular Socialist Party; PPS).

The PSB was originally formed in 1945 by left-wing politicians disenchanted with the Brazilian Communist Party. After the military left power, the PSB was reorganized. The PSB has operated in the shadow of the PT, but the party did better than expected in the 1996 municipal elections. The PSB won in Belo Horizonte, the capital of Minas Gerais, and may be a party of greater importance in the future. Currently, the PSB has 10 representatives in the Chamber of Deputies and 2 senators. The party's leader in the Chamber is Alexandre Cardoso.

The PCdoB was formed in 1962 by a Maoist splinter group from Brazil's Communist Party. The party's leader is João Amazonas. In 1994, the PCdoB elected 10 representatives to the Chamber of Deputies.

The PPS is the new name of the Brazilian Communist Party (PCB). The PCB was formed in 1922 but was legally proscribed for most of its existence between 1922 and 1985. At the PCB congress in 1991, the party elected a "renewalist" leadership and distanced itself from the tenets of Marxist-Leninism. In 1992, the PCB became the

Popular Socialist Party. The PPS is led by Senator Roberto Freire. The party elected only two representatives to the Chamber of Deputies in 1994.

The *Partido Trabalhista Brasileiro* (Brazilian Labor Party; PTB) is more center-right than leftist. The party was formed in March 1979 by the federal deputy Ivete Vargas. The party does not have a clear ideological position. The PTB platform states that the party is "nationalist" and "democratic." Thirty-one politicians under the PTB label won seats in the Chamber of Deputies in 1994. By September 1997, nine had left to join other parties. The number of PTB senators shrank from five to four during the same period.

At the right of the political spectrum, the *Partido Liberal* (Liberal Party; PL) defends free enterprise and "more just" wages. The party elected 14 members to the Chamber of Deputies in 1994, but only 9 representatives continue to belong to the party. The PL is led by Valdemar Costa Neto.

OTHER POLITICAL FORCES

Organized Labor

Two major labor confederations compete to represent organized labor in Brazil. The *Central Única dos Trabalhadores* (CUT) was formed in 1983 by the protagonists of "new unionism." These union leaders emerged from within the corporatist union structures officially recognized by the state, but they were typically members of a younger generation whose union experience was limited to the years of military rule. They demanded to negotiate directly with employers and sought to eliminate the Labor Ministry and Labor Courts as mediators of disputes.

The leaders of "new unionism," known as the *autênticos* (literally "authentic ones"), advocated the formation of a union confederation, independent from the state, that would include opposition unionists and worker associations that lacked legal standing under the existing labor legislation. Meanwhile, the traditional union leadership recommended a national union confederation limited to officially sanctioned unions. In short, they defended a confederation in compliance with existing corporatist structures.

In 1983 two national union confederations were created. The *autênticos* formed the CUT, and the more traditional union leaders created the National Coordination of the Working Class (Conclat), which in 1986 changed its name to *Central Geral dos Trabalhadores* (CGT) and in the 1990s became *Força Sindical*.

The CUT declared itself fiercely independent of the state, espoused socialism, and emphasized that it defended the interests of one class (workers) in plain opposition to another class (employers). Throughout the 1980s the CUT steadfastly opposed calls for "concertation" or a "social pact" among unions, business groups, and the state. The CUT led numerous strikes against the erosion of workers' wages by inflation and opposed the Cruzado Plan and a myriad of other government stabilization efforts. The CGT, meanwhile, participated in several failed attempts to fashion a tripartite "social pact" (in 1987, 1988, and again in 1989). When these economic plans repeatedly ended in ruin, the confrontational style of the CUT proved far more effective than the more conciliatory style of the CGT in attracting union support. The CUT grew prodigiously through the 1980s, while CGT membership remained stagnant.

At the close of the 1980s the CGT leadership began to articulate a *"sindicalismo de resultados"* (literally, "results unionism"). At the heart of this program is the claim that defending profits, free markets, a smaller state, and apolitical unionism is appropriate—even necessary—to reap material gains for workers. In 1991 the formerly moribund CGT became *Força Sindical*.

In the battle to represent Brazil's laborers the CUT is clearly the largest and most representative union confederation. The CUT leadership has softened its rhetoric when compared with a decade ago, but the CUT remains solidly opposed to what it sees as the "probusiness" and "antisocial" reforms pursued by the Cardoso administration.

Organized labor is perhaps stronger in Brazil than in any other Latin American country. However, labor's political clout is less today than it was during the 1970s and 1980s. Union leaders are important interlocutors in legislative debates that directly affect worker interests, but the unions' ability to lead thousands of workers into the streets has diminished. Union members are an essential base of support for the political parties of the left, but these parties are a minority in the Congress.

Landless Peoples' Movement

The *Movimento dos Sem-Terra* (Landless Peoples' Movement; MST) is a grassroots movement that has organized highly publicized land invasions by landless farmers and their families in an effort to force the redistribution of land in Brazil.

Land reform has been a politically hot topic in Brazil for decades. Ownership of land is highly concentrated in Brazil; a few landowners possess tracts of uncultivated land larger than some Central American countries. The state's *Instituto Nacional de Colonização e Reforma Agrária* (National Institute for Colonization and Agrarian Reform; INCRA) has long proved unwilling or unable to implement a significant land reform program over the organized opposition of landowners. However, the MST has galvanized the public's attention and forced the state to dedicate greater time and resources to land reform.

The MST has carried out land invasions in almost every state in Brazil, but primarily in the south and southwest. According to the *Comissão Pastoral da Terra*, more than 480,000 people engaged in the struggle for land in 1996. The MST's capacity for grassroots mobilization and its tenacious challenge to Brazil's social order have captured the attention of the media, the government, landowners, urban unions, and average Brazilians throughout the country. The foremost leader of the MST is José Rainha Júnior. He has been imprisoned and threatened repeatedly for his actions, a fact which only increases his public stature and that of the MST.

The Military

Military officers have long been recognized as vital actors in Brazilian politics. In 1930 the military ended the Old Republic by delivering power to Vargas, whom they kept in power with a coup in 1937, only to depose him in 1945. It was a military manifesto that led to Vargas's suicide in 1954, and it was a "preventive" coup in 1955 that ensured Kubitschek's succession to the presidency. In 1961 military officers led the fight against Goulart's succession to the presidency, and in 1964 the military summarily deposed him.

Since leaving power in 1985, the military has played a much smaller role in Brazilian politics. Ministers of the armed forces appear to enjoy greater autonomy vis-à-vis the government than would be permitted by the heads of other ministerial posts. However, civilians are clearly in charge of Brazilian politics. This is certain to remain true for the foreseeable future, but with the caveat that military intervention in politics has never been fully discredited in Brazil. The military did not commit human rights abuses on the scale of the Southern Cone dictatorships, and the military ruled during the remarkable economic growth of the 1960s and 1970s. Many Brazilians look back with nostalgia on the years of military rule, a sentiment periodically enhanced by news of corruption scandals involving existing politicians.

NATIONAL PROSPECTS

Brazil's continental size and rich natural resources have long encouraged predictions that it is destined to be a major world power. The "miraculous" economic growth rates of the 1960s and 1970s appeared to demonstrate

that Brazil was fulfilling its promise. However, the economic stagnation and political turmoil of the 1980s temporarily quieted these auspicious predictions.

In recent years Brazil has again asserted itself on the international stage. The return of democracy and the stabilization of the economy are achievements to be applauded. Brazil is the leading country in Mercosur (the South American free trade region), and Brazil has also been mentioned as a leading candidate to assume a permanent seat on the UN Security Council. However, Brazil is still a country with colossal social inequalities. The poverty of so many Brazilians can only be reduced substantially over the long term, but there appears to be little political will among the largest parties in the Congress to devote significantly greater resources to public education, health care, or poverty alleviation.

In the short term, much rests on the stability of the currency, which the government doggedly struggles to maintain. The government has argued that constitutional reforms are needed to reduce Brazil's dependence on foreign capital inflows to balance the nation's accounts. However, it has been extremely difficult for the government to persuade Congress—with its numerous and largely undisciplined parties—to approve these reforms. The currency crises that suddenly enveloped Mexico in 1994 and Asia in 1997 are a sober reminder of the kind of calamitous external shock that might befall Brazil.

Further Reading

Baer, Werner. *The Brazilian Economy: Growth and Development*. New York: Praeger, 1983.

Keck, Margaret. *The Workers' Party and Democratization in Brazil*. New Haven, Conn.: Yale University Press, 1992.

Mainwaring, Scott. "Brazil: Weak Parties, Feckless Democracy," in *Building Democratic Institutions: Party Systems in Latin America*. Ed. Scott Mainwaring and Timothy R. Scully. Stanford, Calif.: Stanford University Press, 1995.

Skidmore, Thomas E. *Politics in Brazil, 1930–1964: An Experiment in Democracy*. New York: Oxford University Press, 1967.

———. *The Politics of Military Rule in Brazil, 1964–85*. New York: Oxford University Press, 1988.

Stepan, Alfred. *The Military in Politics: Changing Patterns in Brazil*. Princeton, N.J.: Princeton University Press, 1971.

———, ed. *Authoritarian Brazil: Origins, Policies, and Future*. New Haven, Conn.: Yale University Press 1973.

——— ed. *Democratizing Brazil: Problems of Transition and Consolidation*. New York: Oxford University Press, 1989.

STATE OF BRUNEI, HOME OF PEACE

(Negara Brunei Darussalam)

By Jeffrey K. Hass, Ph.D.

Originally a British colony, Brunei gained some degree of self-rule with the adoption of a constitution in 1959. In 1984, Brunei officially gained independence.

Brunei is a sultanate with no democratic procedures; all power and authority derives from the sultan, Hassanal Bolkiah Mu'izzaddin Waddaulah. The sultan ascended the sultanate throne on October 5, 1967, and has ruled ever since. The political system follows both the traditions of sultanism and the basic teachings of Islamic law and tradition. The sultan is not only the monarchical head of the nation; he is also the prime minister. Both these positions (traditional and formal) confer full decision-making power on the sultan alone. The sultan is aided by a Council of Cabinet Ministers, who are in charge of implementing policies and the day-to-day duties of heading the state bureaucracy. Ministers are mostly members of the royal family and are appointed by the sultan.

The executive bodies are the Religious Council, the Privy Council, and the Council of Succession. The Religious Council, whose members are appointed by the sultan, deals with religious matters. This is an important duty, since politics and society are linked to and guided by Islamic religious laws and norms. The Privy Council—until 1984 the sultan's advisers—was altered in 1984, when the Council of Cabinet Ministers took its place in running the nation. Today the Privy Council, whose members are also appointed by the sultan, are a set of policy advisers rather than administrators. The Council of Succession—again with members appointed by the sultan—serves only to decide on issues of succession to the throne in the case of the sultan's death or incapacitation.

The Legislative Council (*Majlis Masyuarat Megeri*) is a 20-person body responsible only for consultations to the sultan. Originally the Legislative Council was elected; however, after 1970 the sultan reconstituted the body as a consultative organ whose members the sultan appoints. Thus the Legislative Council remains as a historical legacy of the British period but serves no real legislative or other political function in Brunei political life.

The judiciary owes its power and loyalty to the sultan and to Islamic law. At the top of the judicial pyramid is the Supreme Court, which is divided into a Court of Appeal and a High Court; the former is responsible for handling civil disputes and the latter for adjucation on matters of criminal justice and legal interpretation.

As Brunei is a sultanate, there are no elections (the last elections were held in 1962), and political parties are formally banned. Three parties were active in the past but are now banned: the Brunei United National Party, led by Anak Hasanuddin; the Brunei National Solidarity Party (Brunei's first legal political party); and the Brunei People's Party. The Brunei National Democratic Party was allowed to register and organize officially in May 1985, but after the sultan forbade government officials from joining and various quarrels with the government, it was suppressed.

Brunei's sultan has tried to align his country with the Moslem world; he has condemned Israeli actions in the past and supported the Palestinian Liberation Organization's efforts to create a Palestinian homeland. However, in light of Brunei's size and difficulty in raising a serious army, the sultan has also called for nonaggression and peaceful solutions to political problems. Brunei is a member of ASEAN, the United Nations, and the Organization of Islamic Countries.

Brunei faces important choices in its near and middle-range political future. Vast oil reserves have allowed the creation of a welfare state and one of the highest levels of per capita income in the world; yet economic dependence on natural resources may mean modernizing its economy, which could be tricky. Another question concerns democracy in Brunei. While there is a minority of activists who might wish for democracy, Brunei remains a sultanate. However, the 1990s have been the decade of democratization, and this wave has spread even to Asia. How long Brunei can hold out, and whether it can, is still unclear.

Further Reading

CIA World Factbook. Washington, D.C.: Government Printing Office, 1996.

Leake, Jr., David. *Brunei: The Modern Southeast-Asian Islamic Sultanate*. Jefferson, N.C.: McFarland, 1989.

Saunders, Graham. *A History of Brunei*. New York: Oxford University Press, 1994.

BULGARIA

(Republika Balgariya)

By Jeffrey K. Hass, Ph.D.

THE SYSTEM OF GOVERNMENT

Bulgaria, a former member of the Soviet bloc, has witnessed a difficult transition to democracy and a market economy. With a total land area of almost 110,000 square kilometers, Bulgaria lies in the southeast of Eastern Europe, bordering the Black Sea, Romania (northeast), Greece (south), and Serbia (west).

Demographically, the population growth rate is 0.46% per year, due to a net positive migration rate. (The death rate—13.55 per thousand—is greater than the birth rate—8.33 per thousand.) Infant mortality stands at 15.7 deaths per thousand live births; the fertility rate is 1.17 children born per woman. Males make up 49% of the population, and females 51%.

Ethnically, Bulgarians make up 85.3% of the population, with Turks accounting for 13% (important to Bulgarian politics), Gypsies 2.6%, Macedonians 2.5%, and others 1.1%. Bulgarian Orthodoxy is the prevalent religion (85%), with Muslims making up 13% of those practicing religion, Jews 0.8%, Roman Catholics 0.5%, and others 0.7%. Bulgarian is the primary language; the dominant secondary language of a region depends on the ethnic makeup there.

Background

While Bulgaria's political institutions have been stabilizing, the political realm has been one of conflict. After the overthrow of Communist dictator Todor Zhivkov on November 10, 1989, Bulgaria began the precarious transition to parliamentary democracy. In 1990 the Grand National Assembly was called to draft a constitution (passed July 12, 1991). In December 1990, Dimitar Popov was named prime minister, to replace socialist Andrey Lukanov (who would be mysteriously murdered in 1996). Popov's government, associated with the Bulgarian Socialist Party (BSP), maintained a degree of political calm in 1991 and introduced economic reforms (price liberalization, land reform) that led to popular hardships. After the 1991 parliamentary elections Popov was replaced by Filip Dimitrov.

The electoral system is party-based proportional balloting: voters vote for parties, and those that clear a 4% barrier receive seats. In 1991, only three parties cleared the barrier—the Union of Democratic Forces (SDS), the Bulgarian Socialist Party, and the Movement for Rights and Freedoms (DPS). Because the SDS had barely more votes than the BSP, the DPS became the kingmaker and established an uneasy coalition with SDS in 1991 to put Filip Dimitrov in the position of prime minister.

However, by November 1992 this coalition broke apart; Dimitrov, like his fellow SDS members, continued to play a hard anti-Communist line, supporting decommunization of politics and society, attempting to punish those who had worked with the Communist Party by denying them access to politics and high positions. In July 1992 several large strikes resounded, as trade unions objected to the SDS's monetarism. Under pressure from the parliamentary opposition (the BSP), Dimitrov asked for a vote of confidence; the DPS threw its weight with the BSP and both voted against the government. After the 120-111 vote, Dimitrov had to resign, and Lyuben Berov became the next prime minister.

Berov was more sympathetic to BSP programs—populist policies, support for the social safety net, gradualism in regard to restructuring the economy. Initially both the BSP and President Zhelev—consistently at odds with each other—supported Berov. Another odd combination was the BSP–PDS coalition: odd because DPS identified itself in part with minorities that had been subject to Bulgarianization under the Communists, the predecessors to the BSP. As a result of policy weakness, Bulgaria's economy went into decline in 1994, spurring a Cabinet reshuffle and a motion for a vote of confidence (May 1994), which Berov narrowly won. After the May showdown, Berov conceded that with upcoming parliamentary elections in December 1994, his Cabinet would most likely resign; and so Berov turned to more modest policy projects.

The December 1994 parliamentary elections were a shock to the SDS, whose showing was weaker than imagined—from 100 seats to 69, while the BSP went from 106 seats to a parliamentary majority of 125. The harsh, uncompromising anti-Communist rhetoric of the SDS plus economic decline hurt their cause; voters, especially those in small towns and rural areas and those who cared more about their pocketbooks than Communist cleansing, turned to the Socialists and their populist slogans. Zhan Videnov, BSP party leader, became the new prime minister and promised economic recovery without economic pain. Unfortunately, in 1995, banks hovered near crisis and the currency fell, draining reserves; meeting payments on Bulgaria's external debt further hurt government pockets. Crime and corruption continued to climb and became serious issues for the voting public.

In 1996, world grain prices rose; Bulgarian grain, kept at an artificially low price domestically, was exported for profit, and so Bulgarians found themselves standing in breadlines for the first time since the collapse of communism. The grain crisis—which prompted the resignation of several agriculture ministers in succession—led to a vote of no confidence, which Videnov survived, in January 1996. Zhelev, maneuvering for a run at the presidency in 1996 and continuing his war with the Socialists, heaped criticism on the BSP and on Videnov's government. To add to Videnov's headaches, a fault line began to appear within the BSP, between an old guard supporting populism and minimal reform and another group supporting more effective reforms and opposing Videnov on the grounds that he was ineffective as prime minister and would hurt the BSP in future elections.

Toward the end of 1996, presidential elections were held; governmental and parliamentary ineffectiveness helped propel democrat Petar Stoyanov to victory. Videnov and his government resigned, and Stoyanov gave the mandate to the Socialists (still the majority in parliament) to form a new government. However, with calls for new parliamentary elections and massive street demonstrations in the background, Socialist prime minister candidate Nikolay Dobrev eventually gave Stoyanov the option of forming a non-Socialist caretaker government until April 1997, when early parliamentary elections were to be held. Stefan Sofiyanski became the new prime minister, and April 1997 elections gave the parliamentary majority to a non-Communist coalition headed by the SDS.

Executive

The executive branch is run by two people: the president and the prime minister. The president has a vice president to assist in duties; the vice president is elected along with the president on the same ticket, but his duties are unclear.

The presidency is essentially a ceremonial position; real power lies in the legislature. The powers and responsibilities of the president include: scheduling elections for the National Assembly; concluding international treaties; implementing laws; appointing and dismissing diplomatic personnel (upon motion from the Council of Ministers); granting or withdrawing Bulgarian citizenship; is-

suing pardons, granting asylum, and waiving debts to the state; and a few other minor duties. The president enjoys a weak veto: If he disagrees with legislation, he may send it back to the National Assembly with his reasons for disagreement. If the bill receives an absolute majority, it becomes law over the president's objections. When the National Assembly is not in session, the president may issue decrees with the force of law; these decrees must be countersigned by the prime minister.

The president also performs a ceremonial function in the naming of the prime minister and the Council of Ministers: he must give the mandate to form a government to the largest parliamentary party, which then presents a candidate to the National Assembly. Should the parliament fail to approve a government within seven days, then under the constitution the president must give the mandate to the second-largest party. If the National Assembly cannot agree on a prime minister and government, the president can appoint a caretaker government and call for early parliamentary elections to break the deadlock; this is what happened in early 1997, when Dobrev feared he could not garner the parliamentary support—and the president created a caretaker government and called for early elections.

In essence, the president is a weak figure. This is due to the historical legacy of the Stalinist system, where one figure, the general secretary of the Communist Party, was a virtual dictator. Real executive power lies with the prime minister and Council of Ministers, who are approved by the National Assembly and require continued parliamentary support: the prime minister is under threat of a vote of confidence, which he or parliament can bring to motion. Finally, the Council of Ministers must resign before a newly elected National Assembly holds its first convocation.

The power of the prime minister and Council of Ministers lies in their control over the state bureaucracy—the police, the tax authorities, customs authorities, privatization committees, education, foreign policy, agriculture, and so forth. The prime minister and Council of Ministers may introduce legislation for consideration in the National Assembly. Ministers are responsible first of all for day-to-day affairs and must answer for corruption and mistakes within their given ministries; serious mistakes are grounds for no confidence.

Legislature

The legislature, known as the National Assembly (*Narodno Sabranie*), is the most powerful political body in Bulgaria. Made up of 240 members elected according to proportional balloting and party lists, the National Assembly is entrusted with the fate of the nation; Article 67 of the constitution states that "Members of the National Assembly shall represent not only their constituencies but the entire nation. No member shall be held to a mandatory mandate." The powers of the National Assembly include the following (Article 84, constitution): passing, amending, or rescinding laws; passing the state budget; setting tax rates; scheduling the presidential elections; deciding on holding a nationwide referendum; approving and dismissing the prime minister and members of the Council of Ministers; approving and dismissing the head of the Central Bank; approving declarations of war and peace and approving the use of troops; declaring, on request from the president, a state of martial law; setting official holidays; and other responsibilities.

The National Assembly has final control over the government by means of a vote of no confidence. Such a vote can be called in two ways. The prime minister can request it, or such a motion can be seconded by one-fifth of the National Assembly. Once the motion is before the parliament, an absolute majority—121 votes—is required for it to pass. From 1992 to 1995 no-confidence votes were precarious weapons, since the National Assembly was split almost evenly between the Union of Democratic Forces and the Bulgarian Socialist Party; the ruling coalition was whomever the Movement for Rights and Freedoms (the Turkish party) sided with, as became the case in 1992.

The major duty of the National Assembly is legislation: passing bills that are brought up by members of parliament or policies brought up by the Council of Ministers. Such bills must be deliberated (read and voted on) twice before they can pass and must receive a simple majority; in exceptional cases (not defined in the constitution), both votes may occur in a single session. Other acts of parliament that do not become laws—statements, for example—need be voted on only once.

Judiciary

After the collapse of communism, the judicial branch emerged less than gloriously: under communism the courts served as a cloak of legitimacy and as an extension of the power of the Communist regime. Upon coming to power after the 1991 parliamentary elections, the SDS set out to build an independent, competent, Western-style judicial system. While the dearth of qualified, professionally trained jurists, lawyers, and judges will make the functioning of the judicial branch problematic for some time to come, the institutional foundation has been set already.

The judicial branch is composed of three parts: the court system, the Constitutional Court, and the Supreme Judicial Council. The first, the court system, consists of the various courts from the local level up to the Supreme Courts, which engage in dispute resolution, decisions of justice in criminal cases, and dispensing of administrative justice. These courts follow the continental model of jurisprudence. Basically, laws passed by the legislature or issued by the government are considered to be the basis for judicial decisions. The

courts do not add their own interpretations; further, past court decisions have no direct bearing on decisions for different cases, as is the case in Anglo-American common law. Each case for dispute or criminal justice is decided on its own grounds with application of relevant laws and rules. Disputes and appeals may be carried up the hierarchy: municipal courts at the bottom, then district and military courts, then courts of appeal, and finally to the top two courts, the Supreme Court of Cassation and the Supreme Administrative Court.

The Supreme Administrative Court has two roles: first, it oversees the administration of the law for administrative justice (e.g., criminal cases); and second, it rules on challenges to the legality of decisions of the Council of Ministers brought by outside parties. The Supreme Court of Cassation oversees the application of laws to disputes by all lower courts, in essence serving as the ultimate authority for disputes and appeals.

The Constitutional Court stands beyond the normal court system. Only this court has powers of legislative review (the power to declare legislation unconstitutional). Further, the Constitutional Court is empowered to decide on disputes concerning elections and division of powers between the various branches of government; the decision of this court is binding on all branches. The Constitutional Court is composed of 12 justices; 4 are appointed by the president, four are appointed by the National Assembly, and 4 are appointed by the Supreme Court of Cassation and the Supreme Administrative Court.

The Supreme Judicial Council, created in the 1991 constitution, is a body of 25 professional jurists: 3 members are the chairmen of the Supreme Administrative Court and Supreme Court of Cassation and the chief prosecutor; of the remaining 22 (all of whom must have at least 15 years' judicial experience), 11 are elected by the National Assembly and 11 are selected by judicial bodies. These 22 elected members serve a five-year term and may not be reelected to the Council. The mission of this Council is to handle appointments, transfers, and replacements of judges, prosecutors, and investigating magistrates. The Council also appoints the chairmen of the Supreme Court of Cassation and Supreme Administrative Court, after conducting lengthy investigations. To this end the Council has independence from other governmental bodies; its recommendations of chairmen of the two Supreme Courts may be returned by the president for reconsideration only once, and if sent to the president a second time, they must be accepted. The Supreme Judicial Council was set up in August 1991, but after the Council was enlarged in the constitution, more members were added and the Council began work in March 1992. Its first steps were bold and rapid: in March and April the Council replaced 43 judges and prosecutors, reorganized central judicial bodies, and appointed new senior personnel.

Regional and Local Government

Bulgaria is divided into nine provinces (*oblasti*), which are run by local councils. Cities are run by municipal legislatures and by mayors.

THE ELECTORAL SYSTEM

Origins of the Parties

After the fall of Soviet-era crony Todor Zhivkov in autumn 1989, Petar Mladenov was elected by parliament to the presidency, created by constitutional amendment in April 1990. However, after evidence was released in June 1990 that Mladenov had wanted to use military force to crush December 1989 demonstrations, he was forced to resign, and after six rounds of voting, Zhelyu Zhelev, head of the SDS, was elected president. The 1991 constitution made for popular election of the president. The first such election was held in January 1992 and the next in October–November 1996; both times the conservative, promarket candidate has won in the second round.

In 1992, Zhelyu Zhelev came forward as a candidate for Bulgaria's first post-Soviet popular election, with vice presidential running mate Blaga Dimitrova. His main competition was Velko Valkanov and Vice President Rumen Vodenicharov, who were formally independent candidates but were supported by the BSP. After the first round (January 12), Zhelev and Valkanov emerged as the top two winners and proceeded to a second round (January 19), where Zhelev won outright.

In 1996, Zhelyu Zhelev and Petar Stoyanov agreed to hold a primary election to determine who would face the Socialist candidate in the fall elections; neither wanted to compete against the other and split the anti-Socialist vote. The primary, held on June 1, 1996, gave a victory to Stoyanov; Zhelev held by the agreement and declined to run in the fall. The BSP was in a difficult situation due to the infighting in the party, the less-than-successful Videnov government, and economic decline resulting from the government's lack of effective action. Georgi Pirinski was a popular Socialist figure, commanding respect beyond the BSP, and opinion polls showed that he had the best chance of beating Stoyanov in the election. However, the Constitutional Court banned Pirinski from the candidacy; according to the constitution, a president must be a "Bulgarian by birth," whereas Pirinski had been born in the United States. The BSP made noise that it would ignore the Court ruling and run Pirinski anyway but soon backed down, and the Bulgarian Socialist Party nominated Ivan Marazov as its presidential candidate. Stoyanov, as predicted, was the victor; whether he can implement his reform policies remains to be seen, as the president has little political power short of the bully pulpit.

Presidential Elections, January 12 and January 19, 1992	
First Round (1/12/92)	
Zhelyu Zhelev (SDS)	44.58%
Velko Valkanov (BSP)	30.52%
20 others	24.9%
Second Round (1/19/92)	
Zhelyu Zhelev	52.8%
Velko Valkanov	47.01%
invalid ballots	0.47%

Presidential Elections, October 27 and November 3, 1996	
First Round (10/27/96)	
Petar Stoyanov (SDS)	44.1%
Ivan Marazov (BSP)	27.0%
Georgi Ganchev (BBB)	21.9%
Others	4.6%
Second Round (11/3/96)	
Petar Stoyanov	59.7%
Ivan Marazov	40.3%

Source: OMRI Reports; Rada Nikolaev, "The Bulgarian Presidential Elections," *RFE/RL Research Report*, February 7, 1992, 11–15.

Three sets of parliamentary elections have been held since the approval of the 1991 constitution, in 1991, 1994, and 1997 (when elections were called early in order to solve political strife). In 1991 the SDS prevailed, riding a wave of the anticommunism of 1989 and the popularity of the party as reformers. However, stringent anticommunism (when the populace cared more about their pocketbooks) and economic pain hurt the SDS in 1994, and the BSP gained a majority. The BSP's fortunes were hurt by weak economic performance (due to inattention to economic reform), by stories of corruption and crime, and by political conflict within the BSP and with other parties, especially the SDS. In 1997 the SDS returned in a large coalition.

The 240 seats are assigned to parties based on proportional balloting. In an election, a voter casts a ballot for a party. Parties must receive at least 4% of all votes cast to receive the right to representation in the parliament; those that receive less than 4% do not qualify for positions. (An individual may run for parliament but must receive more than 4%.) The number of seats a party receives depends on two numbers: the number of votes received, and the number of votes cast for parties that overcome the 4% barrier. (Essentially, if a party does not gain 4% of votes cast, then all votes it receives are wasted.) The actual delegates for the National Assembly are then drawn from official party lists assembled before

Parliamentary Elections, October 13, 1991

Party	% Votes	Seats
Union of Democratic Forces	34.36	110
Bulgarian Socialist Party	33.14	106
Movement for Rights and Freedoms	7.55	24

Parliamentary Elections, December 18, 1994

Party	% Votes	Seats
Bulgarian Socialist Party	43.5	125
Union of Democratic Forces[a]	24.2	69
People's Union[a]	6.5	18
Movement for Rights and Freedoms	5.4	15
Bulgarian Business Bloc	4.7	13

[a] The People's Union joined the Union of Democratic Forces, hence the SDS effectively had 87 seats in the National Assembly.

Parliamentary Elections, April 19, 1997

Party	% Votes	Seats
United Democratic Forces[a]	52.2	137
Democratic Left[b]	22.0	58
Union for National Salvation[c]	7.6	19
Coalition Euroleft	5.6	14
Bulgarian Business Bloc	4.9	12

[a] Composed of: Union of Democratic Forces, Democratic Party, Bulgarian Agrarian People's Union.

[b] Composed of Bulgarian Socialist Party and Ecoglasnost Movement.

[c] Composed of Movement for Rights and Freedoms and other monarchist and centrist groups.

Sources: Duncan M. Perry, "Bulgaria: A New Constitution and Free Elections," *RFE/RL Research Report*, January 3, 1992, 78–82; Evgenii Dainov, "Bulgaria: Politics after the October 1991 Elections," *RFE/RL Research Report*, January 10, 1992, 12–16; *CIA Factbook, 1996*; Wilfried P.C.G. Derkson, "Elections in Bulgaria," in *Elections around the World* (web site: http:// www.agora.stm.it/elections/election/bulgaria.htm); Stefan Krause, "Socialists at the Helm," *Transition*, March 29, 1995, 33–38.

the elections; if Party A has 30 seats, then the first 30 people on the party list become parliamentary delegates.

THE PARTY SYSTEM

The party system in Bulgaria has been rather stable, although splits and failed coalitions have made the political landscape somewhat disconcerting. Under the constitution, citizens have the right to form political parties, which may then compete in elections and political life. The one major restriction on parties is that they cannot be organized along racial, ethnic, or religious lines, nor

may they seek "violent usurpation of state power" (constitution, Article 11.4). This has not been particularly troublesome except for a brief moment in 1991. The Bulgarian Socialist Party protested that the Movement for Rights and Freedoms, a primarily Turkish-based group claiming to represent the Turkish minority, violated this constitutional prohibition. However, courts did not agree, and the DPS became the founder and largest member of a new 1996 coalition centered on ethnic and minority rights.

Bulgarian parties, with the exception of the BSP, have few grassroots connections to the masses. Instead, parties are essentially groups of elites who try to woo voters with their slogans and programs, rather than trying to mobilize direct support and link their programs to the masses through feedback loops.

UNION OF DEMOCRATIC FORCES

(Sayuz Demokratichni Sili; SDS)

Founded December 7, 1989, SDS was a coalition of 10 smaller parties; several withdrew and newer groups entered the coalition, including the Bulgarian Social Democratic Party, the Democratic Party, the Radical Democratic Party, the Republican Party, and Ecoglasnost (which left later and joined the Socialists in 1997). This union of large and small parties has led to some tension, since larger groups within SDS prefer to maintain some autonomy. For the 1997 elections to the National Assembly, the SDS joined with the Democratic Party (*Demokratichna Partiya*), the Bulgarian Agrarian People's Union (*Balgarski Zemedelski Naroden Sayuz*), and the Bulgarian Social Democratic Party (*Balgarska Socialna Demokratichna Partiya*) to form the supercoalition United Democratic Forces (*Obedineni Demokratichni Sili*), which together won 52.2% of votes cast and 137 of 240 seats. The SDS program follows two lines: anticommunism and monetarist economic reform. Anticommunism was the more important line early on, as SDS pushed legislation that would keep former Communist functionaries out of high political office. After this stance hurt the SDS in 1994, the party has backed away somewhat and although it remains antisocialist, has stressed economic reforms, including privatization, reduction of inflation, and land reform.

BULGARIAN SOCIALIST PARTY

(Balgarska Socialisticheska Partiya; BSP)

Originally founded in 1891 and present heir to the Bulgarian Communist Party, the BSP has espoused populist programs and a gradualist approach to economic change. This means control of prices (especially food prices, which led to the grain shortage of 1996), slow privatization, and resistance to serious structural reforms (e.g., bankruptcy). In 1997 the BSP united with the Ecoglasnost Movement (*Dvisenie Ekoglasnost*) to form the Democratic Left (*Demokratichnata Levica*).

MOVEMENT FOR RIGHTS AND FREEDOMS

(Dvisenie za Pravata Turchite i Balgariya; DPS)

This party, legally founded in January 1990, was originally an organization opposed to forced Bulgarianization of Bulgarian Turks. Since then DPS has come to represent ethnic minorities, most of whom are Turks and live in rural areas. Headed by Ahmed Dogan, DPS joined with other small groups (monarchists and centrists) to form the Union for National Salvation (*Obedinenie za Nacionalno Spasenie*) for the 1997 elections.

MINOR POLITICAL PARTIES

Two others minor parties have landed seats in the parliament: the Bulgarian Business Bloc (*Balgarski Biznes Blok*; BBB) and the Euroleft Coalition (*Koaliciya Evrolevica*; EL). The BBB, founded by Georgi Ganchev, is a populist party oriented toward small property and business owners. The EL is a social democratic party founded as a splinter group off the BSP. Certain delegates and party members of the BSP were concerned both with the inability of Videnov's government to accomplish meaningful change and with the inability of the BSP to field progressive, reform-minded candidates (instead of populist candidates and programs). In 1996 these members split off and created the Euroleft Coalition—dedicated to social democratic principles, maintenance of a social safety net, and concern for social and economic justice, mixed with a realization of the need for economic reform, structural change, and policies to fight crime and corruption.

Other small parties exist and have entered the parliament through union with larger parties. For example, Bulgaria has several agrarian parties; the proreform party united with SDS to gain entry, and the populist, gradualist-oriented agrarian party allied itself with the Socialists. Monarchist parties also have small support but have yet to cross the 4% electoral barrier. Nationalist parties also exist but are rather weak.

NATIONAL PROSPECTS

The Bulgarian transition to democracy and the market has been marred by political strife, in part due to the electoral system. From 1992 to 1994 two opposing parties held equal power, and in 1995 and 1996 the Socialists held the majority, which in 1997 went to the SDS-led coalition. Politics in Bulgaria has been defined by the Communist past and by the pain of economic transformation. On the one hand, the SDS and DPS have defined themselves and their programs around the Communist past: the SDS is primarily an anti-Communist party that does not want socialists in power; and the DPS exists in part as a reaction against Bulgarianization policies of Todor Zhivkov and the Bulgarian Communist Party before 1989. The Socialists, on the other hand, until 1996 had taken a populist stance against painful economic reform.

Bulgaria appears to be well on the way to democracy: parties and presidents have given up power when they were supposed to (e.g., election losses, votes of no confidence). Further, while there are more than 20 parties, 5 have turned out to be of importance: 2 major players (the SDS and BSP) and 3 minor players (Euroleft, BBB, and DPS) that can act as coalition makers. This certainly is a recipe for potential political gridlock, as coalitions can be made and can fall apart soon after; Bulgarian politics, then, may come to resemble Italian politics. The inherent instability in a parliamentary system with more than two parties is well noted and has hindered Bulgaria's economic reforms, especially after the breakdown of the SDS–DPS coalition in 1992.

One other important problem concerns the programs of these parties. The SDS was, and still shows signs of being, anti-Communist, blinding it to other aspects of politics. This virulence cost the SDS its majority in the 1994 elections. The BSP, on the other hand, seems concerned with staying in power rather than effecting change: hence the inattention to structural reform and corruption, the populist streak, and the exit of reform-minded Socialist members to form the Euroleft party.

Bulgaria's primary problem is economic reform; until such reforms take hold and bring development, the population will remain discontented and will provide excellent fodder for the pitched political battles between parties. But to solve this problem, one party must come to dominate long enough to implement a program that brings positive results. Whether the SDS-led coalition can do so remains to be seen; while they have not entirely cast off their anti-Communist rhetoric, they appear to be turning toward a positive program. On the other hand, Bulgarian politicians and political parties have been playing by rules of the game, which appear to have institutionalized. While Bulgaria's economy may not be the envy of Eastern Europe, Bulgaria's democratic roots may be taking hold much deeper than elsewhere.

Further Reading

Andreev, Alexander. "The Political Changes and Political Parties." In *Bulgaria in a Time of Change*. Ed. Iliana

Zloch-Christy. Aldershot, England: Avebury, 1996, 25–43.

CIA Factbook, 1996. Washington, D.C.: Government Printing Office, 1996.

Dainov, Evgenii. "Bulgaria: Politics after the October 1991 Elections." *RFE/RL Research Report*, January 10, 1992, 12–16.

Engelbrekt, Kjell. "Bulgaria's Political Stalemate." *RFE/RL Research Report*, June 24, 1994, 20–25.

Krause, Stefan. "Socialists at the Helm." *Transition*, March 29, 1995, 33–38.

Nikolaev, Rada. "The Bulgarian Presidential Elections." *RFE/RL Research Report*, February 7, 1992, 11–15.

Perry, Duncan M. "Bulgaria: A New Constitution and Free Elections." *RFE/RL Research Report*, January 3, 1992, 78–82.

Web Sites

Open Research Media Institute (OMRI): www.omri.cz

Radio Free Europe/Radio Liberty (RFE/RL): www.RFE/RL.org.

BURKINA FASO

(République Démocratique du Burkina Faso)

By Christopher J. Lee, M.A.

THE SYSTEM OF GOVERNMENT

Burkina Faso is a unitary republic that maintains a constitutional government supported by a multiparty political system. Formerly known as the Republic of Upper Volta, Burkina Faso is located in West Africa to the north of Côte d'Ivoire, Ghana, Togo, and Benin, to the south and east of Mali, and to the west of Niger. With an area of 274,200 square kilometers and a population of 9,889,000 (mid-1994 estimate), the population density is approximately 36 persons per square kilometer. The main ethnic groups include: the Bobo (southwest); Mossi (north); Gourma (east); and the Fulani (north and east). Indigenous religious beliefs are practiced by over 50% of the population. Islam follows next in popular practice, with Christianity placing third.

In December 1958, Burkina Faso, then Upper Volta, became a self-governing republic within the French West African community. It achieved full independence on August 5, 1960.

Executive

Blaise Compaoré is the current president of Burkina Faso. He was elected in 1991 following principles of a constitution approved earlier that year. According to this constitution, executive power is vested in the president and the Cabinet. The president appoints the Cabinet, with approval from the prime minister. The president's term of office is seven years. There is no limit to the number of terms. Presidential election is by universal adult suffrage.

Maurice Yaméogo became the first president of Upper Volta as the leader of the Volta Democratic Union (UDV). The UDV had support primarily from the Mossi, the largest ethnic group in the country at approximately 50% of the population. Other political parties were banned shortly thereafter. In January 1966 a military coup overthrew the government after a period of economic decline. Lieutenant Colonel Sangoulé Lamizana took control

and implemented measures that led to economic improvement. In December 1970 a process began of transforming the government from its military orientation to a more civilian one. Gérard Ouédraogo, leader of the UDV, became head of this civilian administration. With this political shift, other political parties began to form. In 1977 Lamizana introduced a new constitution. Elections took place in May 1978, and a civilian-oriented government controlled primarily by the UDV was installed. All parties, excluding the UDV, the Volta Progressive Union (UPV), and the National Union for the Defense of Democracy (UNDD), were banned.

In November 1980, Lamizana was deposed in a military coup led by Colonel Saye Zerbo after a period of economic decline. A government was formed led by the Military Committee of Redressment for National Progress (CMRPN). After an unstable tenure, the CMRPN was overthrown in November 1982 and replaced with a military council, the Council of Health of the People (CSP), led by Surgeon Major Jean-Baptiste Ouédraogo. This government, divided by radical and conservative military factions, proved to be unstable as well.

In 1983, after the arrest and release of Prime Minister Thomas Sankara and a mutiny by troops supportive of him, Ouédraogo and the CSP were overthrown by Sankara in a military coup. A new government was formed headed by a National Council of Revolution (CNR) led by Sankara. This regime was supported by civilian leftists of the Patriotic League for Development (LIPAD). With this new government, Committees for the Defense of the Revolution (CDR) were established nationwide to encourage the new government's agenda. In August 1984, Sankara changed the country's name to Burkina Faso. Later that same month, Sankara dissolved the government in an attempt to shift away from his earlier Marxist leanings. This move was accompanied by educational and economic reform. However, this new agenda proved controversial.

By 1987, Sankara's power base became fraught with division. Within the CNR, the Union of Reconstructed Communists (ULCR), the party from which he drew his support, suffered a split, which weakened his political standing. In October 1987, soldiers loyal to his rival Blaise Compaoré assassinated Sankara. Compaoré took control and supplanted the CNR with the Popular Front (FP).

This new government pushed a policy of economic liberalization while purging potential political opponents. In April 1989 a new political party was formed, the Organization for Popular Democracy/Labor Movement (ODP/MT). This relatively radical group contrasted with Compaoré's moderation, thus causing tension within the FP. Compaoré later asserted control over the ODP/MT, in April 1990. In March 1990 a constitutional commission was formed by the FP. A draft was finished in October 1990 that sanctioned a multiparty system.

On June 2, 1991, the constitution was approved through a national referendum. A transitional government was established with Compaoré as its head until elections could be held. Despite efforts at creating a diversely represented government, critics contended that the ODP/MT dominated this process. During 1991, conflict arose over Compaoré's refusal to convene a national conference to widen participation in the transition process. Opposition groups formed the Coordination of Democratic Forces (CFD). This coalition of opposition elements led to political resignations and a boycott of the presidential election in December 1991. Compaoré, representing the ODP/MT, won as the sole candidate, though only 25.3% of the electorate voted. On December 24, 1991, he became president of the fourth republic.

Compaoré's first term was characterized by unrest, a result of political centralization and government economic policies. Despite a vocal opposition and an attempted boycott, Compaoré was reelected on November 15, 1998. The participation rate for this election was at 56.1%, with 87.5% voting for Compaoré. This turnout and result have been interpreted as showing an increasing satisfaction with the status quo.

Legislature

The legislative structure is bicameral. The Assembly of Popular Deputies (*Assemblé des Députés Populaires*; ADP) currently contains 111 seats, elected by universal suffrage. Members are elected for five-year terms. The prime minister is appointed by the president, although the ADP can veto the president's choice. The ADP or the executive branch may introduce legislation.

The 1991 constitution also allows for a second representative body, intended as a consultative chamber. This body, known as the Chamber of Representatives (*Chambre des Représentants*), contains 178 appointed members, serving three-year terms.

In 1996, the ruling ODP/MT and 10 other parties joined together to form a new social democratic party, called Congress for Democracy and Progress (CDP). In the general elections to the ADP held on May 11, 1997, the CDP won a sweeping majority of seats, 101 out of 111. This election result was viewed as controversial. The CDP explained that the opposition was divided, but critics from the opposition side accused the CDP of corruption. The next elections are scheduled for 2002.

Judiciary

The judiciary forms an independent branch of the government. However, this independence is questionable. Judges are responsible to the Higher Council, which is chaired by the president.

Regional and Local Government

Despite some past efforts at decentralizing government, local politics largely remains dictated by the climate at the national level. In February 1995, the ODP/MT dominated municipal elections held in major towns nationwide. It gained political control within 26 out of 33 of these municipalities. These elections, in which less than 10% of the voting population had participated, were subsequently contested by opposing parties.

THE ELECTORAL SYSTEM

Despite the 1991 constitution's intent of establishing a multiparty, representative system of government, electoral politics in Burkina Faso has faced two main challenges impeding this process. The first challenge has been a persistent history of shifting authoritarian rule. This history of attempts to centralize control is a reflection of a second challenge, which is the ethnic diversity of Burkina Faso. The French created the geographic territory of Burkina Faso for political reasons. Like those of many other former colonial states in Africa, its state boundaries do not reflect a clear national cohesiveness.

These twin challenges have rendered uncertain the actual meaning of electoral politics in Burkina Faso. Ethnic institutions within local communities remain as a distinct alternative to the central government. Though a sense of national identity and the legitimacy of the central government both have increased, the meaning of representation in electoral politics is still debated, despite a party system with universal suffrage and representation based on a proportion of total votes.

THE PARTY SYSTEM

The general status of political parties has shifted back and forth dramatically since independence. With the establishment of a multiparty political system in 1991, political organizations have flourished in number if not in power. In 1997, 46 political parties were registered

The most prominent political parties are listed below.

Congress for Democracy and Progress (Congrés pour la Démocratie et le Progrés; CDP)

This social democratic party, founded in 1996, aligned the ODP/MT with 10 other parties to form a new foundation of support for Compaoré. It is led by A. Bognessan Yè. This party is assumed to have the most political influence.

United Front for Democracy and the Republic (Front Uni pour la Démocratie et la République; FUDR)

Formed in February 1998, this coalition of 10 opposition parties sought to gather support against Compaoré's presidential reelection campaign for the November 1998 election. The failure to challenge Compaoré's power with a boycott of the election has left status of this coalition is uncertain.

OTHER POLITICAL FORCES

Trade Unions

Compaoré's first term of office was characterized by labor unrest as a result of new economic measures. Trade unions have also grown in strength and influence because of the repression of political parties under the current regime. Over 20 trade unions exist in Burkina Faso. The following are the five most important trade union umbrella organizations: the Burkina Syndicated Confederation, National Confederation of Burkina Workers, the Syndicated Union of Burkina Workers, and the National Organization of Free Syndicates.

NATIONAL PROSPECTS

With the reelection of Compaoré as president in November 1998, his hold on power appears secure. The election turnout and result have placed the opposition in an unclear position. Compaoré's popularity in the future will likely hinge upon the improvement of economic conditions throughout Burkina Faso.

Further Reading

Allen, C., M.S. Radu, and K. Somerville, eds. *Benin, the Congo, Burkina Faso: Economics, Politics, and Society.* New York: Pinter, 1989.

Charlick, Robert, ed. *Rural Development and Local Organization in Upper Volta.* Ithaca, N.Y.: Center for International Studies, 1982.

Englebert, Pierre. *Burkina Faso.* Boulder, Colo.: Westview Press, 1996.

McFarland, D.M. *Historical Dictionary of Burkina Faso*, 2d ed. Lanham, Md.: Scarecrow Press, 1998.

THE REPUBLIC OF BURUNDI

(République de Burundi)

By Christopher J. Lee, M.A.

The Republic of Burundi is located in central Africa, surrounded by Rwanda to the north, Tanzania to the south and east, and Zaire to the west. Lake Tanganyika lies to the west, forming a natural divide with Zaire. Though Burundi is small in area at approximately 27,834 square kilometers, a population of 6,134,000 (1994 estimate) creates a high population density at 220.4 persons per square kilometer. This density has increased pressure on the land, creating related social tensions. The population consists of the following ethnic groups: Hutu (85%); Tutsi (14%); and Twa (1%). Burundi's capital is Bunjumbura.

Burundi as an organized political entity existed for many years prior to European colonial rule. It became a part of German East Africa in 1899. In 1916, Belgium took control over this area and Rwanda under a League of Nations mandate, though a system of indirect rule was maintained. The main features of this system were an aristocratic class and a king, the *mwami*. At this time, the Tutsi, despite being a numerical minority, maintained political control. Under pressure from the UN Trusteeship Council, a process of democratization began in 1948.

Two central parties arose, the Union for National Progress (UPRONA) and the Christian Democratic Party (PDC). The UPRONA, led by Prince Louis Rwagasore, sought to unify all forces into a national coalition. The PDC opted for links with the Belgians. In September 1961, the UPRONA won 58 out of 64 legislative seats in a new national legislature with Rwagasore becoming prime minister. However, he was assassinated in October 1961 by members of the PDC. This event led to a fateful splintering of national coalition efforts.

On July 1, 1962, independence was achieved. This event was coupled with heightened ethnic tensions. The monarchy remained as the basis for balancing diverging interests. The *mwami*, Mwambutsa IV, attempted to equally represent these interests in his government with proportional Cabinet appointments. In January 1965, the Hutu prime minister, Pierre Ngendandumwe, was assassinated and replaced with a Tutsi. Angered by these developments, a Hutu-led coup was attempted in October 1965 and violently repressed, with thousands killed.

In July 1966, Ntare V seized political control from his father, Mwambutsa. Ntare was deposed in November by Prime Minister Michel Micombero. Micombero abolished the monarchy and declared Burundi a republic. Purges of Hutus in politics and the military occurred. After another attempted coup in 1972, an estimated 100,000 Hutu were killed with 200,000 refugees fleeing to neighboring countries.

In November 1976, Colonel Jean-Baptiste Bagaza came to power in a non-violent coup. His goals were national reconciliation and land reform, mainly to improve living conditions for Hutu peasants. Tutsi land control was difficult to dissolve, however. In November 1981, a new constitution established a national assembly with elections by universal adult suffrage. Bagaza was elected president for the first time by universal adult suffrage in August 1984. He was the only candidate. From 1984 to 1987, the government became increasingly oppressive.

In September 1987 Bagaza's government was dissolved by a military coup led by Major Pierre Buyoya, who suspended the 1981 constitution and made himself president. Though the new government aimed at further ethnic reconciliation, little change occurred. Violence erupted in August 1988 with a total estimated death toll at 20,000 along with 80,000 refugees, primarily Hutu, fleeing to Rwanda. In October, Buyoya sought conciliatory measures, appointing Adrien Sibomana, a Hutu, as prime minister. Several Tutsi-led coup attempts occurred in 1989. In 1990, a charter for national unity was presented. This was approved by 89.2% of the vote in a February 1991 referendum but was rejected by the Party for the Liberation of the Hutu People (PALIPEHUTU) and other opposition groups.

In September 1991 a new report was presented to further democratization. The proposals of this report were approved in a referendum held in March 1992 by 90% of the voters. A new constitution based on these proposals was subsequently promulgated on March 13, 1992. This constitution implemented a multiparty presidential-parlimentary system of government with a renewable 5-year presidential term. In June 1993 Melchior Ndadaye, candidate from the Burundi Democratic Front (FRODEBU), won the presidential election with 64.8%

of the vote, becoming Burundi's first Hutu head of state. FRODEBU also captured 65 out of 81 parlimentary seats. Despite these developments, ethnic tensions persisted. Violence gained more international attention in 1992 when the government alleged that Hutu activists had received training across the border in Rwanda.

A Tutsi-led military coup transpired on October 21, 1993. Ndadaye and other Hutu officials were killed. The coup collapsed on October 25, though an internal crisis continued. By request, an international force was deployed by the Organization of African Unity OAU to protect remaining members of the government. In February 1994, Cyprien Ntaryamira became president, elected by the national assembly. Despite efforts at stabilizing the crisis, violence persisted with the Tutsi-controlled military being an active participant despite government efforts to restrain it. Up to 50,000 people, mostly Hutu, died with 800,000 refugees fleeing to neighboring countries.

On April 6, 1994, Ntaryamira was killed when the plane he was in was shot down. Rwandan President Juvénal Habyarimana was the alleged target of the attack. As dictated by the constitution, the Speaker of the National Assembly, Sylvestre Ntibantunganya, became president until elections could be held. Despite an early coup plot, relations between the government and military became closer. In September Ntibantunganya was elected formally as president by special commission. Political stability remained tenuous.

Ethnic tensions increased in 1994 with the violence that was occurring in Rwanda. Approximately 200,000 Rwandan Hutus sought refuge in Burundi. Periodic ethnic violence occurred. In 1995, violent incidents escalating in number prompted further concern locally and internationally. Many civil liberties were suspended. By the end of 1995 the capital was said to be "cleansed" of any Hutu presence. Despite international criticism, the government refused outside intervention to ease the crisis. Regional initiatives were organized in 1995 and 1996 to encourage disarmament and mediate the crisis toward resolution. Debate over the implementation of an intervening international force also took place with Tutsi forces siding against such an action.

In July 1996 a military coup was led by Lieutenant Colonel Firmin Sinzoyiheba. All political activity was suspended, national borders were closed, and a nationwide curfew was implemented. Buyoya was installed as president for an interim period with the professed aim of forming a unity government. Pascal-Firmin Ndimira, a Hutu, was appointed prime minister. Despite such moves, the new government faced international criticism including sanctions. In addition, the military was alleged to be taking violent action against Hutus.

In August 1997, talks held in Arusha between Burundi's various factions failed to accomplish a stable cease-fire. In June 1998 an interim constitution was announced that provided for further sharing of power. The current government fears a backlash against Tutsi interests. Burundi continues to face international scrutiny for its internal legal handling of those suspected of genocide. Ethnic tensions potentially manifested in severe violence remain.

Further Reading

Eggers, E. *Historical Dictionary of Burindi,* 2d ed. Lanham, MD.: Scarecrow Press, 1997.

Lemarchand, R. *Burundi*. Washington, DC: Woodrow Wilson Center, 1994.

———. *Genocide in Burundi*. London: Minority Rights Group, 1974.

———. *Rwanda and Burundi*. London: Pall Mall, 1970.

Mworoha, E. *Histoire du Burundi*. Paris: Hatier, 1987.

Vansina, J. *La Légende du Passé, Traditions Orales du Burundi*. Tervuren: Musée Royale de l'Afrique Centrale, 1972.

Weinstein, W. *Historical Dictionary of Burundi*. Metuchen, N.J.: Scarecrow Press, 1976.

THE ROYAL KINGDOM OF CAMBODIA

(Preahreacheanachakr Kampuchea)

By Carlo Bonura Jr.

THE SYSTEM OF GOVERNMENT

The Royal Kingdom of Cambodia (formerly known as the People's Republic of Kampuchea) is a multiparty parliamentary democracy with a constitutional monarchy. The current constitution took effect in September of 1993, following Cambodia's first democratic elections in May of the same year. These elections took place under the auspices of a major United Nations initiative designed to end Cambodia's costly civil war. After the fall of the disastrous Khmer Rouge–led government in 1979, in which over 1.5 million people were killed by the Pol Pot–led regime, Cambodia experienced an ongoing civil war among the newly installed Vietnamese-supported communist government, the deposed Khmer Rouge, and military forces loyal to Prince Norodom Sihanouk. After over 10 years without any workable solution to the conflict in sight, a monthlong meeting of the Paris International Conference on Cambodia was called in 1989. Two years of strenuous diplomatic effort resulted in the 1991 "Agreements on a Comprehensive Political Settlement in Cambodia," more commonly referred to as the "Paris Accords." Delegations from Australia, France, the United States, China, and Russia all participated in concluding these agreements. The Paris Peace Accords accomplished the unprecedented task of securing agreement from all four major embattled factions: the State of Cambodia forces led by Hun Sen, and the armies of now King Norodom Sihanouk, the Khmer People's National Liberation Front led by Son Sann, and the Khmer Rouge, at the time led by Khieu Samphan.

Pragmatically, the accords led to the formation of the Supreme National Council (SNC), with King Sihanouk as its leader. The SNC constituted a formal mechanism for continued negotiations among the four factions over the future of the peace process. The accords also brought about the withdrawal of Vietnamese troops from Cambodian soil in 1989, a tentative break in the fighting among the above factions, and the beginning of a long and complex transition to democracy.

The Paris Peace Accords also charged the United Nations with the duties of peacekeeping, removal of mines, repatriation of refugees, disarmament of the involved fac-tions, and establishing an environment in which "free and fair" elections could take place in 1993. As a result, the United Nations established the United Nations Transitional Authority in Cambodia (UNTAC), led by Japanese envoy Yasushi Akashi, which began its mission on March 15, 1992. UNTAC consisted of a force of 22,000 peacekeepers, amounting to one-fourth of the UN's total peacekeeping force at the time. Significantly, it included a Japanese contingent, representing the first international deployment of Japanese military troops since World War II.

Although the UNTAC failed in its mandate to completely disarm competing armies, it had, by April 1993, repatriated over 360,000 refugees from camps along the Thai-Cambodian border without major incident or violence against the refugees. This massive effort at repatriation, carried out in just one year, occurred in the shadow of renewed warfare between the Khmer Rouge and government troops. Soon after the arrival of UNTAC the Khmer Rouge reversed its acceptance of the Paris Accords and rejected the conditions for the election in 1993 established jointly by UNTAC and the SNC. The elections held on May 23–28 went forward with the expectation of Khmer Rouge attacks on Phnom Phen and anxieties over the possibilities of a complete Cambodian People's Party (CPP, led by Hun Sen, formerly the Kampuchean People's Revolutionary Party) victory.

To the surprise of many, neither Khmer Rouge strikes nor a CPP victory came to fruition. Instead, 85 to 90% of the Cambodian electorate came out to vote in a peaceful election, choosing the National United Front for an Independent, Neutral, Peaceful and Co-operative Cambodia (FUNCINPEC), led by Norodom Ranariddh, son of King Sihanouk, to lead the country. FUNCINPEC received 45% of the vote, the CPP 38%, Son Sann's Buddhist Liberal Democratic Party (BLDP) 3.5%, the Kampuchean National Liberation Movement (Moulinaka) 1.5 %, and various other minor parties and candidates 6%, while UNTAC authorities marked 15% of the ballots as invalid. The victory came as a shock to CPP leadership, who had suffered losses throughout the country including in provinces the party formerly controlled. The CPP immediately challenged the election results, citing irregularities in the electoral process. UNTAC countered such charges with the announcement, just days after the election, of its success in fostering a "free and fair" atmosphere for the election. The crisis deepened after former FUNCINPEC commander Prince Chakrapong, newly aligned with the CPP leadership, led a failed coup against the new government and the still functioning SNC. In the wake of Chakrapong's abortive coup, King Sihanouk convened a "constituent assembly" of all candidates who won seats in the election. The assembly opened with the sole intent of beginning work on Cambodia's new constitution. In the process of bringing together the Provisional National Government of Cambodia, King Sihanouk guaranteed the CPP a central role in the government by creating a dual prime ministership that would be shared by Norodom Ranariddh as leader of FUNCINPEC and CPP leader Hun Sen. This resolution allowed for the "reunion" of the constituent assembly, with Son Sann as its president, and the successful promulgation of the constitution on September 24, 1993.

Executive

According to the 1993 constitution, the king of Cambodia, "shall reign but shall not govern." Executive power is currently vested in the dual prime ministership arranged prior to the enactment of the new constitution. The constitution, however, only allows for a single prime minister to be selected from the party that secures a majority of votes in the National Assembly. The prime minister(s) are to receive advice from the Council of Ministers, who are nominated by the king with the approval of the prime minister to serve in an executive Cabinet. This Cabinet is also responsible for the administrative control of Cambodia and the execution of it laws.

King Sihanouk, as leader of the transitional SNC, ensured equal representation of major political parties in the Cabinet, although this is not guaranteed by the constitution. The executive is constitutionally responsible to the National Assembly and the judiciary. Cambodia's parliamentary system supplies the National Assembly with a vote of confidence in the executive. Given the present strength of the executive and the lack of any tradition of checks and balances, neither votes of confidence nor strict judicial review of executive actions seems forthcoming in the near future.

Legislature

The 1993 constitution mandates the creation of a unicameral legislature called the National Assembly. The development of the National Assembly occurred under the strict guidelines established in the Paris Peace Accords and through UNTAC oversight. The first election of Assembly members took place in the May 1993 elections. The National Assembly contains 122 members, whose terms are constitutionally limited to five years, though members may be reelected at the end of each term. Seats in the Assembly are assigned by a system of proportional representation in which the number of seats a party receives corresponds to the total percentage of votes a party wins in an election. The constitution mandates two legislative sessions per year. In 1997, however, the Assembly had met less frequently. The National Assembly also has the power of executive review and, as such, it must approve national budgets submitted by the prime minister's office. These checks have rarely come into use because of the strength of the prime ministers and the relative weakness of the legislature. The future of this legislative arrangement is uncertain following an agreement between Norodom Ranariddh and Prime Minister Hun Sen to include Ranariddh in a new government after Hun Sen won the national elections in July 1998. The new proposal would set the National Assembly at 61 seats. Additionally, in December 1998 there were new efforts to establish a Senate separate from the National Assembly.

Judiciary

UNTAC efforts during its mission in Cambodia helped design and institute new legal actors and traditions, including training lawyers and judges and the drawing up of laws concerning investment and a new criminal code. This differs greatly from the judiciary that developed in the 1980s under the authority of the Ministry of Justice. During this period of time, a loose system of provincial courts in addition to a national supreme court was under the close control of the executive branch. The Ministry of Justice had complete authority to review all judicial decisions and revise all laws. Additionally, there existed no right to counsel, and, in fact, Cambodia continues to experience a significant shortage of lawyers and legal professionals.

The 1993 constitution created an independent judiciary. This new court system structure is based on provincial courts and includes a court of appeals and a national supreme court called the Supreme Council of the Majistracy. Because of a lack of trained legal professionals and legal traditions, however, the overall effectiveness of these legal reforms remains uncertain.

Regional and Local Government

Cambodia is divided into 21 provinces. Each province is divided into districts (srok), which provide the basis for the election of members to the National Assembly. Provinces also contain smaller local municipalities, such as villages and towns. Each breaks down into khan and sangkat in diminishing order. Leaders and administrators at the local level are chosen by the prime minister with the approval of the king. The local elections scheduled for 1997 designed to democratically elect local officials have not yet taken place.

THE ELECTORAL SYSTEM

The future of the Cambodian electoral system as established in both the elections and the constitution of 1993 remains in doubt. Actions, amounting to a coup, taken by Second Prime Minister Hun Sen to drive First Prime Minister Norodom Ranariddh from the country in the summer of 1997 had left Hun Sen in complete control of the government. After reaching an agreement with King Sihanouk and Prime Minister Hun Sen, Ranariddh returned to Cambodia to contest elections to be held in July of 1998. The victory of Hun Sen's Cambodian People's Party resulted in major protests from FUNCINPEC and opposition parties, although the elections were formally recognized by the National Election Council in September of 1998. The constitution states that future elections will be held in accordance with an "Electoral Law" drawn up by the National Assembly, but no legal mechanisms have been developed for the carrying out of elections.

NATIONAL UNITED FRONT FOR AN INDEPENDENT, NEUTRAL, PEACEFUL AND CO-OPERATIVE CAMBODIA
(Uni National pour un Cambodge Indépendent, Neutre, Pacifique et Coopératif; FUNCINPEC)

FUNCINPEC, the National United Front for an Independent, Neutral, Peaceful and Co-operative Cambodia, is a royalist party that won a surprising victory in the 1993 elections. King Sihanouk controlled the FUNCINPEC when the organization was purely a military organization fighting communist rule under the People's Republic of Kampuchea. Upon King Sihanouk's taking up the provisional role of president in the transitionary Supreme National Council, command of FUNCINPEC's military forces and leadership of its new political machinery transferred to his son, Norodom Ranariddh. The 1997 coup forced Ranariddh into exile. Between that time and his return in June of 1998, Ranariddh organized a global campaign, meeting with leaders from England, France, the United States, and the ASEAN countries, to diplomatically isolate Hun Sen's government. FUNCINPEC participated fully in the 1998 elections, winning 43 seats in the National Assembly.

CAMBODIAN PEOPLE'S PARTY (CPP)
(Manakpak Pracheachon Kampuchea)

The Cambodian People's Party (CPP) arose out of the Kampuchean People's Revolutionary Party (KPRP). In 1990 party leadership decided to significantly change the party's identity in expectation of the 1993 elections. The party changed its name and renounced communism and expressed full support for multiparty democracy in Cambodia. The KPRP controlled Cambodia's one-party Communist assembly from its origin in 1979 to its own political transformation toward the end of the Paris International Conference. Hun Sen became premier of Cambodia and the de facto leader of the KPRP in 1985 under the Vietnamese-controlled government. He remained in control of the party and directed its changes throughout the UN period of national transition and continues to head the party to this day. At the time of the 1993 elections the CPP claimed 2 million members. In the 1998 elections, the CCP won 63 of the seats in the National Assembly, giving it a majority.

OTHER POLITICAL FORCES
Opposition

There is little effective formal political opposition in Cambodia. The CPP's entrance into a coalition government from 1993 to 1997 successfully prevented the presence of a politically powerful opposition party in Cambodian politics. Furthermore, efforts by FUNCINPEC and the CPP to reduce the effectiveness of opposition parties such as the BLDP and Moulinaka have been successful. These efforts are apparent in a split that arose in the BLDP centering on the longtime political rivalry of two of its leaders, Son Sann and Ieng Mouly. In the fall of 1995, Ieng Mouly successfully ousted Son Sann as leader of the party by calling a party congress that he would control. This action received support from outside the party as both prime ministers, Hun Sen and Norodom Ranariddh, gave permission for the congress to be held. Son Sann reacted by denying the outcome of the congress and held a second party congress. His efforts, however, failed, and Ieng Mouly supporters rioted and shot grenades at the site of the congress in September 1996. The government subsequently barred Son Sann supporters from participating in the congress. Just prior to the September 1997 coup, large numbers of BLDP members defected to FUNCINPEC, thus further reducing the oppositional power of the party.

The government has also taken similar steps to reduce the political power of Moulinaka. In 1994, despite Moulinaka's ability to secure a seat in the National Assembly, the government removed its representative from the Council of Ministers. Other attempts to develop a formal opposition party after the election have been thwarted by the government. Sam Rainsy, the former minster of economics, attempted to form the Khmer Nation Party to oppose the policies of the CPP and FUNCINPEC. The government, however, outlawed this organization. As a result, Rainsy went into self-imposed exile in Thailand. He returned to Cambodia to reenter politics in

November of 1997. Sam Rainsy changed the name of his Khmer Nation Party to the Sam Rainsy Party. In the 1998 election the Sam Rainsy Party won 16 seats in the National Assembly, making it the only opposition party with representation in the Assembly.

Even after its severe defeats in the summer of 1997, the Khmer Rouge still theoretically remains a source of opposition for the government and the political arrangements of the 1993 constitution. After the Khmer Rouge boycotted the 1993 elections, King Sihanouk flatly rejected its request to be included in a national reconciliation government. The Khmer Rouge's reconciliation plan would have included all competing military factions and required an invalidation of the election's outcomes. King Sihanouk's decision to accept the election and not include the Khmer Rouge in the new government marked the beginning of a complete isolation of the Khmer Rouge from Cambodian politics. Its position became worse when in August of 1996, Khmer Rouge leader Ieng Sary defected with 3,000 troops to the CPP seeking asylum and a rapprochement with the coalition government. In 1998, the Khmer Rouge suffered even more setbacks, making it almost completely ineffective as both a political and military force. Pol Pot, the Khmer Rouge's longtime leader, died in April of 1998 after his arrest and subsequent life sentence in July of the previous year. After coming under continued military pressure from the government, other high-ranking Khmer Rouge leaders, such as Khieu Sampah and Noun Chea, surrendered to authorities in December 1998. These arrests have intensified efforts to create an international tribunal to punish leaders of the Khmer Rouge directly involved in the Cambodian genocide.

NATIONAL PROSPECTS

Cambodia's future prospects are divided. In many ways, crippling Khmer Rouge battlefield losses and the death of Pol Pot mark the beginning of the development of a sense of closure concerning the bloodiest time of Cambodian history: the killing of millions of Cambodians committed under the Democratic Kampuchea regime led by Pol Pot from 1975 to 1979. The complete defeat of the Khmer Rouge also represents the end of an incredibly disruptive political force in the current political transitions of a post-UNTAC Cambodia. Cambodia's transition to democracy might prove a smoother and more workable

process with the absence of the Khmer Rouge. The recent return of Sam Rainsy possibly signifies this new moment in Cambodian politics.

The disapproval but relative silence of King Sihanouk regarding Hun Sen's 1997 ouster of the FUNCINPEC leader Norodom Ranariddh, however, suggests how the future of Cambodia's nascent democracy may not prove to be so smooth. Hun Sen used victories by government forces in the northwest of Cambodia against the Khmer Rouge in combination with his successful coup to consolidate his political and military power over almost all of the country. Victories by the CCP in the July 1998 election then allowed Hun Sen to overcome the cold responses that he had universally received from international actors. ASEAN, for example, which had delayed Cambodia's entrance into its organization, once again has listed Cambodia's integration as one of its priorities. Domestically, the veritable lack of violence during the protests that shook Phnom Penh during the summer months of 1998 after the elections also demonstrates a change in the political atmosphere in Cambodia. Moreover, the ability for the CP and FUNCINPEC to reach an agreement on a coalition government following the September opening of the National Assembly proves that for now Cambodia has averted a possible constitutional crisis. In many respects, Cambodia's future prospects still remain in the hands of Prime Minister Hun Sen. His commitment to the 1993 constitution and more broadly to Cambodia's new experiment in democracy awaits the test of time.

Further Reading

Duffy, Terence. "Cambodia since the Election: Peace, Democracy, and Human Rights?" *Contemporary Southeast Asia* 15, no. 4 (March 1994): 407–32.

Heininger, Janet E. *Peacekeeping in Transition: The United Nations in Cambodia.* New York: Twentieth Century Fund Press, 1994.

Hughes, Caroline. *UNTAC in Cambodia: The Impact on Human Rights.* Singapore: Indochina Programme, Institute of Southeast Asian Studies, 1996.

Lizée, Pierre. "Cambodia in 1997: Of Tigers, Crocodiles, and Doves." *Asian Survey* vol. 37, 1 no. 1 (January 1997): 65–71.

Öjendal, Joakim. "Democracy Lost? The Fate of the U.N.-Implanted Democracy in Cambodia." *Contemporary Southeast Asia* 18, no. 2 (September 1996): 193–218.

Um, Khatharya. "Cambodia in 1993: Year Zero Plus One." *Asian Survey* 34, no. 1 (January 1994): 72–81.

REPUBLIC OF CAMEROON

(République du Cameroun)

By Mark W. DeLancey, Ph.D.

THE SYSTEM OF GOVERNMENT

The Republic of Cameroon, a country of 13 million people in west central Africa, is a highly centralized, nominally multiparty state. The major institutions of government are the president and his party, the Cameroon People's Democratic Movement (CPDM, previously the Cameroon National Union; CNU), the bureaucracy, and the legislature. Cameroon was a German colony from 1884 to 1914 and then was a mandate/trust territory under France and Great Britain. The French section gained independence on January 1, 1960, and was joined on October 1, 1961, by the British section.

Executive

The president of the republic serves as head of state and government. He or she is directly elected to a seven-year term by a majority of the votes cast and is reelectable once. President Ahmadou Ahidjo, Cameroon's first president, retired on November 6, 1982, and was replaced by Paul Biya, who had been prime minister. Biya was returned to power in the election of 1984 with 99.98% of the vote and in 1988 with 98.75%. In 1992, the first multiparty elections were conducted; Biya's proportion dropped to 39.9%. The election is considered fraudulent, but Biya has clung to the office in spite of widespread belief that John Fru Ndi of the Social Democratic Front (SDF) had more votes.

The constitution grants great power to the president. He or she is responsible for the conduct of the affairs of the republic and for ensuring national unity. He may initiate legislation and require a second reading of legislation he opposes. All significant legislation originates in the presidency. He is the head of the armed forces, is responsible for negotiating and ratifying treaties, appoints all major civil and military posts, directs the administration, appoints all ministers and vice ministers, and presides over the Council of Ministers. He can proclaim a state of emergency or siege, both of which grant him extraordinary powers.

President Ahidjo ruled the country in a stern fashion. His presidential powers, his position as chairman of the party, and his political skills enabled him to build a system in which all power and authority emanate from the president; the presidency is essentially the government.

Upon taking office Biya moved to open the system to a more democratic mode, but a serious coup attempt in 1984 set him on a different course. He has used the structures and processes established by Ahidjo to return to authoritarian rule. But Biya lacks the political skill of Ahidjo, and he has faced a serious economic crisis. As the democratization movement spread through Cameroon, Biya resisted with arrests and shows of force. In July 1990 he did allow a multiparty system to emerge but continued to fight against the writing of a new, more democratic constitution.

Legislature

Under the 1996 constitution, there is a bicameral legislature. In the first multiparty election since the early 1960s (March 1992), Biya's party, the CPDM, won only 88 seats and had to form a coalition with the Movement for the Defence of the Republic, a tiny northern-based party with only 6 seats. The major opposition party, the SDF, boycotted the election, which was a bad tactical choice for it might have been able to take power. The Assembly meets in two sessions per year, each limited to a maximum of 30 days; the president may call special sessions. Bills may be introduced by the president or by members of the Assembly and require a simple majority vote of members present to become law. The president may require a second reading, and then a majority of all members must vote in favor of passage. Constitutional amendment is the prerogative of the Assembly, requiring a simple majority in favor or a two-thirds majority in the case of a second reading. The president may request a national referendum on an amendment, and he may call on the Supreme Court to judge the constitutionality of any law.

The Economic and Social Council, consisting of 65 members appointed by the president, and a small bureaucracy play an important role in the writing of legislation and in examining (and amending) legislation with respect to its impact on social and economic development.

Certain areas of legislation are reserved to the Assembly, but these may be turned over to the president at his request, unless the Assembly specifically rejects that request. These areas are citizen rights and obligations, labor law, general matters of defense, property law, civil and commercial law, nationality, local government, some aspects of criminal law, taxation, education, economic and social planning, and currency. The Assembly must also approve the budget. All other matters are reserved for the president, who issues statutes in those areas.

The constitution clearly gives the president powerful influence over legislative matters, and through his control of the party, he is in a position to completely dominate the Assembly.

Judiciary

The Supreme Court is appointed by the president. The Court's role is limited, but the constitution does give it certain responsibilities of possible significance. The Court may determine that the president is "permanently prevented from attending to his duties." Also, at the request of the president, the Court can determine the constitutionality of any law. The Court can also decide any disputes on the admissibility of a bill or amendment before the National Assembly. However, in any of the above instances, the size of the Court is to be doubled by the addition of persons designated by the president. There is also a court of impeachment to try cases against the president, prime minister, and ministers for high treason. Its organization and membership are set by law, not by constitution, and are thus amenable to control by the president.

Regional and Local Government

Cameroon is divided into 10 administrative units or provinces, and these are subdivided into *départements* (divisions). A hierarchy of administrators appointed by and reporting to the president governs each of these units. Each ministry has representatives at each of these levels who report to the presidential representative of the same level as well as upward to their ministry. Local governments consisting of locally elected personnel play a very limited role. In rural areas, traditional authorities (derived to some extent from precolonial political systems) are active, although they are largely dependent upon the central government. Local rule is very weak in this highly centralized system.

THE ELECTORAL SYSTEM

The president is directly elected by the nation as a whole, as is the National Assembly. Nominees are from single-member districts based on population. The ballot is secret and suffrage is universal for all persons 21 years or older.

CAMEROON PEOPLE'S DEMOCRATIC MOVEMENT
(Rassemblement Démocratique du Peuple Camerounais; CPDM)

HISTORY

At independence there were numerous political parties of various types in anglophone and francophone Cameroon, including one major organization, the francophone Union of Cameroon Populations (UPC), that had been driven underground and into rebellion by the colonial administration. By 1962, the parties in East Cameroon, the Francophone state, had coalesced voluntarily and under government pressure into the ruling party, *l'Union Camerounaise* (UC), under President Ahidjo. In West Cameroon, a similar process of amalgamation was occurring, with the Kamerun National Democratic Party (KNDP) emerging as the major party. On September 1, 1966, the UC and the parties of the West joined to become the Cameroon National Union (CNU), the single party of the country. This party was an elite party, a union of notables, each of whom brought his followers into the new party.

In March 1985, at the Bamenda Party Congress, the CNU became the Cameroon People's Democratic Movement, symbolizing Biya's assertion of power after the demise of Ahidjo. Although promises of democratization were made—and in part kept by allowing competition in local-level party elections—no structural changes were undertaken. The ties between the CPDM and the government are numerous and in many respects the party and the government are still synonymous.

Over time, the coalition nature of the early party has altered in the direction of a mass party, though powerful individuals still bring their followers into the party.

ORGANIZATION

The cell is the basic structure of the party. Cells are grouped into branches, into subsections, and then into sections. Party sections coincide with the *département*. Each unit has officers elected by its members. The ruling bodies of the CPDM are the Congress, the National Council, the Central Committee, and the National Political Bureau. The Congress meets every fifth year. The reports of these congresses are important documents, for they describe the general policy outlines of party and government. The National Council meets every two years (if called by the president) to supervise the implementation of the decisions of the Congress. The Central Committee is responsible for directing the affairs of the party and for the nomination of all candidates for election. It, too, meets at the request of the president. The National Political Bureau consists of 12 members, nominated by the president from the Central Committee and elected by the Committee. It is the true ruling body of the party and meets at the request of the president.

There are two significant affiliates of the CPDM: the Women's Organization of Cameroon People's Democratic Movement (WCPDM) and the Youth Organization of the Cameroon People's Democratic Movement (YCPDM).

In addition to the reports of the party congresses, the CPDM publishes Biya's speeches; party manuals; and a bilingual monthly magazine, *l'Unité*.

POLICY

The policies of the party are those of the government: national unity, social and economic improvement through "planned liberalism" and "self-reliant development," cultural development, and bilingualism in the domestic sphere; nonalignment, respect for the sovereignty of all nations, African unity, and the liberation of Namibia and South Africa in the international sphere.

National unity is the prime goal in this country where differences in religion (Muslim, Christian, and animist), geographic and cultural affinity (north and south and a welter of ethnic groups), and the French and English languages and other colonial heritages provide plenty of reason for separatist movements and fears of domination by one category or another. In a country with an annual GDP per capita of $820, development is also a prime focus of the government. Planned liberalism—"private initiative within the framework of the conditions of the national development plan"—and self-reliant development—"the determination of the Cameroonian people to depend first and foremost on their endeavors"—are the means to that end. A new policy, communal liberalism, was launched at the Bamenda Congress, but its definition is not yet clear. This is part of President Biya's New Deal policy, in effect, a promise of more liberal economic and political measures to spread the benefits of Cameroon's progress to all of its people.

FINANCING

Revenues are derived from membership fees, annual subscriptions, special contributions from members (especially militants), and proceeds from the sale of publications and other items. Large but unknown amounts of support are provided by government and business by allowing vehicles and other property, as well as personnel, to be used for party activities without charge. No overall financial figures are available.

LEADERSHIP

The prime figure in the CPDM is Biya, from Mvomeka in the central southern part of the country. Born in 1933, he is a Roman Catholic and a member of a small ethnic group, the Bulu. He rose to power as a client of Ahidjo, serving as his prime minister from 1975 until Ahidjo resigned in 1982. Other major figures include Sengat Kuo, who has lost his ministerial position but remains secretary of the party; Ferdinand Oyono, famous as a novelist but powerful as secretary general of the presidency; and Jerome Abono.

OPPOSITION PARTIES

Cameroon Democratic Union (Union Démocratique Camerounaise; UDC)

Adamou Ndam Njoya leads this small party that relies on the Bamoun population for support.

Cameroon Social Union (Union Sociale Camerounaise; USC)

This is one of several small parties from Paul Biya's home area. Like the others, this one, led by Nicole-Claire Okala, tends to support Biya's policies.

Movement for Democracy and Progress (Mouvement pour la Démocratie et le Progrès; MDP)

This splinter group from the UNDP is led by Samuel Eboua and is based on support from his ethnic group, the Mbo.

Movement for the Defence of the Republic (Mouvement pour la Défense de la République; MDR)

Led by Dakole Daisala, this small party is based on support in the Extreme North Province. Its appeal depends upon the personality of its leader.

National Movement for Solidarity and Democracy (Mouvement National pour la Solidarité et la Démocratie; MNSD)

The MNSD is led by Yondo Black. This party has had little electoral success, but it is considered responsible for prodding Biya into agreeing to a multiparty system. It was established in 1989.

National Union for Democracy and Progress (Union Nationale pour la Démocratie et le Progrès; UNDP)

This is at present one of the most significant opposition parties. It is led by Bello Bouba Maigari, the man many believe Ahidjo wished to have take over after his resignation. Many see this party as the true descendant of Ahidjo's party, the Cameroon National Union. The major base of support is in the three northern provinces, although support exists elsewhere. Former Ahidjo loyalists have flocked to the UNDP. In the 1992 legislative elections, the party won 66 seats and thus became the official opposition party. However, in the presidential elections later that year, Bouba placed third behind Biya and Fru Ndi of the SDF.

Social Democratic Front (SDF)

This party, led by John Fru Ndi and founded in 1991, is widely thought to be the strongest opposition party, but due to its boycott of the 1992 legislative elections, its popularity has not been well tested. SDF did participate in the 1992 presidential elections, and although officially its candidate, Fru Ndi, placed second, many believe that he won the election. The main base of support comes from the anglophone population, especially in the Northwest Province, but support is strong throughout the southern coastal area, too. The party has taken a strong anti-French posture and supports the writing of a new constitution to establish a federal system with more autonomy for the anglophone population and strong safeguards for human rights. It is a major supporter of the constitutional draft published in 1993 by the All Anglophone Conference.

Union of Cameroon Populations (Union des Populations du Cameroun; UPC)

This party was founded in 1948 before Cameroon's independence. Its leaders, Reuben Um Nyobe and Felix Moumie, both now dead, wanted immediate independence, a clean break with France, and a socialist system. Banned by the French, one section went into exile and another went underground in Cameroon to engage in a bitter war with the French and then with the Ahidjo government. The UPC was legalized in 1991, and many of its members have returned from exile. It is led by Ndeh Ntumazah.

NATIONAL PROSPECTS

The CPDM and President Biya seem secure in power for only the short term. The government sponsored a new constitutional draft in 1993 that proposed a centralized system with only minor protections of human rights. The president remained very powerful. Opposition arose immediately, and another draft was produced by a group representing the anglophones. This called for a federal system and stringent human rights protections. The widely divergent views have led to an impasse. President Biya has come to depend on an exceedingly narrow base of support, mainly from his ethnic group, and considerable foreign pressure is being exerted to force movement toward democracy. The economy if failing, and there is widespread discontent among almost all elements of society. Violent political change is very possible.

Further Reading

Azevedo, Mario. "The Post-Ahidjo Era in Cameroon." *Current History* 86 (1987).

Bayart, Jean-François. "Cameroon." In *Contemporary West African States*. Ed. J. Dunn and R. Rathbone. Cambridge University Press, Cambridge: 1989, 31–48.

———. *L'Etat au Cameroun*. Paris: Fondation Nationale des Sciences Politiques, 1979.

DeLancey, Mark W. *Cameroon: Dependence and Independence*. Boulder, Colo.: Westview Press, 1989.

———. "The Construction of the Cameroon Political System: The Ahidjo Years, 1958–1982." *Journal of Contemporary African Studies* 6 (1987): 3–24.

DeLancey, Mark W., and Mark D. Delancey. *Cameroon*. Oxford: Clio Press, 1999.

Joseph, Richard A., ed. *Gaullist Africa: Cameroon under Ahmadu Ahidjo*. Enugu, Nigeria: Fourth Dimension, 1978.

Schatzberg, Michael J. , and I. William Zartman, eds. *The Political Economy of Cameroon*. New York: Praeger, 1986.

Takougang, Joseph and Milton Krieger. *African State and Society in the 1990s*. Boulder, Colo.: Westview Press, 1998.

Takougang, Joseph. "The Demise of Biya's New Deal in Cameroon, 1982–1992." *Africa Insight* 23 (1993): 91–101.

Canada

By Robert A. Wardhaugh

The System of Government

Canada (derived from the Iroquoian word *Kanata*, meaning village or settlement) is a nation of over 30 million people with a diverse ethnic composition. According to the 1991 census, Canada's population was composed of 28% British origin, 23% French, 14% British and/or French and other, 4% British and French, and 31% other (made up of 6% aboriginal; 50% European; 20% Asian, Arab, African; 9% Canadian; 3% Black; 2% Caribbean, Latin/Central American; and 10% other). The population is extremely concentrated and highly urban. About 90% live in a 320-kilometer strip along the Canada–United States border; about 60% live in central Canada in Ontario and Quebec; and over 75% live in metropolitan areas.

The system of government is a representative democracy that combines federal structure and constitutional monarchy. The nation consists of 10 provinces and two territories. A federal government serves as the main administrative body, but each province also has its own government that administers to a sphere of local responsibilities as dictated by the constitution. Canadian federalism is not a static division of powers but a process that has undergone considerable and even dramatic transformation (between a centralized and decentralized structure) throughout its history.

Canada's rather unique form of government is a product of the nation's development within the French Empire and then the British Empire and Commonwealth, as well as its location in North America in such close proximity to the United States. In 1763 the French were defeated in the Seven Years' War, and this effectively passed control of their North American possessions to Great Britain. The British were intent on assimilating their new "Canadien" colonists with the Royal Proclamation, but conditions to the south made for poor timing. When the 13 colonies rebelled over a decade later, they assumed that Quebec would join to throw off its new chains of tyranny. They were mistaken. The Quebec Act of 1774 provided the French population with a degree of cultural protection in such spheres as religion, law, and landholding. The British Parliament hoped the offering of tolerance would produce a loyal population. They, too, were mistaken. What it did was guarantee the survival of a distinct French character in the northern half of the continent.

The influx of 40,000 United Empire Loyalists moving into the remaining colonies provided British North America with a strong Anglo and conservative character as well. The British authorities attempted to satisfy both ethnic communities with the Constitutional Act of 1791. The act maintained the 1774 promises to "les Canadiens" but divided the colony in two, both with representative government.

The basic forms of Canadian government emerged over the next century. Over time and as the populations grew, the colonies of Lower Canada (Quebec), Upper Canada (Ontario), Nova Scotia, New Brunswick, and Prince Edward Island were provided a governor, an appointed upper house, and an elected lower house. But the mother country was certain not to allow the same situation to develop as occurred in the United States. As a result, the assemblies were representative institutions with little authority, and de facto power remained with the Crown's representative—the colonial governor—and his elites (the Family Compact in Upper Canada and the Chateau Clique in Lower Canada). Minor rebellions in the late 1830s convinced the British to relax executive control and move toward more responsible government, whereby the governor retained his advisers only as long as they were collectively able to retain majority support in the assembly. The Union Act of 1840 also reestablished the two Canadas as one political unit in the hopes of returning to the plan of assimilating the French minority.

By the 1860s, events south of the border were again forcing change in the political framework of the colonies. The constant fear of American annexation during the American Civil War (and after invasions during the American Revolution and the War of 1812) reached new heights when the British (and Canadians) made it apparent that their sympathies lay with the Confederacy. In fear of an invasion by a triumphant and angry North, the Dominion of Canada was created in 1867. The new political creation would also allow an escape from the French-English squabbling and resulting political deadlock that had befallen the united colony of Canada. The British North America (BNA) Act confederated the colonies of Ontario, Quebec, Nova Scotia, and New Brunswick with a total population of 3.5 million. Despite strong resistance in the Maritimes, the agreement was pushed through the colonial assemblies with the aid of British pressure.

The BNA Act also served as the Canadian constitution, but the situation would remain dominated by a hybrid of both written and unwritten constitutional precedents. The British tradition of an unwritten constitution (such as common-law precedents and the parliamentary form of government) was already established, and the new act contained a provision that Canada was to have a form of government "similar in principle to that of the United Kingdom." There would be no specific mention of the executive roles of the prime minister or the Cabinet. Any amendments to the BNA Act would have to be done with the approval of the British Parliament.

Canada's relationship with Great Britain changed considerably in the 20th century as the dominion moved toward autonomy. Successful efforts were made by the Liberal government of Mackenzie King to thwart pressures toward imperial centralization emerging from the First World War. Canada resisted attempts to have it participate in "imperial" wars and pushed for the right to sign its own treaties with foreign nations. The battlegrounds for many of these developments were the imperial conferences that culminated in the 1926 Balfour Declaration and the 1931 Statute of Westminster. The former cemented the relationship of Britain to the dominions as equal members of the Commonwealth, and the latter allowed the dominion Parliament full power over laws having extraterritorial operation. In 1949 the Supreme Court replaced the British Judicial Committee of the Privy Council as the highest court of appeal and the Canadian Parliament gained the right to amend certain portions (not dealing with provincial interests, the five-year term of Parliament, or the language and educational rights of minorities) of the British North America Act without recourse to London. For fundamental changes, the British Parliament would still have to provide amending legislation.

In 1982 the Constitution Act was passed in Canada and received Royal Assent in Great Britain. The act, it was hoped, would end a long historical process in which the federal and provincial government had sought agreement on an amending formula that would allow for the patriation of the Canadian constitution. Quebec Premier René Lévesque, however, refused to sign the new act on the ground that the agreement did not provide guarantees for the province's cultural survival. Liberal Prime Minister Pierre Trudeau, a French-Canadian federalist, pushed the agreement through ratification regardless.

The Canadian Charter of Rights and Freedoms was part of the April 1982 constitutional package and became the first entrenched comprehensive statement of fundamental values. It outlined democratic rights including fundamental freedoms such as conscience and religion; belief and expression; peaceful assembly; and association. In addition it served to protect equality as a democratic right and in the political sphere to guarantee presumed associated values such as universal suffrage; elections contested by competing political parties; rule of law; majority rule; and minority rights.

In 1984 the new Progressive Conservative prime minister, Brian Mulroney, stepped into the role of national negotiator in an attempt to bring Quebec into the constitution. He sought to appease Quebec's demands: recognition of "distinct society" status that would entail a constitutional veto; control over immigration into the province; financial compensation for nonparticipation in national programs; and involvement in appointments to the Supreme Court. In April 1987, a first ministers conference (gathering of provincial premiers) offered unanimous support for these provisions. The agreement, known as the Meech Lake Accord, failed to be ratified by the provincial legislatures within the required three-year period. Quebec's demands began to face increasing opposition by such groups as anglophones, federalists, and native groups. With the failure of Meech Lake, Mulroney went back to the table and was able to formulate a still more comprehensive package that was unanimously agreed to on October 28, 1992, in the form of the Charlottetown Accord. Facing increasing demands for public input, the government decided to obtain popular approval in a referendum. The deal was rejected by a national majority and by six provinces, including Quebec. Two years later Quebec held its second referendum on independence that resulted in the separatist forces losing by the barest of margins.

Executive

The formal executive in Canada consists of the British crown represented in the capital city of Ottawa by a governor-general and in each of the provinces by a lieutenant governor. As in Great Britain, the monarch's role is formal and its functions are ceremonial. The governor-general and lieutenant governors are officially appointed by the queen, but in practice the selections are made by the Canadian prime minister. The official term of office is six years, but usually the term is five years. The first Canadian to hold the post was Vincent Massy in 1952. Since the appointment of Major General Georges Vanier in 1959, governors-general have alternated between francophone and anglophone. The first woman to hold the position was Madame Jeanne Sauvé in 1984. At present the Canadian governor-general is Roméo Leblanc.

According to the Canadian constitution it is the Queen's Privy Council that serves as the advisory body of the head of state. The Council was originally created to advise the governor-general. Its members are nominated by the prime minister and appointed for life. It includes current and former ministers of the Crown as well as other politically influential figures. In reality the symbolic Council meets rarely, and then only for ceremonial purposes, with its intended political functions being exercised by the Cabinet. The BNA Act makes no mention of the office of prime minister or the Cabinet, yet they play the most significant role in the running of government.

Reflecting the principle of responsible government, the political executive is formed by the political party that enjoys the support of the House of Commons. The prime minister is the leader of this party. Since 1867 Canada has had 20 prime ministers whose average age has been 56. If no party holds a majority of the seats in Parliament, the executive will be formed by the party with the largest number, as long as the government can maintain power by gaining and holding the support of other groups. If a government loses the support of the House, either it will be replaced or Parliament will be dissolved and an election called. Minority governments and coalitions did not become a reality in Canada until 1921 when the traditional two-party system was disrupted. The strength of alternative parties has varied since this time with minority government appearing in 1921, 1925, 1957, 1962, 1963, 1965, 1972, and 1979.

Under normal circumstances the prime minister is the leader of the largest political party in the House of Commons. He or she is selected at a national party leadership convention to which the various constituency organizations send delegates. The first convention was held in 1919. The prime minister, as with all members of Parliament, must win his or her own riding from among the 301 constituencies across the nation.

Upon winning power the prime minister must immediately deal with the usually difficult task of forming the Cabinet. These ministers are usually chosen from among the members of Parliament (MPs), and most will be provided one or more portfolios (government departments). Certain departments are traditionally held by particular regions (Agriculture, for example, is usually held by a westerner). On occasion, members of the Senate may be asked to accept a portfolio to ensure a government representation from all regions. Cabinet selections are based on such factors as regional distribution, talent, experience, and personality. Decisions reached in Cabinet that carry legal force are called orders-in-council.

The size of the Cabinet has varied but increased quite dramatically in the post–World War II period alongside a burgeoning governmental bureaucracy and infrastructure. The general economic recession has led to calls for cost cutting and downsizing. Following the election of October 1993 the Cabinet was reduced to 22 ministers. Signs of economic recovery are now playing a role, and after being elected for a second term in May 1997, Prime Minister Jean Chrétien increased membership to 29. The prime minister and Cabinet are members of both the executive and the legislature simultaneously.

In 1993 the prime minister also introduced a new ministry system based on the British precedent whereby eight secretaries of state are also appointed who serve as chief aides to the ministers. These secretaries are sworn to the Privy Council but attend Cabinet meetings only on request and receive a reduced salary. Parliamentary secretaries play a similar role but have no statutory authority.

Decisions in Cabinet are divided among the various committees that contain ministers, secretaries, and senior civil servants. In the early 1970s two central agencies were formed to help rationalize government operations. The Privy Council Office is an ostensibly nonpartisan agency staffed by civil servants (over 500 officers and support personnel) whose primary function is the coordination of Cabinet activities and Cabinet committee meetings. The clerk of the Privy Council is the top civil servant in the nation. The Prime Minister's Office (PMO) is much more obviously partisan and is composed of appointed staff loyal to the prime minister. This office provides advice, drafts the Speech from the Throne, and does much public relations work. At present the PMO has a budget of over $6 million. Like the Cabinet, these two agencies have no constitutionally defined role and vary in purpose with the desires of the prime minister. The Public Service Commission (civil service) also plays a large role in staffing government departments, even to the level of deputy minister. In theory only ministers and parliamentary secretaries are politicians. Regardless, partisanship remains a strong factor in civil service appointments and there is a considerable amount of change when a new government comes into office.

By the 1980s, decentralized decision making was becoming the norm. Committees such as the Priorities and Planning Committee (chaired by the prime minister), the Operations Committee, the Legislation and House Planning Committee, the Special Committee of Council, the Communications Committee, and the Security and Intelligence Committee, for example, were formed to coordinate policymaking and bring recommendations to the Cabinet. As of 1997 the government functions with four committees: Economic Union, Social Union, Special Committee of Council, and Treasury Board.

The Canadian government establishes what are called royal commissions to investigate issues of public concern and then recommend suitable courses of action. The members of these sources of public policy advice are appointed by the government but are supposed to be experts in the particular field. Usual methods of gathering information include inviting briefs or staging public hearings. While royal commissions have been employed throughout the 20th century, they are often criticized as government ploys to educate the public on action already being taken, thereby creating the "appearance" of action. Probably the most influential commission in Canadian history was the Rowell-Sirois Report on Dominion-Provincial Relations. It reported during the Second World War and was instrumental in restructuring a more centralized federal system after the disaster of the Depression, in which several provinces went bankrupt. One of the most recent reports was that offered by the Royal Commission on Aboriginal Peoples.

Legislature

Canada has a bicameral legislature. The Commons acts as a popularly elected lower house, and the Senate serves as an appointed upper house. Legally, both houses are equal and all legislation must pass both to receive Royal Assent and become law. But as in Great Britain, it is the Commons that deals with the day-to-day handling of government matters and formulates legislation.

The Senate was originally intended to protect the smaller provinces and minorities and to sit as "the House of sober thought," serving as a check on the lower house. It reserves for itself the roles of reconciling legal inconsistencies in Commons legislation and holding hearings on major social and political issues. New members of this body are appointed for life by the incumbent prime minister as a reward for public service. The longer a government remains in power, the more the Senate will reflect this party. A government entering office on the heels of a long-serving administration is forced to face a strongly entrenched Senate of a different political persuasion.

There have long been public opposition to the continued existence of the Senate and serious questions as to its usefulness. It is very clearly a patronage tool to reward older party members even up to the age of 75, the mandatory retirement age. Yet, the House remains intact. More recently, the new constitutional amendment formula has opened the door to Senate reform by depriving it of its veto power over constitutional change. For example, even a move to abolish the Senate can be delayed but not prevented by that body. In recent years the demands for Senate reform have increased, but no new plan has met with approval. The "Triple E" model, standing for elected, effective, and equal, is the most popular and emerges from Alberta, reflecting regional alienation in western Canada. Indeed in 1989 Alberta held an election to select its representative to fill a Senate vacancy. Although Prime Minister Mulroney wanted a list of names, he finally went along with the appointment of the elected candidate. To date, this procedure has not been copied elsewhere.

The distribution of Commons seats is readjusted after each decennial census to take account of demographic changes. The House of Commons has 301 members at present (241 men and 60 women), each member representing a single riding or constituency. The seats are allotted to the provinces in proportion to population. This gives the larger provinces such as Ontario (103) and Quebec (75) considerably more representation than the smaller provinces.

This lack of regional balance is supposed to be compensated for by Senate numbers because the smaller provinces such as Prince Edward Island and Newfoundland are protected against having fewer MPs than senators. Unlike the Commons, the Senate numbers are fixed according to region with 24 from Ontario, 24 from Quebec, 24 from the West (6 from each of the four provinces), 24 from the Maritimes (10 each from New Brunswick and Nova Scotia, 4 from Prince Edward Island), 6 from Newfoundland, and 1 each from the Yukon and the Northwest Territories. Normally total membership in the upper house is 104. The constitution provides, however, for a possible temporary increase to 112 at the discretion of the prime minister. In 1990, this as-yet-unused provision was invoked by Conservative Prime Minister Brian Mulroney to break the opposition of the Liberal majority against the goods and service tax (GST). At present there are 52 Senate seats controlled by the Liberals, 48 by the Progressive Conservatives, and 4 Independents. The first woman to serve in the Senate was Cairine Wilson in 1930.

Parliamentary sessions vary in length depending on the amount of legislation the government is attempting to introduce, but the Commons and Senate can only meet as legislative bodies during one of these sessions. They are usually held twice a year, commencing in October and January. The end of the sessions is not fixed. Parliaments are labeled consecutively, and after the election of 1997 the legislative bodies met for the sitting of the 36th Parliament.

The formal powers of the House of Commons are substantial, but power lies mainly with the prime minister, his Cabinet, and the caucus. It is here that legislation is created and party strategies are decided. General parliamentary committees do exist and members of all parties have places on these bodies, but legislation is generally prepared within a government department and presented to the committees as a fait accompli. Individual members of the governing party without government responsibility (backbenchers) can introduce private member's bills but are expected to follow party directives as indicated by the party whip. This strong sense of party discipline can pit a member's loyalty to his party against his loyalty to his constituents or his own conscience. This contradiction has been a common problem in Canadian political history and has served as part of the justification for third parties as well as ammunition against the traditional party system. Individual opposition to party direction and discipline at times leads to members' "crossing the floor" and switching parties or serving as "independents."

Policy formation is conducted in government through three main avenues— the Throne Speech, the budget, and legislation. The Speech from the Throne is given at the beginning of the session and is meant to provide the general direction of the government by outlining objectives. The budget is meant to provide an accounting of the government's finances and is usually the most controversial issue of the session. Depending on the size of the party's majority, the passing of the budget can provide an opportunity for opposition groups to defeat or "bring down" an administration.

The Commons Speaker fulfils an important symbolic and legislative function. In the past the Speaker was elected by the Commons on the basis of a nomination by the prime minister and seconded by the leader of the opposition. Tradition dictated that the post rotate between an English and a French Canadian. In 1986 a new procedure was introduced whereby the process was opened up to democratic selection. Any MP who does not explicitly withdraw his or her name becomes a candidate. Voting is carried out by secret ballot, and except for the announcement of the victor, results are kept secret. According to parliamentary rules all official comments in the House must be addressed to the Speaker. Members do not speak directly to one another and may not refer to each other by name. Rather, titles must be used (the prime minister, the leader of the opposition, the honorable member).

The effective role of the opposition in the House of Commons varies with the size of the government majority. Its role is to criticize legislation, propose amendments, and resort to obstructionist procedures to gain

concessions. Possibly the most important weapon in the opposition's arsenal is the daily question period. The proceedings are televised to allow voters to evaluate their representatives. Regardless of the number of parties in the House, there can only be one official opposition, known as the Loyal Opposition. This group is usually formed by the second-largest party in the Commons and sits on the benches across the floor from the governing party. The second-largest group, however, is allowed to defer the role if desired. Such was the case in 1921 when the new Farmers' party known as the Progressives burst onto the scene with the second-largest number of seats. The Progressives balked the traditional party system and preferred to sit as a pressure group rather than serve as the official opposition. This role then fell to the party with the next most seats.

Judiciary

The federal structure that dominates Canada's political system is also reflected in its judiciary. The nation has the only integrated system of all federations. The remarkable degree of integration can be seen in the fact that a purely federal judicial power is not even mentioned in the Canadian constitution but instead it provides for a system with federally appointed judges to provincial superior and intermediate courts. The Supreme Court was established as a general court of appeal rather than one limited to federal and constitutional law. Parliament also has exclusive jurisdiction in the area of criminal law, while the provincial legislatures have powers to establish courts of criminal jurisdiction. As a result, provincially established courts administer federal law. There has been a tendency in recent years to move toward a more bifurcated system of dual courts.

The highest court in the land is the Supreme Court, which serves as the final arbiter on civil, criminal, and constitutional cases. Each province has a complete court system for all types of cases culminating in a provincial supreme court (sometimes called the superior court or the court of the queen's bench). Since 1987 these provincial courts have appeal courts as well. The Federal Court of

Percentage Votes in 1993 and 1997
General Elections by Party

Party	1993	1997
Liberal	41.3	38.3
Reform	18.7	19.4
Bloc	13.5	10.7
NDP	6.9	11.1
PC	16.0	18.9
Other	3.6	1.7

1997 General Election Seats by Province

Party	Total	Nfld	PEI	NS	NB	Que	Ont	Man	Sk	Alta	Bc	Y	NWT
Lib	155	4	4	0	3	26	101	6	1	2	6	—	2
Reform	60	—	—	—	—	—	—	3	8	24	25	—	—
Bloc	44	—	—	—	—	44	—	—	—	—	—	—	—
NDP	21	—	—	6	2	—	—	4	5	—	3	1	—
PC	20	3	—	5	5	5	1	1	—	—	—	—	—
Ind	1	—	—	—	—	—	1	—	—	—	—	—	—
Total	301	7	4	11	10	75	103	14	14	26	34	1	2

Canada oversees matters of law, equity, and admiralty.

Criminal law is uniform throughout Canada and determined by federal legislation. Civil law and related judicial matters are controlled provincially; all provinces follow a common-law tradition except Quebec, which uses the *Code Civil du Québec*, a system that has survived since the days of the ancien regime and is based on the *Code Napoléon*.

Canada's Supreme Court was established in 1875, soon after confederation, but it became the final court of appeal only in 1949. Its nine judges are appointed by the governor-general on the advice of the prime minister, and their tenure is relatively secure with a retirement age of 75. They can be removed only by an address to the governor-general by both Houses of Parliament. This would occur only after a formal investigation by the Criminal Judicial Council, including all the chief justices in the land. Such action has never occurred.

As with the Senate, pressure is mounting to make the Supreme Court a representative body. Three judges always come from Quebec and at least one judge comes from the regions outside central Canada. The Supreme Court fulfils all the normal functions of a final court of appeal and provides advisory opinions and judicial review. The first woman to serve on the Supreme Court was Bertha Wilson in 1982 (since 1949 only three judges have been women).

Canada's legislatures have authority over their jurisdiction, but if action is taken that crosses into another realm, the Supreme Court has the ability to demonstrate the federal division of power and declare it ultra vires (beyond jurisdiction). The entrenchment of individual and group rights in the Charter of Rights and Freedoms also limits parliamentary supremacy by protecting these rights. The use of the War Measures Act, which allows the Canadian federal government to exercise extraordinary power by suppressing civil rights in times of war, civil unrest, or natural disaster, is an exception to the rule. The act was last employed in 1970 in Quebec during the October Crisis by the government of the Liberal prime minister Pierre Trudeau to deal with the FLQ (*Front de la Libération du Québec*) terrorist group.

Regional and Local Government

When the Dominion of Canada became a nation in 1867, the architect behind confederation, John A. Macdonald, was intent on creating a strong, centralized federal system to avoid what he perceived as the mistakes that had just recently caused the American Civil War. The resulting federal union was to maintain the influential powers for the federal government while providing only minor local spheres of control for the provinces. The federal government also maintained the power to "disallow" provincial legislation. This overriding power was employed 112 times after confederation but has not been used since 1943. The lieutenant governors were also able to employ royal prerogative and veto legislation, but the power was not used. A power that has been employed, however, is the ability of the lieutenant governors to reserve provincial legislation for federal approval.

In the over 130 years since confederation there has been a continual power struggle between the two levels of government. The provinces usually band together to push for increases in their jurisdictions, but they have not always stood united against federal encroachments into their domain. The glaring lack of balance in Canadian regionalism has led the more prosperous provinces (Ontario, Quebec, and later British Columbia and Alberta) to lead the resistance against increased federalism, while the poorer "have not" provinces (Newfoundland, Nova Scotia, Prince Edward Island, New Brunswick, Saskatchewan, and Manitoba) have, at times, encouraged more federal control.

The issue of federal-provincial relations is further complicated by French-Canadian nationalism in Quebec. For many in the province, any encroachments into provincial jurisdiction by Ottawa is viewed as a threat to Quebec sovereignty. In recent years there has been a shift toward federal devolution of powers in Canada. While the Liberal governments of Pierre Trudeau attempted to be strongly federalist in the 1970s, the Progressive Conservative governments of Brian Mulroney in the 1980s sought constitutional agreement with Quebec and as a result moved toward increased provincial power. This trend toward decentralization continues and can be seen in the changing terminology used to denote Canadian federalism: cooperative federalism (after World War II), executive federalism (1960s–'70s), and contested federalism (1976–'90s).

Not long after confederation the provincial premiers began to gather for conferences to discuss joint issues of concern. These gatherings became known as dominion-provincial conferences and included the prime minister to discuss the distribution of powers and other related matters. Today first ministers conferences are held, often to make interprovincial agreements and to discuss the present constitutional morass.

THE MARITIMES

The region of the Maritimes comprises the provinces of Nova Scotia, New Brunswick, Prince Edward Island, and Newfoundland. The inhabitants are largely of British and Irish ancestry, but there are significant groups of Acadian French centered in New Brunswick. A powerful sense of regional alienation created in large part by economic difficulty dominates Maritime politics. The fisheries remain the staple, and the problems facing this industry, such as the government-imposed cod moratorium, highlight the plight of the populace. The region is deficient in secondary industries, and federal transfer payments make up between 30% and 50% of provincial revenues.

The Maritimes have demonstrated a remarkably strong loyalty to the traditional two-party system dominated by the Liberals and the Conservatives. Regional alienation has led the predominant third parties in the nation (the New Democratic Party and the Reform Party) to target the region as a base of support, but this has not translated into any significant or lasting effect. These efforts have failed largely due to the small "c" conservative nature of Maritime political culture as well as the western orientation of the third-party movements. Distinctly "Maritime" third parties have appeared in the region, but they have also failed to make headway.

Nova Scotia has a population of 937,800. The province's political loyalties have shifted between Liberal and Conservative, but recently there has been some support for the New Democratic Party (NDP) in areas of labor unrest. A Liberal leadership convention in 1997 chose Russel MacLellan, who took over as premier. The Liberals were reelected in March 1998.

New Brunswick has a population of 760,000. The province is officially bilingual with anglophone and francophone communities that are approximately equal in size. The majority of the francophone community are Acadians who perceive themselves as culturally distinct from other French Canadians. To ensure that the bilingual status of New Brunswick cannot be altered by any future provincial government (as occurred in Manitoba), it was provided official status in the Constitution Act of 1982. By 1991, however, an antibilingualism backlash had developed and a new political movement (the Confederation of Regions Party) came into being. But by 1993 its power was waning. Ray Frenette became party leader and premier late in 1997. The Liberals hold 45 seats while the PCs serve as the opposition under Bernard Lord with 9 seats, and the NDP holds 1 seat.

Prince Edward Island is the smallest of the Canadian provinces and has a population of 136,100. In 1997, a bridge and causeway was constructed to link the island to the mainland in New Brunswick. The election of 1996 resulted in a resurgence for the Progressive Conservatives and victory under the leadership of Pat Binns, whose party won 18 seats. The Liberals serve as the opposition under Keith Milligan with 8 seats.

Newfoundland and Labrador have a population of 575,400. The province was the last to join Canada. Prior to a referendum that led to its entrance into the dominion in March 1949, the people had been governed directly from Great Britain. Newfoundland's political culture is dominated by economic difficulty surrounding the troubled cod fishery (a moratorium was placed on cod in July 1992). The province suffers from the highest rate of unemployment and the highest cost of living in the country. Federal fiscal support accounts for as much as 80% of the provincial economy. In 1996 Brian Tobin won victory for the governing Liberals with 36 seats. The opposition

is headed by the PCs under Ed Bryne whose party controls 10 seats.

CENTRAL CANADA

Quebec has a population of 7,334,200, of which about 17% are nonfrancophone. Today, 23% of Canadians claim French as their first language with 83% concentrated in Quebec. The province is one of the nation's most industrialized with agriculture, mining, forestry, hydroelectric power, and construction making up its list of major industries.

The establishment of the province of Quebec in 1867 provided the French Canadians with what they perceived as an autonomous sphere that would ensure their cultural survival. The creation of Canada was believed to have been a compact of the two founding peoples: the English and the French. In recent years this "two-nations approach" has come under scrutiny particularly by those outside Quebec who argue that the dominion is a nation of 10 provinces of which Quebec is only 1. They argue that the two-nations approach does not pay proper attention to the many other ethnic groups that constitute the nation, not to mention the native peoples. Regardless, most Quebecers view the province as the French-Canadian homeland.

Political sentiment in the province is divided between federalists and separatists, and French-Canadian nationalism plays a volatile role in the national unity debate that dominates the political scene at both the federal and provincial levels. The move toward Quebec sovereignty and its separation from Canada has existed to some extent since before World War II but has become the dominant issue particularly since the mid-1970s.

Since confederation Quebec has sought to protect its cultural distinctiveness in both provincial and federal politics. The large number of seats in the province (75), along with the fact that the people usually vote as a bloc, has ensured that a successful party must pay attention to Quebec concerns. In the past, cultural issues have been dominated by religion, education, and military conscription; since the Second World War they have been dominated by the constitution and language.

The Conservative and Liberal Parties controlled Quebec federal politics until 1990 when the forces of separatism emerged in the form of the Bloc Québécois (BQ). Provincial politics, on the other hand, has long been under the influence of French-Canadian nationalism.

Premier René Lévesque held a referendum on "sovereignty-association" (the euphemism of the Parti Québécois for separation but with economic association) in 1980, but it was defeated with a clear majority of 60%. The PQ also passed the controversial Bill 101, declaring the intention to make Quebec a unilingual province. The subsequent years witnessed a decline in PQ power and an increase in support for "renewed federalism." Although it won the election of 1981, the PQ's defeat in 1985 under the leadership of Pierre Marc Johnson brought the return of Robert Bourassa's Liberals, who won 98 seats in the 122-seat legislature. In 1988 Johnson was replaced by Jacques Parizeau, a strong separatist, who returned the PQ to its original mandate for independence. In 1993 Bourassa resigned and was replaced by Daniel Johnson. Parizeau and the PQ won the 1994 provincial election, promising a referendum on sovereignty.

The constitutional rift has caused a dramatic increase in tension between Quebec and the rest of Canada and the most serious threat ever to face national unity. Since 1990 and the death of the Meech Lake Accord, separatist forces inside Quebec have ridden the waves of discontent and frustration. The PQ regained provincial office under Jacques Parizeau in 1994, and a number of Progressive Conservative MPs from Quebec abandoned the party to form the Bloc Québécois under Lucien Bouchard in 1992. The failure of the Charlottetown Accord only widened the gulf between French and English Canada. In the federal election of 1993 the bloc managed to win 54 seats, all in Quebec, and become the official opposition. The climax came on October 30, 1995, when another referendum in Quebec was held on sovereignty-association; this time the federalists won by only the barest of margins with 50.6% voting "No" and 49.4% voting "Yes" (the voter turnout was over 93%). During the campaign the leader of the federal Bloc Québécois became the most popular and influential figure in Quebec. Within days of the referendum, Parizeau resigned and was replaced as PQ leader and premier by Lucien Bouchard. Gilles Duceppe was selected (by mail ballot) as leader of the BQ.

Ontario is the most populous (11,100,300), wealthiest, and most politically influential of Canada's provinces. It is still predominantly of British stock with large numbers of French, Italian, and German ethnic groups, and many others. Together with Quebec, Ontario forms the industrial heartland of the nation. The party that carries Ontario in the federal election has the best chance of winning office. In the 1997 election the Liberals won all but two of the 103 seats, more than half of their parliamentary majority.

The Progressive Conservatives dominated provincial politics in Ontario for 42 years from 1943 until 1985. In 1986 the Liberals formed the government under Premier David Peterson with NDP support. By the following year the Liberals had consolidated their support, but when an early election was called in 1990, the NDP stunned the nation by winning office under Bob Rae with 74 of the 130 seats. This was the first time since the victory of the United Farmers of Ontario in 1919 that a third party had taken power in Ontario. The social democratic government soon experienced difficulties, however, amid economic recession. The Rae government even alienated some of its most loyal and influential supporters when it introduced the "social contract" legislation that overruled the collective bargaining process to reduce or freeze public-sector wages.

By 1995 the Conservatives were returned to power in Ontario. But the cuts, rather than ending, reached new levels. The government of Mike Harris is taking a strong right-wing stance by stressing efficiency and elimination of government waste. The PCs hold 82 seats in the legislature, the Liberals 30, and the NDP 16, and there are 2 Independents.

THE WEST

The Canadian West as a region has changed over the years. Prior to World War II a differentiation was generally made between the Prairie West (meaning the three Prairie provinces of Manitoba, Saskatchewan, and Alberta) and the Pacific West (meaning British Columbia). The Prairie West was viewed as one agricultural region, with minor provincial differences, that contained a diversely mixed population resulting from the immigration boom at the turn of the 20th century. British Columbia with its varying landscape of Pacific coast, Rocky Mountains, and northern forests was a region unto itself.

The West remains Canada's most politically radical region. Due to its relative youthfulness, the immigration influx and ethnic diversity, the strength and influence of the agrarian movements, the great expectations that ended in the disappointment of the "Dirty Thirties," and the domination of central Canada, the region lacks much of the established Liberal and Conservative tradition. The West has served as the experimental site for numerous third-party movements.

Manitoba has a population of 1,137,500. In the first 50 years of its existence the province had a strong Liberal and Conservative tradition. A two-party system has come to dominate Manitoba elections with the Liberals on the periphery. In the provincial election of 1995 the Progressive Conservatives under Gary Filmon won a second term in office with a slim majority. The NDP remains in opposition, led by Gary Doer. Since this contest the Liberals have collapsed into complete dissension and are plagued by party infighting.

Saskatchewan has a population of 1,015,600. The province was long dominated by a Liberal Party whose organization was so powerful and effective that it became known as "the machine." From its creation as a province in 1905 until the landmark provincial election of 1944 that elected the Co-operative Commonwealth Federation (CCF) as the first socialistic government in North America, "the machine" largely controlled the Saskatchewan hustings. The emergence of the CCF on the heels of the Depression and then World War II, however, provided the party with its most solid base in the nation. Like Manitoba, the Progressive Conservatives appeared as the opponent of the recast NDP in what remained a two-party tradition The NDP holds office under Roy Romanow. In 1997, members of the fractured PC Party joined with some disgruntled Liberals and attempted to form an efficient opposition by breaking party lines and forming a coalition group called the Saskatchewan Party. It holds eight seats.

Alberta has a population of 2,747,000. The province has long been characterized by one-party dominance and this is in no danger of changing. Provincial office has been held by the Liberals from 1905 until 1921; the United Farmers of Alberta (UFA) from 1921 until 1935; the Social Credit Party from 1935 until 1975; and the Progressive Conservatives from 1975 to the present. Sentiments of western alienation against central Canada are strongest in Alberta and have blended with a right-wing disposition to create powerful provincial governments that Albertans expect to offer efficient administration while protecting the province's wealth against external (central-Canadian) manipulation.

The PCs often win more than 90% of the legislative seats in Alberta, reinforcing one-party dominance. In the early 1990s, with a recession continuing, deficits rising, and party popularity falling, the party chose Ralph Klein as leader. Klein easily won the election of 1993 on a program of rigorous spending cuts in government payrolls and social programs. At the time, the Liberals were going through one of their apparent rejuvenations under the leadership of Lawrence Decor. Klein's government holds 63 of 83 seats, and the opposition is the Liberal party now led by Nancy MacBeth.

British Columbia, "the West beyond the West," has a population of 3,766,000, the third-largest in Canada. The land is diverse and so is the population, which contains a large number of Asian-Canadians. The exploitation of BC's natural resources, such as timber and the fisheries, along with struggles for native land claims, dominates provincial politics.

A two-party system rules politics in the province, and in recent years power has changed hands between the NDP and the Social Credit Party. Except for a short interval, the Social Credit Party was in office for nearly four decades. This populist group captured the right-wing position and has kept the Liberals and Progressive Conservatives to around only 10% of the popular vote. In 1991, however, amid a series of scandals and internal party strife, the party was defeated under the leadership of Rita Johnston (the first woman premier in Canadian history). Social Credit actually fell to third place behind the resurging Liberals, who became the official opposition. The NDP regained office and is led by Premier Glen Clark, who won the election of 1996 with 39 seats. The Liberals hold 33 seats and are led by Gordon Campbell.

THE NORTH

The land mass north of the 60th parallel forms a region unto itself and is made up of the Northwest Territories and the Yukon Territory. The vast area remains the home predominantly of the indigenous populations (Dene Nation, several Inuit peoples, and Métis). Although there have been efforts to win provincial status for the two territories, they are still under the constitutional authority of the federal government. They do have fully elected assemblies, responsible executives, and a form of delegated responsibility for most of the matters under their jurisdiction.

The Northwest Territories cover the area from Yukon to Baffin Island and have a population of 65,800. The territorial government works out of Yellowknife. There are no parties in elections, and all candidates run as independents. Following the election of 1995, Don Morin was chosen by his colleagues to head the nonpartisan Cabinet.

The Yukon Territory makes up the area in the northwest and borders Alaska. It has a population of 30,100. Partisanship is alive and well in the Yukon. In the 1992 election the territorial government under Tony Penikett was defeated by John Ostashek and his Yukon Party, which previously had been the territorial wing of the Progressive Conservatives. Another election in 1996 saw the defeat of the Yukon Party and the victory of the NDP under government leader Piers Macdonald. The NDP won 11 of 17 seats.

THE ELECTORAL SYSTEM

Canada is a federal state and therefore has two concurrent electoral systems: a national one (which also covers the Yukon and Northwest Territories) and a provincial one. Federal elections used to be conducted on the basis of the provincial regulations, but according to the Canada Elections Act of 1920 these national contests are administered by the independent chief electoral officer and his or her staff. This office is precluded from voting. According to the constitution the Canadian prime minister is obligated to request a dissolution and an election from the governor-general every five years. The prime minister chooses the election date. Elections will occur earlier if the government is defeated, if it resigns, or if it wishes to go to the people to renew its mandate. The election date is always a Monday unless the day is a statutory holiday, in which case it is held on the following day.

Traditionally, there has been no permanent electoral list in Canada, and as a result the government, through the electoral officer (independent official responsible to the House of Commons), has been responsible for enumerating all eligible voters prior to each election. This officer is instructed of the ensuing contest by the Cabinet (officially the governor-in-council). The returning officers in each constituency are issued writs of election and supervise the contest at the riding level. After 1997 a permanent voters' list is being compiled for future use.

All Canadian citizens who are 18 years of age or older are eligible to vote by secret ballot in both provincial and federal elections. Women gained the federal franchise in

1918 (at first this wartime measure was only extended to the wives, sisters, and mothers of servicemen), while the provincial franchise varied from 1916 (Manitoba) to 1940 (Quebec). The native peoples received the right to vote in 1960 (the Inuit gained the right in 1950). Balloting is carried out in the voter's home constituency. Average voter turnout for both federal and provincial elections in Canada ranges from 60% to 85% of registered voters. French Canadians are less active in federal contests than English Canadians but more active in provincial elections.

Candidature for election is open to any individual who files nomination papers with the signatures of 100 other electors and a deposit of $1,000 with a returning officer. The deposit is meant to discourage nuisance candidates, and the money is refundable if the individual submits the required election expenses return and unused official receipts within the prescribed time limit. He or she must also obtain 15% of the ballots cast. Party leaders have a veto over the choice of party candidates, but this interference is rarely employed.

The Canadian electoral system is based on single-member plurality with each member representing one constituency. In a nation of such diverse regional interests, the effect of this structure is twofold: minority political parties or positions that are regionally based become overrepresented, and parties and issues that are both minority-based *and* diffused throughout the country become underrepresented. For example, the New Democratic Party is traditionally viewed as a regional, western-based party. During its history it has received substantial support everywhere except Quebec, garnering 15% to 18% of the vote but only 8% to 12% of the seats in Parliament. In the federal election of 1993 the Progressive Conservative government of Prime Minister Kim Campbell received 16% of the popular vote but only 2 seats in Parliament. In the same contest the Bloc Québécois with only 13.5% of the vote became the second-largest group in the House with 54 seats. This inconsistency has long been debated and calls for a system of proportional representation (usually by those groups that would benefit) have been heard since before the First World War.

When an elected member of either a federal or a provincial house can no longer hold the seat (due to death or resignation), a by-election will be held in that constituency to select a new member. By-elections can be important as indicators of a government's standing or to endanger a government's majority.

The 1997 election witnessed the use of new election rules that reduced the length of the campaign to the new minimum of 36 days from the old standard of 47 days. Redistribution for this contest increased the number of seats from 295 to 301 (4 for Ontario, 2 for BC). Another change was intended to compensate for the varying time zones of the nation that led to polls closing and results being known in eastern Canada long before they had closed in the far West. As a result, ballot counting took place at the same approximate time and results were not announced until the polls closed in the West.

THE PARTY SYSTEM

Origins of the Parties

The traditional party system in Canada evolved from the nation's colonial history and was heavily influenced by the British system. In the years that followed 1867 it was further shaped by the forces of immigration and continentalism and has emerged into a distinctly Canadian system.

Prior to confederation two political groups emerged that reflected the struggle for responsible government in colonial society. The Tories as the dominant group, reflecting the strong influence of the United Empire Loyalists as well as the British imperial establishment, maintained power through an oligarchy, consisting of the governorship, the executive council, and the various ruling cliques. Opposition came from a group known as the Reformers, who took inspiration from both the Whig tradition in Britain and the republican tradition in the United States. The struggle for responsible government, culminating in the Rebellions of 1837–38, cemented the identity of these political groups. In the years leading up to confederation political sympathies became more moderate and took the form of Conservative and Liberal, parties akin to the British system. Mass parties emerged at the end of the century after public voting (which often took up to six weeks to complete) was replaced by the secret ballot and the franchise was expanded.

The two-party system remained intact until 1921 when agrarian protest exploded onto the scene in the form of the western-based Progressives who won enough seats to qualify as the official opposition and force the first minority government in Canadian history. The Progressive Party was short-lived (lasting only two elections), but the traditional party system would never be fully restored. The Great Depression (known as the "Dirty Thirties") once again forced westerners to search for radical alternatives, but this time agrarian discontent coalesced with labor unrest and a burgeoning left-wing intelligentsia to form a more ideologically based social democratic party, the Cooperative Commonwealth Federation. Other protest parties have emerged since this time but the CCF-NDP has remained the enduring third party. Most recently, the Bloc Québécois and the Reform Party have come forward to challenge the traditional two-party system.

The Parties in Law

Political parties are not mentioned in the Canadian constitution. The state registers parties and provides them with financial support if they meet basic requirements. Individual candidates who wish to stand for office need only make an election deposit of $200, which is forfeited if a candidate fails to receive 15% of the vote.

The Election Expenses Act of 1974 altered the basic financing of election campaigns. The act enables the state to subsidize campaigns indirectly by allowing individuals tax credits for gifts up to $500. It also requires that a party have either one representative in Parliament or field candidates in at least 50 electoral districts to be eligible for the indirect subsidies. These requirements are at present met by the Liberal Party, the Progressive Conservative Party, the New Democratic Party, the Bloc Québécois, the Natural Law Party, the Reform Party, and the Marxist-Leninist Party. The act was amended in 1983 with spending ceilings being tied to changes in the consumer price index. Spending is also adjusted to the size of the constituency by allowing an expense of one dollar each for the first 15,000 voters, 50 cents each for the next 10,000, and 25 cents each for the remaining voters. To assist candidates in very large but sparsely populated constituencies, a further 15 cents per square kilometer may be spent. Overall, qualified political parties receive reimbursement for 22.5% of their total allowable election expenses.

Party Organization

In theory the main political parties that exist at both the federal and provincial levels keep their spheres of influence distinct. Party organizations are expected to exist at both levels and be able to function autonomously. While this has occurred to an extent, there is usually considerable cooperation, the level of which often depends on whether the party in question holds federal power. A party in government in Ottawa is usually facing scrutiny in some region or province of the nation. As a result, connections between the federal and provincial organizations may work to the detriment of the latter.

In 1980, the issue of constitutional reform saw each of the three major federal parties at odds with at least some of their provincial counterparts. The federal Progressive Conservatives opposed Prime Minister Trudeau's proposals, but the PC premier of Ontario backed Trudeau because the proposals were popular in Ontario. The NDP premier, Alan Blakeney of Saskatchewan, opposed the proposals despite the federal party's support. In Quebec the provincial Liberal Party came out against the Liberal government in Ottawa. On the other hand, a popular federal party or government may well witness attempts by their provincial counterparts to take advantage of that popularity. Whereas the federal Liberal and Progressive Conservative Parties provide their provincial branches a fair degree of autonomy, the New Democratic Party exerts more control in matters of both policy and financial concern.

Throughout Canadian political history there have been numerous examples of federal parties wielding undue influence in provincial and even constituent situations. It is also common for federal parties to send in their popular members to influence provincial campaigns. This is usually done with the permission and cooperation of the provincial parties.

But the organizational strength of both federal and provincial parties rests at the local level. The constituency associations of the major parties are associations of volunteers who are particularly active in times of elections. The association is responsible for nominating a candidate through a local convention or committee meeting, raising funds for the candidate and party, and canvassing the electorate.

In most cases candidates are residents of the constituencies in which they run for election. Living in the riding helps convince the electorate that the candidate is sensitive to the area's needs. At times, nonresidents will run for election, but this usually occurs in the case of high-profile ("star") candidates who cannot win election in their home constituency or need to provide party representation in a different region or province.

The various branches of a party usually meet in a national party convention (each of the three main parties requires such a convention at least every two years). In general each party has a national council or executive consisting of both provincial and federal representatives that coordinates policy and national election campaigns. A party president, and not the party leader, is responsible for general administration and day-to-day party affairs. This distinction in roles allows the party leader some distance from the potentially troublesome (and scandalous) issue of financing.

The parties and party leaders wield considerable power in Canadian politics. Despite the system's emphasis on individual constituent representation and accountability, a large degree of party discipline is common. This is particularly the case with the mainline Liberal and Progressive Conservative Parties. Criticism of party discipline and calls for elected members to balk the system and answer first to their constituents have long come from the "radical" West and can still be seen in the New Democratic and Reform Parties.

The party leader's power evolves significantly from his or her critical importance to the electoral success of the party. Leadership battles are conducted at party conventions that then become "leadership conventions." The various constituencies are generally able to send delegates who will be provided a vote. A large degree of factionalism usually occurs and runoffs are conducted until only two candidates are remaining and one is proclaimed the leader. The defeated candidates are expected to adhere to party discipline and do what is best for party unity by throwing their weight behind the successful candidate.

Campaigning

Prior to the Second World War, federal election campaigns in Canada severely tested the constitution of the party leaders. The candidates were expected to make whirlwind tours of the massive nation, often crisscrossing its breadth several times by rail and car. Public speaking was the centerpiece of election strategy, and rallies were popular and widely attended. The difficulties in reaching remote areas placed emphasis on the constituent candidates rather than the party leaders. Alterations in media obviously affected this style of campaigning, and since the late 1950s elections have increasingly been staged through the media, particularly television. The media have focused attention on leadership, and increasingly the electorate is selecting personality over party or local candidates. In recent years the televised "leadership debate" has become the most important event in a national campaign, allowing candidates to score points or lose popularity with the populace. The use of opinion polls since the end of the Second World War has also changed the way campaigns are run. The publication of these highly accurate measurements of popular standing undoubtedly influences voting patterns.

Independent Voters

The extent to which both independent and undecided voters play a role in election campaigns differs according to circumstance and region. In the Maritimes, where partisan tradition remains strong, the number of independent voters tends to be quite low. In the West, where skepticism toward the central-Canadian-dominated political system is more pronounced, the independent vote is stronger.

During campaigns Canadian parties are forced to pay considerable attention to what is termed the "swing," or undecided, vote. As a result, crucial areas where this vote is high are targeted and often receive more attention during campaigns. In the 1997 federal election campaign, for example, Ontario with its large number of seats was critical for the success of the Liberal, Progressive Conservative, and Reform Parties. There was a large undecided vote that could swing toward any of the three groups. As it turned out, despite the closeness of the race, the Liberals won 101 of the 103 seats, due to the winner-take-all system.

LIBERAL PARTY OF CANADA

History

The Liberal party emerged as the colonial counterpart of the British Liberal Party after Canada gained dominion status in 1867. The party also emerged from the group of Reformers that had opposed the oligarchical structure controlling the colony after the American Revolution and the Loyalist migrations. This Reform Party drew its support from both French and English segments of the population and was a loosely united but ethnically divided group of "Rouges" (anticlericals in Quebec) and "Clear Grits" (whigs in Ontario).

The Liberal Party based itself on an ideology that advocated reform and an end to corruption, protection of the common man and increased democracy, limited government, dominion autonomy, and freer trade. Through its ability to adapt to changing conditions and even shift itself to meet new needs, the "middle-of-the-road" party has held office so often that it has become known as the "the Government Party." From 1896 to 1984 the party won 18 of the 25 general elections.

Organization

The Liberal Party maintains a strong relationship between the national and provincial party organizations. Although they are separate organizations, the constituency associations of the national party belong to the provincial-level member organizations.

A national party convention meets every two years to set policy and elect national officers. It is broadly representative of party adherents with delegates from Parliament, the provincial organizations, the provincial Legislatures, the constituency organizations, and the various commissions. The delegates to the convention serve as a consultative council between conventions. Party bylaws stipulate that they must be consulted by the national executive twice a year; this consultation is usually done by mail. Recently, efforts to promote the democratic quality of the party have been attempted by various reform commissions. As a result, the traditional procedure of reviewing the performance of the leader by a national convention of delegates was replaced in 1992 by provisions involving all party members in this review.

The 50-person national executive consists of national party officers and the administrative leaders of the provincial party organizations and the youth, women's, and aboriginal people's commissions. The selection of national officers is heavily influenced by the presidents of the provincial member organizations and the three affiliated commissions.

Policy

The Liberal Party has been in power for so much of the 20th century, largely due to its ability to win support in Quebec as well as a wide-ranging distribution of support from English Canada. In both world wars the party opposed conscription and in doing so held Quebec. The most serious question facing the Canadian state has long been national unity and so the Liberals have become the defenders of this notion. They have served as a brokerage party always attempting to walk the tightrope among the various divergent interests in the country. When the CCF was gaining popularity in the 1940s on calls for the establishment of social programs and the welfare state, the Liberals shifted ground and stole the socialist thunder. When recession struck in the 1980s and 1990s, and calls went out for fiscal responsibility and government cutbacks, the Liberals became the party intent on balancing the budget. Their most impressive attribute has been the ability to maintain power.

Membership and Constituency

The party's ability to remain in office at the federal level along with the regional domination of central Canada has given the Liberals traditionally strong bases of support in both Quebec and Ontario. The Maritimes also have a strong Liberal tradition, despite powerful sentiments of regional alienation. "The Government Party" is extremely weak in the West with little hope of a genuine long-term recovery. The Liberals have long been popular with ethnic groups, particularly those who have immigrated to Canada. This has occurred for two reasons: the party has framed itself as the protector of minorities and has fostered the major immigration booms into Canada while in office. The party is also strong in urban areas among middle-class professionals.

Financing

The base of financial support for the Liberal Party comes from corporate sponsorship as well as individual and association donations.

Leadership

The leadership of the Liberal Party has been strong and durable and one of the main reasons for its success and longevity. Due to the overwhelming success of the party, the leader can usually expect to become prime minister. A nonofficial tradition has developed whereby the party leadership takes turns passing between an anglophone and a francophone. After losing two elections in 1984 and 1988, John Turner (who had been prime minister for a short time in 1984) resigned in 1990. The leadership convention in Calgary selected the 1984 runner-up to Turner, Jean Chrétien, on the first ballot. Chrétien returned the Liberals to power in 1993 and won reelection for his party in 1997. According to the constitution of the Liberal Party, a leadership review occurs only during the first national convention after a federal election. In 1992 a policy was approved whereby all party members, and not just delegates to the leadership convention, have a direct say in reviewing the leader's performance.

Prospects

The two election victories by the Liberals in 1993 and 1997, along with high ratings in the polls, would seem to indicate a continuation of Liberal domination in Canadian federal politics. This domination is aided by another constant—the lack of stability within the other parties. Liberal success has been considerably aided by an anti-Conservative backlash against the unpopular Mulroney governments of the mid- to late 1980s and early 1990s. This sentiment will disintegrate as the ire of the populace becomes increasingly directed at the party in office. Most of the discontent will come from the alienated Maritime and western regions that have less political sway, and as a result the prospects of the Liberal Party look promising. Much also depends on the strength of the federalist position in Quebec. Economic prospects seem to be improving as the recession comes to an end, and this upturn will obviously be to the Liberal advantage. Cutbacks in government and social programs, and an obsession to balance the budget, will be replaced by increased spending and tax cuts.

THE PROGRESSIVE CONSERVATIVE PARTY OF CANADA (PC)

History

The Conservative Party governed Canada for most of the first 30 years after confederation. The party was based on the strength of the traditional colonial oligarchies in both French and English Canada. John A. Macdonald became the moving force behind the party in the 1850s and 1860s and was instrumental in bringing about confederation. He maintained a strong alliance with Quebec conservatives and established the Canadian tradition of having an English prime minister from Ontario who governed with an influential French lieutenant from Quebec, in this case George Étienne-Cartier. The leaders of the Conservative Party were heavily involved with the transportation revolution in Canada and became inextricably intertwined with the railway companies and the "big interests" generally.

The Conservative Party came to advocate strong ties with the mother country and the British Empire overall as well as resistance to Americanization by the United States. In the late 1870s Prime Minister Macdonald's "national policy" set out Conservative policy. It called for protectionism in the form of high tariffs against the United States, the maintenance of the British Preference to encourage and protect Canada's favored position in the British market, railway expansion, and immigration into the West.

The oxymoron "Progressive" was added to the party

name in 1942 as a condition for the acceptance of the leadership by the United Farmers of Manitoba premier, John Bracken. The premier, long a figure in the Progressive movement that was so strong in western Canada, argued that the Conservatives had to indicate a desire and ability to change with the times. The renaming was also an attempt to strengthen party fortunes in the West. The party did win power in 1958 under the charismatic westerner John Diefenbaker. The resurgence of the party in 1984 demonstrated the nation's acceptance of the neoconservatism that was also popular in Great Britain and the United States.

Organization

The party's provincial and federal constituency associations are quite separate. The biannual general meeting includes delegates from the federal constituency associations, their youth and women's auxiliaries, and the provincial organizations. The general meeting elects the major party officers. The national executive, which contains 125 members, most of whom are appointed by the party leadership, meets at least once a year. The center of power for the party is the steering committee, which usually has 12 members. It includes the top party officers and meets frequently.

Policy

Traditionally, the Conservative Party stands for law and order, strong government, preservation of the British connection, and economic nationalism. No party in Canadian political history has been forced to change from its original ideology as much as the Conservatives.

The Mulroney era of the mid- to late 1980s and early 1990s demonstrated that the Progressive Conservative Party was no longer Tory in the traditional sense but rather neoconservative and part of the trend toward Thatcherism and Reaganomics. Under Brian Mulroney, a native of Quebec, the party made its first genuine breakthrough in French Canada since the days of John A. Macdonald. The party was now the advocate of free trade with both the United States and Mexico; it supported deregulation and privatization of industry and efficiency in social welfare programs; and it stepped into the role usually reserved for the Liberals as the defender of national unity through attempts to bring Quebec into the constitutional framework.

Membership and Constituency

Under Mulroney, the party managed to solve the gravest defect regarding its membership and constituency: support in Quebec. With this problem solved, the PCs can offer serious opposition to Liberal domination because they hold support in all other parts of the nation, including the alienated regions. The threat facing the party now, however, is the fracturing of the right-wing vote. French-Canadian nationalism in the form of the provincial Parti Québécois and the federal Bloc Québécois, along with western alienation in the form of the Reform Party, is splitting the Right and taking votes away from the Progressive Conservatives.

Financing

The Conservative Party has long had strong funding from large corporations.

Leadership

Leadership has been an enduring problem for the party, and internal divisions in its upper echelons have not helped the situation. The names of Sir John A. Macdonald and Sir Robert Borden are on the list of "great" Canadian prime ministers, but other Tory leaders such as Arthur Meighen, Richard Bennett, John Diefenbaker, Joe Clark, and Brian Mulroney, while reaching the office of prime minister, are some of the most unpopular in the nation's history.

In the face of the impending electoral disaster in 1993, after nine years in office, Prime Minister Mulroney and many of his senior Cabinet ministers retired or accepted patronage positions. The leadership of the party was won by Kim Campbell (the first woman to lead the PCs), who became the first female prime minister. Amid accusations that the new leader was merely left as a sacrificial offering to an anti-Mulroney backlash, Campbell resigned soon after the election. The party then chose the runner-up to Campbell at the last convention, Jean Charest, as leader. The more popular Charest is a French Canadian who was one of only two Progressive Conservatives to win a seat in the 1993 election. In the following four years Charest worked to rebuild the demolished party and led it to win 20 seats in the 1997 contest. During this campaign Charest emerged as the most popular leader of all parties, despite the victory of the Liberals. In 1998 Charest abandoned the party to become leader of the provincial Liberals in Quebec and thereby provide a serious challenge to the separatists under Lucien Bouchard.

Prospects

To have success the Progressive Conservative party must eliminate the Reform Party as a viable option for right-wing voters. This would prevent the traditional conservative vote from being split (particularly in Alberta and Ontario) and rebuild party fortunes in western Canada. The PCs must also continue to represent themselves as the federal option to the French-Canadian nationalists. Time alone will allow the leader to shake the unpopular Mulroney legacy that still lingers with the party. Jean Charest's decision to abandon the party dealt it a serious setback. The search for a new and effective leader will prove difficult.

NEW DEMOCRATIC PARTY (NDP)

History

The New Democratic Party, known prior to 1961 as the Co-operative Commonwealth Federation (CCF), developed in 1933 as an amalgam of farm groups, labor associations, and middle-class intellectuals. It appeared on the Prairies (the first conventions being held in Calgary and Regina) out of the third-party traditions of the Progressives and the United Farmers. Unlike these previous groups, however, the CCF was not so much a populist party as a social democratic party with a definite socialist philosophy. In the wake of the Great Depression and the crisis in capitalism, the movement was more likely to be enduring than previous third parties. The CCF gained popularity in the 1940s, winning office in Saskatchewan in 1944 as the first socialist government in North America. The party became such a threat to the Liberal government of Mackenzie King during the Second World War that it was prompted to implement planks for a social welfare system. The CCF (and then the NDP) has generally maintained its traditional bases of support on the Prairies, in British Columbia, the North, and in northwestern Ontario. It has been unable to break free from its label and identity as merely a regional third party and obtain some form of national status. Occasionally it wins support in the Maritimes as a labor and protest party, but these breakthroughs have not been long-term. Its weakness in Quebec is glaring as well as fatal.

Organization

An individual who joins the provincial wing of the party automatically becomes a member of both federal and provincial constituency organizations. Due to the weakness of the federal party and the strength of particular provincial parties, the two branches work together. The party's biannual federal convention includes delegates from the provincial organizations, the federal constituency associations, the Young New Democrats, and some trade unions and farm groups. The party prohibits its members from belonging to other parties and requires that they pledge support to the constitution and principles of the NDP.

Between conventions, the council is the chief governing authority. Its membership of over 100 includes 20 members who are elected by the convention, 20 elected by provincial party conventions, as well as provincial party officers. The associated trade unions and farm groups also elect members to the council. The council, in turn, elects from among its members the executive of 28 members. The executive is the center of power in the party and meets frequently.

Policy

Over the years the socialist tenets of the New Democratic Party have been weakened. For example, the party supports state control as opposed to ownership of industry. Since 1933 there have been several key struggles within the left-wing movement, involving personality, policy, and ideology, that have divided and weakened its overall success. In the late 1970s the "Waffle," or New Left faction, of the party was expelled.

Generally, the policy of the NDP has been dictated by social democratic principles, conditioned by its agrarian support, and shaped by the third-party tradition in Canada. The party is the main supporter of the nation's impressive social welfare system, including state-funded medical care that the NDP was instrumental in establishing during the 1960s. Thus far, the party has had its greatest effect on policy during periods of minority government when the ruling party has no choice but to rely on NDP support to maintain office. The NDP supports nationalization of industry and is usually opposed to foreign investment and domination by the United States. The party also emphasizes job creation and tax increases on corporations.

Membership and Constituency

The NDP has strong organization in its bases of support in Saskatchewan, British Columbia, Manitoba, Ontario, and most recently in Nova Scotia. It is relatively weak in the rest of the Maritimes and is in a hopeless situation in Quebec. On occasion the NDP has attempted to ally with the Parti Québécois, out of some professed left-wing principles on behalf of the French-Canadian nationalists, but such a marriage has proved impossible due to the very different objectives of the two groups.

Financing

Of all the major Canadian parties the NDP receives the greatest proportion of its finances from individual contributions. Labor unions and small businesses are also crucial sources of income. In recent years the poor showing of the party at the national level led to incurred debts emerging from the federal campaign of 1993 and the national headquarters being put up for sale.

Leadership

Leadership has traditionally been one of the NDP's strong points. From Tommy Douglas to Ed Broadbent the party has been able to produce leaders that have been more popular across the country than the party. On several occasions the NDP leader has been the most popular among all the leadership candidates. But this strength has turned into a weakness since the retirement of Ed Broadbent in 1989. A leadership vacuum developed that was filled by Audrey McLaughlin (the first female leader of a major Canadian party). McLaughlin proved unsatisfactory, and after losing official party status by gaining fewer than 12 seats in the 1993 federal election, she resigned in 1994. The leadership problem remained and was left unsettled for several years while the party attempted to reposition itself on divisive matters of ideology and policy. It then selected Alexa McDonough from Halifax, Nova Scotia. While this choice has strengthened party fortunes to an extent, the leadership problem remains. The NDP has no leadership review procedure, but the leader must seek reelection at the party's biennial national convention.

Prospects

At present the NDP is plagued by crucial problems: a general weakness in the Left; the destructive legacy of Bob Rae's provincial NDP government in Ontario; the failure to gain recognition as a national party; and the consequent erosion of the traditional party strongholds in the West by the Reform Party. The NDP was able to rebound from the 1993 fiasco in the 1997 contest, but with such a poor prior showing, improvements were inevitable.

The selection of Alexa McDonough from Halifax as leader of the NDP is another obvious attempt to break the regional party label and gain national recognition. This has long been the problem and struggle for the party. McDonough's victory in the Halifax riding, along with the good party showing in Nova Scotia and New Brunswick in the 1997 federal election, would seem to indicate that these attempts are meeting success. The question is whether the breakthroughs will be long-term. In its efforts to become a more "national" party the NDP has lost much of its appeal as a regional protest movement, and this ground has been quickly occupied by the Reform Party. If the recent upsurge in Maritime support proves to be fleeting, the NDP may find itself out in the cold.

REGIONAL POLITICAL PARTIES

The pronounced regional characteristics of Canada along with a relatively strong radical tradition have allowed alternative parties to play an important role in the nation's political history. While many have come and gone, the tradition is strong and shows no signs of diminishing.

The Elections Act provides that political parties may have their names officially recorded if they are able to nominate 50 candidates throughout the nation.

Parti Québecois (PQ)

The Parti Québécois is the provincial arm of the French-Canadian nationalist movement. It achieved power first in Quebec in 1976, eight years after is creation, on a separatist platform under its flamboyant leader, René Lévesque. Aside from vying for sovereignty association for an independent Quebec, the party stands committed to ensuring that power in the province is vested in the hands of the Québécois. The PQ government made history in 1980 by holding a provincial referendum on whether the Quebec government could commence negotiations with the federal government on the issue of sovereignty.

The party lost the referendum and the PQ was defeated in 1985 but won office again in 1994 under Jacques Parizeau. Following on the heels of failed attempts by the Mulroney government to form a constitutional deal with Quebec, the new PQ government led the province into another referendum in 1995. This time the growing breach between French and English Canada over the constitutional question was glaring and the "oui" forces were defeated by the narrowest of margins. Parizeau resigned as PQ leader and Quebec premier soon after to be replaced by the popular leader of the federal Bloc Québécois, Lucien Bouchard. Despite the near victory in the referendum, Bouchard must deal with a separatist movement that is again losing steam and energy. He is promising a provincial election to receive another mandate to have another referendum.

Bloc Québecois (BQ)

The Bloc Québécois is the federal wing of the separatist movement in Quebec. It is rather ironic to refer to the party as a federal wing since its mandate is to break apart the federation. However, the bloc was formed in 1990 to provide the separatists representation in the House of Commons. Its first leader, Lucien Bouchard, was a Progressive Conservative Cabinet minister in the government of Brian Mulroney. Bouchard broke from his party over the Meech Lake Constitutional Accord. The bloc contested each of the 75 Quebec seats in the federal election of 1993 and won an impressive 54 constituencies. For decades the Liberal Party had framed its policies to prevent Quebec's falling into the hands of the French-Canadian nationalists. Now, it was a reality.

Due to the impressive Liberal majority and the collapse of the Progressive Conservatives and the NDP, the bloc held the second-largest number of seats and became the opposition. The party worked closely with the PQ government in Quebec, particularly when the Charlottetown Accord was defeated in a national referendum, thereby paving the path toward another Quebec referendum on sovereignty association. Even though it was a provincial referendum, Bouchard was the recognized leader of the "oui" forces. Soon after the referendum Jacques Parizeau resigned as premier and leader of the PQ to be replaced by Bouchard. Gilles Duceppe became the leader of the bloc. In the 1997 election Duceppe and the bloc ran a poor campaign and the party won 44 seats.

Reform Party

It is questionable, considering the recent influence of the Reform Party, whether it should be placed under the heading of regional parties, but it will not shake this label until it succeeds where other western movements have failed and becomes a truly national party or endures long enough to gain the status of a major party. The Reform Party appeared late in 1987 out of the strong Alberta tradition of western alienation and populist protest. At its founding convention the federal party chose as leader Preston Manning, the son of the former Social Credit premier of Alberta, Ernest Manning.

Reform is a party that bases its appeal on the corruption and inefficiency of the main parties; reducing the deficit through responsible spending and the cutting of government waste; reducing government's role in society; reducing taxes; providing incentives to business; reforming the Senate; reducing the power of the House of Commons with devices such as referendum, recall, and initiative; and strong-arm negotiations with Quebec. It claims to be populist, but the neoconservative bent of the party is unmistakable. Reform has been successful in gaining support in western Ontario and to a lesser extent in the Maritimes, but it is still clearly a party based on western alienation.

In the 1988 federal election the party nominated 72 candidates but failed to win a single seat. In the 1993 contest it fielded 207 candidates (but none in Quebec) and elected 51 members (mainly in British Columbia and Alberta). This dramatic breakthrough reflected a backlash against Prime Minister Brian Mulroney and the Progressive Conservative Party but also demonstrated the depth of the electorate's frustration, particularly in western Canada, toward Quebec and central Canada's obsession with "constitutional wrangling." The 1997 campaign pitted Reform against the Progressive Conservatives in a battle to win the right-wing vote. Reform won 60 seats (all in the West) and became the official opposition.

MINOR POLITICAL PARTIES

Canada has several other minor parties that usually place candidates in federal elections. Examples of these small movements that rarely win any seats are the Libertarian Party of Canada, the Marxist-Leninist Party of Canada, the Communist Party of Canada, the Rhinoceros Party (which spoofs the Canadian political tradition), and the environmental Green Party of Canada. In the 1993 fed-

eral election 14 groups ran the required 50 candidates to be officially recognized as a political party.

OTHER POLITICAL FORCES

Aside from the actual parties placing candidates in the field, there are other forces that influence Canadian political life and culture such as environmental, religious, ethnic, women's and agricultural interest groups. In a parliamentary democracy such as Canada, however, with a capitalist economy tempered by a welfare state, the two major forces are the corporate elite and organized labor.

The corporate elite wields considerable political influence through campaign contributions and interlocking corporate directorates that include many prominent former Canadian politicians. The parties and government are well aware that it is in their interest to keep the corporations content.

The largest business association in Canada is the Canadian Chamber of Commerce. There are other large organizations that aim at influencing government policy in such fields as corporate regulation and taxation and freer trade such as the Canadian Manufacturers Association and the Business Council on National Issues. There are various associations attached to particular sectors such as the Canadian Industries Association, the Canadian Nuclear Association, and the Automobile Industries Associations, while the financial interests are represented by such groups as the Canadian Life and Health Insurance Association, the Canadian Bankers' Association, and the Canadian Federation of Independent Business. The Canadian Business and Industry International Advisory Committee is the group that is most significant in influencing government foreign policy.

The Canadian labor movement has long been a force on the political scene. On numerous occasions labor candidates have run in elections. In general, however, the labor movement has maintained a close relationship with the left-wing NDP. In 1961 the Canadian Labor Congress (CLC) was instrumental in the change in party label from the CCF to the NDP. The NDP has had difficulty in central and eastern Canada and this has caused difficulties for national labor support. Recent divisions in the labor movement along with the extreme unpopularity of Bob Rae's provincial NDP government in Ontario have eroded the connection between labor and the NDP and overall effectiveness of labor as a political ally. The CLC usually provides money, volunteer workers, and organizing skills to the New Democrats.

NATIONAL PROSPECTS

Assuredly the dominant issue facing the Canadian polity is the very existence of the federation itself. While the tension has subsided somewhat since the extremely close referendum results on October 30, 1995, Quebec separation remains a very real possibility. At no time since Canada became a nation in 1867 has its breakup been so likely. Instability over this issue will continue despite the narrow victory of the "non" side because the PQ government in Quebec contends that it can hold a referendum every time the provincial government wins a new mandate from the electorate. It is likely that the PQ under Lucien Bouchard will call a referendum after he receives a mandate in an election. The election will be held in 1998 and the referendum probably in 1999 or 2000.

Federal forces hope that time will diminish support for separation, and to an extent this sentiment is being vindicated. Aside from a decrease in separatist support in the polls, the BQ lost its status as opposition to Reform in the 1997 federal election. Both the PQ and BQ leaders have also suffered a decline in their popularity. Questions as to the validity of continuing referendums, as to whether Quebec itself is divisible, as to how the native peoples will be handled, and to the very legality of separation are now being put to the Canadian courts. Yet, regardless of any decline in support for separation, the breach between French and English Canada remains glaring.

The Liberal Party again dominates the federal political scene and this is unlikely to change any time soon. The cautious Liberals under Jean Chrétien are staying away from the volatile constitutional question, even though they will eventually have to face the issue of making a deal with Quebec. Instead, the government is focusing on economic issues and this is popular with most Canadians after at least a decade of recession. In 1996–97 the federal government raised about $135 billion, leaving a federal deficit of approximately $24 billion. The national debt was estimated to be about $603 billion by the end of 1997. Canada's gross domestic product (GDP) was calculated at $806 billion, and the debt was equal to 75% of the GDP. This ranks the nation second-last among the G-7 countries in regard to its total net debt. The Liberals, however, are fortunate to be dealing with a situation where the deficit is almost "under control," meaning revenues are almost equaling spending. Such "control" will allow surpluses to begin going against the debt. This will allow the government to increase spending and reduce taxes.

Perhaps the greatest asset the Liberals possess, as they have through much of Canadian history, is the divisiveness and weakness of the other parties. The Progressive Conservatives are still recovering from the Mulroney years and the fact that they always seem to govern the nation during difficult economic times, thereby incurring inevitable unpopularity. But time heals all wounds and the electorate is often quick to forget. The PCs had a popular leader in Jean Charest and probably would have continued to rebound as they did in the 1997 election. This has all been lost with Charest's move to the leadership of the provincial Liberal party in Quebec.

The existence of Reform is the greatest bane to Progressive Conservative support, and it seems likely that there is only room for one right-wing party in Canada. The question revolves around whether Reform will be able to break its regional label and take the PC position in central and eastern Canada. In this sense the 1997 contest, and the fundamental battle for the many ridings in rural Ontario, was crucial and the very survival and recovery of the Progressive Conservatives are a bad sign for Reform.

The New Democrats are in serious trouble. Under Ed Broadbent in the 1970s and 1980s the party was making gains in Ontario and was a constant threat to force a minority government on either of the other main parties. If the party today had anything like the support it enjoyed during the Broadbent years, it would finally be the official opposition. Instead the NDP has been fraught with splits over ideology, policy, leadership, and overall direction. It has tried to move away from its regional base, but the gains in other areas, such as Nova Scotia, are unlikely to be long-lasting. The party now faces the reality of also losing its regional base to Reform. Changes in party leadership to Audrey McLaughlin and then Alexa McDonough have not been beneficial. Unless the party either returns to its roots or finds a new base, its tenuous position will continue.

A serious issue that all the parties must face is the general populace's growing cynicism toward the political system and process. Only 67% of eligible voters cast their ballots in the 1997 general election—the lowest turnout in over 75 years. While this sentiment has existed in Canada for decades, it has increased from a sense of skepticism to a much deeper sense of cynicism. Studies done since the 1970s have demonstrated this fact, and a 1992 survey concluded that "Canadian political discontent is at its highest since polling began." Respect for political parties dropped from 30% in 1979 to only 9% in 1992. A study in 1991 indicated that 49% of Canadians did not trust the federal government and 52% believed that those running the government were "crooked." All studies seem to demonstrate a lack of confidence in the nation's leadership.

Further Reading

Bakvis, Herman. *Regional Ministers: Power and Influence in the Canadian Cabinet.* Toronto: University of Toronto Press, 1991.

Blair, R.S., and J.T. McLeod, eds. *The Canadian Political Tradition.* Scarborough: Nelson, 1993.

Brooks, Stephen, and Andrew Strich, *Business and Government in Canada.* Scarborough: Prentice Hall Canada, 1991.

Cairns, Alan C. *Charter versus Federalism: The Dilemmas of Constitutional Reform.* Montreal: McGill–Queen's University Press, 1992.

———. *Constitution, Government and Society in Canada.* Toronto: McClelland & Stewart, 1988.

Campbell, Colin, and W. Christian. *Parties, Leaders and Ideologies in Canada.* Toronto: McGraw-Hill, 1996.

Campbell, Colin, and G. Szablowski. *The Superbureaucrats: Structure and Behavior in Central Agencies.* Toronto: Macmillan, 1979.

Chandler, M.A., and W.M. Chandler. *Public Policy and Provincial Politics.* Toronto: McGraw-Hill Ryerson, 1979.

Courchene, Thomas J. *In Praise of Renewed Federalism.* Toronto: C.D. Howe Institute, 1991.

Gibbins, Roger. *Conflict and Unity: An Introduction to Canadian Political Life.* Scarborough: Nelson, 1994.

Jackson, Robert, and Doreen Jackson. *Politics in Canada.* Scarborough: Prentice Hall, 1991.

Knopf, Rainer. *Charter Politics.* Scarborough: Nelson, 1992.

Landis, Ronald G. *The Canadian Polity.* Scarborough: Prentice Hall, 1991.

Rocher, Francois, and Miriam Smith, eds. *New Trends in Canadian Federalism.* Peterborough: Broadview Press, 1994.

Russell, Peter H. *Constitutional Odyssey.* Toronto: University of Toronto Press, 1991.

Smiley, D.V. *The Federal Condition in Canada.* Toronto: McGraw-Hill Ryerson, 1987.

Thorburn, Hugh G., ed. *Party Politics in Canada.* Scarborough: Prentice Hall, 1991.

REPUBLIC OF CAPE VERDE

(República de Cabo Verde)

By Walter Hawthorne

THE SYSTEM OF GOVERNMENT

With a population estimated in 1994 at 449,066 (many emigrants reside abroad), this chain of 10 large and several small islands is situated some 720 kilometers west of Senegal. Cape Verde was discovered by the Portuguese in 1456 and was colonized by them shortly thereafter. It became home to a large African population during the time of the Atlantic slave trade. Portugal administered the islands until 1975, when Cape Verdeans claimed independence.

Cape Verde is a democratic republic. From independence to 1991, the country was ruled by a single party, the African Party for the Independence of Cape Verde (PAICV). In 1991, after constitutional changes and the staging of the country's first multiparty elections, the PAICV lost its hold on power. The Movement for Democracy (MpD) claimed a majority of the seats in the National Assembly, and the MpD's Carlos Veiga became prime minister. With this election, Cape Verde became the first previously single-party state in sub-Saharan Africa to stage multiparty democratic elections. The MpD maintained its dominance of the Assembly in December 1995, when a new round of multiparty elections was held.

Executive

Elected to a five-year term, the president of Cape Verde is head of state. The prime minister is the head of government. The prime minister, who is nominated by the National Assembly, is appointed by the president. The prime minister appoints members of the National Assembly to the Cabinet, or Council of Ministers. In the country's first multiparty elections, António Monteiro, an independent, was elected president. He soundly defeated Aristides Pereira, a leading member of the PAICV and Cape Verde's president since independence. Monteiro was re-elected in 1996.

Legislature

Consisting of the National Assembly, Cape Verde's legislative branch is unicameral. Each of the islands, some of which constitute single electoral districts and some of which are divided into several districts, sends deputies to the Assembly. Further, diaspora residents in Africa, America, and Europe send six deputies, two from each region. Deputies are elected to five-year terms. In the 1991 elections, the MpD won a resounding victory in the Assembly, taking 56 of the 79 seats. The PAICV won the remaining 23 seats. In the 1996 elections, the MpD won 51 of what had become a 72-seat Assembly. The PAICV won 20 seats, and the Party for the Democratic Convergence (PCD) won 1 seat.

Judiciary

Cape Verde's constitution defines the general principles of judicial power. The Supreme Court of Justice is the highest organ of the court system. It is constituted by a minimum of five judges, one appointed by the president of the republic, one elected by the National Assembly, and the remainder appointed by the Supreme Council of Magistrates, a body consisting of the chief justice, judges elected by their peers, and citizens. Judges on the Supreme Court of Justice serve five-year terms. The plenum of the Supreme Court of Justice has the power to decide if one of its judges should be dismissed as a result of a disciplinary matter.

Regional and Local Government

Cape Verde is divided into 16 municipalities. The registered electors of these municipalities elect a mayor and a council to administer local-level public affairs. The MpD captured eight of the mayoral positions in 1996. However, smaller splinter parties with local bases made a strong showing.

THE ELECTORIAL SYSTEM

Elections for both the presidency and National Assembly are held every five years. Through universal and secret balloting, citizens who have registered in the electoral census elect the president of the republic. Should no one receive an absolute majority of the votes, the two leading candidates participate in a runoff election. Cape Verde's 16 domestic and 3 overseas electoral districts send deputies to the National Assembly. The number of deputies that districts send to the Assembly is proportionate to the number of registered electors in each district.

AFRICAN PARTY FOR THE INDEPENDENCE OF CAPE VERDE
(Partido Africano da Independência da Cabo Verde; PAICV)

The successor to the Cape Verdean wing of the African Party for the Independence of Guinea and Cape Verde (*Partido Africano da Independência da Guiné e Cabo Verde*, PAIGC), the PAICV was founded in January 1981. The PAIGC was created in 1956 to lead the people of Cape Verde and Guinea-Bissau in a struggle for independence from Portugal. In Guinea-Bissau, this struggle took the form of a protracted guerrilla war. In Cape Verde, the PAIGC concerned itself with organizing an extensive underground political network that attempted to increase local resistance to the colonial regime. After a coup brought down Portugal's government in April 1974, Portugal began to move toward relinquishing its grip on Guinea-Bissau and Cape Verde. The Portuguese government recognized Guinea-Bissau's independence in September but stalled on the question of independence for Cape Verde. Amid PAIGC-organized strikes and protests, Portugal finally agreed to United Nations–supervised elections for Cape Verde's National Assembly. With 92% of the vote, the PAIGC won that election, and under the PAIGC Cape Verde became an independent nation on July 5, 1975.

Since its founding, the PAIGC had been a binational party with the stated goal of unifying Guinea-Bissau and Cape Verde. However, after a November 1980 coup in Guinea-Bissau raised tensions between the Guinean and Cape Verdean wings of the party, the PAIGC split and plans for a united country were discarded. In January 1981, the Cape Verdean wing of the PAIGC held a congress and changed its name to the PAICV.

Socialist in orientation at its founding, the PAICV created large state-owned and operated enterprises. Internationally, the party pursued a policy of nonalignment. Hoping to increase foreign investment and boost exports, the PAICV began to move toward the gradual liberalization of Cape Verde's economy in 1988. It also began a three-year process of preparing for multiparty elections. Most observers credit the PAICV with ensuring the fairness of those elections and with peacefully stepping aside when defeated by the MpD.

THE MOVEMENT FOR DEMOCRACY
(Movimento para Democracia; MpD)

The MpD was founded and is led by Carlos Veiga, the current prime minister of Cape Verde. Having earned a law degree in Lisbon, Veiga worked as a public prosecutor in Cape Verde before becoming the attorney general of the republic under the PAICV in 1980. Pressing for the party to allow for a more open democratic system, Veiga resigned his post in 1982. From 1985 to 1990, he served on the Special Commission on Constitutional and Judicial Issues of the People's National Assembly. On the commission, he played a key role in moving the country toward a more open electoral system. During this period, a small group of PAICV members began to voice their desires for broader participation in government. Assuming that their movement would be small, the party's leadership revised the national constitution to allow for multiparty elections and permitted the formation of the MpD. Veiga became its candidate for prime minister. With support from the Catholic Church, which opposed the PAICV's stance on abortion, Veiga and the MpD won a shocking election upset in January 1991. In the 1995 elections, their broad-based anti-PAICV coalition proved to be relatively stable.

Under Veiga, the MpD has has moved toward a much faster liberalization of the economy than the PAICV had attempted. Between 1991 and 1996, 13 of 44 state enterprises were privatized, 6 were closed, 11 were restructured, and the rest were in the process of being privatized. With World Bank funds, the MpD-led government has also begun to reform the civil service.

NATIONAL PROSPECTS

In the last decade, Cape Verde has revised its constitution, held two peaceful multiparty elections, and witnessed a smooth transition from PAICV to MpD leadership in the National Assembly. Moving rapidly toward the liberalization of the economy, the MpD has managed to hold together its base of support while allowing for increased debate within the nation's political sphere. Cape Verde does face the problem of severe and recurring droughts and does not have a large endowment of natural resources. However, in recent years, the tourist sector of Cape Verde's economy has grown, as has investment from nationals living abroad. Only time will tell if its plunge into the free market will pay dividends, but, if the last decade is any indication, the prospects are good for the long-term stability of Cape Verde's political system and growth of its economy.

Further Reading
Lobban, Richard. *Cape Verde: Crioule Colony to Independent Nation.* Boulder, Colo.: Westview Press, 1995.
Lobban, Richard, and Marlene Lopes. *Historical Dictionary of the Republic of Cape Verde.* Metuchen, N.J.: The Scarecrow Press, 1995.

CENTRAL AFRICAN REPUBLIC

(République Centrafricaine)

By Thomas O'Toole, D.A.

THE SYSTEM OF GOVERNMENT

The Central African Republic (CAR) is a landlocked, well-watered plateau country of more than 3 million people located in the heart of Africa. Ruled from 1981 by a military regime under General André Dieudonné Kolingba, the CAR made a peaceful transition to a democratically elected government in 1993. The unitary state government combines features of the presidential and parliamentary systems. The current government was formed on October 22, 1993, when Ange-Félix Patassé, the winner of the September 19, 1993, runoff election, was sworn in as president. This is the most democratically chosen government, at least in theory, that the country has had since independence from France in 1960.

The September 1993 election was relatively open and probably represents the will of the voting electorate. The National Assembly convened on November 8 and elected Hughes Dodozendi of President Patassé's Movement for the Liberation of the Central African People (MLPC) as president of the executive bureau.

Executive

The president of the republic is the chief of state, elected by popular vote for a six-year term in a two-round election. The president appoints and dismisses the ministers. Most of the formal business of the executive is transacted in the Council of Ministers. Chaired by the president, the Council of Ministers is composed of the prime minister and other senior members of the government. This body initiates laws.

Legislature

Members of the National Assembly (*Assemblée Nationale*) are elected by universal suffrage for five-year terms. Its members decide on questions submitted to them by an executive committee of the National Assembly, by the president, or by one-third of the deputies. The National Assembly is called by the president of the republic in two regular sessions per year of 60 days each at the most. The executive committee of the National Assembly selects a president of the Assembly to be invested in office by the president of the republic. The final arbiter on constitutional issues is the constitutional court, whose members serve a single nine-year term.

The MLPC won the National Assembly election held in the fall of 1998 with 47 seats to the runner-up Central African Democratic Assembly's 20.

Judiciary

The judiciary consists of regular and military courts, with a presidentially appointed Supreme Court at the apex. In criminal cases, trials are public. The accused have the right to legal counsel, and defendants have the right to be present at their trials. The present constitution has a ban on torture and gives prisoners the right to medical examinations. These safeguards are generally respected in practice, but the judiciary has suffered numerous shortcomings, including executive interference, institutional neglect, inefficient administration of the law, and shortages of trained personnel and material resources. A High Court of Justice created to try political cases has never convened and can be considered defunct.

Regional and Local Government

The Central African Republic is theoretically divided into 16 provinces, all under the direct control of the central government. The provinces are divided into subprovinces and numerous rural communes. Details of regional and local structure are rather vague.

THE ELECTORAL SYSTEM

Direct universal suffrage is mandated for all national and local elections. Both president and parliament are elected in two-round elections. Candidates with more than 50% of the vote are elected in the first round.

THE PARTY SYSTEM

The organization of parties in the period leading up to the September 1993 elections represented rather ephemeral bodies linked to specific leaders. None had strong nationwide appeal and most based their strength on ethnic groups and regions or on various urban groups. Most party activity that took place was limited to Bangui and vicinity and a few larger regional centers. In the year before the elections the Combined Democratic Forces (*Concertation des Forces Démocratique*; CFD), a united front, showed some promise but ultimately could not hold together. Currently 20 to 25 political parties are registered in the country, but only 12 hold seats in the parliament.

CENTRAL AFRICAN PEOPLE'S LIBERATION MOVEMENT
(Mouvement de Libération du Peuple Centrafricain; MLPC)

This is the party of President Patassé and holds 47 seats out of 109 in the National Assembly. It was originally organized by Patassé in Paris in mid-1979. In July 1986 a communiqué released in Paris announced that the MLPC had joined forces with Goumba's party (see Patriotic Front for Progress, below) to present a united front against the Kolingba government. The party was granted legal status in September 1991 and successfully organized among the Sara ethnic groups in the northwest and disaffected elements in the capital.

CENTRAL AFRICAN DEMOCRATIC ASSEMBLY
(Rassemblement Démocratique Centrafricain; RDC)

This is the party of the former head of state André Kolingba. It was launched in May 1986 as the country's sole legal party. At an extraordinary party congress on August 17, 1991, one month after official endorsement of multipartism, then President Kolingba resigned as party president saying he wanted to operate "above politics." The party supported his bid for president in 1993 and holds 20 seats in the National Assembly.

MINOR POLITICAL PARTIES

Liberal Democratic Party
(Parti Libéral Démocratique; PLD)

Headed by Nestor Kombot Naguemon, this party holds two seats and is scarcely a major force in the nation.

Patriotic Front for Progress
(Front Patriotique pour le Progrès; FPP)

This is Dr. Abel Goumba's party. Originally founded in 1981 in opposition to the Dacko government, the Ubangi Patriotic Front–Labor Party (*Front Patriotique Ouban-guien–Parti Travailliste*; FPO–PT) had ties to the French Socialist Party. Sometimes in coalition with the MLPC, this party was a major force in the move to a multiparty system. Often jailed for his activities, Goumba has been the most consistent nationalist and democratic voice in the troubled waters of Central African politics. This party holds seven seats in the National Assembly.

Alliance for Democracy and Progress
(Alliance pour la Démocratie et le Progrès; ADP)

Headed by François Pehoua, who is a former director of the Central African States Bank (*Banque des Etats de l'Afrique Centrale*; BEAC), this party dates to about 1979. With the assistance of Didier Wangue the party gained six seats in the National Assembly in 1993, and it now has five.

Movement for Democracy and Development
(Mouvement pour la Démocratie et le Développement; MDD)

This party, formed in January 1994, holds eight seats and is headed by the former president David Dacko.

Democratic Socialist Party
(Parti Socialist Démocratique; PSD)

The former prime minister Enoch Derant-Lakoue leads this party, which holds six seats.

National Convention
(Convention Nationale; CN)

This is a regionally based party of members of the Banda ethnic group from Grimari and Bambari.

Civic Forum
(Forum Civique; FC)

Holding one seat, this party is led by Timothée Malendoma, who served as minister of national economy in Bokassa's government, minister of state in Dacko's second government, and prime minister in the interim government that closed out Kolingba's rule.

Central African Republican Party
(Parti Républicain Centrafricain; PRC)

Ruth Rolland, the republic's first female party leader, served as minister of social and woman's affairs in Kolingba's government but denounced Kolingba for misappropriation of funds and "tribalism" in 1991.

Movement for Democracy, Renaissance and Evolution in Central Africa
(Mouvement pour la Démocratie, la Renaissance et l'Evolution en Centrafrique; MDREC)

This party is led by Joseph Bendounga.

Movement of Social Evolution in Black Africa
(Mouvement de l'Evolution Sociale en Afrique Noire; MESAN)

This party uses the name of the party founded in 1949 by Barthélemy Boganda, the leader of the country's first political movement.

OTHER POLITICAL FORCES

France

France has at least 1,200 troops stationed in the Central African Republic. These troops provided vital support for the 1993 elections, transporting ballot boxes and monitoring the situation even in remote areas. During the election period French military jets made repeated passes along the Ubangi River, which separates Bangui from Zaire, to dissuade any intervention by troops from neighboring Zaire. A defense pact between the two states permits French intervention in times of "invasion" or outbreaks of "anarchy." French troops intervened on behalf of President Patassé in the late spring of 1996 to quell a military revolt that was followed by widespread urban disorder. Military riots over pay persisted into 1997.

International Monetary Fund (IMF) and World Bank

The nation is virtually bankrupt and depends on subsidies from France to pay government salaries. Consequently, whoever is in power must follow World Bank structural adjustment requirements. In the mid-1980s the government was pressured to follow a structural adjustment program (SAP) supported by the IMF, France, and the World Bank. This SAP strongly encouraged the private sector, supported raising farm productivity, recommended slimming the administration and parastatal organizations, and sought strengthened public finance. However, progress in meeting IMF financial targets fell short because commodity prices for CAR's exports fell, government expenditures were inadequately controlled, state employees resisted job cuts, and social unrest continued. French and World Bank funding continues to support a drifting political economic structure.

NATIONAL PROSPECTS

The stability of any government in the Central African Republic is very uncertain. The economy is in shambles, and even if dreams of a generation of Central African leaders were to come true and uranium, oil, and other minerals were to become important exports within the next few years, severe problems would remain. Corruption, mismanagement, poor health, insufficient food supplies, transportation problems, and a general malaise are so pervasive that the people of this poor landlocked country seem unable to generate self-sustained development. Massive unemployment, a declining rural economy, and generations of instability have created conditions that work against political stability. Even though an elected civilian government has now replaced the military regimes that long dominated the nation's political history, both the army and the urban underclass represent a potential threat to continued stability. There is little likelihood that Patassé can find ways to create sufficient employment and upward mobility to satisfy the distressed urban population's ever-growing demands. Army revolts are a constant threat and are only held in check with French military intervention. Contemplation of the political future of the Central African Republic provides little ground for optimism.

Further Reading

Kalck, Pierre, *Central African Republic*, World Bibliographic Series. vol.152. Oxford: Clio Press, 1993.

———. *Histoire Centrafricaine: Des Origines . . . 1966.* Paris: L'Harmattan, 1993.

———. *Historical Dictionary of the Central African Republic*, 3d ed. Trans. Thomas O'Toole. Metuchen, N.J.: Scarecrow Press, 1994.

O'Toole, Thomas, *The Central African Republic: The Continent's Hidden Heart.* Boulder, Colo.: Westview Press, 1986.

Sy, Ismeila. *Les institutions politique de la République Centrafricaine.* Bangui, Central African Republic: Université de Bangui, 1989.

REPUBLIC OF CHAD

(Republique du Tchad)

By Terry M. Mays, Ph.D.

THE SYSTEM OF GOVERNMENT

Chad has suffered from civil violence and foreign intervention since receiving independence from France on August 11, 1960. The large state consists of 495,800 square miles of territory with an estimated population of approximately 6,495,000. A census has never been conducted in Chad. Officially, Chad is a republic consisting of a president who serves as the head of state, a prime minister fulfilling the duties as a head of government, and a national legislature. In reality, the government is based around whichever faction has managed to gain control of the capital city of N'Djamena and obtain some form of foreign backing, normally from France, to allow it to remain in power. Politics and government in the strife-torn country is based on factional or clan loyalty rather than the ballot box. What appears to be a period of stability is often a lull before another coup.

Political problems in this large Sahelian country stem from colonial attempts at state building. Many diverse groups exist within the artificial borders of Chad as carved out by the French. The Sara (approximately 25% of the total population), largely Christian and animist, live in the southern region of Chad. This area bases its economy on agriculture, and its inhabitants were favored by the French during the colonial period, which lasted from 1900 to 1960. The vast northern region of the country consists of arid and semiarid topography. The people living in the north are predominantly Muslim and are nomadic or seminomadic. The three major groups of people who live in the north are the Toubou (approximately 4% of the total population), the Arabs (approximately 14%), and various "Sahelians" who represent over 13 ethnic groups (approximately 27%). Each is divided into multiple clans. The Sara and their Islamic neighbors distrust each other due to their many differences and the former practice of slave raiding into Sara-populated areas. The population of Chad is classified as being 40% Muslim and 33% Christian, and these religious differences add to the frequent cultural confrontations within Chad. This great diversity of cultures within Chad's borders has stymied all attempts at building a national identity and loyalty to the state. People tend to devote their loyalty to their particular clan or faction at the expense of the state. Thus, Chad has experienced over 35 years of civil disorder, making it one of the poorest countries in the world.

Factional politics in Chad has prevented any one government or power that rules in N'Djamena from exerting effective control over the entire country. An ongoing feature of Chad's political situation, since northerners have risen to dominate the Chadian political system, has been the government's inability to exert total control over the south while constantly fighting new factional opponents in the north or others who are based in Sudanese sanctuaries. Factional politics between clans leads to a "today my friend, tomorrow my enemy" attitude. Clan alliances are fluid as leaders adjust their allegiances to reflect personal benefits.

Chad emerged at independence with French-selected Francois Tombalbaye as president. As Tombalbaye consolidated his power at the expense of other groups, open civil war emerged in the state. A successful coup on April 13, 1975, replaced Tombalbaye with Felix Malloum. Despite the change of government, the civil war within Chad continued between the various factions. A series of conferences brought a loose coalition government to power on March 24, 1979, under Goukhouni Oueddei, who was overthrown by the American-backed Hissein Habre on June 6, 1980. Habre maintained control in Chad until he was overthrown by Idriss Deby on December 2, 1990.

Executive

The president is officially the head of state in Chad. The current president, Colonel Idriss Deby, came to power after ousting fellow northerner Hissein Habre on December 2, 1990. Deby originally held the position of national army commander within Habre's faction. Habre prevented a coup attempt by Deby in April 1989, forcing the latter to escape to Sudan with his supporters. After the successful December 1990 ouster of Habre, Deby appointed himself as president on December 4, 1990. The Sovereign National Council confirmed Deby as president on February 21, 1991, and reconfirmed him on April 6, 1993. A national presidential election held on July 3, 1996, provided Deby with a political victory and a claim to popular support for his regime.

The president of Chad officially serves a 5-year term after being elected and is eligible for reelection once for a maximum of 10 years in the position. Officially, the Parliament has the authority to impeach the president for abuses of his office.

The executive branch of government originally consisted of a Provisional Council of State headed by Deby. The body was dissolved in March 1990 and was replaced by a Council of Ministers and a Provisional Council of the Republic. The government attempted to incorporate members of several new political parties into the Council of Ministers in May 1992. This move can be seen as a continuation of government attempts to ally any potential political opposition with the ruling Patriotic Salvation Movement, the MPS.

The 1996 Chadian constitution retained the Council of Ministers led by a prime minister. Unlike his counterpart in other political systems, the Chadian prime minister functions more as an assistant to the president than the leader of a separate branch of government. Officially, the prime minister serves as the head of government and coordinates the work of the governmental ministries. The prime minister is selected by and serves at the pleasure of the president and can be replaced at any time. The duties of the prime minister include coordination of Chad's economic and social programs. Dr. Fidele Moungar, a southerner, served as Deby's first prime minister. Deby's choice of Moungar illustrated the attempt to incorporate various factions into the government.

Disagreements between Deby and Moungar were followed by the pro-Deby Higher Transitional Council (CST) passing a vote of no confidence against the prime minister and forcing his resignation. Delwa Koumakoye, a member of the National Assembly for Democracy and Progress faction, replaced Moungar on November 6, 1993. Deby forced Koumakoye from office and replaced him with Koibla Djimasta of the Union for Democracy of the Republic faction on April 8, 1995.

Deby's power is based on his ability to maintain factional leadership of the Patriotic Salvation Movement (MPS) and prevent any other group from overthrowing him. Following his sweeping 1996 election victory with 68% of the votes, Deby has been able to officially claim his backing rests with popular support. Another factor that must be considered is Deby's ability to maintain cordial relations with France, which stations over 1,000 soldiers in Chad and has already intervened to prevent a return of Habre to power. Deby also holds the position of military commander in chief.

Legislature

The last true national legislature before the 1996 constitution met in 1971. This body consisted of 105 members elected for five-year terms from single-member districts. Of this total, 54 delegates were elected from the north and 51 from the south, although the latter region held only one-third of the state's population.

Following Deby's assumption of power, the government established what is known as the Sovereign National Council (CNS) in January 1993. The body of pro-government supporters elected a legislature known as the Higher Transitional Council (CST). The CST was a legislature in name only, representing the allies of Deby and not a general electorate of the Chadian people.

The 1996 constitution established a bicameral legislature, known as Parliament, divided into a National Assembly and a Senate. Deputies to the National Assembly serve four-year terms while senators are elected for six-year terms. The Parliament holds sessions in March and October during the year, and each house is led by a President.

Judiciary

Judicial decisions are of a summary nature depending upon which faction controls a certain area. The national judiciary has functioned only sporadically since 1975 and has never been free of political manipulation. The 1996 constitution established a three-layered judicial system.

A Supreme Court sits at the top of the judicial pyramid and consists of three chambers. Sixteen judges, including a president, are assigned to the Supreme Court. Seven of these justices are chosen for their specialties in administrative and budgetary law while the other members must be judges elsewhere in the judicial system. Justices serve for life, unless impeached, and are selected by the president of the republic, the president of the National Assembly, and the president of the Senate. Courts of appeal represent the middle tier of the national judicial system. Local courts and justices of the peace represent the lowest level in the judicial system.

A separate 15-member High Court of Justice was also established by the 1996 Chadian constitution and serves to judge special national cases. Crimes handled at this national-level court include treason against the state, severe violations of human rights, drug trafficking, corruption, and misuse of public funds.

Regional and Local Government

Chad is divided into 14 prefectures, each of which is subdivided into sous-prefectures. Each prefecture is administered by a government-appointed governor. Sous-prefectures are also administered by government appointees. Traditional secular and religious authority figures continue to have some influence in many areas. Towns are governed by government-appointed mayors.

THE ELECTORAL SYSTEM

Deby, facing pressure to legitimize his regime, announced presidential and legislative elections to be held in 1995. Opposition leaders declared that voter registration for the 1995 elections was biased toward MPS supporters. Deby used the criticism as a rationale for postponing the elections and removing Prime Minister Delwa K. Koumakoye. A new timetable called for a presidential election in February 1996. However, the date slipped again to June 1996.

After these delays, Chad held its first presidential election since independence on June 3, 1996. A field of 15 candidates competed in the primary round of the election, resulting in the need for a second round since none of the candidates received over 50% of the vote. The two candidates with the highest percentages of votes selected to compete in the runoff election were Deby with 43% of the vote and Wadal Kamougue with 12%. The July 3, 1996, runoff provided Deby with 68% of the votes cast and an election victory. Voter turnout declined between the June and July elections as many individuals became apathetic with the process and some opposition parties eliminated in the June election boycotted the July vote. Claims of irregularities and the arrest of at least one prominent opposition party member tainted the runoff. In both elections, the government exhibited considerable caution and secrecy as it delayed official announcement of the results for over a week.

THE PARTY SYSTEM

Most Chadian political parties are built around the factional system of the country. The factions derive from the many divisions of traditional society within Chad. As factions form around clans and kinship groups, splinter groups and alliances continually emerge to alter the political scene. Most of the current major political factions were formed after Deby came to power in 1990. Deby granted permission to establish political parties within Chad in October 1991 in response to international pressure. Over 40 political parties currently exist in the Chadian political system.

PATRIOTIC SALVATION MOVEMENT (MPS)

The most important political faction in the country is Deby's Patriotic Salvation Movement, the MPS. Several groups opposed to Hissein Habre formed the MPS in March 1990 with Deby as leader. The MPS alliance included Deby's April 1 Action faction as well as two southern-based groups including the Movement for Chadian National Salvation and the Chadian Armed Forces. The latter organization should not be confused with the national army of Chad. The MPS is officially governed by a national salvation council of 123 members and an executive committee of 13 members.

Political factions and their leaders supporting the MPS include the Union for Democracy and the Republic, founded in March 1992 (Koibla Djimasta and Jean Alingue Bawoyeu), the Movement for Democracy and Socialism in Chad, established in 1988 (Salomon Tombalbaye), the National Alliance for Democracy and Development (Salibour Garba), the Union of Democratic Forces (Ngawara Nahor), and the National Union for Development and Renewal (Saleh Kebzabo).

OTHER POLITICAL FORCES

Minor Political Parties

Political opposition parties and their leaders include the Rally of the Chadian People (Dangbe Laobele Damaye), Movement for Unity and Democracy in Chad (Julien Marabaye), National Assembly for Democracy and Progress (Delwa Kassire Koumakoye), the Collective Parties for Change (Fidele Moungar), and the Rally for Democracy and Progress (Lol Mahamat Choua and Chetti Ali Abbas). Many of these organizations are umbrellas for alliances of smaller political parties.

Rebel opposition factions include the Movement for Development and Democracy, which is a pro-Habre group operating in the Lake Chad region of the country. The organization is led by Mahamat Seid Moussa Medella and Ibrahim Malla Mahamat, while a third important figure, Goukhouni Guet, is jailed in Chad. After initial military success, the replacement of Chadian national forces with French troops helped Deby defeat this faction's attempt to regain governmental control in January 1992. The Chad Liberation Front, led by Alarit Bachar, is another rebel opposition group. Although the organization signed treaties with the government of Deby in 1992 and 1994, many former members refused to abide by the terms of the documents.

The Chad National Liberation Front is a third antigovernment organization. The body is led by a former president and Hissein Habre rival, Goukhouni Oueddei. The group, known as FROLINAT, as been active in Chadian politics and civil strife since 1966. FROLINAT served as the original large umbrella organization for various northern factions in opposition to the southern government installed by France at independence. At one time, even Hissein Habre was a member of FROLINAT.

The National Council for Chadian Recovery represents a fourth rebel movement against the MPS-dominated Chadian government. The organization's president is Hissein Koty, the brother of Abbas Koty, a former minister under Deby charged with plotting a coup against the government. Despite an attempt at reconciliation, government personnel killed Abbas Koty in October 1993, forcing the National Council for Chadian Recovery to renew hostile military operations in southern Chad.

NATIONAL PROSPECTS

Chad is a state in name only. The further one travels from N'Djamena, the less governmental control is present. National authority rests with whichever faction has managed to gain control of N'Djamena and receive international recognition and aid. Although Chad did conduct a presidential election, it is yet to be seen if democracy can really prevail in the country. Irregularities in the process raise many questions as to the legitimacy of the election. President Deby maintains his power through the receipt of French foreign aid and the presence of French soldiers as much as he does from claims of popular support.

The loss of French backing and military assistance could lead to the downfall of the Deby regime. Opposition groups have launched a number of unsuccessful coups against Deby since October 1991. The most serious challenge to Deby occurred with the Movement for Development and Democracy military offensive in late 1991 and late 1992. The timely introduction of French paratroopers allowed Deby to transfer additional Chadian soldiers to halt the rebel offensive. Although the French did not actively participate in combat operations, they assumed security duties throughout the country.

President Deby will continue to be challenged in his efforts to reconcile the multitude of rebel movements as well as political opposition parties and factions. As group leaders are brought into the government in exchange for reconciliation with their factions, splinter groups representing those left out of the government will refuse to honor the agreements and ally with others fighting to gain control of N'Djamena. Many of the factions are led by individuals with strong personalities who exhibit signs of never surrendering their goal of becoming the Chadian national leader. One such individual is Goukhouni Oueddei of the

Chad National Liberation Front and a former president who has been a major player in Chadian politics since independence. Hissein Habre, exiled in Senegal after the collapse of his government, should not be ruled out as a contender. Deby has alienated former members of his government, including Fidele Moungar and Joseph Yodeyman, who lead their own factions.

The Chadian national economy is in shambles and the state is one of the poorest countries in the world. At one point, the most productive nonagricultural industry within the state was the brewing of beer. The government is highly dependent upon foreign aid to survive economically. The one bright spot in the economy is the recent work conducted by Exxon to exploit known oil reserves in the southern region of the country. However, oil income for Chad is still years away. Companies are still conducting tests for oil and mineral reserves in the remote northern regions of Chad. For the near future, economic problems combined with the factional political system almost guarantees a continuation of the instability seen in Chad since 1960.

Further Reading

Bouquet, Christian. *Tchad: Genese d'un conflit.* Paris: Editions L'Harmattan, 1982.

Buijtenhuis, Robert. *Le Frolinat et les revoltes populaires du Tchad, 1965–1976.* Paris: Mouton, 1978.

Chapelle, Jean. *Le peuple tchadien.* Paris: Editions L'Harmattan, 1980.

Decalo, Samuel. *Historical Dictionary of Chad*, 2d ed. Metuchen, N. J.: Scarecrow Press, 1987.

Kelley, Michael P. *A State in Disarray.* Boulder, Colo.: Westview Press, 1986.

Lemarchand, Rene. "Chad: The Misadventures of the North-South Dialectic." *African Studies Review* 29 (September 1986).

———. "The Politics of Sara Ethnicity: A Note on the Origins of the Civil War in Chad." *Cahiers d'Etudes Africaines* 20, no. 4 (1980).

Thompson, Virginia, and Richard Adloff. *Conflict in Chad.* Institute of International Studies. Berkeley: University of California Press, 1981.

Whiteman, Kaye. *Chad.* London: Minority Rights Group, 1988.

REPUBLIC OF CHILE

(República de Chile)

By Jeffrey J. Rinne, M.A.

THE SYSTEM OF GOVERNMENT

The Republic of Chile is a narrow land sandwiched between the towering Andes mountain range and the Pacific Ocean. At its widest point Chile measures only 110 miles; but from its northern border with Peru to the southern tip of South America the country stretches more than 2,600 miles. In area (292,257 square miles) Chile is somewhat larger than France. Chile's population in 1996 was a little over 14 million. The country has a high literacy rate and a relatively large middle class.

From 1973 to 1990 Chile was governed by a brutal military dictatorship headed by General Augusto Pinochet. Chile formerly had enjoyed a long tradition of democratic politics, but the military seized power on September 11, 1973, shut down the legislature, and later banned all political parties and political activity. On October 5, 1988, Chileans were asked in a plebiscite whether then President Pinochet should lead the country for another eight-year term. The victory of the "No" vote (54.7%) marked the start of Chile's transition back to democracy.

Since March 11, 1990, Chile has again been governed by a president and legislature chosen though free elections. However, Chile's current democratic system differs in several important respects from the system that operated prior to 1973. The Pinochet regime wrote a new constitution and decreed additional laws designed to restructure the democratic game. Subsequent elected governments have tried to rescind many of these changes, but as yet most of the changes remain as Pinochet intended.

Chile's democratic tradition originated in the 19th century. After independence from Spain was achieved in 1818, the constitution of 1833 established a presidential system of government with a bicameral legislature. The franchise was highly restricted—limited to literate men of property—and electoral fraud was common, but elections for president and members of the legislature were held regularly. In the 20th century Chilean politics rapidly became more inclusive. The electorate expanded swiftly and political parties worked aggressively to organize these potential voters, first among the urban middle and working classes and later among rural workers. The result was a politically conscious, highly mobilized society.

By the 1940s the Chilean electorate had coalesced around parties of the left, right, and center in nearly equal numbers. Under this arrangement of voter preferences the party (or parties) of the center had substantial leverage because the center could fashion alliances with either the left or right to construct an electoral majority. From the 1920s through the 1950s the Radical Party was the foremost party of the center. On several occasions the Radicals formed an alliance with the worker's parties on the left, but over time the Socialist and Communist Parties grew increasingly dissatisfied with the minimal benefits they gained from this political strategy. In 1956 the parties of the left formed the Popular Action Front (FRAP).

During the late 1950s and 1960s Chilean politics became increasingly divisive. The electorate continued to be almost equally divided into thirds, but the ideological space to craft compromises between the center and left, or center and right, decreased significantly. As the 1964 presidential election approached, the parties of the left, right, and center each prepared to support its own candidate. In March, however, a by-election was held to fill a vacant congressional seat in a traditionally conservative district. Surprisingly, the candidate of the leftist parties won, provoking fear among rightist party leaders that the Socialist presidential candidate, Salvador Allende, might win the upcoming election. To protect against this possible outcome the right decided to endorse the centrist candidate, Eduardo Frei, as the "lesser of two evils."

Frei was leader of the Christian Democratic Party (PDC). During the late 1950s and early 1960s the PDC surged in popularity to replace the Radical Party as the key electoral force of the center. With the support of the right, Frei won the 1964 presidential election with a remarkable (for Chilean politics) 55.6% of the vote. However, the dilemma of the "three thirds" remained. Six years later rightist party leaders were confident of their ability to win the presidency; they were backing a strong candidate, the former president Jorge Alessandri. Thus, in 1970 the left, right, and center each campaigned for a different candidate. The winner of the election was Allende, the perennial candidate of the left, with a slim 36.6% plurality.

It is unlikely that Allende could have won a runoff

election against the second-place finisher, Alessandri. But at that time runoff elections did not exist in Chile. In the event that no candidate received an absolute majority of the popular vote, the Chilean Congress was empowered to choose between the top two finishers. The conservative National Party attempted to block Allende's election in the Congress. However, in the past, many winning presidential candidates had received only a plurality, and always Congress had selected the candidate with the highest number of votes. After first demanding assurances from Allende that he would defend Chile's democratic system, the Christian Democrats, the largest party in the Congress, voted with the Socialist and Communist Parties to elect Allende president.

Once in office Allende attempted what he had always promised: the creation of a socialist economy through democratic means. However, after his first year, the "Chilean Road to Socialism" encountered grave difficulties. Inflation increased sharply and the economy spun out of control. The government also lost *political* control as groups on both the left and the right engaged in an escalating series of protests with increasingly irreconcilable demands. The opposition to Allende pinned its hopes on the 1973 congressional elections, hoping to win the two-thirds majority necessary to overturn Allende's policies. But despite the economic and political chaos in Chile, Allende retained a solid base of popular support. The opposition parties won only 54% of the congressional vote, and the ungovernable stalemate continued.

The possibility of a coup was manifest long before it came. The Allende government made a last-ditch effort at a compromise deal with the Christian Democrats, but there was strong opposition from within both camps. The failure to reach a compromise ended the last possibility of restoring political governability within the boundaries of Chile's democratic system. Soon the crisis reached its tragic conclusion. When the armed forces moved to replace the government, Allende proudly refused to resign; he committed suicide while under attack in the presidential palace.

Many people were surprised to discover that the military junta did not seize power simply to "clean house" and oversee the installation of a new civilian government. The leaders of the coup were determined to effect a rigorous transformation of the Chilean polity and economy. This project began with the violent persecution of leftist party organizations and their members. Chile's Marxist parties were immediately outlawed. Thousands of the regimes opponents were tortured and killed; many were "disappeared." On December 17, 1974, the junta declared Pinochet president of the republic, personalizing the dictatorship and demonstrating clearly that the military intended to remain in power for a long time to come. In 1977, Chile's remaining political parties were banned.

In 1980 the Pinochet regime promulgated a new constitution for the republic. Its "transitory dispositions" en-

sured that Pinochet would remain president until at least 1989, but the new constitution also created a timetable for a possible return to democracy. The 1980 constitution mandated that a plebiscite be held in 1988 to approve (or reject) a candidate chosen by the military to serve as president for another eight-year term. Following the plebiscite, congressional elections would be held—and if a majority of Chileans voted "No" in the plebiscite, elections for president would be held, as well.

To legitimate the new constitution a national referendum was held on September 11, 1980. During the weeks leading up to the referendum the government unleashed a heavy propaganda campaign in support of the new constitution; however, the regime's opponents were permitted little opportunity to campaign against it. The result of the voting was 67% in favor and 30% opposed. The new constitution took effect on March 11, 1981.

In 1988 Pinochet was predictably the choice of the commanders of the armed forces to serve another eight-year term as president. In preparation for the plebiscite the Pinochet regime opened new electoral registries in February 1987 and the following month passed a law allowing non-Marxist political parties to register. This placed the regime's opponents in a difficult position. They were reluctant to legitimate the existing political system by participating in the plebiscite; and yet competing under the rules established by the Pinochet regime was the only strategy available that might restore democratic rule in Chile. Most opposition leaders eventually decided to take part in the plebiscite. Since Marxist parties were still prohibited, the moderate Socialists formed the Party for Democracy (PPD) as a catchall party for those on the left who wished to register and vote in the plebiscite. By August 1988, 9 out of every 10 eligible voters were registered.

The yes-or-no structure of the plebiscite brought the center and left together around a common point of agreement: "No" to Pinochet and his regime. In February 1988 seventeen parties joined forces in the Command for the No. Led by the Christian Democrats and the moderate Socialists, the alliance of parties for the "No" waged a sophisticated and highly effective campaign. Pinochet and his supporters argued that a "No" victory would provoke a return to the chaos of the Allende period, but the "No" campaign skillfully allayed those fears, convincing a majority of Chileans to reject Pinochet.

Following his defeat in the plebiscite Pinochet agreed to observe the timetable established in the 1980 constitution and scheduled congressional and presidential elections for December 1989. In the interim, the government and opposition (with the participation of a new conservative party, National Renovation) negotiated changes in some of the most undemocratic provisions of the 1980 constitution. The two sides eventually reached an agreement on a package of 54 amendments, including an increase in the number of elected senators, elimination of the ban on Marxist parties, expanded participation by civilians on the National Security Council, and an amendment simplifying the process for amending the constitution in the future. The package of amendments was approved in a national referendum on July 30, 1989.

Following their success in the 1988 plebiscite, the parties of the "No" campaign resolved to maintain their alliance for the democratic elections a year later. Renamed the Coalition of Parties for Democracy, the alliance presented a single slate of candidates for the congress and a single candidate for the presidency. The Christian Democrats were the largest party in the Coalition and were therefore entitled to select the presidential candidate. They chose Patricio Aylwin, and in December 1989 Aylwin was elected president with 55.2% of the vote, almost the same percentage as the "No" vote the year before. The Coalition also won 72 of the 120 seats in the Chamber of Deputies and 22 of the 38 Senate seats for which there were elections.

Results of Presidential Elections 1958–1993

1958	
J. Alessandri (Right: Independent)	31.2%
Salvador Allende (Left: FRAP)	28.5%
Eduardo Frei (Center: PDC)	20.5%
Luís Bossay (Center: Radical Party)	15.4%
1964	
Eduardo Frei (Center: PDC)	55.6%
Salvador Allende (Left: FRAP)	36.6%
Julio Durán (Center: Radical Party)	4.9%
1970	
Salvador Allende (Left: FRAP)	36.6%
J. Alessandri (Right: Independent)	34.9%
R. Tomic (Center: PDC)	27.9%
1989	
Patricio Aylwin (Center-Left: Coalition)	55.2%
Hernán Büchi (Right: Democracy & Progress)	24.4%
F.J. Errázuriz (Independent)	15.4%
1993	
Eduardo Frei (Center-Left: Coalition)	58.0%
Arturo Alessandri (Right: Democracy & Progress)	24.4%

The relationship between the Aylwin government and the armed forces was often tense. Pinochet stayed on as commander in chief of the army, refusing all requests that he step down. On December 19, 1990, Pinochet declared a state of alert. All military personnel throughout the country dispersed in battle gear to await further instruc-

tions. They were later ordered back to the barracks, but the message of this "readiness drill" was clear: Pinochet retained the power to limit the actions of the newly elected government.

Despite threats from the military, the human rights record of the Pinochet regime could not be ignored by the new government. In April 1990 the government created the Commission on Truth and Reconciliation to investigate and document human rights abuses committed during the dictatorship. The Commission's report, issued one year later, documented the death or disappearance of 2,279 Chileans at the hands of the military's security forces. Aylwin offered apologies and condolences to the families of the victims, but the government itself did not attempt to prosecute offenders—this was left to private actions in the courts. Pinochet publicly denounced the Commission's report and defended the actions of his men, arguing that they had acquitted themselves honorably in an undeclared war.

The Aylwin government proposed various changes in the constitution inherited from the military regime. However, all but one of these projects stalled in the Senate where the government was unable to muster the necessary two-thirds majority. The 1980 constitution had allowed the outgoing military regime to appoint nine senators, thereby giving the conservative opposition an effective veto against any proposal to reform the political system.

At the next general election, on December 11, 1993, Eduardo Frei Ruiz-Tagle, son of the former president, was elected to succeed Aylwin. Frei was the candidate of the Coalition and triumphed with a remarkable 58% majority in a field of seven presidential candidates. Frei's closest rival was Arturo Alessandri, the nephew of another former president. Alessandri was supported by the Union for the Progress of Chile (UPP), a coalition of parties on the right. The two principal parties of the UPP are National Renovation (RN) and the Independent Democratic Union (UDI). Both emerged during the transition to democracy to represent former supporters of the Pinochet regime.

Executive

Chile's 1925 constitution created a six-year term for the executive, without the possibility of immediate reelection. The 1980 constitution lengthened the presidential term to eight years. But after the victory of the "No" in the 1988 plebiscite, the government and opposition agreed to an exception: the first president elected after the dictatorship would serve only four years. In February 1994, at the end of Aylwin's presidency, the Congress voted to amend the constitution to establish a six-year presidential term without the possibility of immediate reelection.

The 1980 constitution created a runoff election for the

Representation of Chile's Major Political Parties in the National Congress

Political Party	Chamber of Deputies		Senate	
	1993	1997	1993	1997
Coalition of Parties for Democracy	70	70	21	20
Christian Democratic Party (PDC)	37	39	13	14
Socialist Party (PS)	15	11	5	4
Party for Democracy (PPD)	15	16	2	2
Union for the Progress of Chile	50	48	17	18
National Renovation (RN)	29	25	11	7
Independent Democratic Union (UDI)	15	21	3	9

Sources: For 1993, "Latin American Regional Reports—Southern Cone," RS-94-01, February 10, 1994; and for 1997, Chile Interior Ministry. The table presents the results of Chile's two most recent congressional elections: December 11, 1993, and December 11, 1997.

Note: Chile's smaller parties and independents are excluded from the table.

presidency in the event that no candidate receives an absolute majority in the first round of voting. This was the least controversial change from the former 1925 constitution. Runoff elections were included to avert the kind of legitimacy crisis that occurred under Allende. To date no runoff election has been necessary.

The president appoints a Cabinet of 21 ministers. These appointees do not require legislative approval and can be replaced at the pleasure of the president. Administrators for each of Chile's regions and provinces (see below) are also chosen by the president and continue to serve only with the president's approval. The controller general of the republic is another presidential appointee, but the president's choice requires the approval of the Senate. Once approved, the controller general cannot be removed, but he or she must retire at the age of 75.

If the president declares a piece of legislation urgent, then the Congress must act on it within 30 days. If not, the legislation automatically becomes law when the 30 days expire. The president may call Congress into special session and can enact certain laws by decree.

Legislature

Before 1973, legislative power was vested in a bicameral *Congreso Nacional* (National Congress) composed of an upper house, the *Senado* (Senate), with 45 members, and a lower house, the *Cámara de Diputados* (Chamber of Deputies), with 150 members. Senators were elected for eight-year terms and deputies for four years.

The legislature was abolished after the coup and substantially redesigned before the Pinochet regime held elections for a new National Congress in December 1989. The Chamber of Deputies now has 120 members elected from 60 voting districts; 2 representatives are

elected from each district. Deputies are elected from party lists to four-year terms and may be reelected.

The 1980 constitution called for a Senate with 26 elected members and 9 appointed members. However, following the 1988 plebiscite the democratic opposition negotiated a constitutional amendment to increase the number of directly elected senators from 26 to 38. Senators serve eight-year terms and can be reelected. Half of the elected Senate is renewed every four years.

The president of the republic chooses two of the appointed senators (one former minister and one rector of a public university); three are chosen by the Supreme Court (two former justices of the Court and one former controller); and four are chosen by the National Security Council (one former commander in chief of the army, another from the navy, a third from the air force, and a former director of the national police). Before December 1997 all of these appointees—known as "institutional senators"—were chosen while Pinochet was still president. Between December 15, 1997, and December 26, 1997, new institutional senators were selected.

Both the Aylwin and Frei governments have attempted to amend the constitution to eliminate appointed senators. However, thus far, all such efforts have been blocked by the conservative opposition in the Senate. In addition to the nine appointed senators, the 1980 constitution also established that ex-presidents who have served at least six consecutive years may serve as senators for life.

The Congress is empowered to propose and approve legislation. A piece of legislation approved by a majority of both chambers is sent to the executive to be signed into law. If the president vetoes the legislation, it must be sent back to the Congress with the president's comments. The Congress may then either vote to approve the changes (with a simple majority vote in each chamber) or vote to overturn the president's veto (with a two-thirds vote in each chamber). Amendments to the constitution also require a two-thirds vote by both chambers.

The oversight authority of the Chamber of Deputies includes the power to adopt accords or make observations by a majority vote of the members present. The government must then respond to the written document within 30 days. However, the government is not bound to a particular course of action.

The Chamber may initiate impeachment proceedings against the president, a minister, intendant, governor, or a superior or supreme court justice. Charges of impeachment are judged by the Senate. The Senate is also responsible for approving a president's choice for controller general.

Judiciary

Chile's legal system is derived from Spanish law and based on the Code of 1857. The highest court in Chile is the Supreme Court. It is composed of 17 justices. The court elects a president from among its members every three years. Each of the justices has tenure until the mandatory retirement age of 75. However, the Congress is empowered to impeach and remove justices, and in January 1993 the Congress exercised this power. A two-thirds vote of the Senate is required to remove a Supreme Court justice.

When there is a vacancy on the Court the president is entitled to appoint a new justice but must chose from a list of five individuals nominated by the Supreme Court itself. This role for the judiciary in the selection of new judges first appeared in the 1925 constitution as a means of protecting the independence of the courts.

There are nine appellate courts in Chile. Appellate court judges are appointed by the chief executive from a list of three names submitted by the Supreme Court. Local courts have jurisdiction over both civil and criminal cases. Local court judges are appointed by the president from a list of three individuals submitted by the appellate court with jurisdiction in that region.

The Chilean justice system has established a tradition of integrity and independence. However, the courts were severely criticized in the report of the Commission on Truth and Reconciliation for refusing thousands of petitions for habeas corpus during the Pinochet dictatorship. Supreme Court judges were also strongly criticized by the Coalition parties and human rights groups for frustrating the subsequent investigation and prosecution of human rights violators.

Regional and Local Government

Chile is a unitary republic divided into 13 regions. Each region is administered by an "intendant" appointed by the president. The intendant is the "natural and immedi-

ate agent of the president." He is responsible for the coordination and oversight of public services and the maintenance of public order. He serves only with the favor of the president and can be replaced at any time.

Each of Chile's 13 regions is further subdivided into provinces. These are administered by a governor also appointed by the president. Governors take their instructions from the intendant but serve only at the pleasure of the president.

Elected local government functions at the municipal level (*comunas*). Municipal authorities are directly elected for four-year terms in each of Chile's more than 300 municipalities. During the Pinochet regime, locally elected officials were removed and replaced by centrally appointed municipal leaders. In 1991 the Congress approved an amendment to replace these appointed officials with directly elected representatives. The most recent elections for local office were held in 1996.

Municipalities have autonomy to administer their own finances. The sources of municipal finance include transfers from the regional government in which the municipality is located, local fines and fees, and the municipality's participation in the common municipal fund. This fund receives a percentage of monies (stipulated in law) from diverse revenue sources. The money collected is then distributed between Chile's varied municipalities according to criteria of size and equity.

THE ELECTORAL SYSTEM

All Chileans can vote at age 18, and voting is compulsory. Women won the right to vote in 1949. Literacy requirements were officially eliminated in 1970.

Under the 1925 constitution a form of proportional representation was used to elect congressional representatives. Eligible voters cast a single vote for a closed list of candidates; vote totals were then translated into seats using the D'Hondt method. There were nine electoral districts for the Senate, and five senators were elected from each district. Between 1925 and 1973 most of the electoral districts for the Chamber of Deputies coincided with the Chile's 25 traditional provinces. However, the number of electoral districts gradually was expanded over the years (to 28), as well as the number of deputies (from 132 to 150).

Between 1973 and 1988 no elections were held for any public office. Prior to the congressional elections in 1989, Chile's former electoral law was changed to favor the conservative parties expected to be the minority. Instead of proportional representation, the Pinochet regime established two-member districts to elect representatives to the Senate and Chamber of Deputies. There are 19 Senate districts and 60 districts for the Chamber of Deputies. The first seat in each district is awarded to the party (or party alliance) with the largest number of votes.

In order to win the second seat as well, a party (or party alliance) must receive more than two-thirds of the district vote, or twice the number of votes of the second-highest list. If not, the party with the second-highest plurality receives the second seat.

THE PARTY SYSTEM

Origins of the Parties

Organized political parties first emerged in the mid-19th century, principally around the question of church-state relations. Early in the 20th century the growing urban middle and working classes provoked an expansion of the party system as new parties sought to incorporate these emerging political actors. During the 1950s and 1960s party competition was heightened further as parties increased their organizational efforts among rural workers.

As might be expected, the Pinochet dictatorship was a watershed in the history of Chile's political parties. Some parties in contemporary Chile—like the PDC and the Socialist Party—predated the coup and formally reconstituted themselves as soon as they were legalized. Other parties emerged for the first time during the democratic transition. The most important of these recently created parties are, on the right, National Renovation and the Independent Democratic Union and, on the left, the Party for Democracy.

The Parties in Law

Legal recognition of political parties prior to the 1973 coup was relatively easy. To appear on the ballot, the main requirement for a new party was that it submit a petition to the electoral authorities signed by at least 10,000 registered voters. Following the coup, party activities were outlawed by the junta. The electoral registry was ordered destroyed.

The 1980 constitution proscribed Marxist parties, but in March 1987 all other opposition parties were legalized. Non-Marxist parties were permitted to re-form provided they could collect at least 33,500 signatures from registered voters. Marxist parties were legalized again in the July 1990 referendum amending the constitution.

It is relatively easy to register a new political party in Chile, but in order to control the proliferation of minor parties, Chile's party legislation requires that a party dissolve itself if it fails to garner 5% of the vote in a national election.

Party Organization

Chile's political parties have filled the entire spectrum from the revolutionary left to the conservative right. From the 1940s to 1970s the Chilean electorate was roughly divided in thirds among the left, right, and center. However, during this period the parties of the left became increasingly radicalized while the parties of the right experienced a gradual decline in support.

This profile of the Chilean party system was substantially altered by the years of dictatorship. Today, the revolutionary left has virtually disappeared. The right, which had been in decline, has emerged stronger. And the dilemma of the "three thirds" has been replaced (to this point) by competition channeled through two opposing coalitions, one center-left and the other on the right.

The left underwent a profound change during the Pinochet dictatorship. Thousands of the left's partisans were tortured and killed, prompting a critique of the causes of the coup and a revaluation of democratic institutions and the protections they confer. The less extreme parties on the left clearly fared better with the electorate in the 1989 elections. In particular, the Communist Party, which had been one of the largest in Latin America prior to the coup, failed to win a single seat in the legislature.

The rejuvenation of the right is manifest in the solid electoral performance of National Renovation and the Independent Democratic Union. Whereas the National Party was able to attract only about 20% of the popular vote in the 1960s and early 1970s, the new parties of the right have received more than 30%.

The change from proportional representation to the two-member district system for electing representatives created a strong incentive for parties to form broad coalitions. This tendency has been enhanced by the inclination of the Chilean electorate since the return to democracy to reject parties and politicians associated with the political extremes of either the left or right. The center-left Coalition of Parties for Democracy (*Concertación de los Partidos por la Democracia*) has clearly been the dominant force in Chile's electoral politics since it was formed in 1989. The coalition Union for Chilean Progress was formed by the parties on the right to compete with the Coalition.

CHRISTIAN DEMOCRATIC PARTY
(Partido Demócrata Cristiano; PDC)

HISTORY

The earliest predecessor of the Christian Democratic Party was the National Falange, a Catholic reformist group that broke from the ranks of the Conservative Party in 1935. The Falange received meager support: in 1953 the party won only 2.9% of the vote in legislative elections. That same year, the National Falange merged with the Conservative Social Christians to form the Christian Social Federation, which in 1957 became the PDC.

During the late 1950s and 1960s the PDC grew rapidly, attracting voters from both the right and left. Soon the PDC was the dominant party of the center in

Chilean politics, and in 1964 the PDC's candidate, Eduardo Frei, won the presidency. The party's spectacular growth and Frei's success in the election (with the support of the right) led PDC politicians to overestimate their ability to end the division of the "three thirds."

When Allende won a plurality of the popular vote in 1970, the PDC was still the largest party in Congress. The PDC congressional bloc voted to complete Allende's election, but the party staunchly opposed his policies as president. The left wing of the PDC splintered as some groups sympathetic to Allende's program left the party to join the Allende coalition. However, central figures in the PDC leadership initially welcomed military intervention. Many PDC politicians assumed the military would hand over power to them after removing the Allende government. After the coup, however, the PDC was placed in "indefinite recess," and in 1977 the party was formally dissolved.

The PDC reemerged quickly during the transition to democracy to establish itself as Chile's largest party. Patricio Aylwin, former PDC senator, was a central spokesman for the "No" campaign. As the largest party of the Coalition, the PDC has chosen Chile's last two presidents.

POLICY

The Christian Democratic Party's ideological position was strongly influenced by Christian humanism and corporatist thought. The PDC rejected both the individualism of capitalism and the collectivism of socialism, defending a "third way" to development between these two extremes.

The PDC's ideology was given its first serious test during the presidential administration of Eduardo Frei (Sr.). During his presidency Chile's first meaningful land reform program was initiated, but the reach and pace of the program did not satisfy the left. Foreign ownership of Chile's copper mines was another contentious issue during the Frei administration. Frei's solution was a program for the "Chileanization" of copper. The government would not expropriate the mines. Instead, the government would buy a majority stake in the mines through agreements with the foreign companies. Both land reform and "Chileanization" of the copper mines demonstrated the PDC's strong reform impulse and the simultaneous moderation that underlay PDC doctrine and policy.

When a PDC candidate again assumed the presidency in 1990, the Chilean economy was enjoying impressive GDP growth and low inflation. The PDC, at the head of the Coalition, pledged not to make any drastic changes in the orthodox economic model imposed during the dictatorship. To address the "social debt" accrued during the years of harsh military rule and orthodox market reform, the PDC-led government raised taxes somewhat to fund higher spending on education, poverty alleviation, and other social programs. However, the overall structure of the economy and the priority of fiscal solvency were defended and maintained. The same recipe has been followed by Aylwin's successor, Eduardo Frei Ruiz-Tagle.

MEMBERSHIP AND CONSTITUENCY

The PDC is a centrist party with its strongest support among middle-class workers and professionals.

LEADERSHIP

The current president of Chile is a Christian Democrat, Eduardo Frei Ruiz-Tagle. Alejandro Foxley is another prominent PDC leader and has been mentioned for the presidency in 1999. However, Foxley finished second in his district in the 1997 Senate elections. This severely undermines his prospects of receiving the nomination. Enrique Krauss is head of the PDC. Senator Adolfo Zaldívar is vice president of the party.

PROSPECTS

The PDC saw its support fall by 4 percentage points between the 1996 municipal elections and the 1997 congressional elections. The PDC remains the largest single party in Chilean politics, but it is not clear whether the PDC will continue to dominate the Coalition. The combined strength of the PS and PPD (24%) is now slightly stronger than the vote tally of the PDC (23%).

SOCIALIST PARTY
(Partido Socialista de Chile; PS)

HISTORY

The Socialist Party was founded in 1933. During the 1930s and 1940s, the Socialists formed alliances with the centrist (and opportunistic) Radical Party. At that time the Comintern defended alliances of this type. However, in 1956, the Socialists allied with the Chilean Communist Party to form the *Frente de Acción Popular* (Popular Action Front; FRAP).

The Socialist Party reached the height of its power and influence in 1970 when Salvador Allende was elected president. The coup and subsequent repression by the military forced party stalwarts to reassess their positions, producing diverse opinions regarding the role and responsibility of the party. Party factions expressed conflicting views regarding the proper strategy to adopt for the 1988 plebiscite. The moderate Socialists decided to participate actively. Following the presidential and congressional elections in December 1989, the Socialist Party factions reunited.

POLICY

During the Allende years the Socialists supported the expropriation of large private property, irrespective of whether the owners were foreign or domestic. The party advocated massive land reform leading to the formation of agricultural collectives, and management of large industries by workers' committees. In response to the threat these policies provoked from the military, the most militant Socialists advocated arming workers and peasants (a proposal that Allende always firmly rejected). In Chile, the Socialists were far more radical than the Communists.

The experience of the dictatorship has changed the Chilean electorate and transformed the Socialist Party. Today, the Socialist Party in Chile is more akin to social democratic parties of Western Europe. The party advocates greater social spending, but within the confines of fiscal solvency and within a private-market economy.

MEMBERSHIP AND CONSTITUENCY

Urban and rural laborers remain the strongest constituency of the Socialist Party. The party is also supported by professionals and intellectuals with an ideological commitment to greater social equality in Chile.

LEADERSHIP

The Socialist Ricardo Lagos is one of the most articulate and charismatic political figures in Chilean politics today. He is currently minister of public works in President Frei's Cabinet and is a likely presidential candidate in 1999. Although Lagos is most clearly identified with the Socialist Party, he has been registered simultaneously in both the PS and the PPD, despite a law prohibiting dual party membership.

Camilo Escalona is president of the Socialist Party. Juan Pablo Letelier and Francisco Rivas are other prominent members of the party.

PROSPECTS

Support for the PS fell in the 1997 elections. However, Ricardo Lagos has strong popular support, and the vote tally of the PS and PPD combined is now slightly higher than the PDC. This strengthens Lagos's position to claim that he should be the next presidential candidate of the Coalition.

PARTY FOR DEMOCRACY
(Partido por la Democracia; PPD)

HISTORY

The Party for Democracy was formed by Socialist Party dissidents who believed the potential benefits from participating in the 1988 plebiscite outweighed the risks. Since Marxist parties were still illegal at that time, the PPD was formed as a catchall party for those on the left who wished to participate and vote against Pinochet in the plebiscite. It was expected that the PPD would disappear once the Socialist Party was legalized, but instead the PPD has maintained an institutional identity of its own.

POLICY

The PPD proclaims to represent a more "modern" vision of the left. It is not entirely clear what this repeated claim of "modernity" is intended to mean. The PPD appears to have abandoned much of its socialist leaning. The party is a member of the Coalition.

MEMBERSHIP AND CONSTITUENCY

The PPD has a somewhat younger membership than the Socialist Party and a more solidly middle-class constituency.

LEADERSHIP

Prominent leaders of the PPD include Jorge Schaulsohn and Eric Schnake. Senator Sergio Bitar is head of the party.

PROSPECTS

Support for PPD candidates was up slightly in the 1997 congressional elections. In alliance with the PS, the PPD now appears poised to contest the supremacy of the PDC within the Coalition. However, the party is without a strong potential presidential candidate of its own.

NATIONAL RENOVATION
(Renovación Nacional; RN)

HISTORY

National Renovation was founded in 1987 through the merger of the Movement for National Union, the National Labor Front, and the Independent Democratic Union (UDI). The RN split with the UDI over the 1988 plebiscite, but both parties supported the candidacy of Hernán Büchi in 1989.

In 1993 the RN allied with the UDI and the Center-Center Union in the Union for Chilean Progress. This rightist coalition was formed to challenge the electoral dominance of the Coalition.

POLICY

The RN has sought to distance itself from the repression and authoritarian politics of the Pinochet regime while acting as champion for the liberal, free-market economic policies pursued by the military government after 1975. The party promotes itself as the vehicle of "modern" liberal conservatism. The RN emphasizes order, stability, efficiency, and free competition. Far less emphasis is placed on questions of human rights and democratic participation.

MEMBERSHIP AND CONSTITUENCY

Middle- and upper-class businesspeople who fared well under the market reforms advanced during the Pinochet regime are the principal constituency of the RN.

LEADERSHIP

Andrés Allamand is a prominent member of the party who had been mentioned as a possible presidential candidate in

1999. However, he surprisingly lost his bid for the senate in 1997, finishing in fourth place. Alberto Espina is president of the party and a congressional deputy. Alberto Cardemil is vice president of the party and was elected to the Chamber of Deputies in 1997. Sergio Romero is currently president of the Senate.

PROSPECTS

The RN lost 4 deputies and 4 of its 11 senators in the 1997 elections. As a result, the RN is no longer the dominant partner in the Union for Chilean Progress. The two largest parties of the right are now roughly equal in strength: the RN is slightly superior in the Chamber, and the UDI is superior in the Senate. Following the 1997 elections the RN will likely take a more intransigent position vis-à-vis political reform initiatives of the current government.

INDEPENDENT DEMOCRATIC UNION
(Unión Democrática Independiente; UDI)

HISTORY

The Independent Democratic Union emerged as a party of the right during the transition to democracy. In some respects the UDI is a successor of the pre-Pinochet National Party. In 1987 the UDI joined in the formation of National Renovation but withdrew in April 1988 following the expulsion of its founder, Jaime Guzman, from the RN leadership. Guzman was formerly a legal adviser to General Pinochet. He was assassinated on April 1, 1991 by leftist militants of the *Frente Patriótico Manuel Rodríguez* (Manuel Rodríguez Patriotic Front).

The UDI is a member of the rightist alliance, Union for Chilean Progress, with the RN and the Center-Center Union.

POLICY

The UDI supports the economic model implemented during the dictatorship but unlike the RN has not attempted to distance itself from the acts of repression by the Pinochet regime. The UDI has proclaimed itself the trustee of the "protected democracy" ensconced in the 1980 constitution. The party is generally more dogmatic than the RN and less open to negotiating with the parties of the Coalition.

MEMBERSHIP AND CONSTITUENCY

The UDI membership is proud and largely unapologetic for the actions of the Pinochet dictatorship. UDI members may be said to hold a certain distrust of democratic institutions.

LEADERSHIP

Jovino Novoa is president of the UDI. In 1997 he was elected to Congress, though polls listed him as an under-

dog. Joaquín Lavín, mayor of Las Condes, is a popular leader with a strong chance to be the candidate of the Union for Chilean Progress in the 1999 presidential election. His position was strengthened by the weak showing of the RN's Andrés Allamand in the 1997 elections. Juan Antonio Coloma is another prominent UDI leader.

PROSPECTS

In the 1997 congressional elections the UDI was one of the few clear winners. The party strengthened its position on the right, increasing its representation in the Chamber by six and in the Senate by six as well. The party also has a potentially strong candidate for the 1999 presidential elections.

MINOR POLITICAL PARTIES

Social Democratic Radical Party
(Partido Radical Social Demócrata)

The Radical Party was founded in 1863 as the representative of the emerging middle class. However, the party entered into decline during the 1950s and has never recovered. In an effort to restore its image, the party changed its name in 1994 to the Social Democratic Radical Party.

The party is a member of the Coalition, but elected only one senator and two deputies in 1993. In 1997 the PRSD elected four deputies. More significant, perhaps, is that the Radicals' 3% of the vote could prove to be highly significant in swaying the balance within the Coalition between the PDC on one side and the PS and PPD on the other. Will the PRSD maintain its traditional support of the PDC or side with the "progressive bloc" represented by the PPD and PS?

Center-Center Union
(Unión de Centro Centro Progresista)

The Center-Center Union is the creation of the businessman Francisco Javier Errázuriz. Despite its name, the party is not centrist. It is a populist-style party of the right that relies on the personal popularity of its founder. In 1989 Errázuriz ran for president and received a very respectable 15% of the vote. However, the UCC has little representation in the legislature. In 1993 the UCC joined the RN and UDI in the Union for Chilean Progress. In 1997 the UCC elected only one deputy and one senator to the Congress.

OTHER POLITICAL FORCES

The Military

Numerous constitutional and legal changes implemented by the Pinochet regime served to increase the power and influence of the military in Chile's democratic system. Before leaving the executive, Pinochet guaranteed for himself the right to remain commander in chief of the army until 1998. Occupying that powerful position, Pinochet was able to (credibly) declare: "The day any of my men is touched, the state of law is over."

The military holds half the seats on the National Security Council. The president is not commander in chief of the armed forces except during war. And defense spending cannot fall below a specified minimum, including 10% of foreign exchange from copper sales. During the Aylwin government, military courts continued to initiate legal action against civilians for defamation against the honor of the armed forces.

Roman Catholic Church

Nearly 80% of Chileans are Catholic. In political debates that address concerns of the Roman Catholic Church, the church has a prominent voice.

The political role of the church was particularly salient during the Pinochet dictatorship. The church hierarchy opposed the Allende government when it challenged the church's authority in education, and the church did not initially express disapproval when the military intervened to depose Allende. However, the church soon took a firm stand against the human rights record of the military, becoming perhaps the only sphere in civil society that could openly oppose the Pinochet regime. In 1976 the church created the *Vicaría de la Solidaridad* (Vicarate of Solidarity), which provided legal aid and social services for the victims of the dictatorship. The church used its moral authority to speak out against the regime and aided protest groups.

NATIONAL PROSPECTS

Chile's economy continues to post impressive annual growth rates with low inflation and decreasing indices of poverty. Chile's democratic political system has also performed extremely well since 1989. Ironically, this may have contributed to a sharp increase in absenteeism and null or blank ballots in the 1997 congressional elections. The increase has preoccupied many Chilean comentators, but nearly 70% of eligible Chileans voted in 1997, a percentage that compares very favorably with voting rates in the advanced industrial democracies. Today, Chilean politics is duller and more predictable than in the highly charged days of the 1980s and early 1990s. This change has surely contributed to the drop in voter participation, but it is also a change worth celebrating.

The Coalition alliance has dominated Chilean politics since the return of democracy in 1989. However, this dominance was reduced somewhat in 1997. The parties of the Coalition received slightly more than 50% of the total vote, but this was down approximately 5 percentage points from the municipal elections just a year before. The margin of victory between the Coalition and the conservative alliance of the RN and UDI shrank from 22% to 14%.

The 1997 elections did not produce any significant change in the overall constellation of forces in the Chilean Congress. The Coalition retained its comfortable majority in the Chamber of Deputies. However, the Frei government must continue to negotiate with the conservative opposition to approve certain pieces of legislation and to advance any proposal for amending the constitution. The increased stature of the UDI following the 1997 elections makes the prospect of any constitutional change of the political system even more unlikely.

Further Reading

Collier, Simon, and William F. Sater. *A History of Chile, 1808–1994.* Cambridge: Cambridge University Press, 1996.

Drake, Paul W., and Iván Jaksic, eds. *The Struggle for Democracy in Chile.* Lincoln and London: University of Nebraska Press, 1995.

Loveman, Brian. *Chile: The Legacy of Hispanic Capitalism,* 2d ed. New York: Oxford University Press, 1979.

———. "Misión Cumplida? Civil-Military Relations and the Chilean Political Transition." *Journal of Interamerican and World Affairs* 33, no. 3 (fall 1991).

Rabkin, Rhonda. "The Aylwin Government and 'Tutelary' Democracy: A Concept in Search of a Case?" *Journal of Interamerican Studies and World Affairs* 34, no. 4 (winter 1992–93).

Scully, Timothy R. "Reconstituting Party Politics in Chile." In *Building Democratic Institutions: Party Systems in Latin America.* Ed. Scott Mainwaring and Timothy R. Scully. Stanford, Calif.: Stanford University Press, 1995.

Sigmund, Paul. E. *The Overthrow of Allende and the Politics of Chile, 1964–1976.* Pittsburgh: University of Pittsburgh Press, 1979.

Valenzuela, Arturo. *The Breakdown of Democratic Regimes: Chile.* Baltimore and London: Johns Hopkins University Press, 1978.

PEOPLE'S REPUBLIC OF CHINA

(Zhonghua Renmin Gongheguo)

By Donald M. Seekins; revised by Thomas J. Bickford

THE SYSTEM OF GOVERNMENT

The People's Republic of China is, according to its 1982 state constitution, "a socialist state under the people's democratic dictatorship led by the working class and based on the alliance of workers and peasants." It was established formally on October 1, 1949, after the Communist forces under Mao Zedong defeated the Nationalists or Guomindang (Kuomintang) under Jiang Jieshi (Chiang Kai-shek) after four years of civil war.

China's territory can be divided into two geographic and historical regions: the provinces of China proper, located south of the Great Wall, which were unified under the Qin (221 to 207 B.C.E.) and Han (206 B.C.E. to 220 C.E.) dynasties and have been ruled by Chinese or foreign (e.g., Mongol and Manchu) dynasties ever since; and a much larger region consisting of the three provinces of the northeast, Jilin, Liaoning, and Heilongjiang (commonly known as Manchuria), Nei Mongol (Inner Mongolia), Xinjiang, Qinghai, and Xizang (Tibet), all of which were added to the Chinese Empire during the Qing (Manchu) dynasty (1644–1911). China has over 20,000 kilometers (12,400 miles) of land frontier, 6,452 kilometers (4,000 miles) of which form the borders with Russia and the former Soviet republics of Kazakhstan, Kyrgyzstan, and Tajikstan. The border with India runs for over 3,600 kilometers. Border disputes with India and the former Soviet Union have been a major feature of China's relations with its neighbors since the 1950s. While the boundary between Russia and China has now been largely settled, the frontier with India and the Central Asian republics remains in dispute.

In 1993, China's population was estimated to be 1,180,000,000, up from about 580 million in 1953, making it the most populous country in the world. Most of the population is concentrated in the eastern part of the country, especially in the coastal regions, while the vast mountainous and desert regions of Nei Mongol, Xinjiang, Qinghai, and Xizang are only sparsely inhabited. Of the total population, 92% are Chinese (officially known as the Han nationality). The remaining 8% are divided into 55 officially recognized nationalities, of which the most important are the Zhuang, Uygur, Hui, Tibetan, Yi, Miao, Manchus, Mongols, and Koreans. Most of the minority groups are concentrated in the border region, though the Hui can be found in every province in China.

The structure and process of government that evolved during the more than 2,000 years of Imperial rule beginning with the Han (206 B.C.E.) and ending with the fall of the Qing (1911) combined, in a unique fashion, the rational and despotic. At the apex of the system was the emperor (*huangdi*), who embodied the roles of ceremonial head of state with almost divine charismatic powers, chief executive, and supreme legislator. During the Qing dynasty, he made the final decision on all policy matters of importance, enacted laws, and supervised the government bureaucracy at all levels. He was served by a sophisticated and functionally specific hierarchy of civil servants. The historian Albert Feuerwerker estimates that during the 18th century, the high point of Qing power and prestige, a cadre of 20,000 civil servants governed a population of 300,000,000. For most common people, the government was a distant (though often threatening) entity. Lower-level officials had to rely on the cooperation of the local gentry and numbers of often corrupt functionaries in order to maintain public order, raise taxes, and complete public projects such as canals and irrigation works. The constructive influence of even the most enlightened individuals on the villages and hamlets of China was thus much diluted by local interests.

An element of central importance in the continuity of the imperial system was Confucianism, which from the Han dynasty on served as the moral basis of the state and defined the culture and way of life for the ruling classes. As formulated by Confucius (Kong Fuzi, 551–479 B.C.E.) and Mencius (Mengzi, 372–289 B.C.E.) and elaborated by Han dynasty scholars, this body of thought was at once philosophy of human nature, a system of ethics, and a political ideology. For Confucians, society was not an aggregate of self-interested, private individuals but a highly interdependent system consisting of a complex and tightly drawn network of reciprocal, but unequal, social ties. These were regulated by the principles of *ren* (benevolence) and *li* (rites and ceremony).

On the political level, the Confucian ruler, assisted by loyal officials promoted on the basis of merit, was responsible for preserving and promoting this social network, both by providing for the people's basic material well-being and by being a model of Confucian morality. Moral mobilization was especially stressed. Virtuous rulers and upstanding officials could and should, according to Confucian doctrine, inspire people to live up to the ideals embodied in *ren* and *li*, and the empire as a whole would prosper as a result. Superior and inferior were defined sharply, but the right of the former to rule was conditioned by the principle that he possessed superior merit and had an attitude of benevolent paternalism toward the latter. This was an ideal, however, and the growth of the emperor's absolute power in the Ming (1368–1644) and the Qing dynasties led to major abuses of power. For the common people, the repressive aspects of government—harsh laws and punishments, heavy taxes and *corvees*, as well as corruption—were often more apparent than Confucian benevolence.

The inability of the Qing dynasty to maintain internal peace and China's humiliation at the hands of the Western powers, Russia, and Japan in the 19th and early 20th centuries led to the dynasty's overthrow and the dissolution of the imperial system itself in 1911. The period between 1912, when the first Republic of China was formerly established, and 1949 was largely one of disunity and civil war, exacerbated by the Japanese invasion of China in the 1930s. In 1949, the Chinese Communists were finally able to fill the political vacuum that had been left by the fall of the Qing 38 years before.

China has had five state constitutions since the founding of the People's Republic in 1949. In that year, a provisional "Common Program" was adopted by the victorious followers of Mao Zedong. This document was replaced in 1954 by a formal constitution. New constitutions appeared in rapid succession in 1975, 1978, and 1982. This reflects the instability and rapid changes in those years when not only new leaders, but new ideas, were emerging that would profoundly change and reshape China's society, economy, and political system.

The structure of political institutions, as defined in the 1982 state constitution, continues to be based on the Soviet model of a dual hierarchy of party and state organs extending form the center to the local level. In this arrangement, the Communist Party occupies a commanding position as the formulator of policy, while the state administration is charged with implementation. The principle of dual rule, adopted at the Eighth Party Congress in 1956, defines the dominant role of the Chinese Communist Party (CCP) by stipulating that state organs are not only responsible to the state organs above them but are also responsible to the party organ on their own level. For example, the provincial state administration is subordinate to both the central state administration and the provincial party committee. In practice, dual rule has meant that many political leaders at both the national and provincial levels have held both state and party roles. During the Maoist period (1949–76) interchangability of state and party personnel was the norm and lines between the two bureaucracies were frequently blurred. While the 1980s and 1990s have seen attempts to draw a sharper line between party and state, the party remains firmly in control of the state apparatus.

Executive

The 1982 constitution designates the president of the People's Republic of China as the head of state. The president's duties include promulgating laws and decrees, ratifying treaties and other agreements with foreign states, appointing members of the State Council and other important officials, and receiving foreign diplomatic representatives. In all these matters, however, the president is supposed to act on the initiative of the National People's Congress (NPC) or its Standing Committee. The National People's Congress chooses him or her for a five-year term. No president is allowed to serve more than two terms. There is a vice president who replaces the president if the office falls vacant before the NPC can convene to choose a successor. While the state constitution officially gives the right to choose the president to the National People's Congress, in practice the party chooses the candidate in advance and the NPC merely rubber-stamps the choice. In 1997 the president was Jiang Zemin, who concurrently holds the title of chairman of the party.

China's central executive body is the State Council, whose members, as mentioned earlier, are chosen by the president on the recommendation of the National People's Congress. Once again, many, if not all, positions on the State Council are agreed on in advance among party elites. The State Council is headed by the premier, who functions as head of government, and includes a secretary-general, vice premiers, and state councillors (state councillors are equivalent in rank to vice premiers). The number of vice premiers has varied considerably over the years. In 1982 there were 13. Since then the number has ranged from 2 to 4. The number of ministries and commissions under the State Council has also varied considerably over time as China has undergone periodic reorganizations to try to streamline its state bureaucracy. In 1994, the State Council had 40 ministries and commissions with a total staff of approximately 45,000. In 1998 the premier was Zhu Rongji.

The responsibilities of the State Council include submission of draft laws and the budget to the National People's Congress or its Standing Committee and the supervision of the various ministries and commissions under its control. However, even at this level the principle of dual rule applies and the party has precedence on all important matters. An interesting example is that of the two Central Military Commissions, one for the party and one under the State Council. The role of the Central Military Commission is to supervise the armed forces of the country, the People's Liberation Army. Until 1982 there was only one Central Military Commission directly under the Communist Party's Central Committee. The state constitution of 1982 created a separate Central Military Commission under the State Council. This was supposed to help create a sharper distinction between party and state with the party CMC dealing with purely party matters and the state CMC being responsible for issues directly related to the running of government (such as the military budget and strategic doctrine)—and was widely regarded by China specialists at the time as being a significant departure from the Maoist era. In practice, however, membership of the two commissions is identical and has been ever since 1982. The state CMC remains an empty shell, and it is the party CMC that directs all military policy.

Legislature

The National People's Congress, China's equivalent of a parliament, is elected by provincial-level people's congresses and by units of the People's Liberation Army (PLA). In addition to a delegation from each of the provinces and a delegation representing the military, there is a small delegation selected to represent Taiwan, which is regarded as a breakaway province. Delegates to the NPC are supposed to be elected every five years, though this principle has only been observed since 1978. There was a period of six years between the election of the Second NPC in 1959 and the Third in 1965. Ten years elapsed between the election of the Third NPC and the Fourth in 1975. During that ten-year period, no actual sessions of the NPC were held due to the Cultural Revolution. The NPC has been a largely symbolic organization. Its sheer size, over 2,900 delegates, and the fact that it meets for only a few days each year guarantee that it has little role to play in formulating or debating policy.

The Standing Committee of the NPC meets more frequently, but it is mostly a rubber stamp. Nevertheless, in the 1990s the NPC has begun to play a minor role in debating policy and serving as a forum for provincial elites to voice their concerns. In recent years delegates have even questioned parts of the national budget and other legislation presented to them for approval at the annual session. While the National People's Congress still does not function as a true independent legislature, its present role is in marked contrast to its total subservience under Mao Zedong. Many observers attribute the NPC's small

but growing independence to its leadership under Qiao Shi, who has been the chairman of the NPC Standing Committee. However, Qiao Shi failed to win reelection to the Politburo (see below) in September 1997, and with his departure from the highest organ of the Communist Party it is uncertain whether the NPC will continue to show signs of developing into an independent legislature.

Judiciary

The 1982 constitution provides for people's courts on the levels of provincial, county, and local government, and a Supreme People's Court at the center, whose judges are chosen by the National People's Congress or its Standing Committee. Parallel with the court system is the Supreme People's Procurate and its corresponding lower-level branches. It is responsible for seeing that the courts operate in conformity with lawful procedure, and it represents the state in criminal trials. The procurates were abolished during the Cultural Revolution period (1966–76), and their restoration is part of an effort by China's post-Mao leadership to restore and foster a sense of rule by law. Since 1980, China has been slowly developing a criminal code. Progress has been slow and many areas of the law, such as patents, did not have any legal code until the late 1980s or early 1990s. Since the mid-1980s, China has also begun to reintroduce law courses as part of the university curriculum, and a small cadre of trained specialists is beginning to emerge.

Chapter Two of the 1982 state constitution contains 24 articles defining the fundamental rights and duties of Chinese citizens. Guaranteed rights include freedom of speech, assembly, religion, equal rights for men and women, and the right to vote. Article 51 of the constitution, however, states: "Citizens of the People's Republic of China, in exercising their freedoms and rights, may not infringe upon the interests of the state, of society or of the collective. . . . " The Chinese state thus has considerable latitude in interpreting the limits of citizens' rights. The constitution also forbids any actions that might lead to independence for minority areas, stating that it is the duty of every Chinese citizen to preserve the unity of the country. In the 1990s, Chinese dissidents have attempted to use the legal system to push for better enforcement of existing rights. As of 1997, this tactic has met with little success and the judiciary remains subordinate to party goals.

Regional and Local Government

There are three levels of government below the national level. First, the country is divided into 30 provincial-level units: 22 provinces (Anhui, Fujian, Gansu, Guangdong, Guizhou, Hainan, Hebei, Heilongjinag, Henan, Hubei, Hunan, Jiangsu, Jiangxi, Jilin, Liaoning, Qinghai, Shaanxi,

Shandong, Shanxi, Sichuan, Yunnan, and Zhejiang); 5 autonomous regions (Xinjiang, Ningxia, Nei Mongol, Xizang [Tibet], and Guangxi); and 3 municipalities (Beijing, Tianjin, and Shanghai). The 5 autonomous regions are each based on the largest minority group of that region—the Uygurs, Huis, Mongols, Tibetans, and Zhuang, respectively. Note that China regards Taiwan as a Chinese province though no government organization currently exists for Taiwan. It is, however, represented at the National People's Congress.

At a secondary level, the 30 provincial-level units are further subdivided into 2,138 counties, 190 cities, a number of autonomous counties and prefectures, and the districts of the 3 municipalities. At the third level of government are towns, districts within cities, and rural townships (*xiang*). Autonomous districts also exist at these lower levels of government. The term "autonomous" is applied to every unit of regional and local government where there is a substantial minority population. Autonomous areas are normally led by a member of the dominant minority group and enjoy certain privileges and rights aimed at preserving minority cultures and ways of life. The most notable special privilege is exemption from state family planning regulations, a policy that has been the source of considerable resentment on the part of the majority Han. Overall, though, these regions are not truly self-governing.

Government on the three subnational levels essentially parallels organization at the national level. The provincial-level units have people's congresses that are elected for five year terms. County- and township-level governments also have their local people's congresses, elected for periods of three years and two years, respectively. At each subnational level, the people's congress appoints a standing committee that is in turn responsible for selecting a people's government. In cities, there is a network of neighborhood committees, representing between 2,000 and 10,000 families. These are subdivided into residents' committees containing between 100 and 600 families, which are further subdivided into residents' small groups of 15 to 40 families. These units work closely with police and have a social control function. Work units such as factories, offices, and schools are also involved in surveillance and control. City life is thus tightly regulated. There is less control over daily life in rural areas, and the state must rely on relatively small numbers of local leaders to ensure implementation of state polices.

As of July 1, 1997, a new category of regional government, that of Special Administrative Region (SAR), came into being when the British returned Hong Kong to China. A second SAR will be created when the Portuguese return their colony of Macao to China on December 20, 1999. The Hong Kong SAR has the same status as a province. Under this provision, Hong Kong is supposed to be truly self-governing, retaining its own form of government, legal, and monetary system for 50 years. China will take responsibility for defense and for-eign policy, but in all other matters Hong Kong is supposed to enjoy true autonomy. The Chinese government has promised the same type of arrangement for Taiwan under the slogan of "one country, two systems" if Taiwan reunites with China. Exactly how much autonomy the Chinese government will actually allow Hong Kong in political and economic matters in the coming years remains uncertain, but given that Hong Kong is an important part of China's economic strategy and that it hopes to use the return of Hong Kong and Macao as a basis for reunification with Taiwan, China has considerable incentive to ensure that it meets its promises regarding Hong Kong's autonomy.

THE ELECTORAL SYSTEM

Direct popular elections are held at the basic level of town, city district, or township people's congresses, and at the county level for county, city, and municipal district people's congresses. Elections for province-level people's congresses and the National People's Congress are indirect: deputies at each level elect deputies to the next-highest level. Deputies at to the national and provincial-level people's congresses serve five-year terms; those at lower levels serve three- or two-year terms. Suffrage is universal, and the minimum age for voting and running for office is 18.

In 1980, direct popular elections were held at the county level for the first time. Free elections were encouraged, the secret ballot has been introduced, and citizens who are not members of the Communist Party have been encouraged to nominate candidates or run for office themselves. By the 1990s most elections at or below the level of county are at least partially competitive (that is, there are more candidates than positions) and free (in that there are secret ballots), though other political parties have not been allowed to form at the grassroots level. In recent years there has been considerable debate within the Communist Party about the desirability of extending this modest experiment in pluralism to provincial-level and possibly even national elections. Any such extension of competitive, direct elections to higher levels of government is unlikely before the 21st century, if at all, and in any case is unlikely to include free and open competition from other political parties.

CHINESE COMMUNIST PARTY; CCP
(Zhongguo gongchan dang)

HISTORY

The Chinese Communist Party was established in 1921 by a small group of young intellectuals inspired by the

Russian Revolution. During its first years of existence, the CCP concentrated on trying to build a network of support among China's very small working class. Under orders form the Comintern in Moscow, the CCP also formed a united front with the Guomindang, which was lead by Sun Zhongshan (Sun Yat-sen). Sun had been an important figure in the movement to overthrow the Qing dynasty, and the Guomindang were a more powerful organization than the fledgling Communists.

After Sun's death, however, leadership of the Guomindang fell to Jiang Jieshi (Chiang Kai-shek), who opposed Sun's policy of receiving aid from the Soviet Union and alliance with the Chinese Communists. In 1927, after the combined forces of the Communists and Guomindang had successfully defeated a coalition of warlords, Jiang conducted a bloody purge of Communists, virtually eliminating the CCP's organization in the cities. It was at this point that the CCP began to shift away from an urban-based political strategy toward one built upon peasant revolt. Mao Zedong in particular had been a strong proponent of the revolutionary potential of China's peasantry, and by the 1930s Mao had created a strong guerrilla movement, the People's Liberation Army, based in remote areas, that was able to successfully resist the Guomindang and later the Japanese during World War II. The most important base was Yan'an, established in 1935 after the epic 6,000-mile retreat known as the Long March. Yan'an was to serve as the "capital" of the Chinese Communist movement until after the Second World War. Despite a fragile truce between the Communists and the Guomindang in order to resist the Japanese invasion during World War II, fighting broke out between the two political movements in 1945. After a four-year civil war, the Communists emerged victorious. The Guomindang retreated to Taiwan, where they have remained ever since.

The period between 1949 and 1954 was known as the Common Program, and served as a transition period during which China began its recovery from nearly constant turmoil and fighting since the collapse of the Qing in 1911 and during which the CCP consolidated its control over the country. In the countryside a massive land reform was carried out that redistributed land to the poor peasants and broke the economic power of the landlord class. Many landlords were executed in the process. In the urban areas, the Communists gradually took control of industry and in 1953 China began its first five-year plan. The 1950s also saw the defeat of ethnic nationalist movements in Xinjiang and Xizang (Tibet). By 1954 the party had consolidated control throughout the country and the PRC's first state constitution was set up, giving China a Soviet-style regime.

The period between 1954 and 1980 was characterized by major swings between pragmatic policy and revolutionary romanticism resulting in considerable political instability at times. One of the most dramatic, and tragic, shifts was the Great Leap Forward from 1958 to 1960.

Mao, impatient with the slow pace of economic construction, opted for a rapid, ideologically driven push to accelerate economic development and the creation of a socialist society. In the countryside vast communes were set up with the average commune containing 20,000 people. In order to foster socialist solidarity, peasants were no longer to eat in their own homes but were instead to take their meals in huge communal dining halls. With the goal of catching up with Britain in 10 years, the Chinese leadership encouraged the setting up of backyard furnaces to smelt down scrap iron and produce huge amounts of steel. People were encouraged to work day and night to increase production. The result was a disaster. The backyard furnaces produced only poor-quality steel of no value. The communes proved to be unpopular and not economically viable. Combined with three years of bad weather, the policies of the Great Leap led to a major famine in which millions of people died. Between 1960 and 1965, the CCP pursued moderate economic policies allowing some degree of private enterprise and using economic incentives to motivate the peasants to produce more.

The next swing toward radical revolutionary radicalism occurred in 1966 with the start of the Great Proletarian Cultural Revolution. While the worst of the Cultural Revolution's excesses were over by 1969, the political turmoil continued until 1976 and this period is often referred to as the "10 years of chaos" in Chinese publications. The rationale for launching the Cultural Revolution is a matter of some debate. Some analysts feel that Mao launched the Cultural Revolution as a way of reasserting his power after being forced to retreat from day-to-day decision making following the failure of the Great Leap Forward. Others point out that Mao remained the dominant political figure within the party and that the Cultural Revolution was based more on his concerns about the future of Chinese communism. Mao resented the pragmatic economic policies of the early 1960s because he feared they might lead to the restoration of capitalism. He also believed that the Soviet Communist Party had become another elite ruling class and had strayed away from the goals of communism—"revisionism" in the language of Mao. The Chinese party needed to renew itself and to push to a higher level of political consciousness or it too would become just another ruling class. Accordingly, Mao encouraged millions of Red Guards, college students, and other young people to attack the centers of power in the Communist Party and government and drag out those who stood for the status quo and were not sufficiently pure in their revolutionary zeal.

Many pragmatic leaders such as Liu Shaoqi and Deng Xiaoping were removed from office and condemned as "capitalist roaders." The Red Guards spread throughout the country attacking officials who were regarded as too conservative and destroying temples and other relics of the feudal order. At the height of the Cultural Revolution, various Red Guard factions were fighting one another in the streets and many areas were without effective government. In 1969 the army was called in to restore order, and the institutions of government were gradually rebuilt.

Despite the restoration of order in 1969, conflict continued among top party leaders. In 1971 Lin Biao, a radical, head of the People's Liberation Army, and Mao's designated successor, died while attempting to flee to the Soviet Union after his plot to launch a military coup was exposed. Mao rehabilitated Deng Xiaoping, who had been one of the Cultural Revolution's most prominent victims, in order to use Deng to restore order to the military following the death of Lin. From 1972 to 1976 Chinese politics was a seesaw battle between pragmatists lead by Deng Xiaoping and an ailing Premier Zhou Enlai, on the one hand, and the Cultural Revolution radicals lead by the infamous Gang of Four—Mao's wife, Jiang Qing, and her allies Wang Hongwen, Yao Wenyuan, and Zhang Chunqiao. The conflict did not end until Mao's death in September 1976 and the arrest of the Gang of Four the following month.

Between 1977 and 1981, Deng Xiaoping slowly consolidated his power, putting the Gang of Four on trial, rehabilitating Cultural Revolution victims, placing his supporters in positions of power, extending his control over the army, and easing out Mao's last chosen successor, Hua Guofeng. In December 1978, the Third Plenum of the 11th Party Congress endorsed sweeping reforms in the agricultural economy, and in the 1980s reform was extended to the urban economy. December 1978 marks a watershed in the party's history. It represents an end to the radical policies of the Maoist period and the triumph of pragmatic policies. After 1978 the party becomes less and less concerned with ideological issues while economic growth and performance become the most important political goals.

ORGANIZATION

The organization of the party is hierarchical. At the very top is the Standing Committee of the Politburo, usually consisting of six to seven members. These individuals are the most powerful people in the party and are largely responsible for the formulation of policy and defining the regime's goals. The next level is the Politburo. The number of individuals has varied considerably over the years though since the mid-1980s membership has tended to be about 20 full members and between 2 and 4 alternate members. The Politburo is elected by the Central Committee, which is in turn elected by the National Party Congress. As with the National People's Congress, the Party Congress is supposed to be held every five years, though this has not always been the case. It has only been since 1982 that Party Congresses have been routinely held every five years. The most recent Party Congress was the 15th, held in September 1997. The delegates to

the Party Congress, 2,048 in 1997, elect the Central Committee by secret ballot. The elections are not very competitive as delegates are given a preapproved list of candidates and there are usually only a few more names than seats to be elected. The 15th Party Congress was unusual in that there were 10% more candidates than seats to be filled for the Central Committee. This made it the most competitive election in the party's history.

After the 15th Party Congress in September 1997, the members of the Standing Committee were: Jiang Zemin, general secretary of the party and president of China; Li Peng, premier; Zhu Rongji, executive vice premier in charge of economic policy; Li Ruihuan, head of the Chinese People's Consultative Conference; Hu Jintao, member of the Secretariat of the Central Committee, Wei Jianxiang, chairman of the Disciplinary Inspection Commission; and Li Lanqing, vice premier in charge of international trade. In addition to these leaders, 15 ordinary members were elected to the full Politburo, making a total membership of 22. Five of the ordinary politburo members were provincial party secretaries—a significant increase in the representation of regional party interests in the Politburo. Two members of the Politburo were from the People's Liberation Army. There were two alternate members of the Politburo.

The Central Committee usually has over 200 members and therefore is too unwieldy to meet more than once a year, when it endorses policies put forward by the party's leaders in the Politburo. These annual meetings are known as plenums. Hence the Third Plenum of the 11th Central Committee, which marks the beginning of economic reform in China, means it was the third year after the 11th Party Congress elected the 11th Central Committee. The Central Committee elected at the 15th Party Congress has 193 full members (down from 214 in the outgoing Committee) and 151 alternate members. One noteworthy feature of the new Central Committee is that military representation has doubled to 38, reversing a trend since the 1970s of slowly reducing the number of military officers on the Central Committee. At the time of the conference there was considerable speculation that this meant that the military was demanding more say in policy.

The Central Committee also elects several commissions to carry out various party functions. The three most important are the Party Secretariat, the Disciplinary Inspection Commission, and the Central Military Commission. The Party Secretariat is responsible for carrying out the party's day-to-day activities and overseeing personnel issues. It is headed by the general secretary. In 1998 the general secretary was Jiang Zemin, who is also head of the party and president. The Disciplinary Inspection Commission was created in 1978 to look into abuses by members of the party. It is the primary organization concerned with rooting out corruption. In 1998 it was headed by Wei Jianxiang, who is also a member of the Standing Committee of the Politburo. The Central Military Commission is the organization that leads the military. The Commission consists of a chair, a permanent vice chair, and other members. Most members of the CMC are military officers. The chair of the CMC is given to the most powerful person in the party. Mao held the chairmanship of the CMC from 1949 until his death in 1976. Deng Xiaoping was the chairman from 1980 until 1989. Jiang Zemin has held the post since 1989.

Below the national level, party organization parallels the organization of the state. For every provincial-level government there is a party-level congress, committee, standing committee, secretariat, and discipline inspection commission. The party provincial secretary is the head of the provincial party organization and usually takes precedence over the governor, though occasionally the two posts have been held by the same person. Important personages in the people's provincial-level government are also usually on the provincial-level party committee. The pattern is repeated at the county level. At the most basic levels such as villages and neighborhoods there are usually only a small number of party members. In these cases there is usually a party branch or cell. These party branches play a key role in explaining party policy and generating support at the grassroots level. Party committees also exist within various branches of government. The People's Liberation Army, for example, has its own party committees and discipline inspection commissions. Party committees in the PLA extend well down to the regimental level, and political commissars and party branches or cells exist right down to the level of platoon and squad. Party committees and branches also exist in all government-run factories, schools, and other places of work.

POLICY

According to the party's 1992 constitution, the party's official ideology is "Marxism-Leninism-Mao Zedong Thought." At the 15th Party Congress in September 1997, "Deng Xiaoping Thought" was added to the official canon in an amendment to the party's constitution. Marxism provides the philosophical base for all communist parties. It provides an analysis of historical development and predicts a future utopian society brought about by a revolution led by the working class under the guiding principle "from each according to their ability, and to each according to their need." Leninism, with its emphasis on a party of disciplined, professional revolutionaries, provides the justification for leadership of the Communist Party as necessary to lead the working class, seize power, and then begin the task of transforming society in order to bring about the utopian society that Marx predicted. Mao Zedong Thought refers to the application of these universal principles to the specific conditions found in China, the belief that Marxism-Leninism must be modified to reflect the actual political and economic con-

ditions in China. Mao, for example, regarded peasantry as a revolutionary class, which is a major deviation from the ideas of Marx and Lenin, and Mao included peasants in the Communist coalition that was a necessity given the very small size of China's working class. Deng Xiaoping Thought refers to the economic and political reforms that took place under Deng's leadership from the late 1970s until his death in 1997.

Many of the policies pursued under Mao were closely tied to the party's ideology. State ownership of industry and control of the agricultural sector was consistent with the Leninist dictum that the party should command the heights of the economy in order to bring about a socialist transformation of society. In this respect, China followed the same path as other communist regimes. Other features of CCP policy before 1978 reflect the particular nature of the Chinese Communist movement. Mao and other party leaders distrusted hierarchy and were concerned that the existence of status differences impeded progress toward an egalitarian society. This interpretation of Marxism helps explain such policies as the elimination of ranks within the armed forces or sending high-ranking officials down to the countryside to learn from the peasants. Mao and others also preferred ideological incentives to economic incentives as a means of motivating workers in factories to produce more because economic incentives were believed to reinforce feudal or capitalist tendencies. In fact, a tendency to emphasize extreme egalitarianism is a marked feature of many polices adopted under Mao. This is not to say that Mao ignored practical issues or the importance of economic development for a country as poor as China, but Mao did stress the importance of political and ideological goals consistent with the aim of creating a socialist society. Thus there is the constant tendency to move toward radical policies. The Great Leap Forward was an attempt to push China more rapidly toward a utopian, communist society by rapidly speeding up the pace of economic development. The Cultural Revolution involved a wholesale attempt to wipe out vestiges of China's feudal society, destroying many monuments and other historical treasures in the process. Another goal of the Cultural Revolution was to renew the revolutionary zeal of the party and recommit it to its sacred task of building communism. Mao felt that there was a tendency for communist parties in power to become just another ruling class and that therefore a revolution was needed every 10 years or so to renew the party and keep it on the revolutionary path.

With the late 1970s, CCP policy went in a different direction. Post-Mao leaders were primarily concerned with China's low level of development. In addition, Deng and many of his closest associates had been political targets during the Cultural Revolution and were thus determined to prevent any return of the radical agenda. The Communist Party rejected Mao's slogan that class struggle was the key link and instead argued that the key link would be economic development. While the CCP has occasionally worried about ideological issues and political challenges from society, the driving force in Chinese politics since the late 1970s has been economic development. While the party constitution of 1992 states that the ultimate goal of the CCP is the creation of a communist social system, it also states that China is in the early stage of socialism, that this stage will last perhaps a hundred years and cannot be bypassed, and that in this early stage the party's central task must be economic development with all other goals and tasks subordinated to the goal of economic construction. The party constitution further states that this means that the party must uphold an ownership structure that allows for diverse means of ownership, not just state ownership. The CCP's constitution commits it to the principle that some must get rich before others and that people should get paid according to their work, not their needs. The adoption of "Deng Thought" further entrenches the importance of pragmatic economic policy as the most important function of the party.

Economic policy since the late 1970s can perhaps best be described by Deng Xiaoping's famous axiom "black cat, white cat, so long as it catches mice, it is a good cat." He meant that whatever method produces results can been adopted. As a consequence, most of the Soviet-style economy has been dismantled and there is an ever-widening gap between the Marxist-Leninist ideology of the party and its actual policies.

One of the earliest and most dramatic set of reform policies has centered around the agricultural economy. The most successful of these reforms is the household responsibility system. Under this system, individual households contract with the state to produce a certain amount of a given crop. Anything that the household produces above that amount can be sold on the open market, thus providing a market incentive to produce more. Chinese agriculture grew rapidly in the 1980s, and by 1984 China became a net food exporter. The household responsibility system resulted in a significant improvement in the standard of living for peasants with better housing and greater purchasing power to buy household goods such as TVs. Peasants can contract out land for 50 years in some cases and many have become quite rich. The agricultural reforms hastened the disintegration of collective institutions that provided the poorest peasants with economic security and social services. The people's communes have been replaced as an administrative unit by the township (xiang). A second policy that has met with great success has been to encourage small collective and privately owned enterprises, especially in the countryside. Freed from the control of the old commune system, township-owned and other collective enterprises were able to operate independently and become profit-oriented. Industrial output of these rural enterprises grew at an annual rate of 21% between 1979 and 1985 and have

maintained similar rates of growth in the 1990s. Producing a wide range of goods and services, rural enterprises are one of the most dynamic sectors of the economy and employ millions of peasants.

Another area of reform has been China's "Open Door" policy. This refers to a range of policy initiatives in the 1980s and 1990s designed to increase China's trade and attract foreign investment. The initial impetus for these policies stemmed from the perception that China was falling behind in technology and that the only way to change this was to acquire expertise, equipment, and funding from abroad. This was a total rejection of the Maoist policy of self-sufficiency, whereby China engaged in very little trade and economic contact with capitalist countries was illegal. One set of policies has been aimed at attracting foreign investment and technology transfer. Starting in 1980, China has allowed foreign businesses to invest in joint ventures and, in the 1990s, has been increasingly willing to allow wholly foreign-owned businesses to be set up in China. To encourage investment China has introduced many laws to create a legal code to protect such investment, and special economic zones, designed explicitly for foreign investment, were set up in coastal areas. Many other areas have also solicited foreign investment. Joint ventures cover a vast range of activities and include hotels, soft drinks, electronic goods, airplane parts, automobiles, and other manufactured goods. In 1996 China attracted 169 billion dollars in foreign direct investment, making it the largest recipient of investment in the developing world. Chinese trade grew dramatically in the 1980s and 1990s. In 1978 China's total imports and exports were valued at just under 20 billion dollars. By 1993, Chinese imports and exports totaled 196 billion dollars. China has joined the International Monetary Fund and World Bank and in the 1990s entered into negotiations to join the World Trade Organization. A final element of the Open Door policies has been to promote study abroad; China has encouraged tens of thousands of its students to pursue such studies.

Somewhat more problematic have been various reforms aimed at the urban economy. The system of Soviet-style planning has been gradually reduced and very little of the economy is still covered by planning. Stock markets have been created in the cities of Shanghai and Shenzhen. Laws have been passed to enhance legal protection of business and create a better economic environment. Price controls have been removed on most items and by the early 1990s the economy was clearly becoming a predominantly market economy. County-level and other small collective and private enterprises have been encouraged in the urban economy and, like their rural counterparts, have become a dynamic part of the economy and their share of the economy has grown as a result. In 1993 the state sector accounted for only 42% of industrial production. The state-owned industries are the only sector in the Chinese economy that has consistently had a poor economic performance since the beginning of reforms. Estimates as to the number of state enterprises that are running at a loss vary considerably, but the most conservative estimates put them at one-third of the total. Other estimates argue that as many as two-thirds of state enterprises were losing money in the 1990s. While the Chinese have had bankruptcy laws since the 1980s, few state enterprises have been allowed to go bankrupt and the party has been nervous about closing unprofitable enterprises as it fears the unrest that might follow rising urban unemployment. In 1997, Jiang Zemin unveiled plans to sell off many enterprises and convert others to joint stock companies with the state retaining only the largest enterprises under its control. At the time of writing it is too early to tell whether this new policy will be more successful than previous policies at tackling the problem of poor state enterprise performance.

Overall, the economic reform polices have produced dramatic results. The economy has become increasingly marketized, and China has had one of the highest economic growth rates in the world throughout the 1980s and 1990s. Real growth in GNP averaged 8.75% a year between 1979 and 1990. Real growth was a staggering 13.4% in 1993 and was estimated at 9.6% in the first two quarters of 1997. At the same time there are many problems. There have been several bouts of inflation that the state has only been able to control through tough retrenchment policies, creating a boom-and-bust cycle in the economy. Differences in income between individuals have grown, and there is increasing polarization between rich and poor. There is also a growing gap between the rich coastal provinces and the less-developed inland provinces. Crime is on the rise, and there has been a massive increase in corruption. Corruption may be one of the most serious problems facing the party, especially since it played a major role in the downfall of the Guomindang in the 1940s. Between October 1992 and August 1997, some 669,000 officials were disciplined for corruption, and more than 121,000 were expelled from the party.

Political reforms have been a less important part of the Dengist era, being essentially limited to minor changes in the party and state apparatus. The most important set of political changes has been the drive during the 1980s to retire old, poorly qualified officials and replace them with younger, better-educated, and better-qualified officials. Political reform has also meant the introduction of a legal code and the reorganization and streamlining of state bureaucracy. Other changes have included the use of the secret ballot and the introduction of some competition into elections described elsewhere in this article. Political reform has not meant any major move toward democratization despite pressure both within the party and outside it to make politics more democratic.

There is a persistent line within party debate that fur-

ther economic reform will require greater political reform, though its advocates have so far failed in their attempts to persuade the rest of the party to deepen political change. Deng was adamantly opposed to political liberalization, and it appears his successors share his views on the matter. Outside the party, reform has created new social groups and demands for a greater say in affairs. In 1989 frustrations over the pace of economic and political reform combined with anger over corruption and inflation to spark student protests in Beijing's Tiananmen Square. These protests received significant support from the city's population and were brutally put down by units of the People's Liberation Army. Many of the party officials associated with the decision to fire on the demonstrators were still in power as of 1998. It is unlikely that there will be substantial political reform as long as that remains the case. The issue of more democratization is likely to return, however, as pressure groups both within and without the party remain and may not be as weak in the future as they are now.

FINANCING

The basis for party finance is unclear. Some revenue comes from membership dues. The party is known to control a great deal of real estate and other assets.

LEADERSHIP

Deng Xiaoping dominated Chinese politics from 1977 until the last few months of his life, and his death in February 1997 at the age of 93 marks an end to the generation of veteran leaders that had led the Chinese Communist Party since the 1930s. While there were still a few revolutionary veterans left in 1997, most are in retirement and none are at the center of political power. The leadership around Jiang Zemin that emerged from the 15th Party Congress in September 1997 represents the first truly postrevolutionary generation of leaders. They are more technocratic in orientation than their predecessors and are firmly committed to the post-Mao economic reforms. Exactly how this new generation will define themselves is uncertain, however. At the time of writing, China is just emerging from the Dengist era and it is likely that there will be a few years of political maneuvering before any new directions in the development of the party or the political system becomes apparent.

MEMBERSHIP AND CONSTITUENCY

The Chinese Communist Party had 58 million members in 1997, making it by far the largest Communist Party in the world. Even with this size membership, the CCP includes only a tiny fraction of China's nearly 1.2 billion people—despite the party's claim that it is a true party of the people and therefore represents most of the population of China. In fact, members of the CCP form the political elite of China. Most military and other government officials of any importance are members of the party, as are most managers in state-owned industry. Originally, party membership was open to workers, poor peasants, soldiers, intellectuals, and "other revolutionaries." During the Maoist period people from undesirable backgrounds such as rich peasants, landlords and their relatives, capitalists, and those associated with the Guomindang were excluded from membership. In the post-Maoist era entrance standards have become far more lax. The class background of one's parents or grandparents is no longer a factor in recruitment, and in the 1980s and 1990s many of China's new rich were let into the party. Party members are admitted on a one-year probationary basis before becoming full members, and breaches of discipline are punishable by expulsion from the party. Party members are expected to not only be competent and highly motivated individuals but models of virtue and to set a good example for the rest of society. The increase in corruption in the 1990s has been a major source of concern in this regard and has done much to tarnish the party's image.

In the past, the party recruited heavily among workers and poor peasants because they were considered to be the most revolutionary. However, many of these recruits had little or no education and had few administrative skills. In the 1980s and 1990s, the party has made great efforts to improve the quality of its new members and to ensure that skills and knowledge are an important prerequisite for promotion within the party. Most of those who have been promoted to the highest levels of the party since the mid-1980s are technocrats with a university education. This stands in stark contrast to the first generation of Chinese Communist leaders, most of whom had no formal education beyond primary school. Young people are usually recruited through the Communist Youth League, whose members are between the ages of 15 and 25. The Communist Youth League is an important part of the party's efforts to recruit new members and has been the power base for several prominent party leaders over the decades.

MASS ORGANIZATIONS AND "DEMOCRATIC PARTIES"

Mass organizations exist to educate and mobilize the nonparty "progressive" elements in the population and to act as "transmission belts" to important groups in society. Important mass organizations include the All-China Federation of Trade Unions, the All-China Women's Federation, the All-China Federation of Literary and Art Circles, and the All-China Federation of Youth. There are also several religious organizations representing Daoists, Buddhists, Moslems, Protestants, and "patriotic" Catholics. The Chinese People's Consultative

Conference (CPCC) is an organization that plays an advisory role to the central authorities and used to be a key element in governance as it included important representatives from outside the Communist Party. Notable personages who have served in the past have included the Panchen Lama, second only to the Dalai Lama in importance to Tibetan Buddhism, and the younger brother of the last emperor of the Qing dynasty. While the CPCC no longer plays a prominent role, it still exists and its leader in 1997, Li Ruihuan, is a member of the Standing Committee of the Politburo and has been an important leader in the Communist Party throughout the 1990s.

In addition to the mass organizations there are eight small "democratic parties." They include the Revolutionary Committee of the Chinese Guomindang, the China Democratic League, the China Democratic National Construction Association, the China Association for Promoting Democracy, the Chinese Peasants and Workers Democratic Party, The China Zhigongdang (party for public interest), the Jiusandang (September 3 party), and the Taiwan Democratic Self-Government League. These political parties are the remnants of parties that were allied to the CCP when it came to power. They have only a very limited political role and must acknowledge the leadership of the Communist Party. They are allowed to recruit new members and all have branches throughout China. Accurate membership figures are not available, but in 1986 some 5,000 were serving as deputies in various people's congresses at or above the county level and 7 were serving on the Standing Committee of the National People's Congress. In September 1997, the eight democratic parties petitioned the Communist Party to speed up the pace of political reform and develop a more open society.

OTHER POLITICAL FORCES

Military

The role of the People's Liberation Army includes more than national defense. The virtual identification of party and army during the years of revolutionary struggle gave the army political and ideological as well as military functions. This state of affairs continued after 1949. The PLA was heavily involved in national construction projects during the entire Maoist period and was held up as a model of revolutionary virtue in the "Learn From the PLA" campaign the early 1960s. Soldier and martyr Lei Feng was considered the model citizen. During the Cultural Revolution, Marshall Lin Biao, the head of the PLA, was one of the leading radicals around Mao, though other PLA leaders opposed the excesses of the Cultural Revolution.

In the post-Mao era the PLA has become far less involved in ideology and has shed many of its political roles. Efforts have been made to modernize the military, such as the introduction of more modern weapons systems and an improvement in training and officer education. The PLA has also undergone extensive reorganization with deep cuts in manpower (the latest announcement of troop reductions came in 1997), the disbanding of economic units such as the railway construction troops, and the reintroduction of ranks. All these changes have contributed to making the PLA a more modern and professional military force. However, the PLA is still well represented in the highest circles of the Communist Party and has recently increased its membership on the Central Committee, though this is still well below the level it enjoyed in the 1960s and 1970s.

Some Chinese analysts believe that the military's influence over foreign policy has increased in the 1990s, though evidence for this is circumstantial. The PLA has also taken advantage of the reforms to create its own business empire with thousands of small and medium-sized enterprises owned by the PLA generating billions of dollars in sales. However, as of July 1998 the CCP was making an effort to close down many of these enterprises. While the gun does not control the party in China, the PLA is likely to remain a factor in China's politics and the economy for the foreseeable future.

NATIONAL PROSPECTS

The Chinese Communist Party is one of the few remaining communist parties in power. Whether it will continue to remain in power will depend on how it deals with economic and social problems in the coming years. On the one hand, the CCP has enjoyed considerable economic success. China has had one of the fastest-growing economies in the world since the early 1980s. It is a major trading nation and, in 1997, had the second-largest foreign currency reserves in the world. Living standards have improved remarkably, and the major shopping districts of Beijing and other leading cities are full of Chinese with cellular telephones buying VCRs—images that were unimaginable 10 years ago. By some measures China is already the third-largest economy in the world, and it is expected to continue growing with annual rates of 6% to 9% until the end of the century. Inflation in 1997 was under 2%. The economic reforms are firmly in place, and there is absolutely no question of turning back the clock.

On the other hand, many economic challenges remain and China's prosperity has come at the expense of many new social ills. China's state industrial sector remains hugely inefficient with most firms running at a loss. China's financial system is in desperate need of reform and inflation may return. While China has a new middle class, problems such as begging are becoming more common as income gaps continue to widen. Prostitution, crime, and drug addiction are all on the rise in many areas. China's rapid economic growth has brought pollution as well as prosperity: the air in many cities is frequently below world minimum health standards. The worship of money and the rise of materialism have fed corruption, whose increase continues to sap the prestige and legitimacy of the party. Many look back with nostalgia to the Maoist period as an era of clean government.

In addition to these social problems, China's rapid economic growth has created new political and social groups. There is now a private business class, and people are better educated and more aware of what the rest of the world has to offer. More and more nonstate organizations are being set up with the potential to develop into political pressure groups. Peasant protests are not uncommon, and the party's ability to control and mold society has been reduced by its own reforms. There is a more active dissident movement in China, though it is not strong enough to present any serious challenge to the party. Within the party, there are groups that feel that political reform will be necessary to preserve the party and that the system needs to become more open to maintain and preserve the economic reforms. As the 1990s draw to a close the party's most important leaders show little interest in substantive political reform, but that could change. Exactly how China will change in response to these problems and challenges is highly uncertain. But it will change. The Chinese system has been a highly dynamic and flexible one; it is likely to be able to adapt and shift in order to meet its challenges.

Further Reading

Beaufort, Simon de. *Yellow Earth, Green Jade: Constants in Chinese Political Mores.* Harvard Center for International Affairs. Cambridge, Mass.: Harvard University Press, 1978.

Blecher, Marc, and Vivienne Shue. *Tethered Deer: Government and Economy in a Chinese County.* Stanford, Calif.: Stanford University Press, 1996.

Dittmer, Lowell. *China's Continuous Revolution: The Post-Liberation Epoch, 1949–1981.* Berkeley: University of California Press, 1987.

Fewsmith, Joseph. *Dilemmas of Reform in China.* Armonk, N.Y.: M.E. Sharpe, 1994.

Goldman, Merle. *Sowing the Seeds of Democracy in China: Political Reform in the Deng Xiaoping Era* Cambridge, Mass.: Harvard University Press, 1994.

Goodman, David S.G., and Gerald Segal, eds. *China Deconstructs: Politics, Trade, and Regionalism.* London: Routledge, 1994.

Hamrin, Carol Lee, and Suisheng Zhao, eds. *Decision-Making in Deng's China: Perspectives from Insiders.* Armonk, N.Y.: M.E. Sharpe, 1995.

Lee, Hong Yung. *The Politics of the Chinese Cultural Revolution.* Berkeley: University of California Press, 1978.

Lieberthal, Kenneth. *Governing China: From Revolution through Reform.* New York: W.W. Norton, 1995.

Lieberthal, Kenneth, and Michael Oksenberg. *Policy Making in China: Leaders, Structures, and Processes.* Princeton, N.J.: Princeton University Press, 1988.

Naughton, Barry. *Growing Out of the Plan: Chinese Economic Reform 1978–1993.* Cambridge: Cambridge University Press, 1995.

Pearson, Margaret M. *China's New Business Elite: The Political Consequences of Economic Reform.* Berkeley: University of California Press, 1997.

Scalapino, Robert A., ed. *Elites in the People's Republic of China.* Seattle: University of Washington Press, 1972.

Schram, Stuart. *The Thought of Mao Tse-tung.* Cambridge: Cambridge University Press, 1989.

Schurmann, Franz. *Ideology and Organization in Communist China*, 2d ed. Berkeley: University of California Press, 1970.

Teiwes, Frederick C. *Politics and Purges in China*, 2d ed. Armonk, N.Y.: M.E. Sharpe, 1993.

Yan Jiaqi, and Gao Gao. *Turbulent Decade: A History of the Cultural Revolution.* Trans. and ed. D.W.Y. Kwok. SHAPS Library of Translations. Honolulu: University of Hawaii Press, 1996.

REPUBLIC OF COLOMBIA

(República de Colombia)

By Alejandro S. Hope

THE SYSTEM OF GOVERNMENT

Colombia is a nation located at the northernmost tip of South America, covering 445,000 square miles (1,138,914 square kilometers) with coasts on both the Atlantic and the Pacific Oceans and bordering Brazil, Ecuador, Panama, Peru, and Venezuela. Its population of 35 million people makes it the third-most-populous country of both Latin America and the Spanish-speaking world. Its capital, Santafé de Bogotá, has over 5 million inhabitants, and other major cities include Medellín (2.3 millions), Calí (1.7 millions), and Barranquilla (1 million). As a whole, Colombia is over 70% urban and its literacy rate is around 85%. Ethnically, the Colombian people are predominantly of mixed European and Amerindian stock, although there is a significant African presence (around 18% of the total population) and some scattered indigenous groups (around 700,000 people). Roman Catholicism is still practiced by the great majority of Colombians, but other Christian denominations have made significant inroads in recent years.

The politics of Colombia is rife with contradictions: the country is formally a unitary republic, but regional impulses run deep; its system of government is strongly presidentialist, but the power of the chief executive is effectively checked by institutional and extrainstitutional actors; political violence reaches ghastly levels, but it has not disturbed one of the longest stretches of civilian government in Latin America; finally, partisan divisions are deeply entrenched, but so is a culture of consensus that has provided the country 40 years of uninterrupted political stability and economic growth.

The major cleavage in Colombian politics—much stronger than class identification or ethnic rifts—is support for either the Liberal or the Conservative Party. The two traditional parties have overwhelmingly dominated the political landscape since the 1840s (winning over 95% of the electoral positions since 1945). Their rivalries and agreements have shaped the political life of the country and determined the level of violence. On many occasions, their feud for power and patronage resources has engendered bloody civil wars. The most brutal scenes of political strife took place during the War of the Thousand Days (1899–1902) and during the period known as *La Violencia* (roughly 1948–56), in which 100,000 and 200,000 Colombians died, respectively.

As a consequence of *La Violencia*, Colombia experienced the brief populist dictatorship of General Gustavo Rojas Pinilla (1953–57). The return to civilian government came about as a result of a landmark agreement between Conservative and Liberal leaders that created the so-called National Front. Under the accord, Liberals and Conservatives alternated in the presidency and carved up by halves congressional seats and administrative positions during a 16-year period from 1958 to 1974. The coalition significantly reduced the level of political violence, but at the cost of stultifying democratic practices. Since 1974, there has been a gradual return to more competitive politics, but consensus persists on major issues, such as economic policy.

Executive

The president of the Republic is chief of state, head of government, and supreme administrative authority. In typical Latin American fashion, the presidency has extensive formal powers that far surpass the authority of both the legislative and judiciary branches. The president may appoint and remove Cabinet ministers and most public officials without congressional authorization; he or she has extensive veto power over legislation, including a line-item veto over the budget, as well as broad executive decree faculties and, most important, the power to invoke—unhindered by Congress—a "state of internal commotion," during which civil rights and existing legislation are suspended for three months.

Ministers may initiate legislation, participate in congressional debates, and declare a matter urgent. The legislature does not hold firmly the purse strings of the government: if the budget is not approved prior to the beginning of the fiscal year, the budget of the preceding period remains in place (without inflationary adjustment). The chief executive, moreover, has wide authority to determine economic policy: the Central Bank is nominally autonomous, but the government names six of the seven members of its ruling board. The president is also commander in chief of the armed forces and controls directly most police units. He or she can negotiate without congressional oversight with foreign powers, although any foreign treaties must be submitted to the legislature for ratification.

Notwithstanding the wide powers of the presidency, executive authority is limited to a larger extent than in most other Latin American countries. Congress may override a presidential veto with simple majorities (50% +1) in both chambers. The attorney general (*Fiscal General de la Nación*) is appointed by the Supreme Court and has recently shown significant autonomy, particularly during the investigations of the campaign finances of President Ernesto Samper. In Congress, presidential power is limited by factional infighting within the parties and the approval of legislation usually requires intense politicking. On security and defense issues, the armed forces often have a mind of their own and their influence has been growing over the last 15 years as a result of the war against leftist guerrillas and the drug cartels. In some portions of the rugged Colombian countryside, extra-institutional actors (e.g., drug lords, guerrillas) wield more power than governmental institutions. Civil society can also check the power of the president: business groups and the Catholic Church have substantial authority over economic policy and social issues, respectively. The press is significantly free, although threatened by violence, and public opinion can put massive pressure on government, even in nonelectoral periods.

The president is elected for a four-year term in a direct popular election. If no candidate obtains an absolute majority in the first round of voting, a second contest is held three weeks afterwards between the two leading candidates. The president may not seek reelection under any circumstances, even after an intervening term. In the presidential elections of 1994, the electorate could choose among 18 different tickets, none of which obtained more than 50% of the total vote. In the second round, Ernesto Samper Pizano, the Liberal candidate, garnered 50.57% of the vote, whereas Andrés Pastrana Arango, the Conservative candidate, obtained 48.45% of the ballots. The presidential elections of 1998 also went to a second round. Pastrana, who trailed the Liberal Horacio Serpa Uribe slightly in the first round managed a 52%-to-48% victory in the runoff.

Breaking a tradition of more than a century, the constitution of 1991 created the office of the vice presidency. The vice president is chosen by direct popular election, running on the ticket of the president. He or she is the designated successor in the event of the president's ill health, death or resignation and would serve until the end of the term. The vice president may hold administrative functions at the discretion of the head of government, but the constitution does not automatically guarantee him anything other than ceremonial functions. Real power is more often vested in key ministers, such as the minister of the interior (police and internal affairs), the minister of finance (economic policy), and the minister of defense (usually a military officer).

Legislature

The Colombian Congress is a bicameral legislature composed of a Senate (*Senado*) and a House of Representatives (*Cámara de Representantes*). It holds two regular sessions annually, from March 16 to June 20 and from July 20 to December 16, but it may be convened for spe-

Presidents since 1945		
1945–46	Alberto Lleras Camargo	(Liberal)
1946–50	Mariano Ospina Pérez	(Conservative)
1950–53	Laureano Gómez	(Conservative)
1953–57	Gen. Gustavo Rojas Pinilla	(Military dictator)
1957–58	Military Junta	(presided over by Maj. Gen. Gabriel Paris)
1958–62	Alberto Lleras Camargo	(National Front/Liberal)
1962–66	Guillermo León Valencia	(National Front/Conservative)
1966–70	Carlos Lleras Restrepo	(National Front/Liberal)
1970–74	Misael Pastrana Borrero	(National Front/Conservative)
1974–78	Alfonso López Michelsen	(Liberal)
1978–82	Julio César Turbay Ayala	(Liberal)
1982–86	Belisario Betancur Cuartas	(Conservative)
1986–90	Virgilio Barco Vargas	(Liberal)
1990–94	César Gaviria Pérez	(Liberal)
1994–98	Ernesto Samper Pizano	(Liberal)
1998–	Andrés Pastrana Arango	(Conservative)

cial sessions. The Senate has 102 members, elected for a four-year term through a system of proportional representation from a national list. Two seats are reserved for representatives of indigenous communities. The House of Representatives has at present 161 members, serving also four years and elected in two-member districts of 250,000 inhabitants (guaranteeing at least 2 representatives per department); 5 seats are reserved for ethnic minorities. All members of Congress may be reelected indefinitely, and congressional elections are not held concurrently with the presidential ballot.

The formal authority of Congress is quite large in comparison with that of other Latin American legislatures. The elected body has the power of initiation, amendment, interpretation, and repeal of legislation. It must approve the budget and any modification to the tax code, as well as exercising oversight on public spending. Its attributions include ratification of appointments of high-ranking military officers and diplomats. Moreover, congressmen may remove Cabinet ministers through a vote of no confidence in both houses and can initiate impeachment procedures against the president.

The Senate is responsible for conducting impeachment proceedings, at the request of the House of Representatives. Furthermore, it selects the members of the Constitutional Court and the attorney general, as well as ratifying declarations of war and entry of foreign troops. Meanwhile, the lower chamber of Congress has as its specific attributions complete oversight over public spending, as well as the initiation of impeachment investigations against the president, Supreme Court justices, and the attorney general.

In daily practice, congressional power has been significantly reduced in recent years. The constitution of 1991 did away with many prerogatives that buttressed the clientele-building capabilities of congressman. Legislators can no longer hold other public positions simultaneously, nor can alternates be elected to serve temporarily as substitutes: the temporary absence of a congressman results in giving away the position to the runner-up in the election. Nepotism and pork-barrel legislation (auxilios) have been banned. The goal was to reduce the very marked orientation of Colombian congressmen toward regional politics and to strengthen the internal discipline of parties.

Traditionally, factional struggles within parties have been intense, particularly on issues of patronage and electoral legislation. Fiscal policy is often derailed by the attempts of legislators to broker deals favoring their local fiefdoms. Presidents have found it difficult to count on solid congressional majorities: cross-party, single-issue coalitions are not strange occurrences. Nevertheless, there are some indications of growing party cohesiveness in Congress, particularly on issues of crucial importance for the government: for instance, Liberal legislators stood solidly behind President Samper during the recent investigations of his campaign finances and prevented the initiation of impeachment proceedings in the Senate.

In recent congressional elections, the traditional domination of the two major parties has been reified, in spite of the temporary rise of a leftist coalition led by former guerrilla members. The Liberals are increasingly appearing as the dominant party, having defeated the Conservatives in the last four legislative ballots. In the elections of March 1994, the Liberal Party gained an important majority in both houses of Congress (67 senators and 89 representatives) in their most decisive congressional victory in years. The Conservatives saw their share of the vote drop from its customary 35–40% to little more than a quarter of the vote. Meanwhile, the leftist coalition M-19 Democratic Alliance saw its hopes crushed after a surprisingly strong showing in the elections for the Constitutional Assembly of 1991. The Liberals rose to 98 representatives while falling to 51 senators in the March 1998 legislative elections; in both chambers their number of members was double that of the Conservatives.

Judiciary

The Colombian judicial system is founded on Roman law tradition. Juries are employed infrequently, if at all. At the head of the court system stands the Supreme Court of Justice. It serves as the tribunal of last resort in all disputes involving ordinary legislation. It may moreover investigate and bring to trial the president (after impeachment), members of Congress, the attorney general, and other public officials. Justices are selected by the Supreme Council of the Judiciary (Consejo Superior de la Judicatura), although they may be removed by the Senate; they usually serve until retirement age. For administrative matters and questions regarding executive decrees, the highest court is the Council of State. Its members are also selected by the Supreme Council of the Judiciary and serve until retirement age, unless removed by the Senate.

The Supreme Court does not subject legislation to judicial review; that role is reserved to the Constitutional Court. That body rules on the constitutionality of laws, referenda, and international treaties challenged by the chief executive or any citizen. Its eight justices are selected for an eight-year term by the Senate from lists presented by the president and may be removed by the upper house of Congress. Since its inception in 1991, the Constitutional Court has yet to face a major case where the vital interests of the government or other key political actors were at stake, making it difficult to measure its real power. Prior experience, however, points to a long tradition of judicial independence, even in the face of strong executive pressure.

The lower courts are usually overburdened and inefficient, and their integrity has been severely shaken in recent years by violence, corruption, and drug trafficking. The constitution of 1991 introduced a series of reforms to the judicial system that may in the long run improve the administration of justice. The creation of the Supreme Council of the Judiciary is intended to heighten the accountability of judges and reduce inefficiencies in the court system. Moreover, the new constitutional text allows for the election of justices of the peace at the municipal level. Most important, the newly gained autonomy of the attorney general is expected to help restructure the entire criminal investigation system and improve the conditions for the prosecution of crimes.

Regional and Local Government

Colombia is at present divided into 32 departments and the capital district (*Distrito Capital*) of Santafé de Bogotá. Each department is subdivided into municipalities (*municipios*), the lowest level of government. Moreover, the constitution of 1991 allowed for the creation of autonomous indigenous territories, spanning one or more departments. The new constitutional framework also introduced the direct popular election of the governors of the departments and the mayors, including the mayor of Bogotá. Governors and mayors are chosen for three-year terms; the former cannot serve a second term, while the latter may be reelected indefinitely. The departments have popularly elected unicameral assemblies (*Asamblea Departamental*) and the municipalities have elected councils (*Concejo Municipal*), both serving three-year terms. In the elections of 1997, the Liberal Party maintained control of most departments, municipalities, and the local government of Bogotá.

Building on a deeply entrenched tradition of regionalism, the constitution of 1991 greatly strengthened regional and local governments, endowing them with electoral legitimacy and enhancing their faculties and resources. Power, however, is still heavily centralized. The fiscal structure is strongly biased in favor of the central government, and most bureaucrats report directly to Bogotá. Education, health, and most social spending are prerogatives of the national government, limiting the clientele-building capacity of governors. In many provincial towns, municipal councils exist only in name and often do not meet. Mayors must frequently consult on major decisions with the governor of their department, and their financial resources are severely limited.

THE ELECTORAL SYSTEM

Colombians choose their president, vice president, legislators, department governors, mayors, departmental assemblies, and municipal councils in direct popular elections. Every citizen 18 years of age or older may vote,

except for individuals deprived of their political rights by court order. Women obtained the right to vote in 1957, and all property and literacy qualifications were abolished in 1936. Prior registration is not necessary to vote: citizens must only present their *cédula de identidad* (identity card) at their preassigned polling places. Elections are organized by the autonomous National Electoral Council (*Consejo Nacional Electoral*), whose members are selected by the Council of State from lists presented by legally registered political parties. The Electoral Council prints and distributes the official ballots and regularly informs on the vote count during election day. The centralization of electoral organization has been a fundamental political transformation of recent years: prior to 1991, political parties distributed their own ballots and supervised the vote count, opening the door for mutual and frequent accusations of electoral fraud. Elections are always held on Sunday, with polls opening from 8:00 A.M. to 4:00 P.M. Violent clashes between rival party supporters are not uncommon on election day.

The president and vice president must be elected by absolute majority (50% + 1), thus allowing for a second round. At lower levels, executives (governors and mayors) are chosen by a plurality of voters within their respective political division (departments or municipalities). All legislatures (Congress, departmental assemblies, municipal councils) are elected by a list system of proportional representation. Congressmen and departmental assemblypersons are chosen at large within their respective departments; councilors are elected at large within their municipality. Seats are apportioned through a system of electoral quotient, obtained by dividing the total number of valid votes by the number of available positions. The excess seats are distributed by largest remainder in descending order. There is no legally preestablished threshold to obtain representation, but the number of available seats is usually small, thus raising the electoral quotient. In the last congressional election, lists needed to obtain on average 1.3% of the departmental vote to gain seats in the national legislature.

Lists are determined by party directorates at the departmental or municipal levels and then sent to Bogotá for approval by the national directorate. In many instances, factionalism impedes compromise at the local level and several competing lists are sent to the national headquarters. National party leaders may broker a compromise between contending groups or allow the registration of competing lists. The practice of multiple party lists has been in decline in recent years as a result of a change in electoral rules: votes for lists that do not reach the electoral quotient are no longer redistributed to the list with the same party label that has the most votes but to the largest vote winners in strict descending order, notwithstanding their party affiliation. Consequently, internal party cohesion has been enhanced, as well as the relative power of national leaders. Nevertheless, recent elections have still seen an average of

13.2 lists per department. Candidates gain seats by their place on the list and may run outside their department of residence. Key party leaders are often placed in safe districts near the top of the departmental ticket. Since 1991, lists no longer include alternates: in the permanent or temporary absence of a legislator, his or her seat is given away to a member of a competing list.

Voting is not compulsory for Colombian citizens, and abstentionism has become a growing concern. In the congressional elections of 1994, 70% of registered voters did not bother to go to the polls. In the first round of the last presidential election, the abstention rate was a whopping 66%; even in the second and decisive round, more than half of the voters decided to stay away from the polls. Turnout is usually higher in urban than in rural areas and seems to be positively correlated to income and educational level. The most common explanations for the high level of abstentionism include discontent with the party system, the lack of interest generated by traditional elite candidates, and the logistical difficulties of voting (e.g., obtaining a *cédula*, finding the polling place).

THE PARTY SYSTEM

Origins of the Parties

The two traditional Colombian parties trace their origins to the conflict that erupted in the immediate postindependence period between the followers of Simón Bolívar and Francisco de Paula Santander. The two main cleavages separating the two groups were the organization of the State and the role of the Catholic Church within it: the Conservatives, identified with Bolívar, stood for centralism and Catholicism as the state religion; the Liberals, with Santander at their head, championed federalism and anticlericalism. By the 1840s, the terms Liberal and Conservative had become part of common political parlance.

The struggle for power and patronage between the traditional parties has often led to armed conflict. In 1957, after *La Violencia* and the Rojas Pinilla dictatorial interlude, two key political figures, Alberto Lleras Camargo (Liberal) and Laureano Gómez (Conservative), negotiated the crucial Sitges Agreement that gave form to the National Front. The front managed to reduce political violence (although intermittent partisan clashes continued until 1965), as well as avoiding the cycle of instability and military intervention. Since the mid-1980s, the parties have gradually and painfully adapted to more competitive politics. In recent years, their style and organizational features have undergone a process of modernization and campaigns have seemed more "normal," acrimonious affairs. The strong showing of a leftist coalition, led by the former guerrillas of the M-19, in the elections for the Constitutional Assembly of 1991 appeared to signal the end of the two-party system. More

recent results have confounded that expectation: in the first round of the presidential elections of 1994, the Liberal and Conservative candidates obtained a combined total of 90% of the vote. Nevertheless, the conflict over the alleged contributions of drug traffickers to President Samper's electoral campaign has seemingly opened a widening rift between the traditional parties—as well as within the Liberal Party—that could significantly transform Colombian party politics in the near future.

The Parties in Law

Colombian law defines political parties as "permanent institutions that reflect political pluralism, promote and channel citizen participation, and contribute to the formation and manifestation of popular will, with the goal of gaining power . . . and helping influence the political and democratic decisions of the Nation." There are few legal restrictions on electoral participation: to obtain legal recognition and inclusion in the ballots, a party must present to the National Electoral Council a copy of its internal regulations and political platform as well as 50,000 signatures. Since 1986, political parties receive government subsidies (equivalent to 2.16 million dollars in 1994) according to the following formula: 80% of the subsidy is distributed in proportion to the number of seats obtained by each party in the last election; and 20% is distributed in equal shares to all parties. Campaign financing is subject to different regulations. Private contributions are allegedly regulated by the National Electoral Council, but soft, unaccounted money seems to flow easily into the parties. Moreover, the system of patronage has tended to favor the two-party system, notwithstanding the legislative efforts to improve the fairness of electoral processes.

Party Organization

The changes brought by the constitution of 1991 have tended to gradually transfer decision-making power and rent-seeking opportunities from elected officials to the national bureaucracy. For parties, that has meant a strengthening of national directorates at the expense of regional bosses.

Party statutes call for the organization of biennial national conventions, attended by government and party officials. National cadres, including the president or director of the party, are elected on such occasions. Moreover, national conventions serve to nominate the presidential and vice presidential candidates in election years. Even though the conventions are formally democratic, national power brokers tend to dominate the proceedings and departmental representatives usually ratify the decisions previously taken by the leadership. By contrast, national directorates seldom meddle in departmental or municipal conventions and local bosses rule over the selection process of congressional candidates and regional party leaders.

Even though the parties enjoy a strong measure of regionalism and decentralization, major strategic decisions are usually controlled by a handful of top national politicians, the so-called natural bosses (*jefes naturales*). In a pattern reminiscent of the Japanese Liberal Democratic Party (LDP), the natural bosses often do not hold formal positions within the organizational structure of the party. They are usually former presidents or presidential candidates, mostly recruited from the elite and frequently belonging to traditional political families. Their power is a function of their prestige, their access to power, and the size of their clientele. They are regularly called to either head the party during electoral periods or to design the overarching electoral strategy: for instance, former President Alfonso López Michelsen was named national director of the Liberal Party during the presidential and congressional campaigns of 1990.

Campaigning

Long-standing patterns of party identification have traditionally constituted the major source of electoral support for the two traditional parties. The existence of a significant number of so-called hard votes (voters that support a party under all circumstances) has tended to inhibit strenuous campaign activity, centering the efforts of party machines on bringing out the vote. That role has been traditionally assigned to local or regional bosses (so-called *caciques* or *gamonales*), tied to a specific national faction, led by a "natural boss." Electoral results used to depend on the turnout: the winning party was the one better able to bring out its supporters on election day.

In recent decades, however, the Colombian political landscape has seen a rise in the numbers of unidentified voters, more alert to programmatic and/or character issues and capable of important mood swings. Consequently, campaigns have become more intense, seeking to stir interest and capture the "floating vote." Moreover, the two-round system, introduced by the constitution of 1991, has forced candidates to seek absolute majorities, thus enhancing the strategic relevance of independent voters. For instance, according to some exit polls, close to 40% of the voters in the second round of the presidential elections of 1994 were independents; with a very low turnout, their majority support for Ernesto Samper gave him the decisive edge to defeat his Conservative rival, Andrés Pastrana.

Presidential campaigns have tended to gather more interest and organizational resources than congressional contests. Campaigns are usually led by the presidential candidate, in coordination with the national directorate. Candidates go on the stump for a significant portion of the campaign, holding rallies, giving speeches, and meeting local bosses throughout the country. Recent electoral contests, however, have been increasingly fought in the electronic media, particularly on television. In a poll following the 1994 presidential election, 67% of the respondents claimed they had followed the campaign primarily through radio or television. Furthermore, the televised debate between the two leading presidential hopefuls was seen by 48% of the Colombian population, according to an independent ratings agency.

Campaigns are not normally fought in terms of issues. Even though the Liberals tend to be somewhat more to the left on economic matters, the ideological proximity of the two major parties makes it difficult for the electorate to differentiate between the proposals of the leading candidates. In the last presidential election, both the Liberal and the Conservative candidates fundamentally supported the institutional and economic reforms of President César Gaviria (the so-called *revolcón*), although Ernesto Samper called for compensatory measures and increased social spending to mitigate the negative impact of economic liberalization. The main campaign "issues" usually have to do with the character and the record of the candidates and, lately, the question of the drug trade and its social, economic, and foreign policy implications have come to the foreground of political debate.

Campaigns are usually long-drawn and expensive battles, lasting almost a year and straining the financial resources of the parties. Since 1986, government partially reimburses campaign expenses: during the 1994 presidential contest, public subsidies to electoral campaigns totaled 3,700 million Colombian pesos (approximately 3.4 million dollars). Nevertheless, parties and candidates still depend massively on private contributions, and the flow of private resources to electoral campaigns is poorly regulated. Industrialists, coffee growers, and other wealthy party supporters have traditionally been a major source of campaign funds and charges of influence peddling are not uncommon. More disturbingly, drug cartels have apparently begun to pour money into the warchests of major candidates. On the evening of the second round of the presidential elections of 1994, the defeated candidate, Andrés Pastrana, accused his Liberal rival, Ernesto Samper, of receiving 6 million dollars from the barons of the Calí drug cartel. Even though the president has consistently denied the charges, the scandal led to the indictment of a number of campaign officials, including Samper's chief adviser, Fernando Botero, and to a failed impeachment procedure against the chief executive. According to Colombian sources, the question is not whether the campaign received the money, but whether Samper knew about the source of the donation. Some recent polls suggest that a large majority of Colombians have received the president's claims of innocence with growing disbelief.

Independent Voters

The number of independent voters has been growing in recent decades. Party identification has been consistently declining for at least a generation, particularly in urban areas: in 1970, 86% of the inhabitants of Bogotá identified strongly with one of the two major parties; by 1993, the proportion had dropped to 52%. Industrialization and urbanization seem to be the root causes of the declining allegiance for traditional parties. The gradual demise of age-old patron-client networks in the countryside has made it more difficult and more expensive to sustain a permanent support base. The young, more independent of family traditions, mores, and political preferences, have been particularly difficult to recruit as either members or mere sympathizers of the main parties. Moreover, polls suggest that Colombians regard traditional politics with extreme cynicism and hold the political class in very low public esteem.

However, the rise of independent voters does not yet spell doom for the two-party system. In the presidential elections of 1994, the traditional parties still managed to capture 91% of the total vote. Party identification, though decreasing, is still high by Latin American standards and party identifiers still vote massively for their preferred party in every contest. Third parties still face significant formal and informal inequalities, particularly with regard to financial resources and access to the electronic media. The rapid rise and decline of the leftist ADM-19 between 1991 and 1994 (falling from 27% to 3% of the vote within three years) are proof not only of the growing volatility of the Colombian electorate but also of the resilience of traditional political arrangements. Most disgruntled voters are seemingly opting out of the system, not bothering to go to the polls (abstentionism was 66% in the first round of the presidential elections of 1994), instead of looking for new political alternatives in the electoral arena. Ticket splitting is also an option to manifest discontent, although preferences may not be expressed within lists. However, since presidential and congressional elections are not held concurrently, wildly different results may come about within a few months. For instance, the Liberal Party lost 24 percentage points between the presidential contest of 1990 and the elections for the Constituent Assembly of 1991.

CONSERVATIVE/SOCIAL CONSERVATIVE PARTY
(Partido Conservador/Social Conservador)

HISTORY

The Conservative Party has its roots in the Catholic and centralist tradition of the 19th century. In modern times, during the so-called Liberal Republic (1930–46) and the subsequent period of *La Violencia* (1948–58), the internal cleavages of the party gradually emerged, as the organization sought to regain a mass following. The main rivalry was between the supporters of two former presidents, Laureano Gómez and Mariano Ospina.

Gómez, a prominent political figure since the 1930s, was a radical Catholic intellectual, an admirer of the Franco regime in Spain, and a quasi-dictator from 1950 to 1953. Even though he negotiated the landmark Sitges Agreement of 1957, his faction steadfastly opposed the National Front. The group has been led by Alvaro Gómez Hurtado, son of the founder, since 1965 and usually stands slightly to the right of mainstream Conservative thought, even though it has eliminated its early authoritarian proclivities. Successively known as *Laurenistas, Doctrinarios, Alvaristas, Lauro-Alvaristas,* and *Independientes,* the faction currently calls itself the National Salvation Movement (*Movimiento de Salvación Nacional;* MSN) and virtually broke away from the party in 1989, fielding its own presidential candidate (Alvaro Gómez Hurtado) in 1990 and presenting its own list in the legislative elections of 1991 and 1994.

The faction of Mariano Ospina was dominant within the party throughout the National Front period and imposed its candidates in the presidential elections of 1962 and 1970. After the death of Ospina, leadership passed to former President Misael Pastrana. Known as *Ospino-Pastranistas* or *Unionistas,* the faction is ideologically somewhat more moderate than the *Alvaristas* but rallied behind Gómez Hurtado in the presidential elections of 1974 and 1986 and supported Belisario Betancur in 1982. It is important to note that factional infighting is more centered on personality issues and regional politics than on clear ideological or class divides. The *Ospino-Pastranistas* led the transformation of the party in the 1980s, moderating its discourse and changing its name to Social Conservative Party in 1987. It still dominates most of the party's internal decision bodies.

A third contending faction has been on the rise in recent years. In 1990, Andrés Pastrana Arango, son of the *Ospino-Pastranista* leader, founded a personalized movement, the so-called New Democratic Force (*Nueva Fuerza Democrática;* NFD). The group is led by younger, more technocratic cadres and is perceived as the reformist wing of the Conservative Party; it is more inclined toward free-market economics and has sought to attract a younger, more urban electorate. In 1994, the movement managed to rally all the Conservative factions behind the presidential candidacy of its leader and obtained the best electoral result for a Conservative nominee since 1982. And in 1998 Pastrana won the presidency.

ORGANIZATION

The Social Conservative Party, in conjunction with the semidissident MSN and NFD, has organizational presence throughout the Colombian territory. The party has traditionally found its strength in patron-client networks covering rural areas. According to most observers of Colombian politics, the Conservatives have a more comprehensive territorial structure at the municipal level and their machine is usually more effective than the Liberal Party in garnering the "hard vote" on election day. The Conservative organization tends to be extremely hierarchical and centralized, firmly ruled by the leaders of the main national factions in Bogotá. Traditionally, factional struggles were contained by the national directorate and a measure of party discipline existed in spite of intense personal rivalries. Over the last decade, however, infighting has degenerated into open schisms and disputes over nominations have become increasingly acrimonious.

As its Liberal rival, the Conservative Party has attempted to create a network of affiliated social organizations, finding some support in rural areas. The initiative, however, has been less than successful in recruiting social movements. Its constituency in urban areas is maintained by its control of part of the media. In Bogotá, three dailies, *El Siglo* (once run by Laureano Gómez and Alvaro Gómez Hurtado), *La República* (directed by *Ospino-Pastranistas*), and *La Prensa* (the voice of Andrés Pastrana), have a clear Conservative tendency. Several provincial papers, as well as a number of radio stations and television programs, also tend to support the Conservative cause. The party has no formal affiliation with any international organizations, although it has informally attended some Christian Democratic meetings.

The national headquarters of the party are at Calle 36, No. 16-56, Santafé de Bogotá.

POLICY

The Conservative Party has historically stood behind centralism, close ties between church and state, and the preservation of the traditional social order. Until the 1930s, Conservatives opposed the extension of the suffrage, and they had marked authoritarian tendencies up through the 1950s, particularly among the supporters of Laureano Gómez. In recent years, the organization has stood somewhat to the right of center on most social and economic issues. It tends to oppose state interventionism and social welfare measures, even though it supported a moderate ISI development strategy throughout the postwar era. Some of its elected officials, such as former President Belisario Betancur, even showed a slight populist bent and were keen on augmenting social spending. Nevertheless, the party backed the economic liberalization measures of the Gaviria administration, and lately, under the leadership of Andrés Pastrana and the NFD, it has acquired a more technocratic discourse.

On social issues, the party's policies tend to be in accordance with its name. During the 1980s, Conservatives opposed the legalization of divorce championed by the Liberals and were ambiguous regarding birth control policies. However, their differences with their Liberal rivals have been more marked on national security questions. Most Conservative politicians opposed the policy of *sometimiento* of President Gaviria, whereby drug lords obtained a guarantee of nonextradition to the United

States in exchange for their surrender to the Colombian authorities. Moreover, they have steadfastly resisted negotiations with the leftist guerrillas and called for hardline measures against subversive activity. On foreign policy, they have supported the government in its standoff with the United States over the drug trade and have been very critical of the certification process in the U.S. Congress and the overall U.S. drug policy.

MEMBERSHIP AND CONSTITUENCY

The Conservative Party has presence throughout the Colombian territory, but its strength varies by department. Its major strongholds are located in the central valleys of the country, particularly in the departments of Antioquía, Cundinamarca, Caldas, North Santander, and Risaralda, as well as in Narino, on the southern Pacific Coast. It tends to attract more votes in rural areas than in large metropolitan areas, although it outpolled the Liberals in both Medellín and Calí in 1994. The party has a strong appeal among upper- and middle-class voters, as well as among older age groups. Moreover, its constituency has traditionally included rural landowners, provincial industrialists (particularly from Antioquía), the church hierarchy, military officers, and a portion of organized labor (particularly, the Christian-oriented Union of Colombian Workers; CUTC). The Pastrana candidacy, however, was able to attract voters of all ages and class backgrounds in the 1994 and 1998 presidential contests. Since 1945, the party has consistently garnered between 35 and 40% of the national vote, with peaks of 52% in 1998, 48.5% in 1964, and 44.98% in 1994, and a trough of 30.8% in 1972. Figures on membership range from 300,000 to 2 million affiliates.

FINANCING

The party finances its activities from a combination of sources, including government subsidies, membership fees, corporate donations, contributions from officeholders and wealthy private supporters, and fund-raising events. In nonelectoral periods, the financial requirements of the organization are not significant and the permanent staff is small. During campaigns, the party draws heavily from every possible source of funding. In 1994, the government refunded the party approximately 1.7 million dollars for the expenses incurred during the presidential campaign. The scandal that has enveloped the Liberal Party over the alleged contributions of drug traffickers has not left the Conservatives unscathed: in the past three years, the Colombian political milieu has been seething with allegations that drug money filtered into the electoral efforts of the two major parties. (See also, "Campaigning," earlier in this article.)

LEADERSHIP

Party leadership has traditionally been drawn from long-standing political dynasties, such as the Gómez, the Pastrana, or the Ospina. Stability and long-term mandates have been a constant both at the national and the regional levels; many of the present top cadres have been active in politics since at least the 1950s. Nevertheless, the organization has undergone a gradual process of rejuvenation in recent years, and succession now points toward Andrés Pastrana.

Some of the main leaders include:

- **Andrés Pastrana Arango** (born 1954 in Bogotá), son of a former president, Misael Pastrana Borrero, has held the mayorship of Bogotá and a Senate seat. A journalist and a former kidnap victim, Pastrana has his own power base in the NFD and has played up his image of independence, of somehow being above party politics. He was the party nominee in 1994, rallying behind his candidacy all the Conservative factions, and went on to win in 1998.

- **Alvaro Gómez Hurtado** (born 1919 in Bogotá—died 1995) was an old party hand, son of the legendary Laureano Gómez and leader of the *Alvarista* faction since 1965. Until his assassination in 1995, he headed the MSN and, in spite of his age, was still regarded as a powerful force in Colombian politics. He was a presidential candidate in 1974, 1986, and 1990. No clear successor has yet appeared.

- **Belisario Betancur Cuartas** (born 1923 in Antioquía) was president of the Republic from 1982 to 1986 and has been in semiretirement since the late 1980s. Nevertheless, as the last Conservative president, his voice still has considerable authority within the party.

PROSPECTS

The Conservative Party had failed to win a national election since 1982, but its prospects became brighter than at any time since the mid-1980s. In 1994, the Liberals barely edged them in the presidential race, winning by only 2 percentage points in the second round. Since that election, the drug money scandal crippled the Liberal Party and the presidency of Ernesto Samper. Andrés Pastrana, a charismatic leader and a telegenic candidate, took advantage of the division among his Liberal rivals and made a successful presidential run in 1998.

LIBERAL PARTY
(Partido Liberal)

HISTORY

The lineage of the Liberal Party goes back to the struggle between Francisco de Paula Santander and Simón Bolívar in the immediate aftermath of the War of Independence. Descending from Santander, the party has historically been the rallying movement of the urban middle classes and the champion of anticlericalism. The modern factions within the party date back to the period known as the Liberal Republic (1930–46), when moderate elements opposed the allegedly radical reformist efforts of López Pumarejo. The divide between moderates and radicals grew throughout the 1940s, during the brief reign of Jorge Gaitán, the populist mayor of Bogotá, whose murder in 1948 unleashed *La Violencia*.

In the 1980s, the influence of Galán and the *Nuevo Liberalismo* progressively grew, in spite of its failure to secure the Liberal nomination in 1986. His meteoric rise to prominence, however, was cut short in 1989, when gunmen of the Medellín drug cartel killed him during a campaign rally. His murder threw the Liberal Party into unprecedented turmoil and left the younger generation without effective leadership. Nevertheless, the indignation over the crime and the mantle of Galán's legacy was sufficient to guarantee the nomination and electoral victory of César Gaviria, a chief adviser of the murdered politician. His economic and institutional reforms (the so-called *revolcón*) and his soft-line drug policy faced intense opposition within the party, fatally weakening the remnants of the *Nuevo Liberalismo*.

In 1994, Ernesto Samper, a younger member of the orthodox faction, gained the nomination with a center-left discourse that stood in moderate opposition to the economic liberalization measures of the Gaviria administration. His presidency, nevertheless, was consistently sapped by the drug money scandal. Amid deep divisions within the party, Horacio Serpa Uribe, the interior minister, emerged as the Liberal presidential candidate.

ORGANIZATION

Since World War II, the Liberal Party has been beset by virulent factionalism that has weakened the internal discipline of the organization. Regional bosses have played a somewhat bigger role among the Liberals than in the Conservative Party. Leadership has tended to be collegial, even though sitting Liberal presidents are usually seen as the head of the party. Decision making on strategic issues is a complex process, requiring the participation of the president, the national directorate, the heads of the main factions, and some regional leaders. During campaign periods, the party usually names a prominent figure to lead the electoral efforts as sole director (*director único*). For instance, in 1990, the campaign was run by former President Alfonso López Michelsen. At the local level, the Liberals are better organized in the cities than in the countryside and their territorial structure is usually considered somewhat weaker than its Conservative counterpart.

The Liberal Party has a number of affiliated organizations, incorporating mostly urban social movements and some sectors of the middle class. Nevertheless, the links between the fellow traveling organizations and the formal structure of the party remain weak. By contrast, the party has a strong presence in the media, particularly among the printed press. Bogota's two leading dailies, *El Tiempo* (owned by a great Liberal family, the Santos) and *El Espectador*, have marked Liberal tendencies. Many provincial papers also boast Liberal leanings, as do many radio stations and television programs. The party has no international affiliation, although in the 1970s, the possibility of joining the Socialist International was discussed.

The national headquarters of the party are at Carrera 14, No. 36-21, Santafé de Bogotá.

POLICY

In the 19th century and the early decades of the 20th, the main Liberal causes were federalism, the separation of church and state (particularly in the field of education), and the extension of the suffrage. In the post–World War II period, the Liberals have been somewhat on the left on economic and social issues, supporting an ISI development strategy and promoting a measure of state interventionism as well as social welfare measures and legislation favoring organized labor. In the 1960s and 1970s, they championed Keynesian macroeconomics and the growth of the public sector. Since the 1980s, however, they have converted to a moderate free-market creed and during the Gaviria administration, they pushed through an economic liberalization agenda. President Samper turned slightly to the left, but the key economic features of the *revolcón* (privatization, trade liberalization, and such) remained virtually intact.

On social issues, the Liberals stand for continued secularization and religious tolerance: in the 1980s, they supported the legalization of divorce against the firm opposition of the Catholic Church and the Conservatives. Their policy toward the leftist guerrillas and the drug cartels tends to swing between resolute persecution and peaceful incorporation. Nevertheless, they are usually perceived as the dove party: in the late 1980s, President Barco negotiated the surrender of the M-19 guerrillas and their transformation into a legal political party. In the early 1990s, President Gaviria opted for a policy of no extradition and negotiated surrender to deal with the bosses of the drug cartels. Lately, the party has adopted a more hard-line policy toward the guerrillas and the drug trade, partly in response to the drug money scandal and U.S. pressures.

MEMBERSHIP AND CONSTITUENCY

The Liberal Party has been the dominant actor in Colombian politics since the 1930s, obtaining consistently between 45 and 55% of the vote in every national election since 1946. The party has obtained either an absolute majority or a plurality in every congressional election since the war, with the exception of the elections for the Constitutional Assembly of 1991. In the presidential contest of 1994, it obtained 45.3% of the vote in the first round of voting. The organization has presence throughout the Colombian territory, although its main power base has traditionally been located in the more urban and industrialized areas, particularly Bogotá and the departments of Cauca and Valle, as well as in the coastal departments of Córdoba, Atlántico, and Magdalena. The party draws support from all sectors of Colombian society, but it has traditionally been stronger among the urban lower and middle classes. Young voters tend to lean toward the Liberals, even though in 1994, many switched over to the Pastrana candidacy. Its constituency usually includes the major Bogotá industrial groups, a large portion of the intelligentsia, university students, and the biggest labor organization, the Confederation of Colombian Workers (*Confederación de Trabajadores Colombianos*; CTC). There are no reliable figures on membership, although the party is thought to be significantly larger than its Conservative rival.

FINANCING

The Liberal Party finances its activities in much the same way as its Conservative counterpart (although sometimes membership dues are collected), and its financial requirements are equally small in nonelectoral periods. In 1994, the government refunded the party approximately 1.9 million dollars for the expenses incurred during the presidential campaign. The scandal over alleged contributions of drug cartels to Ernesto Samper's warchest severely rattled the country and led to unending speculation about the extent of influence peddling in the upper reaches of the political class. (See also "Campaigning," above.)

LEADERSHIP

As with its Conservative competitor, the Liberal Party draws most of its top leadership from traditional political families, belonging mostly to the upper-middle classes. Former presidents, such as Julio César Turbay and Alfonso López Michelsen, still carry significant weight, but the party has undergone a process of generational renewal over the last decade. The rejuvenation has come mostly from the ranks of the *Nuevo Liberalismo*, although a younger breed of *Oficialista* leaders has also come to the fore of party politics.

The present top leaders include:

- **Ernesto Samper Pizano** (born 1944 in Bogotá), president of the republic from 1994 to 1998, was formerly a representative and a senator, as well as minister of development and ambassador to Spain in the Gaviria administration. A longtime *Oficialista* linked to the López Michelsen faction, Samper is perceived as the standard bearer of Liberal orthodoxy. As president, he was still a decisive actor within the party, but his position and influence were crippled by the political debris of the drug money scandal.

- **César Gaviria Pérez** (born 1949 in Antioquía), president from 1990 to 1994, was the right-hand man of Luis Carlos Galán and carries the mantle of the *Nuevo Liberalismo*. Since 1995, he has served as secretary general of the Organization of American States (OAS) and, as such, he is seen as above daily politics. Nevertheless, is still considered a powerful figure within the party.
- **Humberto de la Calle** (born 1942 in Bogotá), an *Oficialista*, vice president from 1994 to 1996 and minister of government under Gaviria, was implicated in the drug money scandal.
- **Julio César Turbay Ayala** (born 1916 in Bogotá), president from 1978 to 1982, is one of the key figures of the *Oficialista* faction and, in spite of his age, led the electoral efforts of the party as sole director (*director único*) in 1994.
- **Alfonso Valdivieso** (born 1952 in Bogotá) is a prestigious independent lawyer and a former attorney general. Perceived as a maverick, he has little influence within the organization.

PROSPECTS

Although the Liberals retain control of Congress, the party was hard hit by the scandal surrounding the campaign finances of Ernesto Samper. The president's approval rates tumbled, and the economy appeared surprisingly fragile, paving the way for the Liberals' presidential loss in 1998.

MINOR POLITICAL PARTIES

With few exceptions (ANAPO in 1970, M-19 in 1991), minor parties have been unable to break the two-party mold of Colombian politics and usually serve as mere tokens to pluralism. The left has been traditionally prone to extreme sectarianism and personality politics, rarely posing a real electoral threat to the status quo. The main area of strength for third parties usually lies in urban areas, particularly in Bogotá, among the university-educated middle-class voters. All parties listed below have their headquarters in Santafé de Bogotá.

Colombian Communist Party
(Partido Comunista Colombiano; PCC)

The PCC was founded in 1930. The party used to be the main actor in the Colombian left, but since the downfall of the Soviet bloc, its influence and membership have dwindled. It served as the springboard for the Patriotic Union in the 1980s, but lost control of the coalition in

1989. It has not fielded a presidential candidate since 1986. Its secretary general is Gilberto Vieira.

M-19 Democratic Alliance
(Alianza Democratica M-19; ADM-19)

The ADM was founded in 1989. It is the electoral instrument of former guerrilla members, led by Antonio Navarro Wolf. Formed by reconstructed Marxists, the M-19 sustained a decades-long armed struggle against the Colombian government and was responsible for the spectacular and bloody seizure of the Supreme Court building in 1985. It finally signed a peace agreement and became a legal political force in 1989. In the elections for the Constitutional Assembly of 1991, the movement pulled one of the biggest surprises in Colombian electoral history, outpolling both Liberals and Conservatives with 27% of the national vote. Navarro Wolf was minister of health during a portion of the Gaviria administration and had great hopes for the presidential election of 1994. However, the electoral fortunes of the movement came tumbling down in that contest, when it obtained only 3.79% of the vote.

Patriotic Union
(Union Patriótica; UP)

The UP was founded in 1985. The Patriotic Union is the civilian arm of Colombia's largest guerrilla group, the FARC. Originally organized by the Communist Party, it was supposed to serve as a vehicle for the reinsertion of guerrilla fighters into civilian politics. Its members, however, have been targeted by rightist paramilitary forces and the drug cartels (700 militants have been murdered since 1985), and the experiment has floundered. The movement never quite recovered from the assassination of two key members of its leadership, Jaime Pardo Leal and Bernardo Jaramillo Ossa, in 1987 and 1989, respectively. The organization obtained 2.7% of the vote in the presidential election of 1990; it did not field a candidate in 1994.

National Popular Alliance
(Alianza Nacional Popular; ANAPO)

ANAPO was founded in 1961. It was created by former military dictator Gustavo Rojas Pinilla as his personal political instrument. More populist than truly leftist, it stood in constant opposition to the National Front in the 1960s and 1970s and peaked in the presidential elections of 1970, obtaining 39.1% of the vote, just 2 percentage points below the National Front candidate, Misael Pastrana. Since the death of Rojas Pinilla in 1972, the movement has declined, although María Eugenia Rojas, daughter of the founder and a would-be Colombian *Evita*, has attempted to keep the party alive.

Unitary Metapolitical Movement
(Movimiento Unitario Metapolítico)

The Unitary Metapolitical Movement was founded in 1993. It is a colorful fringe group, led by a self-styled witch, Regina Betancourt de Liska, peddling a bizarre New Age discourse. In 1994, it was the fourth-largest vote earner with 1.1% of the total.

OTHER POLITICAL FORCES

Even though there is no consensus on the extent of their influence, it is undeniable that interest group pressure and extrainstitutional actors play a fundamental role in Colombian politics. Traditionally, the Catholic Church and the armed forces, as well as business organizations, have been significant forces in decision-making processes and wielded veto power over some policy areas. Organized labor has seen its influence decrease in recent years but still has some say over economic policy. Interest-group pressure is usually applied through the executive branch, even though lobbies also work through the major parties and the legislature. According to recent evidence, the rise of a relatively insulated technocratic class may have reduced the sway of interest groups, but state autonomy is still significantly limited if faced by concerted societal pressure.

Most interest groups tend to represent upper- and middle-class interests, excluding the peasantry and the large majority of the working class from the policymaking process. Peasant organizations have historically had little influence on the design and implementation of agrarian reform programs and have often opted for direct-action measures, including guerrilla activities. Most workers are not represented by organized labor and have little or no access to decision makers.

Interest-group pressure is usually exerted during policy implementation efforts, coming after government decisions, and seeking mostly redress or exemptions from particular measures. Rarely do lobbies directly participate in policy design within the executive branch, reserving their bargaining power for congressional battles and judicial review processes. They usually do not shy away from confrontational tactics, using boycotts, demonstrations, and strikes as often as necessary. Nevertheless, the relationship between major pressure groups and the political class is embedded in a network of family and personal links and rarely escalates to an open clash.

Business Associations

The most powerful business organization is the National Association of Industrialists (*Asociación Nacional de Industrialistas*; ANDI), comprising the 500 most powerful industrial concerns in the country. It holds considerable financial resources, as well as high visibility, easy access to most relevant policymakers, and official presence in numerous government boards. It champions free-market measures, although it has traditionally supported protectionism and only grudgingly supported the trade liberalization measures of the Gaviria administration. It wields significant influence over economic policy, particularly over taxation and industrial policy areas. The counterpart to the ANDI in the tertiary sector is the National Federation of Merchants (*Federación Nacional de Comerciantes*; FENALCO). The FENALCO is ideologically close to the ANDI, although it is more supportive of free trade. Its extensive organizational structure covers most of the Colombian territory and has substantial financial resources, as well as a well-established network of formal and informal contacts with the political sphere.

Some associations grouping rural interests are also a significant political force. Most particularly, the National Federation of Coffee Growers (*Federación Nacional de Cafeteros*; FEDECAFE), an association of the largest producers and exporters, can extract significant concessions from government in every policy area connected to coffee production and trade. Several Cabinet ministers serve ex-officio on its national board, and it has close ties with both major parties and key bureaucratic agencies. Other agricultural interests are represented in sectoral associations, including sugarcane, rice, and cotton producers, and have some influence over trade and fiscal policy.

Catholic Church

With the possible exception of Chile, the Catholic Church exerts more political power in Colombia than in any other Latin American country, even though its influence has been decreasing in recent years. Prior to the enactment of the constitution of 1991, it had a privileged legal status, protected by a concordat with the Vatican. Under the present constitutional framework, Catholicism is no longer the official religion of the country, although it is still practiced by the vast majority of Colombians, notwithstanding the recent penetration of Protestant denominations. The church hierarchy still has significant influence within the Conservative Party, as well as close ties with the UTC labor federation and considerable power in many policy areas, particularly education and social development. Nevertheless, there is a consensus that its influence is being steadily eroded by the growing secularization of Colombian society. Since the late 1980s, the church has lost two major battles: first, it failed to prevent the legalization of divorce, in spite of its outspoken opposition to the measure; second, it was unable to guarantee its privileged legal position and its dominant role in the educational system in the Constitutional Assembly of 1991.

Organized Labor

The Colombian labor movement has never obtained the institutionalized status or the power of its counterparts in other Latin American countries, such as Mexico, Argentina or Venezuela. Even though two of the three major labor confederations have strong ties with the major parties, their influence over decision making has always been limited by the conservative and probusiness bent of the Colombian political class. Moreover, in spite of significant unionization efforts, organized labor only covers a small and falling fraction of the working class. Legislation favoring labor has been on the books since the 1940s, but the climate for union militancy and development is less than favorable and law enforcement in labor matters tends to be selective and repressive.

Organized labor is divided between the party-aligned confederations and the so-called independents. The biggest "official" organization is the Union of Colombian Workers (*Unión de Trabajadores Colombianos*; UTC), a movement strongly identified with the Conservative Party and right-wing Christian Democratic thought. It is particularly influential among industrial workers in Medellín and Calí.

Its Liberal counterpart is the Confederation of Colombian Workers (*Confederación de Trabajadores Colombianos*; CTC). Slightly more left-wing than the UTC, the CTC is the oldest labor federation in the country (founded in 1934), has quasi-organic ties to the Liberal Party, and dominates most public-sector unions. Among the independents, the field is controlled by the Trade Union Confederation of Colombian Workers (*Confederación Sindical de Trabajadores de Colombia*; CSTC), a militant organization founded by a number of Communist-led unions. Expelled from the CTC in 1966, it is the largest labor federation in the country. Although the CSTC is alleged to maintain some ties to the FARC guerrilla group, its radicalism and confrontational tactics have been gradually abandoned since their peak in the late 1970s.

Military

The Colombian armed forces have traditionally been less infected by authoritarian tendencies than most of their Latin American counterparts. During the independent history of the Colombian state, they have staged only three coups: in 1830, 1854, and 1953. In total, military officers have led Colombia for just six years and only the Rojas Pinilla dictatorship lasted more than one year. Their political role has been limited by a deeply held antimilitarism among both the political class and the general population. For the most part, the military have been content to serve as instruments of civilian politicians, even though they have always had a significant influence in national security matters.

Notwithstanding, the power of the armed forces has steadily grown since the onset of guerrilla activities in the mid-1960s. The Ministry of Defense is usually run by an army general, and it has become common practice to name military officers as departmental governors in particularly violent areas. The military have only grudgingly accepted peace negotiations with the guerrillas and have consistently maintained a hard-line position against subversive groups. In 1985, they forced President Belisario Betancur to order a military operation to dislodge from the Supreme Court building the M-19 commandos who had seized it in previous days. According to several observers, the incident was a "24-hour coup."

The political clout of the armed forces has also grown as a result of the growing militarization of the drug war. The military were decisive in the dismantling of the Medellín and Calí cartels, even though they have been beset by allegations of corruption. In recent years, several generals have been accused of providing protection to drug lords, leading to a number of indictments and damaging the public standing of the armed forces. In general terms, the drug war has opened a widening rift between military officers and civilian politicians. Moreover, the political crisis resulting from the drug money scandal has led to growing calls for direct military intervention. In the aftermath of the failed impeachment proceedings against President Samper, the Colombian political milieu was simmering with rumors of an impending military coup, even though the military leadership repeatedly denied they had any intention of dislodging the elected authorities from power.

Guerrillas

Marxist-inspired guerrillas, mostly of Castroite leanings, have been active in Colombia since the mid-1960s. Their military campaigns have been intermittent, reaching a peak in the late 1960s and the early 1980s. In recent years, they have intensified their war against the Colombian government, concentrating their attacks against oil infrastructure and military facilities in rural areas, particularly in the eastern departments of Casanare and Arauca.

Since the downfall of the Soviet bloc and the suspension of Cuban aid, the guerrillas are thought to finance their activities by obtaining subsidies from drug traffickers and by carrying out kidnappings. At present, the armed groups do not have either the popular support or the military strength to pose a clear threat to political stability and probably have lost the capability to mount spectacular actions in urban areas, such as the 1985 seizure of the Supreme Court building. They are still, however, a constant thorn in the authorities' side and can apply significant political pressure, particularly by destroying strategic infrastructure and by kidnapping prominent figures and military personnel. Government policy toward the guerrillas has fluctuated between repression and negotiation, but since the relative fiasco of the peace process in the late 1980s and early 1990s, hard-liners have prevailed and no political compromise seems in sight.

The main guerrilla groups include the Revolutionary Armed Forces of Colombia (*Fuerzas Armadas Revolucionarias de Colombia*; FARC), the largest active guerrilla movement, grouping some 2,000 fighters. Traditionally, they were perceived as the military wing of the Communist Party and the Patriotic Union; in recent years, both organizations have publicly disavowed the armed struggle. Since their inception in 1966, their ideology has been Castroite, although lately they have played down openly Marxist themes, adopting a more sanitized nationalist discourse. They are particularly active in the department of Casanare, where they mount constant attacks against oil infrastructure. In the late 1980s, they flirted with a possible surrender, but the assassination of numerous Patriotic Union militants reinforced their commitment to guerrilla tactics. In 1996, the FARC humiliated the government and the armed forces by capturing 100 soldiers and forcing a compromise to secure their release.

Another group is the National Liberation Army. The most active clandestine organization in the 1960s, its membership and its power have dwindled in recent years. It still has a presence in some rural areas of eastern Colombia, but it lacks a significant support base. And there is the M-19, which renounced armed struggle in 1989 and has since acted as a legal political force.

Drug Traffickers

Building on the skills and routes of emerald smugglers, Colombian drug traffickers created in the 1970s and 1980s probably the most powerful criminal organizations in the world. By the end of the last decade, the two major groups—the Medellín and Calí cartels—controlled 80% of the world's cocaine trade, obtaining unprecedented financial resources and political clout. More recently, however, the Colombian mafias have gone through hard times. In the late 1980s, the Medellín cartel declared war on the Colombian government on the issue of extradition to the United States. It won a partial victory, gaining nonextradition, but in exchange for the negotiated surrender of its leader, Pablo Escobar Gaviria. After his escape from prison in 1992, the authorities organized a massive manhunt that ended in 1993 with the killing of the legendary drug baron.

After the demise of the Medellín cartel, the government persecuted the Calí barons, in spite of their donations to the presidential campaign of Ernesto Samper. The law-enforcement campaign led to the capture of the Rodríguez Orejuela brothers, kingpins of the Calí drug mafia. According to Colombian sources, the virtual elimination of the cartels has atomized the drug trade, but it

has not reduced its volume. The new generation of drug barons probably does not have the power of its predecessors, but the influence of criminal organizations in the political process remains quite significant. The drug money scandal that enveloped the Samper organization revealed the disturbing closeness between politicians and the criminal underworld, and the ties are probably still binding, in spite of the downfall of the most powerful drug lords.

NATIONAL PROSPECTS

The present trends in Colombian politics point, paradoxically, to both continuity and change. The drug money scandal paralyzed the Samper administration and shook the political system to its foundations. Nevertheless, the crisis did not produce a clear alternative to the domination of the traditional parties. The presidential victory of the Conservative Pastrana was welcomed, especially in the business community, as promising change. Pastrana sought a formula for peace with the guerrillas. He moved to strengthen the economy, proposing legislation to change the tax system and sharply reduce tax evasion.

Change could also come through extrainstitutional actors, but a major modification of the existing regime is highly improbable. Throughout the Samper administration, the Colombian political milieu was rife with rumors of an impending military coup. But the armed forces are most probably not ready to abandon a long tradition of loyalty to the political system; moreover, domestic and international public opinion would not look favorably upon military adventurism. Regarding the guerrillas, it is highly unlikely that they will make significant military inroads, but it is equally improbable that the army will completely suppress them. Peace may be closer on the drug front: the capture or death of a number of major drug barons has probably eliminated the risks of narcoterrorism in coming years. The continued pressure of the U.S. government, however, could reignite the conflict over extradition and obstruct cooperation in the drug war.

Ernesto Samper had sought to bolster his dwindling support base through public spending, leading to an expanding fiscal deficit and accelerating inflationary pressures. The government looked to growing oil exports, resulting from the discovery of the Cusiana oil fields, allegedly the largest in the Western Hemisphere. Guerrilla sabotage, however, has made production and transportation difficult.

In conclusion, the Colombian political system has proved its extreme resilience, enduring the blows of narcoterrorism and guerrilla warfare, as well as a prolonged political crisis. Its major features—bipartisan hegemony, presidentialism, clientelism—will likely carry on into the next century. Nevertheless, winds of reform are blowing in the country: its changing demographic, social, and economic outlook could lead to significant transformations in political style and content over the next decade. Moreover, it would be imprudent to minimize the general disgust felt at the traditional political class and the massive, if nebulous, desire for change. The Colombian people may still confound most analysts in the very near future.

Further Reading

Bushnell, David. *The Making of Modern Colombia: A Nation in Spite of Itself*. Berkeley: University of California, 1993.

Martz, John D. *The Politics of Clientelism: Democracy and the State in Colombia*. New Brunswick, N.J.: Transaction Publishers, 1997.

Pearce, Jenny. *Colombia: Inside the Labyrinth*. London: Latin America Bureau (Research and Action), 1990.

COMOROS

By B. David Meyers, Ph.D.

THE SYSTEM OF GOVERNMENT

The Republic of the Comoros is a federation of three islands, inhabited by approximately one-half million people, located between the mainland of East Africa and Madagascar. On July 6, 1975, the three declared themselves independent; a fourth Comorian island, Mayotte, is claimed by the government but has chosen to remain a French territory.

The March 1996 elections were the first time in its history that the Comoros witnessed the handing of power from an outgoing president to his successor. But this may be deceptive since it was the direct result of a coup d'état and a foreign intervention, both of which have been typical methods of achieving political change in this tumultuous nation.

In early August 1975, less than a month after independence, the nation's first president, Ahmed Abdallah, was overthrown in a coup assisted by French mercenaries. The coup leader, Ali Soilih, was himself overthrown when Abdallah, with support from France, South Africa, and these same mercenaries, returned in 1978. Abdallah declared a one-party state and drove all opposition into exile. In November 1989, he was assassinated by his mercenary guards and replaced by the president of the Supreme Court, Said Mohammed Djohar. In 1990, in an election marked by allegations of widespread fraud, Djohar defeated Mohamed Taki Abdoulkarim for the presidency. Djohar's presidency was marked by absolutism, nepotism, and corruption, which encouraged assassination and coup attempts.

In September 1995, a coup, aided by many of the same mercenaries, ousted Djohar. Under pressure from South African President Mandela, French military forces then intervened. They ended the coup but would not allow Djohar's return until he promised to allow free elections, supervised by a French military contingent. In March 1996, following two rounds of elections, Mohamed Taki Abdoulkarim, who had briefly been installed by the mercenaries, became the country's president.

Political stability has, however, proved illusive, and the fate of the country itself is currently in doubt. In 1997 the islands of Anjouan and Moheli seceded from the federation. The separatists are themselves divided between those who demand reattachment to France and those who prefer to retain some ties to the government on Grande Comore. Meanwhile, Comoran President Taki's inability to reach agreement with the secessionists, together with claims that he had mismanaged the economy and made himself a virtual dictator, caused his unpopularity throughout the country. Taki's sudden death, of a heart attack, in November 1998 leaves the country leaderless.

Executive

Executive authority is vested in a president, elected to not more than two six-year terms. He chooses a prime minister from the largest party in the Legislative Council. There is a Council of Government that includes both ministers chosen by the president and the governors of the three islands. Previous presidents became highly authoritarian and relied heavily on family members and the mercenary-led presidential guard.

In the $2\frac{1}{2}$ years between his inauguration and his death, President Taki frequently replaced his prime minister and ruled virtually single-handedly. An interim president will govern until new elections can be held.

Legislature

Legislative authority is vested in a Federal Assembly, made up of 43 members elected from single-member districts for four-year terms, and a 15-member Senate of 5 members from each island, chosen for six years by each island's legislative council.

Following elections in December 1996, President Taki's party, the National Rally for Development (RND), held a commanding 36 seats in the Legislative Council. The National Front for Justice (FNJ) held three seats and four were held by independents.

Judiciary

The Supreme Court has seven members, two each appointed by the president and the federal legislature, and one by each island's legislative council. The Court is supposed to review decisions of lower courts, decide constitutional questions, and arbitrate in any case where the government is accused of malpractice. In August 1991, the president of the Supreme Court unsuccessfully tried to dismiss, and himself replace, President Djohar.

There are lower courts in the major towns, a superior court in the capital, and religious courts that apply Muslim law in matters relating to social and personal relationships.

Regional and Local Government

Each island has its own governor who is directly elected and a popularly elected legislative council chosen from single-member wards. The councils are responsible for all legislation not specifically granted to the federal government. Many local decisions are made by clan leaders and in the mosques.

ELECTORAL SYSTEM

Both presidential and Federal Assembly elections are held in two rounds with the second a runoff between the two front runners. With the exception of the 1996 presidential elections, there is a long record of disruptions and allegations of fraud.

POLITICAL PARTIES

From 1989, when the ban on opposition parties was lifted, until 1996, the Comoros had numerous political parties. Many of these parties were found on only one island; some had been created to support a single individual.

In 1996, a new constitution established a two-party system. President Taki called for all parties to dissolve and to

join him in creating the National Rally for Development (RND). Most of the political parties that had supported him in the second round of the 1996 presidential elections chose to join. The future of this grouping of previously separate parties, whose primary common ground was support of President Taki, is now in serious doubt.

The only opposition party within the Federal Assembly is the National Front for Justice (FNJ). This is an explicitly Islamic party that has usually worked closely with Taki and the RND.

Most of the political parties opposed to President Taki and his constitutional changes boycotted the 1996 Federal Assembly elections. These parties have formed a coalition, the Forum for the Restoration of Democracy (FRD), led by Abbas Djoussouf, who had been Taki's final opponent in the presidential elections.

NATIONAL PROSPECTS

Optimists had hoped that the 1996 presidential elections might be the start of a new, more democratic, and stable political era for the Comoros. Unfortunately, these hopes were short-lived. The secession of two of the federation's three islands, the failures of the economy, and the continued political instability—only compounded by Taki's death—raise questions concerning the country's continued existence.

Further Reading

Ottenheimer, Martin, and Harriet Ottenheimer. *Historical Dictionary of the Comoro Islands*. Metuchen, N.J.: Scarecrow Press, 1994.

DEMOCRATIC REPUBLIC OF CONGO

(République Démocratique du Congo)

By Timothy P. Longman, Ph.D.

THE SYSTEM OF GOVERNMENT

The Democratic Republic of Congo, known from 1971 to 1996 as Zaire, is a country of 44 million people, with more than 300 ethnic groups. The current government, led by Laurent Kabila, came to power in May 1997 after a seven-month armed rebellion drove longtime dictator Mobutu Sese-Seko into exile.

After gaining independence from Belgium on June 30, 1960, Congo quickly disintegrated into a period of severe social upheaval. Persistent political instability, regional secession, and civil war eventually prompted Mobutu, who was head of the military, to take power in November 1965. While Mobutu successfully consolidated central government control and put an end to most civil unrest, his regime was marked by highly authoritarian rule and extensive corruption. Mobutu's refusal to allow a transition to democratic rule and his attempt to exploit ethnic divisions in the country gave rise to the rebellion that drove him from power. Although Kabila has promised a transition to democracy, the government is currently a military dictatorship.

Executive

Laurent Kabila named himself president of the Democratic Republic of Congo on May 16, 1997, after the rebel movement of which he was leader, the Alliance of Democratic Forces for the Liberation of Congo/Zaire (ADFL), took control of the capital, Kinshasa. Kabila had been a longtime opponent of President Mobutu. In 1960, Kabila was a youth leader in a party allied to Congo's first prime minister, Patrice Lumumba. After Lumumba's assassination in 1961, Kabila joined in several short-lived rebellions in Eastern Zaire—at one point receiving assistance from renowned Argentine-born revolutionary Ernesto (Che) Guevara. In 1967, Kabila founded the Popular Revolutionary Party (PRP), a self-proclaimed Marxist-Leninist party, which established a ministate in the remote hills above Lake Tanganyika. The PRP maintained a gold mine to support its operations and was involved in periodic raids on cities in Eastern Zaire, as well as an infamous kidnapping of four researchers at Jane Goodall's primate center in Tanzania in 1975. In the 1980s, Kabila fled into exile in Uganda and Tanzania, where he met the future Ugandan president, Yoweri Museveni, and the leader of the Rwandan Patriotic Front (RPF) and now vice president of Rwanda, Paul Kagame.

The ADFL was founded in October 1996 when the PRP agreed to support a rebellion by the Banyamulenge, a Rwandan-speaking Tutsi group in South Kivu province who were being threatened with expulsion from Congo (then Zaire). The 1994 genocide in Rwanda and subsequent RPF conquest of the country drove more than 1 million Rwandan refugees into Zaire, the vast majority of them Hutu. The Rwandan Hutu allied with local Zairian ethnic groups to attack Zairian Tutsi and drive them into neighboring Rwanda, which is controlled by the largely Tutsi RPF. While thousands of Tutsi were driven from North Kivu in early 1996, when the violence spread to South Kivu in September 1996, the Banyamulenge Tutsi organized resistance. Leaders of the Banyamulenge and the PRP created the ADFL at a meeting in Lemera in South Kivu on October 18, 1996. They announced the ADFL's intention to drive Mobutu from power, to eliminate the rampant corruption in the Zairian government, and to restore democracy, and they called on all opponents of Mobutu to join in their fight. Kabila initially served as spokesperson of the ADFL but quickly emerged as its leader.

With extensive support from the armed forces of Rwanda and Uganda, the ADFL conquered most of Eastern Zaire by the end of 1996 and from this base pushed rapidly westward toward the capital, Kinshasa. The Armed Forces of Zaire (*Forces Armées Zairoises*; FAZ), demoralized by the declining conditions in the country and their own lack of pay, put up little resistance. The primary opposition to the ADFL's advance came from paid foreign mercenaries and from former Rwandan soldiers who had been living in exile in Zaire since the RPF victory in Rwanda in 1994. Many opponents of Mobutu, such as the Mai-Mai militia in North Kivu, joined the ADFL as it advanced across Zaire. Under pressure from the international community, particularly South Africa, President Mobutu finally agreed to enter negotiations with the ADFL in early May, but by the time Mobutu and Kabila met on May 4, the ADFL had little reason to seek a compromise, since it had conquered more than half the country and was approaching the capital. Two weeks after the meeting, Mobutu fled Zaire for exile in Morocco, where he died of prostate cancer a few months later.

On the day of Mobutu's flight from Zaire, Kabila named himself president and changed the country's name back to its what it had been at independence, the Democratic Republic of Congo. Kabila was formally sworn in as president by the Supreme Court on May 29, 1997, in a ceremony in Kinshasa attended by the presidents of Angola, Burundi, Rwanda, Uganda, and Zambia. As president, Kabila is both head of state and head of government. He also serves as commander in chief of the armed forces and minister of defense. Kabila opted for a presidential form of government in which he enjoys extensive powers despite pressure from Western governments and Congolese politicians to name a prime minister as head of government.

When Kabila took power, he initially received wide support from both the international community, which despite Kabila's Marxist past believed that he would allow economic development, and the Congolese public, which believed that the ADFL victory offered a chance for the country to emerge from decades of political corruption and decline. Kabila promised to hold elections within two years, and he named a government that included members of parties that had been opposed to Mobutu, such as the Union for Democracy and Social Progress (UDPS) and the Patriotic Front (FP), as well as repatriated exiles and a few former associates of slain prime minister Lumumba.

Within days after Kabila's seizure of power, however, opposition to his regime began to emerge. Several demonstrations were held in Kinshasa in May to protest the exclusion from Kabila's Cabinet of major Mobutu opponents, particularly Etienne Tshisekedi, the leader of the UDPS. Kabila quickly outlawed public demonstrations and banned political party activity, arguing that parties divide the population along racial and ethnic lines, and numerous subsequent demonstrations have been violently dispersed. People, particularly in the capital, have objected to the dominance in Kabila's Cabinet and in the leadership of the ADFL of Banyamulenge and people from Kabila's Luba ethnic group and his home region of Katanga (known as Shaba under Mobutu's rule). The continuing presence of Rwandan troops in the country contributed to an impression that Kabila was a puppet of Rwanda and Uganda. To bolster his support, Kabila reshuffled his Cabinet several times within the first six months of his administration. In November 1997, Kabila arrested several Banyamulenge ADFL leaders, including the chief of staff and general secretary, in an attempt to demonstrate his independence and assert his control and apparently to prevent a potential coup.

This move, however, led to an outbreak of fighting between Tutsi, who remain the core of the ADFL, and other soldiers, and it strained relations with Rwanda. Some officers within the ADFL accused Kabila of imitating Mobutu by seeking to concentrate power increasingly in the hands of relatives and trusted people from his ethnic group.

Congo currently has no functioning constitution, since Kabila suspended the constitution after taking office. Kabila promised in his inaugural address to name a constitutional assembly, which would draft a new constitution to be presented for public referendum in 1998, but by late 1997 Kabila had not yet named the promised assembly. In the meantime, the political system that has emerged seems to resemble the no-party movement implemented by Museveni in Uganda after his victory in that country's civil war. With party activity suspended, Kabila has encouraged the formation of "committees" to act as a link between the government and the people, similar to the National Resistance Committees in Uganda. These committees have been created throughout the country, but their exact political role remains ill defined.

Legislature

After taking power in 1965, President Mobutu established a unicameral Legislative Council that served a largely symbolic function, rubber-stamping Mobutu's legislative proposals. In the late 1970s and early 1980s, however, the Legislative Council began to take a more independent role. While Mobutu sought to remove most powers from the Legislative Council, it nevertheless emerged as a center of opposition to the regime. In 1990, members of the Legislative Council joined with leaders of the churches, business, and other social groups in a national conference to chart the future of the country and prepare a transition to democracy. Out of this conference emerged a Transitional Parliament, dominated by Mobutu opponents. Mobutu refused to recognize the Transitional Parliament, and for a time it coexisted alongside the Legislative Council, dominated by Mobutu loyalists. Eventually the two institutions merged into one legislative body, the High Council of the Republic–Transitional Parliament (HCR–PT), divided fairly evenly between supporters and opponents of Mobutu.

When Kabila took office, he suspended the HCR–PT, but he promised that legislative elections would be held in 1999. Many members of the HCR–PT have refused to accept its suspension, and they continue to use their positions as platforms for criticizing the regime. At the same time, Kabila has drawn several of his ministers from the ranks of the HCR–PT. For example, Paul Kinkela Vi Kan'si, the founder of the Patriotic Front (PF) and an influential member of the HCR–PT was named minister of posts and telecommunications and Paul Bandoma of the UDPS was named minister of agriculture.

Judiciary

Under Mobutu, the judiciary almost entirely lacked autonomy. Mobutu appointed judges to the Supreme Court and other courts based on his personal political interests and harassed any who demonstrated independence. Since taking power, Kabila has left the judiciary institutions in place, but their activities have been seriously circumvented. The 22 justices of the Supreme Court presided at Kabila's inauguration but have played little subsequent role. In many locations, the military and government administrators have apparently taken on many of the functions traditionally the domain of the judiciary, such as judging people accused of crimes and determining punishments.

Regional and Local Governments

The Democratic Republic of Congo is divided into 11 provinces, each of which is subdivided into administrative zones, which in turn are subdivided into localities. Although Kabila has returned several provinces to the names they used in the 1960s—Shaba is once again Katanga and Haut-Zaire is again Orientale—he has retained the provincial organization instituted by Mobutu rather than returning to the system of 21 provinces used prior to Mobutu's coup.

As the ADFL advanced across Congo in 1996 and 1997, they held public meetings shortly after capturing territory in which the population was allowed to select new governors, commissioners for the zones, and mayors. This "instant democracy" implemented in ADFL-controlled zones raised popular hopes that the ADFL would quickly move the country to full democracy. Since taking full control of the country, however, the ADFL has held no elections. Vacancies in regional and local posts have been filled by appointment, and Kabila has actively removed those officials whom he suspects of disloyalty.

While most of the regional and local government officials are civilians, many observers claim that regional military officers represent the real centers of power in the provinces. The chief officers in each province, mostly Banyamulenge, Bashi, and Luba who were involved in the beginning of the rebellion that brought the ADFL to power, apparently dictate most policy and ensure that political leaders stay consistent with orders from Kinshasa. In some provinces, Rwandan military officers cooperating with or serving in the ADFL have considerable influence.

Under Mobutu, Zaire was ruled as a unitary state, with policymaking power concentrated in the central government. However, a new constitution that was to have been put before the voters in early 1997 would have changed Zaire to a federal system and devolved substantial power to the provincial governments if it were approved. Kabila has given no indication whether he intends to follow through on plans to move toward a federal system.

ALLIANCE OF DEMOCRATIC FORCES FOR THE LIBERATION OF CONGO/ZAIRE
(Alliance des Forces Démocratiques pour la Liberation du Congo/Zaire; ADFL)

The ADFL does not define itself as a political party but, rather, as a "movement." The ADFL clearly models itself after the National Resistance Movement in Uganda, which established a "no party" political system after taking power in 1986 at the end of a four-year civil war. Like President Museveni of Uganda, Kabila has banned political party activity, claiming that parties are too divisive for a society recovering from war and seeking economic development. Many observers consider the movement system a revised version of the single-party states that were common in Africa until democracy movements in the 1990s demanded the legalization of opposition parties.

HISTORY AND ORGANIZATION

The ADFL was founded as a military and political alliance on October 18, 1996, at a meeting in Lemera in South Kivu. The original members of the ADFL included Tutsi fighters from North Kivu and the Banyamulenge Tutsi militia from South Kivu (several thousand of whom reportedly received military training in Rwanda), Kabila's group *Parti Révolutionnaire Populaire*, and several smaller groups, including the Bashi organization *Mouvement Révolutionnaire pour la Liberation du Zaire*, led by Anselme Masasu Nindanga. As the ADFL expanded, it gained support from members of the Luba ethnic group from Kasai and Shaba (now Katanga), Nande rebels led by André Kissasse, and Mai-Mai and Bangilima militia composed of Nyanga, Hunde, and Nande from North Kivu. In addition, many members of the *Forces Armées Zairoises* deserted to join the ADFL.

Since taking power, the armed wing of the ADFL has converted itself into the new Congolese army, while the political wing has sought to transform itself into a mass political movement. As the ADFL advanced across Congo, Kabila banned political party activity in the ADFL-controlled areas "for the duration of the war." Kabila announced a more general ban on party activity on May 26, prior to his inauguration, but promised during his inaugural address to hold elections within two years. Kabila has not specified whether he will allow parties to compete in these elections or whether they will be organized on a no-party basis. In place of traditional party activity, the ADFL leadership has encouraged people throughout the country to form committees to serve as a liaison between the public and the government. The exact organization and function of these committees were not initially specified by the government, but hundreds of committees nevertheless were created, usually representing a fairly small area. In Uganda, resistance committees have been effectively integrated into the political system as a form of neighborhood government, the lowest level in the National Resistance Movement hierarchy, and many observers believe that Kabila intends to follow this model, bringing the committees under ADFL control and using them both as a means of ascertaining the public will and carrying out government directives and mobilizing the population.

There currently exists no clear distinction between the ADFL movement and the government. By defining the ADFL not as a party but as a movement, Kabila is able to leave its definition and structure conveniently vague.

POLICY

The primary policy objective of the ADFL is clearly reconstruction and development. Despite Congo's remarkable mineral wealth, which includes gold, diamonds, copper, and more than half of the world's cobalt deposits, the country's economy has been in steady decline since the 1960s, largely as a result of official corruption. The Mobutu regime allowed the infrastructure to deteriorate even as Mobutu and other politicians amassed incredible personal fortunes. As a result, Congo now has few passable roads, most areas have no access to power or running water, and the majority of the population lives in extreme poverty. Frustration with Congo's persistent economic decline and plummeting standards of living inspired much of the population to support the ADFL, and the Kabila administration will be judged on its ability to deliver economic development. Despite Kabila's longtime commitment to Marxism, once the ADFL was founded, Kabila turned for support to Western governments such as the United States, and he has welcomed international investment. The exact economic position of the ADFL is not clearly articulated, though it appears to be following a capitalist model of development.

Unifying a country with more than 300 ethnic groups and a history of division and ethnic turmoil is another major task for ADFL leaders. While Mobutu's regime was perceived as favoring Lingala speakers and people from Mobutu's home region, Equateur, the ADFL is seen by many as favoring Swahili speakers and people from Katanga and North and South Kivu. The predominance of people from the Tutsi ethnic group in the ADFL raises concerns for many Congolese: Tutsi constitute a small portion of the population and were frequently scapegoated by Mobutu because of their relative economic prosperity and their suspect nationality, since Tutsi, regardless of their ancestry are characterized as Rwandan. Kabila has attempted to address these concerns by reshuffling his government to include greater ethnic diversity and by removing Tutsi from several prominent government posts. Nevertheless, the ADFL leadership includes few people from Western Congo and continues to be viewed as narrowly focused.

Another major policy concern for the ADFL is combating the culture of impunity that has developed out of the crime and corruption that have run rampant in Congo for decades. Campaigns against gang activity and other forms of criminality have been launched in a number of communities. ADFL leaders have replaced politicians associated with Mobutu throughout the country, and they have made some attempt to reform the civil service. ADFL soldiers and politicians have, however, been accused of engaging in corrupt practices similar to those under Mobutu, lining their own pockets with government funds and appointing relatives and friends to positions. Related to the attack on criminality and corruption, ADFL soldiers and officials have attempted to enforce a code of public morality, which includes a dress code forbidding women from wearing miniskirts and tight pants. Shootings of prostitutes in several communities have been blamed on ADFL soldiers seeking to enforce public morality.

Human rights have been a major concern for the ADFL. Mobutu's refusal to respect freedoms of speech and press and his regime's practice of torturing and killing opponents were factors contributing to public condemnation of his regime and support for the ADFL. However, since taking office Kabila has been reluctant to expand freedoms, claiming that he has to first establish stability. A number of critics of the regime, including journalists and opposition politicians, have been detained. Most damaging, human rights organizations have reported that as the ADFL advanced through Eastern Congo, ADFL and RPF troops slaughtered thousands of unarmed Rwandan Hutu refugees. Kabila's government refused for six months to allow a United Nations human rights team to investigate the massacres. Many foreign governments refused to provide assistance to the Kabila regime until it allowed a full investigation.

MEMBERSHIP AND CONSTITUENCY

Like other movement systems in Africa, the membership in the ADFL is not clearly defined but is generally considered to include the entire population. In contrast to Mobutu's political party, the Popular Movement of the Revolution (*Mouvement Populaire de la Révolution*; MPR), for two decades the only legal party, the ADFL does not require membership dues or issue membership cards. The primary support for the ADFL appears to come from regions that felt excluded from significant power during Mobutu's reign—Katanga, Kasai, Kivu, and Orientale, in particular.

FINANCING

Congo is extremely rich in natural resources. As the ADFL conquered territories with major diamond, gold, and copper deposits in Katanga, Kasai, and elsewhere, major international corporations such as De Beers signed cooperation agreements with the ADFL leadership in which they agreed to pay the ADFL millions of dollars in exchange for the right to exploit the minerals. The ADFL continues to finance its operations through these payments, which are now made to government accounts.

LEADERSHIP

The primary leader of the ADFL is clearly Kabila himself. Kabila was born in 1939 in Likasi (formerly Jadotville) in Katanga province. He is a member of the Luba ethnic group. Kabila studied politics at a university in France, then returned to Congo just before independence in 1960 to become involved in politics. He became leader of the youth league of a party allied with Congo's first prime minister, Patrice Lumumba, and served as a member of the North Katanga assembly. After Lumumba's assassination in 1961, Kabila went into hiding. In 1964 Kabila resurfaced as a leader of a rebellion in Eastern Congo. This rebellion sought to expand another pro-Lumumba rebellion in Western Congo led by Pierre Mulele and has, thus, commonly been called the Mulelist Rebellion. In 1965, this rebellion was expanded and Kabila's forces briefly occupied Kisangani, Congo's third-largest city, but Mobutu crushed the rebellion with support from foreign mercenaries.

In 1967, Kabila founded the Popular Revolutionary Party (*Parti Révolutionnaire Populaire*; PRP), which espoused a Marxist-Leninist philosophy. In the 1970s, the PRP occupied a small territory in the hills above Lake Tanganyika that it declared a "liberated zone" and set up collective farms, schools, and clinics. The PRP gained international notoriety in 1975 when it kidnapped four researchers from Jane Goodall's primate research center at Gombe Stream, just across Lake Tanganyika in Tanzania. In 1977, Mobutu's troops forced Kabila to flee the country, and while in exile in Tanzania, he attended the University of Dar es Salaam, where he made the acquaintance of Yoweri Museveni. Kabila spent much time in Uganda after Museveni took power, and there he apparently developed a relationship with Paul Kagame, future vice president of Rwanda.

As president and head of the military, Kabila enjoys substantial personal power. Nevertheless, he does not dominate the government as completely as his predecessor, who maintained almost complete control over its operations and created a strong public cult of personality to support his rule. Kabila must share power with other officials in the ADFL—the movement that helped bring him to power—who hold key posts in his administration. Mwenze Kongolo, who serves as minister of the interior, is from Kabila's home region of Katanga and lived in the United States before returning to Congo to join the ADFL. Another ADFL officer from Eastern Congo, the deputy minister of interior, General Faustin Munene, apparently exercises considerable power. According to a number of observers, officers from the RPF, the Rwandan army, who remain in the country exercise considerable power in many regions, though they hold no formal positions in the government or military.

In an attempt to consolidate his personal power, Kabila replaced several of the formerly powerful figures in the ADFL after his first six months in office. General Anselme Masasu Nindanga, who is of mixed Shi and Tutsi ancestry, was the second most powerful leader of the ADFL and was very popular with the Tutsi soldiers. He served as deputy president of the ADFL and government chief of staff until his arrest in November 1997, reportedly in connection with a coup plot. Déogratias Bugera, a Banyamulenge Tutsi who served as secretary general of the ADFL, was also arrested in November. Bizima Karaha, a Banyamulenge Tutsi, trained as a medical doctor in South Africa and a close ally of Vice President Kagame was replaced as the minister for foreign affairs.

PROSPECTS

As the ADFL marched rapidly across Zaire, driving Mobutu's troops out of one province after another, huge public crowds thronged city streets to cheer the arrival of the rebels they believed had liberated them from 30 years of authoritarian rule. Shortly after the ADFL took control of the government, however, public opinion began to turn sour. Rather than establishing a broad-based government that included well-respected democracy activists and Mobutu opponents, the ADFL reserved virtually all of the most prominent government posts for its own people, with nearly all Cabinet members drawn from the provinces of Katanga, Kivu, and Kasai. Residents of the capital, where Lingala is the most common language, resented the presence of a largely Swahili-speaking army that acted in many ways like an occupying force despite the population of Kinshasa's years of organized opposition to Mobutu's rule. The continuing presence of Rwandan troops in Congo has been particularly unpopular. The ADFL's ban on party activity, harassment of journalists, human rights activists, and opposition politicians, and increasing concentration of power in the hands of relatives and close associates of Kabila have inspired many Congolese to question whether they have driven out one authoritarian ruler only to replace him with another.

Despite public resentment of the ADFL's authoritarian tendencies, the future prospects of the ADFL are likely to depend more on its ability to rebuild the economy, repair the infrastructure, and raise standards of living than on its respect for civil liberties. Many Congolese may be willing to accept a continued infringement of their freedom provided the country emerges from its precipitous economic decline. However, the ADFL will need to broaden its base of support if it wishes to avoid a disintegration into the ethnic and regional conflict that has long troubled Congo. The renewed ethnically based fighting in North and South Kivu is a troubling reminder of the dangers that await the ADFL if political power and the benefits of economic recovery remain concentrated in the hands of a few ethnic groups and regions rather than being distributed throughout the country.

OPPOSITION

Mobutu founded the MPR as Congo's only legal political party in 1967, and for two decades, the MPR dominated Congolese politics. In the last decade of Mobutu's rule, however, a number of political parties rose up to challenge the dominance of the MPR, and some of them received wide public support. As the ADFL advanced toward Kinshasa, a number of these parties expressed support for the ADFL and organized strikes to urge Mobutu to enter negotiations with Kabila. Nevertheless, Kabila has made little effort to bring the parties into the ADFL. Shortly after naming himself president, Kabila banned all party activity, and although he named a few Mobutu opponents to his Cabinet, he did not include the most prominent opposition politicians. As a result, many of the parties have continued to function, ignoring official restrictions, and have taken up a role as vocal critics of the regime, similar to the role they took under Mobutu. The parties have criticized corruption, nepotism, and foreign influence in the ADFL and have called on Kabila to move toward immediate democracy.

In addition to the political party opposition, several loosely coordinated rebel groups have emerged, primarily in North and South Kivu, where the ADFL rebellion began. While some of these groups supported the Mobutu regime during the civil war, others were allied with the ADFL but have since broken away.

Union for Democracy and Social Progress (Union pour la Démocratie et le Progrès Social; UDPS)

The UDPS is the oldest and most prominent opposition political party in Congo. The UDPS was founded by a group of dissident members of the Legislative Council in 1982, despite the MPR's official monopoly. Because the party's formation was in violation of the law banning other parties, the leaders of the UDPS were imprisoned, and several served lengthy terms. Nevertheless, the party persisted, and Etienne Tshisekedi, the most outspoken critic of the Mobutu regime, emerged as its leader.

The UDPS played a major role in organizing the Sovereign National Conference in 1990. The UDPS joined with other parties opposed to Mobutu to form a party coalition called the Sacred Union (*Union Sacré*) with Tshisekedi as its leader The National Conference appointed Tshisekedi as prime minister in 1992, in a challenge to Mobutu's authority. Many opposition activists hoped that Tshisekedi would oversee a transition to democracy, but Mobutu managed to hang onto power, in part by dividing the opposition. In 1993, Mobutu appointed his own prime minister, but Tshisekedi refused to accept his dismissal, claiming that Mobutu did not have the authority. In 1994, the HCR–PT, the legislative body that combined the National Conference and the Legislative Council, named Kengo wa Dondo as prime minister, but Tshisekedi continued to claim that he was the rightful prime minister. The party became divided as some members of the UDPS and the Sacred Union agreed to serve in the Kengo Cabinet.

In April 1997, Mobutu dismissed Kengo and named Tshisekedi as prime minister. He accepted the position only on condition that he use it to negotiate a peaceful end to the civil war. One week after his appointment, however, Mobutu dismissed him and named his hard-line army chief of staff as prime minister. Many people, particularly in Kinshasa where Tshisekedi is very popular, were distressed that Kabila did not name him to be prime minister or to another prominent post in his government. Tshisekedi has since voiced strong criticisms of Kabila and organized rallies calling for a rapid move toward democracy. At least two other UDPS politicians have, however, been included in the Cabinet. Tshisekedi is a Luba from Kasai.

Union of Federalists and Independent Republicans (Union des Féderalists et Républicans Independents; UFRI)

Nguza Karl-I-Bond, the head of the UFRI, is another longtime political figure. Once a close supporter of Mobutu who served as prime minister and ambassador to the United States, in the 1980s Karl-I-Bond emerged as a major opponent of Mobutu. He was an important figure in the National Conference, but he later served as prime minister, despite objections from others in the opposition. Karl-I-Bond is from Katanga, where UFRI enjoys its main support.

United Lumumbist Party (Parti Lumumbist Unifié; PALU)

PALU is another party that has continued to challenge the Kabila regime to diversify the government, move rapidly toward democracy, and respect human rights. PALU has organized numerous public protests since the ADFL victory, and a number of its members have been arrested. The criticism from PALU is particularly significant, since, like Kabila and the ADFL, PALU claims to follow the political tradition of Patrice Lumumba. PALU is led by Antoine Gisenga.

Mai-Mai and Bangelima

In the province of North Kivu, speakers of the Rwandan language, both Tutsi and Hutu, known collectively as "Banyarwanda," constitute more than 50% of the population. While many Banyarwanda families have been in Congo for centuries, others immigrated during the colonial period, when the Belgian colonial government moved people out of overpopulated Rwanda, or more recently, fleeing ethnic violence. While the Banyarwanda have prospered economically, members of ethnic groups that consider themselves the region's original inhabitants, particularly the Hunde and Nyanga, have dominated political offices. But with a transition to democracy becoming increasingly likely, Hunde and Nyanga feared losing their influence. The Mobutu regime sought to exploit these fears and encouraged Hunde and Nyanga, and to a lesser extent other groups such as Nande and Tembo, to form militia, which came to be known as Mai-Mai or Bangelima. In 1993, the Mai-Mai and Bangelima sought to expel Banyarwanda from the zones of Masisi, Walikale, and Rutshuru and killed several thousand. In 1995 and 1996, fighting broke out again, as Hutu refugees from Rwanda, whose Interahamwe militia had carried out genocide in Rwanda, joined with Congolese Hutu to fight both the Mai-Mai and the Congolese Tutsi.

When the ADFL advanced on North Kivu in late 1996, the Mai-Mai and Bangelima lent their support to the fight against the Zairian army and its Rwandan Hutu allies, but the alliance between the ADFL and the militia was always tenuous. The Mai-Mai remained as distinct groups, with few of their fighters integrated into the ranks of the ADFL, and from the first, ADFL officers had difficulty exercising control over the Mai-Mai. After the ADFL came to power, the non-Rwandan groups in North and South Kivu resented the continuing presence of Rwandan RPF soldiers in the region and the dominance of Tutsi in the new local and regional governments. In August 1997, fighting broke out between Mai-Mai fighters and ADFL soldiers in Masisi and gradually spread to other parts of North and South Kivu. In this more recent fighting, the Mai-Mai and Bangelima appear to have received support from remnants of the Rwandan Hutu Interahamwe and from Congolese Hutu. The goal of the Mai-Mai and Bangelima appears to be to retain Hunde and Nyanga autonomy and resist attempts to impose central government control. Their alliances and enemies have shifted as the threats they perceive to their autonomy have shifted. There appears to be no central command for the Mai-Mai and Bangelima and only limited coordination between various militia groups.

Democratic Resistance Alliance (Alliance pour la Résistance Démocratique; ARD)

The spark that started the war that eventually brought the ADFL to power was violence against the Banyamulenge Tutsi in South Kivu. Attacks on the Banyamulenge, which began in September 1996, involved FAZ troops as well as militia from the Bembe people, known as Simba, the Swahili word for lion. In August 1997, members of the Bembe militia and supporters from other ethnic

groups in South Kivu founded ARD to "liberate Eastern Congo"; however, most Simba militia appear to operate independent of the ARD structure. ARD is based in Fizi zone and is apparently headed by Celestin Anzaluni Bembe, a prominent Fizi politician who was involved in inciting the 1996 violence against the Banyamulenge. The ARD and Simba militia have taken up arms in Fizi and Mwenga zones of South Kivu and appear to have connections with the Mai-Mai and Bangelima in North Kivu and to receive support from Burundian Hutu rebels based in Congo and from Rwandan Hutu.

Congolese Rally for Democracy (Rassemblement Congolais Démocratique; RCD)

Previously unknown, the RCD burst onto the Congolese political scene spectacularly with an attack on Kivu on August 2, 1998. With extensive support from the ADFL's former allies, Rwanda and Uganda, the RCD quickly took control of much of Eastern Congo, following the ADFL's own route to power. In a dramatic move, hundreds of RCD troops were airlifted more than 1,000 miles across Congo in September to the port city of Matadi, from which they launched an offensive on the capital, Kinshasa. Despite initial success, the RCD offensive in the west was eventually crushed by the intervention of troops from Angola, Zimbabwe, and Namibia. At press time, the RCD still occupied a large portion of the east, including the third-largest city, Kisangani, and it was advancing slowly on several fronts.

Led by Ernest Wamba-dia-Wamba, a professor of history at the University of Dar es Salaam in Tanzania and a member of the Kongo ethnic group of Western Congo, the RCD brings together a variety of opponents of Kabila in a loose coalition. The group includes Banyamulenge and other former ADFL soldiers and a number of prominent Congolese politicians, but it has failed to gain much popular support, because many Congolese see the RCD as a puppet of Rwanda and Uganda. For many Congolese, the current fighting is not a rebellion but a foreign invasion, and the RCD offensive has, thus, enhanced Kabila's stature. Were the RCD able to win a military victory, it would have a difficult time gaining the support of the population.

OTHER POLITICAL FORCES

Religious Groups

Congo is a heavily Christian country, with nearly 90% of the population claiming membership in a Catholic, Protestant, or syncretic Christian church. The Catholic Church alone counts more than 50% of the population in its ranks, making it the largest nonstate organization in

Congo. President Mobutu viewed churches as a threat to his authority and implemented policies in the 1970s intended to limit their power and influence. The government passed a law in 1971 regulating churches that recognized as legal only the Catholic Church, the Church of Christ in Zaire (*Eglise du Christ au Zaire*; ECZ, an association that united mainstream Protestant churches), and the Kimbanguist Church (the largest syncretic church). In subsequent years, the government forbade the use of Christian names as part of an attempt to limit the cultural influence of the churches, banned a number of church publications, and nationalized church-run schools. These policies led to a severe conflict with the Catholic Church, which forced Cardinal Malula briefly into exile. In the 1980s, the Catholic Church served as a major source of opposition to the regime, and in 1990, Malula's successor, Cardinal Mosengwo, served as head of the Sovereign National Conference. A number of Catholic clergy were active in the National Conference and in the new political parties that formed. Following the ADFL victory, the Catholic Church has continued to speak out prophetically, calling for greater democracy and condemning the massacre of refugees in Eastern Congo.

During the Mobutu era both the Kimbanguist Church and the united Protestant body, the ECZ, were closely allied with the regime. Bishop Bokeleale, the head of the ECZ, was from Mobutu's home region of Equateur and was a close associate of the president. Because of these associations with Mobutu, the Kimbanguist Church and ECZ are in a precarious position under the new regime and have remained largely silent during the period of transition. Since all Protestant churches were forced into the ECZ by Mobutu's regulations, the very future of the united body, which brings together some 30 different church communities, is in doubt. Various independent Protestant churches and syncretic churches banned under Mobutu may experience greater independence under Kabila and could become a more important political force.

Civil Society Groups

During the 1980s and 1990s, a large number of independent associations emerged in Congo outside the auspices of Mobutu's officially all-encompassing party, the MPR. The most significant of these groups from a political perspective were the new human rights groups. The largest human rights group, the Zairian Association for the Defense of Human Rights (*Association Zairoise pour la Défense des Droits de l'Homme*; AZADHO) became a major thorn in the side of Mobutu during the 1990s, as it regularly denounced human rights violations by the armed forces, police, and government officials. Numerous regional human rights groups also played a role in monitoring government and military abuse. Members of these groups were regularly harassed and arrested, but the number of groups and the extent of their critiques

nevertheless continued to proliferate. Under the ADFL, many of the groups have continued to speak out, and their members continue to face harassment.

The Media

In the final years of the Mobutu regime, a vibrant print media emerged in Zaire, above all in the capital, Kinshasa. The papers publicized information regarding the actual conditions in the country, official corruption, and moves toward democratization. As opposition political parties emerged, many of them created newspapers or received backing from existing papers. The Mobutu regime regularly arrested journalists, but the attempts to subdue the press were largely unsuccessful.

Since the ADFL victory, the press has remained relatively circumspect. Several major newspapers, such as *La Tempete des Tropiques*, *Umoja*, and *Le Phare*, continue to provide frank news coverage, reporting on such issues as the fighting between the ADFL and Mai-Mai in Kivu. They also provide occasional criticisms of the Kabila administration. Kabila has responded by arresting some journalists, but the newspapers have been allowed to continue publishing.

NATIONAL PROSPECTS

The Democratic Republic of Congo has great potential to become a prosperous nation, because in contrast to many African countries, Congo is incredibly rich in natural resources, with substantial reserves of diamonds, gold, cobalt, and copper, vast tropical forests, and a large area of fertile land, only a portion of which is currently under cultivation. More than 30 years of bad economic management, however, have reduced Congo's economy to ruins. The Mobutu regime has been characterized as a "kleptocracy," because of the remarkable extent of official corruption. By funneling profits from mineral exploitation, public taxation, and international development assistance into their own pockets, government officials were able to live lavish lifestyles while the vast majority of the population found themselves struggling to get by. Despite Congo's incredible wealth, the country's infrastructure has almost entirely collapsed, with few roads remaining passable, the systems of education and health care in disarray, and the mining and agricultural industries functioning at only a portion of their capacity. Much of the rural population has reverted to subsistence farming, while urban populations struggle to survive.

The corruption and violence of the Mobutu regime have also left a troubling social and political legacy. Government offices were regarded not as a public trust but as opportunities for personal enrichment. Much of the Congolese population came to view the state as a threat to be avoided, and this legacy of alienation from the state is difficult to overcome. Furthermore, to serve their personal interests, government officials have exploited ethnic and regional differences and created a legacy of deep division that continues to foster conflict. The army and police under Mobutu showed a deep disregard for human rights, widely practicing arbitrary arrest, torture, and summary execution, and extorting money from the population, while almost entirely neglecting the task of stopping crime and maintaining order. The resultant criminality and disregard for the law have created a culture of impunity that cannot be quickly eliminated.

The fall of Mobutu after more than 30 years of authoritarian rule creates a great possibility for Congo to emerge from its current crisis, but the legacy of Mobutu's years in power is a heavy weight on the new regime. The ADFL views economic recovery as its primary initial objective, but this will only be truly possible if the ADFL is able to keep corruption under control. Tolerance by the ADFL of dissent and the diversification of its ranks would help to diminish ethnic resentments and conflict, but to date the ADFL has shown no inclination toward tolerance and diversification. Ultimately, the willingness of Kabila and his movement to move toward democracy may have a large impact on public perceptions and the willingness of the population to support government initiatives. While the task ahead for Congo is immense, the replacement of Mobutu creates the best opportunity since independence for Congo to emerge as an important regional power.

Further Reading

Callaghy, Thomas M. *The State-Society Struggle: Zaire in Comparative Perspective.* New York: Columbia University Press, 1984.

Elliot, Jeffrey M., and Mervyn M. Dymally, eds. *Voices of Zaire: Rhetoric or Reality.* New York: Washington Institute Press, 1990.

Gould, David J. *Bureaucratic Corruption and Underdevelopment in the Third World: The Case of Zaire.* New York: Pergamon Press, 1980.

Gran, Guy, ed. *Zaire: The Political Economy of Underdevelopment.* New York: Praeger, 1979.

Lemarchand, Rene. *Political Awakening in the Belgian Congo.* Berkeley: University of California Press, 1964.

Naipaul, V.S. *A Bend in the River.* New York: Random House, 1980.

Nzongola-Ntalaja, ed. *The Crisis in Zaire: Myths and Realities.* Trenton, N.J.: Africa World Press, 1986.

Schatzberg, Michael G. *Politics and Class in Zaire: Bureaucracy, Business, and Beer in Lisala.* New York and London: Africana Publishing, 1980.

———. *The Dialectics of Oppression in Zaire.* Bloomington: Indiana University Press, 1988.

Willame, Jean-Claude. *Patrimonialism and Political Change in the Congo.* Palo Alto, Calif.: Stanford University Press, 1972.

Young, Crawford. *Politics in the Congo.* Princeton, N.J.: Princeton University Press, 1965.

Young, Crawford, and Thomas Turner. *The Rise and Decline of the Zairian State.* Madison: University of Wisconsin Press, 1985.

REPUBLIC OF THE CONGO

(République du Congo)

By Christopher J. Lee, M.A.

THE SYSTEM OF GOVERNMENT

The Congo is a unitary republic currently maintaining a transitional government. It is located in western Central Africa and is bordered by the Democratic Republic of the Congo (formerly Zaire) to the south and east, the Central African Republic and Cameroon to the north, and Gabon to the west. It has a section of coastline to the southwest on the Atlantic Ocean. With an area of approximately 342,000 square kilometers and a population estimate of 2,516,000 (mid-1994), its population density averages 7.4 persons per square kilometer. The main ethnic groups include the Kongo, the Vili, the Téké, the M'Bochi, and the Sanga. Roughly half of the population practices indigenous religious beliefs. Christianity follows next in popularity with Islam being in third place.

The Republic of the Congo achieved autonomy within the French colonial community in November 1958, with full independence following on August 15, 1960. Its capital is Brazzaville.

Executive

General Denis Sassou-Nguesso became president as of October 25, 1997, having forcefully ousted President Pascal Lissouba from power. With the 1992 constitution suspended, power has remained in the hands of Sassou-Nguesso and his appointed transitional government.

Abbé Fulbert Youlou was elected the first president of the Congo in March 1961. The new constitution granted extensive executive power. Youlou's policies generated ethnic tension and labor unrest. He resigned in August 1963 with a transitional government being created under the leadership of Alphonse Massamba-Débat. Massamba-Débat was elected president in December 1963 shortly after the establishment of a new constitution. Beginning in 1964 with the establishment of the leftist National Movement of Revolution (MNR), the sole political party, tensions developed between the army and government. In August 1968 Captain Marien Ngouabi seized power in a military coup. He officially became president in January 1969. The leftist Congolese Workers' Party (PCT) replaced the MNR. Despite coup attempts in 1972

and 1973, Ngouabi remained in power. After approval of a new constitution in June 1973, a new government was formed in August complete with a National Assembly. Political instability persisted, however, and after a series of power struggles, Ngouabi was assassinated in March 1977. Colonel Jacques-Joachim Yhombi-Opango was appointed president. Despite efforts at improving social conditions, Yhombi-Opango gradually lost support and relinquished control in February 1979. In March, with approval of the PCT, Colonel Denis Sassou-Nguesso became president.

With his leftist political background helping facilitate the adoption of a socialist constitution, Sassou-Nguesso's term was influenced by liberal elements. In 1984, Sassou-Nguesso was elected president for another five years. He also consolidated his power through a new constitutional amendment and obtained further control over the military. Despite these attempts at establishing firmer political control, Sassou-Nguesso faced increasing opposition fueled by economic discontent and ethnic tension. In July 1989, he was again elected president for another five years. The new government implemented policies to further liberalize the economy. In December 1990, the PCT officially dropped Marxism-Leninism and advocated the creation of a multiparty political system. In early 1991, at a national conference intended to reform the political system, the constitution was suspended and the government dissolved. General Louis-Sylvain Goma, who was prime minister, became head of state. In December 1991, a draft constitution was completed that called for an elected National Assembly and a nationally elected president. This constitution was approved in March 1992.

In June and July 1992, elections to the new National Assembly and Senate took place. The Pan-African Union for Social Democracy (UPADS) won a majority of seats in both bodies. In August, Pascal Lissouba, leader of the UPADS, won the two-round presidential election. Lissouba promised economic reform and a decentralization of power from the national to the regional level. Though plans existed for coalition between the UPADS and the PCT, these were discarded by the PCT after Lissouba failed to appoint a Cabinet that met the PCT's expectations. The PCT went on to form a coalition with the

Union for Democratic Renewal (URD), a group of seven parties. This URD–PCT coalition gave a no-confidence vote to the new administration. Lissouba refused to resign, however, and dissolved the parliament. As tensions mounted, the military stepped in to encourage the formation of a transitional government until elections could be held.

Legislative elections in May 1993 brought victory to the UPADS and its allies. The URD–PCT contested the results with violence eventually erupting. In June, the Supreme Court ruled that the elections had been corrupted. A state of emergency existed from July until August with a truce being negotiated. With new elections the UPADS and its allies again won a majority. The URD–PCT, having won more seats than before, accepted the election. Violence erupted, however. Over 2,000 deaths resulted by the end of 1993. A truce was negotiated in January 1994, though violent incidents did continue to occur.

In December 1994, a new attempt at forming a coalition government was pursued. Lissouba signed a truce with opposition leaders Bernard Kolelas, head of the Congolese Movement for Democracy and Comprehensive Development (MCDDI), and Sassou-Nguesso, head of the newly created United Democratic Forces (FDU). A new government was formed in January 1995 with attempts at integrating opposition members, though the FDU refused to participate. In August and September, Lissouba introduced measures to repress union activity and the freedom of the press. In December 1995 an agreement was signed to facilitate the disarmament of opposition militias and the representation of opposition members in the military. Despite efforts at reconciliation that continued into 1996, opposition forces, particularly those associated with the FDU, kept their distance and continued to criticize.

Presidential elections to be held in August 1997 were postponed due to political conflict between Lissouba and opposition forces led by Sassou-Nguesso. After an attempt by Lissouba to form a government of national unity, Sassou-Nguesso forcefully deposed Lissouba in October 1997 after taking control of Brazzaville. Sassou-Nguesso was sworn in as president and established a transitional government.

Legislature

Since the suspension of the 1992 constitution in October 1997, a National Transitional Council was established in January 1998 as a legislative body. This appointed body will exist through a three-year transition period until 2001 when new elections are scheduled. The 1992 constitution had provided a bicameral legislature consisting of a 125-seat National Assembly and a 60-seat Senate. Members were elected by universal suffrage.

Judiciary

Since October 1997, the judiciary system established by the 1992 constitution has been suspended. Prior to this suspension, the court system consisted of two main courts, the Supreme Court and the Revolutionary Court of Justice. The Supreme Court handled cases of civil dispute. The Revolutionary Court of Justice adjudicated cases involving matters of state security.

THE ELECTORAL SYSTEM

The electoral system has been disabled since the October 1997 suspension of the constitution. President Sassou-Nguesso has strong control over government power along with an appointed National Transitional Council. Elections are scheduled for 2001.

THE PARTY SYSTEM

Since the establishment of a multiparty system in 1992, political tensions have developed between parties that have escalated to violence. In the 1992 elections to the new National Assembly and the Senate, the Pan-African Union for Social Democracy (UPADS) won a majority of seats in both bodies. Plans existed for a coalition between the UPADS and the previously powerful Congolese Workers' Party (PCT). Founded in 1969, the PCT was the sole political party until 1990. The coalition plans were discarded by the PCT when President Lissouba of the UPADS failed to appoint a Cabinet that met the approval of the PCT. The PCT instead went on to create a coalition with the Union for Democratic Renewal (URD), a group of seven parties.

Tensions between the URD–PCT coalition and the UPADS led to Lissouba's dissolving the parliament. New legislative elections in May 1993 again brought victory to the UPADS and its allies. The URD–PCT challenged these results, with the Supreme Court eventually ruling in their favor. With new elections, the UPADS and its allies again won a majority. The URD–PCT, having won more seats than previously, accepted the results. Politically influenced violence did occur between both groups, however.

In December 1994, a new attempt at forming a coalition government was pursued with truces being signed with opposition leaders Bernard Kolelas, head of the Congolese Movement for Democracy and Comprehensive Development (MCDDI), and Sassou-Nguesso, head of the United Democratic Forces (FDU). A new government was formed in January 1995, with attempts at integrating opposition members, though the FDU refused to participate. In order to curb violence that threatened political instability, an agreement was signed in December 1995 to facilitate the disarmament of opposition militias and to increase the representation of opposition members in the military. Despite efforts at reconciliation, opposition forces kept their distance and continued to criticize. In October 1997 Sassou-Nguesso forcefully took power, suspending the 1992 constitution and the electoral system. Elections are planned for 2001, after a three-year transition period. Armed militias with party affiliations continue to be a threat to political stability.

The following are the main political organizations in the Congo.

Pan-African Union for Social Democracy
(Union Panafricaine pour la Démocratie Sociale; UPADS)

This social democratic party is the party of Pascal Lissouba and forms his main basis of support.

Democratic and Patriotic Forces
(Forces Démocratiques et Patriotiques; FDP)

Formerly known as the United Democratic Forces, this group, founded in 1994 and renamed in 1996, is the umbrella organization for six allied political parties supporting President Sassou-Nguesso. These include the Congolese Workers' Party (*Parti Congolais du Travail*; PCT), the Convention for a Democratic Alternative (*Convention pour l'Alternative Démocratique*), the National Union for Democracy and Progress (*Union Nationale pour la Démocratie et le Progrès*), the Liberal Republican Party (*Parti Libéral Républicain*), the Union for National Renewal (*Union pour le Renouveau Nationale*), and the Patriotic Union for National Reconstruction (*Union Patriotique pour la Réconstruction Nationale*).

Union for Democratic Renewal
(Union pour le Renouveau Démocratique; URD)

Founded in 1992, this group is an umbrella organization for seven allied democratic parties with some socialist inclinations. The most significant parties are the Congolese Movement for Democracy and Comprehensive Development (*Mouvement Congolais pour la Démocratie et le Développement Intégral*; MCDDI) and the Rally for Democracy and Social Progress (*Rassemblement pour la Démocratie et le Progrès Social*).

NATIONAL PROSPECTS

The current situation in Congo is uncertain. The region as a whole has been shaky politically, and with the recent conflict and shift of power in the Democratic Republic of Congo (formerly Zaire), arms are widely available. Given recent tensions and bursts of violent confrontation, political violence remains a distinct possibility in the near future, even if fair elections are held in 2001.

Further Reading

Allen, C., M.S. Radu, and K. Somerville, eds. *Benin, the Congo, Burkina Faso: Economics, Politics, and Society.* New York: Pinter, 1989.

Decalo, S., V. Thompson, and R. Adloff. *Historical Dictionary of the People's Republic of the Congo*, 3d ed. Lanham, Md.: Scarecrow Press, 1996.

Gauze, R. *The Politics of Congo Brazzaville.* Stanford, Calif.: Hoover Institution Press, 1973.

Young, Crawford. *Ideology and Development in Africa.* New Haven, Conn.: Yale University Press, 1982.

REPUBLIC OF COSTA RICA

(República de Costa Rica)

By Kirk Bowman

THE SYSTEM OF GOVERNMENT

Costa Rica is a presidential system with a strong unicameral legislature and an independent judiciary and has been a vigorous and stable democracy since the Civil War of 1948. One of the immediate results of the Civil War was the permanent and constitutional abolition of the military, which has been a blessing for this small country. With no military, the state has been able to focus on the well-being of the citizenry; health, education, and living standards are well above what would be expected given the country's level of economic development. Elections in the country resemble great celebrations, and voter turnout is about 80%.

Costa Rica is located on the Central American isthmus between Nicaragua and Panama. At 19,575 square miles, the land mass is somewhat smaller than that of West Virginia. The population of 3.4 million is largely Mestizo (although many Costa Ricans erroneously consider themselves to be of pure European descent) and the indigenous population is quite small (about 1%). The other ethnic group is composed of descendants of black Jamaicans who were brought to build the railroads or work on banana plantations. Blacks are concentrated on the Caribbean coast and make up roughly 2% of the population.

Executive

The president is elected every four years by a national secret ballot. The winning candidate must receive a plurality and at least 40% of the vote. If the 40% threshold is not reached, a runoff, which has never been necessary, must be held. A constitutional reform in 1969 limits the president to a single term. In comparison with other presidential systems, the Costa Rican president has limited powers. The president cannot call referenda or issue decrees or control budget writing, although he or she can appoint and dismiss quite powerful ministers without legislative approval. The president has veto power on all legislation except the annual budget, but the veto can be overruled by a two-thirds vote in the Assembly. In 1998 Miguel Angel Rodríquez E., an economist and cattle rancher, was elected president on the Social Christian Unity Party ticket with 46.9% of the vote.

Legislature

The Legislative Assembly (*Asamblea Legislativa*) is a unicameral body of 57 members who serve four-year terms concurrently with the president. Due to the simultaneous elections, the controlling party in the Assembly and the party of the president are generally the same. Costa Rica uses proportional representation at the provincial level (seven multimember provinces) to select legislators. Therefore, regional parties can gain seats with a very small percentage of the national vote and wield significant powers when no party has an absolute majority.

Results of 1998 Elections for Legislative Assembly

Party	Votes	Seats
Social Christian Unity	569,792	27
National Liberation	481,933	23
Democratic Force	79,826	3
Libertarian Movement	42,640	1
Costa Rican Renovation	27,892	1
Alajuela Labor Action	16,955	1
Total	1,383,527	57

The currently ruling Social Christian Unity Party does not have a majority of seats and relies on coalitions with minority parties to push through budget and tax bills. A simple majority is needed to pass all legislation except amendments to the constitution, which require a two-thirds vote. The national budget sets aside 2% for pork barrel projects such as sewage, bridges, and sports facilities. These *partidas específicas* are distributed by the majority party in the Legislative Assembly and are used to build coalitions when no party has an absolute majority.

Judiciary

There are four chambers of the Supreme Court of Justice. The 22 members are chosen by the Assembly to serve eight-year staggered terms that are automatically renewed unless two-thirds of the Assembly vote against. The first chamber (*Sala* 1) reviews commercial, civil, and family matters. The second chamber (*Sala* 2) deals with labor issues. The third chamber (*Sala* 3) judges penal cases. The newly created and controversial fourth chamber (*Sala* 4) addresses constitutional issues. The Supreme Court selects the judges and magistrates of all the lower courts.

Regional and Local

Costa Rica is divided into seven provinces, which are further divided into 81 cantons or municipalities. Provincial governors are appointed by the president, and municipal boards (*municipalidades*) are elected every four years. Almost all funds spent at the local and provincial level originate from the central government in San José, the capital. Regional and local autonomy, budgets, and efficacy are limited.

THE ELECTORAL SYSTEM

In the aftermath of the 1948 civil war, a Supreme Electoral Tribunal (*Tribunal Supremo de Elecciones*) was created to instill confidence in elections. The Tribunal has proved to be so highly effective and publicly popular that it is often referred to as the fourth branch of government. The Tribunal is composed of three magistrates and three alternates selected by the Supreme Court of Justice for staggered six-year terms. The Tribunal has complete autonomy and final authority to oversee and rule on all aspects of elections. During election season, in a largely symbolic gesture, the Tribunal is handed control of the police. Elections are held the first Sunday of February every four years (1994, 1998, 2002), although there has been a movement to change elections to every five years both to save campaign and election expenses and to give the government an extra year to initiate programs and policies. There is universal suffrage in Costa Rica, and at the voting age, 18, one is automatically registered to vote and given a voter identity card (*cédula*). Voting is technically compulsory, but there is no punishment for noncompliance. Polling stations are open from 6 A.M. to 6 P.M., and each voter has two minutes to mark a ballot. In the past, the voter marked the party of choice with a fingerprint, but in 1998 a special pen began to be used, and by 2002 voting will be electronic. People who work on election day are given one hour off to vote. Turnout since the 1960s had averaged about 80%, and the low turnout of only 70% for the 1998 elections raised alarms of public apathy and cynicism toward politics.

Members of the Legislative Assembly cannot be reelected but must sit out one four-year term. Members of the Assembly are elected by proportional representation at the provincial level, and party leaders have traditionally selected the list.

THE PARTY SYSTEM

Origins of the Parties

The modern Costa Rican political system began with the revolution of 1948, which ushered in the Second Republic. Sectors of society allied around Rafael Angel Calderón on one side and José Figueres on the other. Calderón had won the presidency in the 1940 elections as the candidate of the then dominant National Republican Party (PRN). During his tenure, Calderón forged an alliance with the Catholic Church and the Communist Vanguard Party, which together pushed through significant social reforms. Calderón's party won the 1944 elections, which were criticized as fraudulent, and the 1948 elections were flawed and disputed as well. A civil war broke out, and Figueres, assisted by the Guatemalan government and Dominican and Nicaraguan fighters, took control of the country after the war had cost some 2,000 lives. Figueres quickly oversaw the creation of a new constitution, the abolition of the military, and the nationalization of utilities and the banks. He then turned power over to the conservative Otilio Ulate, who had in reality won the 1948 elections.

Figueres, Calderón, Ulate, and their political heirs and sons have dominated Costa Rican politics since 1948. José "Don Pepe" Figueres has twice been elected president and is a near-mythic figure to Costa Ricans. A charismatic and gifted politician, Figueres founded the social democratic National Liberation Party (PLN) in 1951. It has been the dominant political party for nearly a half century.

In 1948, Calderón was exiled from Costa Rica. He subsequently attempted two invasions from neighboring Nicaragua to recapture political power. After years of demonization, Calderonism has been largely rehabilitated and a second competitive party (Social Christian Unity, or PUSC) led by Calderón's son now challenges the PLN. The Unity Party, which was originally formed in 1978 as a product of four smaller parties, evolved into the Social Christian Unity Party in 1983. It appears to be a solid and lasting political organization. Costa Rica currently exhibits a highly competitive two-party system.

Party Organization

Parties are organized in an highly hierarchical fashion with factions at the top battling for control. The Electoral Code mandates that each national party must have an assembly at the district level, an assembly at the canton level constituted of 5 delegates elected from each district assembly, a provincial assembly composed of 5 delegates elected in cantonal assemblies, and a National Assembly with 10 delegates from each of the seven provinces. In reality, a small number of national leaders run the two major parties. Since candidates to the Assembly are elected in proportional representation by province, many provincial parties have emerged. Provincial parties must have similar district, cantonal, and provincial assemblies. These are often controlled by a few people or even a single family.

There has been movement toward a more direct selection of the party lists. The National Liberation Party began holding primaries in the late 1970s, and the Social Christian Unity Party held its first primary in 1997 to help determine candidates for the 1998 election. However, party leaders still largely control the selection of candidates and positions on the party lists. The Supreme Election Tribunal mandated in December 1996 that all party assemblies include at least 40% women. Both major parties are discussing mechanisms to ensure a quota of women in the Legislative Assembly; currently there are 11 women deputies in the 57-seat Legislative Assembly.

Campaigning

The Supreme Electoral Tribunal limits the amount of advertising and public manifestations in the months leading up to the elections. Individuals can contribute up to about $6,000 to a party. With recent revelations of drug money affecting politics throughout the hemisphere, the Tribunal has outlawed contributions from foreigners and requires itemized bimonthly reports of contributors. Party paraphernalia such as visors, flags, and T-shirts proliferate throughout the country during the election season.

Independent Voters

Research has indicated that about 40% of the population are PLN supporters and an equal number are opposed to the PLN. The remaining 20% are the swing voters who largely determine electoral outcomes. There is evidence that both the number of independent voters and the degree of dissatisfaction with the status quo are on the rise. It is easy to form new parties in an attempt to capture the independent voter, but up to now these parties have had limited success on the national stage.

NATIONAL LIBERATION PARTY
(Partido de Liberación Nacional; PLN)

In 1940, a group of progressive intellectuals and students formed the Center for the Study of National Problems and began a dialogue on political and economic challenges facing the country. From this group, the leadership core for the PLN in the post–civil war era emerged; the Center started the Social Democratic Party, which became the PLN in 1951. The party belongs to the Socialist International and is nominally a social democratic party. Under PLN control, the role of the government in economic affairs has grown dramatically as has social welfare provisions such as universal education and health programs.

In the first post–civil war elections, the party founder, José Figueres F., was elected in a landslide, and he served from 1953 to 1958. Control of the presidency was lost in the 1958 elections, but the PLN rebounded with a victory in 1962. After the opposition victory in 1966, Figueres F. won the presidency again in 1970 and has been the only president in modern times to serve two terms. Daniel Oduber, another founding member of the PLN, won the presidency in 1974, thus giving the party its first consecutive terms in office. After losing the 1978 elections, the PLN again won consecutive elections in 1982 (Monge) and 1986 (Árias).

Dr. Oscar Árias S. was the first PLN presidential candidate not associated with the founding of the party. Árias gained international fame and the wrath of the United States for pursuing a peaceful and negotiated settlement of the Central American crises that rocked the region in the late 1970s and 1980s. Largely through Árias's persistence and skilled leadership, peace plans were signed, and Árias won the Nobel Peace Prize in 1987. Árias is still a popular leader, with a 90% favorable rating in public-opinion surveys.

The 1994 PLN presidential primary featured Margarita Peñon (the wife of Oscar Árias) and José Figueres O. (the son of José Figueres F.). In a bruising primary, Figueres captured the nomination and subsequently won the national election with 48.5% of the vote. Going into the primary season for the 1998 elections, the PLN was facing a serious identity crisis. The left-wing faction of the party called for the social welfare policies that were so successful in the past, while the conservative faction countered that the country must accept neoliberal economic prescriptions to succeed in the post–cold war world. The party nominated José Miguel Corrales as its presidential candidate. While Corrales was generally acknowledged as honest, the party was damaged by revelations of fraud in the primary process. The PLN lost the presidency, earning 44.6 of the presidential vote. The PLN currently appears rudderless and factionalized and is deeply in need of ideological coherence and leadership.

SOCIAL CHRISTIAN UNITY PARTY
(Partido Unidad Social Cristiana; PUSC)

This party appears to be the stable and united successor to the host of factionalized opposition parties that have existed since the 1950s, and indeed it has strong links to 1940s Calderónism. For many years, the opposition was able to occasionally win the presidency but without a united opposition party was unable to capture the Legislative Assembly. In 1978, the Unity coalition of parties successfully won the presidency with the candidacy of Rodrigo Carazo O. The coalition changed its name for the 1982 election to Social Christian Unity and ran Rafael Calderón F., the son and namesake of the 1940s president, but it lost the election. The winner of the election, the PLN's Monge, gave the coalition a tremendous boost when he supported changes in electoral laws that allowed four parties to merge into the new PUSC and keep all government campaign financing earned in the previous election. Calderón lost the elections in 1986 to Árias in a campaign in which the PUSC was backed by the United States and the National Endowment for Democracy.

In 1990, Calderón won, and for the first time in modern history the PUSC controlled the legislature. The government implemented drastic IMF–designed economic measures in June 1990, causing widespread protest. During his tenure, Calderón successfully rehabilitated the image of his father as the founder of social policies in the country. Today, Calderón is the second-most-popular political figure in the country and the undisputed leader of the PUSC party.

In 1994, the PUSC lost the election by less than 1% and reran its candidate, Miguel Angel Rodríguez, in the 1998 elections. Rodríquez ran a defensive and cautious campaign, winning the presidency with 46.9% of the vote and outpacing Corrales by 33,326 votes. In an attempt to capture the women's vote, Rodríquez named two women for the vice presidential posts, a move that was countered by Corrales who also named a pair of women.

MINOR PARTIES

Electoral rules that mandate one ballot for the president and a separate ballot for the Legislative Assembly have led to significant ballot splitting and an increase in minor party deputies. The two major parties, the PLN and the PUSC, received 219,269 fewer combined votes for the legislature than for the presidency in 1998. The number of minor parties with legislative representation has grown from three in 1994 to five in 1998, and the number of deputies has grown from four to seven.

There are a total of 12 minor parties at the national level and 9 minor parties at the provincial level. There is occasional talk of minor parties running in a coalition, but prospects remain dim.

The Left

The Left plays a very limited role in Costa Rican politics. The Communist Party was banned after the Civil War and was not permitted to participate again until 1974. Various parties of the Left have emerged since, the latest being Democratic Force (*Fuerza Democrática*), which won two Assembly seats in the 1994 elections and three seats in the 1998 elections, making it the strongest of the minor parties. Democratic Force has since shown signs of splintering, so it is unclear how stable a force it can be in politics.

OTHER POLITICAL FORCES

La Nación

The Nation has been a powerful anti–PLN force since the 1950s and is the only major daily newspaper in the country. The newspaper has a strong neoliberal, pro-free-market slant. This media organization also sponsors forums, speakers, and seminars on issues of importance in the country.

The Catholic Church

The vast majority of the population is Catholic, and the church is an important symbol. The Catholic Church has not been the dominant force that it has been in other Latin American countries. Its symbolic power is best exemplified by the need for José Figueres O. to convert to Catholicism before the 1994 elections. Unlike many other Catholic countries, Costa Rica has legalized divorce, and contraception is widely practiced.

NATIONAL PROSPECTS

With the civil wars and uprisings of Central America at least temporarily resolved, Costa Rican democracy and stability seem assured. The greatest national problems the country now faces are economic, in particular a very high domestic debt. Numerous former politicians, such as Oscar Árias, have proposed the sale of many of the institutions (banks, insurance companies, refineries, alcohol distillers, utilities) that were nationalized after the Civil War and are still owned by the state, to pay off the debt. Others argue that a onetime sale of often-profitable entities is not a long-term solution and is a betrayal of Costa Rica's social democratic exceptionalism. This is the major debate in the country, and its resolution will have major consequences.

Costa Rica, like many other countries, also faces the challenges of opening the country to a free flow of goods and services while simultaneously trying to control the flow of illicit drugs and drug money through the country. Finally, polls have identified an increase in dissatisfaction with the political system in Costa Rica and public support for a third national political force. Many are calling for a new constitution. The PLN is factionalized, and many claim it is in decline. The political system of Costa Rica, while remaining highly democratic, may undergo substantial change in the decade ahead.

Further Reading

Ameringer, Charles. *Don Pepe*. Albuquerque: University of New Mexico Press, 1978.

Booth, John A. *Costa Rica: Quest for Democracy*. Boulder, Colo.: Westview Press, 1998.

Carey, John M. *Term Limits and Legislative Representation*. Cambridge: Cambridge University Press, 1996.

Chalker, Cynthia. "Elections and Democracy in Costa Rica." In *Elections and Democracy in Central America Revisited*. Ed. Mitchell A. Seligson and John A. Booth. Chapel Hill: University of North Carolina Press, 1995.

Edelman, Marc, and Joanne Kenan, eds. *The Costa Rican Reader*. New York: Grove Weidenfeld, 1989.

Honey, Martha. *Hostile Acts: U.S. Policy in Costa Rica during the 1980s*. Gainesville: University of Florida Press, 1994.

Lehoucq, Fabrice Edouard. "Costa Rica: Government and Politics." In *Costa Rica: A Country Study*. Ed. Rexford A. Hudson. Washington, D.C.: Library of Congress, 1997.

————. "The Institutional Foundations of Democratic Cooperation in Costa Rica." *Journal of Latin American Studies* 14, no. 1 (May 1996).

Wilson, Bruce M. *Costa Rica: Politics, Economics, and Democracy*. Boulder, Colo.: Lynne Rienner, 1998.

Yasher, Deborah. "The Historical Foundations of Costa Rica's Competitive Party System." In *Building Democratic Institutions: Parties and Party Systems in Latin America*. Ed. Scott Mainwaring and Timothy Scully. Stanford, Calif.: Stanford University Press, 1995.

REPUBLIC OF CROATIA

(Republika Hrvatska)

By Stephen C. Markovich, Ph.D.

THE SYSTEM OF GOVERNMENT

Croatia is a new country that seceded from Yugoslavia and declared independence on June 25, 1991. As a new country it is undergoing birth pains as it strives to transform itself from a one-party communist republic of the former Yugoslavia into a multiparty democracy and a sovereign nation state. The birth has not been easy. Amid external pressures and internal difficulties, the costs of the birth and transformation have been heavy.

Soon after declaring its independence, Croatia was attacked by Yugoslav-Serbian forces on several fronts. These attacks sparked a war that lasted only a few months but in that short time exacted a heavy toll in loss of land and displacement of peoples. By the time a cease-fire was mediated in January 1992, Croatia had lost one-third of its territories to Serb control and absorbed thousands of refugees from these territories. Three years later, however, the Croats regained most of this territory through counterattacks that not only drove Serbs out of their newly acquired lands but also out of the Croatian Krajina, a region that Serbs had inhabited for centuries. What lands the Croats did not regain by force, they regained by negotiations with the Serbian leaders of the Republic of Yugoslavia. Thus, by the summer of 1997, the Croats had restored all of their lost territory.

In addition to restoring their territory, the Croatian military and diplomatic offensives had forced about 300,000 Serbs out of the country and thereby further increased the domination of the Croats within the nation. When Croatia declared independence in 1991, the total population was 4.8 million. Of this total, over 3.7 million, or 78%, were Croatian, nearly all of them Roman Catholic; 581,000, or 12%, were Serb, nearly all of them Orthodox; and the remaining 10% were "Yugoslavs," Muslims, Hungarians, Italians, Albanians, Czechs, Jews, and others. By 1997, estimates indicate that the number of Serbian inhabitants had been halved, dropping to about 6% of the total; what had been a substantial and vociferous minority had now been marginalized and what had been a minority problem, as far as the Croats were concerned, had now been eliminated. With the Serbs diminished and the Croats inflated, Croats now made up nearly 85% of the population. Essentially the new Croatia has become a homogenous nation.

Through all the turbulence and uncertainty of the early years, Croatia worked to enhance its status as an independent state and to transform itself into a viable democracy. In a new constitution, it set forth the fundamental principles that provide the foundation for the political system. Among the most fundamental of these principles are those dealing with individual rights, the electoral system, the party system, and the governmental system. Individual rights are specifically asserted in over 50 articles and list practically every conceivable right—personal, political, economic, social, cultural. Provisions for free and periodic elections are also laid out in several articles, and the right to form political parties is guaranteed in Article 6. According to the constitution, the government is a mixed presidential-parliamentary system that is framed in a unitary structure and based on the separation of powers, and these powers accordingly are divided among three branches—executive, legislative, and judicial. Should Croatia even begin to live up to these articles, its status as a democracy will be emphatically affirmed.

Executive

The Republic of Croatia has a dual executive comprising the president of the republic, who is constitutionally the head of state, and the prime minister, who is constitutionally the head of government.

While the constitution states that the president is the head of state, in practice he or she is much more than that. His office is by far the most powerful one in the republic; his position and powers more closely resemble those of the American and French presidents in that he is both formal head of state and political leader of the country. According to the constitution the president represents the country at home and abroad. At home he is responsible for the functioning of government, and abroad he is the official spokesperson for Croatia.

In governing the country, the president is expected to work with the prime minister and the legislature, but the system does put him in a dominant position in this governing relationship. The president appoints the prime minister, who must be confirmed by the lower legislative house, and may dismiss him, and he also appoints and dismisses the other Cabinet ministers in consultation with the prime minister. In working with the Cabinet the president may call Cabinet meetings, preside over them, and determine their agendas. This control over agendas enables the president to determine which policies will be initiated and presented to the legislative houses for their consideration, which indirectly permits him to influence the agenda of the legislature. Elections for the two houses are called by the president and dissolution of the lower house is decided by the president in consultation with the prime minister and the chairman of that house. And should the president wish to go beyond the legislature and appeal directly to the people, he may do so through popular referenda. Finally, in addition to dominating the normal governing process, the president's powers are further enhanced by constitutional provisions that make him commander in chief of the armed forces and endow him with extraordinary powers in emergency situations, powers that allow him to rule by decree. All in all, the president's domestic powers are substantial.

In his representation of Croatia abroad, the president's powers are similarly substantial. Simply, he is the sole spokesperson for the country. He does of course work with the ministries of foreign affairs and defense and through his ambassadors, whom he appoints and dismisses, but he is the key decision maker in this area. He is the one who oversees the formulation and implementation of Croatian foreign policy, and he is the one who receives foreign ambassadors and meets with foreign leaders. In fact, in the short time he has been president, Franjo Tudjman has already traveled extensively and often acted as his own ambassador and minister of foreign affairs in dealing with the officials and leaders of other countries.

More than any other man, Franjo Tudjman is poised to influence the practical development of the Croatian political system in its formative years, much as Charles de Gaulle did in the Fifth Republic of France and Konrad Adenhauer in the Federal Republic of Germany. What the constitution prescribes as a political system may be clear in theory, but what actually transpires in practice rests heavily on Tudjman. For the role he played in leading the republic out of communist Yugoslavia and founding an independent Croatia, he is universally honored and respected; his comfortable victories in the presidential elections of 1992 and 1997 attest to this. However, on how he has governed as a sitting president the views are mixed. His supporters, especially those in his own ruling party—the Croatian Democratic Union (HDZ)—continue to praise his efforts and achievements; they claim he has provided Croatia with inspired leadership through difficult times, established a firm foundation for democratic development, and directed the transformation from stagnant socialism to energetic capitalism.

His opponents, of course, have a different assessment. While they admit that Tudjman started out well and with good intentions, they feel that he soon reverted to authoritarian leadership. Even when the country was on a wartime footing, when some authoritarianism might have been accepted, they feel that he went too far, that he simply used the wartime situation to justify his overzealous use of tactics that can only be described as dictatorial. Moreover, they claim Tudjman continued using these tactics well after threats to the country had receded; his control of the media, his intimidation of the courts, his manipulation of the electoral system, his rejection of local election mandates, his tolerance of economic corruption, and his strident belligerence toward political opposition have all been unnecessary. Croatia, the opponents say, has been and still is ready for democracy, genuine democracy, but Tudjman is not. Rather than governing democratically, he is ruling autocratically, and increasingly so. More and more he is reverting to the Titoist authoritarian model, one which he, as a former Communist, finds very familiar and quite comfortable. This presidential authoritarianism, argue the opponents, has to be constantly challenged and limited, primarily in elections and in the legislature, in order to allow the young democracy to survive and progress.

Assisting the president in his executive duties are the prime minister and other Cabinet ministers. As noted above, the president has some say in the appointment and removal of all of these ministers, so much say in fact that the president is clearly the dominant official in the executive. The constitution further underscores this presidential dominance by making the Cabinet responsible to both the president and the legislature. So, it is possible, for example, for the prime minister to be dismissed by the president directly or by the lower house through a vote of confidence. In no way is the prime minister equal to the president; he is not a coleader in the dual executive. The role of the prime minister and his Cabinet is to assist the president in running the country, and they carry out this role mainly by introducing bills and implementing laws. So far this executive relationship has worked as intended, but this may be due largely to the fact that President Tudjman and his party have controlled the political scene; they have controlled both the executive and the legislature.

Legislature

The Croatian legislature, or *Sabor*, is composed of two houses, the House of Representatives and the House of Counties. At present the House of Representatives, the lower house, has 127 members and the House of Counties, the upper house, has 68 members. All members of the lower house are chosen through popular elections, a few of them under special provisions to guarantee representation for minorities; of the 68 members in the upper house, 63 are elected territorially to represent counties and 5 are appointed by the president of the republic as especially deserving citizens.

Although the *Sabor* is set up as a bicameral system, it is one in which the lower house has more power than the upper house. Both houses participate in the proposal of bills, in questioning the executive, and in other legislative matters, but in all of these functions the upper house serves more as a check on the lower house, as the traditional parliamentary brake. When the upper house proposes bills, it does so through the lower house; when it questions the executive, it may question but cannot call for a vote of confidence; and when it receives a bill from the lower house, it can vote to return the bill for reconsideration, but its vote may be overridden by an absolute majority of the lower house. Thus, in all legislative matters where their powers are concurrent, the upper house defers to the lower one.

In addition to being superior in exercising concurrent powers, the superiority of the lower house is further demonstrated in its constitutional powers to adopt the budget, to decide on war and peace, to authorize government by decree, and to call the government to account. This last power is, of course, the ultimate legislative check of the executive, and in the Croatian presidential-parliamentary system members of the Cabinet may be called to account collectively and individually. If an absolute majority of the House of Representatives expresses a lack of confidence in the Cabinet as a whole, that is, in the government, then the prime minister resigns and the government falls. If the House expresses a lack of confidence in the competence of an individual minister, then the prime minister may resign or, less drastically, he may propose to the president that only the minister in question be dismissed. Bear in mind, however, that it is not simply a parliamentary system but a presidential-parliamentary system, one which has adopted the separation of powers, and therefore these legislative checks apply only to the prime minister and other ministers and not to the president, who is elected independently and is the stronger half of the dual executive; consequently, the confidence vote ends up being a limited check on the executive and the presidency remains the key office in the system.

Judiciary

For regular judicial matters the constitution provides for a Supreme Court of the Republic, for the establishment of inferior courts, and for the organization of public prosecutors. For constitutional matters the constitution provides for a Constitutional Court of the Republic of Croatia.

Cases involving regular matters, civil and criminal matters among others, normally are introduced at lower-level inferior courts by plaintiffs and public prosecutors

and rise up the judicial hierarchy only when vital points of law are at stake. In such cases it is the role of the Supreme Court to see that laws are interpreted in a consistent manner and that they are applied uniformly throughout the country and equally to all citizens. Judges and prosecutors in this regular system, from the lowest levels to the highest, are appointed by the High Judiciary Council of the Republic, a council of 15 distinguished legal authorities who are nominated by the House of Counties and elected by the House of Representatives for eight-year terms.

The Constitutional Court is composed of 11 judges proposed by the House of Counties and elected by the House of Representatives for eight-year terms. Once elected, these judges are independent of the legislature that selected them. According to the constitution they determine the conformity of laws with the constitution, decide jurisdictional disputes between the branches of government, oversee the constitutionality of programs and activities of political parties, supervise the legality of elections and referenda, and protect the constitutional freedoms and rights of individuals. With this array of powers the Constitutional Court is in a strong position to defend the constitutional fabric of the country and to play an important role in the stable growth of the nation's legal system and democratic evolution.

Just how a strong a role the judiciary does play will depend on its evolution within the system. So far the results have been mixed. For example, when Tudjman's refusal to accept the opposition's nominee for mayor of Zagreb was challenged in the Constitutional Court, the justices rejected the challenge; on the other hand, when Tudjman ordered the dissolution of the Zagreb city council, the Constitutional Court declared the order null and void. In the lower courts justices refused to be intimidated by Tudjman and acquitted two journalists who had been prosecuted by the government for libel, yet members of the High Judicial Council folded under pressure and removed the chief justice of the Supreme Court on some trumped-up charges. Obviously consistency has not been an early trait of the judiciary and is unlikely to become one as long as Tudjman feels free to intervene in court matters.

Regional and Local Government

Below the national level the country is divided into 21 regional units—20 counties and the city of Zagreb—that function as regional governments for their respective areas and as regional offices for the national administration. Apart from Zagreb with its population of nearly 1 million, the counties vary in size from 70,000 to 470,000. And where Zagreb is governed by a mayor and a council, each of the counties is run by a prefect and a council. Below the county level the units of local government are municipalities and towns, nearly 400 of them for the entire country. They are responsible for covering community needs and interests such as utilities, housing, welfare, culture, and recreation.

THE ELECTORAL SYSTEM

All Croatian citizens, inside and outside the country, who have reached the age of 18 years have the right to vote. On the national level this vote may be exercised in elections for the president and for members of the two houses of parliament. In the pluralistic elections that have been held since the break from communism, voter turnouts have been high but have also been declining, ranging from 85% in the 1990 elections to 69% in the 1995 elections.

The president of the republic is elected by the people for a five-year term and is eligible for a second term. In order to be elected, a candidate must receive a majority of the votes cast; if no candidate receives a majority in the initial election, then a runoff election between the top two candidates is held two weeks later. So far there has been no need for a second ballot as no one has been able to seriously challenge Franjo Tudjman. In the 1992 election, contested by eight candidates, Tudjman handily won on the first ballot with over 56% of the vote, and in the 1997 election, contested by only three candidates, he won even more convincingly with over 61% of the vote, though there were some questions about the democratic quality of this latter election.

The 127 members of the House of Representatives are elected for four-year terms in races that use both the plurality and proportional electoral systems. Under the plurality system, 28 seats are contested in individual constituencies where the candidate with the largest number of votes in each constituency wins the seat; neither a majority nor a runoff is needed. Under the proportional system, 80 seats are contested by the political parties in a national vote; here the electors vote for the party and each party receives the number of seats that corresponds to its percentage of the vote, provided that vote surpasses the 3% threshold. Beyond the 108 seats mentioned above, there are an additional 7 seats elected by minorities in Croatia and 12 elected by the Croatian diaspora. All 12 of these seats have gone to Tudjman's HDZ party since he has insisted that the diaspora includes not only those Croatian living abroad but also the Croatians in neighboring Bosnia and Hercegovina who heavily support Tudjman. What the 12 diaspora seats have done is exaggerate his party's electoral victories. In the 1992 elections the HDZ won 85 of the 138 seats making up the lower house at that time, and in the 1995 elections, called a year early by President Tudjman, it won 75 of the present 127 seats. (See Table 1.) These numbers mean the HDZ holds a 75-to-52 edge over the combined opposition; however, if the diaspora seats are omitted, the majority lead is only 63 to 52, a considerably tighter situation.

Most of the 68 members of the House of Counties are elected directly by the people in the 20 individual counties and the city of Zagreb; 3 representatives are elected in each of the 21 broad constituencies for a total of 63. In these elections too Tudjman's HDZ has dominated; in 1993 it won 37 of the 63 elected seats and in 1997 it won 41 of them. (See Table 2.) Here again Tudjman can exaggerate the electoral majority for the HDZ since he has the prerogative to appoint five additional members to the upper house, and he has not hesitated in exercising this prerogative.

THE PARTY SYSTEM

In many countries that suddenly gained independence and sought rapid transformation from one-party social-

---

TABLE 1
House of Representatives
(following elections in 1992 and 1995)

Political Party	1992 Seats	1995 Seats
Croatian Democratic Union (HDZ)	85	75
Croatian Social Liberal Party (HSLS)	14	12
Social Democratic Party of Croatia (SDP)	6 [a]	10
Croatian Peasant Party (HSS)	3	10 [a]
Other Parties	25	16
Independent Candidates	5	4
Total Seats	138	127

[a]In the 1992 elections the SDP led a coalition of small parties that collectively gained 11 seats, and in the 1995 elections the HSS led a coalition of small parties that collectively won 18 seats; so the numbers for these parties sometimes read differently in electoral reports.

TABLE 2
House of Counties
(following elections in 1993 and 1997)

Political Party	1993 Seats	1997 Seats
Croatian Democratic Union (HDZ)	37	41
Croatian Social Liberal Party (HSLS)	16	7
Croatian People's Party (HNS)	1	0
Social Democratic Party of Croatia (SDP)	1	4
Croatian Peasant Party (HSS)	5	9
Istrian Democratic Assembly (IDS)	3	2
Appointed by President	5	5
Total Seats	68	68

ism to pluralist democracy, the number of political parties rose dramatically, often soaring to large and cumbersome numbers. Such was the case in Yugoslavia before it disintegrated and in Croatia after it declared independence; by 1990 there were some 240 parties in Yugoslavia, and by 1992 there were about 60 parties in independent Croatia. Of course, this number began to diminish once the political system started to operate and elections became competitive. Of the 60 parties in 1992, less than half participated in the elections of that year, only 11 of them won seats in the lower house, and only 2 of these got more than 10 seats each. In the 1995 elections, 12 parties won seats and only 4 of them got 10 seats or more. (See Table 1.) Thus, by the time the electoral smoke cleared from these initial elections, there were but a handful of political parties seriously contending for power and influence in Croatia.

Even these contending parties, it should be stressed, are still adapting and adjusting to the new political system; all of them are still finding their way in the democratic experiment. For the most part they are parties that are five or six years old, that are in the process of organizing their internal governance and recruiting needed members rather than being settled in their structures and established in membership, that are strapped financially and desperately seeking funds, that are seeking broader political manifestos to attract wider support, and that are heavily dependent on their respective leaders who typically were the founders of the parties. For many of these parties the circumstances are difficult and their futures uncertain; some will endure but others will falter and vanish on their own or be subsumed in yet another coalition and emerge under a new name. By the next legislative election, scheduled for 1999, there may be a new array of players in the game. This scenario obviously makes it difficult to describe the political parties in Croatia with any degree of certainty, but fortunately there are some exceptions to the generic model presented above. There are some parties that are surviving the winnowing process, and the most notable of these is the Croatian De-

mocratic Union, the first political party to assume power in an independent Croatia; others that seem to be demonstrating some durability—that can still be termed major parties—are the Social Liberal Party, the Social Democratic Party, and the Peasant Party.

CROATIAN DEMOCRATIC UNION
(Hrvatska Demokratska Zajednica; HDZ)

The Croatian Democratic Union was organized in the spring of 1989 by Franjo Tudjman in opposition to the Communist Party of Croatia. At this time the old Yugoslavia was still in existence but the Communist Parties in the country's six republics were deprived of their power monopolies and competing parties were allowed to organize. Tudjman, who had gone from a member of the Communist Party and supporter of the Titoist regime to a critic of the existing system and a voice for Croatian autonomy, quickly took advantage of the situation and forged ahead of other groups in establishing the HDZ. By the time the first free election was held in the former Socialist Republic of Croatia in the spring of 1990, Tudjman's party was a solid challenger to the incumbent Communist leaders and impressively defeated them in the election—winning over 40% of the votes and over 60% of the seats, earning majority control in the legislative chambers, and gaining the office of president for Tudjman himself. And as noted above, all of these victories were repeated in the postindependence elections. What had begun as a new organization in 1989, just a short time before competitive elections, had rapidly grown into a formidable political party and a legitimate movement for national autonomy.

Croatian autonomy was the major goal of Tudjman and the HDZ. Initially Tudjman was willing to seek this autonomy within a revamped Yugoslav state, specifically a loose confederation, one that would in fact come closer to an economic union than an integrated polity. But the more Tudjman spoke, the more his party and his people leaned toward total autonomy, and subsequently both the temperament of his party and the turbulent political events drove him to proclaim the independence and sovereignty of Croatia on June 25, 1991. In addition to independence, the party program of the HDZ also pushed for a democratic political system, for a free-market economy, and for an orientation toward the West, especially toward Central Europe and Germany. Collectively these policies, according to Tudjman's supporters, make the HDZ a party of the center-right.

Major reasons that the HDZ was able to forge ahead of its competition were its early opportunistic start and its efficient organizational structure. As noted above, Tudjman quickly jumped into the fray when pluralism became accepted and led his party to power. He did so by spreading his party network throughout the nation; before the first election was called he already had party offices in over a hundred townships in Croatia and several in neighboring republics as well. He even went beyond his own country and established branches among the Croatian diaspora in various parts of the world; in the United States alone Tudjman claimed that the HDZ had 35 branches varying in size from 50 to 2,000 members. Not only did this network provide the party with over 200 organized branches and nearly 40,000 official members (as opposed to the hundreds of thousands of supporters the party sometimes claims as members) but it also provided a financial foundation that is generously supported by donations from home and abroad. Since no other party is as well organized and financed as the HDZ, prospects for the party look good. If the party does have a problem at this point, it is grooming a successor for Tudjman, a successor who can keep the party united; there are hints that the party may already be dividing on this question—between a moderate faction led by Mate Granic and a nationalist faction led by Gojko Susak. Should the HDZ in fact split over a new leader, then the opposition parties would have a genuine opportunity to compete more effectively and gain more influence, providing of course that they too can escape internal divisions and fragmentation.

CROATIAN SOCIAL LIBERAL PARTY
(Hrvatska Socijalna Liberalna Stranka; HSLS)

As soon as pluralism was approved in 1989, the Croatian Social Liberal Party immediately registered as an alternative party. Under the leadership of Drazen Budisa and Vlado Gotovac, the party offered a social liberal alternative to the incumbent Communist Party, emphasizing in particular the need for parliamentary democracy and free enterprise.

Initially the party did relatively well. Among the myr-

iad of parties in the early going, the HSLS was not seen as the second party or main opposition, but it steadily improved its position to the point where Budisa came in second in the 1992 presidential election with 22% of the vote, and the party came in second in the first parliamentary elections with 14 seats in the House of Representatives and 16 seats in the House of Counties. While these numbers placed the HSLS a good distance behind the ruling HDZ, they were enough to make the HSLS the main opposition party. In subsequent elections, however, the HSLS has slipped. In the second parliamentary elections, in 1995 for the House of Representatives and in 1997 for the House of Counties, the party dropped down to 12 seats in the lower house and 7 seats in the upper house; and in the presidential elections of 1997 Gotovac came in third in a field of three with 18% of the vote. Even the size of the party, never very large, has dropped below the 10,000 members declared in 1996.

The slippage of the HSLS may simply be a matter of another European liberal party settling at a level of support that hovers around the 10% mark, a rather common level for liberal parties. On the other hand, the slippage in the case of the HSLS may be due to more than that; it may be due to the uncertain leadership that has plagued the party recently. Just as the initial rise and success of the party rested more on the personalities and charisma of Budisa and Gotovac than on any distinctive policy or organizational traits, so its decline may be attributed to these leaders as well. Though the two men have been personal friends and political allies for years, differences between them surfaced and escalated in 1997. By year's end they were exchanging harsh words and quarreling over policy. Fundamentally they differed over the role of the party; whereas Budisa favored cooperating with Tudjman's government, Gotovac wanted a separate road and a distinct identity for the HSLS. After a showdown at a party convention, which elected Budisa as leader, Gotovac threatened to leave with his faction and form his own liberal party. Formally splitting the HSLS into two factions obviously does not bode well for the HSLS or for any factions that derive from that party.

SOCIAL DEMOCRATIC PARTY OF CROATIA
(Socijal Demokratska Partija Hrvatske; SDP)

The Social Democratic Party is the successor to the Communist Party in Croatia. As such it inherited the structural network of the old party that should have given it some advantages in the pluralist electoral campaigns. On the other hand, if there were such advantages, these were more than offset by the burdens of the Communist record; the baggage from the past was a heavy load and, claims of genuine reform notwithstanding, the SDP could not shake this load in the beginning. Thus, though the party espoused commitments to democracy, free enterprise, and a fair deal for workers, the voters did not respond positively in the 1992 and 1993 elections; the party won only 6 seats in the lower house and 1 seat in the upper house, and its presidential candidate came in eighth in a field of eight with less than 1% of the vote. Overall this weak electoral performance was indicative of the difficult times that Communists had in the new republic, and it appeared that their lot was unlikely to improve.

Yet the SDP persevered and has slowly crept back and bettered its position. In the next elections, in 1995 and 1997, the party increased its representation in the lower house to 10 seats and in the upper house to 4 seats, and in the presidential election its candidate came in second to Tudjman, a distant second to be sure with 21% of the vote, yet going from eighth to second and from less than 1% of the vote to 21% was an improvement. While the numbers still were not high, they were at least headed in the right direction. Given the SDP's stable organization, its core membership of 22,000, and its emerging identity, it may yet do more than survive and become a solid opposition force.

CROATIAN PEASANT PARTY
(Hrvatska Seljacka Stranka; HSS)

The Croatian Peasant Party has assumed the name and also attempted to assume the mantle of its popular prewar predecessor. The original Peasant Party, founded in 1904 by the Radic brothers, promoted political democracy and economic practices that served human values. Today the HSS offers a similar platform; it too advocates representative democracy and a market economy that relates to human needs and personal betterment. In sum, it sees itself as a moderate party of the people. Now, assuming the party's traditional name and mantle has been the easy part; attempting to match the success and support of its namesake has been more difficult. Most of the party's support has come from the older generation. Support from the young people has been hard to attract; for many young Croats the party's very name is an anachronism since there are fewer and fewer peasants working the land today, less than 10% of the population, so the party has an uphill climb in generating fresh sources of support.

Nevertheless, despite this difficulty, its overall status with the people seems to be modestly improving. Its small gains with the voters attest to this. Whereas the party won only 3 seats in the House of Representatives in 1992, it won 10 seats in 1995; moreover, in 1995 the HSS not only did well on its own but also did well in leading a coalition of small parties, called the United List, that collectively won 18% of the vote and 18 seats in the House. These 18

seats actually made the United List the largest opposition group in the lower house. In the upper house, the House of Counties, the HSS also strengthened its representation, raising its seat total from 5 in 1993 to 9 in 1997. Party officials, led by Zlatko Tomcic, fully understand that these are not powerful numbers, but at the same time they still believe they have a solid and ascending party, one with 22,000 loyal members and one which will continue to improve its showing in the future, especially when the popular and powerful Franjo Tudjman leaves the political scene. For this rosy belief to become a hard reality, it will take more than Tudjman's leaving; it will take sharp and sustained increases in voter support and legislative representation. At this point such sharp increases for the HSS do not seem to be in the political cards.

MINOR POLITICAL PARTIES

In addition to the political parties described above, there are eight other parties that have a few seats in the House of Representatives. Two of them, the Croatian Party of Rights and the Istrian Democratic Assembly, are minor parties with four seats each; yet, despite their small size, they are parties that do have some significance in the system. The remaining six, two of them with two seats and four of them with one seat, are fringe parties that most likely will remain on the fringe or disappear.

The Croatian Party of Rights (HSP) is an ultranationalist party that was initially led by a young militant, Dobroslav Paraga. The ultranationalism is epitomized in Paraga's dream to extend Croatian territory from the shores of the Adriatic to the outskirts of Belgrade and to take over most of Bosnia and Hercegovina in the process; in effect he wants to build a Greater Croatia. Though the party received some support at home and abroad, about 5% in the 1995 election, most of the voters found its jingoistic positions unacceptable. However, while the support is light, it is also deep, and this has enabled the HSP to advance its nationalistic agenda with gusto and thereby push the other parties and their leaders to the right, including the ruling Democratic Union and President Tudjman. Generally the Party of Rights is comfortable with Tudjman and supports his government so consistently that it can be viewed as an informal coalition partner of the HDZ. What threatens the party, besides its own extremism at times, are internal divisions; clashes at the 1993 party convention saw the removal of Dobroslav Paraga as party leader and the establishment of a collective presidency.

The Istrian Democratic Assembly (IDS) is a viable regional party that has a stable base of support on the Istrian peninsula on the Adriatic coast. It is primarily a Croatian party essentially arguing for more regional autonomy and less centralization in the country. On its own it won three seats in the lower house and three in the upper house in 1992 and 1993 and four seats in the lower house and two in the upper house in 1995 and 1997; in the 1995 election it ran as a coalition partner in the five-party United List that was headed by the Peasant Party. What sustains the IDS at present and will do so in the future is its strength in Istria; it normally attracts over 60% of the Istrian vote, which assures the party of some national representation and complete control of the regional assemblies.

The Croatian People's Party (HNS), which at present has two seats in the lower house, was organized after the 1990 elections by Savka Dabcevic-Kucar, a dynamic and popular leader in Croatia, popular even when she served in the Communist regime. Because of her popularity there were great expectations for her and her new party, but these great expectations have not been realized and the party has been fading; if it does survive, it likely will be as part of a new coalition such as the United List. The Serbian People's Party (SNS), also with two seats in the lower house, claimed in the 1992 election campaign that it was representing the interests of Serbs in Croatia, but this position got it nowhere because so many Serbs chose to boycott that election. By the 1995 election the party's position grew worse rather than better as thousands of Serbs left Croatia under a forced exodus. As a result the future of the party does not look good. The four parties that each have one seat in the House of Representatives are the Christian Democratic Union, a center-right party, the Slavonian-Baranian Party, a regional party, the Independent Democrats, a centrist party, and the Action of Social Democrats, a center-left party. These parties are already weak and fading fast and therefore have little chance of enduring as political entities. Like many of the 60 some parties that mushroomed into existence with the advent of political pluralism in Croatia, they will likely fold into mergers or vanish completely.

OTHER POLITICAL FORCES

It is possible that some of the vanishing parties may reemerge as interest groups or work through traditional institutions. Just what role and influence groups and institutions may have in the new Croatia will depend on the evolution of the political system, more specifically on the democratic evolution of that system. Should groups and institutions become important, then those individuals and organizations that are not satisfied with their influence in political parties may turn to lobbying and critiquing as a political avenue. In this scenario, one can expect business, labor, agricultural, professional, intellectual, ethnic, religious, military, media, and other organizations to join the political scene. Some of these are already increasing their activities; the Roman Catholic Church especially is becoming more vocal and seeking more influence in the system, and the media, though

dominated by Tudjman's government, is not totally under control and consequently critical commentary is being publicly presented.

NATIONAL PROSPECTS

Since the declaration of independence on June 25, 1991, the status of the Republic of Croatia as a nation-state has been internationally and domestically affirmed. Internationally it has been recognized by more than 100 nations, established diplomatic relations with nearly as many, and become a member of the United Nations and other international organizations. Domestically it has survived a war, regained its territorial integrity, and restored internal stability. These are impressive achievements—exceptionally impressive considering the circumstances under which they were achieved. As impressive as these achievements are, however, they do not mean that Croatia is free of problems. Far from it. Unfortunately problems remain, very serious and critical problems at that. Among the most critical are those related to the economic transition to capitalism and the authoritarian style of Tudjman.

Over the past several years, Croats have learned just how difficult and costly the transition from communism to capitalism is. For many of them the transition has been a negative experience; they have seen their standard of living slip considerably and have watched a new class of rich rise rapidly, primarily through blatant corruption in the privatization process and through political connections with Tudjman's party and government. Rather than benefit from the transition, therefore, most Croats have suffered through it. This negative experience has undermined their confidence in the new economy and thereby retarded and possibly even precluded its proper development. Thus, for the young nation to get back on the capitalistic track, the confidence of the people in the economic system has to be restored.

Furthermore, the people's confidence in the economic system has to be restored not only to advance the development of capitalism but also to promote the development of democracy. The synergism between economic pluralism and political pluralism, a synergism so beneficial to both the economy and the polity, is at present missing in Croatia.

As if the economic difficulties themselves have not generated enough obstacles to democratic development in the country, Tudjman has added to them by his authoritarian tactics. Rather than overseeing and encouraging democratic development as a benevolent statesman, he has insisted on controlling the system as a domineering autocrat. He has done this by concentrating power in the executive and marginalizing the legislature and judiciary, by dominating the media and suppressing unfavorable criticism, and by manipulating the electoral system and limiting the role of the opposition parties. What he has in fact done as president of Croatia is incrementally move closer to the old communist ways of governing than he has to the new democratic ways and thereby retarded the healthy evolution of democracy in the country. All in all, he has created an environment that is not good for democracy now or in the future, that is, in the post-Tudjman era. Such an environment has to be changed for Croatia to survive its birth as a democracy. A more hospitable environment is needed for the fragile democracy to take root, for the people to become socialized to the democratic idea, and for the political players to become accustomed to the give-and-take of the democratic process. For democracy to have a chance in Croatia, the present tense and limiting political environment has to be supplanted by a more relaxed and liberal one.

Further Reading

Banac, Ivo. *The National Question in Yugoslavia: Origins, History, Politics.* Ithaca, N.Y.: Cornell University Press, 1988.

Banac, Ivo, Trpimir Macan, and Josip Sentija. *A Short History of Croatia.* Zagreb: Atlantik Papir, 1992.

Cohen, Lenard J. *Broken Bonds: Yugoslavia's Disintegration and Balkan Politics in Transition*, 2d ed. Boulder, Colo.: Westview Press, 1995.

Djordjevic, Dimitrije. "The Yugoslav Phenomenon." In *The Columbia History of Eastern Europe in the Twentieth Century.* Ed. Joseph Held. New York: Columbia University Press, 1992.

Doder, Dusko. *The Yugoslavs.* New York: Vintage, 1978.

Eterovich, Francis H., and Christopher Spalatin, eds. *Croatia: Land, People, Culture.* Toronto: University of Toronto Press, 1964 and 1970.

Lampe, John R. *Yugoslavia as History: Twice There Was a Country.* New York: Cambridge University Press, 1996.

Ramet, Sabrina P. *Balkan Babel: The Disintegration of Yugoslavia from the Death of Tito to Ethnic War*, 2d ed. Boulder, Colo.: Westview Press, 1996.

Rusinow, Dennison. *The Yugoslav Experiment, 1948–1974.* Berkeley and Los Angeles: University of California Press, 1977.

REPUBLIC OF CUBA

(República de Cuba)
By Juan M. del Aguila, Ph.D.

THE SYSTEM OF GOVERNMENT

Cuba is a nation of 11 million people situated approximately 90 miles from the southernmost part of the United States. Cuba is the largest of the Caribbean islands, located at the entrance to the Gulf of Mexico with Haiti and the Dominican Republic to the east and Mexico and Central America to the west and southwest. The island was discovered by Columbus in 1492 during his first trip to the New World, and it remained a Spanish colony until 1898. The United States occupied Cuba between 1898 and 1902 following its defeat of Spain in the Spanish-American War. During its occupation, the United States helped to rebuild Cuba's economy and infrastructure, and it established the foundation of public administration and a national political system.

Subsequently, Cuba and the United States became closely related economically, with approximately 1 billion dollars in U.S. investment going into Cuba's telecommunications, agriculture, industry, and commerce by the late 1950s. Cuba's economic development was substantially dependent on the United States, where Cuba's sugar and other exports found an expanding market. One of the positive aspects of that relationship was the fact that some Cuban products like sugar received preferential treatment in the United States, and U.S. consumer goods were widely available in Cuba.

On the other hand, a close political and economic relationship with the United States was viewed by many Cubans as limiting Cuba's sovereignty and distorting its economic development. While anti-Americanism was not a widespread feeling, U.S. interventions in Cuba in 1906 and 1917 fueled nationalist feelings and a growing desire for greater economic freedom, particularly among the educated elites and some intellectuals. On the whole, U.S. society and culture appealed to many middle- and upper-class Cubans, though others had reservations about the scope of American cultural penetration.

The triumph of Fidel Castro's guerrillas in 1959 over the authoritarian regime of President Fulgencio Batista led to Cuba's change from a capitalist to a socialist country, with the society undergoing major transformations in its political, economic, social, and cultural systems. Castro and the revolutionaries formed a nondemocratic government that relied on Castro's dynamic and charismatic leadership for much of its legitimacy, but the government soon effected redistributive measures that improved the standard of living of Cuba's marginal urban and rural classes.

The revolutionary government confiscated approximately 1 billion dollars of U.S. assets as part of a radical nationalization program in 1960, which led to a break in relations with the United States during President Eisenhower's last days in office. Subsequently, Castro proclaimed the revolution to be a socialist one, proceeding to establish a command economy where all production and practically all property were nationalized. As a result, the state took over the sugar industry, the transportation system, banking, and foreign trade, effectively ending capitalism and prohibiting the individual accumulation of wealth. The commitment to socialism meant that collective values and goals would take precedence over those of private individuals, with the state developing the coercive capability to see that its brand of radical egalitarianism was enforced.

In addition, Cuba became a member of the socialist bloc and a close ally of the former Soviet Union until the latter collapsed in 1991. During the cold war, Cuba received billions of dollars in technical and economic assistance from former Communist countries, and its economy was closely integrated into the communist world's trading and commercial systems. Aiming to extend communist control over parts of Africa and in keeping with (then) Soviet geopolitical goals, Cuban troops fought in several African countries in the 1970s and 1980s. Cuba was also heavily involved in regional politics, providing technical and military assistance to revolutionary forces and governments in Central America in the 1980s.

President Castro, who is now 72 years old, is Cuba's dominant political leader, extending his personal influence over the most significant aspects of Cuba's domestic and foreign policies. At the center of power in Cuba for nearly 40 years, Castro is a highly intelligent, experienced, and skillful leader committed to his own and the revolution's survival at almost any cost. He combines cunning and ruthlessness with a charismatic temperament and ability to adapt, at times suppressing disputes among Cuba's ruling elites while maintaining legitimacy in the eyes of many Cubans. As president, commander in chief of the armed forces, first secretary of the Communist Party, and chairman of the Council of Ministers, Castro exercises direct influence over Cuba's leading institutions. In sum, Castro personifies the revolution and his decisions are final on critical domestic and foreign policy matters.

Executive

Cuba's highest executive and administrative institution is the Council of Ministers (CM), composed of the head of government, all the major ministers, and "others that the law determines." President Castro presides over the Council while his brother Raúl Castro, age 67, is minister of the armed forces and vice president of the Council. Individual ministers are responsible for sectors of the economy and society and are in fact top policymakers in their respective areas. For example, the minister of agriculture (Alfredo Jordán) is responsible for that sector, while the minister of higher education (Fernando Vecino) is responsible for the university system and other institutes of higher learning and training. The minister of labor has overall responsibility for working conditions, seeing to it that Cuba's labor movement remains loyal to the revolution and that workers improve their productivity and efficiency.

The Council is accountable to the National Assembly and can "organize and conduct the political, social, cultural, economic and defense activities outlined by the Assembly." The Council is empowered to conduct foreign relations and trade, maintain internal security, and draft bills for legislative consideration. Ministers are selected for their competence and political loyalty to the revolution and can be dismissed when recurring deficiencies occur that indicate either negligence or failure to discharge ministerial duties properly; for instance, in the 1990s, new ministers have been named for the sugar industry, transportation, and culture.

In short, the Council centralizes top administrative authority in a cabinetlike structure that provides for ministerial leadership of individual areas while remaining subordinate to the will of top political leaders. It is the executive's central bureaucracy, responsible for managing a command economy and integrating social, cultural, and educational tasks.

Legislature

Elected for a period of five years (1976–81, 1981–86, 1986–91, 1993–98) with one exception in the early 1990s, the National Assembly of People's Power is the only national body invested with constituent and legislative authority. During the 1993–98 period, its 589 deputies were elected directly following nominations closely supervised by the Communist Party. Top government officials, including the Castro brothers, were elected to the Assembly, and a former foreign minister, Raúl Alarcón, became its president.

Following changes to the constitution approved in 1992, deputies are elected directly through secret ballot; citizens 16 years of age or older without legal difficulties or mental handicaps are eligible to vote. The government reported a 99% turnout for the 1993 elections from a total pool of 7.9 million eligible voters. President Castro's "unity slate" was approved by 88% of voters, 5% voted for specific candidates, and 7% cast null, void, or blank ballots.

On the other hand, these were not competitive elections because although candidates are not required to belong to the Communist Party in order to be nominated, the process is in fact closely supervised by the party at all times. Second, no parties other than the Communist Party are allowed to nominate candidates for the Assembly, so that all 589 deputies elected were regime supporters. Third, campaigning is highly restricted to publishing individual biographies or discussing a candidate's personal merits and service to the community and the revolution. The mass media are controlled by the state and cannot be used for individual campaigns; in contrast, the government uses the media to encourage participation and to provide "political orientation." Because President Castro believes that campaigns are a sign of "divisiveness, when what the country needs is unity," appealing to voters directly as is common in Western democracies is not permitted.

The composition of the Assembly does not reflect the society's racial, gender, or occupational makeup, making the institution quite elitist. For instance, 23% of the deputies were women and only 3% were peasants. Full-time party functionaries make up a large bloc, as do members of the armed forces and Ministry of Interior. The 48 doctors elected constituted the largest single bloc, with scientists, researchers in various areas, and workers in the sugar, transportation, and construction industries also gaining significant representation. University graduates made up 75% of the deputies, and the average age was 43; overall, 78% of the deputies were under 50 years of age.

Among its powers, the Assembly decides on constitutional reforms, approval of the national budget, declarations of war, and election of the attorney general and judges to the Supreme Court. However, the Assembly fails to exercise legislative initiative and routinely approves measures placed before it by top political leaders. Votes are unanimous or nearly so, and diverging or opposing points of view on substantive issues of domestic and foreign policy are not expressed. Since all deputies either belong to the Communist Party or were approved by the party prior to their election, one cannot expect the Assembly to act as a forum where top political leaders are held accountable.

On the other hand, the Assembly offers a sense of participation to its members and a very limited, somewhat symbolic sense of representation to the masses. Notions of democratic representation common in Western democracies are out of the question, but individual deputies render constituent services and at times demand that government ministers explain problems in a particular area or sector. In sum, the Assembly is neither a policymaking institution nor an equal branch of government; it is inconceivable that it would reverse or disapprove of policies initiated by the political leadership. Deputies are not full-time legislators, and the Assembly as a whole meets only briefly twice a year.

The Council of State (CS) functions as the Executive Committee of the Assembly between sessions. Fidel Castro is the president of the Council and therefore president of the nation; Raúl Castro is the first vice president. Several top officials of the Communist Party are members of the Council, including Carlos Lage, who is in charge of the economy; the foreign minister, Roberto Robaina; the minister of interior, Abelardo Colomé; and José R. Balaguer, an official with extremely important responsibilities in the ideological sphere. In short, the Council reflects quite clearly the continuation of interlocking directorates as a central feature of Cuba's executive, legislative, and party organs.

The CS can issue decrees on its own, exercise legislative initiative, order general mobilization, remove ministers, and issue general instructions to the courts. In times of crisis, it can be called into action by President Castro in order to put its stamp of approval on decisions urged by the political leadership. For example, as the ultimate court of appeal, the Council approved the death sentence and execution of a former division general, Arnaldo Ochoa, and three others in 1989, following their conviction on drug charges and trafficking in stolen property.

Not much is well known of the Council's inner workings, but it is probable that routine decisions are reached through consensus, that is, following some discussion of issues under consideration. As the first among equals, President Castro carries the day once he has made his choices known, particularly in matters of critical domestic importance or involving foreign and security policy. Members do not explain their decisions, nor is accountability something they worry about. Discussions are largely secret; that is, brief reports of Council meetings may be published, but the neither the public nor other institutions have the means to force disclosure.

Judiciary

The People's Supreme Court is the top judicial institution; its decisions can be appealed only to the Council of State. Justices are elected by the National Assembly, as are its president and vice president following their respective nominations by Cuba's president. Under the constitution of 1976, revised in 1992, the Court's objectives are to maintain and strengthen socialist legality and to safeguard the legitimate interests of the state, other institutions, and the masses.

Cuba has 169 municipal courts and 14 provincial courts with jurisdiction over criminal and civil matters; the latter act as appellate courts. Military courts have privileged jurisdiction over some cases, and labor councils provide some quasi-judicial functions. Professional and lay judges are elected to the provincial and municipal courts by the respective assemblies following nominations from the Ministry of Justice.

Courts do not constitute an independent branch of government that could presumably check abuses of executive, legislative, or party authority. Under Article 121 of the constitution, the "courts constitute a system of state organs, structured independently and subordinated to the National Assembly and the Council of State." In other words, the courts are subject to political authority and are not a coequal branch of government.

Neither are the courts charged with protecting rights and freedoms. Citizens are afforded procedural guarantees and have legal recourse when brought before tribunals, but in practice these guarantees are often violated and do not constitute protection against the overwhelming power of the state. Article 62 of the constitution establishes that none of the rights or freedoms (assembly, speech, movement) can be exercised "against the existence or goals of the socialist State," effectively prohibiting all forms of legal dissent and opposition to the government. In short, Cuban courts do not rule against the government or the party on political issues and offer no relief to citizens charged with political crimes.

For instance, in 1996 the Interamerican Commission on Human Rights (an organ of the Organization of American States) found that "the subordination of the administration of justice to political power creates great insecurity and fear among citizens, and that is reinforced by the weaknesses of the procedural guarantees, especially in trials that directly or indirectly could affect the political system." Overall, the Commission reported that the Communist Party is in a position to decide which liberties are exercised and which are prohibited, "effectively eliminating an individual's defense against the state."

In sum, courts sanction criminal behavior but are severely constrained when it comes to performing fairly and impartially in "political trials." Citizens with political grievances cannot use the courts to redress those grievances, nor do courts provide relief from manifestly political abuses by the state. The judicial system is not immune from interference by either the Communist Party or the political authorities and is therefore incapable of rendering judgments that would hold the government accountable for violations of basic civil and political rights.

Regional and Local Government

Since 1976, Cuba has been divided into 14 provinces. The capital city of Havana is a separate province with over 2 million residents. Each province is governed by a provincial assembly, and each one of Cuba's 169 municipalities is governed by a local organ of people's power (OPP). Delegates to municipal assemblies serve for 2 ½ years.

Local governments assume various administrative tasks and are mostly involved in solving local problems and providing some social services. Since the 1970s, local assemblies have supervised schools, clinics, some small industries, and recreational centers. It is also part of their mission to promote cultural, educational, or health-related campaigns intended to mobilize the public toward a specific goal.

Efforts are made by local and provincial assemblies to coordinate some activities with mass organizations like the committees for the defense of the revolution (CDRs) in order to minimize redundancy and duplication of efforts, but these are not always successful. The fact that they are dependent on the central government for some resources means that local assemblies often fail in their tasks because resources are scarce. Operating under severe austerity measures enacted in the 1990s during what the government calls "a special period in times of peace" only makes the situation worse for local assemblies, reducing their overall capability to deliver quality services. Public dissatisfaction with OPP members is evident in some municipalities, and some studies indicate that a significant proportion of OPP delegates are not reelected for second or third terms.

THE ELECTORAL SYSTEM

According to official figures, elections to OPP held in October 1997 registered a 97% turnout among eligible voters, that is, nearly 7.8 million people voted to elect some 14,533 officials of local assemblies. Of those standing for election in 1997, 62% were renominated; women made up 18.5% of all candidates, a slight increase over the 16% who stood in 1995. Quite significantly, 82% of the 31,273 candidates were members of the Communist Party, following nominations by the mass organizations and party assemblies.

Figures indicate that null, blank, or otherwise void ballots were slightly over 7%, with a 3% rate of abstention; the former is a substantial decline from the 11% registered in the OPP elections of 1995. The president of the National Electoral Commission stated that the 10% rate of abstention and null or blank ballots "does not necessarily mean a rejection of the political system," indicating that the government was pleased with the overall results. And President Castro characterized the new officials as "martyrs of the system," urging

them to see to it that everything functions appropriately.

On the other hand, regime opponents able to make their own independent count contend that the number of null, void, or blank ballots was nearly 600,000, or approximately 60,000 more than the government reported. Second, voting in Communist countries cannot in all instances be considered a sign of support for the system, given the lack of choices available to voters and the pressures placed on citizens. On the whole, it appears that between 10% and 15% of voters are dissatisfied with the candidates and/or the system as such and are expressing that dissatisfaction by not voting for anybody.

Changes in the electoral system approved in 1992 call for the mass organizations and party assemblies to nominate candidates to OPP, who need not belong to the party as such in order to be eligible. On the other hand, the party closely monitors the nominating process and informally lets it be known who is acceptable and who is not. Dissenters or opponents need not apply: they will simply not be recognized. A nominee's political behavior, his or her standing in the community, loyalty and service to the revolution, and moral attributes are factors that assemblies take into account when nominating someone.

No campaigning is allowed, much less are alternatives to the system of government or to major domestic or foreign policies articulated. Nominees must get 50% of the vote or higher in order to be elected; if they fail that, a second round follows. Once elected, OPP delegates provide 50% of the delegates to the provincial assemblies, with the balance in turn nominated by the mass organizations. Elections to provincial assemblies and the National Assembly of People's Power were held in January 1998; 601 deputies were elected to the National Assembly and will serve until 2003.

Elections are not meant for citizens to choose among competing policy alternatives, nor can voters choose candidates from several parties. Information reaching the public is tightly controlled and rather than presenting competing points of view tends to emphasize voting as a moral duty of revolutionaries. On election day, activists go from house to house rousing citizens and reminding them of their duty to vote; the government's image is enhanced if it can show a high turnout. In short, the propaganda machine and activist cadres are mobilized around election time, but many citizens have heard it all before and do not take the messages seriously.

The process ensures that only prosystem candidates are elected, that is, persons who are loyal to the system and the political leadership. Not surprisingly, such practices are inherently antidemocratic, limiting choices and preferences to only those within the system. In addition, pressures to vote are substantial, because not voting is seen as a sign of political disaffection or apathy, values contrary to those in the dominant political culture. A revolutionary society urges political participation even in electoral rituals, where voting is one more test of one's political commitment. This is not to suggest that a great majority of Cubans vote against their will or are forcibly coerced into supporting prosystem candidates; rather, it is simply to point out that the costs of nonparticipation are substantial.

CUBAN COMMUNIST PARTY

(Partido Comunista Cubano; PCC)

Castro came to power in Cuba as the charismatic leader of a political movement with substantial popular and middle-class support; for all practical purposes, his guerrilla forces assisted by an urban underground overthrew the Batista regime without the participation of the Communist Party. Subsequently, the party subordinated itself to Castro's leadership, putting aside some of its orthodox views and endorsing his policies and governing style.

The PCC is today a Castroite party that occupies the central role in Cuba's state and governmental institutions. Its primacy is recognized in the constitution, which refers to it as "the organized Marxist-Leninist vanguard of the working class." Presumably inspired by the ideas of José Martí and the example of Fidel Castro, the party constitutes "the highest leading force of the society and the state." Castro himself stated in 1997 that "today the party is the soul of the Revolution," indicating that for him the party is immortal.

HISTORY

Founded in 1925 by Julio A. Mella, Carlos Baliño, and others, the party participated in the nationalistic and anti-imperialistic struggles of the 1920s and 1930s, alongside other social forces. Its activities were often outlawed by governments in the 1930s; by then the party was closely aligned with the Soviet Comintern and espoused ideological orthodoxy. During Cuba's democratic period in the 1940s, the party changed its name to *Partido Socialista Popular* (PSP) and collaborated with Batista's democratically elected government of 1940–44.

The party enjoyed some electoral success in the late 1940s, recruiting from the urban working class and from a growing number of intellectuals disaffected by the growing violence and corruption of the times. On the other hand, party leaders never reached positions of governmental influence after the 1940s; on balance, the PSP had never been a strong electoral competitor for the more traditional parties by the time Castro came to power.

In fact, the PSP denounced Castro's first attack on the Bastista dictatorship, namely his assault on the Moncada barracks in 1953. Characterizing the act as "putschist," the party viewed Castro's 26th of July Movement as a failed bourgeois organization unable to tap the revolutionary potential of the working class. During Batista's government, the party played an ambivalent role, taking advan-

Members Elected to the Political Bureau of the Cuban Communist Party (PCC) during the Fifth Congress (1997)	
Member(s)	Office(s) Held
Fidel Castro	President, Council of State
	President, Council of Ministers
	Commander in Chief, Armed Forces
	First Secretary, PCC
Raúl Castro	First Vice President, Council of State
	First Vice President, Council of Ministers
	Minister, Armed Forces
	Second Secretary, PCC
Ricardo Alarcón	President, National Assembly
	Member, Council of State
Juan Almeida	Vice President, Council of State
	Commander of the Revolution
Concepción Campa	Director, Finlay General Institute
	Member, Council of State
Julio Casas	Division General
	First Vice Minister, Armed Forces
José R. Machado	Vice President, Council of State
Abelardo Colomé	General of the Army Corps
	Minister of Interior
	Vice President, Council of State
Carlos Lage	Vice President, Council of State
	Secretary, Executive Committee of Council of Ministers
Roberto Robaina	Member, Council of State
	Minister of Foreign Relations
Esteban Lazo	Vice President, Council of State
	PCC First Secretary, City of Havana
José R. Balaguer	Member, Council of State
Ulises Rosales	Division General
	First Vice Minister, Armed Forces
	Minister of Sugar Industry
	Member, Council of State
Pedro Ross	Member, Council of State
	General Secretary, Cuban Workers' Confederation
Abel Prieto	Member, Council of State
	Minister of Culture
Marcos Portal	Member, Council of State
	Minister of Basic Industry
Leopoldo Cintra	Division General
	Chief, Western Army
Ramón Espinosa	Division General
	Chief, Eastern Army
Alfredo Jordán	Minister of Agriculture
Yadira García	PCC First Secretary, Matanzas
Juan C. Robinson	PCC First Secretary, Santiago de Cuba
Jorge L. Sierra	PCC First Secretary, Holguín
Misael Enamorado	PCC First Secretary, Las Tunas
Pedro Sáez	PCC First Secretary, Sancti Spíritus

Sources: "Cuba: Escasos cambios políticos y de cuadros en el Congreso del Partido Comunista," ABC (Madrid), October 12, 1997. Reprinted from *El Nuevo Herald* (Miami), Netscape; Granma, October 11, 1997.

tage of the climate of relative freedom to strengthen itself, all the while avoiding political confrontations.

Fidel Castro himself was not a party member at the time, though he had several personal friends who were in fact Communists. His brother Raúl did have open sympathies for the Communists and had traveled to Communist countries. Subsequently, in an effort to move to the winning side, the party sent emissaries to the mountains and established contact with Castro; still, the PSP did not play any significant role in Batista's overthrow and in fact played second fiddle to Castro's guerrillas.

Tactical imperatives rather than ideological commitment or revolutionary comradeship led Castro and the Communists into a political alliance in the early 1960s, as liberal, democratic, and pro-American forces in Castro's own movement were purged, exiled, incarcerated, or killed. There is some evidence that the alliance between Castro and the Communists was forged in secret prior to 1959, but what is clear is that the party accepted Castro's leadership and provided him with a solid organization through which to assert political control.

In addition, the party facilitated contacts between Castro and the (former) Soviet Union that in time led to Castro's formal embrace of Marxist-Leninist ideology and to Cuba's alignment with the Communist bloc. Party leaders and militants began to assume political roles in the 1960s as the transition to socialism was achieved, and Communists acquired influence over education, the mass media, culture, and the mass organizations.

On the other hand, the party's old guard did not respect Castro's ideological conversion, or his anarchistic governing methods and personalization of the revolutionary process. In fact, the party mounted unsuccessful challenges to Castro's leadership in 1962, 1964, and 1968, losing out in the end and suffering purges and humiliation. Still, the party would not break with the revolution, surviving due to the resilience of its cadres and its relationship with the Soviet Union.

Since the late 1960s, the party has assumed a major role in political and state affairs, with its position legitimated in the 1976 constitution. It is the only party allowed in Cuba, and its members enjoy privileged status and access to power. The party remains the faithful custodian and interpreter of Marxist-Leninist ideology and still articulates a view of a future communist society that has little credibility left. In sum, the PCC as one of only four ruling Communist parties left in the world following the collapse of the Soviet empire can claim some continuity with the revolution itself; that is part of the explanation for its longevity.

ORGANIZATION

As is the case with other ruling Communist parties and in keeping with the Leninist method, the principle of democratic centralism governs intraparty affairs. Top organs and leaders decide crucial policy matters, make critical appointments, assess domestic and foreign trends, and then solicit and obtain approval for their decisions from lower party bodies. Structurally, the PCC's top organs are its political bureau, with 24 members, and the central committee, with 150 members. The secretariat was abolished in 1991.

The PCC's first congress was held in 1975 following its cancellation in 1967 and 1969. A second congress was held in December 1980, and a third one in December 1986. The fourth and fifth congresses were held in 1991 and 1997, respectively. At each congress, Fidel Castro delivered the main report to the assembled delegates, usually several hundred men and women elected at the grass roots by the mass organizations and local party bodies. Deliberations at these congresses are largely secret, with the foreign press not allowed to cover them.

Members of the political bureau occupy high positions in government, the armed forces, and the party bureaucracy itself, maintaining the interlocking nature of governance typical of past and present communist regimes. The political bureau is the "elite of the elite," with its members assuming major roles due to their expertise and their loyalty to President Castro. Membership in the political bureau is not permanent, that is, it changes according to circumstances and the will of top political leaders; for instance, following the 1997 party congress, several provincial party secretaries were promoted to the political bureau and four others were dropped.

The central committee is also an important party organ, charged with "electing" top party leaders and representing the overall interest of the party as such. It meets infrequently and on occasion serves as a deliberative body; its primary function is to serve as a channel through which party policy is announced and disseminated to provincial and local party organs. Its work involves internal party organization, economic matters, ideology, and religious affairs. It is organized in several departments, e.g., the department of religious affairs, the department of ideology and revolutionary orientation, and others.

Following the 1997 congress, membership was reduced from 225 to 150 to increase efficiency, reduce costs, and get rid of some "dead wood." A preliminary review of its members indicates that 13% are women and that a minority are black or mulatto. Overall membership is drawn from the party bureaucracy, provincial party leaders, the armed and security forces, and from the ranks of specialists and technocrats involved in economic, financial and managerial jobs. All of the top ministers are members of the committee, and a handful are the leaders of the mass organizations.

Election to the central committee indicates high political status and is in fact something of a prized reward; as is the case with the political bureau, membership is not necessarily permanent. With a few exceptions for top leaders, membership will rotate as younger cadres are promoted and others are shuffled out or given new assignments. Women and blacks are heavily underrepresented at the party's highest levels, and their promotion rates to high positions appear to have leveled off. Finally, the military's representation in the committee is around 17%, a 5% increase from the 1991 congress.

MEMBERSHIP AND CONSTITUENCY

Party membership has risen dramatically since the 1960s. In 1965, total membership stood at 70,000, but it declined to 55,000 by 1969. Membership stood at 202,807 in 1975, reaching some 770,000 in 1997, or roughly 7% of the total population. From 1992 to 1997, membership increased by 232,000, meaning that 30% of all members joined the party in that period. Party documents indicate that the members are drawn "from the mass of manual and intellectual workers, civilian and military, from the city and the rural areas"; in all likelihood, many members belonged at one point to organizations like the Communist Youth Union and others.

Members are urged to "apply Party policy in the workplace and in society, and despite the most difficult and unusual circumstances" set an example of what a good and competent Communist is like. In addition, the party reminds members that "there should be no privilege, only greater discipline and sacrifice, more tasks and responsibilities, motivated by love of country and a limitless loyalty to its people." In short, party membership is defined as a kind of high-minded public service and as a reward for demonstrating loyalty and commitment to revolutionary principles.

On the other hand, membership constitutes an avenue of social mobility for those politically ambitious cadres seeking to move up the political ladder. There is no doubt that members enjoy some privileges unavailable to ordinary citizens and have access to goods and services that would otherwise be more difficult if not impossible to obtain. This is particularly important in a society like Cuba, where austerity, sacrifice, and hardship are the order of the day for millions of people.

Studies from other Communist countries show that party membership opens the way to higher status and facilitates entry into the nomenklatura, a special class of functionaries and officials largely immune from the hardships of daily life. In other words, party members and leaders may be urged to live modestly, set example, and face the same difficulties of ordinary people, but in point of fact membership lifts one to a higher status and allows one to circumvent the rigors of the ration card or other limitations. And for top leaders like the Castro brothers, enjoying a life of opulence and luxury is nothing new.

LEADERSHIP

The party is ruled by Fidel Castro Ruz (born August 13, 1926), who was trained as a lawyer at the University of Havana in the 1940s before he became a professional revolutionary and politician. Second in command and designated successor is Raúl Castro Ruz, minister of armed forces and increasingly active in political and economic affairs. Speculation about who would be third in line often centers on Ricardo Alarcón, the president of the National Assembly and a member of the political bureau, or on younger men like economics czar Carlos Lage or Foreign Minister Roberto Robaina. In any event, there is no good reason to expect Fidel Castro's abdication anytime soon, though (usually false) reports of his declining health surface from time to time.

Following the fifth party congress, 24 individuals make up the political bureau, with the Castro brothers as the first and second secretaries. Candidate membership was eliminated in 1991, so all are full members. In the 1986–91 period, the political bureau had 14 full members and several candidate members, but it appears that membership has stabilized at present levels. Only 2 of the 24 members are women, suggesting that women continue to lag well behind men when it comes to reaching the party's highest organ; the 2 women have been in the political bureau since 1991. There are 3 black members (Almeida, Lazo, and Robinson), indicating that black Cubans also fail to reach the top in proportion to their numbers in the general population.

Only the Castro brothers and Juan Almeida, commander of the revolution, are left from the original political bureau of 1965, showing that rotation at the top is a characteristic of Cuba's ruling elite. Increased participation by the military is noteworthy, with the addition of General Espinosa to the bureau. High-ranking military officers remain loyal to the revolution and the Castro brothers, and several of them joined the political bureau in the 1980s. General Colomé, for example, was named minister of interior in 1989, effectively bringing the security and domestic intelligence services under the control of the regular armed forces.

The military's support would be crucial if any major change in government were to come in the next few years, but what remains clear is that the military as a strategic elite continues to play a major role in the system. Active and retired military officers are involved in some of the economic changes approved in the 1990s and are running quasi-private enterprises in tourism and transportation.

In sum, the political bureau includes "foundational" leaders like the Castro brothers, loyal military officers, some of whom have governmental responsibilities, party secretaries whose turn came up, and younger cadres with major responsibilities in culture, foreign affairs, and the economy. As far as one knows, they are united and committed to the preservation of "the revolution and socialism," and would hardly think of challenging the Castro brothers. Younger members in their 40s or 50s are very much a product of the Communist system, show no inclination of leading a process that would dismantle it, and remain fervently loyal to their mentor(s).

OTHER POLITICAL FORCES

Opposition

There is no organized opposition to the Castro regime in Cuba. The party and government effectively isolate and often repress most manifestations of opposition, using force if necessary to get their message across. For example, the Interamerican Commission of Human Rights found in its 1996 report that "1,173 persons are serving sentence for political crimes" and that "the civil and political rights of Cuban citizens continue to be seriously violated by the State." The Commission recommended that the government "cease its harassment of human rights groups, or others with a political orientation, and legalize them."

Neither the institutions nor the mass media serve as outlets for opponents, and the party itself constantly sees to it that "counterrevolutionaries" stay out of its ranks. For instance, the party warns against the rise of "small groups of annexationists [those allegedly calling for annexation to the United States] financed from abroad" and calls upon the masses to "remain united and show their moral courage" in defense of the revolution and the fatherland.

On the other hand, there is irrefutable evidence not only of growing discontent at the grass roots and massive disaffection among members of the cultural, professional, and educational elites but of political dissidence itself. Some estimates indicate hat there are some 150 active dissident groups in Cuba calling for the rule of law, democracy, constitutional government, and respect for human rights. Second, these organizations form part of a growing national network that includes independent journalists, lawyers, doctors, and other professionals who are completely disillusioned with communism and are organizing grassroots efforts to bring about political change.

In a powerful document released in 1997, leaders of a dissident social democratic movement denounced the regime's violation of human rights and called for a restoration of democracy through internationally supervised free elections. The document, *La Patria es de Todos* (The Nation Belongs to All), stated that "the State does not serve the citizen, rather, the citizen serves the State," something which explicitly contradicts the allegedly egalitarian principles justifying Cuban communism. And the document goes on to say that "the laws fail to respect the rights inherent in a human being, something that is demonstrated by the denunciations of human rights violations that the United Nations has issued against Cuba."

Simply stated, political dissidence is rapidly growing in Cuba, fueled by the economy's near collapse, by a manifest repudiation of one-party politics and commu-

nism itself, and by a sense that a national holocaust is inevitable unless a genuine process of economic and political liberalization takes place. In other words, the regime's and the party's call for "unity" appears to fall on deaf ears; calls for the salvation of "the nation, the revolution and socialism" are increasingly seen as empty slogans designed to deceive and disinform.

Finally, the Catholic Church is out of the shadows and visibly involved more and more in propagating the faith among a new generation of believers. Under the leadership of Jaime Cardinal Ortega, archbishop of Havana, the church at times speaks out against violations of human rights, calling for religious and political freedom. For example, the church has alluded to the "long silence about God" that existed in Cuba for many years, something that "permeated everything, including family life."

Open-air masses are now permitted, and the church has documented a rise in "popular religiosity," namely the interest shown by many Cubans in religious and spiritual matters. Second, Catholic activists are selectively engaged in leadership training, providing moral and ethical interpretations of life that challenge the atheistic postulates of Marxism. Independent publications are distributed in study circles and to a small but highly committed community of religious activists throughout the country, moving debates away from the state-controlled media.

During his five-day visit in January 1998, Pope John Paul II awakened a long-suppressed feeling of religious freedom among the hundreds of thousands of Catholics, believers, and nonbelievers who attended his four public Masses and listened to his homilies. In his homilies, the Pope denounced communist oppression and called for greater religious freedom, insisting that governments should neither violate human rights nor reserve for themselves the education of the young or the provision of basic social services. At the same time, in criticizing the U.S. embargo on Cuba, the Pope restated the church's traditional view that embargos are "ethically unacceptable." In short, the Pope's visit clearly strengthened the Cuban Catholic Church, placing the communist government on the defensive while urging everyone "not to be afraid."

NATIONAL PROSPECTS

Cuba's Communist system confronts major problems in the late 1990s, some of which stem from the collapse of communism and others that are indigenous and exacerbated by the government's refusal to undertake major reforms. The Cuban economy collapsed in the early 1990s, losing nearly 40% of the gross national product from 1989 to 1993. Since then, recovery has been erratic at best. Growth in 1998 will be around 2.5%, and not much higher is expected for the coming years. Sugar production has plummeted to around 4 million metric tons per harvest in the late 1990s, down from an average of some 7.5 million in the late 1980s. In short, the standard of living of the average person is substantially worse than in the 1980s, and the party itself concedes that "the list of problems is enormous."

Furthermore, Cuba no longer receives billions of dollars in subsidies or economic and technical assistance, and it lost its privileged commercial and financial relationships when the Communist bloc imploded. Credits from capitalist countries or financial institutions are obtained only at very high short-term interest rates, given the risks of lending to Cuba, and the government still owes some $12 to $15 billion to Western creditors. Financing production is a major problem for Cuba, and the government finds raising new capital increasingly difficult.

Rather than introducing major structural reforms that would dismantle the command economy and free up resources and encourage private initiative, the government is committed to preserving a Communist model riddled with inefficiency and technological obsolescence. For instance, the party declared in 1997 that "in Cuba there will not be a return to capitalism because the Revolution will never be defeated. The Fatherland will survive and will continue to be socialist."

In conclusion, the last few years of the 20th century shape up as a disaster for a country committed to a model of economy, society, and government that is a proven and colossal failure. There is little hope of reconciliation between the 1.5 million Cubans who have left the island and the 11 million who live under Castro's rule until there are fundamental changes in the nature of governance. And that prospect is remote until the current generation of revolutionary leaders is gone.

Further Reading

Baloyra, Enrique, and J. Morris, ed. *Conflict and Change in Cuba*. Albuquerque: University of New Mexico Press, 1993.

Bengelsdorf, Carollee. *The Problem of Democracy in Cuba*. New York: Oxford University Press, 1994.

Bunck, Julie. *Fidel Castro and the Quest for a Revolutionary Culture*. University Park: Penn State University Press, 1994.

del Aguila, Juan M. *Cuba: Dilemmas of a Revolution*, 3d ed. Boulder, Colo.: Westview Press, 1994.

Horowitz, I.L., and J. Suchlicki, eds. *Cuban Communism*, 9th ed. New Brunswick, N.J.: Transaction, 1998.

Kaplowitz, Donna R., ed. *Cuba's Ties to a Changing World*. Boulder, Colo.: Lynne Rienner, 1993.

Mesa-Lago, Carmelo, ed. *Cuba after the Cold War*. Pittsburgh: University of Pittsburgh Press, 1993.

Pérez-López, Jorge, ed. *Cuba at a Crossroads*. Gainesville: University of Florida Press, 1994.

Pérez-Stable, Marifeli. *The Cuban Revolution*. New York: Oxford University Press, 1993.

Quirk, Robert. *Fidel Castro*. New York: W. W. Norton, 1993.

REPUBLIC OF CYPRUS

(Dimokratia Kyprou [Greek]);
(Kibris Cumhuriyeti [Turkish])

By Keith Legg, Ph.D.
Revised by Deborah A. Kaple, Ph.D.

THE SYSTEM OF GOVERNMENT

The Republic of Cyprus, an island country of nearly 753,000 people (1997 estimate) in the eastern Mediterranean south of Turkey, is approximately 78% Greek and 18% Turkish. Cyprus has been an independent, sovereign state, with a democratic presidential government, since 1960. Both the constitution and the international status of Cyprus derived from a series of accords known as the Zurich-London agreements reached by Britain, Greece, and Turkey in 1959. They were designed as a compromise solution to conflicting aspirations between the Greek and Turkish communities.

The bicommunal 1960 constitution devised by the Zurich-London agreements was never submitted to a referendum by the Cypriots or to ratification by an elected Cypriot legislature. Its complexity and rigidity inevitably led to an impasse in the implementation process. According to the 1960 constitution, Cyprus should have a Greek president and a Turkish vice president elected by their respective communities. Both were granted the power of final veto over any decision of the Council of Ministers or the House of Representatives in matters concerning foreign affairs, defense, and security. Since the president appointed 70% of the ministers, who served at his pleasure, he faced no problems with the Council of Ministers. The veto, therefore, became in essence a vice presidential prerogative. The president recommended in his constitutional proposals of 1963 that the veto power be abolished. He also recommended that the vice president assume the duties of the president in the case of the latter's temporary incapacity or absence. The 1960 constitution provides that it is the president of the House of Representatives (a Greek) who should assume the president's duties. All the constitutional proposals were turned down by the Turkish community. The vice president's post has been vacant since 1964 when the Turks withdrew from the government and established their own representation.

The Greeks of Cyprus once sought to unite the island with Greece. When the British rejected this demand, they fought a guerrilla war in the mid-1950s in order to unite with Greece. The Turkish Cypriots opposed unification with Greece. They preferred either the status quo or partition of the island between the two communities. The 1959–60 Zurich-London Agreement expressly prohibits both *enosis* (union) with Greece and *taksim* (partition).

Since independence the Greek Cypriots (a small right-wing faction excepted) seem to have turned away from the idea of *enosis*, for several reasons. First, they thought it was not feasible even if it was desirable. Second, as Cyprus began to modernize and prosper as an independent state, they realized the advantages of independence. The feeling was that given the small size of Cyprus, the central government was more immediately and directly involved with problems that would have to wait if Cyprus were part of Greece and only one of many districts of another country. People began to realize that it was not absolutely essential for them to be part of the state of Greece in order to be Greeks. Thus, a more sophisticated definition of Greekness began to emerge that distinguished between cultural and political identities. Finally, the military junta that ruled Greece from 1967 to 1974 was not attractive to the democratic Cypriots.

The Turkish Cypriots never believed that the Greeks had given up the idea of *enosis*, and their suspicion played a major role in shaping their policies. The Turkish Cypriots interpreted the constitution as guaranteeing them the status of an equal partner in the government. They regard themselves as one of two communities in the island with equal claim to political power. The constitution was indeed bicommunal and gave the Turks disproportionate power relative to their numbers. The Greeks felt they were discriminated against. After the constitutional crisis and the intercommunal violence of the 1960s, both sides recognized the need for revising the 1960 constitution. That was the purpose of the 1968–74 intercommunal talks. Although no concrete, final agreements were reached, substantial progress was made on various important issues. Everything was changed with the events of 1974 when Turkey invaded Cyprus.

Unlike the Greek Cypriots, who were independent of Greece in their policymaking, the Turkish community depended heavily on Ankara for political direction and economic aid, illustrated by the history of the intercommunal talks of 1968–74. In January 1974, the Turkish prime minister in Ankara announced that the new structure in

Cyprus should be along federal lines. This was a major reason for the disruption of the talks.

In mid-1974, the military junta that ruled Greece instigated a coup against the Cypriot government of Archbishop Makarios. The Turkish government responded to the apparent move toward *enosis* by invading the island and occupying the northern third of it. It then instituted a massive population transfer in which all Greeks in the Turkish occupied area were forced to move south, while Turks in the south fled north to escape the possibility of a Greek backlash. The island has remained rigidly partitioned since then.

After the 1974 invasion, Turkey declared the occupied area to be the Turkish Cypriot Federated State and refused to recognize the Republic of Cyprus as legitimate. Its successor, the Turkish Republic of Northern Cyprus, proclaimed in November 1983, claims sovereign independence but is recognized only by Turkey. The 1960 constitution, as amended, is still the legitimate legal structure of Cyprus even though it does not operate in the north. Internationally, Cyprus continues to be represented by the Greek-controlled government. And despite the efforts of a number of international organizations in the 1980s and 1990s to come to some agreement between the two, the Greek and Turkish portions of Cyprus continue to be separate.

Executive

The 1960 constitution calls for a joint administration of the affairs of Cyprus, but since the creation of a separate Turkish Cyprus in the northern part of the island in 1974, each community has administered its own affairs. The Greek Cypriot government claims to be the government of Cyprus, and it is generally recognized as such without the approval of Turkey. The northern area is controlled by "The Turkish Republic of Northern Cyprus," and each side has its own president, vice president, and Council of Ministers.

The president of the republic is the head of state and government. He is elected by universal suffrage for a five-year term, with no limit on the number of terms he may serve. Executive powers are exercised by the president through a Council of Ministers appointed by him and serving at his pleasure. There is no prime minister, since the constitution calls for the post to be occupied by a Turkish Cypriot. The Council has executive power on all matters except those expressly reserved for the president, i.e., appointment of ministers, the attorney general, and other high officials and the granting of pardons and clemency. The president may convene meetings of the Council, set the agenda, and preside over them. He does not have the right to vote in such meetings.

The Council's powers include the general direction and control of the government; direction of general policy; defense and security; foreign affairs; the coordination and supervision of all public services; consideration of bills to be introduced in the legislature; consideration of the budget, and so on. The decisions of the Council are taken by absolute majority. They are binding on the president, but in practice, since the Council serves at the president's pleasure, it also serves as his instrument.

Archbishop Makarios was president from 1960 until his death in 1977. He dominated the political life of the country and commanded widespread support. Makarios was succeeded by Spyros Kyprianou, leader of the Democratic Party (DIKO). In 1988, Georghios Vassiliou, who was officially an independent but unofficially supported by the Communist Party, won the presidency. In 1993, Glavkos Klerides, the leader of Democratic Rally (*Dimokratikos Synagermos*; DISY) won the presidency; he was elected again in 1998.

Legislature

The legislative body of the republic is a unicameral House of Representatives, elected for a term of five years. The 1960 constitution provided for a House of Representatives of 50 members, 35 elected by the Greeks and 15 by the Turks. The latter have boycotted the House since 1964. In 1985, a constitutional amendment increased the size of the House of Representatives to 80 seats, with 24 reserved for Turks. In reality, only the 56 seats reserved for Greeks are filled.

House of Representative Elections, May 26, 1996	
Party	**56 Seats**
Democratic Rally (DISY)	20
Liberal Party (KF)	—
Progressive Party of the Working People (AKEL)	19
Democratic Party (DIKO)	10
Socialist Party of Cyprus (EDEK)	5
Movement of Free Democrats (KED)	2

In addition, representatives elected by the Maronite Christians, Latins (Cypriot ethnic group), and Armenian communities on Cyprus may participate in discussions when legislation affecting those communities is under consideration. According to the constitution, the president (Speaker) of the House is elected by the Greek legislators.

A simple majority vote of those members present and voting is required for all laws and decisions to pass. The power to veto or return for consideration any law or decision is vested in the president with regard to foreign affairs, security, and defense. Although this limits the power of the House, the independence of the legislature is expressly recognized and protected by the constitution. For example, the president of the republic does not have the power to dissolve the legislature.

The last legislative elections took place in May 1996. The three main parties took all but 7 of the seats. These include 20 seats for Democratic Rally (DISY), 19 seats for the Progressive Party of the Working People (AKEL) and 10 seats for the Democratic Party (DIKO).

Judiciary

The 10-member Supreme Court is the highest appellate court for all criminal and civil matters. It also adjudicates exclusively and finally on all matters of constitutionality. The judges are appointed by the president and may be impeached by the House. The assize courts have unlimited criminal jurisdiction. The district courts exercise original civil and criminal jurisdiction. The Supreme Council of Judicature (the attorney general, the judges of the Supreme Court, and a member of the Cypriot bar) is entrusted with appointment, promotion, transfers, termination, and disciplinary control over all judicial officers, other than the judges of the Supreme Court.

There are also Greek ecclesiastical and Turkish family courts.

Regional and Local Government

Administratively, Cyprus is divided into six districts: Nicosia, Paphos, Larnaca, Limassol, Famagusta, and Kyrenia. The last two have been under military occupation by Turkey since 1974. The administrative center for each district is the principal city of the district and has the same name. Most of the departments of the central government have offices in these cities. Each district is administered by a district officer appointed by the Ministry of Interior. He is the coordinator of all government activities in his district, including the supervision of all elections. His general duties include advice and guidance to local authorities, i.e., municipal corporations, village improvement boards, and village commissions.

The mayors and councils for the municipalities are appointed by the central government. Village affairs are administered by five-member commissions appointed by the Ministry of Interior. Recent legislation provides for the election of these authorities.

THE TURKISH REPUBLIC OF NORTHERN CYPRUS

All of Kyrenia, most of Famagusta, and parts of Nicosia make up the Turkish Republic of Northern Cyprus, which was proclaimed on November 15, 1983. From the Turkish invasion in summer 1974 until this proclamation, the area was known as the Turkish Federated State of Cyprus. Only Turkey has recognized the proclamation; other states view the action as illegal. Regardless, a new constitution has been approved and presidential and legislative elections were held in 1985. The constitution

provides for a president, prime minister and Cabinet, a legislative assembly, and a separate judiciary. Rauf Denktash was elected president in June 1985, and again in 1996, with over 60% of the vote. The legislative assembly (*Temsilciler Meclisi*) has 50 members, elected for a five-year term. Four parties shared seats; although a number of other parties gained votes, they did not meet the 8% barrier needed for legislative representation.

Legislative Assembly Elections, 1993		
Party	% of Total	Of 50 Seats
Party of National Unity (UBP)	29.8	17
Democratic Party (DP)	29.2	15
Republican Turkish Party (CTP)	24.1	13
Communal Liberation Party (TKP)	13.3	5

Despite its nominal independence, the Turkish Republic of Northern Cyprus relies upon Turkey for support. Indeed, Turkish military forces are still stationed on its territory. The Turkish government has resettled some Turks from the less productive parts of Turkey on Cyprus as well.

There are four major political parties of the Turkish community. The Party of National Unity (*Ulusal Birlik Partisi*; UBP) was established in 1975 by the Turkish-Cypriot leader Rauf Denktash. The UBP is a right-of-center party that advocates a bicommunal federal state in Cyprus. The Democratic Party (*Demokrat Parti*; DP) was founded in 1992 by former members of UBP. The Republican Turkish Party (*Cumhuriyetci Turk Partisi*; CTP) is a leftist party with an anti-imperialist stance. The Communal Liberation Party (*Toplumcu Kurtulus Partisi*; TKP) wants a solution of Cyprus problems as an independent, nonaligned, bizonal federal state.

THE ELECTORAL SYSTEM

Voter registration and voting are compulsory for all citizens 21 years of age and older. Voter turnout is usually high. Voting is by secret ballot. The president is elected through universal suffrage by an absolute majority. If no candidate receives more than 50% of the vote, a second round of elections takes place between the top contestants.

For legislative elections Cyprus is divided into six electoral districts: Nicosia, Famagusta, Limassol, Paphos, Larnaca, and Kyrenia. Each is allocated a number of seats based on population. Greeks who formerly lived in Famagusta and Kyrenia vote for the representatives from those districts.

A new and complex proportional representation system was used for the first time in the 1981 elections for the House. In the first round of counting, seats are distributed within each district to parties that gather more votes than the district's electoral quotient (the total votes divided by the seats available). Parties with less than 10% of the total vote (8% if one of their candidates gets elected) are eliminated. In a second round of counting, surplus votes are added together and the remaining seats are distributed on the basis of a new quotient (the total number of surplus votes divided by the number of seats remaining). The leftover votes from the second distribution are used to allocate the remaining seats. Seats are then allocated to parties for the districts in which they polled best, ensuring that all elected legislators represent the districts in which they run as candidates.

THE PARTY SYSTEM

All parties are essentially the creatures of their founders and reflect the personality and orientation of their leaders. They are supported by membership dues and donations. Although regional and local branches exist, they are centrally controlled. Reliable data on party membership and finances are scarce.

Party rallies in the squares of the big cities and extensive speechmaking by the party leader and candidates are the major modes of political campaigning. While there is no political advertising on television or radio, party leaders are invited to debate their views through these media. Most newspapers are party instruments and promote their party's candidates.

DEMOCRATIC RALLY
(Dimokratikos Synagermos; DISY)

DISY was organized by Glafkos Clerides (born 1919) in 1976 after a disagreement with Archbishop Makarios. It is a right-wing party with some extremist members in its ranks. It favors a pro-Western policy, contending that only the United States and the European community can pressure Turkey to make concessions on Cyprus. It supports a free-enterprise system and is favored by the business community. DISY has been critical of the handling of the intercommunal talks by the government, accusing it of missing opportunities to come to an agreement.

PROGRESSIVE PARTY OF THE WORKING PEOPLE
(Anorthotikon Komma Ergazomenou Laou; AKEL)

The oldest and most effectively organized party, AKEL, succeeded the Communist Party of Cyprus in 1941. Until

1989 a pro-Moscow party, it follows a pragmatic domestic program. It has traditionally supported nonalignment and prefers welfare reformism within the free-enterprise system rather than revolutionary transformation of society. It claims the support of more than half of organized labor, and its following is fairly evenly distributed geographically.

AKEL's leadership is the oldest of all parties and, like the party itself, represents an element of continuity and stability in the country's political history. Until the fall of the USSR, AKEL participated in international Communist conferences and promoted cultural exchanges between Eastern bloc countries and Cyprus. Still Marxist-Leninist in orientation, it supports a demilitarized, non-aligned and independent Cyprus.

DEMOCRATIC PARTY
(Demokratico Komma; DIKO)

The DIKO was founded by former president Spyros Kyprianou in 1976 and follows the policies of Makarios. Kyprianou (born 1932) served as foreign minister and president of the House of Representatives before becoming president of the republic. He is a moderate-centrist and politically pragmatic. He was supported by the Communists in his 1983 bid for the presidency and until late 1985 they supported him in the House of Representatives. Kyprianou works closely with Greece on questions of policy for solving the problem of partition. Today DIKO supports the settlement of Cyprus's problems based on UN intervention.

UNIFIED DEMOCRATIC UNION OF THE CENTER
(Eniea Demokratiki Enosis Kyprou; EDEK)

This socialist party was founded in 1969. It is anti-NATO, favors nonalignment, and strongly opposed the interference of the Greek junta (1967–74) in Cyprus. It advocates a long struggle to liberate Cyprus from foreign influence. It has called for the nationalization of foreign-owned mines and banks and favors socialized medicine. It attracts noncommunist leftist youth and intellectuals. EDEK is active internationally, especially in Third World forums. It is a consultative member of the Socialist International and a member of the Afro-Asian People's Solidarity Organization. Vassos Lyssarides, born 1920, EDEK's founder and leader, is the finest political orator in Cyprus. He has strong affiliations in the Arab countries and is anti-Moscow. A daily paper, *Ta Nea* (The News), and a weekly paper, *Anexartitos* (Independent) are the party instruments.

OTHER POLITICAL FORCES

Ethnic Groups

Turks and Greeks lived in partially intermingled communities for years under the British with little ethnic tension but without ever developing a distinct Cypriot identity. Each group retained a primary identification with its homeland and culture.

The Greek community may be roughly characterized as urban and cosmopolitan with extensive business dealings throughout the Mediterranean. Greek Cypriots have generally been more prosperous, better educated, and more inclined to expend the energy and take the risks required by entrepreneurship. Nearly all the Greeks have an Orthodox Christian background.

The Turkish community, once associated with the Turkish rulers of the island until it was ceded to Britain in 1878, have traditionally been more rural, less prosperous, and less educated than the Greeks. Conservative in lifestyle and inclined to fatalism, they have not been as self-assertive as the Greeks. The Turks are generally Sunni Moslem.

Approximately 4% of the population is made up of three other ethnoreligious groups—Armenians, Maronites, and Latins, all Christians. Most Maronites are of Lebanese Arab descent, while the Latins are largely of Italian origin. All three groups have harmonious relations with the Greek community.

United Nations

Following Turkey's invasion in 1974, the Cyprus government worked through the United Nations peacekeeping forces to restore the unity of the country and free the northern third from Turkish control. General Assembly Resolution 3212, the basic document, was adopted unanimously (including Turkey) on November 5, 1974. It called for the withdrawal of all foreign troops and the safe return of all refugees to their homes. Neither this nor any other UN resolution on Cyprus has been implemented. A UN peacekeeping force controls a buffer zone of about 3% of the island between the two communities.

NATIONAL PROSPECTS

The problem of divided Cyprus defies easy solution. Fundamentally, it involves the dilemma of balancing the rights of the majority (the Greeks) with the rights of a minority (the Turks). However, it is not merely a question of political power but of economic power as well. Before partition, economic power was largely in the hands of Greeks; the Turks were involved in agriculture. In addition, the historical animosity between Greece and Turkey carries over to Cyprus.

After several rounds of intercommunal negotiations under United Nations auspices, no agreement has been reached. A bizonal, bicommunal, federal state appears to be the only solution. Unfortunately, tentative agreement on general principles is always undermined by conflict over specifics. The longer the "temporary" division of the island continues, the more likely that the partition will be permanent. This is a "solution" that pleases none of the immediate participants. It may, however, be satisfactory to both the United States and other interested outside observers. Almost all who are familiar with the problems of Cyprus recognize that nearly any other result will alienate Greece on the one hand or Turkey on the other.

Further Reading

Calotychos, Vangelis, ed. *Cyprus and Its People: Nation, Identity, and Experience in an Unimaginable Community, 1955–1997.* Boulder, Colo.: Westview Press, 1998.

Joseph, Joseph S. *Cyprus—Ethnic Conflict and International Politics: From Independence to the Threshold of the European Union.* New York: St. Martin's Press, 1997.

Mirbagheri, Farid. *Cyprus and International Peacemaking 1964–1986.* New York: Routledge, 1998.

Salem, Norma. *Cyprus: A Regional Conflict and Its Resolution.* New York: St. Martin's Press, 1992.

Solsten, Eric, ed. *Cyprus: A Country Study.* Federal Research Division of the Library of Congress. Government Printing Office: Washington, D.C., 1993.

Streissguth, Thomas. *Cyprus: Divided Island (World in Conflict).* Minneapolis: Lerner, 1998.

CZECH REPUBLIC

(Ceská Republika)
By William D. Pederson, Ph.D.

THE SYSTEM OF GOVERNMENT

The Czech Republic became an independent nation on January 1, 1993, when the former Czechoslovakia separated peacefully into two sovereign parts (see Slovakia). The new republic consists of the Czech Lands of Bohemia and Moravia and part of Silesia. Its 10.4 million people are located at the heart of Europe with Poland to the north, Germany to the west, Austria to the south, and Slovakia to the east. The constitution, adopted on December 16, 1992, established a parliamentary democracy with a bicameral legislature, presidency, and supreme court.

Five phases may be identified in the Czech historical development from medieval to modern times: (1) the incorporation into the Austro-Hungarian Empire from the 16th and 17th centuries until the early 20th century; (2) the establishment of the independent Republic of Czechoslovakia after World War I until World War II; (3) the Nazi Germany occupation; (4) the Communist takeover shortly after World War II that lasted until the "velvet revolution" in late 1989; and (5) the transition from a restored free Czechoslovakian republic until the "velvet divorce" in 1992. Each of these phases in the country's past contributes to understanding its present situation.

In 1620 the medieval Czech state was incorporated into Austria and remained a part of the Hapsburg Empire for more than 300 years. The area benefited from a moderate form of Austrian rule during the second half of the 19th century while it served as the center of the Austro-Hungarian Empire's industrialization. Economic development led to urbanization and a subsequent flowering of Czech culture in the late 19th century.

After the fall of the Austro-Hungarian Empire in World War I, Czech philosopher Thomas G. Masaryk visited the United States and proclaimed the Republic of Czechoslovakia through the support of President Woodrow Wilson and the Allies. The new nation became the most industrialized and prosperous economy in Eastern Europe.

However, the new republic was short-lived after Adolf Hitler's rise to power in 1933. Agitation in the Sudetenland (an area in northern Bohemia inhabited by some 3 million German-speaking people) offered an excuse for Hitler to pressure the major European prime ministers to cede him Czech land. The remainder of Czechoslovakia was invaded in 1939 and the Nazis established a protectorate in Bohemia and Moravia. After Nazi Germany's defeat, the pre-1938 frontiers of Czechoslovakia were restored and nearly all the German-speaking inhabitants were expelled.

Soon after World War II, the Communist Party gained control of Czechoslovakia and it became a rigid Stalinist state. The country was renamed the Czechoslovak Socialist Republic in July 1960. Only after Joseph Stalin's death in 1953 did the country see the beginnings of some relaxation. Post-Stalin moderation was evident by January 1968 when Alexander Dubcek became the secretary of the party. Yet the more independent and moderate policies adopted during the "Prague Spring" were crushed soon after invasion by Warsaw Pact forces. Gustav Husák replaced Dubcek as the last head of the country during the 20-year demise of Communist rule.

Only one reform from the Prague Spring was continued. In January 1969, the Czechoslovak unitary state was transformed into a federation, with separate Czech and Slovak republics, each having a National Council and government. A federal government was established and the legislature was restructured into a bicameral Federal Assembly. The implementation of this single reform from the Prague Spring may be explained partially by the fact that both Dubcek and Husák were Slovaks.

Both the fall of the Communist regime and the velvet divorce were accomplished rapidly. Demonstrations against the Communist government, triggered by reforms in the Soviet Union, began in 1988. The "velvet revolution" took place from November 17 to 28, 1989, signaling a dramatic, yet primarily peaceful political change. An informal alliance known as Civic Forum, in the Czech republic, and the Public Against Violence, its Slovak counterpart, emerged at this time. A month later, Václav Havel replaced Husák as the president of Czechoslovakia. Alexander Dubcek was elected chairman of the Federal Assembly, and the Communist Party lost its majority in the legislature.

Executive

The executive branch of the government includes the president, the prime minister, the deputy prime ministers, and other ministers within the Council of Ministers. The administration (or government) is the supreme executive power of the Czech Republic. The president appoints the prime minister and other members of the administration, which is accountable only to the Chamber of Deputies. Yet the key governmental figure is the prime minister. While the constitution empowers the president to appoint members of the government, it assumes that the presidential appointments are made only at the suggestion of the prime minister, who actually determines the government's composition.

The president of the republic is the head of state. A candidate for the position must be at least 40 years old and be nominated by a minimum of 10 deputies or senators from the legislature; election requires approval by a simple majority of deputies and senators in a joint session of the legislature. The president is elected for a five-year term and may be reelected for a second consecutive term.

The president represents the republic in foreign affairs, receives the heads of diplomatic missions, and serves as the supreme commander of the armed forces. The president also appoints the members of the council of the Czech National Bank.

In terms of legislative powers, the president appoints, dismisses, and accepts the resignation of the prime minister and other members of the Council of Ministers. As noted, the president appoints the members of the Council of Ministers based on the recommendation of the prime minister. The president convenes sessions of the Chamber of Deputies and calls legislative elections. The president has the power to return adopted constitutional laws to the legislature as well as to initiate laws. For example, after a public outcry, President Havel vetoed an amendment to the customs law that exempted custom officials from searching the personal belongings of legislature deputies at the border.

The president's quasi-judicial powers include naming judges of the Constitutional Court, its chairman, and deputy chairman. The president also had the right to grant amnesty.

The first president of the Czech Republic is Václav Havel, the leader of the 1989 "velvet revolution" that freed Czechoslovakia from the Soviet bloc. He had served as the president of Czechoslovakia beginning in late December 1989. Though he was reconfirmed for another term in July 1990, Havel resigned his post two years later in an effort to forestall the breakup of the 74-year-old nation founded by Thomas G. Masaryk, the president of the Czechoslovak Republic from 1918 to 1937. The Czech Parliament elected Havel president on January 26, 1993. Though Havel aligns himself closely with Masaryk's nonideological approach to democratic politics, Masaryk's stature as the nation's founder allowed him to maneuver as if he were in charge of a presidential system rather than a parliamentary democracy. Havel, originally a dissident playwright, has not been afforded that latitude.

In his election as president of the Czech Republic by the new Czech legislature Havel obtained 109 votes against two opponents. As president, he is not a member of a political party. He is viewed as remaining above political struggles, fulfilling a ceremonial and moral role in the state. On the other hand, he has been a strong voice for greater regional representation, a bicameral legislature, and a role for religion in the Czech Republic—issues that divided him from the prime minister.

Havel also continues to be concerned with issues of human rights and justice. The president can issue a pardon during any time in the state's prosecution of criminal suspects, similar to the practice in other European states. Without a constitutional requirement to justify his pardons, Havel has been willing to act against public opinion. After taking office as the Czechoslovakian president in December 1989, he declared a broad amnesty that released more than 20,000 prisoners. In 1995, he granted 107 pardons and in 1996, 77 pardons, out of the 2,500–2,700 annual requests. On January 20, 1998, Havel was reelected president.

Legislature

The Czech constitution, adopted on December 16, 1992, by a vote of 172 to 16 with 10 abstentions, provides for a bicameral legislature as the highest organ of state authority in the republic. The Parliament enacts the constitutions and the laws, approves the budget, supervises the activities of the government (administration), approves the electoral laws and international agreements, and decides upon the declaration of war. At a joint session of both legislative chambers, it elects the president of the republic.

The lower house, which has 200 members, is called the Chamber of Deputies, and members must be at least 21 years old. They serve four-year terms. Elections to the Chamber of Deputies are based on a system of proportional representation. Political parties must receive 5% of the electoral vote to achieve parliamentary representation. The first representatives were elected on June 5–6, 1992. With 105 seats, the ruling coalition commanded an absolute majority. The coalition consisted of four political groups: the Civic Democratic Party, the Civic Democratic Alliance, the Christian Democratic Union–People's Party, and the Christian Democratic Party.

Ex–Prime Minister Václav Klaus (of the Civic Democratic Party), a former minister of finance, was the architect of Czechoslovakia's neoliberal economic program. He was elected leader of the Civic Forum in the fall of 1990, when it grew more conservative. His high approval rating matched that of Václav Havel, the president of the

Council of Ministers

Position	Occupant	Area of Responsibility	Party
Prime Minister	Milos Zeman		CSSD
Deputy Prime Ministers	Pavel Mertlik	Finance, Industry, Transportation, Agriculture	CSSD
	Egon Lansky	Foreign Affairs, Defense, Interior	CSSD
	Pavel Rychetsky	Legislation, Justice, Local Development	CSSD
	Vladimir Spidla	Culture, Education, Health, Environment, Labor and Social Affairs	CSSD
Ministers	Jan Fenci	Agriculture	CSSD
	Ivan David	Health	CSSD
	Jan Kavan	Foreign Affairs	CSSD
	Ivo Svoboda	Finance	CSSD
	Otakar Motejl	Justice	CSSD
	Pavel Dostál	Culture	CSSD
	Jaroslav Basta	Without Portfolio	CSSD
	Vladimir Vetchý	Defense	CSSD
	Eduard Zeman	Education	CSSD
	Jaromir Cisar	Local Development	CSSD
	Vaclav Grulich	Interior	CSSD
	Antonin Peltrám	Transportation	CSSD
	Milos Kuzvart	Environment	CSSD
	Miroslav Gregr	Industry and Trade	CSSD

Czech Republic, until a campaign finance scandal forced his resignation in late 1997.

The 81 member upper house of Parliament is called the Senate. The constitution describes the Senate's powers in great detail. Every two years one-third of the Senate is up for election. Senators must be at least 40 forty years old. They serve six-year terms. Unlike the lower Chamber of Deputies, the Senate cannot be dissolved, and it is designed to perform some of the legislative tasks of the Chamber when the latter has been dissolved or is not in session. The Senate is empowered to debate laws by the Chamber and has the right to return a law to the Chamber if a majority of the senators vote against it. The first Senate was elected in November 1996. Ex–Prime Minister Klaus was reluctant to have a Senate for fear his party might not control it. Moreover, a group of 21 leftist deputies (Czech Social Democratic Party, Liberal Soviet Union, and Left Block) and the extreme right-wing Republican Party wanted the Senate abolished, while President Havel and others remained committed to it.

Judiciary

Judicial power in the Czech Republic is exercised by independent civilian courts under the Ministry of Justice and military courts under the Minister of Defense. The civilian court system consists of several levels in the tradition of the first Czechoslovak Republic. The Supreme Court interprets law to serve as a guide to other courts and acts as a court of appeal. Decisions are made by a panel of three judges who are appointed for life. The Supreme Administrative Court is concerned with administrative regulations and mediates jurisdictional conflicts; the Constitutional Court decides broad constitutional issues.

Regional courts handle serious cases and act as appellate courts for the district courts. Cases are usually decided by a five-member panel, two judges and three associate judges.

The district court cases are decided by panels usually comprising a judge and two associate judges. Qualifications for the associate positions include citizenship and a minimum age of 25. They are elected to four-year terms.

The Constitutional Court is a judicial body charged with upholding the constitution of the Czech Republic. It consists of 15 judges each appointed to 10-year terms by the president of the republic with the consent of the Senate. The Court has broad powers to rule on the constitutionality of proposed laws and disputes among levels of government, as well as on electoral laws. The Parliament established the Court in June 1993.

Regional and Local Government

Though the Czech constitution does not specify the number of regions for administrative purposes, the republic is divided into eight lands (*Kraj*): central, southern, western, northern, eastern Bohemia; southern, northern Moravia; and the capital Prague (*Praha*). These units are governed by elected representative bodies that promulgate ordinances. The lands or regions are further subdivided into municipalities empowered to raise local taxes for roads, schools, utilities, and public health. The issue of territorial division remains sensitive. Deputies from Moravia and Silesia have demanded that both regions be given the status of a "land" and the right to establish their own representative bodies.

In June 1994, the government agreed to establish 17 "higher administrative" units (similar to county councils) at the local level. Though the prime minister and deputy prime minister (Jan Kalvoda) were reluctant to accept this approach and favored having fewer units to dilute possible minority opposition, the Parliament approved the plan for greater representation.

THE ELECTORAL SYSTEM

The electoral system emerged from its Czechoslovakian history. The constitution provides for universal suffrage and a secret ballot. Citizens 18 years of age or older are eligible to vote. In February 1990, the Czechoslovakia Federal Assembly passed a new electoral law based on the principle of proportional representation. Only registered parties were permitted to compete in the June 8–9, 1990, elections, which were the first free elections held since 1946. The Communist Party and its former allies (the Czechoslovak People's Party, the Czechoslovak Socialist Party, and the Slovak Freedom Party—formerly the Slovak Renaissance Party) were considered formal parties and therefore were not required to register. The same applied to the Civic Forum and its Slovak counterpart, Public Against Violence. The electoral law stipulated that lists of candidates could be presented only by parties and movements composed of at least 10,000

members. Candidacy requirements were citizenship and a minimum age of 20. The parties had to poll a minimum of 5% of the total vote to achieve representation in the legislature. State financial assistance encouraged a proliferation of parties; any party that obtained at least 2% of the vote received .15 crowns per vote. More than 20 parties finally competed in the June 1990 elections. The 5% electoral threshold necessary to obtain parliamentary representation tended to stabilize later election results.

THE PARTY SYSTEM

One of the legacies of Communist Party rule was that it gave the name "party" a bad connotation. Its bureaucratic mindlessness perpetuated by a cadre of self-serving careerists resulted in a reluctance by new politically affiliated groups to call themselves a party. Some political organizations use synonyms, such as *hnuta*, loosely translated as a "movement," "tendency" or "group." Nonetheless, the Czech Republic has developed a multiparty system as it had during the interwar period.

The June and November 1990 elections confirmed the transformation from a Communist regime to one with free elections. The elections served more as a referendum and social consensus to reject the Communist past than to stress partisanship. More than 60 parties and groups were registered by the end of February 1990; some 20 fulfilled the conditions to participate in the June 8–9, 1990, election. At the federal level, Civic Forum–Public Against Violence emerged as the dominant political force with about half of the total vote. Seven parties or movements exceeded the 5% threshold necessary for parliamentary representation. The November local elections further confirmed the mass rejection of the Communists.

During the next two years Civic Forum and Public Against Violence began disintegrating into competing parliamentary factions. The initial seven parties in Parlia-

Political Parties in the Chamber of Deputies

Name	Party Initials	% of Vote June 1992	% of Vote June 1996	% of Vote June 1998
Civic Democratic Party	ODS	28	27	28
Czech Social Democratic Party	CSSD	6	26	32
Communist Party of Bohemia and Moravia	KSCM	14	10	11
Christian Democratic Union	KDU	6	8	10
Czechoslovak People's Party	CSL			
Association for the Republic	SPR	6	8	
Czechoslovak Republican Party	RSC			
Civic Democratic Alliance	ODA	6	6	
Freedom Union	US			

9

ment had splintered into 19 parliamentary factions by the eve of the June 1992 elections. The future of the federal Czechoslovakian state became a major theme throughout the election campaign. The breakup of the dual republic is linked to the parties opposing each other after their common enemy, the Communist state, was vanquished. Though polling data suggest that the majority of the people favored the old union, inexperienced politicians were not capable of dealing with their common problems.

In early April 1997, the Constitutional Court supported the election law requirement that parties must obtain 5% of the electoral vote to be represented in the Chamber of Deputies. Without this requirement, 16 political parties would have been represented in the Chamber as a result of the 1996 election. Following is a brief discussion of the political parties that have achieved national importance.

CIVIC DEMOCRATIC PARTY
(Obcanská demokratická strana, ODS)

The Civic Democratic Party grew out of the fall 1991 split within the Civic Forum (*Obcanske forum*), which had formed two years earlier as an informal alliance in opposition to the Communist regime. The ODS is a center-right party that advocates continuation of the move toward a free-market economy and a limited role for the state.

In the June 5–6, 1992, parliamentary elections, the CDP won nearly one-third of the Czech vote in coalition with the small Christian Democratic Party. The Civic Democratic Party was part of the party coalition in control of the Czech Parliament. After the June 1996 Chamber of Deputies elections, the Christian Democratic Party (KDS) merged into the ODS. It controlled 68 of the 200-seat Chamber and a majority of the positions in the Cabinet. In the November 1996 Senate elections, it also became the strongest party with 32 seats. Yet in the June 1998 parliamentary elections the ODS lost to the CSSD. The party has 35,000 members.

The chair of the party is Václav Klaus, the first prime minister of the Czech Republic. He has earned a reputation for arrogance and an inability to accept criticism. By training, the 54-year-old Klaus is an economist, a conservative who admires America's Milton Friedman and Britain's Margaret Thatcher. He graduated from Prague's School of Economics in 1963 and did graduate work in Italy and the United States (Cornell University in 1969). He previously served as the first post-Communist finance minister. Though a strong free-enterprise partisan, who plays down civic and religious concerns, Klaus continued to cushion the economic blows during the transition to a free-market economy by allowing exchange controls, wage controls, and rent controls during his massive privatization campaign. He served as prime minister until late 1997.

Party headquarters are located at Snemovni 3, 110,000, Prague 1.

COMMUNIST PARTY OF BOHEMIA AND MORAVIA—LEFT BLOCK
(Komunistická strana Cech a Moravy, KSCM)

In 1921 the left wing of the Social Democratic Party formed the Communist Party of Czechoslovakia. Though it called for the revolutionary overthrow of the democratic government, it was the only Communist Party in Central and Eastern Europe openly allowed during the interwar period. It became the strongest Communist Party outside the Soviet Union. After gaining control of the country in 1948, it remained a totalitarian force until 1968, when for the first time in world history a ruling Communist Party was challenged from within by reformers, a short-lived challenge crushed by the Warsaw Pact invasion in August 1968. The party's peaceful demise occurred quickly in 1990 after the "velvet revolution."

The Communist Party of Bohemia and Moravia (CPBM) emerged in 1991 as a result of the reorganization of the former Communist Party of Czechoslovakia. The Left Block (a coalition of the CPBM and a small group called the Democratic Left) obtained 14% of the vote in the June 1992 election; 10% of the vote in the June 1996 election; and 11 % of the vote in the June 1998 election. Though a smaller party in the Czech Parliament, its members often show more skill than other parliamentarians. The party accommodates several factions among its 380,000 members.

Its former leader was Jirí Svoboda, a relative moderate who was less ideological and willing to enter into coalitions with other leftists. He had to contend with several factions within the party. There were a number of hardline Stalinists who formed the "Platform for Socialism" in January 1993 and who oppose any party reforms, and there were other conservative factions both within the parliamentary delegation and the party's leadership. At the June 1993 party congress Svoboda was replaced by his former conservative deputy chairman, Miroslav Grebenicek, who had refused to cooperate with him. The reform-minded members of the party split from the neo-Stalinist core to form the party of the Democratic Left.

Party headquarters are located at Politicky vezna 9, 100 00 Prague 1.

CZECH SOCIAL DEMOCRATIC PARTY
(Cseká strana sociálne demokratická, CSSD)

Formed in 1878, the Czechoslovak Social Democratic Party has a long history. Its heyday was in 1918 when it won electoral victory and the leader of the party was made prime minister. Within the ruling governmental coalition the party was left-wing on the political spectrum. Its electoral success was short-lived. After World War II, the party eliminated its conservative wing and adopted a Marxist-Leninist ideology. In June 1948 it merged with the Communist Party. Twenty years later some social democrats tried to reactivate the party during the Prague Spring.

The party finally was fully revived in November 1989, after more than 40 years of underground existence. Its newly elected leader, Slavomir Klaban, was critical of the Civic Form, claiming it was too broad a coalition and lacked a clear political program. In 1990 the party had more than 10,000 members. In the June 1992 election, the CSSD obtained 7% of the vote. Its presence in Parliament serves to balance the stronger nonextremist right-wing parties. The CSSD has a commitment to social welfare, and as do other Czech leftist parties, it advocates close relations with Slovakia.

There are moderate and radical factions within the party. The better-known moderates are Pavel Novak, elected deputy chair of the party in 1993; Ivan Fisera; Rudolf Battek, affiliated with the Association of Social Democrats; and Jirí Horak, who had headed the party in 1992 after his return from exile in the United States, where he had spent his time during the entire Communist period. The more radical leaders of the party include Jirí Paroubek and Robert Dostal, affiliated with "the Rakovnik group," as well as Milos Zeman, who unexpectedly was elected chair of the party at its 1993 congress. Younger than Horak, Zeman is a blunt, flamboyant character who wants to move the party further to the left, though he does not want to cooperate with the Communists. He wanted to attack the government's ruling coalition directly to unite the nation's left-wing parties into an informal coalition, a proposal that only the Liberal Social Union found agreeable. Polls indicate that he is the most popular left-of-center political leader. In June 1998 the CSSD for the first time won a plurality of the vote and Zeman became prime minister. Party headquarters are located at Lidovy dam, Hybernská 7, 110 00 Prague 1.

CZECH SOCIALIST PARTY
(Ceská strana socialistická, CSS)

Founded in 1897 as the Czechoslovak National Socialist Party (no relationship to the interwar German party of the same name), the party supported socialist reforms and national unity while disassociating itself from the notion of a Marxist class struggle. The party contained those who favored democratic socialism and others who advocated traditional liberal democratic values. In 1948, the left wing established itself as the Czechoslovak Socialist Party. Its membership included mostly Czech white-collar workers and the urban middle class, reflecting the membership of the prewar party. Its last leader was Bohuslav Kucera. The party published a

daily paper called the *Svobodné slovo*. The party continued to exist after the dissolution of Czechoslovakia. During the Communist regime its membership was limited by statute, though it was believed to have about 10,000 members.

The current chair of the party is Ladislav Dvorák. The party contains divisive factions that threaten Party unity. A former chair of the party, Jirí Vyvadill, heads a "liberal" caucus against the party's leadership.

Party headquarters are located at nam. Republiky 7, 111 49 Prague 1.

AGRARIAN PARTY
(Zemedelská strana, ZS)

The original Agrarian Party was established in 1899 and became strongest during Masaryk's rule. Its political program glorified the role of peasants in society. During the late 1930s, the party was captured by its conservative wing, which called for authoritarian solutions. The party was banned during the Communist era since it was an adversary. In 1990, the new agricultural party was established to defend the interests of the cooperative farms. The party seeks compensation for farmers whose property was confiscated during the collectivization.

The party's chairman is Dr. Frantisek Trnka, who concurrently serves as chairman of the Liberal Social Union (LSU).

GREEN PARTY
(Strana Zelenych, SZ)

Formed in 1989, the Green Party is the most influential of the various Green movements in the Czech Republic. Though it has considerable differences with farmers, the party advocates rural values within a modern context. Its chair is Jan Jecmínek. Party headquarters are located at nam. Republiky 7, 111 49 Prague 1.

CHRISTIAN DEMOCRATIC UNION
(Krestanská a demokratická unie, KDU)

The Christian Democratic Union, formed in 1992, is composed of two small center-right parties: the Christian Democratic Party (KDS) and the Czech People's Party (CSL). It was part of the ruling coalition in the Czech Republic and was rewarded with posts in the government until the CSSD won in 1998. The party generally stresses the importance of social issues. Jan Kasal is the acting leader of the KDU–CSL.

CHRISTIAN DEMOCRATIC PARTY
(Krestanská strana demokratická, KDS)

The small Christian Democratic Party was formed in December 1989. The party advocates a religious dimension to political issues. Its founding leader was former dissident Václav Benda, one of the Charter 77 signatories—the most influential dissent group, founded in January 1977 by intellectuals and others to campaign for civil and political rights. He entered the party into a coalition with Václav Klaus's Democratic Party in the June 5–6, 1992, parliamentary elections. The party supports the family, restrictions on divorce, and opposes abortion. It obtained 6% of the vote and held 10 Chamber seats. In December 1993, the party congress replaced Benda with the younger Ivan Pilip. In 1996 the KDS merged into the Civic Democratic Party (ODS), and Pilip was made the minister of education. Party headquarters are located in Sokolská 39, 120 00 Prague 2.

CZECH PEOPLE'S PARTY
(Ceská strana lidová, CSL)

The original Czechoslovak People's Party was founded in 1918 and was based in the Czech Republic. It was later recognized as one of the three official satellite parties during the Communist reign. The CSL tends to be a center-right Catholic party with its strongest support in Moravia and southern Bohemia. Zbynek Zalman was the party's last chairman before the "velvet revolution." He was replaced by Josef Bartoncík, who subsequently was charged with collaborating with the secret police. The acting chair is Jan Kasal. Party headquarters are located at Revolucni 5, 110 15 Prague 1.

ASSOCIATION FOR THE REPUBLIC–CZECH REPUBLICAN PARTY
(Sdruzení pro republiku–Republikánská strana Ceská)

The Association for the Republic and the Czech Republican Party have allied for electoral purposes. They occupy the extremist right-wing position on the political spectrum. Though the alliance failed to cross the threshold in the 1990 election, it won 6% of the vote for Parliament in the June 5–6, 1992, elections. Miroslav Sládek, an outspoken militant nationalist, chairs the alliance. He has called for the return of Ruthenia, which was annexed by the Soviet Union during World War II. The party favors economic protection, withdrawal of support for the United Nations, law and order (reintroduction of capital punishment), and cuts in the government. Corruption and racist charges undermined the party, resulting in its loss of parliamentary representation after the June 1998 election. Party headquarters are located at U zemepisného ústavu 1, 160 00 Prague 6.

CIVIC DEMOCRATIC ALLIANCE
(Obcanská demokratická aliance, ODA)

The Civic Democratic Alliance grew out of the late 1989 Civic Forum (*Obcanské forum*), which later split up. Formed in 1991, the ODA is conservative in orientation and close to Václav Klaus in its policy goals but lacks the grassroots organization of the Civic Democratic Party (ODS). Though it was unsuccessful in winning representation in the Czechoslovakian Federal Assembly, it won 6% of the vote in the June 5–6, 1992, elections, which qualified it for 14 seats in the Czech National Council, and then in the Czech Parliament. It was part of the ruling ODS coalition. Because the ODA shares a similar party platform with the Civic Democratic Party, it often challenged the ODS to gain media attention. Jan Kalvoda, a popular politician, was formerly chair of the party who served along with a fellow party member and deputy ODA chairman, Vladimir Dloughy, the minister of industry and trade who resigned from the Cabinet on May 26, 1997. Because of his charisma, pragmatism, and noncontroversial approach to his job, Dloughy received the highest approval rating among Czech political leaders. True to his pragmatic nature, he had belonged to the Communist Party prior to the "velvet revolution." But trade deficits and investment fund scandals forced him to step down from his Cabinet position. Another ODA leader was Milan Uhde, who served as the parliamentary Speaker. The current ODA chairman is Michael Zantovsky. Party headquarters are located at Stefánikova 17, 150 00 Prague 5.

MOVEMENT FOR AUTONOMOUS DEMOCRACY OF MORAVIA AND SILESIA
(Hnutí za samosprávnou demokracii Moravy a Slezska, HSD–SMS)

The Movement for Autonomous Democracy of Moravia and Silesia (formerly called the Movement for Autonomous Democracy–Society for Moravia and Silesia), campaigned in the June 1990 parliamentary elections for regional autonomy. A self-described liberal party, its constituency is limited to the two Moravian areas in the eastern half of the Czech Republic. The party advocates establishment of a self-administered republic of Moravia and Silesia within the Czech Republic. Despite a lack of nationwide appeal, it was one of only two parties in addition to the Civic Forum and the Communists to succeed in crossing the 5% threshold.

In the June 5–6, 1992, elections it again won nearly 6% of the vote. Dr. Jan Krycer, the party chairman, is regarded as a moderate leader since he favored forming a strong centrist group within the Parliament. He has considered forming a broader new party by joining the Entrepreneurs' Party, which is chaired by Rudolf Beranek. Party headquarters of the HSD–SMS are located at Frantiskánská 1-3, 600 00 Brno.

CIVIC MOVEMENT
(Obcanské hnuti)

The Civic Movement formed in 1991 resulted from a split within the Civic Forum, the new umbrella opposition group to Communist rule that had emerged in November 1989. The Civic Movement, a centrist liberal party on the political spectrum, has members who are Communists and were active in the dissident movement. Presenting itself as a party for intellectuals, it was unable to attract many voters in the 1992 parliamentary elections. As a result, it plays no active role in Czech politics at the national level, although it is represented in communal and municipal governments. The former chair of the Civic Movement was Jirí Dienstbier, a former Czechoslovak foreign minister who has expressed interest in forming an informal coalition of left-of-center parties as advocated by Milos Zeman (CSSD). Dienstbier is at present the chair of the Free Democrats. He remains a centrist and a popular political leader.

OTHER POLITICAL PARTIES

There are a number of other smaller parties in the Czech Republic, though they have not gained parliamentary representation. For example, the Czech-Moravian Party of the Center (CMSS) favors a return to the regional administrative system dismantled in 1949 by the Communists; and the Entrepreneur's Party is chaired by Rudolf Beranek. In the June 1998 election Pensioners for Secure Living (DZJ) won 3% of the vote.

NATIONAL PROSPECTS

Economics and political tradition suggest a bright future for the Czech Republic. As expected, the "velvet revolution" was conducted peacefully while the subsequent division of Czechoslovakia is often described as the "velvet divorce." Though data suggest that the public was against the separation, in retrospect it is apparent that the inexperience of newly emerged political leaders made the change almost inevitable. Most of the new leaders were political unknowns prior to 1993.

Overall, the economy remains strong, despite trade deficits and investment scandals. There is a skilled labor force with a strong industrial tradition. The government inherited a low level of external debt and has cushioned the transition to a free economy. The Czech Republic enjoys one of the highest standards of living in Eastern Europe.

Its foreign affairs are similarly stable. Both the Czech Republic and Slovakia belong to the Visegrad Four (along with Poland and Hungary) and the Council of Europe; are associate members of the European Union and the Western European Union; and have joined NATO's Partnership for Peace program.

The governing coalition stabilized the transition to political independence and a market economy. The 1996 elections both reinforced and reminded the dominant party that it wanted prudent political leadership. The uncertain condition of the opposition parties matches the tension between the two Václavs in power who struggle to provide direction for the new state.

Ironically, Klaus's loss of the prime ministership in late 1997 was matched by personal crises for the president. Václav Havel lost his first wife, Olga Havlova, to cancer on January 27, 1996, and then he faced death from pneumonia and a malignant lung tumor. He then married the Czech stage and screen actress Dagmar Veskrnová.

Both the ideologically prone but politically practical Klaus and the morally courageous but politically inexperienced Havel have bounced back. Klaus entered into an agreement on July 9, 1998, with the CSSD to allow Milos Zeman to form a government in exchange for allowing the ODS to occupy the premier leadership offices in the lower house of Parliament. The public reminds them that after the twin experiences with fascism and communism, a vibrant democratic state requires prudent politicians. The outlook for democratic leadership appears optimistic for the political development of the Czech Republic.

Further Reading

Bankowicz, Marek. "Czechoslovakia: From Masaryk to Havel." In *The New Democracies in Eastern Europe: Party Systems and Political Cleavages*, 2d ed. Ed. Sten Berglund and Jan A. Dellenbrant. Brookfield, Vt.: Edward Elgar, 1994.

Batt, Judy. *Czecho-Slovakia in Transition: From Federation to Separation*. London: Royal Institute of International Affairs, 1993.

Bryant, Christopher G., and Edmund Mokrycki, eds. *The New Great Transformation? Changes and Continuity in East-Central Europe*. New York: Routledge, 1994.

Cottey, Andrew. *East-Central Europe after the Cold War*. New York: St. Martin's Press, 1996.

Crawford, Keith. "Problems of Institutionalization of Parliamentary Democracy: The Federal Assembly of the Czech and Slovak Federative Republic, 1990–1993." In *Working Papers on Comparative Legislative Studies*, Ed. Lawrence D. Longley. Appleton, Wisconsin: Research

Committee on Legislative Specialists, International Science Association, 1994.

Dubcek, Alexander. *Hope Dies Last. The Autobiography of Alexander Dubcek*. Ed. and trans. Jiri Hochman. New York: Kodansha International, 1993.

Economist Intelligence Unit. *Czech Republic; Slovakia*. London: Economist Intelligence Unit, 1993.

Krejci, Oskar. *History of Elections in Bohemia and Moravia*. East European Monographs. New York: Columbia University Press, 1995.

Kriseova, Eda. *Václav Havel. The Authorized Biography*. Trans. Caleb Crain. New York: St. Martin's Press, 1993.

Leff, Carol S. *The Czech and Slovak Republics: Nation versus State*. Boulder, Colo.: Westview Press, 1997.

Olson, David M. "Political Parties and Party Systems in Regime Transformation: Inner Transition in the New Democracies of Central Europe." *American Review of Politics* 14 (winter 1993).

Pridham, Geoffrey, and Tatu Vanhanen. *Democratization in Eastern Europe: Domestic and International Perspectives*. New York: Rutledge, 1994.

Weiner, Robert. *Change in Eastern Europe*. Westport, Conn.: Praeger, 1994.

Wolchik, Sharon L. "The Politics of Ethnicity in Post-Communist Czechoslovakia. *Eastern European Politics and Societies* 8, no. 1 (winter 1994).

Wrightman, Gordon. "The Czech and Slovak Republics." In *Developments in East European Politics*. Eds. Stephen White, Judy Batt, and Paul G. Lewis. Durham, N.C.: Duke University Press, 1993.

———, ed. *Party Formation in East-Central Europe: Post-Communist Politics in Czechoslovakia, Hungary, Poland and Bulgaria*. Brookfield, Vt.: Edward Elgar, 1994.

DENMARK

(Kongeriget Danmark)

By Alastair H. Thomas.

THE SYSTEM OF GOVERNMENT

Denmark, as one of the Nordic countries, has close linguistic and historical affinities to Norway and Sweden. Its main territory is a geological extension of the north-German plain. The unitary constitution applies to Denmark itself—the Jutland (*Jylland*) peninsula and numerous islands of which Funen (*Fyn*) and Zealand (*Sjælland*) are the two largest—and also to "North Atlantic Denmark:" the Faroe Islands and Greenland. Denmark has a culturally homogeneous population of 5.2 million (1995). The Faroe Islands north of Britain (with 45,000 inhabitants) have been a "self-governing community within the Danish realm" since 1948, with a distinctive Nordic language. Greenland (55,000 inhabitants), with a mainly Inuit people and language, has been "an equal part of the kingdom" since 1953, with home rule since 1979. Their sparse populations depend heavily on fishing.

The oldest kingdom in Europe, Denmark dates from well before the Viking King Knud I (Canute) united Denmark and England in 1018–35. The national flag *Dannebrog*, a white cross on a red ground, dates from 1219. Their Viking-age link ended with Iceland's independence in 1944. Earlier Danish kings were elected, but the 1665 constitution introduced hereditary absolute monarchy. King Frederik VII conceded constitutional monarchy in 1848. After the second Schleswig-Holstein War of 1864 ended in disastrous loss of territory to Prussia, Christian IX reverted to monarchy, choosing politicians of the right for his advisers despite rising liberal strength. With the right reduced to 7% of the *Folketing* seats, the "Change of System" was made to parliamentary democracy and constitutional monarchy in 1901. This principle survived the Easter Crisis of 1920 and Nazi German occupation in 1940–45 and has flourished since.

Supreme authority is located formally with the queen but is exercised through ministers who are politically responsible to parliament. The constitution of 1953 remains unchanged. With broad agreement it created a single-chamber parliament, the *Folketing*, by abolishing the upper house, and it introduced referendums in specified circumstances. An ombudsman investigates citizen complaints of maladministration. As the result of a change in the law of succession in 1953, Queen Margrethe II succeeded her father, King Frederik IX, in 1972.

Executive

The constitution requires that "No Minister shall continue in office after the Folketing has expressed no confidence in him." This negative formulation does not require a vote of confidence before a government takes office and permits the many minority governments to continue without challenge. The Cabinet of about 20 ministers is headed by the prime minister (*statsminister*). It is officially appointed by the monarch after hearing the views of all parties in the *Folketing*. Party groups make recommendations based on the prospects of forming a government that will include themselves and their allies. After assessing their advice, the queen commissions a party leader to try to form a majority government. If this proves impossible in the prevailing complex multiparty relationships, the commission may be amended. A minority or single-party government may finally be accepted as the only real possibility.

Politically the main limit on a government is imposed by the multiparty system, which has given no single party a majority since 1906. Cabinets usually include two or more parties, and on most issues they seek wider support in parliamentary committees and plenary votes. Since 1945 there have been majority governments only in 1957–64 (Social Democrats, SD; Radical Liberals, RV; and Justice Party), in 1968–71 (RV, Venstre, and Conservatives), and in 1993–4 (an SD-led center-left coalition). Minority coalitions were formed in 1950–53 (Venstre and KF), 1978–79 (SD and Venstre), 1982–93, and 1994–98 (see Table 2). Otherwise, single-party minority Cabinets have been formed. Most minority Cabinets have support arrangements with other parties for specified policies.

Additional limits on executive power involve the referendum provisions in the 1953 constitution. These come into play if any sovereignty is ceded to an international authority unless there is a five-sixths majority in the *Folketing*; to change the voting age; as a legislative veto, on the request of one-third of *Folketing* members, to oppose a bill after its third reading; and to amend the constitution, when the amendment must be passed twice by the *Folketing* in the same form with an intervening election. A referendum is then held requiring a "Yes" vote by a majority of voters that must also constitute at least 40% of the electorate. During 1953–98, 15 referendum votes were held: 5 on issues of European integration; 6 lowering the voting age from 25 in 1963 to 18 in 1978; and 4 in 1963 to veto laws on landholding (see Table 1). Financial and nationality legislation is excluded from this referendum procedure.

The most controversial referendum was the narrow rejection of the Maastricht Treaty of European Union in 1992, which required ratification by all 12 member states for the treaty to take effect. A "national compromise"

agreed upon by seven parties ranging from the Socialist People's Party (SF) to the Conservatives (but excluding the Progress Party) and opt-outs agreed upon at the EC summit in December 1996 proved sufficient to secure a referendum majority in 1993.

In addition to overseeing Cabinet formations, Queen Margrethe II presides over the Council of State, a formal meeting of the Cabinet that assents to legislation. Her other functions are ceremonial and representational, but she enjoys great popularity and respect, both as monarch and as an accomplished artist and designer. Constitutionally, legislative power is vested jointly in the monarch and the *Folketing*, executive power in the monarch, and judicial power in the courts. In legal reality, executive power is exercised by civil servants acting within laws signed by the queen, countersigned by a minister, and authorized by a Cabinet responsible to the elected parliament. The judiciary act independently of legislature and executive.

TABLE 1
Referendums in Denmark

Year	Issue	Result	% of Electorate Voting Yes	Turnout %	Valid Votes Yes	Valid Votes No
1916	Sale of Danish West Indies (Virgin Islands) to U.S.A.(Consultative)	Approved	63.2	23.0	57.4	44.1
1920	Constitutional Amendment following Reunion with Northern Slesvig	Passed	47.5	49.0	96.9	3.1
1939	Constitutional Amendments (Including Lower Voting Age and Abolition of Landsting [Upper House])	Rejected	44.46 (45% Required)	48.4	91.85	8.15
1946	(In the Faroes) on Independence	Rejected	48.6	66.4		
1953	New Constitution	Passed	45.76	59.1	78.75	21.25
1953	Reduce Voting Age from 25 to 23 or 21 (All over 21 Entitled to Vote)					
	For 23	Passed	25.0			
	For 21	Rejected	30.0			
1961	Reduce Voting Age from 23 to 21	Passed	20.3	36.9	55.0	45.0
1963	Land Laws:					
	Inheritance of Farms	Rejected	27.7	72.2	38.4	61.6
	State Small-Holdings	Rejected	27.9	72.2	38.6	61.4
	Municipal Compulsory Purchases	Rejected	28.7	72.3	39.6	60.4
	Nature Conservation	Rejected	30.8	72.3	42.6	57.4
1969	Reduce Voting Age from 21 to 18	Rejected	13.6	63.4	21.4	78.6
1971	Reduce Voting Age from 21 to 20	Passed	47.4	83.9	56.5	43.5
1972	Denmark to Join European Community	Passed	56.7	89.6	63.3	36.7
1978	Reduce Voting Age from 20 to 18	Passed	34.2	63.2	53.8	46.2
1986	Danish Ratification of Single European Act (SEA) (Advisory Referendum)	Passed	42.0	32.7	56.2	43.8
1992	Maastricht Treaty of European Union	Rejected	40.4	83.1	49.3	50.7
1993	Maastricht Treaty with Derogations	Passed	63.0	86.5	56.7	43.3
1998	Amsterdam Treaty	Passed	41.6	75.6	55.1	44.9

Sources: Kauffeldt 1972; Holt 1988; Keesings 1993: 39483; Bille 1993:412; Bille 1994: 281.

Legal basis: 1916, 1953 (voting age), 1986: specific legislation; 1920, 1939, 1953: constitution of 1920, paragraph 94; 1972, 1992, 1993: constitution of 1953, paragraph 20, s. 1; 1961, 1969, 1971, 1978: constitution of 1953, paragraphs 29 and 42; 1963: constitution of 1953, paragraph 42.

TABLE 2
Danish Governments 1968–98

Years	Cabinet Parties	Support %[a]	Prime Minister
1968–71	Radical Liberals, Liberals (Venstre), Conservatives	56	Hilmar Baunsgaard (RV)
1971–72	Social Democrats	40	Jens Otto Krag (SD)
1972–73	Social Democrats	40	Anker Jørgensen I (SD)
1973–75	Liberals (Venstre)	13	Poul Hartling (V)
1975–78	Social Democrats	30	Anker Jørgensen II (SD)
1978–79	Social Democrats, Liberals	49	Anker Jørgensen III (SD)
1979–81	Social Democrats	39	Anker Jørgensen IV (SD)
1981–82	Social Democrats	34	Anker Jørgensen V (SD)
1982–84	Conservatives, Liberals (Venstre), Center Democrats, Christian People's Party	34	Poul Schlüter I (KF)
1984–87	Conservatives, Liberals (Venstre) Center Democrats, Christian People's Party	44	Poul Schlüter II (KF)
1987–89	Conservatives, Liberals (Venstre), Center Democrats, Christian People's Party	40	Poul Schlüter III (KF)
1989–90	Conservatives, Liberals (Venstre), Radical Liberals	38	Poul Schlüter IV (KF)
1990–93	Conservatives, Liberals (Venstre),	34	Poul Schlüter V (KF)
1993–94	Social Democrats, Radicals, Center Democrats, Christian People's Party	51	Poul Nyrup Rasmussen I (SD)
1994–96	Social Democrats, Radicals, Center Democrats	43	Poul Nyrup Rasmussen II (SD)
1996–98	Social Democrats, Radicals	39	Poul Nyrup Rasmussen III (SD)
1998–	Social Democrats, Radicals	40	Poul Nyrup Rasmussen IV (SD)

[a]Cabinet support is the percentage of parliamentary mandates held by the parties represented in the Cabinet. From this it is clear that since 1968 there were majority governments only in 1968–71 and 1993–94.

TABLE 3
Denmark: Party Shares of Cabinet Office, 1848–1998

Period			% of Period That Each Party Was in Office								
From	To	Length in Years	SD	RV	Nat Lib	DR	V	KrF	Right/KF	CD	Others
3/22/1848	7/11/1864	16.3			81				53		
7/11/1864	7/24/1901	37.1			14				100		
7/24/1901	4/30/1929	27.8	10	27			63				
4/30/1929	11/7/1945	14.9	100	100			25		25		3
11/7/1945	12/5/1973	28.1	69	39		12	31		23		
12/19/1973	3/13/1998	24.2	55	34			52	26	43	43	

Notes: Rows do not sum to 100 because in coalitions two or more parties are in Cabinet together.

For key to party names see text. Nat Lib–National Liberals. Others–During the liberation government of May 5–November 7, 1945, the Communists and *Dansk Samling* were also in the Cabinet. The 1929–45 period excludes 1.7 years (8/30/43 to 5/5/45) during the 1940–45 German occupation when Cabinet government was suspended.

Legislature

The maximum *Folketing* term is four years, but elections have been held about every three years. The 179 members include 2 each from the Faroes and Greenland. Its presidium of a chairman and 4 deputies is elected from the five largest parties. It convenes autonomously on the first Tuesday in October and following each election. It normally sits until the end of May with recesses at Christmas and Easter and for sessions of the transnational Nordic Council, which meets in rotation in one of the five Nordic parliaments. About one-third of the members are women. The largest category of members come from public-sector white-collar occupations. Only 8% were law graduates, and a qualification in political science was more likely.

Judiciary

Judicial review of legislation is a logical consequence of the codified constitution, but in each of about ten 20th-century cases the Supreme Court found the law to be constitutional. This happened in 1998 when a group of citizens failed in their challenge to the authority of the prime minister to sign the Maastricht Treaty. Executive orders that do not conform to the enabling legislation have been struck down, but the courts cannot override discretionary executive decisions unless the influence of extraneous considerations can be shown. The judiciary assert their independence by maintaining an apolitical stance.

The constitution includes an impeachment procedure under which a minister may be tried before the High Court of the Realm (*rigsret*) on a charge of "maladministration of office" brought by the Crown or the *Folketing*.

The most effective remedy available to citizens in dispute with the administration is through the ombudsman, whose opinions are usually accepted. An official with legal training, he has extensive powers to investigate administrative decisions at the national and local levels and reports to the *Folketing* Justice Committee. Most cases concern the Ministries of Justice or Social Policy and their attached agencies.

Regional and Local Government

Since extensive amalgamation of small administrative units in 1970 Denmark is administered by 275 municipalities (*kommuner*). In population they range from 2,700 to 500,000 but average 18,500. They run most local services, including primary schools, social security, primary health care, children's day care, assistance to the elderly including care homes, local roads, and the environment. They keep a population and electoral register and raise property taxes. They receive block grants from the state and are fully reimbursed by the state for the pensions they pay to the elderly and the early-retired.

Fourteen second-tier counties (*amtskommuner*) range in population from 47,000 to 630,000, but half have between 200,000 and 300,000. They run major roads, secondary schools, and hospitals (except a few specialized facilities run by the state—there are no private hospitals). Primary health care is paid for mainly by the counties, while doctors work as private practitioners paid on a fee-for-service basis. Health insurance is compulsory, and all hospital treatment and most other health services are free

---

TABLE 4
Denmark: *Folketing* Elections 1971, 1973, 1984–98

	1971		1973		1984		1987		1988		1990		1994		1998	
	vote %	seats	vote %	seats	vote %	seats	vote %	seats	vote %	seats	vote %	seats	vote %	seats	vote %	seats
KP	1.4	0	3.6	6	0.7	0	0.9	0	0.8	0	—		—			
VS	1.6	0	1.5	0	2.7	5	1.4	0	0.6	0	—		—			
FK							2.2	4	1.9	0	1.8	0	—			
RG											1.7	0	3.1	6	2.7	5
SF	9.1	17	6.0	11	11.5	21	14.6	27	13.0	24	8.3	15	7.3	13	7.5	13
SD	37.3	70	25.6	46	31.6	56	29.3	54	29.8	55	37.4	69	34.6	62	36.0	63
RV	14.4	27	11.2	20	5.5	10	6.2	11	5.6	10	3.5	7	4.6	8	3.9	7
DR	1.7	0	2.9	5	1.5	0	0.5	0	—		0.5	0	—			
KrF	1.9	0	4.0	7	2.7	5	2.4	4	2.0	4	2.3	4	1.9	0	2.5	4
CD			7.8	14	4.6	8	4.8	9	4.7	9	5.1	9	2.8	5	4.3	8
KF	16.7	31	9.2	16	23.4	42	20.8	38	19.3	35	16.0	30	15.0	27	8.9	16
V	15.6	30	12.3	22	12.1	22	10.5	19	11.8	22	15.8	29	23.3	42	24.0	42
DF															7.4	13
FP			15.9	28	3.6	6	4.8	9	9.0	16	6.4	12	6.4	11	2.4	4
Ind														1		
T/o	87.2		88.7		88.4		86.7		85.7		82.8		84.3		86.0	

Note: This table of *Folketing* elections shows the five-party system (**in bold**) that existed 1958–71 and the effect of the 1973 "earthquake" election. For reasons of space it omits results of elections in 1975, 1977, 1979, and 1981, which were printed in earlier editions of this Encyclopedia.
Parties: Socialist block: KP–Danish Communist Party. VS–Left Socialists. FK–Common Course. RG–Red-Green Unity List. SF–Socialist People's Party. SD–Social Democrats. *Center parties*: RV–Radical Liberals. DR–Justice Party. KrF–Christian People's Party. CD–Center Democrats. *Parties of the right*: KF–Conservative People's Party. V–Venstre, Denmark's Liberal Party. *Protest parties*: FP–Progress Party. DF–Danish People's Party. Ind–Independent candidate. T/o–turnout (% of electorate voting).

TABLE 5
Danish *Folketing*: Occupational Categories of Members

Occupation	Members	Population
Independent Occupations	15.5	7.4
White-Collar Employees, Private Sector	34.9	13.2
White-Collar Employees, Public Sector	41.7	17.9
Workers, Private Sector	2.3	5.6
Workers, Public Sector	1.1	15.6
Other Employed	1.1	3.5
No Occupation	3.4	36.7

Source: Hans Peter Hilden, ed., *Folketinget efter valget 1990* (Copenhagen: Folketinget).

of charge to the patient. Local government collectively spends funds equivalent to one-third of GNP and employs around one-fifth of the workforce. Elections for county and municipal councils are held every four years. These elections are not contested by many of the smaller parties. A mayor (*borgmester*) chairs the council and leads its work but is not the chief executive. The large cities have collective leadership, with mayors chairing each of the major departmental committees.

The Faroe Islands have had home rule since 1948, while the Danish government retains authority over foreign policy, defense, justice, police, and the church. There is an elected *Løgting* of 32 members and an executive (*Landsstyr*) headed by a *Lagmand*. In 1998, an independence majority was elected favoring a more clearly defined relationship to Denmark. The Danish state is represented by the *rigsombudsmand*, exercising prefectorial powers. The islands have two representatives in the *Folketing*. Similar arrangements have applied in Greenland since 1979, with powers transferred progressively.

THE ELECTORAL SYSTEM

The *Folketing* is directly elected using a complex party-list proportional method. The threshold for representation is 2%. Parties may use three types of list and can use different types in different districts. Voters can cast a personal vote for a candidate, and this allowed the rare election in 1994 of an independent (nonparty) candidate on a "nonsense" program. Since 1953 Sainte Laguë rules (but with a first divisor of 1.4) have been used to allocate 135 mandates in 17 voting districts, averaging 7.9 representatives per district. A further 40 supplementary seats are allocated by largest remainder, based on each party's total national vote, taking into account the 135 mandates previously allocated. The results score 99 on a proportionality index that rates perfect proportionality at 100. Casual vacancies are filled by the next candidate on the list, so the *Folketing* party balance remains fixed between elections unless a party splits.

The ballot shows a list of candidates grouped under party names. The lists are lettered for identification (A for SD through Z for the Progress Party). Parties use these letters when campaigning. Candidates are nominated from one of 103 nomination districts within the 17 electoral districts, so candidates keep a territorial link. Nonparty candidates can also be nominated. Blank or invalid votes are no more than 0.6% of the poll. The electoral register is renewed every January and includes all qualified residents known to the *folkeregister* (almost all the eligible population). Turnout ranges between 80 and 90%.

There has been universal adult suffrage since 1915. The voting age has been 18 since 1978. All permanently resident Danes may vote, unless declared incapable of managing their affairs. Since 1981, foreigners resident in Denmark for three years before a local election may vote or run as a candidate in these elections. The three-year limit does not apply to citizens of the EU, Iceland, or Norway.

THE PARTY SYSTEM

The party system originated in 1848. Initially the Right and National Liberals shared office, then alternated it between them. From 1905 there was a four-party system: Social Democrats, Radical Liberals, Venstre Liberals, and Conservatives, with the Social Democrats the largest party from 1924. In 1959 the Socialist People's Party became the fifth significant party in the system. Since the 1973 "earthquake" election at least 10 parties have been represented in the *Folketing*, with a broad central core of "responsible" parties forming governments, criticized by a periphery of noncoalitionable parties. On a left/right scale the parties in the 1990s can be ordered: Red-Green Unity List, Socialist People's Party (SF), Social Democrats (SD), Radical Liberals (RV), Center Democrats (CD), Venstre Liberals (V), Christian People's Party (KRF), Conservatives, and Progress Party (FP). Refugees and immigration have been sensitive issues since the mid-1980s, and on a pluralism/assimilation scale the order is similar except that RV and CD are more pluralist than SD. The Progress Party and its successor, the Danish People's Party, are most opposed to "foreigners."

The Parties in Law

The 1953 constitution requires *Folketing* members to be bound solely by their own consciences and not by any directions given by their electors. Parties are not mentioned in the constitution but are regarded as voluntary and private associations. There is a constitutional right to form associations for any legal purpose without prior permission. Political associations can be dissolved only by

Supreme Court decision. Their voluntary character ensures the absence of obligations on members beyond payment of dues and the requirements not to join another party and to support their own party's policies. SD members are additionally expected to join a trade union, and officers must subscribe to the affiliated newspaper.

Parties may contest elections if they obtained parliamentary representation at the previous election and continued to be represented when the election is called, or if they give notice to the Interior Ministry 15 days before the election. The latter parties require nominations on an official form from a number of electors equal to 1/175th of the total of valid votes at the previous election. Following the 1994 election, this required 19,015 valid signatures for a new party. A candidate must consent to nomination and requires party approval. A nonparty candidate requires the nomination of between 150 and 200 voters from the nomination district. Parties have substantial freedom to determine their own structures and regulations.

State subventions to political parties were legislated in 1986, and the rates were increased in 1995. The central office of a national party is paid 19.50 kroner (up from 5 kroner) per year per vote cast for the party at the last parliamentary election. Regional party organizations are paid 2.50 kroner (up from 2 kroner) for a vote at the last county election, and local party organizations are paid 4 kroner (up from 3 kroner) per vote at the last municipal elections.

Although state subventions were initially intended to support *Folketing* activity, in practice they become general party income to a party secretariat. SF, FP, and RV locate their central party offices in the *Folketing*, and it is impossible to distinguish money spent by the parliamentary group from spending by the party headquarters. Parties also receive donations, but these do not attract tax concessions, so personal donations are usually not large. Another 1995 law required publication of party accounts and the names of donors of 20,000 kroner or more per year to party funds. Special-interest organizations are important donors: trade unions to SD, industry and employers to the Conservatives, and agrarian organizations to Liberals. Donations are usually specifically for an election or publicity campaign. The possibility that, for example, union donations might go to SF rather than to SD may be a significant sanction in the hands of organizations.

Membership dues are fixed locally and vary between areas. The financial significance of individual members has declined drastically and the importance of direct state subventions has increased correspondingly in 1986–96.

Party Organization

Parliamentary groups actively negotiate and compromise with their counterparts, especially in parliamentary committees, and policy support arrangements extend well beyond the span of the parties represented in Cabinet. In these daily interactions it is impractical to take orders from or even consult national party organizations, so the national committee is briefed only after an agreement is reached. Parliamentary groups keep party discipline generally high by a strongly held norm of party solidarity. This requires dissident views to be reported and justified to the group meeting held before each day's parliamentary session.

Direct party membership totals declined from almost 600,000 in 1960 to just over 250,000 in 1989, with SD and the Liberals feeling the decline most sharply from earlier high figures. The greater number of parties after 1973 did little to counter the trend.

Campaigning

Voters rate television as much the most important channel of political communication, followed by newspapers. Radio, personal communication, and books or magazines together account for less than 30% of election information. Some public election meetings are held, and politicians seek to meet the people in public places, but there is no canvassing door to door.

Television time for each party is strictly allocated in equal shares to each party, even in the final evening-long broadcast before the poll. This favors the smaller parties. There is extensive newspaper coverage and advertising, and leaflets are also delivered to households. The "four old parties" used to publish their own daily newspapers in most large towns, but concentration of ownership has greatly reduced their number.

Party Support

Of working-class voters, 75% supported the Social Democrats in 1953, while under 20% supported "bourgeois" parties and under 10% supported the left (then the Communist Party). Their support for SD declined to just over 40% in 1988, while support for the left (principally SF from 1958 but also the Left Socialists and other small parties) rose to over 20%. Working-class support for nonsocialist parties has increased even more, to just under 40% in 1988.

Office workers have voted predominantly for nonsocialist parties. Support for parties of the left by office workers rose from 3% in 1957 to 16% in 1971, fell to 12% in 1973, then rose steadily to 27% in 1987, then fell to 21% in 1988.

Economically independent people in urban occupations overwhelmingly support the nonsocialist parties, the proportion fluctuating between 75% and 80% during 1953–56 and lying between 80 and 90% from 1968, ending at 81% in 1988. SD support from this category declined from 24% in 1953 to 14% in 1988. Their support for left-wing parties peaked at 9% in 1987 but fell to 4% in 1988.

Farmers overwhelmingly support nonsocialist parties, principally Venstre, with a dip to 94% in 1979, a rise to

TABLE 6
Denmark: Party Membership 1960, 1969, 1979, 1989

Party	Category	1960	1969	1979	1989
SF		3,334	4,433	4,424	8,797
SD	Direct	259,459	179,609	109,389	98,000
	LO	772,262	894,350	1,212,048	1,412,767[a]
	Youth Org	21,069		14,975[a]	
	ARF				200,000[a]
RV	Direct	35,000	25,000	13,000	9,900
	Youth Org			1,500[a]	1,500[a]
KrF		—[b]		10,810	9,629
	Youth Org			1,400	1,525
CD		—[b]		1,575	2,141
V		192,629	149,164	98,482	79,425
	Youth Org	53,306	16,340	3,744	4,000
KF	Also Total	108,751	139,855	44,000	40,392
	Youth Org			4,317[a]	8,360[a]
FRP		—		6,500	6,400
	Youth Org			2,100[a]	1,650[a]

Source: Lars Bille, "Denmark," in *Party Organizations: A Data Handbook on Party Organizations in Western Democracies, 1960–90*, ed. Richard S. Katz and Peter Mair (London: Sage, 1992).

Affiliated organizations: youth organization. ARF: Workers' Radio and Television Association. LO: Federation of Danish Trade Unions.

a Figures are highly unreliable.

b Party did not exist.

99% in 1984, and a fall to 92% in 1988. Such support as remains goes to SD.

Students show a distinctive pattern of party support. In 1964, four out of five students voted for nonsocialist parties, but after almost unbroken decline, with sharp falls in 1968 and 1971, this figure was down to one-fourth in 1979. At that point almost two-thirds voted for one of the left-wing parties, which in 1964 had been supported by only 5% of these voters. Their support for SD has been around 10%, with a peak of 18% in 1977.

CENTER DEMOCRATS
(Centrum-Demokraterne; CD)

HISTORY

CD was formed when Erhard Jakobsen, mayor of the Copenhagen suburb of Gladsaxe and a member of the Folketing since 1953, broke from SD and precipitated the 1973 election. CD is a nonsocialist party of the center that seeks cooperation between nonsocialists and SD to secure the stability of a Danish society of high quality, both for those who can work and for those who need help. CD was in the Conservative-led coalitions of 1982–88, where it saw itself as the social guarantor in a center-right government. In 1993–96 CD participated in SD-led governments, rationalizing its role as retaining de-

cision making in the center and acting as a bridge to the other nonsocialist parties.

ORGANIZATION

From the start CD gave the parliamentary party predominance and independence from the national organization. Erhard Jakobsen, its public persona, was its effective leader as national chairman, able to overrule the chairmen of the national party and the parliamentary group. The chairman and secretary are elected from the national conference of branch delegates, and these two constitute the presidium together with MPs, MEPs, and the national executive. Local branches, 150 initially, declining to 118 in 1989, send voting delegates to regional organizations and the national conference, which also includes MPs and MEPs plus candidates for both these offices, plus representatives from county and municipal councils. Parliamentary candidates are chosen within a year after each election by a procedure that makes it easy to include new nominees. The structure encourages members to participate in choosing representatives and discussing issues but imposes few constraints on MPs or the leader.

Party headquarters are at Ny Vestergade 7, DK-1471 Copenhagen K.

POLICY

The party locates decision making authority with its parliamentary group, the better to negotiate policy agreements with other parties. It supports a mixed economy of private capitalism and initiative together with a well-functioning public sector, and it considers that Danish private commerce is better served by the welfare state than is its counterparts in other countries. CD opposes the trade union influence exerted through SD and wants a balance between the rights of employers and employees. It wishes to replace competitive provision of hospital specialty services by state planning.

CD argues that Danish freedom and democracy, together with the vital interests that the country shares with other countries, must be defended. But to build security, defense policy must be supplemented by economic, trade, and aid policies and an active role in the European Union, NATO, the UN, and other international organizations. Denmark has a major obligation to aid developing countries, which is best done by investment and freer trade. CD supports the European Union unconditionally as the best means of securing European economic and foreign policy. It supports the Maastricht Treaty but regrets the 1992 reservations and hopes to see them removed. It would like a stronger European foreign and security policy and a wider Europe to include countries of Eastern and Central Europe.

MEMBERSHIP AND CONSTITUENCY

Membership grew to about 1,500 in the 1970s and was over 2,000 for most of the 1980s. At about 1%, this is the lowest ratio of members to voters of any Danish party, although its close links with the association Active Listeners and Viewers, which campaigned on media policy, supplemented its organizational base. CD attracts middle-class supporters with some social democratic values who want the economic independence of house ownership.

FINANCING

In 1988 a total income of 1.1 million kroner was derived 72% from state subventions, 15% from members and branches, 4% from donations, and 9% from other sources. Almost all went in direct expenses by the parliamentary group.

LEADERSHIP

Erhard Jakobsen (1917–) led the party until 1989. He was also a member of the European Parliament 1973–87 and 1988–94. His daughter Mimi Jakobsen (1948–) followed him as party chairman and leader from 1985. She was minister for culture 1982–86, minister for social policy 1986–88, and briefly minister for Greenland and also served as a leading member of Poul Nyrup Rasmussen's Social Democrat governments 1993–96. The party's political spokesman and chairman of the parliamentary group is Peter Duetoft (1950–).

PROSPECTS

As a splinter party, CD was not expected to survive long, but from 1982 it established itself as one that can form coalitions; it also managed the transfer of leadership from its charismatic founder. As a nonsocialist party of the center it is in contest with RV but has outrun the Christian People's Party. It transferred support from Conservative-led Cabinets in the 1980s to the SD-led Cabinets of 1993–96 but withdrew to give higher priority to the party's survival than to its retention of Cabinet office.

THE CONSERVATIVE PEOPLE'S PARTY
(Det konservative Folkeparti; KF)

HISTORY

The Right (Højre) originated in 1876 as a parliamentary group to counter the liberal party, Venstre. It lost power in 1901 and re-formed as the Conservative People's Party in 1915 but had to wait until 1950 to enter government. In minority coalition with Venstre and with conditional parliamentary support from SD, this government successfully carried through major constitutional reforms in 1953, including abolition of the upper house. KF returned to the Cabinet in 1968–71, when the party served with Venstre in a majority Cabinet led by the Radicals. But Poul Schlüter, prime minister 1982–93, was the first Conservative to head a Cabinet since 1901.

ORGANIZATION

KF is branch-based, but direction of its affairs is centralized. Local branches elect constituency organizations and send delegates to the national conference. Branches are intended as meeting places for conservatives and a base for spreading the party's policy. The large national council (repræsentantskab) comprises representatives from branches, regional organizations, the youth and women's organizations, Folketing members and candidates, the conservative press, and the conservative foundation. The parliamentary group proposes lines of party policy for debate by the national council, which is the party's highest authority. It elects its own director and the party chairman. The national committee (hovedbestyrelsen) implements party policy and is the highest authority between meetings of the national council. This body, approaching 100 in size, appoints the party secretary and is chaired by the party chairman. KF headquarters are at Nyhavn 4, Postboks 1515, Dk-1020 Copenhagen.

POLICY

As one of only two European parties named Conservative, KF has tried to avoid the reactionary label that this implies. Aiming to attract SD voters at the 1984 election, Schlüter admitted to being Conservative, "but not so much that it mattered." Although there were signs of Thatcherite influence in the party's rhetoric, initial ambitions to reduce the scope of the public sector met little success. Instead, KF's aim became a modernized and effective public sector, with bureaucracy abolished wherever possible and decision making decentralized.

With its close links to business and industry, KF favors individual enterprise but sees an important role for the state in improving education and research. Education should develop knowledge, insights, and skills that can be measured against standards of achievement. Effective production helps to resource a fine-meshed social security net and to secure a welfare society that has the needs of the individual at its center. KF defends the values of the nuclear family and the country's Lutheran Church and its national Christian-humanist cultural heritage. KF has always favored strong Western European collaboration in the EU, squaring this with national sovereignty by emphasizing the subsidiarity principle to ensure that only decisions of international importance are taken at the EU level. KF has always favored strong national defense, wants an active part for Denmark in the UN and NATO, and seeks to raise the country's status within the Western European Union from observer to full member.

MEMBERSHIP AND CONSTITUENCY

Membership peaked in 1967 with 143,455, or 27% of the party's 1966 vote, but is lower now, at 40,392 in 1989 (7.8% of the 1988 vote). These figures include members of the women's committee and highly unreliable figures for the youth organization. The Conservatives have rivaled Venstre for leadership of the nonsocialist bloc since the 1940s.

KF is strongly supported by urban employers, professionals, the self-employed, and office workers, especially those in the better-paid private-sector jobs. Supporters once were better educated than average, but this distinction has almost disappeared. They are still likely to have above-average income and own a house on its own land. Supporters are probably aged over 40.

FINANCING

KF does not publish its accounts. Like the other Danish parties, it depends heavily on state subventions, annually receiving 7.7 million kroner for the parliamentary group, 3.2 million kroner for the central organization, and almost 2 million kroner for the local and regional organizations (1990 figures).

LEADERSHIP

Poul Schlüter became leader in 1974 and reunited the party after damaging leadership disputes since 1968. As prime minister from 1982 he effectively brought together the center-right parties. His enforced resignation in January 1993 left his successors a major task of recovery. Hans Engell, leader 1995–97, resigned following an alcohol-driving incident but retained the parliamentary group chairmanship.

Then Per Stig Møller led KF for a year before giving way to Pia Christmas-Møller (1961–), who faces a major task in reviving the party's electoral fortunes.

PROSPECTS

The Conservatives made a generational change of leadership in 1993–97 and repaired their relations with Venstre, the largest of the nonsocialist parties. They need a high-profile leader and effective campaigning to recover prominence on the right. Instead, they lost credibility in the 1988 election.

DANISH PEOPLE'S PARTY
(Dansk Folkeparti; DF)

HISTORY

In October 1995 Pia Kjærsgaard and three colleagues left the Progress Party (FP) and formed the Danish People's Party in reaction to the organizational and policy chaos of FP's autumn national conference. With an SD government in office they were confined to opposition but made a significant impact at the 1998 election.

ORGANIZATION AND LEADERSHIP

DF's leader is strongly placed to exert a firm grip on the party. Its central body, the party executive, chose the leading election candidates in 1998, decided the districts where they would be nominated, and used a hierarchical party list to ensure a parliamentary group committed to Pia Kjærsgaard as leader. A small staff included her husband, Henrik Thorup, in charge of presentation, and Kristian Thulesen Dahl as chief ideologue and chairman of the election committee. As organizer, Peter Skaarup led DF's successful assault on the Copenhagen city council, and was elected to the *Folketing* in 1998. Søren Espersen, previously a tabloid journalist, had charge of publicity. The party is organized at the county level and has a youth organization. This well-oiled and professional machine contrasted with FP's anarchy. Its origin as a breakaway from FP gave it a *Folketing* presence and base for its office: Christiansborg, 1240 Copenhagen K.

POLICY

DF is a party of xenophobic protest, especially against the small population of refugees and immigrants in Denmark. In almost every year since 1960 there have been more immigrants than emigrants, mostly Europeans, but the biggest visible groups include Turks, Iranians, Pakistanis, Sri Lankans, and Somali refugees. Yet all foreigners constitute only 4.5% of the population, and only 17% of the population see them as a problem. The party insists it is not racist or fascist, but it sees Muslims as a problem and wants to return immigrants to where they came from. Its views on foreigners link to its opposition to "the foreign," represented by the European Union, which it equally opposes and links to the open borders of the Schengen and Amsterdam Treaties. On other issues it looks back to the "old virtues" of 1960s conservatism, for example, supporting parents' right to beat their children. Its economic policies promise to combine dramatic tax reductions with more money for pensioners and hospitals but omit to say where the cuts will be made to finance these. Its "anxiety" about a multiethnic society is the basis of its electoral appeal. Its name allows the slogan "Vote Danish."

CONSTITUENCY

The November 1997 local elections showed that DF was especially attractive to men over 50 in skilled or unskilled manual occupations, previously traditional supporters of SD. DF became the fourth-largest party in the Copenhagen city council. It probably drew much of its 1998 support from disillusioned Conservatives. In early 1998 DF claimed about 2,800 members.

PROSPECTS

DF influenced the anti-EU referendum vote in May 1998 and the 1999 European Parliament vote. In domestic politics its xenophobic protest is more successful than FP's, but both parties remain peripheral on the right wing.

PROGRESS PARTY
(Fremskridtsparti; FP)

HISTORY

The Progress Party began as a populist protest. Mogens Glistrup, its founder in 1972, is a tax lawyer who claimed that he and his clients paid no income tax. He demanded an end to taxation, bureaucracy, and "paper-shuffling jacks-in-office," with a defense policy consisting of a phone-answering machine with the message "We surrender!" in Russian. Largely ostracized, FP has never been in the Cabinet, but its presence has compelled the other parties to take account of its demands for tax reforms. In 1995 a "responsible" group broke away to form the Danish People's Party.

ORGANIZATION

Its populism initially led FP to operate with a small and informal organization but no formal structure or membership. But local organizations were soon necessary to raise money and campaign support. The Progress Party's headquarters are in the parliament building, Christiansborg, 1240 Copenhagen K.

MEMBERSHIP AND CONSTITUENCY

In 1973 FP drew support from all categories of voters and all the established parties. Later its support came more specifically from the self-employed. But it has also succeeded in drawing support from manual workers, and initially also from better-educated middle-aged people. When Glistrup launched his first attack against foreigners in 1979, the better-educated left the party and have never returned. Among young voters, FP supporters are the poorest educated. Among older voters, there is no difference in educational profile from the other bourgeois parties. In 1988, half the occupationally active FP voters were manual workers, the same proportion as for the Social Democrats and considerably higher than in all other parties. FP derives much of its strength from the decline of working-class culture and has benefited from political dealignment. It draws little support from public employees, who are predominantly nonmanual wage earners.

POLICY

Although on the far right of the Danish party spectrum, FP is not extremist. Although populist, FP is neither antimodernist nor anticapitalist nor nationalistic. The label comes from Glistrup's appeal to the baser instincts of tax avoidance, chauvinism, an antistate individualism, and a neoliberal belief in market forces. This is not the neoliberalism of the upper strata. FP has always demanded increased expenditure on public-sector health care and state pensions and has supported the unique flat-rate Danish pension system. The spending cuts it wants are in areas unpopular with the lower strata—culture, refugees, and foreigners. Rather than subsidize the Faroe Islands or Greenland, Glistrup proposed selling these territories to the highest bidder, hardly the views of a nationalist. FP's proposals for a lower income tax have entailed higher tax-free allowances rather than lower marginal tax rates.

FINANCING

Income is very largely from state subventions, especially to the parliamentary group and the central party organization, so FP is heavily dependent on its electoral success.

LEADERSHIP

Plagued from the start by defections and internal rifts between those favoring Glistrup's provocative, uncompromising style and adherents of a more conventional bourgeois line, there were fewer tactical disputes after Glistrup and three colleagues were expelled from the parliamentary group in 1990 and from the party in 1991. They formed *Trivselspartiet* (the Prosperity Party), but it failed to collect sufficient signatures to qualify for the ballot. Instead Glistrup agreed on a joint list with the left-wing Common Course Party, with little success. The 1994 election changed the internal balance of the party, and Pia Kjærsgaard was fired as party spokeswoman (see Danish People's Party). In 1995–96, the party chairman was Johannes Sørensen, the group chairman was Kim Behnke (born 1960, an electronics consultant), and the political spokeswoman was Kirsten Jacobsen (an estate agent, born 1942).

Although never a potential government partner, at its height FP pulled policy rightward. Weakened by internal splits, it was marginalized in 1998 by the Danish People's Party.

RED-GREEN UNITY LIST
(Enhedslisten-De rød-grønne)

HISTORY

The List advocates policies to the left of the Socialist People's Party. Formed in 1989, its sponsors were the Left Socialists, the dwindling Danish Communist Party, and the Socialist Labor Party. It has attracted unattached left-wingers and developed its own momentum with some local election successes, including four on the Copenhagen city council. Its first parliamentary success was in 1994, with six *Folketing* representatives. Its leaders supported Rasmussen to form a government, implying qualified parliamentary support for the SD government. It claims not to be an "all-or-nothing" party and is willing to support policies that will improve conditions for ordinary people and their environment.

ORGANIZATION

Not a conventional party, the List uses electoral law to present candidates prepared to support a set of democratic socialist policies. It claimed 1,500 members in 1995. Members in local branches elect an annual conference, which is the List's highest authority. It chooses an executive and the candidates to lead the electoral list. The List's headquarters are at Studiestræde 24, 1455 Copenhagen K, and its parliamentary secretariat is at Christiansborg, 1240 Copenhagen K.

CONSTITUENCY

Too small to have a distinctive constituency, the List appeals to voters who share its postmaterialist values. They are mostly in the capital city and are young and well educated.

POLICY

The List opposes the European Union, especially for its external tariffs against trade with developing countries and its support of capital against the interests of ordinary people in Europe and abroad. Instead it wants interstate cooperation among all European states, East and West, while allowing each to retain its independence. It opposes NATO and WEU, attributing "security problems" to social and economic inequalities that are best solved by disarmament, democracy, social development, and conflict prevention. It seeks a socialist society but considers that the defunct Eastern European regimes were neither democratic nor socialist.

FINANCING

A significant reason for contesting elections is to qualify for the state subventions to parties achieving representation.

LEADERSHIP

There is a seven-person collective leadership chaired by Bruno Jerup.

PROSPECTS

Occupying a peripheral space on the left of Danish politics, the List's prospects are threatened by the 2% representational threshold. It depends on a Social Democratic government that it can criticize and on not being outflanked by the Socialist People's Party, especially on European union.

RADICAL LIBERALS
(Det radikale Venstre; RV)

HISTORY

One of the "four old parties," RV split from the Venstre Liberals in 1905 with three objectives: abolition of vested interests, a more just distribution of land and taxes, and lower military expenditure. Although one of the smaller parties, from its central position RV has influenced both SD and the parties of the moderate right. It has succeeded in maintaining a center-based consensus and opposing the polarizing plans of the Progress Party or the Socialist People's Party.

ORGANIZATION

Constituency organizations elect regional organizations and send voting delegates to the national conference. The national committee is elected from regional and national levels and in turn elects a national executive and a standing committee. The parliamentary group sends voting delegates to the national committee and the national executive, whose chairman is chosen by the standing committee. Local branches and links to affiliated organizations were abolished in 1970, but the youth organization was revived in 1994. RV has retained a national chairman who is generally not a member of the parliamentary party.

RV's organizational base is in parliament, Christiansborg, DK-1240 Copenhagen K.

MEMBERSHIP AND CONSTITUENCY

After a steep decline in the 1960s, RV membership in the 1980s remained stable around 10,000. Electoral support comes from the population broadly but fluctuates quite widely. It has attracted a significant "green" vote.

POLICY

RV is a social-liberal party, equidistant from socialism and unrestrained liberalism and striving for the interests of society as a whole. Radicals stand for intellectual, personal, and political freedom and oppose vested interests. Radicals emphasize cooperative democratic values and the practical approach to policymaking that has contributed much to modern Denmark. The results it claims include people's active involvement in their social care, a well-balanced economy, and secure individual rights. Educational reforms aim to develop individual competencies, both in children and adults. RV has supported action plans and taxes to conserve resources and reduce environmental damage. Its cultural policy encourages variety. In foreign policy RV aims for closer cooperation in a wider post–Warsaw Pact Europe, with greater use of the defense budget for peacekeeping and humanitarian purposes.

Financing

Just over half the party's expenditure derives from state subventions.

Leadership

Niels Helveg Petersen (born 1939 and a political science graduate) has been a leading figure in the party since the 1970s, serving as economics minister 1988–90 in the Conservative-led government and as foreign minister since 1993 in SD-led governments. The party has also held the portfolios for Economics, Nordic Cooperation, Education and the Church, and Culture—all areas of traditional concern. The party chair since 1995 is Margrethe Vestager, and the parliamentary group chair is Jørgen Estrup.

Prospects

Radical leaders have been adept at using their central placing to maintain the cooperative style of politics that is their ideal. This strategy has been emulated by the Christians and CD.

Social Democrats
(Socialdemokratiet; SD)

History

The party was founded in 1871 on Marxist principles, although with little initial contact with other socialist parties. It achieved its first parliamentary representation in 1884. By 1913, SD had more votes than any other party. Observer status in the Cabinet in 1916–20 and the predominance of the parliamentary over the union wing from the 1920s attracted voters more widely than from just industrial workers. These developments made it the largest *Folketing* party since 1924 and the only significant socialist party until the 1960s. SD formed its first Cabinet in 1924–26, but the coalition with the Radical Liberals of 1929–40 carried through extensive social reforms and the foundation of the welfare state. Collaboration of RV and SD lasted to the mid-1960s and was re-

vived in 1993. SD has given Denmark 8 of its 15 prime ministers, from Thorvald Stauning (1929–42) to Poul Nyrup Rasmussen since 1993.

Throughout that period it has been the predominant government party and has shaped the country's political culture. It claims credit for reducing class-based social divisions and building a society with equal access to publicly provided education, health, and social services. These achievements rest on center-oriented pragmatism, not dogmatic ideology.

Organization

SD's highly developed organization builds on some 660 local branches throughout the country, with just under 100,000 direct members. It also has close links with the trade union movement (*Landsorganisationen i Danmark*; LO), the Workers' Radio and Television Association, and a youth sports association. SD is represented on the trade union, cooperative, youth, arts, leisure, press, and workers' educational wings of the labor movement. A paid staff of 78 (in 1989) was employed, mostly in the parliamentary and central offices. The national congress meets every fourth year and is the party's highest authority, electing the president, the party chairman, two vice chairmen, and the party secretary. After debate in branches, it approves the party's program of principles. A national committee (*hovedbestyrelsen*) is the highest authority between congresses and includes representatives of regions and linked organizations, plus the 11-member national executive (*forretningsudvalg*). The latter meets twice a month. Party members may not hold mandates simultaneously in the *Folketing*, the European Parliament, or county or local councils. The party office is at Thorvaldsensvej 2, DK-1780 Copenhagen, and its parliamentary secretariat is at Christiansborg, 1240 Copenhagen K.

Membership and Constituency

Party membership has declined nationally. This trend has especially affected SD because of its membership-based structure. Growing union membership does not fully compensate, since less than half of union members vote SD. In 1977, 52% of SD voters were blue-collar workers, 43% were white-collar workers, and 4% were professionals, and the breakdown has remained very similar since. SD voters are likely to have only a secondary education, include a high proportion of the elderly, and live in provincial towns.

Policy

The core of SD policies has been to develop a secure welfare society resting on equal opportunities achieved through equal and free access to well-functioning health, education, and social services. This involves effective measures against unemployment, including leave for training or parenting, in turn creating short-term vacancies for work experience for the young or long-term unemployed. SD gives high priority to environmental protection in all its policies and planning.

The cornerstones of SD foreign policy have been membership in NATO and the European Union, through which a small country such as Denmark can best exercise influence. The EU is seen as a peace project capable of resolving shared economic and political problems, and SD therefore wishes to see the EU extended eastward, with priority given to employment and the protection of consumers and the environment. But SD opposes the "ever-closer union" of a single European currency and wishes to see greater clarity in the allocation of functions between national and European levels of decision making.

FINANCING

As the party with the largest representation at all levels, SD benefits most from state subventions. Members' subscriptions are indexed to inflation, with a reduction for pensioners. They are higher than those of any of the bourgeois parties, making SD the best-financed party in the country.

LEADERSHIP

Poul Nyrup Rasmussen was chosen as party chairman in 1992 after RV made clear that it could not work with his predecessor, Svend Auken, and another potential rival, Ritt Bjæregaard, became the Danish member of the European Commission. The parliamentary group is chaired by Pia Gjellerup, and its political spokesman (floor leader) is Torben Lund.

PROSPECTS

Electoral volatility has decreased since 1973, but no party can be complacent. After opposition in the 1980s, SD returned to government in 1993, but its vote has eroded. Its ability to stay in government depends on maintaining an alliance of the center-left against a center-right alliance based on Conservatives and Liberals.

SOCIALIST PEOPLE'S PARTY
(Socialistisk Folkeparti; SF)

HISTORY

The party was founded in 1959 by Aksel Larsen (1897–1972). He had led the Danish Communist Party (DKP) for 26 years, but he and others who formed SF were expelled for advocating socialism on Danish lines rather than as laid down from Moscow. The new party eclipsed the DKP and has won substantial *Folketing* representation ever since. After the 1992 referendum result opposing the Treaty of European Union, SF helped to broker the "national compromise" of exceptions, which paved the way for the "Yes" referendum vote in 1993. SF also helped to keep SD in office during 1996–98. These

are reasons to see SF as part of the responsible "core" of parties in the 1990s, rather than part of the anticonsensual periphery.

ORGANIZATION

SF achieved far greater electoral success with a mass party structure that allowed real democratic participation than did its Communist predecessor. One cost was factionalism: the Left Socialists broke away in 1967, and in 1974 and 1976 there were disagreements between the parliamentary group and the membership that led to leadership changes. Whereas the 1960 structure gave no distinct status to the parliamentary group, the 1990 structure makes the chairman of the parliamentary group ex officio chairman of the national executive. The parliamentary group has been highly disciplined. The party's headquarters, with its parliamentary secretariat, are in the *Folketing*, Christiansborg, 1240 Copenhagen K.

MEMBERSHIP AND CONSTITUENCY

SF membership peaked at 7,803 in 1967, then declined sharply as the party split that year. There was further decline to 4,400 in 1979. Conservative government in the 1980s brought substantial growth, to over 9,000 in 1988. SF appeals more successfully than SD to white-collar and service employees and has attracted young and well-educated voters, including public-sector professionals. SF recruitment of trade unionists increased in the late 1980s. Its strength is concentrated in the Copenhagen area. Its environmental policies have made a significant "green" appeal to voters inclined toward postmaterialist values.

POLICY

SF aims to achieve democratic socialism within Danish realities and only with active majority participation. Although drawing on Marxist theory, SF specifically rejects the communist idea of an elite avant garde seizing power on behalf of the working class and argues that the application of theory must be constantly revised to serve the best interests of wage earners. Since the mid-1970s SF has successfully integrated green and environmental values into its program; consequently no Green party has gained representation. SF has also made effective links to the women's movement and hopes for a red-green majority with SD.

SF is antimilitaristic, argues for disarmament and freedom from alliances, and opposes block politics. Specifically it has opposed U.S. wars in Vietnam and Nicaragua and Soviet invasions of Czechoslovakia and Afghanistan. SF opposed Danish membership in the EC in 1972 and since then has worked for Danish sovereignty and greater social and environmental justice within the EU. Thus SF opposed economic and monetary union, common EU defense, union citizenship, and supranational legal and police cooperation, securing broad agreement for these reservations as the "national compromise" that was accepted at the EU summit in December 1992 and by the

"Yes" majority in the 1993 referendum. While opposing a "united states of Europe," SF supports cooperation across the whole of Europe on environmental improvement and wants countries to choose the level of their commitment. In 1998, it was divided in its recommendation on the Amsterdam Treaty.

In domestic policies SF gives priority to reducing unemployment, for example, by shorter working hours; environmental improvement, with tax incentives and collective transportation; energy saving; and democracy extended to the economy, investment, and workplaces, with more influence for consumers and employers.

FINANCING

Unusually among Danish parties, SF sets its subscriptions in three bands related to the member's income. A party tax is levied on representatives' salaries, producing 16% of party income. Other major sources of income are state subventions (31%) and subscriptions (31%), but there are no donations (1989 figures).

LEADERSHIP

The party chairman and political spokesman is Holger K. Nielsen (born 1950 and a representative since 1981). The parliamentary group chairman is Steen Gade (born 1945, a teacher elected since 1981).

PROSPECTS

Positioned on the left, SF can only achieve influence through cooperation with SD, an aim that the parties of the center (especially RV) and right are dedicated to prevent. SF also risks being outflanked by formations like the Red-Green Unity List. In the 1980s SF achieved center-left agreement on several more stringent environmental standards, and in 1992 it brokered the "national compromise" on European integration. In 1993–98 the SD governments relied on SF support at times.

VENSTRE, THE DANISH LIBERAL PARTY
(Venstre, Danmarks liberale Parti; V)

HISTORY

Venstre (meaning Left) originated in 1870 when liberal and agrarian individuals and groups, but not the National Liberals, joined to form the United Left. Its aims included responsible parliamentary government and universal franchise. Until the 1970s a strong agrarian element was a vital feature of the party.

ORGANIZATION

Venstre maintains local, constituency, regional, and national levels of organization. Representatives in the *Folketing* and (since 1980) the European Parliament and candidates for both parliaments are members ex officio of the national conference, which is otherwise composed of voting delegates from constituency organizations. It elects a national executive and a national committee, which also includes the chairmen of elected standing committees. The national committee discusses and negotiates policy with the parliamentary group. It can also expel party organizations or members. The annual national conference, as the party's highest authority, debates policy and passes the party's program. A youth organization is based in Copenhagen, as is a parliamentary secretariat. Venstre's national organization is at Søllerødvej 30, DK-2840 Holte.

MEMBERSHIP AND CONSTITUENCY

Venstre retains a large and loyal individual membership, second only to SD. Until the 1970s this was based on its representing farmers' interests. While historically important, the agricultural sector produces only 3.5% of GDP (1993). Venstre has broadened its base to include rural communities generally and significant urban support from white-collar and business sectors, but these votes are more volatile. Previously labeled agrarian liberal, Venstre is the Danish counterpart of the agrarian parties in Finland, Norway and Sweden. While they changed their names to Center Party, Venstre added Denmark's Liberal Party to its name in 1970. Venstre retains close links to the large agricultural and food industry organizations and still has important support from provincial newspapers.

POLICY

During the 1980s, in Cabinet with the Conservatives, Venstre developed clearer free-market positions and influenced its coalition partners in this direction. Venstre has always been interested in education policy and emphasized the values of personal development and initiative in the 1994 School Law. Venstre's guiding principles begin with the personal freedom to think, believe, and speak and to choose one's own way of life and work. The right to private property should be shared as widely as possible.

These freedoms imply personal responsibility for the consequences of choice. The individual exists in a community of family, friends, and work colleagues, for whom he or she is coresponsible. An open society works for human rights for all, open borders, and free trade. But environmental problems know no borders and are best resolved by international cooperation. The EU environmental policy should therefore be strengthened.

FINANCING

Venstre does not publish its accounts and opposed the June 1995 law requiring publication of names of donors of 20,000 Kroner to political parties.

LEADERSHIP

The party chairman 1985–98 was Uffe Ellemann-Jensen (1941–). A journalist until elected in 1977, he was foreign minister throughout 1982–93 and was the leading opponent of the 1993–98 SD governments. In the 1998 elections, however, the party did not make the widely predicted gains, so he resigned and was replaced by Anders Fogh Rasmussen (born 1953), an economist who was tax minister 1987–93. The parliamentary group is chaired by Ivar Hansen (born 1938).

PROSPECTS

Venstre's vote has fluctuated between 10 and 23% since 1973. It became the second-largest party (after SD) in 1994, despite a declining rural constituency. Venstre rivals the Conservatives for leadership of nonsocialist opinion. These two parties can dominate the right but need additional support from the center parties to carry their policies. In 1994 Venstre was willing to work with FP, but this strategy alienated center voters.

OTHER POLITICAL PARTIES AND MOVEMENTS

The Christian People's Party (Kristeligt Folkeparti; KRF)

Founded in 1970, KRF is a party of religious and moral protest and cultural defense, more like similarly named parties in Norway, Finland, and Sweden than the catchall Christian Democrats that form a large moderate right in Germany. Initial support came from the evangelical Inner Mission, but the party draws on other wings of the national Lutheran Church as well as Catholics and the free churches, and on rural voters. KRF policies emphasize respect for life, peace, and property in a just society that recognizes the importance of the family. Its three basic principles are the Christian perspective, which gives unlimited value to each person; a good-neighborliness, which requires each person to care for family, society, and especially for its weaker members in illness and poverty; and stewardship of the environment, resources, and animal life, for the good of all mankind and future generations.

In 1994 it failed to surmount the 2% threshold, but it regained representation in 1998. KRF was a junior partner in the Conservative-led coalitions of 1982–88, holding portfolios for Environment, Nordic Affairs, and Housing. It was also in the SD-led Cabinet of 1993–94 with responsibilities for Energy, Housing, Nordic Cooperation and Baltic Affairs, and Church Affairs.

With a greater emphasis on individualism and responsibility than when KRF was formed, and with 87% (1994) of the population in the national church, KRF's

prospects are marginal.

The party's leader since 1990 is Jann Sjursen (born 1963), a trained teacher whose main career has been as a politician. Its office is at Bernhard Bangs Allé 23, DK-2000 Frederiksberg.

The People's Movement against the European Community (Folkebevægelsen mod EF)

The June Movement (Junibevægelsen)

Not strictly parties, these organizations attract cross-party support for anti-European opinion at referendums and European Parliament (EP) elections. The People's Movement was formed in April 1972 to oppose Danish membership in the European Community (EC) in the October referendum. Although the result was a "Yes" majority, the organization continued to exist and has campaigned in subsequent referendums. In each of the 1979, 1984, and 1989 EP elections it obtained 4 of Denmark's 16 seats.

The June Movement was formed for the June 1992 referendum on the Maastricht Treaty of European Union (TEU) by those who accepted membership in the (economic) EC but opposed the objectives of political union in the treaty. The TEU was narrowly rejected in 1992 and passed in 1993 (see Table 1 for referendum voting figures). At the 1994 EP election the movements each obtained 2 seats, the People's Movement with 10.3% and the June Movement with 15.2% of the vote.

THE FAEROE ISLANDS PARTIES

A nationalist movement was led by Jóannes Patursson (1866–1946), and after his electoral defeat in 1906, the Home Rule Party was formed to oppose the Unionist Party, which was in power until World War II. In 1936, however, the Home Rule Party lost heavily to SD. After the war agitation grew for outright independence, and a referendum on the issue was held in September 1946. The result was so indecisive that fresh *Løgting* (assembly) elections were called. Those favoring independence were defeated, but the Faroes were granted home rule in March 1948 with the *Løgting* wholly responsible for internal affairs and a *rigsombudsmand* to represent the state. Since 1953 the Islands have had two representatives in the Danish *Folketing*.

Lavish investment in the fishing industry in the 1980s brought heavy indebtedness. Then a decline in the catch and depressed prices resulted in an economic recession in 1989. In 1992 the Danish government made a large loan to prevent the collapse of the Faroese banks, conditional on a reduction in the fishing fleet and higher taxes. In 1993 unemployment rose to 20%, setting off emigration, often to Denmark. Despite an improving economy, the 1998 election indicated a wish for greater independence from Denmark.

After the election one representative of the Islands sat with the Conservative group and one with SD. In the 1998 *Løgting* elections a majority (Republicans, People's Party, and Independence Party) favored a more sharply defined relationship with Denmark.

The Faroese Unionist Party (Sambandsflokkurin)

Founded in 1906, this liberal party pursues progressive policies based on Christian cultural values. It wishes to retain the link with the Danish kingdom and, within this, to work for the stable development of the Faroese people, constitutionally, economically, and culturally. After the 1998 *Løgting* election it had six seats, a loss of two. In the *Folketing* it was represented by its chairman, Edmund Joensen, who was attached to the Venstre parliamentary group.

The Home Rule Party (Sjálvstýrisflokkurin)

The Home Rule Party was founded under the leadership of Jóannes Patursson in 1906 to oppose the Unionist Party. It has advocated the greatest autonomy for the islands and equal status for the Faroese language with Danish. It held 2 of the 32 seats in the *Løgting* in the 1998 elections on 7.7% of the vote.

The Faroese Social Democratic Party (Javnaðarflokkurin)

This party was founded in 1925. The party believes that the Islands and their resources belong to their people. It wishes to keep the link with Denmark, but with full freedom on either side to decide on the transfer of policy responsibility to the Faroes home government. It supports national self-determination and Nordic cooperation. Led by Joannes Eidesgaard, in 1998 it had seven representatives in the *Løgting*, an increase of two. Its *Folketing* representative sits with SD.

The People's Party (Folkáflokkurin)

The People's Party, founded in 1940, is a conservative party formed by the leading Faroese nationalist Jóannes Patursson after breaking with the Home Rule Party, largely over economic policy. It won a quarter of the seats

in the *Løgting* in 1940 on a program of full independence. The party stands for a Christian culture, a just society, and democracy and seeks independence for the Faroes with legislative authority to the *Løgting* on all policies and membership in NATO independently of Denmark. The party chairman is Anfinn Kallsberg. The party gained eight seats in 1998. Oli Breckmann, its representative in the Danish *Folketing*, works with KF.

The Republican Party (Tjódveldisflokkurin)

The Republican Party, founded in 1948, wants a republican constitution for the Islands, arguing that no foreign power should have the right to own or dispose of the country's resources. In the 1998 elections it doubled its strength to eight seats under its new leader and *Lagmand* (prime minister), Høgni Hoydal.

The Christian People's Party and Fishing Industry Party (Kristligi Fólkaflokkurin–Føroya framburðs og Fiskivinnuflokkurin)

Formerly the Progressive and Fishermen's Party, it changed its name for the 1984 elections. It argues for cooperation with the EU based on trading and fishery agreements. It supports NATO membership, which it sees as "securing peace and freedom for the Western world." Led by Niels Pauli Danielsen, it lost its two *Løgting* seats in the 1998 elections.

The Center Party (Miðflokkurin)

The Center Party was formed in 1991 following internal dissent in the Christian People's Party and Fishing Industry Party, with which it shares much, including a Christian perspective and active support for the family. Led by Alvur Kirke, in the 1998 elections it lost the two members elected to the *Løgting* in 1994.

The Labor Front (Verkmannafylkingin)

This party first contested an election in 1994. In its view the old parties have lost all connection with or respect for the trade unions and wage earners. It argues that the exceptional difficulties (recession and low catches) facing the Faroes require broad political cooperation to get their society functioning again, since social cohesion is threatened by current social changes. The party seeks to secure the people's rights, economically, politically, socially, and generally. It is led by Óli Jacobsen and in 1998 lost the three *Løgting* seats it had taken in 1994.

THE GREENLAND PARTIES

Akulliit Partiiat

This Center Party, formed in 1991 and led by Bjarne Kreutzmann, aims to privatize the large enterprises owned by the Greenlandic home rule authority. It has two seats in the *Landsting*.

Atassut (Solidarity, or The Link)

Atussut is a liberal group that was founded as a movement in 1978; in 1981 it became a political party and has since been the main opposition. It favored home rule, wished Greenland to remain in the European Community, and advocates constitutional unity with Denmark. Its economic policy favors greater privatization of commerce, in contrast to the prevalent extensive public control of the economy. Its representative in the *Folketing* works with Venstre. In 1995 it gained two seats. Its leader is Daniel Skifte.

Inuit Ataqatigiit (Inuit Brotherhood or Human Fellowship)

Inuit Ataqatigiit is a socialist party. Founded in 1978, it wants to confine Greenland citizenship to people of Inuit parentage. It opposes the 1979 Home Rule Law, wants complete independence from Denmark by 2000, and stands for a progressive tax system. It also opposed European Union membership. In 1995 it won six *Landsting* seats. Its leader is Josef Motzfeldt.

Siumut (Forward)

Siumut is a social democratic party dating from 1971. It became a party in 1977 with the long-term aim of maximum autonomy for Greenland, although in the 1990s it has supported the Home Rule Law of 1979. In 1979 it won 13 of the 21 *Landsting* seats and formed a government under its chairman, the Lutheran pastor Jonathan Motzfeldt. In 1982 it successfully campaigned for Greenland to leave the European Community in 1985. Its *Folketing* representative works with SD. Motzfeldt remained prime minister until 1991, when he was replaced by Lars Emil Johansen, who succeeded as the party's leader. In the 1991 elections Siumut won 37.3% of the vote and 11 of the 27 seats, increasing its number of seats to 13 in 1995. Siumut's *Folketing* representative is Hans-Pavia Rosing.

NATIONAL PROSPECTS

Venstre and KF repaired the rift in their relationship caused by the 1992 Tamil affair, but Venstre remained the stronger in public opinion. In the 1998 election they challenged SD with a center-right coalition that avoided the 1994 mistake of including the far right, thereby attracting the label "the black Cabinet," but their task of constructing a coherent opposition was complicated by the flow of votes to the Danish People's Party. SD retained its governing status, able to draw on parliamentary support from socialist and center parties.

The Treaty of European Union, rejected in 1992, was accepted in 1993. Although Danes still have reservations about European political union, their political leaders are generally more enthusiastic. With EU membership for Finland and Sweden from 1995, Denmark's bridging task between the EU and her Nordic sister countries is no longer so large, although it is still useful to Iceland and Norway. The prominence of the "foreigner" issue in the 1998 election raised doubts whether Denmark will proceed with the Schengen Agreement to end border controls before the end of the 20th century. Danes want the "wider" Europe that follows from expansion of NATO and the EU to include some of the countries of Central Europe, bringing new trading opportunities that Denmark is well placed to exploit. In the Danish view, both international organizations provide a desirably wider context in which to manage relations with their large and powerful southern neighbor, Germany.

Further Reading

Bille, Lars. "Denmark." In *Party Organizations: A Data Handbook on Party Organizations in Western Democracies, 1960–90*. Ed. Richard S. Katz and Peter Mair. London: Sage, 1992.

———. "Denmark: The Decline of the Membership Party?" In *How Parties Organize: Change and Adaptation in Party Organizations in Western Democracies*. Ed. Richard S. Katz and Peter Mair. London: Sage, 1994.

Cave, William, and Per Himmelstrup. *The Welfare Society in Transition: Problems and Prospects of the Welfare Model*. Copenhagen: Danish Cultural Institute, 1994.

Christiansen, Niels Finn. "Denmark: End of an Idyll?" In *Mapping the West European Left*. Ed. Perry Anderson and Patrick Camiller. New York: Verso, 1996.

Hix, Simon, and Christopher Lord. *Political Parties in the European Union*. London: Macmillan, 1997.

Jones, W. Glyn. *Denmark: A Modern History*. London: Croom Helm, 1986.

Lyck, Lise, ed. *Denmark and EC Membership Evaluated*. New York: St. Martin's Press, 1992.

———, ed. *Socio-economic Developments in Greenland and in Other Small Nordic Jurisdictions*. Copenhagen: Copenhagen Business School, New Social Science Monographs, 1997.

Miles, Lee, ed. *The European Union and the Nordic Countries*. London and New York: Routledge, 1996.

Miller, Kenneth E. *Friends and Rivals: Coalition Politics in Denmark, 1901–1995*. New York: University Press of America, 1996.

Pedersen, Mogens N. "The Danish 'Working Multi-Party System': Breakdown or Adaptation?" In *Party Systems in Denmark, Austria, Switzerland, the Netherlands and Belgium*. Ed. Hans Daalder. London: Pinter 1987.

Pedersen, Mogens N., and Lars Bille. "Public Financing and Public Control of Political Parties in Denmark." In *The Public Purse and Political Parties: Public Financing of Political Parties in Nordic Countries*. Ed. Matti Wiberg. Helsinki: The Finnish Political Science Association, 1991.

Svensson, Palle. "Denmark: the Referendum as Minority Protection." In *The Referendum Experience in Europe*. Ed. Michael Gallagher and Pier Vincenzo Uleri. New York: Macmillan and St. Martin's Press, 1996.

REPUBLIC OF DJIBOUTI

By Yomi Durotoye, Ph.D.

The Republic of Djibouti, which became independent on June 27, 1977, was formerly known as French Somaliland and later the French Territory of the Afars and the Issas. The official languages are Arabic and French. This small and semiarid country by the coast occupies 8,880 square miles and is strategically located at the southern entrance of the Red Sea. Ethiopia bounds it on the west and southwest, while Somalia is to the southeast and the Republic of Eritrea to the north. There are two main ethnic groups in the country: the Issa, who are a Somali clan, constitute 50% of the 580,000 population (1995 estimate), while the Afar, who are of Ethiopian origin, constitute 40%. The remaining 10% of the population are the Arab, Issaq, and Gadabursi minorities. The Issa and Afar, who are Muslims, both speak related Cushitic dialects.

Djibouti at independence adopted the French presidential system of government. Thus, the president holds the executive authority and is nationally elected for a six-year period. Legislative functions are carried out by a 65-member, unicameral Chamber of Deputies, elected for a five-year tenure, while the Council of Ministers, led by a prime minister, administers the country.

Hassan Gouled Aptidon, an Issa and the leader of the interethnic political movement that spearheaded the demands for independence, the African People's League for Independence (*Ligue populaire africaine pour l'independence*; LPAI) became the first president of the republic on June 27, 1977. The hopes that Djibouti would remain a competitive democracy and that the LPAI would continue to serve as a unifying force for all ethnic groups were dashed when Gouled replaced the LPAI with the Popular Rally for Progress (RPP), which he personally dominated. Within months, most senior Afar ministers resigned. After this, violence between the Afar and Issa erupted.

In October 1981, the RPP was officially declared the sole legal party after Gouled won another six-year term in a presidential election in which he ran unopposed. Opposition to Gouled led to years of fighting, and by April 1991, Afar resistance movements had coalesced into a more powerful armed opposition group called the Front for the Restoration of Unity and Democracy (FRUD), which signaled the beginning of a civil war in earnest.

Attempts at reconciliation yielded mixed results. In

September 1992, the government accepted the results of a referendum, which was boycotted by the opposition, in which 96% of the voters were said to have ratified a new constitution. By March 1994, military pressures on the FRUD resulted in its split, and subsequently a branch of it led by Ougoureh Kifleh Ahmed and Ali Mohamed Daoud entered into a rapprochement with the Gouled regime. The two won Cabinet positions, and the FRUD was officially recognized in March 1996.

Nevertheless, opposition to the regime grew. Between May 1995 and May 1996, the regime had to contend with several union-inspired demonstrations against government economic policies. Some of these were violently repressed. In 1996, the struggle for succession among leading members of the government, such as President Gouled's nephew Ismael Guelleh and the justice minister, Moumin Farrah, led to a split in the ruling party. To contain this crisis, President Gouled sacked some of the ambitious officials and announced that he intended to remain in office until 1999.

The head of state is the president and commander in chief of the armed forces. Hassan Gouled Aptidon has occupied this position since June 27, 1977. The head of government is the prime minister, who heads the Council of Ministers, which has 15 other members. Barkad Gourad Hamadou holds this post and concurrently serves as the minister of planning.

In accordance with the 1992 constitution, four political parties are officially recognized.

Popular Rally for Progress (*Rassemblement populaire pour le progres*; RPP) is the ruling party, and until 1992, it was the sole party in the country. Formed in March 1979 in an attempt by LPAI to broaden its popular support, the RPP is socialist in its programs and organization. The party is run by a political bureau selected by the party chairman, who also happens to be the state president, Hassan Gouled Aptidon. Prime Minister Barkat Gourad is the first deputy chairman of the party.

The Front for the Restoration of Unity and Democracy (*Front pour la restauration de l'unite et de la democratie*; FRUD) is composed mainly of the Afar. FRUD is a political and military organization that was founded in 1991 as an armed group against the government. It is dedicated to promoting multipartism and democracy as well as vigorously resisting ethnic domination of national politics. It has since split over strategy. Its leader is Ali Mohammed Dauod.

The Party of Democratic Renewal (*Parti de renouveau democratique*; PRD) was founded and led by Mohamed Djama Elabe in 1992 and is committed to the establishment of democracy in Djibouti. It was the first official opposition party recognized by the government and the only party to contest the ruling RPP party in the legislative elections of December 1992. It won 25% of the vote but was allocated no seats.

The National Democratic Party (*Parti national democratique*; PND) was founded in 1992 by Aden Awalleh. It seeks to terminate one-party rule and stands for the formation of a government of national unity to be followed by multipartism. It is led by Aden Robleh Awalleh.

In addition to these four parties, several mostly officially unrecognized opposition groups exist. The Front for the Restoration of Right and Equality (*Front pour la Restauration du Droit et de l'Egalite*; FRDE), which was founded by Mohammed Soule in 1991, seeks the forceful removal of the ruling government. The Djibouti Democratic Union (*Union Democratique Djiboutienne*; UDD), founded in 1992, is led by Mahdi God and Mohammed Moussa. It promotes a national conference of all political groups in order to draft a new constitution and organize elections. The Front of Democratic Forces (*Front de Forces Democratique*; FFD) was founded by Omar Kareem, who is an Issa. The Democratic Union for Justice and Equality in Djibouti (*Union Democratique pour la Justice et l'Egalite Djiboutienne*; UDJED) is an armed resistance party founded by Abdallah Deberkaleh Ahmed

in 1988. It is allied with the FRUD. The Djibouti People's Party (*Parti Populaire Djiboutienne*; PPD), which was founded in 1981, attracts mostly the section of Afar leadership that seeks cooperation with the Issa-dominated regime. Hence, members have included such well-known Afar figures as the former prime ministers Mohammed Issa, Moussa Idris Ahmed Dini Ahmed, and Abdallah Kamil.

The ethnic composition and geographic location of this small country have made it of strategic interest to powerful neighbors and extracontinental powers. Since shortly after independence, the Afar and the Issa have engaged in conflicts that were largely generated by the cold war–inspired tensions in the Horn of Africa, discriminatory French colonial policies, and the struggle for power by the Issa and Afar political elite.

The civil wars have left the economy bankrupt, and recent changes in French policy toward Africa have led to a decline in foreign aid. However, this development does not pose any threat to President Gouled's regime and his plan to hand over power to his nephew Ismael Omar Gelleh, nor does the opposition, which is in disarray. It is reasonable to predict that in the long run, a combination of domestic political, military, and economic pressures as well as political changes in the region will enforce political liberalization on the country.

Further Reading

Schraeder, Peter J. *Djibouti*. Oxford University Press: Oxford: Clio Press, 1990.

Thompson, Virginia McLean. *Djibouti and the Horn of Africa*. Stanford, Calif.: Stanford University Press, 1968.

DOMINICA

By Thomas D. Anderson, Ph.D.

THE SYSTEM OF GOVERNMENT

Dominica is an island country of 740 square kilometers that lies in the Windward Islands of the Caribbean between Guadeloupe and Martinique. Its population of about 88,000 is largely black and English-speaking with an annual growth rate of 1.4% and a literacy rate of 94%. It is a parliamentary democracy that became independent from Britain in 1973, after more than a decade of self-rule as an Associated State. It is a volcanic island with a largely rural population, although only about 20% of the area is devoted to crops. Bananas are the chief export.

Executive

The head of government is a president elected to a five-year term by the House of Assembly after being jointly nominated by the leaders of the majority and opposition parties. The powers of the president are largely formal. Real executive power belongs to the prime minister, who is the leader of the House majority.

Legislature

The legislature is unicameral, with a House of Assembly that has 21 members elected to five-year terms and nine appointees. Five of the latter are appointed by the prime minister and four by the leader of the opposition. The number of elected members can be changed by an independent Constituency Boundaries Commission. Party discipline is strict and government bills in the House seldom are voted down.

Until June 1979, power had been held by the Dominican Labour Party (DLP), a democratic socialist party led by Patrick John. A series of scandals up to that time caused John to step down, and the House chose Oliver Seraphin, a John associate, to lead a caretaker government and prepare for new elections. By the time elections were held in July 1980, the Seraphin government also was tainted by scandal. The Democratic Freedom Party (DFP) led by Eugenia Charles then won overwhelmingly, capturing 17 of the 21 seats. The remaining four seats were split between independent candidates and Seraphin's Dominican Democratic Labour Party (DDLP). The discredited DLP was shut out.

In the July 1985 elections, the DFP remained in control despite a strong challenge from a reunited DLP. The DFP won 59% of the vote but lost two seats to the DLP, which won five seats.

Judiciary

The judicial system is based on English common law and is part of the Eastern Caribbean Supreme Court, one of whose judges sits in Dominica.

Regional and Local Government

The only subnational governments are partially elected town and village councils that manage local affairs.

THE PARTY SYSTEM

The first election to be contested by political parties was in 1961. The oldest party, the DLP, had its origins in the organized labor movement. The Democratic Freedom Party developed largely in reaction to the policies of the DLP, particularly advocacy of land reform and independence. Party organization has been relatively loose, and parties do not have formal membership. This casual approach appears to be changing, at least within the DFP. Images, if not the realities, of the the two oldest parties are that the DLP is more sympathetic to communist governments (read Cuba), whereas the DFP is criticized for "slavish" ties to Washington.

DEMOCRATIC FREEDOM PARTY (DFP)

The DFP draws its leadership from the middle classes and traditionally has represented landowners. In the 1980 election it successfully appealed to the rural poor with promises to improve the economy. Founded in 1970, it consistently supported pro-Western, anticommunist policies. As prime minister, Eugenia Charles was a leader in organizing the 1983 armed overthrow of the Marxist government of Grenada. Early in 1995, Charles, at age 76, turned over party leadership to Brian Alleyne. The party's financial strength and influence with the press provide ample leverage at election time.

DOMINICAN LABOUR PARTY (DLP)

The DLP was founded by Phyllis Shand Allfrey, a Fabian socialist who drew considerable inspiration from the British Labour Party. Its initial electoral success was based on promises of land reform and improvement of conditions on banana plantations and docks. Two other of its charismatic leaders were Edward O. LeBlanc (1970–75) and Patrick John (1975–80). In 1981, John was arrested on charges of conspiring to overthrow the government, a coup that was to be carried out by hired American soldiers of fortune. He was replaced as party leader by Michael Douglas. Following his arrest, John founded the United Dominica Labour Party (UDLP) as a vehicle of his personal ambition and was its sole candidate in the 1985 elections. Even though he won a seat in the House, he later was sentenced to 12 years in jail on the charge of conspiracy to overthrow the government.

UNITED WORKERS PARTY (UWP)

The UWP, a comparatively recent party, is headed by Edison James, whose policies lie somewhat between the two traditional parties. His party swept to power in the June 1995 general election, ending 15 years of rule by Eugenia Charles and the DFP. By winning 11 of 21 elected seats, the UWP received a clear mandate, but an even split between the other two parties complicated matters because the constitution states that only one party can be the officially designated opposition. This issue finally was settled with the designation of the Dominican Labour Party (DLP), and its head, Rosie Douglas, became opposition leader of the House.

NATIONAL PROSPECTS

The victory of the UWP can be attributed, at least in part, to the country's economic uncertainty during the mid-1990s. International pressures to end import privileges for West Indian bananas into Europe threatened one of the country's main foreign exchange earners, and the still-unsettled status of the NFTA has inhibited attraction of outside investments. In addition, a poorly developed road network and lack of a large modern airport have hampered expansion of a competitive tourist industry. Dominica is poor (GDP per capita of $2,990 US) and is likely to remain so.

Further Reading

Caribbean Week: The Regional Newspaper of the Caribbean. St. Michael, Barbados.
CIA World Factbook. Washington, D.C.: Government Printing Office, various years.

DOMINICAN REPUBLIC

(República Dominicana)

By Rolando A. Alum, Jr.
Revised by James Wessman, Ph.D.

THE SYSTEM OF GOVERNMENT

The Dominican Republic, a Caribbean nation of over 7 million people, occupies the eastern two-thirds (over 44,000 square kilometers) of the island Columbus named Hispaniola, which it shares with the Republic of Haiti. Across the Mona Passage to the east lies Puerto Rico. Almost three-fourths of the population is of mixed descent; about 16% are Caucasian and 11% are Black. In spite of a moderately high birth rate and low death rate, the population is in slight decline, due to emigration. An estimated 90% of the population is Roman Catholic, but there are other Christian denominations such as Evangelical and Adventist Churches, as well as Jewish synagogues. Some Dominicans practice African religions, often simultaneously with these other religions.

This country, a unitary, multiparty, democratic state with a strong president, has had a history of political instability, undergoing foreign domination and invasions, native dictatorships, civil wars, and revolutions. Despite remarkable stability and social and economic development achieved between the mid-1960s and the mid-1980s, the last decade has been especially difficult, with pent-up internal pressures stemming from over 60 years of fairly continuous political rule, running from Trujillo (1930–61) through Balaguer (1966–78, 1986–96).

The United States occupied the Dominican Republic from 1916 to 1924. There followed six years of relatively democratic experimentation, until a mulatto army officer of humble origins, Rafael Trujillo, took power in 1930 with the support of the army and a coalition of political forces. Trujillo, while preserving a facade of constitutional legitimacy, ruled with an iron fist for 31 years, with a single political party, the Dominican Party. In May 1961, he was assassinated by underground opposition forces.

Trujillo's dictatorship was followed by a succession of temporary governments, notably the election of Juan Bosch in 1962, and various provisional civilian-military juntas until April 1965, when a new coup triggered a civil war that was largely limited to the capital city of Santo Domingo on the southern coast. The fratricidal conflict ended when joint military forces of the Organization of American States (OAS) and the United States intervened.

In new elections held in 1966 under close international supervision, Dr. Joaquín Balaguer, head of the Reformist Party (PRef), an intellectual and Trujillo protegé, defeated Bosch by a two-to-one margin, thus inaugurating the 12-year "pax Balagueriana." Balaguer was reelected in 1970 and 1974 but lost in 1978 to a renewed PRD, which also won the 1982 elections.

Antonio Guzmán became the first presidential candidate of the PRD to gain the presidency since Juan Bosch. Guzmán's administration suffered the international financial crisis of the late 1970s that forced his administration, as well as that of his successor, Salvador Jorge Blanco, to adopt strict measures that led to popular unrest. Guzmán pledged not to seek reelection, and shortly before leaving office, he committed suicide. Jacobo Majluta served briefly as president, handing the office over to Salvador Jorge Blanco, also of the PRD, in 1982. Blanco's administration was plagued by corruption, and after leaving office, he was convicted of corruption; in 1992 he was sentenced to 20 years in prison.

Balaguer returned to power in 1986 as the candidate of the reorganized Reformist Social Christian Party (PRSC) and remained president until 1996. In that year, Dr. Leonel Fernández, representing the Party of Dominican Liberation (PLD), formed by Bosch in 1973 after his split from the PRD, was elected, defeating PRD candidate José Francisco Peña Gómez in a runoff.

Executive

Executive power is exercised by the president with the assistance of a vice president and various secretaries of state, the latter named by the president. These secretaries of state, however, are defined by law and therefore may change in number and identity over time. Typically, there are about 15 secretaries of state.

The president is head of public administration and commander in chief of the armed forces and police corps. The president has a great deal of power, in part through the initiative of proposing the budget but also due to the heritage of the Trujillo-Balaguer years. Balaguer, for example, directly controlled about half the national budget. It remains to be seen what will happen when the president's political party does not control either body of Congress.

Starting with the 1996 election, to be victorious a presidential candidate requires 50% plus one vote of the votes cast. Otherwise, a second round is required, pitting only the top two candidates against each other. As indicated above, a second round was required in 1996, in which a candidate with little support in Congress was elected.

Legislature

Legislative power is exercised by a bicameral Congress consisting of a Senate and a Chamber of Deputies. Legislators are elected directly for four-year terms and may not simultaneously hold any other public office. The Senate has 30 members, 1 for each province and the National District, Santo Domingo. The 120 deputies are elected from the provinces, with at least 2 from each province, in the ratio of 1 deputy for each 150,000 inhabitants or fractions of more than 25,000. Both chambers convene on February 27 and August 16, both national holidays, for legislative periods of 90 days, which may be extended.

Senators elect the president and other members of the Central Electoral Board (*Junta Central Electoral*), as well as members of the Chamber of Accounts (*Cámara de Cuentas*). They must act on diplomatic nominations from the executive branch and on accusations formulated in the Chamber of Deputies against public officials.

Proposed laws can be introduced by senators, deputies, the president, the Supreme Court (in judicial affairs), and the Central Electoral Board (in electoral affairs). Traditionally, legislative initiative has come from the president, but this may change now that the Trujillo-Balaguer era is at an end.

Judiciary

The Supreme Court consists of at least 11 judges, named by the National Council of the Magistrate, which is presided over by the president, with representatives from the Senate and Chamber of Deputies and the Supreme Court itself. The Supreme Court elects its own president. As noted above, the Supreme Court may initiate legislation in judicial matters. In addition, there are nine Courts of Appeal, a Land Tribunal, courts of first instance in each judicial district, and judges of the peace.

Regional and Local Government

Each of the provinces is headed by a governor appointed by the president. There are no provincial legislatures, and the provinces have little financial independence. The provinces are subdivided into municipalities, each headed by a *síndico* (mayor) and a municipal council, both elected every four years.

The National District, which has almost 30% of the national population, is a separate entity, also headed by an elected *síndico*. It has great influence in national affairs, as evidenced by the prominence of Jorge Blanco and Jacobo Majluta as senators who became president and vice president, respectively, of the republic and by José Francisco Peña Gómez, who served as *síndico* of Santo Domingo and in several campaigns stood as the presidential candidate of the PRD.

THE ELECTORAL SYSTEM

Elections for national and local offices are held concurrently every four years on May 16. All citizens 18 years of age or over (or those younger if married) are eligible to vote. It is estimated that at least 90% of eligible voters are registered, a high proportion by Latin American standards. According to the constitution, voting is compulsory, but this provision apparently is not enforced. Turnout commonly runs above 73% of registered voters.

Election days are national holidays, and the people treat the event as a festive occasion. Selected police and military personnel are assigned to safeguard the polling places and the ballots; all other military personnel are confined to barracks. Active members of the armed forces and police may not vote.

Voters are presented with two ballots for each party—one for local offices, the Chamber of Deputies, and the Senate and one for the presidency. The ballots are color-coded to indicate the party; this practice continues from times when most adult Dominicans were illiterate. Senators and deputies are elected by direct vote.

The electoral system suffered a conjunctural shock after the bitter 1994 presidential election. Balaguer was induced to limit his term to two years. Consequently, a new president was elected in 1996, but congressional elections were held in 1998. At some point, the two elections, congressional and presidential, must be returned to the same four-year cycle.

THE PARTY SYSTEM

Origins of the Parties

Political parties began to develop in the late 19th and early 20th centuries, but foreign intervention and Trujillo's one-party system prevented the full development of other political parties. Although some of the contemporary parties claim to have roots in pre-Trujillo times and some were founded during the Trujillo period, none became effectively functioning entities until after the Trujillo dictatorship. Furthermore, most have gone through sweeping changes in leadership and cadre so that with the partial exception of the PRD, the present parties cannot be clearly associated with those existing before 1961. In the 1980s, the Dominican Republic seemed headed toward a two-party system (PRef and PRD), but in the 1990s the PLD established itself as a contender, winning the presidency in 1996.

The Parties in Law

The constitution declares that the organization of political parties shall not be restricted. A party may register with the government and appear on the ballot by the relatively simple process of filing a petition with a minimal number of signatures of qualified voters. A party must win at least 10% of the popular vote or repeat the petitioning process. These parties may appear, disappear, and reappear at four-year intervals.

Party Organization

The major parties are effectively organized, with dues-paying members in localities nationwide, and run candidates in local elections. Most parties also have a formal structure with democratic procedures for the naming of delegates to the national conventions and for choosing candidates for office. In practice, the parties have been dominated for significant periods by individual leaders—the PRef and PRSC by Balaguer, the PLD by Bosch. All parties have been rocked by internal dissension that has sometimes resulted in public scandals and/or the creation of new parties.

Another feature of the Dominican system is the appearance in election years of alliance parties and of parties established as the independent personal vehicles of politicians usually associated with one of the major parties. In the 1982 elections, for example, six leftist parties established the Unified Left (*Izquierda Unida*) with Rafael Tavares as their presidential candidate. José Rafael Abinader, normally associated with the PRD, used the Social Democratic Alliance (*Alianza Social Democrática*) to support his presidential candidacy; after the election he was appointed finance minister in the new PRD government.

In recent years, the political parties have moved away from their earlier formulations, in which ideology remained vague and the personal views of their leaders, rather than the formal party platform, determined the parties' positions along the left-right spectrum. Members of the national elite may be found in the top leadership of all the parties, no matter how radical. All social classes are represented in all the parties.

Campaigning

Campaigning has become strident, expensive, and professionalized. Vast amounts are spent on marketing strategies based on polling. Radio and rallies constitute the primary means for reaching voters. Caravans, posters, and party decorations make campaigning quite colorful. In recent decades, Dominican parties have sought the prestige of political figures from abroad to support their campaigns. Most campaigns and elections have been marked by violence and judicial and electoral irregularities, although these appeared in decline after the late 1970s until the contentious 1994 presidential election.

REFORMIST PARTY/REFORMIST SOCIAL CHRISTIAN PARTY

(Partido Reformista; PRef)

(Partido Reformista Social Cristiano; PRSC)

The PRSC is the result of the amalgamation of the old Reformist Party, which Balaguer represented as president in the 1960s and 1970s, and the Revolutionary Social Christian Party. The net result in name was to substitute "reformist" for "revolutionary." To comprehend this political entity, it is necessary to know something about the histories of the respective parties that came together to form the PRSC.

The Reformist Party was founded by Balaguer while in exile in New York in 1964. The party grew rapidly, won the 1966 elections, and increasingly consolidated its power during the 12 years of Balaguer's rule, leading up to 1978. Nevertheless, rampant corruption and ostentation, neglect of the needs of the countryside, police and military heavy-handedness, and Balaguer's dominating style, age, and ill health caused party support to decline before 1978 and to diminish still further in 1982.

Although the party has maintained a representative democratic structure rising from local party organizations to the national conference, for most of its history it was effectively dominated by Balaguer, whose personality and political astuteness held the party factions together. Balaguer's dominant position was clearly illustrated in 1978, when Fernando Alvarez Boegart was nominated as the party's vice presidential candidate by democratic processes, only to be later replaced at Balaguer's order. In 1982, Alvarez Boegart again won the party's nomination, but Balaguer was not able to unseat him a second time.

The PRef's ideology was vaguely centrist and democratic. In 1981, Balaguer declared the party to be Christian Democrat, which facilitated the merger with the old PRSC. Factions within the party ran all the way from former Trujillo supporters to democratic socialists, although moderates were the strongest force. Balaguer's administrations emphasized rapid economic development, which was largely based on foreign aid and investment. The program benefited urban areas but neglected crucial rural interests.

The PRef's greatest liability was the unwillingness of its founder to permit the development of a capable leadership to succeed him. Joaquín Balaguer, born in 1908, became partially blind, deaf, and in evident ill health. The merger with the old PRSC provided new options for leadership, but the party's 1996 presidential candidate, Jacinto Peyando, ran a poor third behind Fernández and Peña Gómez.

The Revolutionary Social Christian Party emerged after Trujillo's assassination in 1961. Heavily influenced by the most progressive elements of Catholicism, the party's ideology was a complex center-left doctrine that rejected the excesses of both capitalism and Marxism-Leninism. The party developed close ties with the Autonomous Confederation of Christian Syndicates (CASC), which controls the all-important unions of sugar workers. A multiclass party, the PRSC also had great appeal to intellectuals and students, and it was noted for the efforts it made to impart its ideology to youth. In spite of its strong Catholic background, many of the PRSC leaders were Protestants.

In the 1960s, it appeared that the PRSC was going to become a significant force in Dominican politics. However, from a solid third place in the 1962 elections, it slipped to a poor fourth place in 1978, as the electorate polarized behind the PRD and the PRef. During Balaguer's last term in the 1970s, some PRSC leaders accepted government positions, especially in the diplomatic corps, and Balaguer then proposed a merger of the PRef and PRSC. Although the party supported Balaguer in the 1982 elections, the merger did not occur until the 1986 elections. The political marriage brought the ideology and international connections of the old PRSC together with the voting support of the PRef.

Balaguer obviously benefited from this merger in the 1986 and 1990 elections, but the party did not develop visible successors to Balaguer. A costly and controversial symbol of his declining years was Columbus Lighthouse in Santo Domingo, built to attract visitors to the island in 1992 in commemoration of the Columbian Quincentenary. Although Balaguer again won for the PRSC in 1994, this election was so controversial, with widely believed accusations of fraud, that Balaguer was forced to accept an abbreviated term of office, with a new election in 1996 under a new constitution and electoral rules.

In this election, Balaguer withheld his support of Jacinto Peyando, the PRSC candidate, so that he ran a distant third in the first round of the election in May and was eliminated from the second round. Subsequently, Balaguer worked out an alliance with the PLD, called the National Patriotic Front, in which the PRSC sup-

ported the PLD's candidate, Leonel Fernández, in the second round. This campaign featured joint appearances of Balaguer and Bosch with Fernández, with the old bitter rivals embracing at the end of the program. Although some have questioned Balaguer's motives and strategy, it is clear that his actions kept José Francisco Peña Gómez from reaching the nation's highest office. In addition, the PRSC had 50 deputies and 14 senators, so that the National Patriotic Front had a majority in the Chamber of Deputies and exactly half the membership of the Senate.

In contrast, the PRD had the same number of deputies as the PRSC, and 2 fewer senators, but with its allies came close to matching the National Patriotic Front. The congressional elections of May 1998 tested the alliance between the PRSC and the PLD. In that election, the PRD won clear majorities of seats in the Chamber of Deputies (83 of 149) and the Senate (24 of 30), while the PRSC was reduced to a poorly performing third party. Fernández's party, the PLD, won almost a third of the deputies (49) but only 4 senatorial seats. Thus the PRD is well poised for the presidential election to be held in 2000.

DOMINICAN REVOLUTIONARY PARTY
(Partido Revolucionario Dominicano; PRD)

The PRD was founded in Havana in 1939 by a group of anti-Trujillo exiles, among whom was Juan Bosch. It was in more than one way a copy of the populist Cuban Revolutionary Party (PRC), better known as the *Auténticos*, which reached power in 1944. The PRD became the PRC's protégé until Batista's coup in 1952. When Rómulo Betancourt won the presidency of Venezuela in 1959, most of the PRD leadership went there.

The PRD did not become active on Dominican soil until after Trujillo's demise. In the first free elections (1962), Bosch became the winning presidential candidate against the National Civic Union (*Unión Cívica Nacional*; UCN). His administration received the enthusiastic support of U.S. President John F. Kennedy. Bosch imported foreign talent from among his Latin American friends, including Cubans exiled by Fidel Castro. After the military coup that deposed him in 1963, Bosch went to Puerto Rico as a guest of Governor Muñoz Marín. Bosch returned after the civil war of 1965, in which the PRD was an active participant, and ran unsuccessfully against Balaguer in 1966.

In 1970, the PRD abstained from the elections, claiming lack of civil liberties. By then Bosch had repudiated the traditional idea of representative democracy and proposed a "dictatorship with popular support." This policy alienated many PRD members, especially the founders. In 1973, Bosch finally walked out of the PRD, founding the

PLD. The PRD leadership fell to its secretary general, José Francisco Peña Gómez.

For the 1974 elections, the PRD organized an opposition coalition called the *Acuerdo* [Accord] *de Santiago*, embracing seven parties. Guzmán was the candidate for the presidency and General Elías Wessin for the vice presidency. Wessin had been the leader of the anti-Bosch coup in 1963 and of the anti-Constitutionalist and anti-Bosch forces in the 1965 civil war. At the last minute, the coalition, with the exception of one group, withdrew from the elections, charging Balaguer with "colossal fraud." In 1978, the party finally defeated Balaguer by itself with a wide margin that elected Guzmán president and Majluta vice president.

The PRD that came to power in 1978 was very different from the earlier party. The well-dressed *Perredeistas* (PRDers) who paraded or drove expensive cars along Santo Domingo's ocean drive, waving the PRD's symbolic white flag in celebration, little resembled the *campesinos* who followed Bosch in 1962 or the students who revolted in 1965.

After the return of Joaquín Balaguer to the presidency in 1986, PRD's opposition focused on Dr. José Francisco Peña Gómez, "the Dominican Horatio Alger." Peña Gómez rose from humble roots to become a radio commentator, first on sports and later for the PRD. After following Bosch into exile in 1963, Peña Gómez returned to Santo Domingo as secretary-general of the PRD. Active in the rebellion in 1965, Peña Gómez again went into exile in 1966, when Balaguer was elected, and did graduate work in France.

Peña Gómez was elected mayor of Santo Domingo in 1982 and served in the 1980s as a vice president of the Socialist International. He seemed to have a bright future in Dominican politics, in spite of the fact that he is Black. Rumors of Haitian ancestry and even of a desire to unite Haiti and the Domincan Republic politically have been particularly damaging in a society in which fear and distrust of Haitians have been a major theme.

In 1994, Peña Gómez ran for the presidency of the Dominican Republic, losing to Balaguer, now representing the PRSC. This election was marked by irregularities that led to a congressional ruling limiting Balaguer's term to two years. Peña Gómez again was the PRD candidate in 1996 and won more votes than any other candidate in the first round of the election, but he failed to obtain the required majority. In the runoff or second round, the alliance of the PRCS and the PLD gave the election to Leonel Fernández.

Late in 1996, Peña Gómez became seriously ill and was hospitalized in the United States. In order to prepare his party for the 1998 congressional elections, Peña Gómez decided not to seek further public office, thus opening the way for other PRD candidates to make themselves better known across the country. He died in May of 1998.

DOMINICAN LIBERATION PARTY
(Partido de la Liberación Dominicana; PLD)

Bosch founded the PLD after abandoning the PRD in 1973. For much of its history, the PLD was dominated by Bosch. Because the party seemed a personalistic organization, it was given little chance of achieving major status in Dominican politics. The party received only 18,000 votes in the 1978 election and had to go through the registration process again to reestablish its legal status. In the 1982 elections, however, the PLD won nearly 10% of the vote and emerged as a third force in Dominican politics. In 1986, the PLD received 18% of the popular vote for president, and in 1990 it did very well, but it fell to 13% in 1994. New party leadership brought the PLD to its victory in the 1996 presidential election.

The 1996 election was the first in Dominican history in which the winner had to receive at least 50% plus one vote. Since the PRD's Peña Gómez failed to achieve that number in the first round, a second round was held, also for the first time in Dominican history. Leonel Fernández, who was the PLD's vice presidential candidate in 1994, won the presidency in 1996 with 51% of the popular vote, but he is not supported by corresponding majorities in Congress. His vice president is Jaime David Fernández Mirabal (no relation), a nephew of the Mirabal sisters murdered during Trujillo's regime.

Fernández provides a new model for Dominican leadership. Not only has he inherited a party created in the old personalistic mode, but he spent part of his early years in the United States and speaks fluent English. His priorities—to modernize and globalize the Dominican Republic—establish him as a technocrat. One sign of his leadership has been the emphasis upon collecting taxes due the government, which is not an issue with high voter appeal. Although he has been besieged in Congress by opposition parties, his international participation, such as his speech to the United Nations, suggests that he will find it easier to collaborate with other leaders in the Caribbean and Latin America than was the case with Balaguer.

The PLD followed the example of the PRD in creating a strong hierarchical organization that demands a great deal of its members. The party offers study circles (*C'rculos de Estudio*) to provide political education for members and has base committees and intermediate committees, as well as a political committee of 11 members and a central committee of 105 members. Its congress meets every four years to select members of the central committee.

MINOR POLITICAL PARTIES

The 1994 and 1996 elections established the PRSC, PLD, and PRD as the primary parties of Dominican politics, and the rules of the game will make it difficult for minor parties to have much say. These parties, however, were among those that participated in the May 1996 presidential election.

Independent Revolutionary Party
(Partido Revolucionario Independiente; PRI)

The PRI is a splinter party from the PRD, founded by Jacobo Majluta in 1985. Majluta was Guzmán's vice president and served briefly as president after Guzmán's suicide. Although the PRI has no deputies or senators, it achieved enough votes in the presidential election to remain registered as a political party. Majluta remains its leader.

Democratic Unity Party
(Partido de la Unidad Democrática; UD)

Democratic Unity supported the PRD in 1994 with seven deputies and three senators. It also made a respectable showing in the May 1996 presidential election, with over 66,000 votes, roughly the difference between the PRD and the PLD. Its leader is Luis Homero Lájara Burgos.

Christian People's Party
(Partido Popular Cristiano; PPC)

The PPC, which has one deputy in the Dominican Congress, won fewer than 7,000 votes in May 1996.

Democratic Quisqueyan Party
(Partido Quisqueyano Demócrata; PQD)

General Elías Wessin y Wessin, leader of the anti-Bosch forces in 1963 and 1965, founded the PQD in 1968. (Quisqueya is the indigenous name of the island.) Implicated in a plot to overthrow Balaguer in 1973, Wessin was exiled for five years. In 1974, he ran as the vice presidential candidate of the Santiago Accord alliance. In 1982, running alone, Wessin received less than 2% of the vote. Although he had some support in the officer corps, this declined with the passing of time.

Currently the PQD has one deputy in the Congress but performed poorly in the 1996 presidential election. Its leaders are Pedro Bergés and Dr. Elías Wessin Chávez, the latter the son of the party's founder.

Other parties participating in this election are the Institutional Democratic Party (*Partido Democrático Institucional*; PDI), the National Party of Veterans and Civilians (*Partido Nacional de Veteranos y Civiles*; PNVC), and the Dominican Social Alliance Party (*Partido Alianza Social Dominicana*; ASD. In addition, the Social Democratic Institutional Block (*Bloque Institucional Social Demócrata*; BIS) and the Democratic Arrangement (*Concertación Democrática*; DC) fielded candidates. The latter two also have representation in the Chamber of Deputies, as do the National Progressive Force (*Fuerza Nacional Progresista*; FNP), the Dominican Workers' Party (*Partido de los Trabajadores Dominicanos*; PTD), and "The Structure" Liberal Party (*Partido Liberal la Estructura*; PLE).

OTHER POLITICAL FORCES

Considering the fairly late development of political parties in the Dominican Republic, perhaps it is not surprising that other political forces have also been late in emerging. The Roman Catholic Church has not been as powerful as in other Latin American countries. The military, of course, is remembered for its role in the downfall of Juan Bosch and the subsequent civil war. More recently, nongovernmental organizations have been established, such as the Institute for Research, Documentation and Human Rights (*Instituto del Investigación, Documentación y Derechos Humanos*; IDH-RD) and the Action Group for Democracy (*Grupo de Acción por la Democracia*; GAD). The former was founded in 1986 and its executive director is Dr. Ramón B. Martínez Portorreal. The latter consists of representatives from business, unions, universities, and other associations. The growth of nongovernmental organizations, as elsewhere in the region, reflects the search for alternatives that do not depend exclusively on the political process.

NATIONAL PROSPECTS

Since 1966, the Dominican people have shown themselves capable of using their democratic freedom effectively to regularly elect governments by popular vote according to their own perceptions of their best interests. The principal parties seem to be committed to democratic procedures, civil rights, and peaceable alternation in power. While military figures and radical leftist groups have stood ready to take advantage of any serious crisis, the stability of the present system appears to be secure through the end of the century.

Much of the country's future depends upon the economy. The republic has been self-sufficient in basic needs and is potentially rich, but it suffers seriously when the prices of its export products decline. The worldwide recession of the early 1980s slowed the country's ability to deal with its social problems—illiteracy, poor public health facilities, substandard housing and housing shortages, unemployment, and the like. Sugar continues to dominate agriculture. President Reagan's Caribbean Basin Initiative offered little hope. There were street riots in 1984, which were replicated in neighboring Haiti, leading to the demise of the Duvalier regime.

The early 1990s represented a prolongation of the transition from dictatorship to democracy, with aging and infirm Joaquín Balaguer holding tenaciously onto power until 1996. But like the period between 1978 and 1986, the current situation seems to offer manifold opportunities for change. For example, the Central Electoral Board has proposed that Dominicans living abroad should be able to vote in presidential elections. Should this come to pass, the country's diaspora, especially the large Dominican population in the United States, could play a pivotal role in national politics, considering that the last presidential election was decided in a runoff by only 3 percentage points.

Of course, there are other dangers that are peculiar to Dominican politics. In order to force Balaguer from office, the Dominican Congress adopted a policy of no reelection for presidents, but forces within the PRSC have recently brought this question back to the table. The PRD has renewed its commitment to this principle, which seems necessary to guarantee peaceful alternation of power as vested in the presidency of the republic.

Another danger involves drug trafficking that uses the island for transshipment to markets in the United States and elsewhere. In an affront to Dominican sovereignty, the United States has sought to extradict drug dealers who, facing arrest on the mainland, have fled to the island. Thus the Dominican Republic faces both internal and external threats that will have a great deal to do with how it enters the 21st century.

Further Reading

Black, Jan Knippers. *The Dominican Republic: Politics and Development in an Unsovereign State.* Boulder, Colo.: Westview Press, 1990.

Cambeira, Alan. *Quisqueya La Bella: The Dominican Republic in Historical and Cultural Perspective.* Armonk, N.Y.: M.E. Sharpe, 1996.

Ferguson, James. *Dominican Republic: Beyond the Lighthouse.* New York: Monthly Review Press, 1992.

Kryzanek, Michael J., and Howard J. Wiarda. *Politics of External Influence in the Dominican Republic.* New York: Praeger, 1988.

Moya Pons, Frank. *The Dominican Republic: A National History.* Armonk, N.Y.: Hispaniola Books, 1994.

Palmer, Bruce. *Intervention in the Caribbean: The Dominican Crisis of 1965.* Lexington: University of Kentucky Press, 1990.

Vedocato, Claudio. *Politics, Foreign Trade, and Economic Development: A Study of the Dominican Republic*, vol. 1. New York: St. Martin's Press, 1986.

Wiarda, Howard J., and Michael J. Kryzanek. *The Dominican Republic: A Caribbean Crucible.* Boulder, Colo.: 1992.

REPUBLIC OF ECUADOR

(La República del Ecuador)

By David W. Schodt, Ph.D.

THE SYSTEM OF GOVERNMENT

Ecuador, a nation of 12 million people, is a republican, presidential democracy and a unitary state divided administratively into provinces, cantons, and parishes. There are separate executive, legislative, and judicial branches of government. Traditionally politics has been characterized by chronic instability and strong regional antagonisms. Since independence in 1830, Ecuador has had 18 constitutions; the most recent version was adopted in 1998[1]. Prior to the 1970s, Ecuador's weak political institutions and the generally low regard for democratic process among its elites led to a situation in which the average president served less than three years of what was a nominal four-year term. The petroleum boom of the 1970s dramatically transformed Ecuador's economy and ushered in a democratically elected government after nine years of nonconstitutional rule. Per capita incomes rose dramatically, and political participation broadened. In 1984, in spite of severe economic stress, this government presided over the first constitutional transfer of power from one democratically elected government to another since 1960. Subsequently, Ecuador has successfully navigated five successive democratic transitions. Nevertheless, the persistent weakness of Ecuador's democratic institutions, particularly of its party system, and the continuously elusive goal of sustainable economic growth pose considerable challenges for the country's political leaders. In 1997, elected president Assad Bucaram was removed from office and the country thrown into a constitutional crisis of succession.

Executive

The president of Ecuador is chosen by majority vote in direct popular elections for a four-year term and can be reelected only after a lapse of one term. Presidents must be Ecuadorian by birth, in full possession of citizenship rights, and at least 35 years of age at the time of election.

[1]The 1978 constitution was modified significantly in 1984 and 1996. These are referred to here as the 1984 and 1996 constitutions.

The vice president is elected simultaneously with the president and is subject to the same requirements. Following the adoption of the 1998 constitution, the future president will assume office on January 15 of the year following the election, a change from the traditional date of August 10.

The most recently elected president is Jamil Mahuad Witt (DP), who was sworn into office on August 10, 1998. His successful inauguration followed a period of deep political crisis, precipitated by the removal from office in 1997 of Assad Bucaram (PRE). Bucaram had been sworn into office on August 10, 1996, along with his vice president, Rosalia Arteaga. He served less than a year until February 1997, when his erratic personal behavior, escalating levels of administrative corruption, and his sharp policies of economic austerity led to his removal. Congress invoked an obscure provision in the constitution allowing for removal of a president on grounds of "physical or mental incapacity" declared by a simple majority vote of its members. A formal impeachment vote would have required a two-thirds majority vote by Congress.

The vote by Congress to remove Bucaram from office set off a constitutional crisis over succession, severely threatening Ecuador's democratic institutions. While the 1984 constitution had identified a line of succession that included the vice president, the president of Congress, and the president of the Supreme Court (although the order was not clearly specified), the 1996 constitution was strangely mute on the subject. The latter document specified a clear line of succession only in the event that a president is temporarily unable to perform his or her duties but said nothing about the situation where a president leaves office permanently before completing his term. As a consequence, Ecuador experienced a brief period following Bucaram's removal when three individuals—Bucaram, Vice President Arteaga, and the president of Congress, Fabián Alarcón—each claimed to be the country's legal president. In the end, Arteaga served three days as Ecuador's first female president, after which time Congress appointed Alarcón, a member of the Radical Alfarist Front (FRA), to serve as interim president until August 1998. A national referendum held in June 1987 showed 75% of voters confirming Bucaram's dismissal and 68% ratifying Alarcón's appointment as interim president,

TABLE 1
1998 Presidential Election Results

| | | Vote (%) | |
| | | Round 1 (May 31, 1998) | Round 2 (July 12, 1998) |
Name	Party		
Jamil Mahuad Witt	Popular Democracy	35. 3	51. 3
Alvaro Noboa Ponton	Ecuadorian Roldosista Party (PRE)	26. 9	48. 7
Rodrigo Borja Cevallos	Democratic Left (ID)	15. 9	
Freddy Ehlers Zurita	Movimiento Unidad Plurinacional Pachakutik-Nuevo Pais (MUUP-NP)	14. 3	
Rosalia Arteaga	Movimiento para una República Auténtica (MIRA)	5. 2	
Maria Eugenia Lima	Movimiento Popular Democrático	2. 4	

Source: Tribunal Supremo Electoral.

and initiated a process for reform of the 1996 constitution. A National Constituent Assembly (*Aaemblea Nacional Constituyente*), headed by the former president Osvaldo Hurtado, drafted a new constitution, which was approved on June 5, 1998, in Riobamba. This constitution introduced a number of important changes, among which was the specification of a clear line of presidential succession. If the president is unable to complete his term of office, the vice president succeeds him. If the vice president is unable to assume the office, the president of Congress assumes power for a maximum of 10 days, during which time Congress must elect a new president of the republic.

Legislature

The National Congress (*Congreso Nacional*) is unicameral. (It was bicameral until the constitution of 1978). Its 121 members (deputies) are selected by province in direct popular elections. To be eligible for election, deputies must be natives of the province or have resided in the province for the preceding three years, and they must be 25 years of age. They are chosen from lists of candidates presented by legally recognized parties in proportion to the number of votes earned. Elections for congressional deputies are held concurrently with the first round of the presidential elections. Since the 1996 constitution, deputies may be reelected.

In an effort to reduce the disproportionate influence of small parties in Congress, the 1998 constitution changes the procedures for selectin the president of Congress. Each two years, Congress elects a president and vice president. For the first two years following the national election, its president is elected from the party with the largest representation (the DP in 1998) and its first vice president from the party with the second-largest representation (the PSC in 1998). The second vice president is elected from among the minority parties and movements.

For the next two years, the president and first vice president are elected from the parties with the second-largest and largest majorities respectively.

TABLE 2
Congressional Election Results and Seat Distribution (May 19, 1998)

Political Party	Seats
Popular Democracy (DP)	32
Social Christian Party (PSC)	27
Ecuadorian Roldosista Party (PRE)	24
Democratic Left (ID)	18
Movimiento Unidad Plurinacional Pachakutik-Nuevo Pais (MUUP-NP)	9
Radical Alfarist Front (FRA)	5
Ecuadorian Conservative Party (PCE)	3
Popular Democratic Movement (MPD)	2
Concentration of Popular Forces (CFP)	1
Total	121

Source: Tribunal Supremo Electoral.

Until the 1998 constitution, the legislature met each year from the 1st of August to the 9th of October. When the legislature was not in session, The Plenary of Legislative Commissions (*Plenario de las Comisiones Legislativos*; PCL) functioned in its stead. The 1998 constitution attempts to professionalize the legislature by stipiulating that it meet for the entire year, with only two periods of recess, each a month long.

Until 1998, any member of the legislature had the authority, through a process called "*interpelación*" (censure), to call a government official before Congress for questioning and censure, after which a majority vote could result in the official's dismissal. This tactic has been used with increasing frequency by Congress in recent years to block and show disagreement with presidential initiatives. During the presidency of Rodrigo Borja (1988–92), Congress dismissed six government ministers using *interpelación*. Borja's minister of agriculture, Marcos Espinel, had to appear before Congress 28 times in 24 months to defend himself against censure initiatives. The constitution of 1998 restrains congressional recourse to *interpelación* by requiring approval by at least a quarter of the members of Congress to initiate the process. A successful vote of censure (requiring a majority) still results in the immediate removal of the official from office, except in the case of ministers of state, who may continue in office at the discretion of the president.

Women are underrepresented in Congress. Following the elections in 1988, only 3 out of 71 deputies were women. In 1996, the number of women who were deputies remained the same, although the number of deputies had increased to 82. The 1998 elections saw a significant increase in the number of women delegates, to 21, out of a total of 121.

Judiciary

The highest court is the Supreme Court of Justice, which presides over the judiciary. At the province level there are superior courts (intermediate appellate courts) and penal tribunals (trial courts for all serious crimes); at the sub-province level there are criminal courts (*juzgados*), as well as courts for civil, landlord-tenant, labor, and traffic cases. Another set of officials (*Tenientes Políticos, Comisarios de Policía, Intendentes,* and *Subintendentes*), whose duties include processing minor infractions, had been responsible to the executive branch but with the adoption of the 1998 constitution, are moved to the judicial branch.

The Constitutional Tribunal (*Tribunal Constitucional*, formerly the Tribunal of Constitutional Guarantees, TGC), established by the 1996 constitution, monitors compliance with the constitution. It consists of nine members, chosen by the Congress, who serve four-year terms and who may be reelected. Its members must meet the same requirements as those for Supreme Court justices. In practice, the TGC has been a weak institution, frequently accused of becoming overtly politicized.

The judicial branch of government has been relatively weak and, in recent years, has become increasingly politicized as the Court became part of the political spoils to be distributed following the election of a new Congress. In an effort to provide the Court some insulation from political pressures, the 1996 constitution restored the terms of Supreme Court justices to six years, from the four years that had prevailed since the constitutional reforms of 1983. The 1998 constitution continues the movement toward increased judicial independence by mandating that the Supreme Court justices be appointed

for an indefinite term. Appointments of new justices to fill vacancies on the Supreme Court are made by a two-thirds vote of the sitting justices.

The 1996 constitution also created a judicial oversight body, the National Judiciary Council (*Consejo Nacional de la Judicatura*),. an institution that is preserved in the 1998 constitution.

Regional and Local Government

There are three subnational levels of government: 21 provinces, including the Galapagos Islands, and, at the subprovince level, cantons or municipalities, and parishes.[2] Government is a mixture of appointed and elected officials. Officially, the president appoints provincial governors, canton political chiefs (*jefes politicos*), and parish political lieutenants (*tenientes politicos*). In practice, provincial governors normally make appointments to the last two offices.

In rural areas, the appointed officials, especially the *tenientes politicos*, are important sources of authority. In urban areas, elected officials play a more important role. All provincial capitals have an elected mayor who presides over an elected council (*consejo*) whose members are called *consejales*. The mayors of Quito and Guayaquil exercise considerable national as well as local power. Each province also has an elected council made up of provincial councillors (*consejeros*), presided over by the provincial governor.

Except for Quito and Guayaquil, local government plays a clearly subsidiary role in the Ecuadorian political system. Yet regional interests, as expressed through organizations such as the chambers of production (*Cámaras de la Producción*) and Congress, continue to exert a profound influence on national politics. Regionalism has contributed to the lack of national vision in Ecuadorian politics. Presidential candidates rarely exhibit broad national appeal, drawing their support primarily from either the coast or the sierra. Regional demands on the public budget lead to multiplication, and duplication, of local public works projects.

The Electoral System

The Supreme Electoral Tribunal (*Tribunal Supremo Electoral*; TSE) is charged with directing and overseeing the electoral process. It has seven members representing the parties that have received the largest number of votes in the most recent national election. Its members are elected by a majority vote of the Congress. Administratively beneath the TSE are the provincial electoral tribunals (*Tribunales Provinciales Electorales*; TPE) and the vote-receiving committees (*Juntas Receptoras del Voto*; JRV).

[2]As of January 1995, there were 196 cantons and 770 rural parroquias.

The TPEs are formed by the TSE in each province to oversee and direct the electoral process. The JRVs, whose members are selected by the respective TPEs, manage the actual polling process on election days.

The president and vice president are chosen directly in popular elections. A candidate must secure an absolute majority of the vote to win. If no candidate is able to win an absolute majority in the first round of voting (typically held in May), a runoff election between the top two candidates is required. The 1998 constitution adds the proviso that there will be no second-round election, if the first-place candidate wins greater than 40 but less than 51% of the total valid vote and that vote total is more than 10% greater than that of the second-place candidate. For example, in the 1998 presidential elections, no candidate won an absolute majority: the two leading candidates, Jamil Mahuad and Alvaro Noboa, won 35.3 and 26.9% of the first-round vote, respectively. Since the vote difference (8.4%) was less than 10%, a second-round election was required. In the runoff election held in July 1998, Jamil Mahuad won with 51.3% of the vote.

TABLE 3
Participation Rates in Presidential Elections
(Percent of Population)

Year	%
1888	3. 0
1924	11. 0
1931	3. 1
1932	4. 2
1933	3. 1
1948	9. 1
1956	15. 8
1960	17. 8
1966	11. 0
1968	14. 7
1979	21. 0
1984	31. 0
1996	42. 0

Representatives to the National Congress are chosen in the following way: At least two are elected from each province, with an additional representative elected for each 200,000 provincial residents or fraction greater than 150,000 residents (e. g. , a province of 555,000 people would have five representatives). Voters choose among ranked lists of candidates presented by legally recognized parties. Where more than two seats are to be filled, they are allocated by a simple proportional system.

In an important change from previous systems of representation, the 1978 and subsequent constitutions eliminated functional representatives. Since the constitution of 1929, functional representation had given disproportion-

ate representation to special interest groups such as agriculture, commerce, industry, labor, and the military. Under the 1967 constitution, for example, 15 of the 54 senators in the upper house were selected by a form of electoral college to represent different special interests.

The 1996 constitution allowed candidates for office to run as independents for the first time since 1978.

All Ecuadorians 18 years of age or over have the right to vote; literates under age 65 are required to vote. Illiterates were given the vote for the first time in the constitution of 1978 and exercised that right for the first time in the municipal and provincial elections in 1980. Qualified voters must register to vote and can vote only in the parish in which they register. A change in residence must be communicated to the Electoral Tribunal 30 days prior to an election in which the individual wishes to vote.

A significant feature of Ecuadorian politics has been historically low levels of political participation. The literacy requirement in a country where, as recently as 1974, national rates of illiteracy were in excess of 25%, the low level of economic development, and various other legal restrictions have effectively disenfranchised large sectors of the population. Recently, however, the abolition of the literacy requirement, rising income levels, and increasing urbanization have all contributed to rising levels of electoral participation.

Poverty, language differences, low levels of education, and discrimination have contributed to the political marginalization of indigenous groups. In recent years, however, the level of organization and political participation of indigenous groups has increased markedly. Organizations such as the Confederation of Indigenous Nationalities of the Amazon (CONFENIAE) and the Confederation of Indigenous Nationalities of Ecuador (CONAIE) were formed in 1980 and 1986, respectively. Although early political participation by indigenous groups took place largely outside of electoral politics, in the 1996 presidential and congressional elections, a new party, the New Country Movement-Pachakutik (MNNP), emerged as a vehicle for indigenous interests. Its presidential candidate won 11 out of 21 provinces to secure third place in the first-round voting. In May 1996, the party captured seven seats in Congress. In 1998, the party (now named *Movimiento Unidad Plurinacional Pachakutik/Nuevo Pais*) captured five seats.

THE PARTY SYSTEM

Origins of the Parties

Ecuador's traditional parties emerged in the latter half of the 19th century. Their ideological orientations reflected the theocratic debates of the period and the regional conflicts that have continued to characterize Ecuadorian politics. The Conservative Party represented the interests of the sierra landowning aristocracy, supporting close relationships between the Catholic Church and the state, centralized government, and state regulation of economic activity. The Liberal Party drew its primary support from coastal (*Costa*) commercial and financial interests, particularly those of Guayaquil. It was anticlerical and advocated decentralized government along with laissez-faire economic policies. By the end of World War II, anticlericalism had ceased to be an important issue. Differences between the two parties were drawn largely along regional lines. The coast was the center of economic activity; most imports and exports passed through Guayaquil. The sierra produced primarily for the domestic market; the national government in Quito drew its resources principally from taxes on foreign trade.

Politics in the latter half of the 20th century saw the progressive displacement of traditional parties by emerging populist movements and an increased fragmentation of parties as numerous splinter parties appeared at the left and right ends of the political spectrum. Neither Conservative nor Liberal candidates have won the presidency since the 1956 victory of Conservative Camilo Ponce Enríquez. Highly personalistic politics, always a feature of Ecuadorian political competition, became even more prominent. No one better exemplified this characteristic than José María Velasco Ibarra (1893–1979), who held the presidency five times between 1933 and 1972. Velasco was a spellbinding orator with a charismatic appeal for the masses but with little ability to govern once elected, as evidenced by his successful completion of only one of his five terms in office. Although supported by the Conservative Party during his early career, he resisted formal party affiliation until he formed the *Federación Nacional Velasquista*, a party that served only as a vehicle for its leader's personality.

Ecuador's second major populist movement also casts a long shadow over the country's political life. The Concentration of Popular Forces (*Concentración de Fuerzas Populares*; CFP) was established in Guayaquil under Carlos Guevara Moreno in 1949. The CFP firmly controlled Guayaquil politics, but it was never able to compete successfully in national elections. Guevara Moreno ran for the presidency in 1953 but was defeated by the rightist candidate, Camilo Ponce. With this defeat, Guevara Moreno gradually withdrew from active political life. Unlike *Velasquismo*, however, the CFP survived its founder's political demise.

Assad Bucaram assumed control of the CFP in 1960 and was elected mayor of Guayaquil in 1962. Under Bucaram, the CFP began to emerge as a significant national political force. One indication of the CFP's growing national strength was its capture of 5 of the 16 provincial seats in the National Congress in 1968. Bucaram was widely regarded as a certain victor in the presidential elections of 1978, but he was disqualified by the military on the grounds that neither of his parents was born in Ecuador. The CFP selected Jaime Roldós Aguilera

(nephew-in-law of Assad Bucaram), the ultimate victor, as its candidate, and Bucaram was elected president of the National Congress. However, feuding between the two men that split the party into rival factions, Jaime Roldós's untimely death in an airplane accident in May 1981, and Assad Bucaram's demise six months later dealt a severe blow to the party's aspirations.

Following Roldós's death in 1982, his brother-in-law, Abdalá Bucaram, took some members of the CFP to form a new party, the Roldosista Party of Ecuador (PRE). The PRE's candidate, Abdalá Bucaram, finished second to the Democratic Left's Rodrigo Borja in the 1988 presidential elections. In the 1992 legislative elections, the PRE won 15 of 77 seats; in the 1996 elections, the party won 21 of 82 seats and its leader, Abdalá Bucaram, was elected president.

The return to democracy in 1978 saw the emergence of center-left parties, such as Popular Democracy (DP), the Democratic Left (ID), and the Democratic Party (PD). While the last of these has disappeared as an electoral force, the first two continue as important actors in Ecuadorian electoral politics. Emphasizing issues-oriented, responsible politics, these parties have their strongest support among public-sector workers, the new middle class, and professionals, groups whose electoral importance increased greatly with the socioeconomic changes accompanying the petroleum boom. Both parties draw their support disproportionately from the sierra, reflecting the continuing regional divisions of the country's politics.

With the virtual disappearance of the traditional parties of the political right, the Conservatives and the Liberals, the Social Christian Party (PSC) emerged as the standard-bearer for these interests. In Congress, the conservatives have been joined at opportunistic moments by the populist right. In 1978, PSC candidate Sixto Durán Ballén, a former mayor of Quito, ran second in the presidential elections and the party took 3 out of 69 seats in the legislature. In 1984, PSC candidate León Febres Cordero won the presidency and the party captured 29 out of 71 seats in the legislature. Sixto Durán again ran unsuccessfully for president in 1988 but finally emerged victorious in 1992, when he ran at the head of his own party, the Republican Union (PUR), a splinter from the PSC, against PSC candidate Jaime Nebot. Although both candidates represented conservative interests, they differed in both personality and the regional bases of their support: Durán Ballén was strongest in the sierra and the Amazon; Nebot drew his strength from the coast. In 1996, PSC candidate Jaime Nebot won the first-round vote but came in second to Abdalá Bucaram in the second round. The elections of 1998 saw the emergence of an alliance between the PSC and the DP.

The Parties in Law

The 1978 constitution and the accompanying Laws of Parties and Elections took steps to restrict the growth of splinter parties and to increase their accountability in an effort to reduce the role of individual personalities, such as Velasco Ibarra. For example, independent candidates were explicitly barred from running for office (in 1996, independents were again allowed to run). Nevertheless, no fewer than 17 parties registered for the 1984 elections, 12 parties contested the 1996 elections, and aproximately 18 parties were invoved in 1998.

The Law of Parties establishes the conditions under which a party will be recognized. A party wishing to compete in elections must submit information to the Supreme Electoral Tribunal, the most important of which includes the following: a declaration of ideological principles; a detailed government plan indicating the policies the party would undertake if successful in the presidential elections; certification of membership equal to at least 1. 5% of the registered voters in the last elections; and evidence of national support demonstrating the existence of the party in at least 10 provinces, including 2 of the 3 most populous provinces, which are dominated by the cities of Guayaquil, Quito, and Portoviejo. A party must submit this information and be qualified six months prior to an election it wishes to contest. This requirement does not apply to coalitions formed within six months of an election.

According to the 1998 constitution, parties or political movements that fail to earn a minimum of 5% of the valid votes cast in two successive national elections are eliminated from the electoral register.

Party Organization

Party organization in Ecuador has traditionally been weak, reflecting the elite character of politics and the lack of articulation between party leaders and voters. Personalistic domination of many parties has hindered the development of programmatic policies, and parties are not characterized by consistent ideological positions. Parties tend to appear before elections, campaign furiously, and disappear until the next round of elections, if not forever. Party membership is limited. Until the 1980s there had been virtually no effort to create mass-based organizations. The party with the strongest mass base prior to this time was the Concentration of Popular Forces (CFP), which sought to build an organization among lower-class voters in Guayaquil. More recently, the Democratic Left (ID), the Popular Democracy (DP), and the Social Christians (PSC) have invested heavily in party building. Yet, despite these efforts, voter identification with parties remains weak. Although party activity is intense, it takes place among small groups of elites and tends to involve Byzantine political maneuvering for short-term advantage. This tendency, when combined with the large number of parties, sets the stage for constantly shifting coalitions and alliances. The continuing fragmentation of parties points to the persistent weakness of the party system.

Campaigning

Campaigns are characterized by intense periods of political activity and traditionally have relied heavily on the oratorical skills of the candidates. Velasco Ibarra, an unparalleled performer in this arena, is said to have boasted: "Give me a balcony and the people are mine. " Beginning in the 1950s with the rise of populist leaders like Velasco Ibarra, the campaign tour became a feature of campaigns. Personality and the sweeping promises of populist rhetoric continue to characterize most campaigns, although some parties, notably those of the center-left, have endeavored to emphasize issues. Television has begun to play an increasingly important role, with the advantage this expensive medium gives to well-financed candidates, traditionally those of the Ecuadorian political right. However, in the 1996 and 1998 presidential elections, television personality Freddy Ehlers made a strong showing as the head of a loose coalition of indigenous, labor, and environmental groups.

Independent Voters

Party identification in Ecuador is weak. The majority of voters have learned that whichever party holds office, it has little concrete impact on their lives. Most of these voters tend to vote for personality rather than party, or for patronage opportunities. For the small group of elites who stand to gain or lose from the policies of different parties, there is somewhat greater party identification, but even this is largely opportunistic.

DEMOCRATIC LEFT PARTY
(Izquierda Democratica; ID)

The ID is a moderate left-wing, social democratic party that is affiliated with the Socialist International. The ID was formed in 1970 after dissatisfaction within the Liberal Party over its support of Velasco Ibarra in 1969 and later disagreement over candidates for mayor and municipal council of Quito in 1970 led to the defection of the bulk of the Liberal's Quito leadership. The ID fielded its own candidates for the first time in the 1970 elections for Congress and won strong representation. Following the return to democracy, the ID won 12 seats in the congressional elections of 1979, making it the second-largest delegation. The ID's main base of support is the province of Pichincha (Quito), but its influence has grown in other parts of the country, as witnessed by its strong showing in the 1984 and 1988 presidential and congressional elections. In 1984, ID candidate Rodrigo Borja Cevallos won the first round of the presidential elections, only to lose narrowly in the second round to Leon Febres Cordero. In the first round of the presidential elections, Rodrigo Borja won 18 of the 20 provinces, failing to carry only the coastal provinces of Guayas (Guayaquil) and Los Rios, where the ID has traditionally been weak. The party won 24 seats in the congressional elections that year. In 1988, Rodrigo Borja was elected president, and his party took 20 of the 71 seats in Congress. In 1992, with Rodrigo Borja constitutionally barred from running for reelection, the ID took 8 out of 21 seats.

Prospects for the ID are uncertain. Rodrigo Borja's decision not to contest the 1996 presidential elections (possible under the recent constitutional reforms allowing reelection after a lapse of one term) caused divisions to develop within the party. The ID won only 3 seats in the 1996 congressional elections. Borja's relatively poor showing in the 1998 elections decreases the likelihood he will run again. In Congress, the ID improved its position, winning 18 seats.

NEW COUNTRY MOVEMENT-PACHAKUTIK
(Movimiento Nuevo País-Pachakutik; MNPP) (1996)

Movimiento Unidad Plurinacional
(Pachakutik/Nuevo País; MUUP-NP) (1998)

This movement emerged for the first time in the 1996 elections, taking advantage of the change in the electoral laws allowing individuals to stand for election without being nominated by a legally recognized political party, as had been the case. Freddy Ehlers, a television journalist who had earned a reputation for investigating issues, such as official corruption, the environment, and social problems, ran as its candidate for president, winning a surprising 21% of the first-round vote to place third. Ehlers was a former member of ID and media adviser to Rodrigo Borja during the latter's 1988 presidential campaign. Labor, environmental, and indigenous groups organized earlier as the *Coordinadora de Movimientos Sociales* to protest the political establishment in general and the economic policies of Durán Ballén in particular supported his campaign. Of these groups, the most important was the 2. 5-million-member *Confederación de Nacionalidades Ind'genas* (CONAIE), which represents indigenous groups and which had been assembling a list of indigenous candidates for the upcoming elections.

The political durability of this movement is probably limited. What is unlikely to disappear is the new political voice of Ecuador's previously marginalized indigenous communities.

POPULAR DEMOCRACY
(Democracia Popular; DP)

The DP is a center-left party that is affiliated with the Christian Democratic International. The DP claims as its fundamental objective that of serving as a means of political expression for rural and urban popular organizations. It advocates "popular democracy" as opposed to "formal democracy": in the latter the people choose from an agenda presented to them by the dominant groups in society, while in the former, the agenda supposedly rises from the grass roots. The DP is the most committed to programmatic politics of any of the parties.

The DP was formed from an alliance of the Christian Democratic Party and the Progressive Conservative Party in early 1978. The former was originally organized in 1964 by reform-oriented university students, faculty, and young professionals who had become disillusioned with the conservative Social Christian Party. At the time of the alliance, it was led by Osvaldo Hurtado, who was elected vice president in 1979 and became president on Roldós's death in 1981. The DP has established itself as a national force in a remarkably short time, due largely to the recognition it achieved under Osvaldo Hurtado, although since the end of his presidency the party has been without strong nationally recognized leadership. In 1984, the DP won 4 seats in the National Congress. Its presidential candidate, Julio César Trujillo, ran seventh out of a field of nine, earning 4. 7% of the valid vote. In 1996, the DP made its largest electoral gains when its candidate, Rodrigo Paz, captured 13. 5% of the first-round vote and the DP won 12 out of 82 seats in Congress. The DP made a very strong showing in the 1998 elections, when its candidate, Jamil Mahuad, the former mayor of Quito, captured the presidency and the party took 32 seats in the Congress.

The DP has its base in the sierra urban professional class, whose numbers greatly increased during the petroleum boom. The party has had difficulty reaching beyond this constituency and is particularly weak on the coast. In 1966, Rodrigo Paz only won more than 25% of the first-round vote in Pichincha province (Quito); in no coastal province did he win over 10%. The party's alliance with the PSC, should it prove durable, may give the DP a new strength on the coast.

SOCIAL CHRISTIAN PARTY
(Partido Social Cristiano; PSC)

The PSC is a right-wing party that is unabashedly free-market-oriented, advocating a restricted role for government in the economy and economic liberalization.

The PSC was established in 1951 as the Social Christian Movement (MSC), an organization intended to further the political ambitions of its founder and leader, Camilo Ponce Enríquez, a leading rightist politician. In 1956, Ponce Enríquez was elected president of Ecuador, the first conservative president in over 60 years. His administration was distinguished by fiscal conservatism and increased foreign investment. In the 1960s, the MSC endeavored unsuccessfully to affiliate with Christian Democracy. Dissident members left to help form the Christian Democratic Party in 1964, denouncing what they viewed as Ponce's efforts to cloak his basic conservatism in Christian Democratic clothing. In 1976, Ponce Enríquez died. His movement became the party of Ecuador's conservative business elites, drawing its support principally from the coast. In the 1978 presidential elections, the PSC candidate, Sixto Durán Ballén, finished second. In 1984, the party's candidate, the former Guayas chamber of industry president León Febres Cordero, was elected president of Ecuador. He ran as the candidate of an alliance of right-wing parties called the National Reconstruction Front (FNR). In 1998, the party chose bot to run a presidential candidate, but it did win 27 seats in Congress, the second-largest block.

The party has become the principal electoral vehicle for Ecuador's political right wing. Unlike the center-left of the political spectrum, where a number of parties compete for voter allegiance, the PSC has no significant challengers on the right.

THE ROLDOSISTA PARTY OF ECUADOR
(Partido Roldosista del Ecuador; PRE)

The PRE is a populist party with little ideological consistency. A highly personalistic creation, it was formed in 1982 by Abdalá Bucaram, nephew of CFP leader Assad Bucaram, becoming the principal vehicle for the political fortunes of the Bucaram family. Abdalá Bucaram drew on the old CFP organization and on the patronage resources available to him while he was mayor of Guayaquil to create an organization that allowed him to capture the presidency in 1996. As with the CFP, the PRE's electoral base is on the coast, particularly among lower-class voters in Guayaquil.

The PRE's prospects for the future are, at best, uncertain. Abdalá Bucaram's removal from the presidency in 1997 and his subsequent flight to Panama leave this personalistic party without its charismatic leader and the pivotal lower-class Guayaquil vote up for grabs. Nevertheless, the party's second-place showing in the 1998 presidential elections under its standard-bearer, Alvaro Noboa, a wealthy coastal businessman and its capture of 24 seats in Congress point to the enduring appeal of populist candidates among Ecuadorian voters.

CONSERVATIVE PARTY
(Partido Conservador Ecuatoriano; PC)

The Conservative Party, Ecuador's oldest political party, was founded in 1883 by followers of the assassinated for-

mer president, Gabriel Garcia Moreno, an autocratic leader who dominated Ecuadorian politics until his assassination in 1875. It has traditionally represented the landed elite of the sierra. The party has suffered from considerable factionalism in recent years. In 1976, the party split into left and right wings, with the former organizing as the Progressive Conservative Party, which later joined with another party to form Popular Democracy–Christian Democratic Union (DP). The party's prospects for an expanded electoral role are poor. Its presidential candidates in 1956 and 1960 polled barely 9% of the coastal vote. In recent years, the party has not been a serious contender for the presidency. In 1992, it captured five seats in Congress, revitalized somewhat by its being chosen by Alberto Dahik (vice president under Sixto Durán Ballén) as the electoral vehicle for his ambitions. Dahik's alleged misuse of public funds and his subsequent flight from the country have probably squandered whatever renewed vitality he might have brought to the party. In 1996, the party won only two seats in Congress, an accomplishment it barely managed to replicate in 1998.

CONCENTRATION OF POPULAR FORCES
(Concentración de Fuerzas Populares; CFP)

The CFP has traditionally been a personalistic, not an ideological, movement that has represented itself as strongly opposed to the privileges of the oligarchy. A statement of CFP philosophy emphasizes "its essence, which is profoundly democratic, progressive, antifeudal, contrary to the caciquismo of cliques and influential bigwigs, republican, law-abiding, and supportive of large-scale social and economic transformation. " In spite of these claims, however, the CFP has demonstrated little ideological consistency. In the 1984 Congress, for example, the CFP under Averroes Bucaram entered into an alliance with the political right against the president. The stronghold of CFP support has traditionally been the Guayaquil lower classes. The party's unexpectedly strong showing in the 1984 first-round presidential elections attests to its organizational base in Guayaquil. With the deaths of Roldós and Bucaram, the party was left without a strong leader; in recent years it has captured only one or two seats in Congress. Voters who had been the CFP's traditional base have largely deserted the party for the PRE.

DEMOCRATIC POPULAR MOVEMENT
(Movimiento Popular Democrático; MPD)

This far-left party is the electoral vehicle for the Maoist Marxist-Leninist Communist Party (PCML), a breakaway from the official Ecuadorian Communist Party. In the first round of the 1984 presidential elections, MPD candidate Jaime Hurtado Gonzalez finished a surprising fourth with 7.3% of the valid vote, but generally the party has only limited, and declining, electoral appeal. In 1996, MPD candidate Juan José Castello ran a distant seventh out of a field of nine in the first round. The party captured two seats in Congress in the 1998 elections.

ALFARIST RADICAL FRONT
(Frente Radical Alfarista; FRA)

This populist party, named after Ecuadorian hero Elroy Alfaro, was founded when Abdón Calderón split from the Liberal Party in 1972. Calderón was the party's candidate in the 1978 elections. Several months after the election he was assassinated in Guayaquil. The FRA candidate in the 1984 presidential elections, Jaime Aspiazu, won only 6.8% of the valid vote; the party won six seats in the national Congress. The FRA has had some success mobilizing former CFP voters in Guayaquil. The party is center-right in orientation. The FRA is unlikely to increase its appeal to voters (in the 1990s, the party has won only one to three seats in Congress each election), although FRA member Fabián Alarcón's assumption of the presidency in 1996 may boost the party's fortunes. Despite this advantage, the party won only five seats in the 1998 congressional elections.

RADICAL LIBERAL PARTY
(Partido Liberal Radical Ecuatoriana; PLRE)

The dominant party in the first decades of the 20th century, the PLRE has declined greatly in electoral importance. Numerous internal disagreements and defections have weakened the party, which has a center-right orientation. The party won four seats in the 1984 congressional elections. It contested the 1996 presidential elections in coalition with the Alfarist Radical Front (*Frente Radical Alfarista*; FRA) but won only 3% of the first-round vote. The party appears spent as an electoral force.

ECUADORIAN POPULAR REVOLUTIONARY ACTION
(Acción Popular Revolucionaria Ecuatoriana; APRE)

APRE originated in 1970 as the National Guevarista Party, founded by a group of CFP members who had been followers of the CFP founder, Carlos Guevara

Moreno. In 1978, the APRE joined other parties in a coalition called the Constitutional Front to back the presidential candidacy of Sixto Durán Ballén. In 1988, following the national attention gained from his leading a revolt against President León Febres Cordero two years earlier, a retired air force general, Frank Vargas Pazzos, became the standard-bearer for this party. In the 1996 first-round elections for the presidency, APRE candidate Frank Vargas took 4.93% of the vote for a distant fourth-place finish. The party won two seats in Congress. APRE is center-left and populist.

OTHER POLITICAL FORCES

Military

Historically, the military has played an active role in Ecuadorian politics; prior to the 1960s, over 30% of Ecuador's presidents had been army officers. About six times as many military officers are from the sierra as from the coast and tend to come from middle-class families. Typically, the military has remained in power only briefly, viewing its role as caretaker and defender of the constitutional order. Even without direct involvement, the military plays a significant role since the threat of military intervention does much to shape the course of politics.

Since 1960, however, military juntas have ruled Ecuador for longer periods on two separate occasions. The first military junta took power in 1963, using the threat of Cuban communist intervention to justify its action. Its proposed policies were reformist. Its most notable achievement was the establishment of Ecuador's first land-reform legislation, although little reform was actually realized. The military withdrew from power in 1966, under heavy criticism from nearly all sectors of society. In 1972, the military again entered politics, this time in response to its perception of threats of destabilization created by Ecuador's new petroleum wealth and the almost certain victory of the populist leader Assad Bucaram in that year's presidential elections. The second junta proclaimed itself reformist and nationalist in the style of the Peruvian military at that time. Severe internal disagreements over the proper political model for the military and strong opposition from civilian elites prevented the realization of any significant reforms. Again under heavy criticism, the military withdrew from power in 1979.

Badly tarnished after its two recent episodes in power, the military's reputation within Ecuadorian society was given new luster by its performance in the 1995 border war with Peru. Public enthusiasm for the military's conduct during that conflict led the defense minister, General José Gallardo, to resign in order to run as an independent candidate in the 1996 presidential elections. He won only 1.22% of the first-round vote to finish in next-to-last place.

The military's commitment to democracy was severely tested in the constitutional crisis surrounding President Abdalá Bucaram's removal from office in 1997. As public order broke down and massive protests swept Quito, the military high command eschewed its interventionist past in favor of supporting democratic process. The military withdrew its support for Bucaram, refused to name the next president, and brokered a solution to the ensuing succession dilemma by insisting that Congress pass changes to the constitution that would allow the transition to take place according to the rule of law.

Students

Students in Ecuador, while not well organized, have often mounted major demonstrations that have served as the catalysts in every nonconstitutional change of government but one since 1944. Both secondary and university students are highly political and generally leftist in their political orientation. The two major student organizations are the Federation of University Students of Ecuador (*Federación de Estudiantes Universitarios del Ecuador*; FEUE) and the Federation of Secondary Students of Ecuador (*Federación de Estudiantes Secundarios del Ecuador*; FESE). Students at the Central University (several public campuses) tend to be the most radical and active.

Organized Labor

Labor unions in Ecuador have traditionally been weak, owing in large part to the low level of industrialization and the fragmentation of organized labor along both regional and ideological lines. Union membership represents less than 18% of all workers and is divided among three competing national organizations and numerous local ones. An important development during the 1970s was the emergence of an alliance of the three major unions, the Unitary Workers Front (FUT), which has successfully organized a series of national strikes. However, organized labor has not yet been particularly important either in deciding the agenda of politics or in supporting parties.

Interest-Group Organizations

The economic elites in Ecuador play a very important political role. Indeed, until very recently politics was a game played almost exclusively by these classes. Although the landowning sierra aristocracy still wields considerable influence, the most important group today is undoubtedly the commercial, financial, and banking elite of the coast. Both these groups exercise political influence through the chambers of commerce, industry, and agriculture. The 1984 victory of León Febres Cordero was largely orchestrated through these organizations. In recent years, indigenous groups have become increasingly important political actors, as have some nongovernmental organizations, particularly those active in the environmental area.

NATIONAL PROSPECTS

The successful navigation of five democratic transitions since the late 1970s and the recently demonstrated military support for democracy are encouraging signs in a country that has suffered from a long history of political instability. Nevertheless, the persistent weakness of the party system, the high degree of conflict between the legislature and the executive, and the constraints imposed on public spending by the need for policies of economic adjustment contribute to a highly volatile political environment. Expanded political participation has placed increased demands on the state at a time when it must implement policies that, at least in the short run, impose costs on large sectors of society. Ecuador's highly fragmented party system will be severely challenged to mediate the ensuing distributive conflicts.

Further Reading

Chinchilla, Laura, and David W. Schodt. *The Administration of Justice in Ecuador.* San José, Costa Rica: Center for the Administration of Justice/Florida International University, 1993.

Conaghan, Catherine M. "Party Politics and Democratization in Ecuador." In *Authoritarians and Democratics: Regime Transition in Latin America.* Ed. J. Malloy and M. Seligson. Pittsburgh: University of Pittsburgh Press, 1987.

Fitch, John Samuel. *The Military Coup D'État as a Political Process: Ecuador 1948–1966.* Baltimore: Johns Hopkins University Press, 1977.

Hurtado, Osvaldo. *Political Power in Ecuador.* Albuquerque: University of Mexico Press, 1980.

Isaacs, Anita. *Military Rule and Transition in Ecuador, 1972–92.* Pittsburgh: University of Pittsburgh Press, 1993.

Martz, John D. *Ecuador: Conflicting Political Culture and the Quest for Progress.* New York: Allyn and Bacon, 1972.

Reyes, Beatriz, and Ramón Gorriarán, eds. *Vote Sabiendo.* Quito: Corporación Editora Nacional, 1983.

Rodr'guez, Linda A. *The Search for Public Policy: Regional Politics and Government Finances in Ecuador, 1830–1940.* Berkeley: University of California Press, 1985.

Salgado, Hernan. *Instituciones Pol'ticas y Constitución del Ecuador.* Quito: ILDIS, 1987.

Schodt, David W. *Ecuador: An Andean Enigma.* Boulder, Colo.: Westview Press, 1987.

Tribunal Supremo Electoral. *Análisis de los Procesos Electorales.* Quito: Corporación Editora Nacional, 1990.

ARAB REPUBLIC OF EGYPT

(Gumhuriyat Misr al-Arabiya)

By Joel Gordon, Ph. D.

THE SYSTEM OF GOVERNMENT

With 65 million people, Egypt is the most populous nation in the Arab world and commands the largest military force in the region. Located in the northeast corner of Africa, the country has historically been a crossroads for commerce, ideas, and conquerors. The Nile Valley, stretching for 750 miles north to south, is one of the cradles of ancient civilization. The great pharaonic dynasties of antiquity consolidated control over both the upper and lower capitals of Thebes and Memphis, creating a unified power base from which they exerted authority over the eastern Mediterranean and Red Seas. Egypt's fortunes have risen and fallen ever since, but the Nile Valley has fostered a sense of common identity that laid strong foundations for modern nationalism in the late 19th and 20th centuries.

Muhammad Ali (1805–48), the maverick Ottoman governor, established a semiautonomous state and a hereditary line that would last until 1953. Embarking upon ambitious development projects, including the Suez Canal, which was completed in 1869, his successors found themselves saddled with enormous foreign debts. Increasing European economic domination sparked an independence movement that heralded the cry "Egypt for the Egyptians. " The Khedive Ismail (1863–79) allowed a consultative assembly to sit but was dismissed by the Ottoman sultan under European pressure. In 1882 Britain defeated nationalist forces and occupied the country. At the same time, Egypt became a haven for Arab intellectuals and artists and a center of Arab cultural production. The Arab League, promoted by King Farouk (1936–53) and backed by the British during World War II, was originally headquartered in Cairo, and in the postcolonial era Egypt has remained an axis of regional leadership.

Egypt covers 385,000 square miles, of which only 3. 5% is arable. The overwhelming majority of the population thus lives in the Nile Valley (which in parts of upper Egypt is only 1. 5 miles wide). The population is slightly less than half urban. One-third of all Egyptians, some 16 million, live in the Cairo metropolitan area. The population is also predominantly young: 44% of Egyptians are 15 years old or less. A majority of Egyptians are Muslim and Islam is the state religion. A significant Coptic Christian minority (8–10%) has played an important social and political role, and national symbols have often included both crescent and cross.

Egypt today is a "socialist democratic" republic ruled by an authoritarian president, Hosni Mubarak, who has governed for the past 17 years under emergency measures. In the past decade Egyptians have undertaken a dramatic reevaluation of the 1952 military coup that ushered in a social revolution and put the present political structures in place. Since the late 1970s the country has experimented with greater democratization, but facing challenges from an Islamist current that rejects key foundations of the state, it has yet to truly open up the political process.

Egypt has been a republic since June 18, 1953, when the Revolutionary Command Council (RCC), the military junta that seized power on July 23, 1952, abolished the monarchy and appointed its figurehead leader, Muhammad Nagib, Egypt's first president. The July Revolution was the culmination of the independence struggle against British occupation. Britain declared a protectorate in 1914, formally severing Egypt's links to the Ottoman Empire. Following the 1919 nationalist uprising, Britain granted Egypt nominal independence, reserving the right to intervene in domestic affairs, and oversaw the establishment of a constitutional monarchy. Under the yoke of a monarchy with unbridled power to dismiss parliament and a British residency loath to accede to nationalist demands for "total independence," Egyptian liberalism foundered. Between 1924, when Egyptians first held elections, and 1952, the leading nationalist party, the Wafd, was allowed to rule only four times, for a total of less than seven years. In 1936 Britain granted Egypt formal independence but retained treaty rights to maintain a military presence in the Suez Canal zone and to intervene to preserve internal and external security. With the outbreak of World War II, the British reoccupied Egypt and in 1942 imposed a Wafdist government upon Farouk. In such a dispirited political culture, extraparliamentary antiestablishment forces emerged that further undercut democratic idealism and promoted aspirations for a benevolent dictatorship.

The secret Free Officers movement led by Gamal Abdel Nasser was an outgrowth of this political malaise.

The movement seized power on July 23, 1952. The junior officers intended to institute sweeping reforms and restore "sound" democracy. But resistance to land reform, the hesitancy of political parties to purge their ranks, and the encouragement of civilian allies who feared a return to politics as usual persuaded the officers to consolidate their authority over the state. In December 1952 they abrogated the 1923 constitution. A month later they abolished all political parties and formed a single mass party. In June 1953 the RCC proclaimed a republic. In March 1954 the regime weathered its most significant challenge when the ouster of Muhammad Nagib provoked a massive outcry for the military rulers to step aside. The RCC marshaled street forces and successfully cast its opposition as reactionary. Thereafter the regime acted to bring labor unions, the press, professional organizations, and the universities under rigid control. In 1956 a new constitution was acclaimed by popular referendum and Nasser was elected president. He held this office until his death in September 1970.

Under Nasser the state experimented with three mass parties (Liberation Rally, 1954; National Union, 1958; Arab Socialist Union, 1961), and in the 1960s embarked on a series of socialist reforms, creating a large public sector and nationalizing finance, heavy industry, and the media. Few Egyptians today would dispute that Nasser ruled with dictatorial powers, yet many recall the era with fondness as one of national unity, hope, and prestige and as a golden age of popular and fine arts. Socialist reforms remain highly debated. Many supported the dramatic turn toward privatization engineered by Nasser's successor Anwar Sadat (1970–81). Nasserist foreign policy produced a similarly mixed legacy. The nationalization of the Suez Canal in July 1956, a move lauded by virtually all Egyptians, provoked the tripartite Anglo-French-Israeli aggression. Despite suffering enormous military setbacks, Nasser was able to parlay the Suez War into a diplomatic triumph and emerged a regional superstar. His call for Arab unity led to union with Syria—the United Arab Republic,—between 1958 and 1961. A decade of escalating tension with Israel culminated in the disastrous June 1967 Six-Day War in which Israeli forces captured Gaza and the Sinai peninsula. A subsequent War of Attrition (1968–70) kept Egypt militarized, but Nasser's death in September 1970 left his successor with the immense burden of restoring Egyptian territory and national pride.

Anwar Sadat set out quickly to fashion his own identity and distance himself from Nasserist "centers of power" that sought to dominate him. In his May 1971 "corrective revolution" he purged Nasserist loyalists from the Arab Socialist Union (ASU) and high state offices. In the 1973 October War the Egyptian army restored a susbstantial amount of national pride and Sadat won great public acclaim, after which he set out to liberalize the economy. His open-door policy (*infitah*), pro-

claimed in October 1974, was followed by a sincere but wavering desire to open the political process. In 1976 Sadat promoted the division of the ASU into three platforms (*minabar*), representing a left, center, and right. After the formal legalization of political parties in 1977 these platforms were refashioned into a new ruling party, the Egyptian Arab Socialist Union (later the National Democratic Party), the leftist National Progressive Unionist Party (NPUP or Tagammu), and the conservative Liberal Socialist Party. The new election law sanctioned the formation of any party that could muster 20 representatives within the People's Assembly.

In 1978, in a stunning move, Sadat permitted the rebirth of the Wafd under the leadership of Fuad Sirag al-Din, heir apparent to party leadership in the early 1950s and scion of one of Egypt's largest prerevolutionary landowning families. Sirag al-Din's aggressive challenge to the legitimacy of the July Revolution, however, led the government to pass legislation barring from politics anyone who had held a ministerial post prior to July 23, 1952. With its leader disqualified, the New Wafd disbanded in protest.

Sadat's final years were marked both by great diplomatic success, highlighted by the 1978 Camp David accords and subsequent Egyptian-Israeli peace treaty, and by increasing instability at home, largely the result of economic travails. Losing his grip on power, Sadat retreated from his political reforms, ordering sweeping arrests of opponents across the political spectrum. In September 1981 security forces detained 1,500 political prisoners. On October 6, Sadat was assassinated by Islamist militants at the ceremony marking the crossing by Egyptian troops of the Suez Canal eight years earlier in the October 1973 war against Israel.

Hosni Mubarak, Sadat's vice president, was sworn in as president on October 13, 1981. Mubarak, who has ruled ever since, has overseen a dramatic march toward greater democratization. He has done so in the shadow of emergency measures decreed in the wake of Sadat's murder and extended by parliamentary approval thereafter. Nonetheless, Mubarak has allowed a greater number of parties to emerge, has honored judicial rulings invalidating electoral procedure, and has fostered a press, official and opposition, that is, despite restrictions, far freer than it had been since the 1952 revolution. Although he has, against stated desire, held office for three consecutive six-year terms, never appointing a vice president or designating an heir, Mubarak has overseen four rounds of parliamentary elections and tolerated opposition calls for curbs on presidential powers.

Executive

Ultimate power in Egypt resides in the president, who is chief executive and leader of the ruling National Democratic Party (NDP). The president is not elected by popular vote but rather is nominated by two-thirds of the People's Assembly (*Majlis al-Shaab*), then approved by popular referendum. The president must be of Egyptian parentage and at least 40 years old. The 1971 constitution promulgated by Sadat set the presidential term at six years and made provisions for another term. A 1980 constitutional amendment stated that the president may serve additional terms. Mubarak has subsequently been reapproved twice, in 1987 and 1993.

The issue of succession has surfaced increasingly in recent years. Mubarak's two predecessors died in office, one at assassins' hands. Sadat's killing was intended to spark nationwide insurrection, but the only manifestation of this, an attack on police cadets in the upper Egyptian city of Asyut, was contained. While the relatively peaceful transition underscored for many a fundamental institutional stability, cynics despair at ever seeing a standing president retire. As Mubarak's second term ended, opposition forces put forth proposals for a popularly elected chief executive. Supporters argued that Mubarak needed a third term to carry out his political agenda and maintain stability. Generally speaking, the president remains above and beyond the scope of official and unofficially expressed public criticism. While government ministers up to and including the prime minister are constant targets of a lively press, even the opposition press exercises self-censorship in refraining from any critique of the president.

Legislative

The People's Assembly (National Assembly before 1971) approves general policy, the national budget, and development plans. It also nominates the president. It may vote no confidence in any government minister, deputy minister, or deputy prime minister but has no power to vote no confidence in the prime minister. It may bring complaints against the prime minister before the president, who may then put the issue to a popular referendum. If the referendum fails, the president may dismiss the Assembly. This prerogative may be exercised at any time but must be followed by a popular referendum within 60 days.

The People's Assembly is currently composed of 454 deputies (numbers have fluctuated slightly since the 1980s). Each of Egypt's 222 legislative districts is represented by two deputies. The legislative term is five years and polling occurs in two stages with provisions for runoffs. Voters cast ballots for a party list divided between professional and worker/peasant candidates. Each district must be represented by one from each category. The outgrowth of Nasser-era striving for social justice and broad representation, this last feature is today a cause for cynicism. A cartoon in an opposition paper after the 1995 elections depicted the parking lot designated for worker/peasant representatives full of luxury

vehicles. The remaining 10 members of the Assembly are appointed by the president, who usually uses this prerogative to ensure greater representation by women and Coptic delegates.

In 1980 the Shura Council (Advisory Council), was established to replace the former ASU central committee. The Council oversees and approves broad matters of policy but has no legislative authority. At present 140 of its 210 members are elected; the remaining members are presidential appointees. Elections to the Shura Council, held every three years, closely mirror elections to the People's Assembly. The opposition boycotted elections in 1983 and 1986, then ran candidates in 1989, only to see the NDP sweep. In 1995 two independents were elected in a round in which several opposition parties offered candidates.

Judiciary

According to the 1971 constitution, Islam is the state religion and the *Sharia* (Islamic legal code) the principal source of legislation. As in other parts of the Ottoman Empire, however, the judicial and legal system has been modeled on European lines since the late 19th century. The jurisdiction of Sharia judges was curtailed as new criminal, civil, and commercial codes were drafted and a new legal establishment was trained along Western lines.

The judiciary in Egypt is divided between courts of general jurisdiction and administrative courts. Sitting atop the system is the Supreme Constitutional Court that reviews the constitutionality of legal measures and resolves constitutional disputes. Courts of general jurisdiction begin at the district level. At least one tribunal of first instance, with civil and criminal chambers, is located in each of Egypt's 26 governorates. Appellate courts, also with separate civil and criminal chambers, have jurisdiction over one or more governorates. Topping the system is the Court of Cassation in Cairo, which hears petitions from criminal and civil appellate courts. Administrative courts hear cases involving governmental agencies. The State Council, an independent judicial body, is empowered to render decisions in administrative disputes and cases within the legal system. The Supreme Judicial Council, abolished in 1969, then reinstated in 1984, is consulted with regard to draft laws that organize the affairs of other judicial bodies.

The high court has on numerous occasions rendered decisions curbing executive and legislative authority. In 1985 the court overturned key provisions of the "Jihan" personal status laws, passed in 1979 and named for Sadat's wife. In rescinding the laws, which granted women greater rights in matters of divorce and child custody, the court accepted arguments raised by Islamist lawyers that the legislation had been illegally promulgated. The decision proved a pyrrhic victory for democratic forces that championed the court's exertion of power over the executive, yet bemoaned the rescinding of legislation that they supported in principle. The court has played a particularly influential role in the realm of political participation, as will be discussed below.

Regional and Local Government

Until the mid-1970s regional and local affairs were heavily dominated by the national government. In accord with the Sadatist program of political liberalization, the government in 1975 passed legislation promoting administrative decentralization. Further laws have augmented the powers of Egypt's 26 governorates, and popularly elected local councils have been allowed greater policy-making authority.

THE ELECTORAL SYSTEM

All citizens aged 18 or over can vote, with the exception of those serving in the armed forces or working overseas. Women gained the vote in 1956 and have served in parliament and the Cabinet ever since. Egyptians are not required to register to vote, and somewhat over half have not. In 1987, the official turnout was 54%, an increase over 1984. Literacy is not required to vote; individual candidates are assigned one of 100 licensed symbols in order to facilitate electoral participation. Cynics note that progovernment officials are assigned symbols with positive connotations (e. g. , crescent, camel, palm tree), while opposition candidates are often assigned unsavory symbols such as pistols and swords.

Under Hosni Mubarak, elections have been energetically contested and a true opposition has emerged. That opposition, despite philosophical differences, has often stood as a bloc on behalf of greater democratization and civil liberties. Although the NDP has retained a consistent majority and nominates the Speaker of parliament, who has broad powers to guide and at times constrict discussion, parliamentary debate is lively and is widely covered in the print media.

The process has undergone dramatic developments since the early 1980s. The May 1984 elections, the first since Sadat's killing, were held under provisions of a new electoral law passed the previous July that rescinded the ban on prerevolutionary Cabinet ministers but stipulated that a party must receive 8% of the popular vote in order to seat representatives in the Assembly. The number of representatives was also increased from 392 to 448, and 48 large constituencies replaced the earlier 175. Parties wishing to stand for election were required to offer lists in every constituency. Prior to the elections the New Wafd had been recertified and allowed to stand for office.

In an election with an estimated 43% turnout, the NDP captured 73% of the vote, good for 389 seats. The Wafd polled 15% and sat 59 delegates, constituting a siz-

able opposition. Fueling controversy, the Wafd had aligned with the illegal but officially tolerated Muslim Brotherhood. Due to fundamental philosophical differences the pact did not survive. Many in fact speculated that the alliance cost the Wafd votes among some secularist and Coptic voters who otherwise harbored great sympathy for the party's prerevolutionary liberal legacy and looked to the party as a credible opposition force.

Opposition outcry against the inability of independents to stand for election and speculation that the Supreme Court would rule the 1984 elections illegal led to promulgation of a new electoral law in December 1986. The new law provided for 48 seats to be held by independent candidates, 1 per electoral district. By overwhelming margin in a popular referendum, the Assembly was dissolved in February 1987, and elections were held in April. For this round the Muslim Brotherhood struck an alliance with the Socialist Labor Party (SLP) and the Liberal Socialist Party (LSP). With a 54% turnout, the NDP won 346 seats. The alliance won 17%, good for 60 seats, 37 of which went to Muslim Brother candidates (in 1984 the SLP had scored 7%, too low to gain any seats). The Wafd polled 11% to control 35 seats. Independent candidates landed 7 seats. Overall, opposition candidates made up approximately 20% of the chamber. In July, President Mubarak was nominated for a second term, for which he was approved by referendum in October.

Despite significant gains by the opposition, its leaders raised new challenges, and in May 1990 the Supreme Court ruled the 1986 law unconstitutional, again on grounds of discriminating against independents. The new election law invalidated the 8% threshold for party representation in parliament and established the current structure of 222 constituencies with 2 representatives each, and 10 presidential appointees. In October 1990 voters elected to dissolve the Assembly (57% turnout; 94% support). Elections were held in the shadow of the Iraqi occupation of Kuwait and the assassination in October of the controversial Speaker of the Assembly, Rifat al-Mahgub, who had run the Assembly with an iron fist, provoking an unprecedented number of walkouts by opposition delegates.

Now, despite greater opening of the process—the abolition of the 8% requirement in particular—most opposition parties determined to boycott the elections, protesting the extension of emergency measures. Voter turnout reached only 20% to 30%, down significantly from the prior two elections. The Wafd, SLP, LSP, and Muslim Brothers did not contest; several members who ran as independents were dismissed by their parties. The NDP captured 77% and 348 seats. The Tagammu polled 1. 5% to win 6 seats and lead the parliamentary opposition. In addition, 83 independents won seats. Of these 56 were affiliated with the NDP, 14 with the Wafd, 8 with the SLP, and 1 with the LSP. Election to 7 seats was suspended, and the president for the first time appointed 10 additional delegates.

Egypt's most recent elections were held in November–December 1995. The background to these elections was the intensification of the confrontation between state security forces and militant Islamists. In January 1995, 87 people died in clashes in Upper Egypt, the highest monthly total in three years. The government lashed out at the Muslim Brotherhood, accusing it of aiding and abetting political violence. In addition, the government gave the judiciary wide powers to intervene in elections to professional associations that had come under Brotherhood control and to prevent Brothers from standing for office. In June, Mubarak survived an assassination attempt in Addis Ababa, where he was attending the Organization of African Unity (OAU) summit. In September the government announced that Brotherhood leaders arrested earlier in the year would be tried before special military tribunals.

The most recent elections, therefore, while offering great promise—4,109 candidates contested seats, compared with 2,681 in 1990—were also held at a time of increased tension. Earlier that month Israeli Prime Minister Yitzhak Rabin had been assassinated. After the first round, no opposition candidates had secured their constituencies, including individuals who had been consistently elected since the 1980s. In the second round a small opposition emerged, but many cried foul and it seemed as if the regime had determined to punish any and all critics. The focal point of controversy remained the Islamist opposition. Still not recognized as a legal party, the Muslim Brotherhood nonetheless ran a large list of independents. Several days prior to the polling many on the list were arrested, throwing their candidacy into disarray. In the end the NDP won 316 seats, down significantly from prior rounds. This number was bolstered, however, by the victories of 115 independents, most of whom proved to be surrogate NDP candidates (most immediately joined or rejoined the party). The true opposition controlled far fewer seats than has become the standard: the Wafd netted 6, the Tagammu 5, the Liberals and Nasserists 1 each. Leading opposition parties raised a legal suit in the courts contesting the results; the Tagammu, however, holding down a small opposition in parliament, refused to back the challenge, further splintering the opposition.

THE PARTY SYSTEM

As noted above, the current political party system is the outgrowth of electoral reform initiated by the Sadat regime and advanced much more forthrightly under Mubarak. Since the early 1980s Egyptians have witnessed a proliferation of parties that constitute a credible opposition, if not one that can command enough electoral support to form a government. In order to be licensed and contest elections, parties must be certified by the quasi-governmental Political Parties Commission, although most opposition parties have been certified only after appealing negative decisions to the judiciary. In addition to standing for election, most parties publish newspapers, mostly weeklies, that constitute a lively, if at times quasi-tabloid, opposition press. The opposition press serves as gadfly, printing stories that will not be covered in the official media, at times stretching the truth in a system where libel is loosely defined. Still, Egyptians who follow politics read all the major opposition papers as a matter of course.

In addition to widening printed political discourse, announcing scandals, and decrying state authority, opposition papers serve as platforms to advance the political agenda of non-NDP candidates and their parties, as well as to announce and cover campaign appearances and rallies. Political campaigning is restricted by law; demonstrations or marches are illegal, and campaign rallies must be approved by authorities. Campaign activities are not covered by the mainstream press. There is no paid political advertising in the print or broadcast media. Recent campaigns have, however, been marked by lively displays of hand-painted banners and a proliferation of campaign posters (candidates prepay the municipality a cleanup fee). Private vehicles festooned with campaign placards cruise the streets, and campaign volunteers distribute leaflets in the streets. Those more savvy to American tactics have in recent years distributed wallet-sized calendars and bumper stickers.

Voting irregularities have been endemic, and charges of hooliganism and vote fraud resound afterward. In 1987 opposition forces charged that three-quarters of the polling stations lacked proper observers. In 1995 an independent Egyptian commission oversaw polling and condemned irregularities by both government and opposition campaign workers. In earlier years elections had been marred by instances of violence that occasionally resulted in several deaths. Government officials have held that in such cases elections served as a cover to mask the settling of scores unrelated to the elections.

NATIONAL DEMOCRATIC PARTY (NDP)

(Hizb al-Watani al-Dimuqrati)

The ruling NDP is the outgrowth of the Nasser-era Arab Socialist Union. Consistently dominating parliament, the NDP has controlled the highest offices of state, from Speaker of parliament to the presidency. In the most recent (1995) elections it appeared to lose some ground, but most of the 115 independents elected proved to have links to the NDP. Speculation held that some of these candidates ran as independents as a way of garnering political experience. NDP ideology is reflected in state policy, which speaks to the legacy of the July Revolution—Revolution Day, July

23, remains a government holiday and the occasion for a major presidential address—even while furthering many of the economic reforms initiated by Sadat.

SOCIALIST LABOR PARTY (SLP)
(Hizb al-Amal al-Ishtiraki)

The SLP is the outgrowth of the old prerevolutionary Socialist Party that was, in turn, an outgrowth of the Young Egypt youth movement founded in the early 1930s. Despite its antiestablishment orientation, the Socialist Party was banned in 1953 along with other old-regime parties. Currently led by Ibrahim Shukri, a deputy in the last prerevolutionary parliament, and Magdi Husayn, the son of Young Egypt's founder, the SLP advocates greater social equity—but not in the Marxist terms advanced by the Tagammu—and civil liberties. Its social policies are conservative and leaned toward the Islamist position well before the electoral alliance with the Muslim Brotherhood (and Liberals) in 1987. SLP members accounted for just under half of the 60 seats won by the alliance, and Ibrahim Shukri led the parliamentary opposition. Mirroring the party's rise in influence, its weekly, Al-Shaab (The People) has transformed itself into a powerful and widely read opposition organ.

NEW WAFD PARTY
(Hizb al-Wafd al-Jadid)

The New Wafd is the reincarnation of the leading prerevolutionary nationalist party and is still led by Fuad Sirag al-Din, although due to his advanced age he is largely a figurehead. His younger brother Yas leads the parliamentary bloc. In terms of social and economic policy, particularly its support for greater privatization, the party has at times been labeled a proregime opposition party; in terms of promoting a more open electoral process and greater civil liberties and decrying the emergency measures still in force, however, the Wafd clearly fits an opposition bill. An early electoral alliance with the Muslim Brotherhood collapsed after the 1984 vote, and the party returned to its traditional secular-nationalist orientation. Its newspaper, Al-Wafd, quickly gained national attention and succeeded in transforming itself into a widely read daily.

NATIONAL PROGRESSIVE UNIONIST PARTY (NPUP)
(Hizb al-Tagammu al-Watani al-Taqaddami al-Wahdawi)

The NPUP, or Tagammu, is the outgrowth of the leftist strand within the ASU. Its members, many of whom served the Nasserist state, describe themselves alternatively as Nasserists and Marxists. The party president, Khalid Muhyi al-Din, the "red major," was a cofounder of the Free Officers movement and a close colleague of Nasser. The secretary general, Rifat al-Said, a respected historian, recently served on the Shura Council. Leading figures in the party such as Milad Hanna, a specialist in housing issues who has been appointed to the People's Assembly, Muhammad Sid-Ahmad, and Lutfi al-Khuli, are highly respected intellectuals and social critics and lend the party weekly, Al-Ahali (The People), greater weight than circulation figures might indicate. The party has remained the most outspoken champion of social reform, labor rights, and preserving the foundations of the socialist state. It has gained support among industrial workers, yet its influence has always far outweighed its electoral base. In recent years it has thrown itself in league with the government in combating religious extremism. In the 1995 elections the Tagammu emerged as the leading party of a tiny opposition. Party leaders opted not to join other opposition forces in filing a suit protesting irregularities.

NASSERIST ARAB DEMOCRATIC PARTY
(Hizb al-Arabi al-Dimuqrati al-Nasiri)

The Nasserist Democratic Arab Party is a more recent arrival, having been certified, after nearly two decades of denial, in April 1992. The party, which first constituted itself as the Nasserist Arab Socialist Party pursuant to Sadat's 1976 electoral reforms, seeks to promote the legacy of the Nasser era with a much less critical reevaluation than Tagammu counterparts, who also claim Nasserist credentials. The party's stated challenge—and the challenge of critics—is to find relevance in the policies of an earlier era, particularly one characterized by a lack of democracy, and in an individual who remains an icon but with contested legacies. The Nasserist Party has consistently faced internal factionalism. The party chief, Dia al-Din Daoud, who served as minister of social affairs in the late '60s, has been challenged in recent years by younger members for party leadership. The party's weekly, Al-`Arabi (The Arab), is less influential than other opposition papers but during the 1995 election season was published twice a week.

LIBERAL SOCIALIST PARTY (LSP)
(Hizb al-Ahrar al-Ishtiraki)

The LSP, heir to the right-wing platform of the ASU, has been led since its formation in 1976 by Mustafa Kamil Murad. The party is viewed largely as a shadow of the NDP, supporting privatization and foreign policy initiatives. Neither it nor its paper, *Al-Ahrar* (The Liberal), are accorded much interest. With Murad's death in August 1998, the party's future remains uncertain.

MINOR POLITICAL PARTIES

A variety of smaller parties have been licensed in recent years, none as yet exerting any significant influence on the polity. These include the Green Party, the Democratic Unionist Party, and a revived Young Egypt. A reconstituted Liberal Constitutionalist Party has been envisioned by descendants of the prerevolutionary minority party.

OTHER POLITICAL FORCES

The Military

Since the 1952 revolution the military has remained the ultimate guarantor of state power. Shortly after the July 23 coup, junta leaders acted to distance the Free Officers movement from direct political activity, arresting former comrades who continued to meet and attempt to influence policy. In 1953 the military high command was reshuffled. An RCC member and close Nasser confidant, Abdel Hakim Amer, was appointed commander in chief. During the March 1954 crisis triggered by Muhammad Nagib's dismissal, dissident members of the armor corps were arrested and further dismissals effected. In 1956, members of the RCC, Amer excepted, resigned their commissions and joined civilian ranks. Nevertheless, during the Nasser era the military emerged as a new elite, garnering special privileges and a fast track to high office. In the aftermath of the 1967 war, the military lost much of its prestige. Students demonstrated when senior officers escaped blame for the debacle and official responsibility fell on more junior colleagues. Fearing a military coup, Nasser ordered Amer placed under house arrest, and the field marshall died under mysterious circumstances.

The army regained popular acclaim in the October 1973 war, during which it first demonstrated a great degree of professionalism and battlefield competency. The Egyptian-Israeli peace led some to speculate that the military would lose political influence and social privilege. Combined maneuvers with Western alliance nations in regional strategic initiatives (Bright Star) and participation in the 1991 Gulf War (Desert Storm) have helped ensure an important place for the military. In 1986 the army had to be called in to quell riots by cadets in the central security forces (a branch of the Interior Ministry), provoked by rumors of extended service requirements. The rising tide of militant Islamic activism has led many to reassert the importance of the military as the ultimate foundation of state authority.

The military has kept its distance from direct political activity but remains the training ground for attaining the highest state offices. Hosni Mubarak, a flight instructor in 1952, represents the ascension of a second generation of military men to wield power. He rose to command the air force prior to the October War, and Sadat subsequently appointed him vice president. Many of his chief ministers and advisers hail from the officer corps. His defense minister, Abdel Hamid Abu Ghazala, a man long held to be the second-most-powerful individual in the country, was forced to resign in 1989 after being implicated in a scheme to smuggle U. S. missile technology to Egypt, yet remained a close adviser to the president. Safwat al-Sharif, Mubarak's minister of information since 1982 and one of his most prominent associates, rose from the ranks of military intelligence, as have many of Egypt's prime ministers.

Professional Organizations

Given the steps taken since the 1980s to open the political process and liberalize the economy, the role of professional organizations, once strictly supervised by the state, has grown in importance. The bar association, press syndicate, doctors' association, and other professional organizations have become centers of political opposition and vocal exponents of civil society. By the early 1990s they also became heavily influenced by Islamist elements with links to the Muslim Brothers. The state has acted in recent years to curb this influence through legal means, but the constitutionality of such measures remains questionable. In 1996 the government declared elections to the bar association illegal and placed the organization under judicial sequestration. Student government associations on the major campuses in Cairo, Alexandria, and provincial capitals became dominated by Islamists during Sadat's reign. The universities remain sites of frequent protests, most often relating to foreign affairs (the Gulf War, Palestinian-Israeli negotiations), but have not erupted in the kind of turmoil that characterized the campuses prior to the July Revolution.

Print and Broadcast Media

The official print media and all broadcast media are state-owned, funded, and directed. The *Al-Ahram* publications in particular are viewed as authoritative organs of government policy and are widely read throughout the region. A host of weekly news/arts magazines such as *Ruz al-Yusuf*, *Al-Musawwar*, and *October*, express varying degrees of political criticism, but always within the fold of regime approval. Political opposition has received greater coverage in recent years, but this coverage remains minimal and highly selective. The print media include an opposition press, primarily affiliated with opposition parties, but they too are inextricably linked to the state. Opposition newspapers use government-owned presses to print their product. This reliance on state institutions, in addition to restrictions on expression, promote self-censorship as a survival strategy, curbing the extent to which the opposition papers will speak out against state policy or individuals in government. Nonetheless, opposition papers are read by people who follow political, economic, and social developments, and readership is not limited to a partisan audience. There have been efforts in recent years to establish privately funded newspapers without links to political parties or state institutions, but these have not been approved.

Yet in a country known for its plethora of newspapers and journals, the real contest for influence is engaged in broadcast media, television in particular. Television programming in Egypt is fully state-produced. News broadcasts are still characterized by a protocol that runs the presidential calendar of events as the lead. Opposition viewpoints are rarely expressed. All of this has become increasingly complicated with the advent and spread of cable and satellite television in the 1990s. An estimated 200,000 television sets (4%) in Egypt are able to receive satellite transmission. Unlike some other Middle Eastern governments, the Egyptian government has not banned satellite dishes, but the control of information and the rampant pirating of state-produced products are a paramount concern.

With the formation of the Egyptian Radio and Television Union (ERTU) in 1970, all broadcast, from writing to production, fell under the auspices of the Ministry of Information. Prior to that it had shifted between Communication and Culture. In the early 1990s the government established as ERTU subsidiaries two satellite channels and a cable network, CNE, which subcontracts other Arab cable channels. In April 1998 Egypt launched its first telecommunications satellite, Nilesat. This is in part an effort to maintain Egypt's dominance over broadcast production throughout the Arab world. A new 300-million-dollar Media Production City outside Cairo is intended to bolster a sagging film industry and to lure Arab television producers back into Egyptian studios.

Certain nonnews programming, dramatic serials especially, have increasingly become stages upon which state policy is articulated. While state-produced dramas have been allowed to criticize social and economic trends—often couched in historical settings but sometimes set in the present—television drama has focused increasingly on the contest between the state and the religious opposition. Most social dramas now include Islamist characters who are generally misguided if not outright evil and who pay a heavy price when they attempt to quit their brotherhood. Such figures are the only outwardly devout characters portrayed. In this way, television plays an active role in promoting a secular-oriented public culture, and television producers and writers are engaged in trying to shape a public consensus with regard to the most serious issue facing the state.

THE ISLAMIC CURRENT AND PROSPECTS FOR THE FUTURE

The most important nonparty political force in the country—perhaps the most important overall—is the still-illegal Muslim Brotherhood. Founded in 1928, the movement promoted national liberation within a socially conservative religious framework that defined modern Islamism throughout the Arab and broader Islamic world. Caught in a cauldron of political violence, the movement was outlawed in 1948 and again by the Nasser regime in 1954 (after a period of collaboration with the RCC). After an unsuccessful attempt on Nasser's life in October 1954, the movement was crushed. A military tribunal tried and sentenced to death the assailant and five Brotherhood leaders implicated in the plot. Anwar Sadat restored a degree of official legitimacy to the movement, freeing Muslim Brother prisoners and allowing exiled Brothers to return and the movement to publish a weekly journal. Many reemerged on the political scene to promote a gradualist program of social conversion, seeking to opt into the political process as a legal participant, a goal that has remained elusive despite the compromises struck with the state.

At the same time, two decades of political repression bred a radical wing that came to define the secular state as apostate and embarked upon militant stratagems to overthrow the regime and spark revolutionary change. The Sadat government attempted to use Islamist movements to offset the power of more rooted Nasserist organizations on campuses, in professional organizations, and the bureaucracy. This proved a dangerous gambit, particularly as Sadat embarked upon closer relations with the West, peace with Israel, and economic policies that promoted a previously unseen consumerism replete with foreign/Western trappings well out of the financial reach of most Egyptians. Islamist activists were among the many arrested in September 1981. Followers of Muhammad Islambuli, leader of the militant Jihad movement and one of those detained, assassinated Sadat in 1981.

The Mubarak regime has approached the Islamist current with a carrot-stick policy, allowing the Muslim Brothers to participate in the political process under the auspices of legal parties and striking with force against radical splinter movements. Brotherhood figures have sat in parliament and promoted greater civil liberties along with an Islamist social agenda. At the same time they have spoken out consistently against the repression of more radical Islamist counterparts, blaming the state for fomenting violence.

Islamism remains an issue that sorely divides the body politic. Popular sentiment runs strongly against both state security forces and Islamist militancy. Yet the ability of Islamist organizations to provide basic services, often more efficiently than the state, garners public support in poorer neighborhoods. In the past decade the Islamist current has made great inroads into basic organs of civil society, winning control over trade unions and professional organizations. The state has responded by confronting Islamism in popular media: print, television, cinema, and theatrical drama. Many champions of greater political liberalism find themselves supporting the government crackdown on Islamist forces, even to the extent of election engineering that successfully kept Islamist candidates—along with other opposition forces—from sitting in the current parliament. Others argue that the regime should allow the Muslim Brothers more voice in governing in order to bolster mainstream nonmilitant Islamist confidence in the political process and foster a greater stake in promoting civil order.

The decentralization of radical Islamist movements has stymied government efforts to decisively eliminate them. In 1997 imprisoned leaders called for a halt to violent acts, but the extent of their authority over operatives at large is uncertain. Recent acts of political violence targeting security forces and tourists—a serious blow aimed against domestic and foreign confidence in the state as well as a major source of national income—belie government claims to have suppressed militant forces and un-derscore the extent to which Egypt remains a nation still in search of pluralistic stability.

Further Reading

Abdalla, Ahmed. "Egypt's Islamists and the State. " *Middle East Report*, July–August 1993, 28–31.

Abu-Lughod, Lila. "Finding a Place for Islam: Egyptian Television Serials and the National Interest. " *Public Culture 5* (1993): 493–513.

Baker, Raymond. *Sadat and After: The Struggle for Egypt's Soul*. Cambridge, Mass. : Harvard University Press, 1990.

Gordon, Joel. "Secular and Religious Memory in Egypt: Recalling Nasserist Civics. " *The Muslim World* 87, no. 2 (April 1997): 94–109.

Al-Sayyid, Mustapha K. "A Civil Society in Egypt?" *Middle East Journal* 47, no. 2 (spring 1993): 228–42.

Springborg, Robert. *Mubarak's Egypt: Fragmentation of the Political Order*. Boulder, Colo: Westview Press, 1989.

Waterbury, John. *The Egypt of Nasser and Sadat: The Political Economy of Two Regimes*. Princeton, N. J. : Princeton University Press, 1983.

Zubaida, Sami. "Islam, the State, and Democracy: Contrasting Conceptions of Society in Egypt. " *Middle East Report*, November–December 1992, 2–10.

THE REPUBLIC OF EL SALVADOR

(República de El Salvador)

By Kristin Marsh

THE SYSTEM OF GOVERNMENT

El Salvador is a small Central American country bordering Guatemala to the northwest and Honduras to the northeast. With the highest population density in the region, El Salvador's 21,041 square kilometers sustain nearly 6 million people, 56% of whom live in rural areas dominated by export agriculture. Today, 94% of Salvadorans are mestizo, 5% are Indian, and 1% are white. The religious makeup of the country roughly reflects the region as a whole: 75% of Salvadorans are Roman Catholic, although Protestantism is on the rise.

El Salvador is one of the top five sources of U. S. immigration. In 1995, for example, more than one-third of Central Americans entering the United States legally were from El Salvador. And only Mexico surpasses El Salvador as a source of illegal immigration to the United States. Today, the reasons for migration are economic rather than political. Immigration represents an important supplement to El Salvador's stagnant economy. Immigrants send approximately $1. 25 billion each year to families in El Salvador.

According to the 1983 constitution, El Salvador's republican form of government is made up of the executive, the legislative, and the judicial branches of government. Although formally independent, the three branches remained highly politicized and intertwined throughout the 1980s, and many constitutional guarantees were suspended under the frequent states of emergency called during the civil war period.

Much of El Salvador's recent political history has been dominated by social unrest and political conflict, escalating in the 20th century to a series of revolts, military dictatorships, heightened repression, and protracted civil war. Beginning in the mid-1800s, the Salvadoran government supported and directed the development of an export-oriented agricultural economy based predominantly on coffee and increasingly controlled by a few wealthy families. Heightened levels of poverty and inequality fueled a climate of rebellion, which culminated in Agustin Farabundo Martí's organized revolt at the beginning of the Depression in 1931. The landed oligarchy, supported by the military government, met rebellion with repression and managed to force reformists either underground or into quietude. Approximately 25,000 Indian peasants were massacred, and Martí was executed. Because most of the victims of the 1932 government-directed peasant massacre were Indians, the indigenous population was drastically reduced. Since public officials were usually members of the aristocracy, the landed oligarchy (popularly known as *los catorce*) traditionally held political as well as socioeconomic power. But the 1930s marked a transition in the character of Salvadoran power sharing. The military co-opted political power in its 1931 coup and justified its position by achieving the necessary social stability to see the economy and the country through the Depression. The resulting uneasy alliance characterized the Salvadoran power structure for 50 years: while the landholders retained their economic position, the military ruled politically.

Nevertheless, a strengthening guerrilla opposition worked to unite peasants, workers, and students; it also heightened instability in the traditional power structure. In a military coup staged by junior officers, General Carlos Romero was overthrown in October 1979. However, the resulting military-civilian junta was no more successful in achieving real reform or restoring stability. Civil war escalated dramatically in the early 1980s and continued virtually unabated until 1992 when negotiated settlement finally brought the stalemated civil war to a close. The peace process started in Geneva with the April 1990 framework agreement. By 1991, the parties agreed to a series of changes in the constitution that guided later reforms in the armed forces, the judiciary, and the electoral system.

The two major parties to the conflict—the Salvadoran government/armed forces and the Farabundo Martí National Liberation Front (FMLN)—signed the Peace Accords on January 12, 1992, in Chapultepec, Mexico. The settlement, made possible by a persisting stalemate in the intransigent conflict, represented a compromise on both sides. The government conceded points on political procedure and security concerns, in effect agreeing to simultaneous demilitarization of the government and democratization of the political process. The FMLN, on the other hand, conceded its demands for socioeconomic restructuring, thereby postponing battles over land distribution, income inequality, and development. These issues could be worked out through newly opened institutional political channels. The period between 1992 and the 1994 elections was dedicated to the transition from civil war to stable republic, and the period between 1994 and 1997 has helped consolidate the fragile peace.

Executive

Most political and economic matters in El Salvador fall under the jurisdiction of the executive office, which is made up of the president, vice president, and Council of Ministers. The president, who holds the authority of chief of state and head of government, selects Cabinet members and serves a single five-year term. The March 1994 general election resulted in a runoff for president between Armando Calderón Sol (ARENA) and Ruben Zamora Rivas (CD/FMLN/MNR). Calderón won the April runoff with 68% of the vote. The mayor of San Salvador, Hector Silva (FMLN), and a former president, Alfredo Cristiani (ARENA), are possible candidates for the 1999 race.

Legislature

National parliamentary and municipal elections are held every three years, and the 84 seats of the National Assembly are filled by proportional representation. ARENA, the leading party on the right, took 39 seats in the National Assembly in 1994. The FMLN, participating in elections for the first time, won 21 seats in coalition with the National Revolutionary Movement (MNR) and the Democratic Convergence (CD). The Christian Democratic Party (PDC) was pushed into third place, with 18 seats, and the Party of National Reconciliation (PCN) followed in fourth, with 4 seats.

The March 1997 elections advanced the FMLN. Results for the National Assembly were very close for ARENA and the FMLN. Out of a possible 84 seats, ARENA won 28, FMLN won 27, the PCN won 11, the Christian Democrats won 7, and the PD obtained only 3 seats. Because neither party dominates the Assembly, both sides have been forced to seek alliances and work toward consensus on legislative issues. Following the 1994 elections, for example, the split legislature came to an impasse over the election of supreme court justices. The country went for a month without a supreme court before a political compromise allowing the necessary two-thirds majority could be obtained.

Judiciary

Because human rights abuses and judicial scandal were highly entrenched problems in El Salvador prior to and throughout the civil war period, reform of the justice system has been one of the most important and most problematic concerns of the peace process. The Supreme Court, El Salvador's highest judicial authority, determines the constitutionality of laws and regulations. It encompasses the divisions of constitutional law, civil law, penal law, and litigation. Lower courts include courts of the second instance, courts of the first instance, and courts of peace. Fourteen Supreme Court magistrates are elected to staggered nine-year terms by a two-thirds majority in the Legislative Assembly. Historically, the Court was often selected on the basis of suggestions of the executive, with little debate within the legislature. With the greater political diversity introduced in the 1994 elections, the makeup of the Court now reflects legislative debate and compromise. The Court has a more balanced makeup and greater independence from partisan politics.

However, the power of the judiciary remains highly concentrated in the Supreme Court, despite attempts at reform. For example, the National Council of the Judiciary (*Consejo Nacional de la Judicatura*; CNJ) nominates and evaluates Supreme Court magistrates, lower judges, and justices of the peace. Theoretically independent, the relationship between the CNJ and the Supreme Court contributes to its vulnerability to Supreme Court control.

Regional and Local Government

El Salvador is divided into 14 departments and 262 municipalities. Unlike the proportional representation at the national level, the simple-majority electoral system gives the winning party 100% representation on each municipal council. In 1994 ARENA held full control over 207 municipalities, followed by PDC (29), the FMLN (15), and PCN (10). With only 44% of the vote, ARENA obtained 79% of the municipal councils, while the FSLN, with 24% of the vote, obtained only 6% of municipal councils. In the March 1997 elections, however, ARENA kept only 161 municipalities. The FMLN won 48 municipalities outright in 1997; it also won another 7 races in alliance with other leftist parties. Importantly, the mayoralty of San Salvador, considered the nation's second-most-influential post and a stepping-stone to the presidency, was won by Hector Silva (FMLN).

THE ELECTORAL SYSTEM

The electoral system in El Salvador is based on universal suffrage for all citizens 18 years of age or older. Because illiteracy is high, the secret ballot uses party symbols and colored ballots to facilitate broad participation. Historically, elections were so consistently fraudulent that the left and center-left parties refused to participate. One of the central accomplishments of the implementation of the 1992 Peace Accords has been the opening up of the electoral system. The FMLN participated for the first time in 1994, and again in 1997. Both of these elections, while problematic in some respects, were internationally recognized as generally free and fair.

For the 1994 elections, the Supreme Electoral Tribunal (TSE) was established to head the electoral process, thereby replacing the Central Elections Council (CCE). The TSE, made up of one magistrate from each of the four main parties in the General Assembly and one president elected by the General Assembly, was overseen by a board composed of representatives from all parties. For the 1994 elections, therefore, the FMLN was represented on the oversight board but not on the TSE itself. Local elections boards were also set up to represent all political parties.

Reform of the electoral system has contributed directly to increases in registration, although voter turnout has not improved since the 1980s. Voter turnout in 1994 was 55% in the first round and 46% in the runoff, representing a slight increase since 1991 but a decline in participation compared with 1982 and 1984. The 1997 election, which did not involve a presidential race, had only a 40% participation rate.

THE PARTY SYSTEM

Historically, El Salvador's political party system has been characteristically exclusionary. Leftist opposition parties were often banned (the constitution disallows armed political parties), and their members and leaders became victims of violent repression. And government parties stayed in power even against centrist parties such as the PDC through political repression and fraudulent elections.

The general elections of March 1994 marked the opening of the electoral system to include political parties of the left. Nine parties participated: three parties representing the ideological right (ARENA, MAC, and PCN), three representing the center-right (PDC, MSN, and MU), and three representing the left (MNR, CD, and FMLN). The parties of the left formed the coalition MNR–CD–FMLN for the presidential race. This expanded inclusiveness has allowed for greater political polarization, with considerable support for both the left and right and decreasing support for moderate and center-right parties.

NATIONALIST REPUBLICAN ALLIANCE

(Alianza Republicana Nacionalista; ARENA)

ARENA emerged in 1981 as the rightist party led by Major Roberto D'Aubuisson. D'Aubuisson, former chief of intelligence for the National Guard, has been implicated in the 1980 killing of Archbishop Oscar Romero and other human rights abuses. Under D'Aubuisson, ARENA sup-

ported a military solution to the civil war and opposed the reform program sought by the United States. As the main rival of the PDC throughout the civil war period, the majority of ARENA's support came from big business, the military, and various segments of the rural population.

Responding to political defeat in the 1985 legislative elections, ARENA's political strategy took a more moderate tack. Under the leadership of Alfredo Cristiani and Armando Calderón Sol, the new platform emphasized neoliberal economic reform and played down the importance of political solutions to the conflict. The strategy paid off electorally in 1988, when ARENA's Alfredo Cristiani took the presidency with 55% of the vote. Once in office, Cristiani put a new emphasis on the problem of civil war and initiated negotiations with the FMLN.

ARENA remains the leading political party of the right. In 1994, ARENA's showing was strong: Armando Calderón Sol won the presidency and ARENA took 39 seats in the National Assembly race. In 1997, ARENA's representation in the National Assembly declined somewhat to 27 seats. The 1994 results have been interpreted as a rejection of ARENA's neoliberal economic policy, which has failed even to sustain the already poor standard of living of most people.

FARABUNDO MARTÍ NATIONAL LIBERATION FRONT

(Frente Farabundo Martí para la Liberacion Nacional; FMLN)

The FMLN was established in 1980 as a Sandinista-style guerrilla fighting arm of the leftist opposition (whose political wing at the time was the once-legal FDR). The FMLN served to coordinate the several leftist parties and emerged as the leading leftist opposition party, both during and in the aftermath of the civil war. When the FMLN was formed, it was thought that the civil war could be quickly brought to a close militarily. Even with considerable regional support, however, the guerrillas were not strong enough to overpower the military forces.

Citing electoral fraud and repressive political conditions, the FMLN refused to participate in any of the elections of the 1980s. Although the electoral system went through formal reforms, the FMLN's abstention undermined the legitimacy of the elections. The Democratic Convergence, a coalition of leftist parties, participated in 1989 but had considerable difficulty mobilizing without the active support of the FMLN.

The first elections of the post–civil war period ushered in a new, legitimate, political role for the FMLN. In 1994, the FMLN had a strong showing, and the legislative elections of March 1997 mark the left's first victory at the polls. FMLN participation exemplifies the new openness of the political system and the institutionalization of oppositional politics in El Salvador.

PARTY OF NATIONAL RECONCILIATION

(Partido de Conciliacion Nacional; PCN)

Colonel Julio Adalberto Rivera created the PCN in the 1960s as the official government party. The PCN ran official candidates and controlled elections, thereby ensuring victory for its presidential candidates through 1979, including Colonel Fidel Sanchez Hernandez (1967), Colonel Arturo Armando Molina (1972), and General Carlos Humberto Romero (1977). Although the PCN is widely recognized as having resorted to election fraud, at first the system was relatively open to participation by opposition parties, particularly in local and National Assembly races. After the 1979 military coup, the PCN lost its influence among the armed forces. Support for the PCN waned through the 1980s, as the Christian Democrats and ARENA took center stage.

CHRISTIAN DEMOCRATIC PARTY

(Partido Democrata Cristiano; PDC)

Under the leadership of the mayor of San Salvador, Jose Napoleon Duarte, the PDC emerged in the 1960s as the major opposition party to the PCN regime. In the aftermath of the highly fraudulent 1970 National Assembly elections and in anticipation of the 1972 presidential elections, the PDC, the socialist National Revolutionary Movement (MNR), and the communist National Democratic Union (UDN) formed a leftist alliance party, the *Union Nacional Opositora* (UNO). Duarte ran for president under the UNO and clearly won the 1972 elections. But the military declared victory for Molina, the PCN candidate. After a defeated coup attempt that Duarte had been persuaded to support, he was forced into exile by the Molina government.

The continuation of electoral fraud through the 1970s, coupled with worsening economic conditions and continued rigidity in the government (especially repression of the peasantry), led to increasing popular discontent. To avoid the possibility of a leftist revolutionary overthrow similar to that experienced in Nicaragua, a group of junior army officers staged a coup in 1980 against General Romero that was intended to be progressive and achieve moderate reform. The new government was highly divided, however, and collapsed within months. Almost immediately, a new government was announced that represented an agreement between the military and the PDC, whereby the PDC would reorganize the new government and the security forces would retain their autonomy.

Duarte returned from exile in December 1980 as the newly appointed president. In 1985, presidential elections resulted in a PDC majority in the National Assembly (after a poor showing in 1982) and a victory for Duarte's presidency. As a centrist party, the PDC has suffered a decreasing constituency in the 1990s. With the political system increasingly open, voters are polarizing in their party alignment.

MINOR PARTIES AND PARTY COALITIONS

Major opposition parties in El Salvador frequently strengthen their voting bloc through strategic alliances with one or more ideologically compatible minor parties. In the 1994 presidential race, for example, the leftist coalition FMLN–MNR–CD backed the FMLN candidate. At the local level, leftist coalitions were built around four different types of alliances: FMLN–MNR–CD, FMLN–MR, FMLN–CD, and CD–MNR. In most local races and in the National Assembly race, however, each party ran alone. Other minor parties represented in the 1994 legislative elections included Unidad and the rightist Christian Authentic Movement (MAC).

OTHER POLITICAL FORCES

The Military

As a central political actor, the military in El Salvador has controlled the state administration for much of the 20th century. Rather than establish an open military dictatorship as was more common in South America, the military in El Salvador sought a facade of legitimacy by setting up the PCN as its political party and holding formally open elections. Military generals held the position of president until the 1979 coup.

Operating under a strongman *caudillo* system, the military controlled the country through high levels of repression by the security forces. During the 1980s, the United States influenced a measure of reform by supporting Duarte's civilian presidency and emphasizing human rights. The number of political disappearances and the use of torture against political opponents declined somewhat. But the military remained powerful, its personnel retained impunity, and the level of general violence against the civilian population increased. Salvadoran society was highly militarized.

The 1992 Peace Accords outlined the demobilization process for both parties to the conflict, the Salvadoran armed forces and the FMLN. It also called for far-reaching structural changes in the military: the complete demobilization and disarmament of the FMLN and reintegration of its members into civilian society; the separation of the armed forces and civilian police, involving the establishment of a new police force; the dismantling of the security forces and the army's "shock troops"; an overall cut in the number of enlisted military personnel; and the replacement of military intelligence by a civilian intelligence service. Army personnel lost impunity through the establishment of the Salvadorean Ad Hoc Commission and the non-Salvadorean Truth Commission, both of which were charged with investigating human rights abuses. Agreeing to complete demilitarization of the government and of civilian society was one of the state's biggest compromises of the negotiations. In short, the military, once at the center of El Salvador's protection racket state, is now virtually excluded from the internal security arena.

The National Commission for the Consolidation of Peace (Comision para la Consolidacion de la Paz; COPAZ)

COPAZ was established in 1991 in order to ensure civilian participation in the implementation of the peace agreement. During the transition period, COPAZ provided an arena for multiparty dialogue and consensus building. The FMLN was represented on COPAZ, as was the government and each political party represented in the Assembly. COPAZ also filled a legislative function, having the authority to accept or reject any law considered by the Legislative Assembly. COPAZ was intended to operate through completion of the peace implementation. In the aftermath of the 1994 elections there was considerable debate about whether COPAZ was still useful. In 1995, COPAZ disbanded, and the government of Calderón Sol took over responsibility for any pending items of the Peace Accords.

Organized Labor

The labor movement in El Salvador benefited from the strong economy of the 1950s and 1960s. Both membership and numbers of organizations grew during this period. But starting in the late 1970s and continuing through the civil war, repression hit the labor unions particularly hard.

The peace process afforded organized labor an institutionalized voice in economic policy through representation on the Forum for Economic and Social Consultation. The Forum brought members of labor together with representatives of the government and business on issues of post–civil war economic readjustment, urban poverty, and labor legislation. While the Forum has had limited success overall, its success in the area of labor legislation has been considerable. Despite resistance from the business sector, initial success in achieving individual worker rights was followed eventually by the adoption of gains in trade union rights, which were formalized in Labor Code reform in April 1994.

External Forces

Various external parties have exerted substantial influence on El Salvador's political events, although none has played a decisive role. The U. S. government's interest in El Salvador increased with escalation of the civil war in the 1980s. Fearing a FMLN takeover similar to that of the FSLN in Nicaragua, the United States strongly supported the Duarte presidency and the military, but it also pressed for political and military reforms. However, human rights abuses were continuing, the civil war had clearly reached stalemate, and the communist threat had receded. By 1990, the U. S. position had shifted in support of a cease-fire.

The FMLN's external support came from regional neighbors, particularly Nicaragua and Honduras. Again, outside influence was not decisive. The FMLN was unable to win the civil war with FSLN support. Yet when that support lagged in the late 1980s, the guerrillas were still able to hold their own.

The UN played a major role in mediating the negotiations, implementing the settlement, and consolidating the peace. The United Nations Observer Mission in El Salvador (ONUSAL) provided multidimensional support for the implementation of the peace settlement. Initially deployed as a verification mission for human rights reforms, ONUSAL's mandate expanded with the signing of the final Chapultepec Agreement. Military and police divisions were added to the human rights division, and the mandate was interpreted broadly to encompass active monitoring and verification of all aspects of the Peace Accords. Much of the success of the transition period has been attributed to the creative deployment of the ONUSAL mission.

NATIONAL PROSPECTS

Twelve years of civil war cost 75,000 Salvadoran lives, devastated the fragile economy, and depleted or destroyed core natural resources such as soil and water. The 1992 Peace Accords brought a welcome end to the violent conflict. It also set the stage for free elections, a general democratization of politics, an end to human rights abuses, and reform of the military and police forces. The years since have been dedicated to the process of peace consolidation, including implementation of the terms of agreement within a peaceful transition period.

How stable is post–civil war El Salvador? During the early transition period, prospects for a lasting peace appeared tenuous, at best. The compromising nature of the Accords and continuing economic hardship point to unmitigated grievances that may or may not flare up in conflict in the future. And the question remains whether

ARENA and the upper classes will accept a political back seat when and if political democracy eventually allows for a left-dominated government.

On the other hand, the 1994 general elections and the March 1997 local and National Assembly elections have each strengthened an optimistic outlook for El Salvador's political stability. In 1994, the left participated, for the first time, in a campaign and elections that international observers recognized as free and fair. And in 1997, the left enjoyed a major advance in the National Assembly and local elections. So far, ARENA has accepted this political setback. Prospects for lasting peace and a stable democracy appear increasingly strong.

Socioeconomically, the situation for most Salvadorans has not improved with the end of civil war. Economic reforms were not a condition of the final agreement. Since most attention has been directed to implementing the Accords' specific terms, El Salvador remains a poor and highly stratified society. The strategy for the left is now to bring about socioeconomic reforms through institutionalized political power. Now that the FMLN has a real voice in the Assembly, it remains to be seen how successful it will be in achieving greater equality and improved living standards, either in the short or the long run.

National prospects are certainly brighter today than they have been at almost any other period in the country's relatively short history. Whether or not political democracy and civil rights are strong enough advantages to allow this small state to finally prosper, it is clear that peace and increasing political stability are providing a significant move in the right direction.

Further Reading

Anderson, Thomas P. *Matanza: El Salvador's Communist Revolt of 1932.* Lincoln: University of Nebraska Press, 1971.

———. *Politics in Central America: Guatemala, El Salvador, Honduras, and Nicaragua.* New York: Praeger, 1988.

———. *The War of the Dispossessed: Honduras and El Salvador.* Lincoln and London: University of Nebraska Press, 1981.

Armstrong, Robert, and Janet Shenk. *El Salvador: The Face of Revolution.* Boston: South End Press, 1982.

Boyce, James K. *Economic Policy for Building Peace: The Lessons of El Salvador.* Boulder, Colo. : Lynne Rienner, 1996.

Doggett, Martha. *Death Foretold: The Jesuit Murders in El Salvador.* Washington, D. C. : Georgetown University Press, 1993.

Dominguez, Jorge I. , and Abraham F. Lowenthal, eds. *Constructing Democratic Governance: Latin America and the Caribbean in the 1990s.* Baltimore: Johns Hopkins University Press, 1996.

Dunkerly, James. *The Long War: Dictatorship & Revolution in El Salvador.* London: Junction, 1985.

Johnstone, Ian. *Rights and Reconciliation: U. N. Strategies in El Salvador.* Boulder, Colo. : Lynne Rienner, 1995.

Lernoux, Penny. *Cry of the People: The Struggle for Human Rights in Latin America—The Catholic Church Conflict with U. S. Policy.* New York: Viking Penguin, 1982.

Stanley, William. *The Protection Racket State: Elite Politics, Military Extortion, and Civil War in El Salvador.* Boulder, Colo. : Westview Press, 1996.

Thiesenhusen, William C. *Broken Promises: Agrarian Reform and the Latin American Campesino.* Boulder, Colo. : Westview Press, 1995.

REPUBLIC OF EQUATORIAL GUINEA

(República de Guinea Ecuatorial)

By T. Bruce Fryer

Equatorial Guinea, formerly Spanish Guinea, is a small country with a resident population of about 522,400 in 1997. Its chief of state is President Teodoro Obiang Nguema Mbasogo, elected February 25, 1996, to a seven-year term. The country includes two principal geographical divisions. The first division, Río Muni on the continent of central west Africa, is bounded by Cameroon on the north and Gabon on the east and south. The second consists of two major islands, the larger of which is Bioko, and several smaller islands. Both the continental and the insular portions were part of Spanish colonization in the Gulf of Guinea. The capital of the republic, Malabo, is located on the island of Bioko and has a population of around 80,000.

The republic officially gained its independence from Spain on October 12, 1968, and had its first presidential elections in August. Francisco Macías Nguema Negúe, a colonial civil servant, was elected president. By mid-1970, Macías had created a single-party state through the elimination of opposition leaders, and by 1972, he had assumed the title of president for life. The country was converted into a military-dominated police state with ties to Moscow and Havana. An unknown number of people were killed (perhaps as many as 35,000), and an estimated 100,000 went into political exile. Eventually Macías's personally established party, the National Workers' Party (*Partido Unico Nacional de Trabajadores*; PUNT) had eliminated all other political parties within the country. Forced labor was provided to the cocoa and coffee plantations.

Macías, or *Papa Gallo* (Father Gamecock) as he was known, was overthrown in a palace revolt led by his nephew on August 3, 1979. The coup leader, Lieutenant Colonel Teodoro Obiang Ngueme Mbasogo (born 1942), is currently the head of state. Most all of the nation's leaders, including Obiang, are from the Fang, the dominant mainland ethnic group from around Mongomo. The new constitution (The Fundamental Law, 1982) called for a seven year presidential term. Obiang began his first term as the first president of the Third Republic of Equatorial Guinea on October 12, 1982.

During the first term of Obiang's presidency, the office of prime minister was created and was given the power to coordinate internal policy, although he could be appointed, dismissed, or granted power by the president. A legislature was organized by 1983 with 15 members appointed by the president and 45 elected by citizens. The judicial system was headed by the head of state and judicial advisers, thus forming the Supreme Court. This body allowed traditional laws to be in force as long as they did not conflict with the national laws. The Chamber of the People's Representatives (*Cámara de Representantes del Pueblo*) could not function without approval of the president.

By 1987, Obiang Nguema and his supporters had established a national political party, the Democratic Party of Equatorial Guinea (*Partido Democrático de Guinea Ecuatorial*; PDGE), and political exiles were invited to reenter the country for a promised open presidential election in 1989. In June 1988, some exiles returned to run in the election, but the pledge to multiparty elections was not honored, and Obiang was elected to office without opposition in June 1989.

The presidential election in February 1996 again overwhelmingly supported Obiang in the presidency. The results of that election were not well received by the Spanish press, by opposition leaders, or by international observers. There is some indication from recent elections in Equatorial Guinea, however, that the Joint Opposition Party (*Plataforma de Oposición Conjunta*; POC) may have won at least nine municipal elections, indicating broader support than reported.

Between July and August of 1998, there were reports of continued arrests of oppostion party members with activists being detained for short periods of time and being ill-treated to get them to pay fines or join the PDGE. The elections originally scheduled for October 1998 were rescheduled for December 1998.

The government of Obiang has been encouraged to seek additional financial investment from the United States. This may have begun with Walter International, an American-based company that signed an agreement in 1990 to develop an oil deposit north of the island of Bioko. In March 1995, Mobil Corporation and United Meridien Corporation announced the extraction of significant quantities of crude oil under the agreement off shore Zafiro. How this new revenue source will be administered by the government is of critical importance to the economic future of residents and emigrées of Equatorial Guinea and to the future course of national political directions within the country.

Further Reading

Fegley, Randall. *Equatorial Guinea: An African Tragedy.* New York: Peter Lang, 1989.

Lininger-Goumaz, Max. *Guinea Ecuatorial: Bibliografia general, X.* Geneva: Les Éditions du Temps, 1998.

———. *Guinée Equatoriale: 30 ans d'État délinquant nguemiste.* Paris: L'Harmattan, 1998.

Roig, Joan. *Guinea Ecuatorial: La dictadura enquistada.* Bilbao, 1996.

ERITREA

(Ertraa)

By Jon Abbink, Ph. D.

THE SYSTEM OF GOVERNMENT

Since April 1993, Eritrea has been an independent state, the first one to emerge from the fold of an existing African state in the postcolonial era. The country, with an estimated 3. 5 million inhabitants, was forged in war. From 1962 to 1974, the country was engaged in armed struggle with the autocratic regime of emperor Haile Sellasie, and from 1974 to 1991, with the dictatorial Marxist regime of Mengistu Haile Mariam in Ethiopia. In May 1991 it ended with the victorious entry of the Eritrean Peoples' Liberation Front (EPLF) troops into Asmara, the Eritrean capital. The EPLF, as the dominant and best-organized resistance movement in the country, took power and installed a provisional government. Eritrea declared independence after a referendum in April 1993.

At present, Eritrea is a virtual one-party state led by the Popular Front for Democracy and Justice (PFDJ), which is the political successor party to the EPLF. After a unilaterally proclaimed four-year transition period (1993–97), Eritrea was scheduled to be transformed into a multiparty state. The government is made up of an executive State Council, supervised by a National Assembly. The role of the president (chairman of the party, of the Council, and of the Assembly) is dominant.

History

The political history of Eritrea in the past century cannot be understood apart from that of Ethiopia. Eritrea—the name and the territory—was created as an Italian colony in 1889, after the Italians gained a foothold on north Ethiopian territory in 1869 (around the port city of Assäb and extended it in 1885 to Mis'iwa). Emperors Yohannis and Minilik II did not succeed in dislodging the Italians from the coastal area, despite the resounding military victory of Ethiopia over expansionist Italian troops in 1896 at Adua.

In 1941, Eritrea was liberated by the British, and became a UN-mandated territory until 1952. It saw political reforms and the beginnings of a more democratic political culture. From 1952 to 1962 Eritrea was federated with Ethiopia. Eritrea's autonomy was, however, accepted nei-

ther by Emperor Haile Selassie nor by Eritrean leaders of the reigning Unionist Party, and in 1962, through a controversial vote in the Eritrean Parliament, Eritrea was "integrated" with Ethiopia as a province.

Around that date, an armed struggle was taken up to regain autonomy, and later independence, by the (mainly Muslim-supported) Eritrean Liberation Front (ELF) and later the EPLF (supported by Muslim and Christian groups). After the Ethiopian revolution of 1974, the struggle continued, because of the increasingly rigid unitary standpoint of the Ethiopian Provisional Military Administrative Council (PMAC). A peaceful opening made by the then chairman of the PMAC, General Aman Andom, in December 1974, was sabotaged by the pro-Mengistu faction in the PMAC and led to the assassination of General Aman and to the death of the peace option.

Due to its strong internal organization and high morale, the EPLF—with some foreign support—held its ground in the war even in critical times, captured sizable quantities of enemy weapons, and instituted a new social, medical, and economic infrastructure behind the frontlines, while keeping strict political discipline. This experience was essential in preparing the EPLF for the exercise of political control in the period after May 1991. The rival ELF had been decimated in internal fighting during the 1970s and 1980s and did not play a major role in the later years of the armed struggle, nor in the postliberation period after May 1991. In May 1993, after two years of "provisional" rule, Eritrea was declared an independent state following a referendum in which 99. 81% voted "Yes" to independence after a vote in which saying "No" (i. e. , maintaining a bond with Ethiopia) would mean being ostracized. Friendship and kinship relations exist between Eritrean and Ethiopian leaders, most of whom come from the same region and population group (Tigrinya). Economically, Eritrea has difficulty managing without the Ethiopian hinterland, although it has received substantial assistance and facilities from the Ethiopian government, partly as compensation for war damages. A big advantage is that Eritrea has no external national debt to international banks or donor countries: this was taken over by Ethiopia.

Executive

After the declaration of independence on May 25, 1993, a "Transitional Administration" was installed, replacing the Provisional Government. The postindependence political structure that was valid for the period 1993–97 was defined by Government Decree Number 37.

A nonelected 130-member National Assembly (Baito) was created, consisting of the 70-member Central Committee of the EPLF and 60 other representatives from various regions, groups, and walks of life. Apart from the National Assembly, the government in 1994 appointed a 50-member National Constitution Commission to prepare a draft constitution. In mid-1996, this Commission finished its work, and the constitution was adopted in May 1997.

The president of Eritrea since June 8, 1993, is the chairman of the EPLF, Issaias Afäwärk'i (who was already leader of the provisional government). He also acts as commander in chief of the armed forces.

The government is formed by the "Consultative" or "State Council" of Eritrea, which consists of the 14 Cabinet ministers, 11 heads of government commissions and authorities, and the provincial governors. The Consultative Council is the replacement for the Executive Council of the provisional period, which consisted of the president, the 10 regional administrators, the 5 top military and naval commanders, and "secretaries" for 12 government departments. In all these political organs, the EPLF/PFDJ is the dominant political force, while key posts such as Defense, Foreign Affairs, Interior, Finance, and Information are occupied by its "Politbureau" members.

Legislature

The National Assembly was seen as the supreme legal authority in the present four-year transitional period up to 1997 and also thereafter. It holds sessions only with large intervals, during which the State Council led by the president runs daily business. This Council has 35 members, among them the 14 Cabinet members. The National Assembly was not elected in democratic elections but appointed, and is dominated by the Central Committee of the EPLF/PFDJ, which firmly leads the building of Eritrean state structures. Policy is prepared and submitted to the Assembly for discussion, amendment, and ratification by the party leadership according to its ideological guidelines.

Judiciary

The judiciary has been going through a reform period, created after the announcement in Decree Number 37 of May 1993. A new court structure, the development of new law codes (partly going back to the inherited system of Ethiopian law and partly taken over from the EPLF's own law system developed when still a guerrilla movement), and formalization of military tribunals and local courts all are being worked out. Guaranteeing the independence of the judicial system vis-à-vis the executive and legislative bodies is a stated aim but will be difficult.

The incorporation of customary law codes and Islamic law is being investigated, although the traditional social and legal notions are deemphasized and devalued by the PFDJ government. Social and cultural changes promoted by the EPLF during the period of armed struggle and in the liberated areas since the 1970s have undermined the applicability and acceptance of traditional law (e. g. , with regard to the land question, inheritance, and customary family law).

Regional and Local Government

Eritrea is now organized in six administrative regions, which do not (in contrast to Ethiopia) derive from ethnic group names. Seeing the signs of instability in neighboring states seriously divided by ethnic loyalties and with the state's territorial identity being based on the Italian political boundaries, the government has no intention of making ethnicity the criterion of administrative organization and national policy.

Below the level of the National Assembly, the units of government are the assemblies on the provincial (region), district, and village levels, which were not elected in open elections but appointed by local EPLF units in consultation with the party hierarchy and the local communities.

THE ELECTORAL SYSTEM

So far, no elections have been held in the transitional phase, or thereafter (since June 1997) for the National Assembly, only for regional and other administrations in mid-1997, won by the PFDJ. In view of the perceived or assumed national consensus and the period of transition, national and presidential elections will probably not be held soon. Details about electoral procedure and the nature and number of parties are not known yet but are to be determined by the present PFDJ government. The Constitution is silent about multiparty elections. To assess the performance of administrators, periodic judgmental meetings are held during which people failing to meet their duties can be removed.

POPULAR FRONT FOR DEMOCRACY AND JUSTICE (PFDJ)

Party Organization

The reigning and so far only significant party is still the EPLF, which in February 1994 was renamed PFDJ (see above). It is well rooted in the wider Eritrean population and so far has no serious competition. In the current transition period, no other political parties are allowed to be active.

The original rebel movement, the Eritrean Liberation Front (ELF), was founded in 1962; supported primarily by Muslims, it started as a group inspired by Marxist ideology. In 1970, the Eritrean People's Liberation Front (EPLF) split off from this parent organization. It was also Marxist-socialist in orientation and drew support from both Tigrinya highlanders and Muslim lowlanders (Beni Amer, Tigré) and other groups. The ELF and its various split-offs still exist. They do not have part in the EPLF/PFDJ government but cannot but recognize its leading role and authority. Many former ELF leaders have, however, joined the EPLF. One other small opposition group is the Democratic Movement for the Liberation of Eritrea (DMLP).

The EPLF had a communist party structure, with a central committee, a politbureau, and local cells. This structure is being transformed because of EPLF's new role as the broad, leading political party in an independent Eritrea. A third and last EPLF conference was held in February 1994, during which the conversion of the EPLF into a civil political party with a national unity and development program took place. The new Popular Front for Democracy and Justice, though similar to the EPLF in personnel and policy, has drawn up a charter serving as its program (as distinct from the government's). It is thus also (formally) separated from the government in terms of leadership, policy, and financing. The new party has offices in five designated regions of the country. Although it is officially not part of the governmental system, it intends to act as a "catalyst" in national policy. The PFDJ's program emphasizes nation building, economic development, social justice, and political restructuring.

Political organization (apart from the EPLF/PFDJ) is tightly controlled, and any future party based on ethnicity or religion will be prohibited. Violent opposition, including the incursions from several small Islamic fundamentalist groups (e. g. , Ansar-el-Sunna or the Eritrean Islamic Jihad movement) operating from Sudan is quelled with force. There have also been reports of political assassinations and disappearances of other declared opponents or of collaborators with the previous Ethiopian regime. Calls from opposition groups (e. g. , the ELF–RC) to broaden the composition of the national government have not been accepted. Eritrea thus has remained in effect a one-party state.

NATIONAL PROSPECTS

During the past few years, Eritrea has internally been one of the more peaceful and stable countries in eastern Africa, partly because of a cultivated "national consensus" after

1991 on building up the new, free country and partly because of strict control of the EPLF/PFDJ government on political activity, the press, and social and religious institutions. The three greatest challenges of this war-damaged country are the rebuilding of the infrastructure, economy (agriculture, mining, and industry), and energy supply system; the involvement of and respect for all ethnic groups in national development; and the gradual absorption of around 750,000 refugees, the majority of whom are in Sudan and an educated minority in Western Europe, Canada, and the United States. (Tens of thousands have already returned, although a further massive influx in a short time span is discouraged by the government.) Support from the United Nations, the World Bank, and other international agencies and Western governments (Canada, the United States, and Germany) has been obtained, but this does not yet provide structural solutions to the problem of how to productively absorb all the returnees. In order to get the economy going and to generate surplus, the government has also opened the door for substantial foreign investment.

Eritrea's rebel experience with disciplined self-organization and single-minded devotion to national tasks could serve as an important factor in building up the country, even with scarce resources and limited international recognition and assistance. But prospects of short-term food self-sufficiency are bleak, due in part to unreliable ecological factors such as erratic rain, locust plagues, and the effects of erosion. The same problem of dependency and limited resources holds for most other domains.

Democratic representation, freedom of expression and organization (so far lacking), and productive redeployment of many of the nearly 85,000 fighters will be essential preconditions for long-term social stability of the country. Questions of Eritrean national identity and ethnic relations may also have to be addressed in the future.

In terms of international relations, Eritrea has tried to assert itself in the wider region. It cut diplomatic links with Sudan in 1995 after the border incidents with Islamic fundamentalists in attacks launched from Sudan, and has called for the removal of the present Sudanese regime. It has also fought with Yemen over the Hanish Islands. Official political relations with Ethiopia were good up to early 1998, as the EPRDF-led government in Addis Ababa always had sympathy for Eritrean nationalist aspirations. (The EPLF and EPRDF were allies in the military struggle against the Mengistu regime.) When by late 1997 relations between the two countries came to be based more on business criteria (which Ethiopia was forced to apply due to mounting domestic pressure and its own economic problems) than on a past common cause, friendship, and preferential treatment, relations became more strained. Eventually this led to a border conflict in May 1998 in which thousands died and tens of thousands were displaced. In November 1998 no solution to this unexpected conflict was in sight. Even if peace would be restored, Eritrea's close links with and perhaps even dependency on Ethiopia will be there for many years to come.

Further Reading

Gebre Hiywet Tesfagiorgis, ed. *Emergent Eritrea: Challenges of Economic Development.* Lawrenceville, N. J. : Red Sea Press, 1994.

Eyassu Gayim. *The Eritrean Question: The Conflict between the Right of Self-Determination and the Interest of States.* Uppsala: Iustus Förlag, 1993.

Iyob, Ruth. *The Eritrean Struggle for Independence: Domination, Resistance, Nationalism, 1941–1993.* Cambridge: Cambridge University Press, 1995.

Tekeste Negash. *Eritrea and Ethiopia: The Federal Experience.* New Brunswick, N. J. : Transaction; and Uppsala: Nordiska Afrika Institutet, 1996.

ESTONIA

(Eesti Vabariik)

By Jeffrey K. Hass, Ph.D.

THE SYSTEM OF GOVERNMENT

Estonia, the northernmost of the three former Baltic republics of the Soviet Union, with a 1995 population of 1. 49 million people, is not a homogeneous country. While ethnic Estonians make up 61. 5% of the overall population, Russians come in a strong second with 30. 3%; Ukrainians account for 3. 2%, Byelorussians 1. 8%, Finns 1. 1%, and other ethnicities 2. 1%. Lutheranism is the prevalent religion, although Russian Orthodoxy also has a significant number of followers. Estonian is the official language, but Russian, Latvian, and Lithuanian are significant as well.

Estonia has enjoyed a relatively stable transition to democracy and a market economy. While political parties have yet to tap deep roots into society and some scandals have marred political life, Estonia is further on the way to a Western-style political and economic system than most of the former Soviet republics.

Economically, Estonia has been the *wunderkind* of the former Soviet republics since its economy reached bottom in 1993. Experts suggest this is due to economic discipline and strong adherence to orthodox economic reform. Since 1992 monthly inflation has been under 5% (at 2% for 1995), and GDP growth for 1995 was around 6%. While unemployment has been rising and wages in many sectors have not risen with inflation, privatization of small- and medium-sized firms is complete and large-scale privatization is proceeding apace. Further, Estonia has oriented its economy to trade with the West, solidifying this link by managing to obtain association status within the European Union.

Executive

The executive is made up of the president, the prime minister, and the deputy ministers who head the state bureaucracy.

Estonia's president is a weak president, essentially a figurehead who represents Estonia in international forums. Another of his major duties is appointing and recalling diplomatic personnel. The president does enjoy some formal powers over internal policy and legislation.

While the president is expected to proclaim as law those bills that pass the Parliament, he can exercise a weak veto, which involves sending back to the Parliament legislation he considers faulty. If the Parliament passes the bill a second time (by simple majority vote), the president can bring the law to the attention of the National Court (the highest court of the land) to rule on its constitutionality. Further, in moments when the Parliament cannot convene, the president may issue decrees that have the force of law; these decrees must be confirmed when the Parliament is able to convene if they are to remain in force. Finally, the president presents candidates for high governmental positions (e. g. , prime minister), who must then be confirmed by the Parliament.

Lennart Meri, the first and current president of the Estonian republic, has tried to make the presidency a more forceful office, partially through use of the position as a bully pulpit and partially through his own initiatives in the international arena. For example, without prior approval of the Parliament and at his own initiative, Meri negotiated and signed an agreement with Russia over removal of the latter's troops from Estonian soil. However, such acts are the exception rather than the rule, due to constitutional restrictions.

The prime minister and his deputy ministers are the heads of the government bureaucracy, making the PM and the Council of Ministers as important as, if not more important than, the president within the executive. In fact, by the constitution, the prime minister is the chief executive. The biggest responsibility of the prime minister and the Council of Ministers is the day-to-day operations of government and implementation of policy. The prime minister and the Council of Ministers answer for their actions to the Parliament rather than to the president; when called upon they have to appear before Parliament to answer questions and provide requested information.

Estonia has had four prime ministers since Edgar Savisaar left and the constitution was ratified in 1992. The first PM, Mart Laar, held office from October 1992 (after the presidential and parliamentary elections) to October 1994, when two scandals (involving a transfer of a large sum of money to Chechnya and arms sales to Israel) forced him out of office. Laar's government, whose policies of tax cuts and fiscal discipline set a course to make Estonia the economic miracle of the former Soviet republics, suffered scandals due to inexperience or ineptitude. For instance, an economics minister resigned after it became apparent he could not handle his responsibilities, the defense minister in 1993 allowed Russian troops to enter the country during negotiations with Russia over troop withdrawals, and a law on noncitizens was suggested that provoked severe criticism from Russians in Estonia and from Western countries (the law would have required noncitizens, such as ethnic Russians, to reapply every two years for residency permits without guarantee of reacceptance).

In 1994 Laar was replaced by Andres Tarand, who held the office until the March 1995 parliamentary elections. At that point Meri proposed Tiit Vahi as prime minister. Vahi's tenure was marked by problems with Parliament—namely, lack of confidence in the economics minister, Liina Tonisson, and a scandal involving bugging telephone conversations between prominent politicians. Vahi resigned but was soon reappointed by Meri and remained in office until 1997, when Meri proposed Mart Siiman as prime minister.

Legislature

In Estonia, the Parliament (*Riigikogu*) is the supreme political power. A unicameral body composed of 101 delegates, Parliament wields the power of legislation. Policymaking is delegated to the prime minister and government, but the government is beholden to Parliament and must account for its actions and results before the legislative branch. Passing legislation requires a majority of 51 votes; legislation may be introduced by the president or through the Parliament. The Parliament also controls the purse strings, as the state budget requires majority support within the *Riigikogu* before it is official.

The *Riigikogu* exercises control over the prime minister through votes of no confidence. For example, after several political mishaps the *Riigikogu* passed a vote of no confidence in Mart Laar. However, if the Parliament is too strongly taken to infighting and cannot pass a state budget or cannot approve a prime minister (after "prolonged delay"), the president can dissolve the Parliament and call for new elections. Further, the president can also dissolve the Parliament after a vote of no confidence in the prime minister and Cabinet; however, because the Parliament elects the president, the president must take care that the incoming Parliament will not be inclined to seek revenge in the next presidential "election. "

Judiciary

As for all former Soviet republics, the Estonian judicial system is undergoing change, which is not surprising considering that the judiciary was subordinate to the Com-

munist Party and requires the laws and procedures of an independent court in a democracy. The court system currently follows a continental, rather than an Anglo-American, model: courts are arbitrators between parties rather than interpreters. Legal interpretations are not set by courts, and precedent does not play an important role in Estonian jurisprudence, meaning that every case has to be argued from the basis of the law and context of conflict, rather than on the basis of past decisions.

Estonia has three levels of courts. The first level is local, for cities and rural regions. The next level, the district courts, is for appeals from the local level. Both levels decide on criminal cases and on legal conflicts between parties. Appeals may be made up the hierarchy. At the top of the pyramid is the National Court, which decides on constitutional issues and has the final say on appeals that have worked their way up from the local and district levels.

Regional and Local Government

With its capital in Tallinn, Estonia is comprised of 15 counties (*maakonnad*), each of which is run by county councils elected for three-year terms.

THE ELECTORAL SYSTEM

According to the constitution, the president is chosen by the Parliament. To "win," a presidential candidate must receive two-thirds of the votes cast by parliamentary deputies (e. g. , 68 votes). Parliament has three rounds to select a president; if no candidate receives the necessary two-thirds support, then an "electoral college" decides. This electoral college is composed of the 101 parliamentary delegates plus 273 representatives of local governments.

The exception to this procedure was in 1992, when the first post-Soviet Estonian president was to be selected by popular vote. In this case, a candidate had to receive more than 50% of votes cast on the first ballot; otherwise, the top two vote getters would face a runoff in the Parliament. In 1992, none of the four candidates received a majority; Arnold Ruutel (a former Communist and head of the party Secure Home, the successors to the Communist Party) and Lennart Meri (a former writer) received 42. 7% and 28. 8% of votes cast. Hence, both candidates went to the Parliament, which proceeded to select Meri (the second-place candidate) as president; Meri received 59 votes in Parliament to Ruutel's 31. (Apparently, several parliamentary groups had agreed ahead of time to select any candidate except the communist candidate, Ruutel.) In August 1996, Ruutel and Meri came forward again as presidential candidates; this time the voting was done in Parliament only, rather than in a popular election. In the first round of voting only 95 of the 100 deputies present cast votes: 45 went to Meri, 34 went to Ruutel, and 16 were either blank or invalid. In the second and third rounds of voting Meri received 49 and 52 votes; however, he could not reach the 68-vote threshold, and no alternative to Meri and Ruutel who could receive 68 votes could be found. Meri's proactive presidential style—in a polity where the Parliament holds supreme power and the president only nominal figurehead status—apparently annoyed many delegates, while Ruutel's Communist past made him a less-than-satisfactory choice. The electoral college convened at the end of September and chose Meri for a second term as president.

In the 1992 popular-vote presidential election, Arnold Ruutel of the Secure Home Party took 42. 7% of the vote; Lennart Meri of Pro Patria, 28. 8%; Rein Taagepera of the Popular Front, 23. 8%; and Lagle Parek of the Estonian National Independence Party (ENIP), 3. 85%. Because no candidate won an outright majority, the two candidates with the most votes were considered by Parliament, which selected Meri over the former Communist Ruutel.

THE PARTY SYSTEM

Political parties in Estonia, as in the other Baltic states, have had a more difficult time in forming than in other post-Soviet states. Parties have been forming and reforming, creating and breaking coalitions and parliamentary factions, making solidification of a small number of parties difficult. Few parties have any history and thus any legacies, nostalgia, or party apparatus to organize and maintain both image and discipline. Even the parties that had some history, such as the Pro Patria and ENIP Parties, which were active in anti-Soviet mobilization in the late 1980s, have suffered in local elections in 1993 and parliamentary elections in 1995. This has reduced any impetus to solidification or hegemony these parties may have had. And while the Communist Party found its successor in Secure Home, this party is not trying to be a direct descendant, as in other post-Communist nations; further, former Communist functionaries are spread throughout other parties as well.

Another reason that parties have not solidified in Estonia is that voters in Estonia do not readily identify with parties; they instead identify more closely with candidates who have a "clean" past (untainted by Soviet history). Voting is for individual candidates, rather than for parties; while the electoral system does favor party formation through elections (by rewarding parties whose candidates do well), the individual basis of voting does not appear to impress party identification on voters' minds. Finally, as in the United States, Estonian parties do not appear to differ strongly in their political platforms, so that promarket reforms, independence, and integration into Europe (NATO, the EU) are common goals among most platforms.

While any grouping of parties as "right" or "left" has limited utility in the former Soviet republics, it does serve to group together those parties that are more committed to market reforms and to Estonian nationalism (in muted form) and those that prefer a more gradual approach and may be less antagonistic toward Russia.

THE PARTIES

Parties to the Right

These parties support market reforms (privatization and land reform, trade liberalization), fiscal responsibility, and muted nationalism. The earliest was ENIP, the Estonian National Independence Party (*Eesti Rahvusliku Sõltumatuse Partei*), formed in 1988 against the Soviet/Russian occupation of Estonia. ENIP has been plagued since its early days by factionalism, which has hurt its strategic decision making and helped its decline in elections in 1993 and 1995. The second major rightist party was Pro Patria (Isamaa), which began in 1992 as a coalition of five parties that decided to form a united party.

Parties to the Left

These parties formed the opposition after the 1992 elections. Especially in their pre-1992 embryonic forms, they tended to support conciliation and compromise with Russia and the Russian-speaking population (while maintaining an orientation to Europe rather than the CIS) and have been less enamored with radical economic reform, preferring instead gradualism and protection of agriculture, industry, and the social safety net. One major leftist party, the Center Party (*Rahva Keskerakond*), was a coalition of social and liberal democrats and the pre-1992 Popular Front; the "Center" in the name was an attempt at moderating its image away from its leftist and conciliational past.

Three other leftist parties formed a coalition called "Secure Home" (*Kindel Kodu*) for the 1992 elections, but it has since split back into three. One member party was the (Estonian) Rural Union (*Eesti maalit*), formed originally by collective farm bosses and a champion of land reform by local initiative (rather than through state-led nationwide privatization). The second party, the (Estonian) Coalition Party (*Eesti Koonderakond*), was originally formed by enterprise managers who wished to retain their positions during reform and privatization and by reform Communists. The Coalition Party billed itself as procapitalist but in practice has championed more moderate reform. The third member of Secure Home was the Estonian Democratic Justice Union (*Eesti Demokraatlik Õigluslitt*), originally formed as a pressure group to protect the rights of pensioners and invalids. The Coalition Party and the Rural Union joined with three other small parties (the Estonian Country People's Party, the Farmers' Assembly, and the Estonian Pensioners' and Families League) to form Coalition Party–Rural Union, the 41-seat victor in the 1995 *Riigikogu* elections.

The Moderate Parties

Between the right and left are moderates, led by the Moderates Party (*Mõõdukad*), itself created by the merger of the Social Democrats and the Rural Center Party in January 1992, both of which were themselves formed by the union of several social democratic groups. The Moderates have, as their name implies, favored more gradual economic reform, with the Rural wing calling for more protection of Estonian agriculture. However, they differ from other parties only in degree rather than in content of reforms and policies for development.

NATIONAL PROSPECTS

Estonia's economy is on the road to recovery, and most political parties appear to hover around a middle ground, sharing the conviction that Estonia needs economic reform and should be part of Europe; differences involve the means to these ends, political conflict being more a function of political ambition and normal politics than of ideological differences. While citizenship and ethnic problems—particularly concerning Russians living in Es-

tonia—will be a sore spot for years to come, the government does not appear intent on purposely antagonizing the Russian population; while there have been moments of intolerance or prejudice, these have been minor and rare. With practices of democracy institutionalizing and with market recovery under way, Estonia may serve as the textbook case of how to build democracy and a market.

Further Reading

Arter, David. *Parties and Democracy in the Post-Soviet Republics. The Case of Estonia* (Aldershot, England: Dartmouth,1996).

CIA Factbook, 1996. Washington, D. C. : Government Printing Office, 1996.

Iwaskiw, Walter R. , ed. *Country Studies: Estonia, Latvia, and Lithuania.* Washington, D. C. : Federal Research Division, Library of Congress, 1995.

Kionka, Riina. "Free-Market Coalition Assumes Power in Estonia. " *RFE/RL Research Report* 1, no. 46 (November 20, 1992): 6–11.

Open Media Research Institute (OMRI). Daily reports and analytic reports. Back issues of daily reports can be found at http://www. omri. cz.

Radio Free Europe/Radio Liberty. Several sources of information offered. The daily reports and occasional analytic papers are available at http://www. rferl. org.

Transitions. This journal began publication in 1995 and functionally continues the type of work previously done by the *RFE/RL Reports.*

ETHIOPIA

(Itiyop'iya)

By Jon Abbink, Ph.D.

THE SYSTEM OF GOVERNMENT

Ethiopia, a nation of over 59 million people, was proclaimed a "federal democratic republic" on August 21, 1995, after a four-year transitional phase that followed the overthrow of the Marxist-Leninist dictatorship of Mengistu Haile Mariam on May 28, 1991. In the phase of transition (which took more than 4 years instead of the originally declared period of 2. 5 years) the groundwork for a new political system was laid. The Transitional Government of Ethiopia (TGE) active in that period was led by the Ethiopian Peoples' Revolutionary Democratic Front (EPRDF), the dominant resistance movement emanating from the northern Tigray region.

After its takeover of power (coinciding with that of its ally the EPLF, or Eritrean Peoples' Liberation Front, in Eritrea), the EPRDF initiated the transition by calling a National Conference of Peace and Stability in June 1991 in Addis Ababa. Most major rebel movements and ethnoregional groups were represented. The conference led to a "Transitional Charter," which became the supreme law for the period of transition, and to the appointment of a president, a Council of Ministers, and a (nonelected) Council of Representatives with 87 members taken from the various ethnic and political movements. Groups said to oppose the EPRDF, e. g. , those accused of planning "violent opposition," were excluded. During this period, the president, the EPRDF leadership, and the Council of Ministers were the dominant players.

The policy of centralist control has remained the same under the new Federal Democratic Republic of Ethiopia (FDRE), though it is now formally a parliamentary system with periodic elections. The chairman of the EPRDF occupies the most important political position in the FDRE, that of prime minister.

Background

Ethiopia is the oldest independent state in Africa; save only for an Italian occupation from 1936 to 1941, it was never a colony. It was an autocratic monarchy under Haile Selassie until he was deposed by military rebels in September 1974. Although much respected as an elder statesman by other African leaders, Haile Selassie had lost much of his support because of his failure to deal with the Eritrean and Somali secessionist movements and with the country's chronic economic underdevelopment and rural exploitation. Ethiopia always suffered under periodic centrifugal (regional or sometimes ethnic) tendencies. Haile Selassie's two constitutions (of 1931 and of 1955), while creating a first legal framework of a country in dire need of modernization and reform, did not create an adequate basis for the construction of a stable national state or of democratic representation of the population at large.

Ethiopia's history over the last 30 years, especially since the military came to power in 1974, has been marked by violence, not only of armed struggle against the attempted secession of the province of Eritrea (1961–91) and against Somalian irredentism in the west (in the 1977–78 war) but also of local revolts, rebellions, and urban terror.

The revolution erupting in February 1974 was based on widespread civil discontent. But hopes for a democratic process of change were dashed with the "hijacking" of the revolution by the military in September 1974. After this date, and especially since December 1974, when the first serious shootout within the ruling provisional military council (*Derg*) occurred, the revolutionary process became dictatorial and violent. Civilian political parties and occupational organizations were prohibited or suppressed. Political opponents from other leftist revolutionary parties such as the All-Ethiopian Socialist Movement and the Ethiopian People's Revolutionary Party were ruthlessly eliminated in a "Red Terror" period (1977–79) during which arbitrary arrests, torture, and executions were the order of the day. This period caused deep and still-unhealed wounds in Ethiopian society.

The Mengistu regime had its international allies in the "Socialist" camp, especially Cuba, North Korea, and the Soviet Union, which supplied arms, experts, and ideological advice on party building and administration. In the course of years, Mengistu increasingly became a dogmatic Marxist-Leninist out of touch with Ethiopian realities. The villagization effort, the collectivization of agriculture, and the "nationalities" policy were all copied from the Soviet model. The change in ideological orientation in March 1990, under the pressure of the domestic economic and military crises, came too late to prevent the demise of a thoroughly discredited regime.

The EPRDF—whose core party TPLF (Tigray People's Liberation Front) was also a carrier of communist ideals in the 1970s—had abandoned this ideology (especially in the economic sense) in the year before its entry into Addis Ababa, although there is still a leadership core of the TPLF nominally referred to as "The Marxist-Leninist League of Tigray."

Executive

The FDRE is headed by the president of the Tigray People's Liberation Front (TPLF) within the EPRDF, Melles Zenawi, acting as prime minister. With the institution of the FDRE, he moved from the position of president to prime minister, leaving the president's office to Negasso Gidada of the EPRDF's "Oromo party," the OPDO. The former prime minister Tamrat Layne, chairman of the Amhara National Democratic Movement (ANDM), the Amhara part of EPRDF, became one of the deputy prime ministers and minister of defense but was dismissed and jailed in 1996.

Executive power lies not in the hands of the Council of Ministers but in those of the prime minister and his important body of advisers and special committees within the prime minister's office. The executive has the authority to appoint and ban members of the judiciary and the legislature. In practice, it also can overrule decisions and proposals of the Council of Ministers.

Legislature

In the transitional period, the 87-member Council of Representatives, appointed in 1991, was the formal legislative body. Since August 1995, this has been called the Council of People's Representatives, and it has a solid EPRDF majority. There is a second chamber called the Council of the Federation, with members appointed by the regional assemblies of the nine "regional states." This Council, a largely ceremonial body with little lawmaking capacity, meets infrequently. Ethnic groups are represented here on the basis of their numerical strength nationwide.

The EPRDF obviously dominates the lawmaking process. Its five-year plan of 1994 is the basis for policy. Lawmaking has been slow and laborious and mainly concerned with solidifying the power basis of the regime, the new regional-political structures, economic policy, revenue collection and distribution, and education policy. Legislation on socioeconomic, demographic, and environmental matters has been lagging behind and has had little effect so far.

Judiciary

The legal system has also been reformed (mainly in its personnel) but still functions partly on the basis of structures of the previous regimes. There are local courts (*woreda*), people's courts, a High Court, and a Supreme Court consisting of a president and two other judges. It has appellate jurisdiction but also supervises juridical proceedings throughout the country. The High Court is the most important court in the land. Ethiopia also has been using military tribunals; there is no appeal against the decisions of the Supreme Military Tribunal. Many of its powers, such as the power to detain opponents for up to six months without trial, were inherited from the previous regime. Cases of extrajudicial torture by security forces are reported by human rights organizations.

A large number of former officials from the previous regime (well over 3,000) are in prison awaiting trial, many of them not yet formally charged. Since 1993, a mass trial against the most important top-ranking politicians and officials has been going on at low intensity, with many delays and interruptions. The proper judicial structure to deal with these cases took a long time being installed. Since 1994, they have been handled by a Special Prosecutor's Office.

The judiciary in general is susceptible to informal political pressure and cannot be considered fully independent of the government.

Regional and Local Government

While the Mengistu regime had reorganized Ethiopia in 1987 into 24 new regions and five "autonomous" regions, the FDRE has again rearranged the map in line with its intention to make regions predominantly inhabited by one majority ethnic group the basis of administration. The first map, which was drawn in October 1991 and formally discussed and only slightly amended by the Council of Representatives in June 1992, became effective that same year. It designated 14 new regions, called *killils*, including the "special status" cities of Harar and Addis Ababa. In 1994, 5 southern *killils* were merged, yielding the present 9 regions. A new special region was the city of Dire Dawa. Within the *killils*, zones were distinguished, in their turn divided into districts (*woredas*), many of which again have the old boundaries that were abolished in the 1987 reform.

In urban areas, the EPRDF government has worked through the existing structure of the urban dwellers' associations (*k'ebeles*), of which there are several thousand. They have also changed all personnel of the old regime. The *k'ebeles* were initially under the authority of the newly instituted "peace and stability committees," but have now merged with them. In the countryside (with 85% of the population) the existing peasants' associations, which were state conduits of administrative and judicial authority, were also kept in place, but again with new, loyal appointees. In addition, on the local and regional levels many ethnic political associations have been created, meant to become representative organs of the ethnic groups.

THE ELECTORAL SYSTEM

Ethiopia has put in place an electoral system under which parties and independent candidates are in principle allowed to run for office. The system is, however, not to be compared with a Western liberal democracy. Ethiopia's system is very intricate. Broad national parties are not registered, and elections are held in every ethnoregion, where only parties can run who have a kind of ethnic basis there. This means that an Oromo party could not run in the Tigray region. Thus, the system is not nationwide with proportional representation but is based on district or regional parties that are allied to the existing EPRDF power and party structure.

This system (at one remove) tends to secure the reproduction of the dominant power structure. This was obvious in the various rounds of elections held so far: the 1992 regional elections, the 1994 Constituent Assembly elections, the 1995 National Assembly elections, and the *woreda* elections of early 1996. While some seats did go to opposition and independent candidates, EPRDF usually won with a large majority.

Ethiopia's democratic system and civic culture have not yet taken root. Moreover, they are kept in check by the government's frequent action against trade unions, the teacher's association, and the independent press. Non-EPRDF parties and candidates are often actively discouraged from running, and several important opposition groups have opted out of the elections, complaining of violent intimidation of activists and voters and interference with party activities, especially in the rural areas.

THE PARTY SYSTEM

Origins of the Parties

Under the dictatorial, one-party system system of the previous regime, two parties dominated Ethiopian politics. From 1984 to 1990, it was the Workers' Party of Ethiopia, and from 1990 to 1991, the Ethiopian Democratic Unity Party. After the regime was overthrown in 1991, a plethora of ethnoregional groups emerged.

Some of these already existed, and several, such as the parties, or "self-organizations," of various ethnic groups

like the Gurage, Hadiya, Kämbata, Gedeo, and Käfa were founded after 1991. There were at least 100 groups in existence in 1994. Some parties have disappeared or become dormant, others have tried to build up their organizational structure. However, opposition groups have been hampered by obstruction from the government. They are also prohibited from receiving financial support from outside Ethiopia. Those that are EPRDF allies are partly funded by the government and/or the EPRDF.

ETHIOPIAN PEOPLES' REVOLUTIONARY DEMOCRATIC FRONT (EPRDF)

Ethiopia's leading party, EPRDF, is composed of four main groups: the Tigray People's Liberation Front, or TPLF, the Amhara National Democratic Movement, or ANDM, the Oromo People's Democratic Organization, or OPDO, and the Southern Ethiopian Peoples' Democratic Front, or SEPDF. The EPRDF understandably receives the lion's share of government party financing, but detailed information on party finances is not available.

Organization

The TPLF is the core party and was the main fighting force. It created satellite parties among the two largest ethnic groups, the Oromo and the Amhara, and later among the "southerners" so it could say it had a broad basis and fought for the liberation of "all the peoples and nationalities of Ethiopia." The party constituency is probably small, although in Tigray all people have to be TPLF.

The most important party, the EPRDF (and within it the TPLF) was originally set up on a Marxist-Leninist model. Its structure has now been adapted, although personnel is largely the same and periodic expulsions and demotions of deviant members occur. The party has its power base in the northern regions, where no other party apart from the TPLF is allowed, but it has loyal support parties elsewhere in the country.

Ethnicity, which is usually related to a language and region of origin, is the basis of party organization, not only of the EPRDF. In the transition phase, the Transitional Government would not allow parties without a clear ethnoregional basis into the Council of Representatives nor could one be registered for elections. This pattern has been continued in the elections for the Council of Representatives of the Federal Democratic Republic.

Membership and Constituency

The EPRDF (as TPLF) has its main constituency in the Tigray region and among Tigray people in the rest of the country. Similarly, it has urged the formation of other parties and movements on the basis of region and ethnicity as well. During the last year of the armed struggle, this already led to the setting up of parallel parties among the Oromo (OPDO) and the Amhara (ANDM) people and among the SEPDF (Southern Ethiopian Peoples' Democratic Front). They all are to represent their respective ethnic groups, according to the ideological formula of the TPLF that ethnic identification (on a political basis) is the key to real democracy. For several widely dispersed ethnic groups for whom "ethnic allegiance" in itself is a problematic concept, ethnic party organization is especially difficult. Membership of the various parties is unknown but is not massive.

Leadership

Leader of the EPRDF (and of the TPLF faction) is the current prime minister, Melles Zenawi, born in Tigray. The first prime minister, Tamrat Layne, previously leader of the ANDM faction in the EPRDF and probably from northern Gondar was suddenly dismissed in 1996 on corruption charges. He was replaced by Teferra Waluwa, an unknown ANDM politician. The OPDO is led by the current president of the Oromia region, Kuma Demeksa.

OPPOSITION PARTIES

Many opposition parties exist, the most important ones being the Southern Ethiopian Peoples' Democratic Front (SEPDF); the broad front CAFPDE (Council of Alternative Forces for Peace and Democracy); the All-Amhara Peoples' Organization, the AAPO, which represents the Amhara people; the Oromo OLF, which was part of the TGE from July 1991 to June 1992, but has been dwindling ever since; and Afar and Somali parties. Parties do not have complete freedom of movement, and leaders and activists are occasionally detained. Most of the dozens of parties are not represented in the parliament.

OTHER POLITICAL FORCES

Organized Labor

The farmers' organization, the All-Ethiopian Peasants Association (AEPA), set up and controlled by the previous government, has been reformed. It has no important political role and no public profile.

The former All-Ethiopian Trade Union (AETU), with about 330,000 industrial workers, was also a creation of the WPE government and politically subservient to it. Its successor is a new organization that began with a relatively independent status, the CETU (Confederation of Ethiopian Trade Unions). But the government has now taken over the organization and replaced its chairman,

Dawi Ibrahim, and chances for its continued independent functioning are slim.

Religious Groups

The country is nearly equally divided between Ethiopian Orthodox Christians (about 50%) and Muslims (about 35%), with smaller groups of other religions (Catholics, Evangelical Protestants, and traditional religions, mainly in the south and west). While Amharic-speaking Christians (of various backgrounds) have dominated the Ethiopian government for a long period (as exemplified in the Haile Selassie era, when Ethiopian identity was projected as a largely Christian one), religion as such has never played a major organizing role in politics. No parties or pressure groups were based on an exclusively religious constituency. Partly this was due to suppression of religion (alongside regional or ethnic identity) as a political force by both Haile Selassie and the *Dergue*, but partly also to an emphasis on political programs of development and modernization held to apply to the country as a whole. In the final phases of the anti-*Dergue* military struggle (1987–91), ethnic and religious elements became stronger as ideologies of opposition.

NATIONAL PROSPECTS

Politically, the EPRDF government is struggling with the problem of finding a new democratic formula for ethnoregional diversity, representation, and economic development of the country as a whole. Economic concerns are foremost in the minds of virtually all Ethiopians and increasingly in the mind of the government. But the latter at the same time mainly concentrates on creating a stable political power structure as a means "to create conditions" for economic development.

The strict economic policies of the previous regime have been modified, the aim being an open, mixed economy with room for private initiative and foreign investment (local business circles complained of certain privileges given to foreign business). Tight controls and taxes on imports, particularly with regard to development projects, machinery, cars, consumer electronics, luxury items, and so on, are enforced as before. A strict monetary policy is followed to maintain Ethiopia's relatively good reputation as a debtor country.

Enduring problems exist in the agricultural sector. Continued vulnerability to droughts, underdeveloped technology, and disastrous demographic pressure are inhibiting the expansion of agricultural production, despite the fact that in the last few years rains and harvests have been good and marketing has been liberalized. For many years to come, Ethiopia will be dependent on extra food donations. Ethiopia's industrial sector is small and needs quick expansion. There is a substantial and well-edu-cated middle class waiting to realize its potential.

Internationally, Ethiopia is supported by the United States and accordingly tries to style itself as a stable government in the Horn of Africa, with Somalia and Sudan in shambles. A serious complication has been the eruption of a bloody border conflict with Eritrea in May 1998, which in November 1998 had not been resolved. Ethiopia's assumption of a leading role in the region will ultimately depend on the resolution of problems of domestic unity and reconciliation, economic improvement, and real democratic representation.

Further Reading

Abebe Zegeye, and S. Pausewang, eds. *Ethiopia in Change.* London: British Academic Press, 1994.

Andargatchew, Tiruneh. *The Ethiopian Revolution, 1974–1987.* New York: Cambridge University Press, 1993.

Tecola W. Hagos. *Democratization? Ethiopia (1991–1994): A Personal View.* Cambridge, Mass. : Khepera, 1995.

Young, J. *Peasant Revolution in Ethiopia: The Tigray People's Liberation Front, 1975–1991.* Cambridge: Cambridge University Press, 1997.

Fiji

By Eugene Ogan, Ph.D.

In 1987 Fiji experienced the first military coup in the history of the Pacific Islands. The decade that followed was filled with political uncertainty. All of these developments were related to conflict between ethnic Fijians (*Taukei*) and the descendants of indentured laborers who had come from India to work in sugar plantations. The constitutional changes that were adopted in 1997 created a new political system, the consequences of which will be seen in the future.

The Republic of the Fiji Islands consists of numerous islands, about 100 of which are inhabited. The population in 1996 was 72,655; of whom, 51% were indigenous Fijians, about 44% Indians, and the remainder of part-European, Chinese, and other descent. This represents a shift since 1987, because many Indians chose to emigrate after the coup.

A faction of Fijian chiefs ceded the islands to Great Britain in 1874. British colonial administrators were careful to preserve Fijian rights, especially in land. The political conflicts that have developed since independence was gained in 1970, and most particularly the coup, have been triggered by Fijian fears of losing their political pre-eminence in the face of a growing Indian population. A Constitution Review Commission was established in 1995 to create a system that would deal with these issues appropriately. Their recommendations were adopted unanimously by Parliament in July 1997. The structure described below is based on these recommendations, though at this writing they have yet to be made completely operational. For example, elections under the new system have not yet been held.

The president is head of state and must be an indigenous Fijian. The vice president must be from a different ethnic community. The Great Council of Chiefs nominates three to five candidates for president; each nominee is required in turn to nominate a running mate. An electoral college consisting of the Great Council and members of the Upper House of Parliament selects one of the pairs for a term of five years. They may be reelected for a second term, but no more. The president's role is parallel to that fulfilled in the past by the governor-general.

Parliament consists of two houses. The Lower, where all legislation must originate, has 70 members: 12 seats are reserved for Fijians, 10 for Indians, 1 for a member from the island of Rotuma (whose inhabitants are culturally distinct from other Fijians), and 2 for other ethnicities. Only members of the relevant ethnic communities can vote in the reserved seat contests. There are 45 seats open to any candidate, to be elected from 15 three-person constituencies. The Upper House comprises 35 members, 2 elected from each of the 14 provinces and 1 elected from Rotuma. The remaining 6 are appointed by the president to represent communities and groups otherwise inadequately represented. All citizens may vote at the age of 18 but must be 21 to stand as a candidate. The maximum term of Parliament is four years after a general election, though it can be dissolved by the president acting on the advice of the prime minister.

Effective power of government lies in the Lower House. The president is to appoint a prime minister from that House who appears to command the support of a majority of its members. In turn the prime minister recommends to the president a Cabinet of not more than 15 ministers, drawn from elected members of Parliament. Not more than a quarter of the Cabinet should be from the Upper House.

The Great Council of Chiefs is a distinctive feature of Fijian government that acknowledges both tradition and Fijian ethnic identity. It consists of 46 members. The president, the heads of three traditionally recognized confederate communities of indigenous Fijians, and the minister for Fijian affairs serve ex officio. Twenty members are appointed by the heads of the three traditional confederacies. Five are nominated by the council chair and approved by the Council as a whole. Fifteen members are elected, one by each of the provincial councils and the council of Rotuma. Elected and appointed members serve for three years. The Council has particular responsibility for all matters relating to ethnic Fijians.

Judicial power in the republic is independent of other government authority and is vested in a Supreme Court, a Court of Appeal, and a High Court. Appointment to these courts is by the president, following the recommendations of an independent Judicial Services Commission. Parliament may establish other courts by law.

It is clear that the recommendations of the Constitu-

party holding at least one seat in the Parliament or by a petition signed by 20,000 eligible voters. Until 1988 the president was elected to a six-year term by a 300-member electoral college, which itself was selected by popular vote based upon proportional representation. During this period, the electors were not legally bound to support any particular candidate, and while no formal discussion was allowed, tough and extended negotiations between ballots frequently occurred. This process, in turn, made it difficult to defeat incumbent presidents. Since there were no limits on the number of terms a president could serve, relatively long tenure in the office has been the rule; only four individuals have held the office since the end of World War II. Regular constitutional procedures for the election of the president have sometimes been bypassed. Most recently, in January 1973, the Parliament voted 170 to 28 (just over the five-sixths majority needed) to postpone the 1974 presidential contest, giving Kekkonen a four-year extension in office to allow him to conduct lengthy economic negotiations with the European Community. Earlier, in 1919, 1944, and 1946, the president was elected by the Parliament, and in 1940 and 1943 the president was chosen by the same electoral college that had convened in 1937.

In 1987, a two-stage election procedure was enacted, but it was applied only in the 1988 election. In the first stage, voters chose directly among the legally nominated candidates but at the same time selected 301 electors, who would elect the president if none of the candidates won a majority of the popular vote.

The current election procedure took effect in 1991 and was used for the first time in the 1994 election. If only one presidential candidate is designated, that candidate becomes president without an election. If there are competing candidates, the first round of voting takes place on the third Sunday in January of an election year. If one of the candidates receives a majority of the popular vote, that candidate is elected president. Otherwise, a second round is held on the third Sunday after the first round between the two candidates receiving the most votes in the first round. The candidate who then receives the most votes is elected president. In the event of a tie, the election is resolved by lot. The Council of State confirms the outcome of the election and, if necessary, conducts the drawing of lots. In the same electoral reform of 1991, the president is limited to two consecutive terms; President Martti Ahtisaari, elected in 1994, is the first to whom this limitation applies.

Ahtisaari was the nominee of the Social Democratic Party. He built his career as a diplomat and negotiator with the United Nations, winning considerable acclaim for his successful mediation of Namibian independence. Some commentators indicated that Ahtisaari had the good fortune to be out of the country when a major recession hit, thus avoiding blame for skyrocketing unemployment. Of the 11 candidates running in the first round on January 16, 7 nominated by parties and 4 by voters' association (VA) petitions, Ahtisaari won 25.9% of the

vote. In the ensuing runoff election held three weeks later, Ahtisaari won with 53.9% over Elizabeth Rehn, the sitting defense minister and nominee of the Swedish People's Party, who received 46.6%.

1994 Finnish Presidential Election, January 16, 1994

Candidate	Number of Votes	% of Votes
Martti Ahtisaari (SDP)	828,038	25.9
Elisabeth Rehn (RKP)	702,211	22.0
Paavo Väyrynen (KESK)	623,415	19.5
Raimo Ilaskivi (KOK)	485,035	15.2
Keijo Korhonen (VA)	186,936	5.8
Claes Andersson (VAS)	122,820	3.8
Pertti Virtanen (VA)	95,650	3.0
Eeva Kuuskoski (VA)	82,453	2.6
Toimi Kankaanniemi (KRIST)	31,453	1.0
Sulo Aittoniemi (SMP)	30,622	1.0
Pekka Tiainen (VA)	7,320	0.2

Total Number of Votes: 3,195,953, or 78.4% of those eligible.

No candidate received the required majority of the votes cast in the first round. The results of the second round on February 6, 1994, were:

Candidate	Number of Votes	% of Votes
Martti Ahtisaari	1,723,273	53.9
Elisabeth Rehn	1,476,506	46.6

Total Number of Votes: 3,199,779, or 78.7% of those eligible.

The State Council (*Valtioneuvosto*), or Cabinet, consists of a prime minister, deputy prime minister, and no more than 15 other ministers. Its primary functions are to prepare legislation for submission to the Parliament and to supervise the implementation and administration of policies by the civil service. Over 90% of Finland's enacted bills originate with the State Council, whose legislative program is worked out in cooperation with the president. The State Council occupies a precarious position: it is appointed and dismissed by the president, but also needs the confidence of the fractious, multiparty Parliament. As a result, Finland averaged about one government per year over the first 65 years of the republic. However, government durability has seen marked improvement in recent years; the nonsocialist coalition that left office after the 1995 elections was the third consecutive coalition to complete its four-year term. The abolition in 1992 of several antiquated supermajority voting rules in favor of simple majoritarianism should further contribute to this trend.

Nearly all Finnish governments have been coalitions of three or more parties. Between the end of World War II and 1966, center-right coalitions prevailed. Between 1966 and 1983, governments became almost exclusively center-left in composition (the "Red-Green Alliance").

The right-wing Finnish Rural Party was brought into the government in 1983, and in 1987 the center-right coalition reasserted itself for two terms.

Due to the strength of the presidency and the principle of collegiality (equality of all ministers), the Finnish prime ministry is weaker than that of most parliamentary systems. The prime minister leads the day-to-day work of the State Council and serves as the government's spokesperson in parliamentary debates and interpellations but does not have the authority to command his or her ministers, that power being reserved to the president.

Legislature

Legislative power is vested in a 200-member unicameral Parliament known as the *Eduskunta*. Since 1955, its maximum term has been set at four years, one year more than previously. In recent years, it has met virtually throughout the year. Members are chosen by direct, secret election based on proportional representation. The president of the republic opens the parliamentary session. There are also formal ceremonies at the end of the parliamentary term. The body selects its own Speaker, who is then expected to drop his or her partisan role and cannot vote. The Speaker since 1995 has been Riitta Uosukainen. The *Eduskunta* usually convenes for its annual regular session at the beginning of February. The annual session is divided into a spring term and an autumn term. At the beginning of the parliamentary term the committees of Parliament are appointed to deal with the preparation of parliamentary business. There are at present 13 parliamentary standing committees: The Committee for Constitutional Law, The Legal Affairs Committee, The Foreign Affairs Committee, The Finance Committee, The Administration Committee, The Transport and Communications Committee, The Committee for Agriculture and Forestry, The Defense Committee, The Committee for Education and Culture, The Social Affairs and Health Committee, The Economic Affairs Committee, The Committee for Labor Affairs, The Environment Committee. In addition, a Future Committee has been appointed for the current electoral period.

These committees each comprise 17 members of Parliament, apart from the Finance Committee, which has 21 members. A further parliamentary committee, The Grand Committee, has 25 members and meets once a week. Committee meetings are not normally open to the public. The committees meet from one to four times per week, depending on the volume of work to be done. The Speaker of Parliament and deputy Speakers, together with the chairpersons of the parliamentary committees, constitute the Speaker's Council. The main task of the Speaker's Council is the planning of parliamentary business.

The ordinary plenary sittings of Parliament are usually held on Tuesdays and Fridays, but if necessary they may also be held on Wednesdays and Thursdays. Plenary sittings are chaired by the Speaker of Parliament or by one

of the deputy Speakers. The chair neither contributes to the debate nor casts a vote. The plenary session debates are open to the public unless Parliament decides otherwise. A voting machine is usually used during the plenary sessions, except in the case of the election of functionaries, which is always conducted by secret ballot.

Exceptions to a Fundamental Law can be enacted, as in the 1973 extension of President Kekkonen's term in office. However, the procedure required is the same as for enacting a Fundamental Law: namely, a two-thirds majority after a five-sixths declaration of an "urgent question" or two successive two-thirds majority votes with an intervening general election. Such exceptions have been much more common than formal amendment of a Fundamental Law. Other than the limits of Fundamental Laws, there are in principle no restrictions on the powers of the *Eduskunta*, but in practice its powers are exercised primarily at the behest of the president and State Council. Individual members may introduce legislation, but in recent years only 7% of members' bills have been approved, compared with 80% of those submitted by the government.

Current representation in the *Eduskunta* is based on the March 1995 elections, presented in the accompanying table, with changes from the 1991 election in parentheses [e.g., (-2) means the party lost two seats in the 1983 election]. The results constituted a victory for the two left-wing parties that had been in opposition since 1991. The Social Democrats received more votes and seats than in any other election since World War II and reclaimed from the Center Party the position of being the largest single party.

Eduskunta Representation after 1995 Elections			
Party	Votes	Percent	Seats
Finnish Social Democratic Party	785,637	28.3	63 (+15)
Finnish Centre Party	552,003	19.8	44 (-11)
National Coalition Party	497,624	17.9	39 (-1)
Left Wing Alliance	310,340	11.2	22 (+3)
Green Party	181,198	6.5	9 (-1)
Swedish People's Party	142,874	5.1	12 (0)
Finnish Christian League	82,311	3.0	7 (-1)
Young Finns' Party	78,066	2.8	2 (+1)
Finnish Rural Party	36,185	1.3	1 (-6)
Ecology Party	7,865	0.3	1 (+1)
Others	106,818	3.8	0 (0)

The turnout was 68.5%. The average age of members is 47. There are 67 women members, down from 77 in 1991.

Judiciary

Finland's legal system finds the bulk of its heritage in its 700-year history as a province of Sweden. Sweden's first written codes were compiled in the Middle Ages. The ethical and judicial rules compiled by Olaus Petri in the 16th century can still be found in Finnish law books, and some parts of the Swedish Codification of 1734, the first of its kind in Europe, remain in force in Finland today.

The "Russification period," which lasted from 1809 until 1917, was marked by czarist efforts to impose royal absolutism on Finland. However, these attempts were countered in Finland with a steadfast reliance on the law and the rule of law. The saying *Maa on lailla rakennettava* ("By law shall this country be built") crystallizes one of the basic principles of Finnish history, reflected in the constitutional provision that "there shall be strict compliance with the law in all official functions."

Judicial authority today is exercised through a system of general courts, special courts, and administrative courts. The Finnish constitution guarantees to everyone the right to have his or her case heard appropriately and without undue delay by a court or other public authority. Everyone also has the right to have a decision affecting his rights and duties reviewed by a court or other judicial organ. The constitution also contains the basic provision on good government. The main principles guaranteeing good government are the publicity of proceedings, the right to be heard, the right to receive a decision on stated grounds, and the right to appeal against the decision. The independence of the judiciary is constitutionally guaranteed. The courts are under the sole obligation of applying the law in force, without further restrictions. The judges are appointed by the president of the republic. Most appointments are made upon a nomination from within the judiciary. A judge cannot be dismissed except by court order, e.g., if he has been convicted for an offense. The compulsory retirement age for judges is 67.

The decisions of the Courts of Appeal remain usually final, as appeal to the Supreme Court must be granted by the Supreme Court itself. However, the cases that a Court of Appeal hears in first instance are subject to appeal in the Supreme Court without restrictions. An appeal must be lodged within 60 days of the decision of the Court of Appeal. The Supreme Court is the court of final instance in the country and grants appeals in cases where a precedent is necessary for purposes of the correct application of the law, where a serious error has been committed in proceedings before a lower court, or where there is another special reason in law. Its most important task is to hand down precedents, thus giving directions to the lower courts on the application of the law. The procedure in the Supreme Court is usually written. Oral hearings can, however, be held if this is deemed necessary.

The Supreme Court consists of a president and 23 permanent justices. As vacancies arise, they are filled by the president from among legally trained and experienced candidates. The Supreme Court fulfills its ordinary duties in sections. Only matters considered to be of highest principle or the trial of a sitting president for treason are heard in plenary session. Most notable of the rights and duties not granted to the Supreme Court is the judicial review of the constitutionality of legislation, which is left to the *Eduskunta*'s constitutional committee to decide.

District court judgments are subject to appeal in a Court of Appeal. There are six Courts of Appeal in Finland: those of Turku, Vaasa, eastern Finland (located in Kuopio), Helsinki, Kouvola, and Rovaniemi. When a district court hands down its judgment, it at the same time gives appeal instructions to the parties. An appeal must be lodged within 30 days of the judgment. The procedure in a Court of Appeal has until recently been predominantly written. It is, however, undergoing changes that will considerably increase the use of oral hearings. In the future, to ensure a fair trial, the Court of Appeal has to arrange an oral hearing when a party so requests. This reform is intended to enter into force in 1998.

There is a general right of administrative appeal in Finland. It can only be restricted by a specific legislative provision to that effect. The administrative courts hear the appeals of private individuals and corporate bodies against the acts of the authorities. In certain cases the state and municipal authorities also have a right of appeal. An appeal is usually heard first by a County Administrative Court; there are 11 such courts in Finland. In the autonomous province of Åland there is no county administrative court, but instead an administrative court attached to the Åland district court. These courts hear tax cases, municipal cases, construction cases, social welfare and health care cases and other administrative cases. In certain of these, the appeal must be preceded by a complaint to a separate lower appellate body. The procedure in a county administrative court has thus far been predominantly written. Oral hearings are, however, increasing. An oral hearing must be held whenever it is necessary for the resolution of the case. In addition, an oral hearing must generally be held when a party so requests.

The Supreme Administrative Court is the final arbiter of the legality of the acts of the authorities. The bulk of its caseload consists of appeals against the decisions of the county administrative courts. Usually no leave to appeal is required. The main exception to this rule is an appeal against a decision in a tax case, for which leave is required. It is the Supreme Administrative Court itself that grants the leave. The Supreme Administrative Court consists of a president and 20 justices of the Court. In addition, expert members participate in the hearing of water and patent cases. The procedure is usually written. The Court may also hold oral hearings and conduct inspections. The new Act on Administrative Judicial Procedure will also increase the number of oral hearings in the Supreme Administrative Court. In addition to its purely judicial tasks, the Supreme Administrative Court supervises the lower judicial authorities in the field of administrative law and participates in the development of the administrative court system.

There are four land courts in Finland: those of southern

Finland, eastern Finland, northern Finland, and Vaasa. They hear disputes and appeals relating to the demarcation of plots of real estate. The decisions of the land courts are subject to appeal in the Supreme Court. The decision-making power in permits concerning water legislation is vested in the specific water courts (three in all). The water courts are competent also in private law suits and a few criminal suits. The appellate courts for the permit procedures are the superior water court (in Vaasa) and ultimately the Supreme Administrative Court. The Supreme Court is the highest instance in some matters of private or criminal law nature. The market court can prohibit misleading or improper advertising and unreasonable contract terms. Its decisions are not subject to appeal. The labor court hears disputes relating to collective agreements on employment relationships and on civil service relationships. Its decisions are not subject to appeal. Disputes relating to individual employment relationships are heard by the general courts, and those relating to individual civil service relationships by the general administrative courts. The insurance court considers certain cases falling within the field of social insurance, e.g., accident insurance and pensions. Such cases are usually first heard by an appellate board, whose decisions are then subject to appeal in the insurance court. Its decisions are not subject to appeal. The prison court considers the incarceration of dangerous recidivists and the enforcement of sentences involving the deprivation of the liberty of young offenders. The High Court of Impeachment, which has been convened only a few times, hears criminal cases relating to offenses in office allegedly committed by a member of the Council of State, the chancellor of justice, or a member of either the Supreme Court or the Supreme Administrative Court. In such cases the prosecution is handled either by the chancellor of justice or the parliamentary ombudsman.

There is no special constitutional court in Finland, but the Constitutional Committee of Parliament has been entrusted with the advance supervision of the compatibility of new legislation with the constitution. In addition, the courts and other authorities are under an obligation to interpret legislation in such a way as to adhere to the constitution and to respect human rights.

In 1995 Finland acceded to the European Union. This has naturally brought new elements into the Finnish legal system, but as a member of the European Union Finland is able to participate in the enactment of new European legislation. The Finnish judiciary now applies not only Finnish but also European law.

Regional and Local Government

Although Finland is essentially a unitary state, its constitution recognizes a certain measure of local self-government, in accordance with practices extending back many centuries. Today, there are three such basic units, collectively known as communes: 49 cities (*kaupungi*), 29 towns

(*kaupplat*), and 443 rural communes (*maalaiskunnat*). Communal authority is vested primarily in a communal council, consisting of between 13 and 77 members, depending on the commune's population, directly elected by proportional representation every fourth year. This council selects an executive body, the communal board. The commune's authority is exercised in matters delegated to it by the *Eduskunta* or not specifically assigned to other bodies: maintenance of order, local highways and transportation, primary and special schools, public health, social welfare, public works employment, and land settlement. Communes are permitted to levy local taxes, primarily income taxes, to finance their activities. In recent years, total communal revenues have equaled about one-half of state revenues. Party identification has been less clear-cut in communal elections than in national elections but is becoming increasingly apparent. In recent years about one-third of the communes have been led by socialists, with two-thirds ruled by nonsocialists. Finland's 13 provinces also have their own provincial governments, each headed by a governor. These, however, function essentially as administrative units operating under the direction of the State Council. Since 1951 the Aaland Islands have constituted an autonomous province, which, while still subject to overall state control, enjoys broader self-governing authority than any other area in Finland.

THE ELECTORAL SYSTEM

All three types of elections (presidential, parliamentary, and communal) are conducted in much the same way. All begin as direct, secret ballots based on proportional representation. For the two national elections, Finland is divided into 15 electoral districts. These districts vary considerably in population, so that before each election the State Council apportions the number of seats in each according to census figures (rather than size of the electorate). For the 200-member *Eduskunta*, the number of seats per district ranges from 9 to 21, except for the Aaland Islands, a separate district electing just 1 representative. Two or more parties may join together to form an election bloc, but they still present separate lists. The voter casts his ballot for an individual candidate, but it is also tallied for the party list on which it appears. The number of votes for each list and/or bloc is recorded. Each candidate of a unified voting group (list or bloc) is then assigned a "comparison number" based on the following formula: the person who garners the most votes in each bloc is assigned the total vote of that bloc, the second-leading individual is assigned one-half the total vote of that bloc, the third receives one-third, and so on. Once these computations are made for each bloc, all candidates are ranked according to these figures, and the available seats are assigned on the basis of this ranking.

In effect, then, the vote for the individual candidate

helps determine his ranking within the bloc, while the simultaneous vote for the party list helps determine the party's proportion of the available seats. This system does discriminate somewhat against the very small parties, but it has not prevented 8 to 10 or even more parties from being represented in the *Eduskunta* in recent years.

All citizens who have reached age 18 before the election year may vote. Registration is conducted by local election boards on the basis of the previous year's census. Voter turnout as a proportion of those eligible has been declining, especially in parliamentary elections. For example, in 1962, 85.1% of those eligible voted, while the figure for 1995 had fallen to 68.5%. In contrast, turnout for both rounds of the 1994 presidential election exceeded 78%. Advance voting in post offices has become quite common, accounting for over 40% of the votes cast in recent elections.

THE PARTY SYSTEM

Origins of the Parties

Modern party organizations date from the mid-19th century. The original impetus was provided by ethnolinguistic divisions between Finnish- and Swedish-speaking Finns. Later, class and urban-rural cleavages also emerged, so that with Finland's first modern elections in 1906, a distinct multiparty system was evident. This pattern has persisted until today, with many Finns believing that this multiplicity of parties is preferable to what they would consider an "unhealthy" polarization of politics.

The Parties in Law

Political parties are not mentioned in any of the Fundamental Laws and thus are generally considered civil organizations with the same legal status as other associations. There are no special state restrictions, except when extreme parties have been banned, as with the Communist Party in 1928 and the profascist People's Patriotic League (IKL) in 1944. Since 1970, nomination of candidates for the *Eduskunta* has been a legally recognized function of registered political parties. Legally defined seating in the Parliament is also by party grouping. Overall, there is a minimum of legal apparatus surrounding party formation or activity.

Party Organization

Today, all the major parties in Finland are considered mass parties, with large dues-paying memberships. However, they have not evolved into catchall parties on the American, British, or West German models. Rather, they remain rather narrowly based. For the most part, Finnish parties share the same basic pyramidal structure, with a large number of local base units, district (provincial) units, and the national party congress, executive organs, and central bureaus. The local units, usually defined residentially rather than functionally, have as their main tasks the recruitment of new members; the organization of meetings, study clubs and courses, and entertainment events; and the distribution of party literature. Local activities peak at the time of communal or national elections. The district or provincial organization serves to coordinate and support the work of the base units and to link the base units with the party's central leadership. Authority is vested in district meetings, to which each base unit sends one representative. This meeting elects a district executive committee of 10 to 20 members to direct the day-to-day work of the district organization.

The national party congress is the primary source of the party's program, rules, and finances. The delegates are chosen at the local and district levels either at meetings or by membership vote, the latter being more characteristic of the socialist parties. The congress also elects the executive council or board that exercises authority between congresses and that, in turn, chooses an even smaller committee to handle day-to-day affairs.

The left parties tend toward a more centralized administration coupled with emphasis on democratic participation by the rank and file. The nonsocialist parties lean more toward territorial decentralization, but with greater passivity of members and reliance on party officials at various levels. Each party also sponsors parallel women's, youth, and auxiliary organizations. The relationship between a party's members and its parliamentary bloc also tends to vary along the ideological spectrum, with the independence of the member of Parliament (MP) being greatest in the rightist parties and least on the left. Overall, it is still safe to say that the MPs represent their party organizations more than their electoral constituencies. Candidate lists are drawn up by the district party organizations, with the left parties seeking more and the center and right parties less rank-and-file participation.

Party leadership dominated by outstanding individuals is relatively rare in Finland. It is unusual for anyone to become the undisputed leader of a Finnish party. Thus, in the case of a Cabinet crisis, a given party may well have several candidates of near-equal stature for prime minister.

Campaigning

Campaign activity is centered on the permanent party organization, supplemented by special election committees and support organizations. Propaganda for candidates is conducted at all levels, but with a recent tendency toward centralized, uniform party propaganda. The shift to single-name candidate lists in 1965, however, has led to a significant growth in separate electioneering by individual candidates and voters' associations. Campaign activities include speeches, rallies, newspaper and journal articles, mass mailings, door-to-door canvassing, posters, print media advertising, and broadcast debates.

Independent Voters

The number of independent voters, those not identifying with one particular party, is estimated at about 15% of the electorate. Even in the least-partisan elections, those for the communal councils, the party affiliation of most candidates can be discerned and voted upon. Given conditions of partisan stability and multipartism, elections are now often effectively won or lost with these floating independents, found disproportionately within the urban upper middle class.

Party Financing

As largely unregulated civil associations, Finnish parties were not required to divulge their sources of funds until changes in the campaign laws in 1986 required the parties to itemize campaign expenses in their statements of accounts. Data presented since then indicate that campaign spending by the major parties has approximately quadrupled since 1975. The leftist parties rely more heavily on membership dues than do the others, but even here dues make up less than 10% of revenues. Private contributions, raffles, entertainment, business activities, and income from publications and auxiliary organizations supplement state financing, which since 1967 has been set at 10 million marks (about $2.38 million) annually. This sum is distributed to parties on the basis of 50,000 marks (about $12,000) per MP.

CENTER PARTY
(Keskustapouloe)

Although the Center Party was the biggest loser in the 1995 elections, dropping 4.9% in its share of the popular vote and 11 seats in Parliament, its showing was still the second-strongest posted since it changed its name from the Agrarian Party in 1966. It also regained in 1995 its position as the strongest nonsocialist party in the *Eduskunta*, a position it had ceded to the Conservatives through most of the 1970s and 1980s. With by far the largest formal membership of any Finnish party (about 300,000 members) the Center is the strongest party in the four western and northern constituencies of Vaasa, Kuopio, Oulu, and Lapland. Its electoral support today is about evenly divided among farmers and white-collar and blue-collar workers. Since 1976 it has markedly increased its support among younger (18–40) white-collar workers. The Center Party does better with women voters than the socialist parties but not as well as the more conservative parties.

Significantly, in 1995 it lost its only MP from Helsinki, which it had gained in 1983.

The party was founded as the Agrarian Union in 1906 and adopted its present name in 1965. Until the 1970s it was consistently the leading nonsocialist party, with *Eduskunta* representation ranging from 60 seats in 1929 to 35 in 1972. It has also served as the nearly indispensable pivot in coalition formation, having served in over 90% of the noncaretaker governments since 1918. Similarly, it has supplied more presidents and prime ministers than any other party. However, with the sharp demographic decline of the farming population following World War II, the party's change of name in 1965 signaled its awareness of the need to broaden its appeal, which has been at least reasonably successful, although the party's center of gravity remains in rural Finland.

Eskimo Ho, prime minister from 1991 to 1995, is the party leader.

LEFTIST ALLIANCE (LA)
(Vasemistoliitto)

After going through a difficult period of rancor and division surrounding the dissolution of the Soviet Union, Finland's leftists (a coalition of communists and radical socialists) rebounded in 1995 to record their best result since 1983. As before, the LA's major strength was among older blue-collar voters and the three rural districts of central northern Finland, characterized by economic marginality and high levels of long-term unemployment. Although the LA bitterly opposed Finland's entry into the European Union, its backwoods stronghold is a major recipient of European Union "Zone Six" economic support.

The Leftist Alliance formed in 1990 is the successor to several other groups and coalitions dating back to the founding of the Finnish Communist Party by a revolutionary group in exile in 1918. Its adherents returned to Finland with the general amnesty of 1922. By 1929, its militancy had helped arouse the fascist Lapua Movement, which, through legal pressure and illegal terror, crushed the Communist Party and eliminated it as an institutional force until 1944. In that year, dissident Social Democrats, independent socialists, and Communists formed the Finnish People's Democratic League (SKDL), which served as an umbrella electoral vehicle for these groups until 1990. The Finnish Communist Party (*Suomen Puolu*; SKP) was the leading group within the SKDL, but a significant role was given to non-Communists and to the League's other two constituent organizations, the Democratic League of Finnish Women and the Socialist League of Students. The SKDL enjoyed considerable electoral success between 1944 and 1966, receiving between 23.5 and 20.0% of the vote in seven consecutive elections. Between 1966 and 1983, the SKDL participated in all but two of the noncaretaker governments of that period. Starting in 1970, however, SKDL popularity declined, and its *Eduskunta* representation fell steadily, from a peak of 50 in 1958 to 20 in 1987. Deep ideological divisions led to the dissolution of the SKDL in 1990 and its replacement by the new alliance, based on the model of the Danish Socialist People's Party. While the 1995 vote was encouraging to the Alliance, it has yet to achieve its desired "red-green" image and faces a severe challenge of generational renewal, as fully 76% of its 1995 voters reported being over 40 years old.

The leader of the Leftist Alliance is Claes Andersson.

NATIONAL CONSERVATIVE PARTY (NCP)
(Kansallinen Kokoomus)

After serving eight years as part of Finland's ruling coalitions, the Conservatives' losses in 1995 were more modest than those of the Center Party, dropping just 1.4% of the popular vote and one seat in parliament. Partly as a result, the *Kokoomus* was included in a historic coalition along with the winning Social Democrats, the Swedish People's Party, the Leftist League, and the Greens. This marks the first time in Finnish history that *Kokoomus* and the Leftist League have served in the same government. Still, the *Kokoomus* share of the 1995 vote was down 5.2% from its all-time high of 23.1 in 1987. In 1995 the Conservatives also failed to regain their position as the leading nonsocialist party, a position they had held continuously between 1971 and 1991. The Conservatives have been losing some ground to the Social Democrats, Greens, and Young Finns among the growing urban-based service sector (the "New Middle Class") of southern Finland that had recently served as the core of its electoral base. Indeed, in 1995 the Conservatives conceded to the Social Democrats the position of leading party in Helsinki and Uusimaa.

The *Kokoomus* was founded in 1918 as a continuation of the preindependence "Old Finns," a Finnish-language group less hostile to Russification than the "Young Finns." For decades, its electoral support was limited to less than 20% by its image as a rather extreme right-wing party. This image was reinforced by its support for the Lapua Movement, stopping just short of endorsing the attempted Lapuan coup d'état of 1932. However, other sources of strength gave it power far beyond that indicated by the election results. With its leader, P. E. Svinhufvud, serving as president from 1931 to 1937, the *Kokoomus* was largely able to implement its probusiness program for meeting the Great Depression. It participated in most governments between 1925 and 1946, supplying 10 prime ministers. It was also included in three governments between 1953 and 1966, but then was shut out of government until its smashing victory of 1987.

Historically, membership and voting support came from big business, large landowners, and portions of the upper middle class (e.g., top bureaucrats). Since 1987 the party has made gains in the new middle class of the larger southern cities and towns, with 77% of its 1991 voters categorizing themselves as "officials and managers." Many first-time voters and disgruntled supporters of the smaller nonsocialist parties have also rallied to the *Kokoomus*. Traditionally, interest-group support was a more significant contributor to *Kokoomus* power than membership or voters. As the party has become more mass-based and catchall in nature, this balance has shifted. Still, the Federation of Finnish Industries, the Confederation of Finnish Employers, the Central Chamber of Commerce, the Confederation of Agricultural Producers, and various university alumni and veterans organizations maintain close, if informal, financial and political ties to the *Kokoomus*.

Sauli Niinistö, MP, minister of finance, deputy prime minister, is the party chairman. Vice chairmen include Pirkko-Liisa Ollila (chair of the women's league of NCP); Kirsi Piha, MP; and Juha Rintamäki (chairman of the youth league of NCP). The secretary-general is Maija Perho, MP.

SOCIAL DEMOCRATIC PARTY (SDP)
(Suomen Socialidemokraattinen Puolue)

The Social Democrats scored a resounding victory in 1995, gaining their largest proportion of the vote (28.3%) and number of seats (63) in any election since World War II. They also regained from the Center Party their historic position as the largest party in the *Eduskunta*. Gaining 15 seats over 1991, the SDP profited from a rare "national swing" to win a plurality in 10 of the 14 mainland constituencies. Traditionally strong among the more prosperous and secure blue-collar workers and increasingly attractive to the white-collar segments, the SDP did especially well in the Helsinki hinterland of Uusimaa, eastern and southeastern Finland. Especially in the south, there is evidence that the SDP benefited from a crossover vote from disgruntled Center Party voters. Holding both the presidency (Martti Ahtisaari) and prime ministership (Paavo Lipponen) for the first time since 1987, the SDP is in a position to consolidate these new supporters with a solid performance in office.

The party was founded in 1899 as a direct outgrowth of the nascent labor movement. It rejected a reformist approach in favor of an uncompromising commitment to class struggle, as reflected in the radical Forssa Program of 1903. When the czar allowed elections to the 200-member Finnish Diet to be conducted by universal adult suffrage in 1907, the Social Democrats astonished nearly everyone by winning 80 seats, 21 more than any other party. In 1916, it won 103 seats, an absolute majority not nearly matched by any party since. (The czar refused to convene the Diet following this election.)

With the collapse of the Russian Empire in 1917, the highly polarized Finnish political system erupted in civil war, with the Social Democrats leading the nearly victorious Red forces. With their defeat, the most radical Social Democrats were forced into exile, where they formed the Finnish Communist Party. The more moderate remnants of the Social Democratic Party reconstituted themselves under the control of its reformist wing, led by Vaino Tanner. In the first postindependence elections, the party again won 80 seats, almost twice as many as any other party. Since World War II, the SDP has had to face renewed competition on its left first from the SKDL and now from the Leftist Alliance. A period of intraparty tension culminated in 1958 when a group of more radical dissidents was expelled from the party. They formed the Social Democratic League of Workers and Small Farmers (TPSL), which was able to win seven *Eduskunta* seats in 1966, before fading away in the early 1970s. From its all-time low of 38 seats in 1962, the SDP quickly rebounded and headed most governments between 1966 and 1987. In the 1970s and 1980s, the SDP profited from the popularity of its leader, Mauno Koivisto, who became prime minister in 1979 and served two terms as president between 1982 and 1994. From 1991 until its major victory in 1995, however, the SDP was in opposition.

The party chairman is Paavo Lipponen, the general secretary is Kari Laitinen, and the vice chairpersons are Antero Kekkonen and Liisa Jaakonsaari.

SWEDISH PEOPLE'S PARTY
(Ruotsalainen Kansanpuolue)

The durability of this smaller party's appeal was demonstrated yet again in 1995. Standing in the first instance for the defense of the cultural and linguistic interests of the 6% of the population of Swedish language and heritage, this party seemed on the decline when its proportion of the vote dropped below 5% in 1979 and 1983. Since then, however, it has rebounded by constructing a disparate coalition of anti–European Union farmers in the northwest, southwestern fishermen, and progressive economic liberals in Helsinki and environs. While some portions of its electoral base are aging (71% report being age 40 or above), it has recently attracted support from younger "bilinguals," that is, mixed Finnish- and Swedish-speaking couples. Of its voters in 1991, 77% reported being white-collar workers, with the remainder composed primarily of Swedish-speaking farmers, fishermen, and blue-collar workers.

During the period of Swedish rule of Finland (1323–1809), thousands of Swedes became residents in Finland and established themselves as an elite. By the mid-19th century, the language and culture of this group had become dominant at the top of Finland's upper class. The party was founded in 1906 as the institutional continuation of the Swedish interest group (*Svecomen*) in the Diet and was aimed explicitly at promoting the interests of the Swedish-speaking minority. Even by the time of its founding, however, the language issue had been largely settled in favor of Finnish. Nevertheless, the Swedish People's Party was able consistently to obtain between 10% and 14% of the vote through the 1930s. After the war, its popularity declined steadily, reaching the lowest total in its history in 1979. Since then, by broadening its appeal as described above, the party has been able to stabilize its support at around 5.5% of the electorate. Swedish-speaking Finns, if still somewhat privileged, are no longer considered a threat by the Finnish majority. The party has been included in almost all the ruling coalitions since 1968, including the current "rainbow" coalition. It has never contributed a prime minister or president, however.

FINNISH GREEN LEAGUE
(Vihreä Liitto)

Despite losing fractional voting support and one seat in the 1995 elections, the Finnish Green League still cemented its status as probably the most successful party of its type in the world. Unique not only in winning continuous parliamentary representation since 1983, its inclusion in the current "rainbow" coalition makes it the first Green party ever to be included in a European government. Clearly a youth-oriented party, three-quarters of its voters report being under 40, and over half live in Helsinki or neighboring Uusimaa, where it is now the third-largest party. The challenge for the Greens will be to use their representation in government to retain current supporters as they age and perhaps lose some of their youthful idealism, while continuing to attract new generations of young voters.

The Green League of Finland grew out of the environmental movement of the 1970s as it merged with kindred movements promoting alternative ideas in social policy and rejuvenating grassroots democracy. The Green League first took part in parliamentary elections in 1983, running a handful of independent candidates. Contrary to most forecasts, 2 Green MPs were elected. In the 1987 elections the number of Green MPs doubled to 4. In the local elections of 1984 and 1988, Green candidates still ran as independents, gaining council seats mainly in the larger cities. The Green League was finally registered as a political party in 1988 after a lengthy debate about the pros and cons of a formal electoral vehicle. The first comprehensive Green Manifesto was drafted and approved in 1990, and the successful 1991 parliamentary elections brought the number of Green MPs to 10 with 6.8% of the vote. The upward trend continued in the 1992 local elections. Public opinion polls taken in the run-up to the 1995 elections were extremely favorable to the Greens, and though the actual vote was disappointing, with the League chairman, Pekka Haavisto, losing his seat, a subsequent two-thirds vote in the National Council confirmed Haavisto as environment minister in the new "rainbow" government.

The executive committee chair is Satu Hassi, and the deputy chairs are Kirsi Ojansuu, and Erkki Pulliainen.

FINNISH CHRISTIAN LEAGUE
(Suomen Kristillinen Liitto)

Winning *Eduskunta* representation for over a quarter century, the Christian League is the second-most-durable party of its type in the Nordic region. While it suffered a marginal loss of votes and one seat, this was largely due to its failure to work out an electoral alliance with the anti-EU Free Finland Union that likely would have won it two additional seats. The League's pledge "to restore respect for basic values" and "to strengthen the values of the traditional family and its restoration as a God-fearing institution" appeals to farmers and blue-collar and white-collar workers in roughly the same proportions they represent in the general population. Geographically, its strongest representation is in the Pietist strongholds of Vaasa and Mikkeli. The Christian League faces perhaps the most acute challenge of all the parties from an aging electoral base; no fewer than 83% of its voters report being 40 years or older.

The League was founded in 1958 in an attempt to give partisan expression to the Lutheran pietist tradition. It gained its first *Eduskunta* representative in 1966, expanding to four seats in 1972 and nine in 1976. In the 1979 election, the party increased its popular vote but still won just nine seats. In 1983 it was outflanked on the right by the Finnish Rural Party in the 1983 elections, losing six of its nine seats. It rebounded in 1987 and in 1991, back up to eight seats, and was included in the Center Party–led government. The League has never aspired to be a permanent fixture on the political scene, stating that a more overt Christian orientation in the Center or National Coalition parties would render its existence superfluous.

However, these parties have demurred. Following the surge to power by the Finnish Rural Party in 1983, it was thought that the latter's success might threaten the existence of the League. By 1995, however, the durability of the Christian League has made the reverse seem more likely.

The present chairman is Toimi Kankaanniemi.

FINNISH RURAL PARTY
(Suomen Maaseudun Puolue)

Born in 1956 as a protest party of the Poujadist variety, the Rural Party has seen its fortunes wax and wane in volatile fashion ever since. However, its disastrous showing in 1995, when it lost three-fourths of its voters and six of its seven *Eduskunta* seats, may finally signal the end of its turbulent but colorful history. The party's program always sought to combine seemingly incongruous socialist and nonsocialist elements accompanied by constant reference to rooting out the misuse, abuse, and corruption of public power by the older parties. Its voters were generally small businesspeople and impoverished smallholders geographically centered in the eastern provinces, especially Kuopio and Pohjois-Karjala. In times of economic hardship or perceived corruption by the established parties, voters from all walks of life turned to the Rural Party as a protest vehicle. But this pattern changed in 1991 and 1995, when protest was channeled through one of the established parties, the Center in 1991 and the Social Democrats in 1995.

The Finnish Rural Party was founded in 1956 by a group of dissident Agrarian (Center) Party members led by the colorful and outspoken Veikko Vennamo, who charged that the Agrarians were selling out the interest of the small farmers, laborers, and small businesspeople, especially in the remote areas. The Rural Party achieved a stunning breakthrough in the *Eduskunta* elections of 1970, winning 10.5% of the vote and 18 seats. It held this total in the 1972 poll. In 1975, however, it fell dramatically to 3.6% and 2 seats. The 1979 elections represented something of a comeback for the party, paving the way for another major breakthrough in 1983, when the party was included in the government for the first time. When the party leadership passed to Vennamo's son, Pekka, policy positions became more moderate and predictable but may have lost some of their flair as well.

The party chair is Pekka Vennamo.

YOUNG FINNS
(Nuorsuomalainen Puolue)

Replacing the Rural Party and the Liberal People's Party as vehicles for antiestablishment protest may be this revival of the famous 19th- and early-20th-century liberal-republican party. Spearheaded by a special adviser in the Defense Ministry, Risto Penttila, the Young Finns attack the allegedly outmoded party democracy and the "old thinking" on which it is based. They propose drastic budget cuts, including all party, agricultural, and corporate subsidies; a shift from income to consumer taxes; and teaching all Finns to use the World Wide Web. Two-thirds of their parliamentary candidates listed their occupations as students, entrepreneurs, mangers, or mothers, and the party won almost 22% of the vote at the Helsinki University of Technology. Overall, they picked up two seats in Helsinki and Uusimaa, where they polled between 5% and 6% of the vote.

Founded in 1994, the Young Finns are a revival of a 19th-century party of the same name. The original Young

Finns disappeared when they merged into the Finnish People's Party, which itself merged into the Liberal People's Party in 1965. Penttila, having narrowly failed to become secretary of the Conservative Party, bolted to form this revived "reformist center" party.

The present party chairman is Risto Penttila.

ECOLOGY PARTY

This party is largely a vehicle for Pertti Olavi Virtanen, a maverick therapist who considers himself the therapist, prophet, and promoter of the Finnish identity. Having tried his hand as a composer, writer, psychologist, hypnotist, troubadour, and master of debate, Veltto ran in the 1994 presidential election, getting 3% of the vote. He then decided to run for the *Eduskunta* and was successful in winning a seat from south-central Häme province.

MINOR POLITICAL PARTIES

The Liberal People's Party, the Joint Responsibility Party, the Women's Party, For Peace and Socialism–Communist Workers' Party, Pensioners for the People, Finnish Pensioners' Party, and the Natural Law Party are all parties that fielded candidates but failed to win *Eduskunta* representation.

NATIONAL PROSPECTS

The fall of communism in Eastern Europe and the dissolution of the Soviet Union marked the end of an extremely perilous era for Finland. Whether one agrees or disagrees with the pejorative connotations of the concept of "Finlandization," and there is a deeply searching debate over it taking place in Finland, there can be no doubt that Finland's control of its own destiny is much greater than at any time since World War II. Perhaps paradoxically, one of the first exercises of its new-found sovereignty was to vote fairly comfortably (57% to 43%) in 1994 to apply for membership in the European Union.

At the same time, the collapse of the Soviet Union and its East European satellites had a devastating effect on Finland's economy, which had relied on those countries as its biggest customers. The resulting downturn, which saw unemployment skyrocket to 20%, was the primary cause of the defeat of the Center Party in 1995. The outsized "rainbow coalition" led by Prime Minister Paavo Lipponen has designated itself "The Government of Employment and Joint Responsibility" and has set itself the objective to halve unemployment in Finland by the year 2000 and meet the convergence criteria of the European Monetary Union, which will require serious budget cutting. While these challenges are indeed formidable, with the major threat to Finland's sovereignty removed and with the country firmly enmeshed in the institutions of democratic Europe, the Finnish people have every right to face the future with cautious optimism.

Further Reading

Alapuro, Risto. "Finland, Thrown Out into the World Alone." *Scandinavian Studies* 64, no. 4 (fall 1992): 699–709.

Anckar, Dag. *Parties and Law-Making in Finland*. Åbo: Åbo Academy, 1989.

Arter, David. *Bumpkin against Bigwig: The Emergence of a Green Movement in Finnish Politics*. Tampere: University of Tampere, Institute of Political Science, 1978.

———. "The March 1995 Finnish Election: The Social Democrats Storm Back." *West European Politics* 18, no. 4 (October 1995): 194–205.

———. *Politics and Policy-Making in Finland*. New York: St. Martin's Press, 1987.

Borg, Sami, and Risto Sänkiaho, eds. *The Finnish Voter*. Tampere: The Finnish Political Science Association, 1995.

Halliday, Fred. "Letter from Helsinki." *New Statesman and Society* 7, no. 285 (January 14, 1994): 11–12.

James, Anthony. "A Northern Paradox: How Finland Survived the Cold War." *Contemporary Review* 264, no. 1538 (March 1994): 113–23.

Keränen, Marja. *Gender and Politics in Finland*. Aldershot, England: Avebury, 1992.

Mylly, Juhani, and R. Michael Berry, eds. *Political Parties in Finland: Essays in History and Politics*. Turku: University of Turku Department of Political History, 1984.

Sänkiaho, Risto, et al. *People and Their Polities: Festschrift for Pertti Pesonen*. Helsinki: Finnish Political Science Association, 1990.

Ståhlberg, Krister. *Politics and Administration in Finland*. Åbo: Åbo Academy, 1989.

Popular Presidential Elections under the Fifth Republic

1965	1st Round	2d Round		1st Round	2d Round
de Gaulle (G.)	10,828,523 (44.6)	13,085,407 (55.2)	Chirac (G.)	5,225,846 (18.0)	
Mitterrand (S.)	7,694,003 (31.7)	10,623,247 (44.8)	Marchais (Comm.)	4,456,922 (15.3)	
Lecanuet (Cen.)	3,777,119 (15.6)		Others	3,626,876 (12.5)	
Others	1,954,909 (8.1)		**1988**		
1969			Mitterrand (S.)	10,367,220 (34.1)	16,704,279 (54.0)
Pompidou (G.)	9,763,428 (44.0)	10,686,498 (57.6)	Chirac (G.)	6,063,514 (19.9)	14,218,970 (46.0)
Poher (Cons.)	5,202,271 (23.4)	7,870,601 (42.4)	Barre (Cons.)	5,031,849 (16.5)	
Duclos (Comm.)	4,781,838 (21.5)		Le Pen (NF)	4,375,894 (14.4)	
Defferre (S.)	1,128,049 (5.1)		Others	4,567,561 (15.0)	
Others	1,335,136 (6.0)		**1995**		
1974			Jacques Chirac (G.)	6,278,557 (20.7)	15,654,234 (52.6)
Giscard d'Estaing (Cons.)	8,326,774 (32.6)	13,396,203 (50.8)	Lionel Jospin (S.)	7,061,300 (23.3)	14,114,715 (47.4)
Mitterrand (S.)	11,044,373 (43.2)	12,971,604 (49.2)	Edouard Balladur (Cons.)	5,616,885 (18.5)	
Chaban-Delmas (G.)	3,857,728 (15.1)		Jean-Marie Le Pen (NF)	4,564,776 (15.1)	
Others	2,309,761 (9.0)		Robert Hué (Comm.)	2,631,173 (8.7)	
1981			Others	4,141,626 (13.7)	
Mitterrand (S.)	7,505,960 (25.8)	15,714,598 (51.8)			
Giscard d'Estaing (Cons.)	8,222,432 (28.3)	14,647,787 (48.2)			

G. = Gaullist, S. = Socialist, Cons. = Conservative, Cen. = Centrist, Comm. = Communist, NF = National Front.

deputies elected to their Assembly offices by its membership. The constitution requires that the Assembly president be "elected for the duration of the legislature." That officer is chosen from the chamber's political majority and ensures the orderly conduct of its business, as well as performing other important functions. The vice presidents represent the major parties in the governance of the Assembly. The Assembly's agenda is prepared by the Conference of Presidents, which includes the president of the Assembly, its vice presidents, the committee chairs, the party caucus chairs, and the member of the Finance Committee responsible for reporting bills. A representative of the government may attend its meetings. In fact, under the constitution, the government controls the agenda by requiring priority consideration of its bills.

The Assembly meets for no more than 120 plenary sessions on Tuesdays, Wednesdays, and Thursdays during nine months each year beginning the first Monday of October. One meeting each month is reserved for private members' bills. Most legislative work of the Assembly is prepared by six standing committees, a number specified by the constitution. Their subjects are culture, family, and social affairs; production and exchange; constitutional law, legislation, and general administration; foreign affairs; finance, the economy, and planning; and national defense and the armed forces. They range in size from 70 to 140 members and usually are chaired by the government's supporters. Most bills are referred to those committees.

Partisan affairs in the Assembly are managed by caucuses, called parliamentary groups. Caucuses require at least 20 members. Five caucuses have formed in all recent Parliaments: Communist, Socialist, Gaullist (RPR), conservative (UDF), and centrist or radical. Some independent deputies affiliate with these caucuses. The caucuses are represented proportionally on the committees and other Assembly organs and in the distribution of debating time.

Parliament controls the government formally by defeating it on votes of confidence or motions of censure, by committee work, and through debates and questions. The National Assembly of the Fifth Republic has voted out a government only once. In October 1962, the Assembly censured the Pompidou government over President de Gaulle's plan to revise the constitution by popular referendum. De Gaulle dissolved the rebellious Assembly, and his supporters won a record majority in the new one. Since then, MPs have grumbled, groaned, and occasionally defected, but they have not censured any government. Through the 1993 elections, 49 motions of censure had been submitted in the National Assembly, an average of 1.4 per year. Only votes favorable to a censure motion are counted, avoiding a distinction between negative votes and abstentions. Except for the 1962 motion, none was adopted and very few have come close. The most nearly successful failed by three votes in 1989.

The total time spent in committee sessions averaged 578 hours annually, from 1978 to 1996, mostly in work on government bills. The use of investigative committees increased dramatically during the 1988 legislature. Until then, the National Assembly had formed 23 such committees in 30 years. During the next 5 years, it appointed 11, plus 5 "missions" of information or evaluation. Their effect in controlling the government is difficult to assess, but none has endangered its survival. Plenary sessions of the National Assembly devote some 140–150 hours to exercising direct control over the government. This is about 17% of the total time (850 hours, 1978–96) in public sessions. Parliamentary questions take several forms. Nearly 20,000 written questions are posed some years and about 90% are answered, also in writing. The Thursday afternoon sitting is reserved for oral questions—mainly on parish pump issues—to which the ministers must respond immediately. Also, during the two first hours of each Tuesday and Wednesday sitting, deputies quiz ministers with brief, spontaneous questions to which the ministers respond. The Tuesday and Wednesday sessions are televised. Several hundred oral questions of all types are posed and answered each year.

The French upper house is principally a "chamber of reflection" and a means of ensuring representation of the provinces. It has somewhat less legislative authority than the lower house and no direct power to vote down governments. In 1958, de Gaulle and Michel Debré (a senator in the Fourth Republic) conceived of the Senate as one means to protect governments from the National Assembly. In fact, throughout the Fifth Republic, whatever the partisan orientation of the governments, the Senate has tended to be less favorable to the governments than has been the Assembly and, thus, has not served its intended purpose.

Number of Senators, by Party, after Each Election, 1986–98					
	1986	1989	1992	1995	1998
Communists	15	16	15	15	16
Socialists	64	66	70	75	78
Radicals	35	23	22	24	22
MRP/Center	70	68	67	59	52
Independents	54	52	47	47	47
Gaullists	77	91	90	94	99
Other	—	—	12	7	7
Total	319	321	321	321	323

The internal structure of the 323-seat Senate resembles that of the Assembly. The subject areas of the standing committees are slightly different, and neither special committees nor investigative committees have been used as much. Usually, six party caucuses are formed: Communist, Socialist, Radical, Centrist, Conservative, and Gaullist.

Because of its higher age requirement (35), its less political character, and the longer terms of its members, the Senate tends to attract local "notables," rather than more active, ambitious politicians. Also, the partisan lineup in the Senate has been quite different from the Assembly. Neither the Gaullists nor the Socialists have ever held as many as 30% of the Senate seats, despite their clear majorities in the Assembly. Rather, the Senate's composition has remained remarkably similar to that of its Fourth Republic predecessor.

At the call of the president of the republic, the Assembly and Senate meet together, as "the Congress," to adopt constitutional amendments approved by the chambers separately. They had done so eight times through 1998. Their most significant amendment authorized 60 deputies or 60 senators to bring cases to the Constitutional Council (1974). Also, the constitution was amended by popular referendum to introduce direct popular election of the president (1962) and, by a separate amending process involving the former French overseas possessions, to facilitate their decolonization (1960).

Judiciary

The 1958 constitution created, for the first time in France, a quasi-judicial institution—the Constitutional Council—that can invalidate legislative and executive acts on grounds of unconstitutionality. Its authority is much more closely prscribed than is that of the U. S.Supreme Court, but it has become somewhat more important than expected as a result of some of its decisions and a constitutional revision.

The Council is composed of nine appointed members. The president of the republic, the president of the Senate, and the president of the National Assembly each makes one appointment every three years. Members serve nine-

The 13 departments and territories with 1 seat each choose senators by the majority system with single-member districts and a runoff ballot the same day if no candidate wins a majority in the first round. The 15 most populous departments with at least 5 seats each (a total of 98 seats) use proportional representation. The remaining departments with from 2 to 4 seats each (198 seats) use the majority system with multimember districts and a runoff ballot. Finally, the 12 senators who represent French citizens living abroad are nominated by an official governmental advisory council composed of representatives of their local associations. Its choices are ratified routinely by the Senate. *Suppléants* for the candidates in the departments using the majority electoral systems are nominated as their running mates. In the departments that use proportional representation, the highest-ranking unsuccessful candidate on the senator's party list is the replacement.

The original 1958 constitution provided that the president be elected for a seven-year term by an electoral college dominated by local elective officials. A 1962 constitutional amendment replaced the electoral college with direct popular election. A majority of the votes cast is required for election on the first ballot. If no candidate receives a majority, a second round of balloting is held two weeks later. Only the two top first-round candidates who choose to remain in the running are eligible for the second balloting.

Another form of national popular consultation is the referendum. De Gaulle introduced this institution after World War II, but the Fourth Republic dropped it. De Gaulle revived it in the 1958 constitution. Referenda played an important role in the early Fifth Republic. De Gaulle held five referenda, giving each a plebiscitary character by threatening to resign if his proposal was defeated. The fifth time (1969), the voters said "No" and de Gaulle retired. Since then, the referendum has faded badly. It was used only three times in 28 years: in 1972 on expansion of the European Community, in 1988 on eventual independence for New Caledonia, and in 1992 on the Maastricht Treaty. None of those referenda was treated as a plebiscite, and they aroused relatively little voter interest. Only in 1969 was a referendum vote negative.

All French citizens at least 18 years old are eligible to vote. The government registers all voters by mail. Registration lists are available for public perusal, verification, and correction well in advance of each election campaign.

Generally, voting turnout has been high. Of the 25 national-level consultations, 18 have drawn between 75% and 85% of the registered voters in at least one round of balloting. The exceptions have been the 1981, 1988, 1993, and 1997 Assembly elections, in which turnout was 74.5%, 69.9%, 69.2%, and 68.3%, respectively, and the 1972, 1988, and 1992 referenda (60.2%, 36.9%, and 69.8%). French turnout figures are somewhat inflated, as about 5.5% of the eligible voting-age population is not registered.

THE PARTY SYSTEM

Origins of the Parties

Organized political parties appeared in France after the 1789 revolution. However, today's party system evolved from one that emerged about 1900. The Third Republic had an extreme multiparty system with no party ever winning as many as one-quarter of the votes cast. The centrist Radical Socialist Party was the most important during that period. Hardly a government could be formed without support from a substantial part of that faction-ridden and undisciplined, but strategically placed, party. Multipartism was less extreme during the Fourth Republic, but the general configuration of the system survived and the Radicals remained pivotal.

The ideological character of the party system underwent substantial change from the Third to the Fourth Republic. The Marxist Socialists and Communists were the only Third Republic parties to profess anything approaching systems of doctrine. The Radical-Socialists rarely united on anything except resistance to the church and the state, and the rest of the political landscape was occupied by pragmatic, personalist cliques. The ideological parties were joined in the Fourth Republic by the Christian democratic Popular Republican Movement (*Mouvement Républicain Populaire*; MRP) and the nationalist Gaullists. Those four parties held 65% to 75% of the Assembly seats in the first three postwar Parliaments (1945–56), but their strength and ideological commitment waned late in the Fourth Republic.

The Parties in Law

Parties are virtually extralegal institutions. The 1958 constitution departed from French tradition by dealing explicitly with parties. Article 4 reads: "Parties and groups take part in the exercise of the suffrage. They may form and engage in their activities freely. They must respect the principles of national sovereignty and democracy."

The clause has been almost a dead letter. The last sentence was directed at the Communist Party because of its close ties to the Soviet Union and its authoritarian internal structure. However, neither the Communists nor any other party has been required to abide by its terms. In fact, the only application of Article 4 yet made was a Constitutional Council ruling that struck down parliamentary rules of order that restricted the freedom of MPs to form party caucuses. No laws or decrees rest on the authority of Article 4, nor has the Constitutional Council applied that provision to parties outside Parliament.

Few laws deal expressly with parties as organizations. However, parties are covered by a 1901 statute that governs all associations. Also, legislation regulating campaigns and elections refers to parties. For instance, certain types of parties are recognized as organizations eligible to receive governmental support in campaigns such as controlled access to radio and television and free mailings of candidates' flyers. Neither the associations' laws nor the campaign laws restrict the behavior of parties significantly. The former are very permissive, and the latter are easily and frequently evaded. An exception is a 1994 law requiring parties to submit their financial records to a national governmental commission, which publishes them but cannot verify their accuracy. The same law forbade corporate contributions to parties.

Political parties receive state subsidies. Half of the available fund (about $97.5 million annually for the 1993 legislature) was distributed among the parties that fielded at least 50 candidates in proportion to their share of the popular vote in the preceding parliamentary elections. The other half was distributed among the parties in Parliament in proportion to their share of the seats. For instance, in each full year of the 1993 Parliament, the Gaullists received about $26.4 million, the Communists about $6.5 million, and the various environmentalist parties a total of about $5.5 million. These subsidies stimulated the rapid formation of new parties. The 29 that applied for aid in 1990 had grown to 160 by 1993. Also, in common with nonparty associations, parties have some tax advantages as nonprofit associations, their candidates get electoral campaign subsidies, and their newspapers benefit from press subventions. However, the amount of this aid to the parties is quite modest.

Candidates for the National Assembly file declarations at the prefecture of the appropriate department and pay deposits of 1,000 francs ($150), which are refunded to all candidates receiving at least 5% of the vote. A presidential nomination requires the signatures of 500 elected officeholders from at least 30 different departments.

Party Organization

Historically, French political parties followed two basic patterns of organization: the Center and Right were loosely organized and based on committees of leaders. The Left had well-articulated, mass-membership parties.

That dichotomous structural pattern was broken in the early Fourth Republic by the Christian democratic MRP and the Gaullist Rally of the French People (RPF). Both were Center or Right parties that built mass-membership organizations somewhat similar to those of the Left. As they declined late in the Fourth Republic, both movements adopted committee structures. Nevertheless, when Gaullism rebounded in the Fifth Republic, it resumed its mass-membership orientation. Also, after 1977, that model was followed, though less successfully, by what was the largest component of the UDF, the Republican Party (now Liberal Democracy). Thus, all three

major parties today are, more or less successfully, mass-membership organizations, though the minor parties—except the Communists—tend to remain in the committee mold.

The activities of all French political parties center on elections. They spend most of their organizational time and effort working in local, parliamentary, and presidential campaigns: preparing for them or raising money to pay for them. Other activities, such as regular business meetings and conventions and discussion sessions, have the primary purpose of keeping the organization in shape for the next election. The Communist Party engages in a somewhat broader range of activities.

The parties vary considerably in the relationship between the membership organizations and the parliamentary caucuses. The Communists see their MPs as infiltrators into enemy territory and treat them like potential defectors. Communist MPs are strictly accountable to the membership organization. Party policies and strategies are decided by the national committee and national bureau, and the MPs are expected to put them into effect loyally.

The Socialists subscribe to the same principle of authority, but usually Socialist MPs control the leading organs of the membership party. Thus, membership-party decisions differ little from those that the parliamentary caucus would make on its own. When the two branches conflict, the caucus prevails. That relationship is complicated by the faction-ridden character of the party. The resultant struggle for party unity leads to compromises that modify parliamentary dominance.

The highly authoritarian structure of the Gaullist Rally for the Republic (RPR) determines the relationship between its membership and parliamentary wings. Party founder Jacques Chirac dominates both the membership organization and the parliamentary caucus, though his control has declined somewhat since Philippe Séguin became President of both organizations in 1997. A similar situation existed in the Republican Party, when Giscard d'Estaing was president of the republic. The Centrist and Radical membership parties have little say in the behavior of their caucuses.

Most parliamentary candidates are nominated by political parties. In all parties, the decisions on parliamentary candidates are made through consultations within the local party, among local and national party leaders, and by negotiations among the parties. The amount of influence of the local party in the nominating process is roughly proportionate to its strength. In a party's weakest districts, its main task is finding suitable candidates willing to run and the national party often takes the initiative. At the other extreme, a strong local party with a well-entrenched incumbent deputy who wants reelection is virtually immune to national party intervention. Also, the parties vary greatly in the degree of centraliza-

dues of about 1% of the member's annual income. An equal amount comes from special fund drives and donations, about 25% from state subsidies, and the remainder from the party's MPs and other elected officials, who contribute the difference between their salaries and the average annual wages of a skilled worker. In addition, the party earns profits on some publishing, commercial, and financial enterprises. Before the collapse of the Soviet Union, it received about $2 million a year in subsidies from that source. It spends about half its income on propaganda and one-fourth each on administrative expenses and salaries and benefits for its 600 regular staff members.

LEADERSHIP

The Frencer Communist Party leaders include Robert Hué, born 1946, national secretary (1994–), protégé of Marchais, a nurse by profession, judo champion, mayor of Montigny, a Paris suburb, elected deputy in 1997; André Lajoinie, born 1930, 1988 presidential candidate and secretariat member responsible for elections; Louis Viannet, born 1924, CGT general secretary, national committee member, national bureau member (1982–96); Alain Bocquet, born 1946, president of the PCF group in the National Assembly, Hue's main rival for the leadership in 1994, leader (with Marchais) of the antireformist wing of the party; Maxime Gremetz, born 1940, member of national bureau (1976–), deputy, editor, of *France Nouvelle*, leads "conservative" party faction; and Francis Wurtz, born 1947, head of the PCF list in the 1994 European Parliament elections and responsible for international affairs on the national bureau.

PROSPECTS

Long-term prospects for the PCF seem bleak, though the failure of the Socialists to win an absolute majority of the National Assembly seats in 1997 increased its political leverage. Its share of the vote in recent elections has remained below 10%, leaving it consistently in fifth place. Membership has shrunk. The Socialists dominate the French Left, and even the right-wing National Front outpolls it. The once-great party seems doomed to remain marginalized, more likely to survive as an historical artifact than as an important political force.

SOCIALIST PARTY
(Parti socialiste; PS)

HISTORY

Modern French socialism dates to 1905, when most of the movement united as the *Section francaise de l'internationale ouvrière* (SFIO). Although the party was reformist in practice, its policy program proclaimed it a "class party whose goal is to transform capitalist society into a collectivist or communist society." That split between action and rhetoric marked the SFIOfor the next 64 years.

From 1920 until 1969, the SFIO was dominated by Leon Blum (1920–46) and Guy Mollet (1946–69). During that time, the party withered in membership, voting strength, and doctrinal integrity, despite brief periods of government leadership (1936–38; 1946). By the timeMollet served as premier for 16 months in 1956–57, the SFIO had become so "bourgeois" that the government's policies were virtually indistinguishable from those of the conservatives.

The Socialist revival began in 1969 when Alain Savary became general secretary and changed its name to the French Socialist Party. Most party leaders at all levels were replaced by 1971 when François Mitterrand brought his confederation of political clubs into the PS, became first secretary, and reoriented French socialism decisively leftward. Mitterrand pursued the "Union of the Left" strategy he had followed consistently since 1958 to unite the traditional parties of the Left (Socialist, Radical, Communist) against Gaullism.

By 1972, he had negotiated a Common Program with the PCF and the Left Radicals. That alliance increased leftist strength in the 1973 parliamentary and 1974 presidential elections but fell apart in the 1978 parliamentary elections. His strategy finally triumphed in 1981. Mitterrand won the presidency with the essential help of Communist votes, and the PS outvoted the PCF more than two-to-one in the parliamentary elections. Socialists received a larger share of the poll than any Left party in French history. The PS, with the PCF in harness, drove the Right from all the bastions of power.

Since then, the Socialist record has been mixed. Excessive zeal in socializing the economy in 1981–83 produced high inflation, high unemployment, and low growth, costing them their parliamentary majority in 1986. They recovered in 1988, slumped in 1993 and the 1994 European Parliament elections, and lost the presidency in 1995. However, their alliance with the Communists won the 1997 parliamentary elections and their leader, Lionel Jospin, formed the government.

ORGANIZATION

The French Socialist movement has always been highly factionalized. For instance, in 1995 the 19 "political" members of the national secretariat represented 11 factions. The main factional leaders were Jospin, Henri Emmanuelli, Laurent Fabius, and Michel Rocard. The factions are represented in the leadership organs in numbers proportionate to their support among the party members.

The basic units of the PS are 1,500 local sections. They require at least five members and may be formed by residence, workplace, or university. Sections send delegates to the 102 departmental federations in proportion to the size of their membership. Federation representation in the regional coordinating committees, national congresses, and national conventions has similar bases. Traditionally, the four largest federations (Nord, Bouches-du-Rhone, Pas-de-Calais, and Paris) have dominated the national party. The members of the federations elect some 600 delegates and an equal number of alternates to the national congresses that meet biennially as the sovereign decision-making body of the party and to the conventions that meet at least twice a year on specific policy issues. The congresses elect a first secretary and 204 members of the national council. The federation secretaries, who are elected in each department by the rank-and-file members, join the national council by right. The council makes the major decisions between congresses and elects from among its members by proportional representation a national bureau of 59 members that meets each Wednesday and supervises the day-to-day management of the party. The first secretary appoints from the majority faction or coalition the national secretariat, with which he runs the party. The secretariat numbers 15 to 20 members, each with specified policy or administrative responsibilities. The PS is a member of the Socialist International.

The PS has no official national party daily newspaper, although *Libération* (circ. 230,000) tends to be sympathetic to it. *Le Provençal* (circ. 155,000) in Marseilles and *Nord-Matin* (77,000) in Lille are the leading (unofficial) Socialist dailies in the provinces. *L'Unité* and *Vendredi-Idées* (weeklies) and *Combat Socialiste* (monthly) are official party periodicals, *Le Poing et la Rose* is its house organ, and *La Nouvelle Revue Socialiste* is its theoretical journal.

The largest organization associated with the PS is the 550,000-member CFDT, the third-biggest French trade union federation. Although its ties are looser than those of the CGT to the PCF, Socialists dominate its leadership and form the largest bloc of members; the two organizations are reciprocally influential. Similar affinities bind the PS to other trade unions, especially the largest teachers' organizations and the largest general-labor confederation (FO, *Force ouvrière*; Workers' Force). Also, the party sponsors youth, women's, and farm associations.

POLICY

The PS has moved away from the radical socialist reformism of the early 1980s, with its stress on nationalization and major changes in labor-management legislation, and has renounced Marxism in favor of a "mixed economy." It proposes to ease unemployment by reducing the workweek without loss of purchasing power. The party is a fierce protector of social welfare programs and of the public education system. It resists privatization but advocates no further nationalization. Internationally, it supports a European approach to protection, both economi-

cally and militarily. It prides itself on its commitments to civil liberties and to aid to the Third World.

MEMBERSHIP AND CONSTITUENCY

The party claimed about 109,000 members in 1996. It declined steadily from a peak of about 355,000 in 1945 to a low of perhaps 15,000 in the late 1960s (although it never admitted to fewer than 75,000). Under Mitterrand's leadership, it recovered to about 250,000 members shortly after its 1981 election victory. In the 1997 parliamentary elections, its candidates drew nearly 70 votes for each member.

Support for the PS remains most solid among certain categories of state employees (teachers, postal employees, railroad workers), industrial workers in some regions (the north and Provence) and sectors (light and medium manufacturing), and farmers in the center and south. Overall, it is weakest among farmers and small businesspeople. However, the party has been successful in recent years in broadening its appeal to some categories of the French, especially practicing Catholics. The party is strongest in the north, parts of the east, and Provence. It does better south of the Loire River than north of it. It draws less than its share of women and more than its share of the young.

FINANCING

The annual PS budget totals about $40 million. Revenues come mainly from four sources. One substantial item is the state subsidy, which amounts to about $12 million a year. Another is membership dues, which produce about $8–10 million annually for the national party. A third substantial amount comes from a levy on its MPs. Finally, the party collects considerable sums in special fund drives and individual contributions. The amounts received from each source depend on electoral success and size of membership.

LEADERSHIP

PS leaders include Lionel Jospin, born 1937, prime minister 1997– , diplomat and educator, first secretary, 1981–88, 1995–97, minister 1988–92, member of European Parliament 1984–89, deputy 1981–93, presidential candidate 1995; François Hollande, born 1954, first secretary 1997– , high civil servant, government spokesman 1983–84, deputy 1988–93, 1997– ; Jacques Delors, born 1925, president of the European Union Commission (1985–95), minister of finance (1981–85), "social" Catholic trade unionist, leader of the social democrat wing of the party; Michel Rocard, born 1930, minister 1981–85, prime minister 1988–92, PS first secretary 1993–94, senator 1995– , deputy 1969–73, 1978–81, 1988–93, leader of moderate reformist wing, former PSU leader; Laurent Fabius, born 1946, first secretary, 1992–93, prime minister 1984–86, president PS National

Assembly group 1995–97, National Assembly president (1988–92, 1997–); and Henri Emmanuelli, born 1945, banker, deputy 1978–81, former minister, former national secretary convicted of party finance illegalities 1996.

PROSPECTS

The 1997 parliamentary elections gave the French Socialists an almost miraculous second chance. The 1981 triumph of the Socialists had been pyrrhic. The economic program on which they had been elected failed, forcing an embarrassing about-face. This and Mitterrand's Machiavellian penchant produced bitter infighting and recriminations, frequent leadership changes, and a frantic search for new ideas and proposals. The emergence of a significant environmentalist movement complicated its task further. Also, Jospin was seen as a colorless, lackluster leader. However, the unpopularity of the Chirac-Juppé government, resulting from the public perception of Juppé as cold and arrogant and from the persistence of a high unemployment rate, paved the way for a Socialist recovery. The party's future depends heavily on the success of the Jospin government.

RADICAL SOCIALIST PARTY
(Parti Radical Socialiste; PRS)

This minor party is a junior partner of the PS in electoral alliances, in Parliament, and in left-wing governments. It began in 1972, with the name Left Radical Movement (MRG), as a band of Radical Socialists disgruntled by the decision of their party to form an alliance with centrists. It signed the Common Program with the Communists and Socialists in July 1972 and fought the 1973 parliamentary elections allied with them and the 1978 elections in concert with the Socialists. Its delegation to the National Assembly has hovered between 6 and 13 in elections since 1978. It claims about 9,000 .

The Baylet family, based in Toulouse, has been a major force in the Radical Socialist movement since 1930. Jean-Michel Baylet, born 1946, party president and senator, is publisher of the *Depeche du Midi* and former national secretary of the MRG. Other top leaders are André Rossinot, delegate to the UDF; Michel Crépeau, born 1930, lawyer, mayor of La Rochelle, deputy 1973–81, 1986–93, 1997– , leader of Radical parliamentary group, presidential candidate 1981, minister 1981–86, leader of the left wing of the Radical Socialist movement; Roger-Gérard Schwartzenburg, born 1943, law professor and political scientist, deputy since 1986; Emile Zuccarelli, born 1940, engineer, elected deputy 1993, 1997, civil service minister in Jospin government, member of leading Corsican political family; Bernard Kouchner, born 1939, physician and founder of Doctors without Borders, minister several times.

NATIONAL FRONT
(Front national; FN)

This nationalist party was founded in 1972 by Jean-Marie Le Pen, who remains its president. Le Pen was a paratrooper in the Algerian war and briefly a deputy late in the Fourth Republic. The Front entered Parliament in 1986 with 2.7 million votes (9.7%) and 35 deputies. However, when the PR electoral system was dropped, it retained only 1 seat in 1988, none in 1993, and 1 in 1997 despite polling 9.7% of the vote in 1988, 12.5% in 1993, and 14.9% in 1997. Le Pen won 15.3% of the 1995 presidential vote. The Front has more than 2,200 members in regional and local councils and 11 in the European Parliament.

The party structure includes a quadrennial congress open to all members (2,200 attended in 1996); a 100-member central committee elected by the congress as the main decision-making body between congresses; a 40-member political bureau, appointed by the president from the central committee, that manages the party through monthly meetings; and a national council composed of the central committee, the political bureau, the national and regional elected officials, the departmental secretaries, and appointed "personalities" that meets two or three times a year to debate the general orientation of the party. Finally, the president, 4 vice presidents, delegate general, treasurer, and general secretary form an executive bureau that manages the party on a day-to-day basis.

The National Front attracts support mainly for its anti-immigrant stance, although its policies also include tough anticrime positions, suspicion of European integration, advocacy of "popular capitalism," ultranationalism, trade protectionism, defense of "traditional values," and hostility toward rigorous tax enforcement. It claims 80,000 members. Its strongholds are in the east, especially the southeast, and among repatriated Algerian settlers, workers in areas with large numbers of immigrants and the unemployed. Its voters are more masculine, less Catholic, and less well educated than the electorate as a whole.

FN auxiliary organizations include a national youth front that claims 15,000 members, a student renewal organization for university students, over 20 special-interest "circles," and several small labor unions. It also has a "security service" of 3,000–7,000 members trained to use firearms. It publishes a bimonthly "Letter" from Le Pen. Publications close to the FN include the daily *Présent*, and the weekly *National Hebdo and Rivarol*. The FN is largely financed by annual dues of about $45, a levy on its members who win elective office, and a $6.3 million annual state subsidy. Besides Le Pen, born 1928, top party leaders are general secretary, Bruno Gollnisch, born 1950, delegate general, Bruno

Mégret, born 1949 (member of European Parliament and of a regional council), and MP Jean-Marie Le Chevallier, born 1936, mayor of Toulon.

RALLY FOR THE FRENCH REPUBLIC
(Rassemblement pour la République; RPR)

HISTORY

The RPR, which also calls itself simply Le Rassemblement (The Rally), is the "orthodox" Gaullist party. Itoriginated in the program of democratic nationalism and strong central leadership of General Charles de Gaulle. The Gaullist movement's first party, the Gaullist Union (1946), was soon absorbed by de Gaulle's own Rally of the French People (RPF), which quickly became the largest party in France with a million members and 120 deputies (1951). Nevertheless, the party failed to effect constitutional reform and declined precipitously in the early 1950s. When de Gaulle retired from politics in 1955, only 80 deputies remained faithful to him.

With de Gaulle's return to power, the party revived as the Union for the New Republic and won 188 seats in the 1958 elections. It led the Assembly for the next 20 years. In 1974, after the party's candidate lost the presidential election, Prime Minister Jacques Chirac took over the party, now called the Union of Democrats for the Republic, to make it more aggressive. After Chirac resigned as premier in 1976, he assumed the party's presidency, changed its name to the RPR, centralized its structure, and launched a massive membership drive. Nevertheless, the party lost its leadership of the Assembly in 1978 and was reduced to an opposition role in 1981. Since then, it has alternated between being the largest opposition party (1981–86, 1988–93, 1997–) and the largest party (1986–88, 1993–97). It has fought all recent elections in alliance with the Union for French Democracy, and when the National Assembly has a conservative majority, the RPR and UDF serve together in the government. In 1998, the PRP president, Philippe Séquin, and former UDE leader François Leotard formed a loose coalition of moderate conservative parties, called the Alliance, to contest the 1999 European Parliament elections. Besides the RPR and UDF, the Aliance includes the Liberal Demacracy Party of Alain Madelin.

ORGANIZATION

The Rally (RPR) is a mass organization, claiming about 150,000 members. It has always had centralized leadership, but the authority of its top leader was further enhanced in its 1998 by-laws revision. The President is elected for three-year terms by general vote of the membership. He chairs its national bodies and appoints the general secretary and executive committee, who assist him in managing the organization. He sets the size of the executive committee and the task assignments of its members.

National conventions (assises rationales), composed of several thousand delegates, meets biennially to "define the general action and policy orientation of the Rally" and choose 100 national councilors. Each constituency federation elects a number of delegates proportionate to the size of its membership. National councillors, MPs, and economic and social councilors are ex officio members.

Between conventions, management of the party is reviewed by a national council that must meet at least annually. Its members are the policy committee members, RPR MPs, departmental secretaries and presidents, and the 100 members elected by the convention. The policy committee may add constituency secretaries to the council.

A policy committee "defines the policy orientations of the Movement . . . under the authority of the president and in accordance with the directives of the convention and the national council." Its members are one-fifth of the RPR MPs chosen by their colleagues; one representative elected by each departmental federation; an additional representative for each of the 20 largest federations; ten representatives each of the party's youth, women's, and syndic organizations; the policy bureau; and former RPR prime ministers, presidents, and general secretaries, and parliamentary caucus chairs.

Chirac was elected initially by 11,500 to 0, with 400 abstentions and spoiled ballots. His leadership was not seriously challenged for 20 years, but he yielded the presidency to his protégé Alain Juppé in preparation for his 1995 candidacy for the presidency of the republic. Then, after the party's debacle in the 1997 elections that he had called early, Philippe Séquin ousted Juppé with 78.9% of the vote.

The main party units below the national level are departmental federations and constituency associations. The former are headed by secretaries appointed by the party's president and ratified by the departmental committee and by presidents elected by the departmental committees at least two-thirds of whose members are elected by the constituency members plus, ex officio, the main RPR elected officials. The constituency associations are led by a secretary elected by the membership and by a committee composed in the same way as the departmental committees.

The party distributes a daily newsletter, *La Lettre de la Nation*, and publishes monthly *Democrates* and fortnightly *Les Cahiers* magazines and a monthly internal newsletter, *La Lettre des Compagnons*. The RPR has few auxiliary organizations. On the other hand, it has made a considerable effort to build up party schools for its activists and candidates.

POLICY

The RPR professes to advocate policies in line with those pursued by de Gaulle. He pursued foreign policies intended to promote national independence and "grandeur." That meant a defense policy based on a French nuclear striking force, aversion to NATO's military system or any international organization not controlled by France, and special ties with former French colonies and other French-speaking areas. It meant commitment to a strong, centralized state and domestic policies designed to cement French unity and strength, such as "participation" of workers in management, economic modernization, and hostility to ethnic particularism. The RPR–UDF electoral alliances have compromised some traditional Gaullist policy positions. It now favors sweeping privatizations, including enterprises nationalized by de Gaulle, and it advocates closer integration in the European Union and NATO and greater decentralization of the French state than did de Gaulle. Its economic policies resemble those of the monetarists in the United States and Great Britain more closely than those of de Gaulle. Also, it has toughened its stand on immigration restrictions, apparently responding to the challenge on its right from the National Front.

MEMBERSHIP AND CONSTITUENCY

The RPR made good use of its opposition interlude to strengthen its internal organization, raising its membership total to about 850,000 in 1985, but it fell again to about 150,000 in the late 1990s. Its ratio of members to voters in the 1997 elections was about 1:28.

RPR supporters are predominantly masculine, middle-aged, middle-class, northern, and Catholic. The largest occupational category is "businessmen, tradesmen, and members of the fee-earning professions," followed by white-collar workers, middle management, workers, farmers, and upper management, in descending order. The party is strongest north of the Loire Valley, especially in Paris and its middle-class suburbs. Other areas of strength are such traditional Catholic regions as Alsace, Lorraine, and Brittany. Throughout France, practicing Catholics support Gaullism disproportionately.

FINANCING

The RPR is very well financed, with an annual budget of about $60 million. As the largest party in the 1993 elections, it drew about $27 million per year from the public treasury. Given the size and relative affluence of its membership, it also receives a substantial income in members' dues and contributions. In addition, it can call on many prosperous French who choose not to join the party. Finally, its supporters are well able to donate time, effort, and physical resources. The 1994 law banning corporate contributions hit the RPR the hardest, costing it nearly $10 million in income. Nevertheless, the movement does not suffer from lack of funds. For instance, in the nonelection year of 1991, it spent over $8 million on propaganda and communications alone. Especially when it holds national office, its regular income is supplemented through the diversion of state resources such as staff time.

LEADERSHIP

Leaders of the RPR include Jacques Chirac, founder and only national president until 1995, born 1932, prime minister 1974–76, 1986–88, principal opposition leader 1981–86, Paris mayor 1977–95, 1981, and 1988, presidential candidate, president of the republic 1995– ; Philippe Séguin, born 1943, president 1997– , high civil servant, deputy 1978– , minister 1986–88, president of the National Assembly 1993–97, president of National Assembly group 1997– , leader of nationalist-protectionist faction; Edouard Balladur, born 1930, prime minister 1993–95, protégé of Georges Pompidou, prime minister 1993–95, conservative candidate for president 1995; Alain Juppé, born 1946, former general secretary, president 1995–97, foreign minister 1993–95, prime minister 1995–97; Charles Pasqua, born 1927, minister of the interior 1986–88, 1993– , deputy 1968–73, senator 1977–86, president of the RPR Senate group 1981-86, ally of Séguin; and Jean-Francois Mancel, born 1948, high civil servant, deputy 1978– , general secretary 1995– .

PROSPECTS

The prospects for the RPR dimmed considerably after its electoral triumphs of 1993 and 1995. The failures of the governments it dominated to solve such persistent problems as the chronic unemployment and the personal unpopularity of Chirac and Juppé undermined its electoral base seriously. Furthermore, its 1997 loss precipitated a leadership crisis. Balladur had already been shunted aside because he dared challenge Chirac for the presidency, and Juppé was discredited by the failures of his government. Also, the RPR risks losing its distinctive Gaullist identity, as it moves ever further from the principles of its founder. Nevertheless, it remains the largest, best-organized and most well financed party on the rRght.

UNION FOR FRENCH DEMOCRACY
(Union pour la démocratie francaise; UDF)

Centrist and Right-Center parties have formed electoral alliances as the UDF for every national election since 1978. Most of their deputies join a parliamentary caucus of the same name. They numbered 63 in 1998. The sovereign decision-making body is the national council of some 1,700 delegates elected by the departmental federations of the constituent parties, proportionately to their respective membership sizes. For instance, in 1996 (before the renaming and defection of the PR), the numbers were PR 513, FD 565, PPDF 160, Radicals 192, direct members 205, and unaffiliated UDF 86. The council chooses 18 members of the political bureau, the main factions represented proportionately. The political bureau also includes two persons selected by each constituent unit, the current and former UDF presidents, the general secretary, and the presidents of the parliamentary caucuses. The political bureau runs the UDF between national council meetings. The UDF in 1996 claimed 300,000 members, including 25,000 direct members. However, that total included 190,000 members claimed by the PR, most of whom left the UDF in 1998 as the DL. Its headquarters are at 25, avenue Charles Floquet, 75007 Paris. Recent leaders are François Bayrou, president and FD leader; Francois Léotard, former president and co-founder of the Alliance; Alain Lamassoure, Republican Independent leader; Jean-François Calzat, general secretary; Philippe Douste-Blazy, president of National Assembly caucus; Radical party leader André Rossinot; and Pierre-André Wiltzer, leader of the direct members. The ratio of members to voters in 1997 was 1: 12.

The largest occupational category of UDF voters is "inactives," those who are not in the labor force because they are retired, have independent means, or are homemakers. White-collar workers are next, just ahead of workers and a group identified as high-level administrators, fee-earning professionals, industrialists, and big businessmen. Farmers and farm workers and small shopkeepers and tradesmen are also disproportionately represented. This pattern parallels closely that of the RPR, the main differences being that the UDF draws fewer workers and more "inactives." The UDF is the most elderly and feminine of the three major parties. Of its electorate, 48%are 50 or older and only 26% are under 25. Women constitute 54% of its supporters.

The member-parties of the UDF are Democratic Force, Popular Party for French Democracy, Radical Party, and Republican Independent and Liberal Group.

POPULAR PARTY FOR FRENCH DEMOCRACY
(Parti populaire pour la démocratie francaise; PPDF)

This is the Giscardian rump of the old Republican Party. When Giscard d'Estaing was forced out of the PR leadership in 1995, he merged his Perspectives and Reality political clubs with his remaining PR followers. Initially, they included 40 MPs, but only 6 survived the 1997 elections, compared with 41 as UDF–PR and 43 as UDF–FD. Giscard himself ran simply as UDF.

The main leaders of the PPDF are Valéry Giscard d'Estaing, founding president, born 1926, high civil servant, president of the republic 1974–81, chair of the National Assembly foreign affairs committee; Henri de Charette, general delegate, born 1938, high civil servant, former foreign minister, deputy, PPDF representative to UDF, principal party administrator; Jean-Pierre Raffarin, deputy general delegate, former minister, former leader of young Giscardians.

REPUBLICAN INDEPENDENT AND LIBERAL GROUP
(Groupe Independant Republicain et Libérale)

This small party is another UDF fragment of the old Giscardian Republican Party. When Alain Madelin j and the bulk of the DL defected from the UDF in 1998, Alain Lamoussoure organized this faction to defect from the DL and remain in the UDF. They disagreed mainly with Madelin's belief that the best way to deal with the National Front is to offer policies that will lure away its supporters. Rather, they want to avoid any appearance of sanctioning NF policies.

DEMOCRATIC FORCE
(Force Démocrate; FD)

The FD was founded in 1995 by a merger of the Center of Social Democrats (CDS) and the Social Democratic Party (PSD). The CDS had, in turn, been formed in 1976 by two centrist parties: the Democratic Center and the Center for Democracy and Progress. The PSD was a splinter group, headed by Senator Max Lejeune, that left the PS when it formed an alliance with the PCF in 1972.The CDS elected 49 deputies in 1988 and 57 in 1993. In 1993, it claimed 43,500 members. The CDS branch of the FD is the current heir to the once-powerful Christian democratic movement in France. It abandoned its trademark clericalism when it merged with the PSD but, in return the PSD accepted Catholic social doctrine. The FD is the most consistent promoter of European integration among French political parties.

Its principal national leaders are François Bayrou, born 1951, president, minister 1993–97, deputy; Dominique Baudis, vice president, born 1947, journalist, mayor of Toulouse, deputy, Pierre Méhaignérie, born 1939, president 1976–94) and senior minister in several conservative governments; André Santini, general secretary, born 1940, lawyer, former general secretary of PSD, former minister; Claude Goasguen, spokesman and general secretary, born 1945, educator, former CDS deputy general secretary, deputy and former minister; René Monory, president of the Senate.

RADICAL PARTY
(Parti radical)

This group is the remains of the powerful Radical Socialist Party of the Third and Fourth Republics after the MRG (now PRS) defected in 1972. Its principal leaders are André Rossinot, born 1939, president 1983–88, 1994– , mayor of Nancy; former presidents Yves Galland (1988–94) and Didier Bariani (1979–83); and General Secretary Ayméri de Montesquiou. The party won 3 seats in the 1988 and 1997 elections and 15 in 1993. It has 15,000 to 20,000 members.

THE RIGHT
(La Droite)

A small, right-wing fraction that was expelled from the Alliance for suspected sympathy with the National Front in 1998. It advocates free-market economics and restrictive immigration policies and is lukewarm on European integration. Its leader is Charles Millon.

LIBERAL DEMOCRACY
(Démocratie libérale; DL)

HISTORY

The Republican Party, from which the DL emerged in 1996, had a dual origin. It belonged in the tradition of Orleanist conservatism, the moderate, reasonable, adaptable branch of the French Right. Yet, its existence, growth, and early success derived solely from the ambition of one man, Valery Giscard d'Estaing.

Giscard founded the Independent Republicans to organize the 31 traditional conservative deputies who had survived the Gaullist triumph in the parliamentary elections of 1962 by remaining loyal to de Gaulle. Except during the 1968–73 Assembly, their successors have been an essential but distinct part of all the non-Socialist governmental coalitions of the Fifth Republic. They sometimes vote differently from the orthodox Gaullists but never endanger conservative governments.

The Independent Republicans were the basis for the organization that became the Republican Party in 1977. Meanwhile, Giscard's fidelity to de Gaulle softened steadily until his defection provided the decisive votes in the 1969 referendum that forced the Old Hero's retirement.

Although Giscard supported Pompidou in the ensuing elections and served in his governments, he launched his own presidential campaign, which succeeded in 1974 after Pompidou's death. After his defeat for reelection in 1981, Giscard gradually lost control of the PR. In July 1995, he was forced to resign as PR president and Lotard replaced him. The party was reorganized, renamed, and after the conservative loss in the 1997 elections, taken over by Alain Madelin. Despite the name change, DL candidates ran in the 1997 elections under the old PR label. In 1998 it defected from the UDF over the issue of relations between the moderate Right and theNational Front. A small rump remained in the UDF.

ORGANIZATION

The DL leadership structure is dominated by MPs. It includes an honorary president, president, and 10 vice presidents. Day-to-day party administration is supervised by a general secretary (Pascal Clément), general delegate (Hervé Novelli), and treasurer (Thiérry Jean-Pierre). Other prominent national leaders are José Rossi, Jean Puech, Jean-Claude Gaudin, and Laurent Dominati. The DL has no regular national newspaper or periodical, getting along with internal newsletters and campaign literature.

The most important auxiliary organization of the PR was the Perspectives and Reality club system. However, in July 1995 it merged with Giscardian PR dissidents to form the PPDF (see below)The DL has an active youth auxiliary, called Social and Liberal Generation (*Génération Sociale et Libérale*; GSL), but no viable women's affiliate. Madelin heads a political club called Idées-Action.

POLICY

The PR combined the modern liberal stance of its founder with the more traditional conservativism of the bulk of its members. Since Madelin took control, the DL has become oriented much more toward supply-side, free-market economics. It promotes individual enterprise with as little governmental restraint as is compatible with the requirements of social order. The DL is more European, more Atlanticist, less centralist, and more parliamentarist than the RPR. Also, the DL is less committed to social welfare programs and to such Gaullist policies as the nuclear striking force, worker "participation," and the referendum. It is more outspoken on privatization and the elimination of various economic controls. The differences between the two parties have diminished in recent years, largely by alignment of the RPR with the DL. However, any description of the DL's program must be qualified by observing that it is essentially a pragmatic party.

MEMBERSHIP AND CONSTITUENCY

The DL claims 190,000 members, but that figure is probably inflated. The GSL has perhaps 15,000 members. Of course, those numbers include a lot of overlap. Probably, the DL structure rests on no more than 150,000 to 160,000 individuals.

FINANCING

The DL relies heavily on its state subsidy, which runs about $23 million per year. Its national offices probably receive less than $250,000 in dues annually. The rest of its income comes mainly as donations from wealthy sympathizers and corporations. Also, some income may come from questionable financial manipulations, and when the party is in power, personnel is loaned to the party from government ministries.

LEADERSHIP

The leadership of the Giscardians underwent a very perceptible evolution during their years in power. Initially, the Independent Republicans were a group of conservative MPs with local power bases united by a wish to support de Gaulle without joining his party. Giscard brought them together and was the most prominent of them but was little more than the first among equals. As the movement became more structured and bureaucratized and as Giscard's career soared, he acquired greater authority over the party and brought it under the control of young, ambitious technocrats whose political careers depended on Giscard's personal patronage. After his 1981 defeat, his control gradually slipped until his ouster in 1996.

Current leaders are Alain Madelin, president 1997– , born 1948, lawyer, party functionary, protégé of Giscard d'Estaing, finance minister, 1993–95; François Léotard, born 1942, honorary president 1997– , PR general secretary 1982–95, PR president 1995–97, high civil servant, deputy 1978– , former defense minister, mayor of Fréjus 1977– ; José Rossi, born 1944, president of the parliamentary caucus, vice president, former president and general secretary, deputy and former minister; Jean-Claude Gaudin, born 1939, schoolteacher, Socialist Marseilles city councilor, defected to CNIP, then PR, former deputy; Laurent Dominati, born 1960, national political secretary, deputy from Paris; Gilles de Robien, born 1941, leader of internal opposition to Madelin, mayor of Amiens, deputy, former UDF group leader in the National Assembly.

PROSPECTS

The DL is one of the principal components of the conservative movement in France. Also, the support of its MPs is essential to the survival of any conservative government. Nevertheless, it has much less power than when its leader was president of the republic. In the immediate future, the DL seems to be cast more in the role of followers and possible spoilers than as first-rank leaders in the conservative movement.

MINOR PARTIES

Environmentalists

The environmentalist movement came late to France and is badly divided. The eight "ecologists" elected to Parliament in 1997 have four different party affiliations. The most important of their political parties are the Greens (*Verts*), and Ecological Generation (*Génération écologiste*; GE).

The Greens are a militant, leftist movement of some 5,600 members, based on environmentalism but with other left-wing causes on their agenda. The GE is more moderate, more sharply focused on environmental issues, and more open to collaboration with other parties, especially the Socialists. Smaller environmentalist parties are the left radical Red and Green Alternative (AREV); the Alliance for Ecology and Democracy (APED); the Convergence Ecology Solidarity (CES) of GE defector deputy Noël Mamère; the Independent Ecology Movement (MEI) of Green defector Antoine Waechter; and the Alternative for Democracy and Socialism (ADS) of dissident Communist Marcel Rigout. The Greens and GE formed an electoral alliance in 1993 but not in 1997. Although the environmentalists won their first—8—seats in the National Assembly in the 1997 elections, their share of the popular vote actually declined from 1993. The percentages were Greens 4.0 in 1993, 3.6 in 1997; GE 3.6 in 1993, 1.7 in 1997; other ecology candidates 2.5 in 1993, 2.7 in 1997; totals 10.1 and 8.0.

The "sovereign body" of the Greens is the biennial ordinary general assembly. It meets first in regional sections open to all party members. They elect delegates to the second-phase federal assembly that meets the following month. The general assembly decides the general policy orientation of the party and elects for two-year terms the members of the inter-regional national council (CNIR), 90 by the regional sections and 30 by the federal assembly. Extraordinary general assemblies may be called by the CNIR, 20% of the members, or five regional councils. A national "forum" with limited competence meets in off-years. The CNIR is the governing body of the national party with responsibility for implementing the decisions of the general assemblies, meeting every two months. Day-to-day manager is an executive college composed of the national secretary, three deputy secretaries, the treasurer, four spokesmen, and six other members elected by the CNIR. The Greens publish a review, *Political Ecology*. Their most prominent leader is Dominique Voynet, born 1958, physician, presidential candidate 1995, member European Parliament, deputy since 1997, and minister for territorial development and the environment in the Jospin government. The other three spokespersons are Marie-Anne Isler Béguin, Philippe Boursier, and Alain Lipietz and the other four deputies are André Aschièri, Marie-Hélène Aubert, Guy Hascoët, and Yves Cochet.

The GE organization consists of a national council of 64 members and a small executive council appointed by the president. Brice Lalonde, born 1946, journalist, former minister, 1981 presidential candidate, is much the most prominent GE leader.

Citizens' Movement (Mouvement des Citoyens; MDC)

This party was founded in December 1993 by PS defector Jean-Pierre Chevènement, born 1939. Its members come mainly from the CERES, formerly the left wing faction of the PS. He is a deputy, was defense minister under Mitterrand until he resigned over the Gulf War, and is interior minister in the Jospin government. The party's structure includes a sovereign congress open to all 800 or so party members that elects a president, seven vice presidents, a general secretary, and 14 members and three alternates of a national secretariat that also has five ex officio members. The MDC elected seven members to the 1997 Parliament. Other leading members are president Jean-Jacques Karman and vice presidents Max Gallo, member of the European Parliament, and Georges Sarre, dissident Socialist deputy.

Revolutionary Communist League
(Ligue communiste révolutionnaire; LCR)

The LCR is a Trotskyite communist party, led by Alain Krivine, born 1941, claiming about 1,500 members. Its address is 2 rue Richard Lenoir, 93108 Montreuil.

Movement for France
(Mouvement pour la France; MPF)

Well-financed right-wing anti-European nationalist party led by aristocrat Philippe de Villiers, born 1949, high civil servant, deputy 1987–94, 1997– , European deputy 1994– .

National Center of Independents and Peasants
(Centre national des indépendents
et paysans; CNI)

Traditional conservative movement, powerful in the Third and Fourth Republics but very weak now. Its president is Olivier d'Ormesson, born 1918, wealthy, aristocratic journalist; general secretary, Pierre Olivier Mahaux, born 1959. Headquarters:146 rue de l'Université, 75007 Paris.

Convention for a Progressive Alternative
(Convention pour une Alternative
Progressiste; CAP)

Radical left-wing group formed in 1994 mainly by dissidents from various other leftist parties. Its most prominent leader is a former Communist minister, Charles Fiterman. It claims 1,600 members and publishes a monthly newsletter, *Confluences*. Its headquarters are located at 17-19 rue des Envierges, 75020 Paris.

NATIONAL PROSPECTS

Politically, France approaches the near future in better shape than at any time in its modern history. Its governmental institutions are anchored solidly in a consensus that includes all significant political movements. The last remaining institutional question mark was erased by the willingness of all major parties—right and left—to accept the "cohabitation" of a president of one political orientation with a government and Parliament of the opposite persuasion in 1986–88, 1993–95, and 1997– .

The political parties have shown similar adaptability, easing much of the traditional ideological tension in French politics. The Gaullists have softened the edges of their nationalism, and the Socialists have abandoned their revolutionary rhetoric—including their commitments to nationalization of industry and to a secular monopoly on education. The PCF has been marginalized, and the National Front seems locked in a single-issue stance. Recent accommodations of the parties reflect a rising consensus in the general public. One survey found that popular consensus exists on 70% of the issues, an unprecedented situation in modern France. As a result, much of the legislation introduced by the Socialist governments survived the conservative returns to office in 1986 and 1993 and the Socialists did not fight bitterly for the rest.

In short, France seems to have joined—at long last—the mainstream of Western democracy. While French politics is, in no sense, a carbon copy of the American, British, German, or Scandinavian models, it shares their basic managerial, pragmatic, consensual orientation.

However, two persistent problems undermine French confidence in their governmental system. One is the pervasive political-financial corruption. Major political figures, including the president of the National Assembly (Henri Emanuelli), a former prime minister (Laurent Fabius), the former UDF president (François Léotard), the maverick businessman-politician Bernard Tapie, and mayors of several large cities have been deeply implicated in serious scandals. The second is the intractable unemployment that no government seems capable of reducing.

Mitterrand left behind a very mixed record. His early socialist economic programs engendered high unemployment and low growth rates that seem to have become endemic. Much more successful and durable was the decentralization program of his interior minister, Gaston Defferre. His sweeping transfer of functions, authority, and resources from the national to the regional and local levels of government has transformed the French state irreversibly and was accepted loyally by his conservative successors.

The French state has also yielded authority to the European Union. As with its partners in that enterprise, its national prospects are bound up very tightly with those of the EU. Despite recent expansions of the EU, France and Germany continue to dominate its affairs. The times, under de Gaulle, when France blocked progress toward integration are long past. France now benefits too greatly from the Union to sabotage it. Because economic protectionism continues to hold sway in French political economic circles, French influence often works to the detriment of world trade and—inevitably—the long-term health of the French economy. So long as that continues, the French economy will remain shaky, with the usual political and governmental repercussions. The French commitment to the European Monetary Union may rest on the hope that the EMU will ensure that the robust German and British economies will prop up the French.

Further Reading

Cole, Alistair, *François Mitterrand: A Study in Political Leadership*. London: Routledge, 1997.

Elgie, Robert. *The Role of the Prime Minister in France, 1981–91*. Basingstoke, England: Macmillan, 1993.

———, ed. *Electing the French President: The 1995 Presidential Election*. Basingstoke, England: Macmillan, 1996.

France, Ministére des affaires etrangéres. *The Institutions of the Fifth Republic*. Paris: Ministry of Foreign Affairs, 1995.

Frears, J. R., *Parties and Voters in France*. New York: St. Martin's, 1991.

Hayward, J. E. S., and Martin Harrison, eds. *De Gaulle to Mitterrand: Presidential Power in France*. London: Hurst, 1993.

Huber, John D. *Rationalizing Parliament: Legislative Institutions and Party Politics in France*. Cambridge: Cambridge University Press, 1996.

Knapp, Andrew. *Gaullism since de Gaulle*. Brookfield, Vt.: Dartmouth, 1994.

Marcus, Jonathan. *The National Front and French Politics: The Resistible Rise of Jean-Marie Le Pen*. Basingstoke, England: Macmillan, 1995.

Safran, William. *The French Polity*, 5th ed. New York: Longman, 1997.

Web Sites

Greens:http://www.verts.imaginet.fr

National Assembly:http://www.assemblee-nationale.fr

National Front:http://www.front-nat.fr

Radical Socialist Party:http://members.aol.com/Mainate/-radical.htm

RPR:http://www.rpr.org

Socialist Party:http://www.parti-socialiste.fr

UDF:http://www.sdv.fr/udf

Government:http://www.admifrance.gouv.fr

In US:http://www.info-france-usa.org

INDEX

A

Abacha, Sani, 816–817, 818, 820, 822, 984

Abashidze, Aslan, 393, 397

Abbas, Abul, 850

Abbas, Chetti Ali, 193

Abbas, Farhat, 17

Abboud, Ibrahim, 1041, 1044, 1046, 1047

Abdallah, Ahmed, 232

Abdallah, Ali Hamisi, 1092

Abdildin, Serkbolsyn, 606, 608, 609

Abdul Aziz, 961, 962, 963, 964, 965, 967

Abdul Aziz bin Fahd, 963

Abdul Aziz bin Salman, 963

Abdullah, 604, 962, 963

Abdullah, David, 1115

Abdullah, Farooq, 499

Abdullah, Mohammed, 499

'Abdullah, 919

Abdullah al-Sulayman, 964

Abdullojonov, Abdumalik, 1086, 1088, 1089

Abdul Muhsin, 963

Abdul Rahman, 962, 963

Abessole, Paul M'Ba, 387, 389

Abinader, José Rafael, 307

Abiola, Moshood, 816, 817, 820, 821, 822

Abubakar, Abdulsalami, 817, 818, 819, 820, 822

Abuhatzeira, Aharon, 550

Abybajarm Abdyksakanu, 816

Achakzai, Mahmud Khan, 844

Acheampong, I. K., 414

Action Committee for Democracy and Pension Justice (Aktiounskomitee fir Demokratie a Rentegerechtegkeet; ADR) (Luxembourg), 687–688

Action Committee for Renewal (Comite d'Action pour la Renou-veau; CAR) (Togo), 1110–1111

Action for Change (Action pour le Changement; AC) (Mauritania), 725–726

Action for the Republic (Acción de la República) (Argentina), 36

Action Front for Renewal and Development (FARD) (Benin), 109, 110

Action Group for Democracy (Grupo de Acción por la Democracia; GAD) (Dominican Republic), 310

Action of Social Democrats (Croatia), 258

ACT New Zealand, 798

Adalberto Rivera, Julio, 335

Adams, David, 1180

Adams, Gerry, 1177

Adams, Grantley, 91

Adams, John Michael Geoffrey "Tom," 91

Adams, Tom, 430

Adelsohn, Ulf, 1063

Adenauer, Konrad, 252, 404, 405, 406

Adiahenot, Jacques, 388

Adji, Boukary, 813

Adjovi, Severin, 110

Adolat Social Democratic Party of Uzbekistan, 1213

Advani, L. K., 489, 490

Afäwärk'i, Issaias, 341

Afghanistan, 1–8

Afghan National Liberation Front (Jabba-ye-Milli-ye-Afghanistan), 2

Aflaq, Michel, 527, 1073, 1076

African Christian Democratic Party (ACDP) (South Africa), 1018–1019

African Democratic Rally (Rassemble-ment Démocratique Africain; RDA) (Ivory Coast), 575

African Forum for Reconstruction (Forum Africain pour la Reconstruc-tion; FAR) (Gabon), 389

African Independence Party (Parti Africain de l'Independence; PAI) (Senegal), 975

African Liberation Forces of Maurita-nia (Forces de libération africaine do Mauritanie; FLAM), 726

African National Congress (ANC) (South Africa), 1010, 1011, 1012, 1013, 1014–1016, 1018, 1019, 1020, 1047

African National Congress (Zambia), 1257

African National Congress (Zim-babwe), 1264

African National Union (Zimbabwe), 1265

African Party for the Independence of Cape Verde (Partido Africano da In-depêndencia da Guiné e Cabo Verde; PAICV), 186, 187

African Party for the Independence of Guinea and Cape Verde (PAIGC) (Partido Africano da Independência da Guiné e Cabo Verde) (Guinea-Bissau), 187, 443, 444, 445

African People's League for Indepen-dence (Ligue populaire africaine pour l'independence; LPAI) (Dji-bouti), 301

African Rally for Progress and Democ-racy, 110

Afro-Shirazi Party (ASP) (Tanzania), 1093

Agboyibo, Yaovi, 1110, 1111, 1112

Agenda for Zambia, 1259

Agondjo-Okawé, Pierre Louis Agondjo, 389

Agrarian/Center Party of Norway, 825

Agrarian Democratic Party (Moldova), 744, 745

Agrarian Labor Party (Panama), 855

Agrarian League (Norway), 826

Communist Party of Japan (JCP) (Nihon Kyosanto), 587, 593, 594–595, 597

Communist Party of Jordan (JCP) (Hizb al Shuyu'i al-Urduni), 601

Communist Party of Kazakhstan (Kommunisticheskaya Partiya Kazakhstana; KPK), 605, 606, 607, 608, 609

Communist Party of Kyrgyzstan, 639

Communist Party of Latvia, 646, 647

Communist Party of Leban (Al-Hizb Ash-Shuyu'i Al-Lubnani; LCP), 659, 660

Communist Party of Luxembourg (Kommunistesch Partei vun Letzeburg; KPL), 687

Communist Party of Malta, 719, 722

Communist Party of Mexico (Partido Comunista de México; PCM), 737

Communist Party of Moldova (CPM), 743, 744, 745

Communist Party of Mongolia, 749, 750, 751

Communist Party of Mozambique, 764

Communist Party of Nepal-Leninists, 776, 778

Communist Party of Nepal-Marxist, 778

Communist Party of Nepal-Unified Marxist Leninists (UML), 776, 777, 778

Communist Party of Nicaragua (Partido Comunista de Nicaragua; PCdeN), 808

Communist Party of Norway (Norges Kommunistiske Parti; NKP), 825, 830, 831

Communist Party of Palestine, 849

Communist Party of Paraguay (PCP), 868, 869, 871

Communist Party of Poland, 893, 895, 897, 899

Communist Party of Portugal (Partido Comunista Portugues; PCP), 904, 905, 908

Communist Party of San Marino (Partito Comunista Sammarinese; PCS), 958

Communist Party of Serbia (Yugoslavia), 1249

Communist Party of Slovakia (Komunisticka strana Slovenska; KSS), 993, 995, 997, 1001

Communist Party of Soviet Ukraine, 1147

Communist Party of Spain (Partido Comunista de España; PCE), 1024, 1028

Communist Party of Sweden, 1060

Communist Party of Syria, 1073, 1077

Communist Party of Tajikistan (CPT) (Hizbi Communisti Tojikiston), 1089

Communist Party of the Netherlands (CPN), 786, 787

Communist Party of the Republic of Moldova (Partidul Communist Republica Moldovei), 745

Communist Party of the Russian Federation (CPRF) (Kommunisticheskaia partiia Rossiiskoi Federatsii), 933, 934, 938, 939, 941, 942, 943

Communist Party of the Soviet Union (CPSU), 1131, 1132

Communist Party of the Soviet Union (Uzbekistan), 1212

Communist Party of Tunisia (Parti communiste tunisien; PCT), 1118, 1119

Communist Party of Turkmenistan (CPT), 1131, 1132

Communist Party of Ukraine (CPU), 1144, 1146

Communist Party of Uruguay, 1208, 1209

Communist Party of Uzbekistan (CPUz), 1211, 1212–1213

Communist Party of Venezuela (CPV) (Partido Comunista Venezolana; PCV), 1222, 1223, 1225, 1226, 1228

Communist Party of Vietnam (VCP) (Dang Cong San Viet-Nam), 1231, 1232, 1233–1236

Communist Party South Africa (SACP), 1013, 1018

Communist Refoundation (Rifondazione Comunista; RC) (Italy), 567–568

Communists-Workers' Russia, 941

Communist Vanguard Party of Costa Rica, 247

Community Party of Lithuanian, 682

Comoros, 232–233

Compaoré, Blaise, 153, 154

Concentration of Popular Forces (Concentración de Fuerzas Populares; CFP) (Ecuador), 318, 320, 321

Concepción de Gracia, Gilberto, 916

Concerned Citizens Movement (CCM) (Saint Kitts), 951

Condé, Alpha, 441

Confederación de Nacionalidades Ind'genas (CONAIE) (Ecuador), 319

Confederation of Bolivian Workers (Confederación de Obreros Bolivianos; COB), 120

Confederation of Colombian Workers (Confederación de Trabajadores Colombianos; CTC), 229

Confederation of Ethiopian Trade Unions (CETU), 351

Confederation of Kazakh Trade Unions, 606

Confederation of Mexican Workers (Confederación de Trajabadores de México; CTM), 734

Confederation of Regions Party (Canada), 173

Conference of Ulema of Islam (Jamaat al-Ulema-i-Islam; JUI) (Pakistan), 844

Conference of Ulema of Pakistan (Jamiat-i-Ulema-i-Pakistan ; JUP), 843–844

Confrontation Front (Lebanon), 659

Confucious, 205

Congo, Democratic Repbulic of, 234–242

Congo, Republic of the (République du Congo), 243–245

Congolese Movement for Democracy and Comprehensive Development (Mouvement Congolais pour la Démocratie et le Développement Intégral; MCDDI), 244, 245

Congolese Rally for Democracy (Rassemblement Congolais Démocratique; RCD) (Congo), 240

Congolese Workers' Party (Parti Congolais du Travail; PCT), 243, 244, 245

Congress for Democracy and Justice (Congrès pour la démocratie et la justice; CDJ) (Gabon), 389

Congress for Democracy and Progress (Congrés pour la Démocratie et le Progrés; CDP) (Burkina Faso), 154–155

Congress for the Second Republic (CSR) (Malawi), 704

Congress of National Democratic Forces (CNDF) (Ukraine), 1148

Congress of Russian Communities (Kongress Russkykh Obshchestv; KRO), 938, 939, 941, 944

Korzhakov, Aleksandr, 934
Koskotas, Georgios, 423
Kotalawala, John, 1038
Koty, Abbas, 194
Koty, Hissein, 194
Kouchner, Bernard, 378
Koumakoye, Delwa, 192, 193
Kountché, Seyni, 812
Kovác, Michal, 994, 1001
Kovác, Roman, 993
Kozhakhmetov, Hasan, 608
Kpoleh, Gabriel, 667
Kpormikor, David, 666
Krajcí, Gustav, 1001
Krajisnik, Momcilo, 124, 125
Krastins, Andrejs, 647
Krauss, Enrique, 201
Kravchuk, Leonid, 932, 1141, 1142,
    1143, 1146, 1147, 1148
Kreisky, Bruno, 66, 67
Kreituse, Ilga, 646
Kreutzmann, Bjarne, 299
Krishak Praja Party (Farmer's People's
    Party) (Bangladesh), 85–86
Krishak Sramik Party (KSP; Farmer's
    and Worker's Party) (Bangladesh),
    86
Krishak Sramik Party (Pakistan), 842
Kristiansen, Kaare, 828
Krivine, Alain, 384
Kromah, Emmanuel, 668
Kromah, Alhaji, 667, 668
Krycer, Jan, 281
Kubitschek, Juscelino, 132
Kucan, Milan, 1002, 1003, 1006
Kucera, Bohuslav, 279
Kuchma, Leonid, 1141, 1142, 1146,
    1149
Kufuor, J. A., 416
Kuipers, Kirsten, 787
Kukan, Eduard, 997
Kukrit Pramoj, 1107
Kuljis, Ivo, 115, 119
Kumar, Nitish, 498
Kumaranatunga, Chandrika Ban-
    daranaike, 1035, 1039
Kunaev, Dinmukhammed, 609
Kunio, Hatoyama, 592
Kuo, Ahidjo, 165
Kurdish Democratic Party (Iran), 523
Kurdish Democratic Party (Iraq), 531
Kurdish Democratic Party (Lebanon),
    661
Kurdish Democratic Party-Provisional
    Leadership (Lebanon), 661
Kutan, Recai, 1126

Kuwait (Dawlat Al-Kuwayt), 632–636
Kuwaiti Democratic Forum, 634
Kwasniewski, Aleksander, 892, 893,
    894, 896, 899
Kwayana, Eusi, 450
Kyprianou, Spyros, 270, 272
Kyrgyz Republic (Kyrgyzstan),
    637–640
Kyrkos, Leonidas, 427

L

Laar, Mart, 344—345
Labor Front (Verkmannafylkingin)
    (Denmark), 298
Labor Party of Australia, 44, 46, 47, 48
Labor Party of Israel, 545, 549, 551,
    554, 555
Labor Party of Mauritius, 728, 729
Labor Party of Mozambique, 764
Labor Party of Norway (Det Norske
    Arbeiderparti; DNA), 825, 827,
    829—830, 831, 832
Labor Party of Panama (Partido La-
    borista), 852, 854, 855
Labor Party of the Netherlands (Partij
    ven de Arbeid; PvdA), 782, 783,
    785—786, 788
Labour Party Democracy of Kenya,
    614
Labour Party of Ireland, 537, 538, 540
Labour Party of Malta, 719, 720—721,
    722
Labour Party of Northern Ireland,
    1171
Labour Party of Saint Kitts (LP), 951
Labour Party of United Kingdom,
    1158, 1161, 1164, 1167
Lacalle, Luis Alberto, 1204, 1207,
    1208
Lachmon, Jaggernath, 1050
Ladin, Osama bin, 7
Lafontaine, Oskar, 412
Lage, Carlos, 262, 266
Laghari, Sardar Farooq Ahmad, 837
Lagos, Ricardo, 202
Lahhud, Emile, 662
Lahnstein, Anne Enger, 826, 827
Laino, Domingo, 866, 870
Laitinen, Kari, 363
Lajoinie, André, 376
Lak, Robert, 863
LAKAS-EDSA (Philippines), 889
LAKAS-NUCD (Philippines), 888
LAKAS (Philippines), 885, 890

Lak Group (Papua New Guinea), 863
La Kha Phieu, 1238
Lal, Devi, 496
Lalonde, Brice, 383
Lamassoure, François, 381
Lambanya, Lubwe, 1259
Lamizana, Sangoulé, 153
Lamoussoure, Alain, 381
Landless Peoples' Movement (Movi-
    mento dos Sem-Terra; MST)
    (Brazil), 143, 144
Landsbergis, Vytautis, 680, 682, 683
Lange, Anders, 831
Lange, David, 794
Lange's, Anders, Party for Substantial
    Reduction in Taxes, Duties, and
    Governmental Interference, 831
Langos, Ján, 1000
Lanka Sama Samajaya Party (LSSP)
    (Ceylon Equal Society Party) (Sri
    Lanka), 1039
Lanotte, Johan Vande, 101
Lao Front for National Construction
    (Naeo Lao Sang Xat), 643
Lao Patriotic Front (Naeo Lao Sang
    Xat), 642
Lao People's Democratic Republic
    (Sathalanalat Paxathipatai Paxaxon
    Lao), 641—644
Lao People's Revolutionary Party (Phak
    Paxaxon Pativat Lao), 641, 642
Lapshin, Mikhail, 943
Larkin, James, 539
Larsen, Aksel, 295
Lassalle, Ferdinand, 411
Latvia (Latvijas Republika), 645—649
Latvian Farmers' Union, 646
Latvian National Independence Move-
    ment, 647, 648
Latvian Socialist Party, 648
Latvian Unity Party, 648
Latvia's Way (Latvijas Cels), 646, 647,
    648
Laugerud, Kjell, 435
Laurel, Salvador, 882, 889, 890
Lauría, Carmelo, 1224
Lauro, Achille, 850
Lavalas Family (La Famille Lavalas)
    (Haiti), 454
Lavalas Political Organization (Organi-
    sation politique Lavalas; OPL)
    (Haiti), 454
Lavian National Independence Move-
    ment, 647
Lavilla, Landelino, 1028
Lavín, Joaquín, 203

Q

AAFU–see Anti-Communist and Anti-Imperialist Front of Ukraine

AAPO–see All-Amhara People's Organization (Ethiopia)

ABVP–see All-India Students Organization

AC–see Action for Change (Mauritania)

ACDP–see African Christian Democratic Party (South Africa)

ACLM–see Antigua Caribbean Liberation Movement (Antigua and Barbuda)

AD–see Democratic Alliance (Guatemala)

AD–see Alleanza Democratica (Italy)

AD–see Democratic Action (Venezuela)

ADA–see Democratic Alliance of Angola

ADEMA–see Alliance for Democracy in Mali-The African Party for Solidarity and Justice

ADERE–see Democratic and Republican Alliance (Gabon)

ADFL–see Alliance of Democratic Forces for Liberation of Congo/Zaire (D. Rep. Congo)

ADM-19–see M-19 Democratic Alliance (Colombia)

AND–see Nationalist Democratic Action (Bolivia)

ADP–see Alliance for Democracy and Progress (Benin)

ADP–see Assembly of People's Deputies (Burkina Faso)

ADP–see Alliance for Democracy and Progress (Central African Republic)

ADP–see Arab Democratic Party (Israel)

ADR–see Action Committee for Democracy and Pension Justice (Luxembourg)

ADS–see Alternative for Democracy and Socialism (France)

ADSR–see Alliance of Democrats of the Slovak Republic

AEEM–see Association of Pupils and Students of Mali

AEPA–see All-Ethiopian Peasants Association

AETU–see All-Ethiopian Trade Union

AFC–see Alliance of Forces of Change (Niger)

AFD–see Alliance of Free Democrats (Hungary)

AFD–see Alliance For Democracy (Nigeria)

AFKM–see Congress Party for the Independence of Madagascar

AFKM-Renewal–see Congress Party for Madagascar Independence-Renewal Party

AFL–see Armed Forces of Liberia

AFL-CIO–see American Federation of Labor-Congress of Industrial Organizations (U.S.A.)

AFORD–see Alliance for Democracy (Malawi)

AFPFL–see Anti-Fascist People's Freedom League (Myanmar)

AFRC–see Armed Forces Revolutionary Council (Sierra Leone)

Agaleu–see Ecologist Parties (Belgium)

AGP–see Assam Peoples Council (India)

AIADMK–see All-India Anna-Dravida Munnetra Kazhagam

AICC–see All-India Congress Committee

AICP–see All-India Communist Party

AID–see Agency for International Development (U.S.A.)

AIS–see Islamic Salvation Army (Algeria)

AKAR–see People's Justice Movement (Malaysia)

AKEL–see Progressive Party of the Working People (Cyprus)

AKPML–see Workers' Communist Party Marxist-Leninist (Norway)

AL–see Awami League (Bangladesh)

AL–see Liberal Alliance (Nicaragua)

AL–see Awami League (Pakistan)

ALF–see Arab Liberation Front (Palestinian Authority)

ALN–see National Liberation Army (Algeria)

ALO–see Austrian Alternative List

ALP–see Australian Labor Party

ALP–see Antigua Labour Party (Antigua and Barbuda)

AMAL–see Detachments of the Lebanese Resistance

AMP–see Association for Muslim Professionals (Singapore)

AMU–see Arab Maghreb Union (Libya)

AMU–see African Mineworker's Union (Zambia)

AN–see Alleanza Nationale (Italy)

ANAGAN–see National Association of Ranchers (Panama)

ANAPO–see National Popular Alliance (Colombia)

ANC–see Conservative National Action (Nicaragua)

ANC–see African National Congress (South Africa)

AND–see National Democratic Group (Andorra)

ANDDS-Zaman Lahiya–see Nigerian Alliance for Democracy and Social Progress-Zaman Lahiya (Niger)

ANDI–see National Association of Industrialists (Colombia)

ANDM–see Amhara National Democratic Movement (Ethiopia)

ANL–see National Liberating Alliance (Brazil)

ANM–see Armenian National Movement

ANP–see Alliance for New Politics (Philippines)

AOV and UNIE 55+–see General Union of the Elderly (Netherlands)

AP–see Popular Action (Peru)

AP–see Popular Alliance (Spain)

AP5–see Popular Alliance 5 (Guatemala)

APAI–see Israel Workers Party

APC–see Popular Conservative Alliance (Nicaragua)

APC–see All People's Congress (Sierra Leone)

APED–see Alliance for Ecology and Democracy (France)

APEDE–see Panamanian Association of Business Executives

APK–see Worker Party Communists (Sweden)

APMU–see All-Popular Movement of Ukraine

APNI or AP–see Alliance Party of Northern Ireland

APP–see All People's Party (Nigeria)

APRA–see American Popular Revolutionary Alliance (Peru)

APRC–see Alliance for Patriotic Reorientation and Construction (Gambia)

APRE–see Ecuadorian Popular Revolutionary Action

APU–see United Peoples Alliance (Portugal)

ARD–see Democratic Resistance Alliance (D. Rep. Congo)

AREMA–see Vanguard of the Malagasy Revolution (Madagascar)

ARENA–see National Renovating Alliance (Brazil)

ARENA–see Nationalist Republican Alliance (El Salvador)

AREV–see Red and Green Alternative (France)

ARF–see Armenian Revolutionary Federation

ARLN–see Revolutionary Army of Liberation of Northern Niger

ARMM–see Autonomous Region of Muslim Mindanao (Philippines)

ARP–see Anti-Revolutionary Party (Netherlands)

ASD–see Dominican Social Alliance Party

ASEAN–see Association of Southeast Asian Nations

ASI–see Federation of Labor (Iceland)

ASIS–see Alliance of Small Island States (Maldives)

ASP–see Afro-Shirazi Party (Tanzania)

ASU–see Arab Socialist Union (Egypt)

ASU–see Arab Socialist Union (Libya)

ATC–see Association of Rural Workers (Nicaragua)

ATLU–see Antigua Trades Labour Union (Antigua and Barbuda)

AV/MRDN–see And Jeff: Revolutionary Movement for the New Democracy (Senegal)

AVI–see Work Finished by Solidarity (Madagascar)

AWARE–see Association of Women for Action and Research (Singapore)

AWS–see Solidarity Electoral Action (Poland)

AYD–see Alliance of Young Democrats (Hungary)

AZADHO–see Zairian Association for the Defense of Human Rights (D. Rep. Congo)

BAKSAL–see Bangladesh Krishak Sramik Awami League

BAMCEF–see All-India Backward and Minority Communities Employees Federation

BBB–see Bulgarian Business Bloc

BCP–see Basotho Congress Party (Lesotho)

BDF–see Botswana Defense Force

BDG–see Gabonese Democratic Group

BDP–see Bahamian Democratic Party

BDP–see Botswana Democratic Party

BDS–see Senegalese Democratic Bloc

BIP–see Citizen's Initiative Parliament (Austria)

BIS–see Social Democratic Institutional Block (Dominican Rep.)

BITU–see Bustamante Industrial Trade Union (Jamaica)

BJP–see Bhanatiya Jawata Party (India)

BKU–see Bhanasiya Kisan Union, Punjab (India)

BKU–see Bhanatiya Kisan Union, Uttar Pradesh (India)

BLDP–see Buddhist Liberal Democratic Party (Cambodia)

BLP–see Barbados Labour Party

BN–see National Front (Malaysia)

BNA Act–see British North America Act (Canada)

BNF–see Botswana National Front

BNG–see Galician Nationalist Bloc (Spain)

BNP–see Bangladesh National Party

BNP–see Basotho National Party (Lesotho)

BPC–see Basic People's Congress (Libya)

BPF–see Belarusian Popular Front "Adrazennie"

BPP–see Bechuanaland People's Party (Botswana)

BQ–see Bloc Quebecois (Canada)

BRA–see Bougainville Revolutionary Army (Papua New Guinea)

BSB–see Burkina Socialist Bloc

BSP–see Bulgarian Socialist Party

BSP–see Bhutan Samas Party (Party of Society's Maturity) (India)

BSPP–see Burma Socialist Program Party (Myanmar)

C–see Center Party (Sweden)

C90–see Change 90 (Peru)

CAC–see Argentine Chamber of Commerce

CACIF–see Coordinating Committee of Commercial, Industrial, and Financial Associations (Guatemala)

CADE–see Annual Conference of Business Executives (Panama)

CAFPDE–see Council of Alternative Forces for Peace and Democracy (Ethiopia)

CAN–see Authentic Nationalist Central (Guatemala)

CAP–see Convention for a Progressive Alternative (France)

CASC–see Autonomous Confederation of Christian Syndicates (Dominican Rep.)

CAUS–see Council for Union Action and Unity (Nicaragua)

CC–see Christian Way (Nicaragua)

CC–see Canarian Coalition (Spain)

CCD–see Christian Democratic Center (Italy)

CCD–see Democratic Constituent Congress (Peru)

CCE–see Central Elections Council (El Salvador)

CCF–see Co-operative Commonwealth Federation (Canada)

CCM–see Concerned Citizens Movement (Saint Kitts)

CCM–see Revolutionary Party (Tanzania)

CCOOs–see Worker's Commissions (Spain)

CCP–see Chinese Communist Party

CD–see Center Democrats (Denmark)

CD–see Democratic Convergence (El Salvador)

CD–see Center Democrats (Netherlands)

CD–see Democratic Coordination (Nicaragua)

CD–see Democratic Change (Panama)

CD–see Democratic Center (Spain)

CDA–see Christian Democratic Appeal (Netherlands)

CDJ–see Congress for Democracy and Justice (Gabon)

CDP–see Congress for Democracy and Progress (Burkina Faso)

CDP–Convention of Democrats and Patriots (Senegal)

CDPA–see Democratic Convention of African People (Togo)

CDPP–see Christian Democratic People's Party (Hungary)

CDRs–see Committees of the Defense of the Revolution (Burkina Faso)

CDRs–see Committees for the Defense of the Revolution (Ghana)

CDS–see Social Democratic Center (Angola)

CDS–see Center of Social Democrats (France)

CDS–see Social Democratic Center Party (Portugal)

CDS–see Party of the Social Democratic Center (Portugal)

CDS–see Social Democratic Center (Spain)

CDS-Rahama–see Democratic and Social Convention-Rahama (Niger)

CDT–see Democratic Labor Confederation (Morocco)

CDU–see Union of Christian Democrats (Italy)

CDU–see United Democratic Coalition (Portugal)

CDU–see Unified Democratic Coalition (Portugal)

CDU/CSU–see Christian Democrats (Germany)

CEA –see Argentine Episcopal Conference

CEC–see Central Executive Committee (Singapore)

CEMC–see Central Election Management Committee (South Korea)

CEN–see National Executive Committee (Mexico)

CEN–see National Executive Committee (Venezuela)

CES–see Convergence Ecology Solidarity (France)

CETU–see Confederation of Ethiopian Trade Unions

CFD–see Coordination of Democratic Forces (Burkina Faso)

CFN–see Coordination of New Forces (Togo)

CFP–see Concentration of Popular Forces (Ecuador)

CG–see Galician Centrist (Spain)

CGEM–see General Economic Confederation of Morocco

CGT–see General Confederation of Labor (Argentina)

CGT–see General Confederation of Labor (France)

CGT–see General Confederation of Workers (Nicaragua)

CGTI–see Independent General Workers Confederation (Nicaragua)

CGTP–see General Central of Workers of Panama

CGUP–see Guatemalan Committee of Patriotic Unity

CHU–see Christian-Historical Union (Netherlands)

CIA–see U.S. Central Intelligence Agency

CIDOB–see Indigenous Confederation of the East, Chaco, and Amazonia of Bolivia

CIPRODEH–see Center for the Investigation and Promotion of Human Rights (Honduras)

CIS–see Commonwealth of Independent States

CiU–see Convergence and Union (Spain)

CLC–see Canadian Labor Congress

CLR–see Convention of Reformist Liberals (Gabon)

CLSTP–see Liberation Committee of Sao Tome and Principe

CM–see Council of Ministers (Cuba)

CMC–see Central Military Commission (China)

CMEA or COMECON–see Council for Mutual Economic Assistance (Vietnam)

CMLN–see Military Committee of National Liberation (Mali)

CMRPN–see Military Committee of Redressment for National Progress (Burkina Faso)

CMS–see Supreme Military Council (Niger)

CMSS–see Czech-Moravian Party of the Center (Czech Rep.)

CN–see National Convention (CAR)

CNC–see National Peasant Confederation (Mexico)

CND–see National Development Council (Rwanda)

CNDF–see Congress of National Democratic Forces (Ukraine)

CNE–see National Electoral Council (Venezuela)

CNI–see National Center of Independents and Peasants (France)

CNID–see National Congress of Democratic Initiative (Mali)

CNIR–see Inter-Regional National Council (France)

CNJ–see National Council of the Judiciary (El Salvador)

CNOP–see National Federation of Popular Organizations (Mexico)

CNR–see National Council of Revolution (Burkina Faso)

CNS–see Sovereign National Council (Chad)

CNS–see National Unity Commission (Rwanda)

CNT–see National Workers Federation (Mexico)

CNTP–see National Worker's Central of Panama

CNU–see Cameroon National Union

COB–see Confederation of Bolivian Workers

COD–see Coalition of Democratic Opposition (Togo)

CODE–see Democratic Coordinator (Peru)

CODEH–see Committee for the Defense of Human Rights in Honduras

COFADEH–see Committee of the Families of the Detained and Disappeared in Honduras

COMELEC–see Commission on Elections (Philippines)

CONAIE–see Confederation of Indigenous Nationalities of Ecuador

CONAPRODEH–see National Commission for the Protection of Human Rights (Honduras)

CONCAMIN–see Confederation of Industrial Chambers (Mexico)

CONCANACO–see Confederation of National Chambers of Commerce (Mexico)

CONCLAT–see National Coordination of the Working Class (Brazil)

CONDEPA–see Conscience of the Fatherland (Bolivia)

CONEP–see National Council of Private Enterprise (Panama)

CONFENIAE–see Confederation of Indigenous Nationalities of the Amazon (Ecuador)

COPAZ–see National Commission for Consolidation of Peace (El Salvador)

COPCON–see Continental Operations Command (Portugal)

COPE–see Committee on Political Education (U.S.A.)

COPEI–see Christian Social Party (Venezuela)

COSATU–see Congress of South African Trade Unions

COSEP–see Superior Council of Private Enterprise (Nicaragua)

COSU–see Coordination of the United Senegalese Opposition

COTU–see Central Organization of Trade Unions (Kenya)

CP–see Popular Coalition (Spain)

CPBM–see Communist Party of Bohemia and Moravia (Czech Rep.)

CPC–see Central People's Committee (North Korea)

CPCC–see Chinese People's Consultative Conference

CPD–see Citizens for Democracy (Guatemala)

CPDM–see Cameroon People's Democratic Movement

CPI–see Communist Party of India

CPIB–see Coordinator of the Indigenous Peoples of Beni (Bolivia)

CPM–see Communist Party of India (Marxist)

CPM–see Communist Party of Moldavia (Moldova)

CPML–see Communist Party of India

CPN–see Communist Party of the Netherlands

CPP–see Cambodian People's Party

CPP–see Communist Party of the Philippines

CPP–see Convention People's Party (Ghana)

CPRF–see Communist Party of the Russian Federation

CPSA–see Conservative Party (South Africa)

CPSU–see Communist Party of the Soviet Union (Tajikistan)

CPSU–see Communist Party of the Soviet Union (Turkmenistan)

CPT–see Communist Party of Tajikistan

CPT–see Communist Party of Turkmenistan

CPU–see Communist Party of Ukraine

CPUz–see Communist Party of Uzbekistan

CRA–see Argentine Rural Confederations

CRA–see Coordination of Armed Resistance (Niger)

CRM–see Citizens Rights Movement (Israel)

CRN–see Council of National Reconciliation (Mali)

CROC–see Revolutionary Federation of Workers and Peasants (Mexico)

CRP–see Circle for Renewal and Progress (Gabon)

CS–see Council of State (Cuba)

CSDDM–see Committee for the Support of Democracy and Development in Madagascar

CSE–see Supreme Electoral Council (Nicaragua)

CSL–see Czech People's Party

CSN–see Council of National Health (Niger)

CSP–see Council of Health of the People (Burkina Faso)

CSP–see Christian Social Party (Luxembourg)

CSR–see Congress for the Second Republic (Malawi)

CSS–see Czech Socialist Party

CSSD–see Czech Social Democratic Party

CST–see Higher Transitional Council (Chad)

CST–see Sandinista Workers Confederation (Nicaragua)

CSTC–see Trade Union Confederation of Colombian Workers

CSU–see Christian Social Union (Germany)

CSUTCB–see United Syndical Confederation of Bolivian Peasant Workers

CTC–see Confederation of Colombian Workers

CTM–see Confederation of Mexican Workers

CTN–see Social-Christian Nicaraguan Worker's Confederation

CTP–see Republican Turkish Party (Cyprus)

CTRP–see Confederation of Workers of the Republic of Panama

CTSP–see Transition Committee for the Health of the People (Mali)

CTV–see Confederation of Venezuelan Workers

CUAS–see Chief of Army Staff (Pakistan)

CUF–see Civic United Front (Tanzania)

CUG–see Citizen's Union of Georgia

CUT–see Central Union of Workers (Brazil)

CVP–see Civic United Front (Tanzania)

CVP–see Christian Democratic People's Party of Switzerland

CVP–see Christian Democratic Parties (Belgium)

CWC–see Congress Working Committee (India)

CWC–see Ceylon Workers Congress (Sri Lanka)

CYL–see Congress Youth League (South Africa)

D66–see Democrats 66 (Netherlands)

DA–see Democratic Renewal (Greece)

DA–see Democratic Alternative (Macedonia)

DAC–see Democratic Action Congress (Trinidad & Tobago)

DAP–see Democratic Action Party (Malaysia)

DC–see Democratic Arrangement (Dominican Rep.)

DC–see Democratic Convergence (Guatemala)

DC–see Christian Democratic Party (Italy)

DC–see Deputy Commissioner (Pakistan)

DC–see Christian Democracy (Spain)

DCG–see Christian Democrats (Guatemala)

DDCs–see District Development Councils (Sri Lanka)

DDLP–see Dominican Democratic Labor Party (Dominica)

DEMOS–see Democratic Opposition of Slovenia

DEMYC–see Democratic Youth Community of Europe

DEPOS–see Democratic Coalition of Serbia (Yugoslavia)

DF–see Danish People's Party

DFLP–see Democratic Front for the Liberation of Palestine

DFP–see Democratic Freedom Party (Dominica)

DFPE–see Democratic Front For Peace and Equality (Israel)

DIKKI–see Democratic Social Movement (Greece)

DIKO–see Democratic Party (Cyprus)

DISK–see Confederation of Revolutionary Workers' Unions (Turkey)

DISY–see Democratic Rally (Cyprus)

DJAMA–see Masses (Guinea)

DJP–see Democratic Justice Party (South Korea)

DL–see Liberal Democracy (France)

DLF–see Liberal People's Party (Norway)

DLP–see Democratic Labour Party (Barbados)

DLP–see Dominican Labour Party (Dominica)

DLP–see Democratic Liberal Party (South Korea)

DM–see District Minister (Sri Lanka)

DMC–see Democratic Movement For Change (Israel)

DMK–see Dravidian Progressive Federation-Dravida Munnetra Kazhagam (India)

DMLP–see Democratic Movement for the Liberation of Eritrea

DMOs–see Democratic Mass Organizations (Tanzania)

DN–see National Directorate (Nicaragua)

DNA–see Labor Party (Norway)

DOLA–see Department of Local Administration (Thailand)

DOP–see Declaration of Principles (Israel)

DP–see Democratic Party (Cyprus)

DP–see Popular Democracy (Ecuador)

DP–see Democratic Party (Kenya)

DP–see Democratic Party (Uganda)

DP–see Democratic Party (Luxembourg)

DP–see Democratic Party (Seychelles)

DP–see Democratic Party (Zimbabwe)

DP–see Democratic Party (South Africa)

DPJ–see Democratic Party of Japan

DPP–see Democratic Progressive Party (Taiwan)

DPS–see Movement for Rights and Freedoms (Bulgaria)

DPSCG–see Democratic Party of Socialists of Montenegro (Yugoslavia)

DPT–see Democratic Party of Tajikistan

DPT–see Democratic Party of Turkmenistan

DPU–see Democratic Party of Ukraine

DRC–see Democratic Republic of Congo

DRP–see Democratic Republican Party (South Korea)

DRY–see Democratic Republic of Yemen

DS–see Democratic Party (Slovakia)

DS–see Socialist Democracy (Spain)

DS–see Democratic Party (Yugoslavia)

DTA–see Democratic Turnhalle Alliance (Namibia)

DUP–see Democratic Unionist Party (Sudan)

DUP–see Democratic Unionist Party (Northern Ireland)

DUS–see Democratic Union of Slovakia

DVU–see German People's Union (Germany)

DZJ–see Pensions for Secure Living (Czech Rep.)

EA–see Basque Solidarity (Spain)

Ecolo–see Ecologist Parties (Belgium)

ECOMOG–see Economic Community of West African States Cease-Fire Monitoring Group

ECOWAS–see Economic Community of West African States

ECZ–see Church of Christ in Zaire (D. Rep. Congo)

EDEK–see Unified Democratic Union of the Center (Cyprus)

EDP–see Erk "Will" Democratic Party (Uzbekistan)

EDU–see European Democratic Union

EE–see Basque Left (Spain)

EEA–see European Economic Agreement

EEC–see European Economic Community

EGLE–see Every Ghanian Living Everywhere

EGP–see Guerrilla Army of the Poor (Guatemala)

EL–see Euroleft Coalition (Bulgaria)

ELF–see Eritrean Liberation Front

EMU–see Economic and Monetary Union

ENIP–see Estonian National Independence Party

EOP–see Executive Office of the President (U.S.A.)

EP–see European Parliament

EPLF–see Eritrean People's Liberation Front

EPP–see Evangelical People's Party (Netherlands)

EPRDF–see Ethiopian Peoples' Revolutionary Democratic Front

EPRLF–see Eelam Peoples' Revolutionary Liberation Front (Sri Lanka)

EPS–see Sandinista Popular Army (Nicaragua)

ERC–see Catalonian Republican Left (Spain)

ERC–see Catalan Republican Left (Spain)

ERTU–see Egyptian Radio and Television Union

ESNS–see Coexistence (Slovakia)

ET–see Ethics and Transparency (Nicaragua)

ETA–see Basque Nation and Liberty (Spain)

EU–see European Union

EVP–see Protestant People's Party (Switzerland)

FAA–see Angolan Armed Forces

FAR–see African Forum for Reconstruction (Gabon)

FAR–see Rebel Armed Forces (Guatemala)

FAR–see Royal Armed Forces (Morocco)

FAR–see Front of Associations for Renewal (Togo)

FARC–see Revolutionary Armed Forces of Colombia

FARD–see Action Front for Renewal and Development (Benin)

FATAs–see Federally Administered Tribal Areas (Pakistan)

FAZ–see Armed Forces of Zaire (D. Rep. Congo)

FBP–see Progressive Citizen's Party (Liechtenstein)

FC–see Civic Forum (CAR)

FCC–see Federal Communications Commission (U.S.A.)

FCD–see Civic Democratic Front (Guatemala)

FD–see Democratic Force (France)

FDA–see Angolan Democratic Forum

FDCs–see Forces Defence Committees (Ghana)

FDF–see French-Speaking Democratic Front (Belgium)

FDIC–see Front for the Defense of Constitutional Institutions (Morocco)

FDN–see National Democratic Front (Mexico)

FDNG–see New Guatemalan Democratic Front

FDN-Mountounchi–see Nigerian Democratic Front-Mountounchi (Niger)

FDP–see Democratic and Patriotic Forces (Rep. of Congo)

FDP–see Free Democratic Party (Germany)

FDP–see Radical Democratic Party of Switzerland

FDR–see Democratic Front of Renewal (Niger)

FDU–see United Democratic Forces (Rep. of Congo)

FEDECAFE–see National Federation of Coffee Growers (Colombia)

FEDEMU–see Federal Democratic Movement of Uganda

FENALCO–see National Federation of Merchants (Colombia)

FESE–see Federation of Secondary Students of Ecuador

FEUE–see Federation of University Students of Ecuador

FEUU–see Federation of Uruguayan University Students

FF- see Front of Democratic Forces (Djibouti)

FFS–see Socialist Forces Front (Algeria)

FI–see Forward Italy

FIDA–see Palestinian Democratic Union Party

FIM–see Independent Clean Government Front (Peru)

FIS–see Islamic Salvation Front (Algeria)

FL–see Free List Party (Liechtenstein)

FLAA–see Liberation Front of Air and Azaouad (Niger)

FLAM–see African Liberation Forces of Mauritania

FLEC–see Front for the Liberation of the Cabinda Enclave (Angola)

FLING–see Front for the Liberation and Independence of Guinea

FLN–see National Liberation Front (Algeria)

FLOSY–see Front for the Liberation of Occupied South Yemen

FLQ–see Quebec Liberation Front (Canada)

FLT–see Liberation Front of Tamoust (Niger)

FMG–see Federal Military Government (Nigeria)

FMLN–see Farabundo Marti National Liberation Front (El Salvador)

FN–see National Front (Belgium)

FN–see National Front (France)

FN–see National Front (Spain)

FNC–see Federal National Council (United Arab Emirates)

FNDR–see National Front for the Defense of the Revolution (Madagascar)

FNJ–see National Front for Justice (Comoros)

FNLA–see National Front for the Liberation of Angola

FNM–see Free National Movement (Bahamas)

FNP–see National Progressive Force (Dominican Rep.)

FNR–see National Reconstruction Front (Ecuador)

FNT–see National Worker's Front (Nicaragua)

FNTC–see National Front of Workers and Peasants (Peru)

FO–see Worker's Force (France)

FORD–see Forum for Restoration of Democracy-Kenya-Asili

FP–see Popular Front (Burkina Faso)

FP–see Patriotic Front (D. Rep. Congo)

FP–see Progress Party (Denmark)

FP–see Progressive Federation (Spain)

FP–see Federal Party (Sri Lanka)

FP–see Liberal Party (Sweden)

FPD–see Front for Democracy (Angola)

FPD–see Free Democrats (Germany)

FPI–see Ivorian Popular Front (Ivory Coast)

FPLS–see Patriotic Front of Liberation of the Sahara (Niger)

FPO–see Freedom Party (of Austria) or Freedomites (Austria)

FPP–see Patriotic Front for Progress (Central African Republic)

FPR–see Rwanda Patriotic Front

FPT–see Ivorian Popular Front (Ivory Coast)

FRA–see Afarist Radical Front (Ecuador)

FRAP–see Popular Action Front (Chile)

FRD–see Forum for the Restoration of Democracy (Comoros)

FRDD–see Front for the Restoration and Defense of Democracy (Niger)

FRDD–see Front for the Restoration and Defense of Democracy (Niger)

FRDE–see Front for the Restoration of Right and Equality (Djibouti)

Frelimo–see Front for the Liberation of Mozambique

Frepaso–see Front for a Country in Solidarity (Argentina)

FRG–see Guatemalan Republican Front

FRODEBU–see Burundi Democratic Front

FROLINAT–see Chad National Liberation Front

FRUD–see Front for the Restoration of Unity and Democracy (Djibouti)

FSB–see Bolivian Socialist Falange

FSB–see Federal Security Council (Russia)

FSLN–see Sandinista National Liberation Front (Nicaragua)

FSN–see National Salvation Front (Romania)

FSTMB–see Bolivian Mineworkers Syndical Federation

FSTSE–see Federation of Unions of Workers in the Service of the State (Mexico)

FTC–see Federal Trade Commission (U.S.A.)

FUDR–see United Front for Democracy and the Republic (Burkina Faso)

FULRO–see United Front for the Struggle of Oppressed Races (Vietnam)

FUN–see National Unity Front (Guatemala)

FUNCINPEC–see National United Front for an Independent, Neutral, Peaceful and Cooperative Cambodia

FUR–see United Revolutionary Front (Guatemala)

FUSA–see United Front for the Salvation of Angola

FUT–see Unitary Workers Front (Ecuador)

GA–see Green Alternatives (Austria)

GAD–see Action Group for Democracy (Dominican Rep.)

GAD–see Grand Alliance for Democracy (Philippines)

GAO–see General Accounting Office (U.S.A.)

GDF–see Guyanese Defense Force

GDK Azat–see Freedom Civil Movement of Kazakhstan "Azat"

GDP–see Guyana Democratic Party

GE–see Ecological Generation (France)

GGG–see Good and Green Georgetown (Guyana)

GIA–see Armed Islamic Group (Algeria)

GMMLU–see Grenada Manual and Mental Labourer's Union

GN–see National Guard (Nicaragua)

GNP–see Gross National Product

GPA–see General Peace Agreement (Mozambique)

GPC–see General People's Congress (Libya)

GPC–see General People's Congress (Yemen)

GPRA–see Provisional Government of the Republic of Algeria

GPS–see Green Party of Switzerland

GPV–see Reformed Political Association (Netherlands)

GRCs–see Group Representation Constituencies (Singapore)

GST–see Goods and Service Tax

GULP–see Grenada United Labour Party

GURN–see Government of Unity and National Reconciliation (Angola)

GURN–see Government of Unity and National Reconciliation (Palestinian Authority)

HAMAS–see Movement for an Islamic Society (Algeria)

HB–see United People (Spain)

HBP–see People's Unity Party (Uzbekistan)

HCR–see High Council of the Republic (Togo)

HCR-PT–see High Council of the Republic-Transitional Parliament (D. Rep. Congo)

HD–see Grand National Party (South Korea)

HDF–see Hungarian Democratic Forum

HDP–see People's Democratic Party (Uzbekistan)

HDZ–see Croatian Democratic Union

HDZ–see Croatian Democratic Union (Bosnia and Hercegovina)

HFP/PFH–see Humanist Feminist Party (Belgium)

HNS–see Croatian People's Party

HSD-SMS–see Movement for Autonomous Democracy of Moravia and Silesia (Czech Rep.)

HSLS–see Croatian Social Liberal Party

HSP–see Hungarian Socialist Party

HSP–see Croatian Party of Rights

HSS–see Croatian Peasant Party

HZ–see Farmer's Movement (Slovakia)

HZDS–see Movement for a Democratic Slovakia

I–see India National Congress

IAF–see Islamic Action Front (Jordan)

ICJ–see International Court of Justice

ICP–see Indochinese Communist Party (Vietnam)

ID–see Democratic Left Party (Ecuador)

IDF–see Israeli Defense Force

IDH-RH–see Institute for Research, Documentation and Human Rights (Dominican Rep.)

IDN–see National Democratic Initiative (Andorra)

IDS–see Istrian Democratic Assembly (Croatia)

IEC–see Independent Electoral Commission (South Africa)

IEPES–see Institute of Political, Economic and Social Studies (Mexico)

IFE–see Federal Electoral Institute (Mexico)

IFES–see International Foundation for Election Systems

IFLB–see Islamic Front for the Liberation of Bahrain

IFLRY–see International Federation of Liberal & Radical Youth

IFP–see Inkatha Freedom Party (South Africa)

IGNU–see Interim Government of National Unity (Liberia)

IKL–see People's Patriotic League (Finland)

ILO–see International Labor Organization

IMF–see International Monetary Fund

IMRO-DPMNU–see Internal Macedonian Revolutionary Organization-Democratic Party of Macedonian National Unity

INCRA–see National Institute for Colonization and Agrarian Reform (Brazil)

INF–see National Front of Iran

INLA–see Irish National Liberation Party (Northern Ireland)

INPFL–see Independent National Patriotic Front of Liberia

INTU–see Indian National Trade Union Congress

IP–see Independence Party (Iceland)

IP–see Independence Party (Morocco)

IPD–see Impulse to Progress and Democracy (Benin)

IRA–see Provincial Irish Republican Army (Northern Ireland)

IRP–see Islamic Renaissance Party (Uzbekistan)

IRPT–see Islamic Renaissance Party of Tajikistan

IRSP–see Irish Republican Socialist Party (Northern Ireland)

ISP–see Independent Smallholders' Party (Hungary)

IU–see United Left (Bolivia)

IU–see United Left (Peru)

IU–see United Left (Spain)

IZG–see Independent Zimbabwe Group

JADP–see Jordanian Arab Democratic Party

JAPBP–see Jordanian Arab Progressive Ba'th Party

JASBP–see Jordanian Arab Socialist Ba'th Party

JCP–see Japan Communist Party

JCP–see Jordanian Communist Party

JD–see People's Party (India)

JDPUP–see Jordanian Democratic Popular Unity Party

JI–see Islamic Assembly (Bangladesh)

JI–see Islamic Assembly (Pakistan)

JLP–see Jamaica Labour Party

JNE–see National Board of Elections (Peru)

JP–see Jatiya Party (Bangladesh)

JRM–see Society of Combatant Clergy (Iran)

JRV–see Vote Receiving Commitees (Ecuador)

JRV–see Polling Places (Nicaragua)

JSC–see Judicial Service Commission (Sri Lanka)

JTI–see Islamic Assembly (Student Wing) (Pakistan)

JUDP–see Jordanian United Democratic Party

JUI–see Conference of ULEMA of Islam (Pakistan)

JUL–see Yugoslav United Left

JUP–see Conference of ULEMA of Pakistan

JVP–see People's Liberation Front (Sri Lanka)

KADU–see Kenya African Democratic Union

KAMPI–see Supporters of the Free Philippines

KANU–see Kenya African National Union

KAU–see Kenyan African Union

KBL–see New Society Movement (Philippines)

KCIA–see Korean Central Intelligence Agency (South Korea)

KD–see Christian Democrats (Sweden)

KDH–see Christian Democratic Movement (Slovakia)

KDS–see Christian Democratic Party (Czech Rep.)

KDU–see Christian Democratic Union (Czech Rep.)

KF–see Conservative People's Party (Denmark)

KF–see Cooperative Movement (Sweden)

KKE–see Communist Party of Greece

KKE-Interior–see Greek Communist Party of the Interior

KMT–see Nationalist Party (Taiwan)

KNDP–see Kamerun National Democratic Party (Cameroon)

KNUT–see Kenya National Union of Teachers

KPA–see Korean People's Army (North Korea)

KPB–see Party of Communists of Belarus

KPD–see Communists (Germany)

KPK–see Communist Party of Kazakhstan

KPL–see Communist Party of Luxembourg

KPO–see Communist Party (Austria)

KPRP–see Kampuchean People's Revolutionary Party (Cambodia)

KPU- see Kenya People's Union

KRF–see Christian People's Party (Denmark)

KrF–see Christian People's Party (Norway)

KRO–see Congress of Russian Communities

KRRS–see Karnataka State Farmers' Association (India)

KSCM–see Communist Party of Bohemia and Moravia-Left Bloc (Czech Rep.)

KSOOR–see "Republic" Coordinating Council of Public Associations (Kazakhstan)

KSP–see Farmer's and Worker's Party (Bangladesh)

KSS–see Communist Party of Slovakia

KTPI–see Indonesian Party of High Ideals (Suriname)

KUP–see Catholic People's Party (Netherlands)

KWP–see Korean Workers' Party (North Korea)

LA–see Leftist Alliance (Finland)

LAA–see Local Administration Bill (Zambia)

LABAN–see People's Force (Philippines)

LAKAS-NUCD–see People's Power-National Union of Christian Democrats (Philippines)

LAMMP–see Fight of the Free Filipino Masses Party

LAP–see Liberal Action Party (Liberia)

LC–see Latvia's Way

LCD–see Lesotho Congress for Democracy

LCP–see Lebanese Communist Party

LCR–see Revolutionary Communist League (France)

LCR–see The Radical-Cause (Venezuela)

LCs–see Local Councils (Uganda)

LCS–see League of Communists of Yugoslavia (Slovenia)

LD/MPT–see Democratic League/Popular Labor Movement (Senegal)

LDLP–see Lithuanian Democratic Labor Party

LDP–see Democratic Filipino Struggle

LDP–see Liberal Democratic Party (Japan)

LDP–see Liberal Democratic Party (Macedonia)

LDP–see Liberal Democratic Party (Malaysia)

LDPR–see Liberal Democratic Party of Russia

LDS–see Liberal Democracy of Slovenia

LdU–see Alliance of Independents (Switzerland)

LF–see Liberal Forum (Austria)

LIPAD–see Patriotic League for Development (Burkina Faso)

LIPE–see Guinean League for the Protection of the Environment

LKDS–see Farmer's Union/Christian Democratic Union/Latgale/Democratic Party Coalition (Latvia)

LLA–see Lesotho Liberation Army

LMI–see Liberation Movement of Iran

LN–see Northern League (Italy)

LNNK–see Latvian National Conservative Party and Green Party

LNTG–see Liberian National Transitional Government

LO–see Norwegian Trades Union Federation

LO–see Swedish Confederation of Trade Unions

LOPPE–see Law of Political Organizations and Electoral Processes (Mexico)

LP–see Liberal Party (Philippines)

LP–see Labor Party (Saint Kitts)

LPAI–see African People's League for Independence (Djibouti)

LPP–see Law of Popular Participation (Bolivia)

LPP–see Liberia People's Party

LPRP–see Lao People's Revolutionary Party (Laos)

LRF–see National Farmer's Association (Sweden)

LSAP–see Socialist Workers' Party (Luxembourg)

LSP–see Latvian Socialist Party

LSP–see Liberal Socialist Party (Egypt)

LSSP–see Ceylon Equal Society Party (Sri Lanka)

LSU–see Liberal Social Union (Czech Rep.)

LTTE–see Liberation Tigers of Tamil Eelam (Sri Lanka)

LU–see Liberal Union (Andorra)

LUP–see Liberian Unification Party

M–see Moderate Party (Sweden)

M.G.R.–see M.G. Ramachaudran (India)

MA–see Melanesian Alliance (Papua New Guinea)

MAC–see Christian Authentic Movement (El Salvador)

MAFREMO–see Malawi Freedom Movement

MAKI–see Israel Communist Party

MAPAM–see United Workers Party (Israel)

MAS–see Solidarity Action Movement (Guatemala)

MAS–see Movement toward Socialism (Venezuela)

MAUDR–see Angolan Democratic Unity Movement for Reconstruction

MBL–see Movement for a Free Bolivia

MBPM–see Maurice Bishop Patriotic Movement (Grenada)

MCA–see Malayan Chinese Association

MCDDI–see Congolese Movement for Democracy and Comprehensive Development (Rep. of Congo)

MCP–see Malawi Congress Party

MCPC–see Central African People's Liberation Movement

MCs–see Municipal Councils (Sri Lanka)

MDA–see Movement for Democracy in Algeria

MDB–see Brazilian Democratic Movement

MDC–see Malawi Development Corporation

MDC–see Citizen's Movement (France)

MDD–see Movement for Democracy and Development (Central African Republic)

MDN–see National Democratic Movement (Guatemala)

MDP–see Malawi Democratic Party

MDP–see Portuguese Democratic Movement

MDP–see Movement for Democracy and Progress (Cameroon)

MDP–see Movement for the Defense of the Republic (Cameroon)

MDP–see Democratic Popular Movement (*Senegal*)

MDR–see Democratic Republican Movement (Rwanda)

MDREC–see Movement for Democracy, Renaissance and Revolution in Central Africa

MDS–see Movement of Social Democrats (Tunisia)

MDS–see Democratic and Social Movement (Morocco)

MDU–see Malawi Democratic Union

MEI–see Independent Ecology Movement (France)

MEP–see People's Electoral Movement (Venezuela)

MESAN–see Movement of Social Evolution in Black Africa (Central African Rep.)

MFA–see Armed Forces Movement (Portugal)

MFDC–see Movement of Democratic Forces of Casamance (Senegal)

MFP–see Marematlou Freedom Party (Lesotho)

MHRA–see Mauritanian Human Rights Association

MIC–see Malayan Indian Congress

MILF–see Moro Islamic Liberation Front (Philippines)

MINUGUA–see UN Verification Mission (Guatemala)

MIR–see Movement of the Revolutionary Left (Bolivia)

MIRT–see Movement for the Islamic Revival of Tajikistan

MISK–see Confederation of Nationalist Labor Unions (Turkey)

MK–see Member of Knesset (Israel)

MKDH–see Hungarian Christian Democratic Movement (Slovakia)

ML–see Liberty Movement (Peru)

MLA–see Martial Law Administrator (Pakistan)

MLN–see National Liberation Movement (Uruguay)

MLN–see National Liberation Movement (Guatemala)

MLPC–see Central African People's Liberation Movement

MLSTP–see Liberation Movement of Sao Tome and Principe

MMD–see Movement for Multiparty Democracy (Zambia)

MMM–see Mauritanian Militant Movement

MMP–see Mixed-Member Proportion (New Zealand)

MNDP–see Malawi National Democratic Party

MNLF–see Moro National Liberation Front (Philippines)

MNPP–see New Country Movement (Ecuador)

MNR–see Nationalist Revolutionary Movement (Bolivia)

MNR–see National Movement of Revolution (Republic of Congo)

MNR–see National Revolutionary Movement (El Salvador)

MNR–see Mozambique National Resistance

MNR/Renamo–see Mozambique National Resistance

MNSD–see National Movement for Solidarity and Democracy (Cameroon)

MNSD-Nassara–see National Movement for a Society of Development-Nassara (Niger)

MNU–see Movement for National Unity (Saint Vincent and the Grenadines)

Modin–see Movement for Dignity and National Independence (Argentina)

MOJA–see Movement for Justice in Africa (Liberia)

MOLIRENA–see Liberal National Republican Movement (Panama)

MOPOCO–see Colorado Popular Movement (Paraguay)

MORENA–see National Renovation Movement (Panama)

MORENA-B–see Movement for National Regeneration-Woodcutters (Gabon)

MOTION–see Movement For Social Transformation (Trinidad & Tobago)

MOVERS–see Movement for Responsible Public Service (Philippines)

MP–see Member of Parliament

MP–see Popular Movement (Morocco)

MP–see Motherland Party (Turkey)

MP–see Ecology Party (Sweden)

MP's–see Members of Parliament

MpD–see Movement for Democracy (Cape Verde)

MPD–see Democratic Popular Movement (Ecuador)

MPF–see Movement for France

MPLA-PT–see Popular Liberation Movement of Angola (Labor Party

MPR–see Popular Movement of the Revolution (D. Rep. Congo)

MPR–see Patriotic Movement for Renewal (Mali)

MPRP–see Mongolian People's Revolutionary Party

MPS–see Patriotic Salvation Movement (Chad)

MQM–A–see Mutahida Qaumi Movement (Altaf) (Pakistan)

MQM–H–see Mutahida Qaumi Movement (Haqiqi) (Pakistan)

MRD–see Movement for the Restoration of Democracy (Pakistan)

MRG–see Left Radical Movement (France)

MRM–see Assembly of Combatant Clerics (Iran)

MRND–see National Revolutionary Movement for Development (Rwanda)

MRNDD–see National Republican Movement for Democracy and Development (Rwanda)

MRP–see Popular Republican Movement (France)

MRS–see Senegalese Republican Movement

MRS–see Sandinista Renovation Movement (Nicaragua)

MRTA–see Tupac Amaru Revolutionary Movement (Peru)

MRTKL–see Tupak Katari Revolutionary Liberation Movement (Bolivia)

MSC–see Social Christian Movement (Ecuador)

MSI–see Italian Social Movement

MSM–see Mauritian Socialist Movement

MSN–see National Salvation Movement (Colombia)

MSP–see Movement for a Peaceful Society (Algeria)

MST–see Landless Peoples' Movement (Brazil)

MTD–see Togolese Movement for Democracy

MTDP–see National Revival Democratic Party (Uzbekistan)

MTI–see Islamic Tendency Movement (Tunisia)

MUN–see Mission of National Unity (Panama)

MUZ–see Mine Workers Union of Zambia

MVR–see Fifth Republic Movement (Venezuela)

MYP–see Malawi Young Pioneers

NA–see New Alliance (Slovakia)

NABR–see National Alliance for Belizean Rights

NAF–see Norwegian Employers' Association

NAFTA–see North American Free Trade Agreement

NAP–see National Awami Party (Bangladesh)

NAP–see New Aspiration Party (Thailand)

NAP–see Nationalist Action Party (Turkey)

NAR–see National Alliance for Reconstruction (Trinidad and Tobago)

NATO–see North Atlantic Treaty Organization

NBM–see New Beginnings Movement (Jamaica)

NCC–see Our Common Cause(Benin)

NCCR–see National Convention for Constitutional Reform (Tanzania)

NCF–see Nordic Youth Center Association

NCGUB–see National Coalition Government Union of Burma (Myanmar)

NCMPs–see Non-Constituency Members of Parliament (Singapore)

NCNC–see National Council of Nigeria and the Cameroons (Nigeria)

NCNP–see National Council for New Politics (South Korea)

NCP–see National Constitutional Party (Jordan)

NCP–see National Convention Party (Ghana)

NCP–see Nepalese Congress Party

NCP–see National Conservative Party (Finland)

ND–see New Democracy (Andorra)

ND–see New Democracy (Greece)

ND–see New Democracy (Yugoslavia)

NDA–see National Democratic Aliance (Sudan)

NDC–see National Democratic Convention (Ghana)

NDC–see National Democratic Congress (Grenada)

NDC–see National Defense Commission (North Korea)

NDF–see Namibian Defense Force

NDM–see National Democratic Movement (Jamaica)

NDP–see National Democratic Party (Antigua and Barbuda)

NDP–see New Democratic Party (Canada)

NDP–see National Democratic Party (Egypt)

NDP–see New Development Policy (Malaysia)

NDP–see National Democratic Party (Saint Vincent and the Grenadines)

NDP–see National Development Party (Trinidad and Tobago)

NDP–see Nationalist Democracy Party (Turkey)

NDP–see New Democratic Party (South Korea)

NDP–see New Democratic Party (Suriname)

NDP Zheltoksan–see December National Democratic Party (Kazakhstan)

NDPL–see National Democratic Party of Liberia

NDRP–see New Democratic Republican Party (South Korea)

NDS–see National Democratic Party (Slovakia)

NDU–see National Democratic Union (Argentina)

NEC–see National Election Commission (Nigeria)

NEP–see New Economic Policy (Malaysia)

NERP–see New Economic Recovery Program (Zambia)

NF–see National Front (UK of Great Britain)

NFD–see New Democratic Force (Colombia)

NFP–see New Frontier Party (Japan)

NFSL–see National Front for the Salvation of Libya

NGOs–see Non-Governmental Organizations (India)

NIF–see National Islamic Front (Sudan)

NIO–see Northern Ireland Office

NIP–see National Independence Party (Ghana)

NJAC–see National Joint Action Committee (Trinidad and Tobago)

NJM–see New Jewel Movement (Grenada)

NKK–see People's Congress of Kazakhstan

NKP–see Communist Party of Norway

NKP–see New Korea Party (South Korea)

NLD–see National League for Democracy (Myanmar)

NLF–see National Liberation Front (Yemen)

NLM–see National Labour Movement (Saint Lucia)

NM–see New Majority (Peru)

NMPs–see Nominated Members of Parliament (Singapore)

NNDP–see Nigerian National Democratic Party

NNLC–see Ngwane National Liberatory Congress (Swaziland)

NNP–see New National Party (Grenada)

NORAID–see Irish Northern Aid Committee (Northern Ireland)

NP–see Nacionalista Party (Philippines)

NP–see National Party (South Africa)

NPA–see New People's Army (Philippines)

NPC–see National People's Congress (China)

NPC–see Northern People's Congress (Nigeria)

NPC–see National People's Coalition (Philippines)

NPD–see National Democratic Party (Germany)

NPF–see National Policy Forum (UK of Great Britain)

NPFL–see National Patriotic Front of Liberia

NPH–see New Party Harbinger (Japan)

NPP–see New Patriotic Party (Ghana)

NPP–see National Patriotic Party (Liberia)

NPS–see Suriname National Party

NPUP–see National Progressive Unionist Party (Egypt)

NRA–see National Resistance Army (Uganda)

NRC–see National Resistance Council (Uganda)

NRC–see Nuclear Regulatory Commission (U.S.A.)

NRC–see National Republican Convention (Nigeria)

NRM–see National Resistance Movement (D. Rep. Congo)

NRM–see National Resistance Movement (Uganda)

NRP–see National Reconciliation Party (Gambia)

NRP–see National Religious Party (Israel)

NRP–see Nevis Reform Party (Saint Kitts)

NRP–see Nevis Reformation Party (Saint Kitts)

NSC–see National Security Council (Tunisia)

NSC–see National Security Council (U.S.A.)

NSP–see National Solidarity Party (Singapore)

NSS–see Nature Society of Singapore

NTC–see National Transition Council (Algeria)

NUCD–see National Union for Christian Democrats (Philippines)

NUP–see National Union Party (Sudan)

NUP–see National Unity Party (Myanmar)

NUPRG–see New Ulster Political Research Group (Northern Ireland)

NVU–see Dutch People's Union (Netherlands)

NWFP–see Northwest Frontier Province (Pakistan)

NWU–see National Workers' Union (Jamaica)

NYM–see Nigerian Youth Movement

NZLP–see New Zealand Labour Party

OAAB–see Austrian Association of Workers and Employees

OAPEC–see Organization of Arab Petroleum Exporting Countries

OAS–see Organization of American States

OAU–see Organization of African Unity

OBB–see Austrian Farmer's Association

OBCs–see Backward Castes (India)

ODA–see Civic Democratic Alliance (Czech Rep.)

ODP/MT–see Organization for Popular Democracy/Labor Movement (Burkina Faso)

ODS–see Civic Democratic Party (Czech Rep.)

ODU–see Civic Democratic Union (Slovakia)

OECD–see Organization for Economic Cooperation and Development

OHR–see Our Home Is Russia

OIRA–see Official Irish Republican Army (Northern Ireland)

OLF–see Oromo (Ethiopia)

OMB–see Office of Management and Budget (U.S.A.)

OMUG–see Organizations for the Exploitation of the Gambia River (Guinea-Bissau)

OMUS–see Organizations for the Exploitation of the Senegal River (Guinea-Bissau)

ONA-JPU–see Uruguayan National Organization of Retirees' and Pensioners' Associations

ONM–see National Organization of Veterans (Algeria)

ONR–see Organization for National Reconstruction (Trinidad and Tobago)

ONUSAL–see United Nations Observer Mission in El Salvador

OPC–see Ovambolamo People's Congress (Namibia)

OPDO–see Oromo People's Democratic Organization (Ethiopia)

OPEC–see Organization of Petroleum Exporting Countries

OPG–see Official Parliamentary Group (Pakistan)

OPL–see Lavalas Political Organization (Haiti)

OPL–see Organization of the Struggling People (Haiti)

OPP–see Organ of People's Power (Cuba)

ORA–see Organization of Armed Resistance (Niger)

ORPA–see Armed People's Organization (Guatemala)

OSCE–see Organization for Security and Cooperation in Europe

OUP–see Official Unionist Party (Northern Ireland)

OVP–see Austrian People's Party

OWB–see Austrian Economic Association

OYAK–see Army Mutual Assistance Foundation (Turkey)

PA–see Palestinian Authority

PA–see People's Alliance (Iceland)

PA–see Arnulfista Party (Panama)

PA–see People's Alliance (Sri Lanka)

PAC–see Civilian Self-Defense Patrol (Guatemala)

PAC–see Pan-Africanist Congress (South Africa)

PACIA–see Angolan Party of African Identity Conservative

PACs–see Political Action Committees (U.S.A.)

PAD–see People's Party for Democracy and Development (Ghana)

PAGS–see Socialist Vanguard Party (Algeria)

PAI–see Angolan Independent Party

PAI–see African Independence Party (Senegal)

PAICV–see African Party for the Independence of Cape Verde

PAIGC–see African Party for the Independence of Guinea and Cape Verde (Guinea-Bissau)

PAIS–see Open Politics for the Social Country (Argentina)

PAJOCA–see Party of the Alliance of Youth, Workers, and Farmers of Angola

PAL–see Progressive Alliance of Liberia

PAL–see Angolan Liberal Party

PALA–see Labor Party (Panama)

PALI–see Neo-Liberal Party (Nicaragua)

PALIPEHUTU–see Party for the Liberation of the Hutu People (Burundi)

PALU–see United Lumumbist Party (D. Rep. Congo)

PAM–see Peoples Action Movement (Saint Kitts)

PAMSCAD–see Program of Action to Mitigate the Costs of Adjustment (Ghana)

PAN–see National Advancement Party (Guatemala)

PAN–see National Action Party (Mexico)

PAP–see People's Action Paarty (Papua New Guinea)

PAP–see People's Action Party (Sierra Leone)

PAR–see Aragonese Regionalist Party (Spain)

PARENA–see Party for National Renewal (Mali)

PARM–see Authentic Party of the Mexican Revolution

PAS–see Pan-Malaysian Islamic Party

PASOC–see Socialist Action Party (Spain)

PASOK–see Pan-Hellenic Socialist Movement (Greece)

PATAs–see Provincially Administered Tribal Areas (Pakistan)

PAV–see Public Against Violence (Slovakia)

PAVN–see People's Army of Vietnam

PBDS–see Sarawak Dayak People's Party (Malaysia)

PBS–see United Sabah Party (Malaysia)

PC–see Progressive Conservative Party of Canada

PC–see Conservative Party (Ecuador)

PC–see Center Alliance Party (Poland)

PC–see Carlist Party (Spain)

PCB–see Brazililian Communist Party

PCB–see Communist Party of Benin

PCB–see Bolivian Communist Party

PCB–see Belgian Communist Party

PCC–see Colombian Communist Party

PCC–see Cuban Communist Party

PCD–see Liberal Democratic Party (Angola)

PCD–see Party for the Democratic Convergence (Cape Verde)

PCD–see Democratic Conservative Party (Nicaragua)

PcdeN–see Nicaraguan Communist Party

PcdoB–see Communist Party of Brazil

PCE–see Spanish Communist Party

PCF–see French Communist Party

PCI–see Italian Communist Party

PCL–see Plenary of Legislative Commissions (Ecuador)

PCM–see Communist Party of Mexico

PCML–see Maoist Marxist-Leninist Communist Party (Ecuador)

PCMR–see Presidential Council for Minority Rights (Singapore)

PCN–see Conservative Party of Nicaragua

PCN–see Party of National Reconciliation (El Salvador)

PCP–see Palestine Communist Party

PCP–see Portuguese Communist Party

PCP–see Communist Party (Paraguay)

PCS–see San Marino Communist Party

PCT–see Congolese Workers' Party (Republic of Congo)

PCT–see Tunisian Communist Party

PCV–see Venezuelan Communist Party

PD–see Democratic Party (Ecuador)

PD–see Democratic Party (Romania)

PDA–see Angolan Democratic Party

PdA–see Swiss Labor Party

PDB–see Party of German-Speaking Belgians

PDB–see Democratic Bolivian Party

PDC–see Christian Democrat Party (Argentina)

PDC–see Christian Democratic Party (Brazil)

PDC–see Christian Democratic Party (Burundi)

PDC–see Christian Democratic Party (Chile)

PDC–see Christian Democratic Party (El Salvador)

PDC–see Christian Democrat Party (Honduras)

PDC–see Peace and Development Council (Myanmar)

PDC–see Christian Democratic Party (Panama)

PDC–see Christian Democratic Party (Paraguay)

PDC–see Christian Democratic Party (Rwanda)

PDCI–see Democratic Party of Ivory Coast

PDCN–see Democratic Party of National Cooperation (Guatemala)

PDCs–see People's Defence Committees (Ghana)

PDCS–see Christian Democratic Party (San Marino)

PPBB–see United Traditional Bumiputra Party (Malaysia)

PPC–see Christian People's Party (Dominican Rep.)

PPC–see Popular Christian Party (Peru)

PPD–see Djibouti People's Party

PPD–see Doctrinaire Panamenista Party

PPD–see Party for Democracy (Chile)

PPD–see Popular Democratic Party (Puerto Rico)

PPDF–see Popular Party for French Democracy

PPE–see Papa Egoro Party (Panama)

PPI–see Italian People's Party

PPM–see Party of the People of Mauritania

PPM–see Popular Monarchist Party (Portugal)

PPN–see Niger Progressive Party

PPN-RDA–see Niger Progressive Party-African Democratic Rally

PPOs–see Primary Party Organizations (Kazakhstan)

PPP–see People's Progressive Party of Malaysia

PPP–see Palestine People's Party

PPP–see People's Progressive Party (Gambia)

PPP–see People's Progressive Party (Guyana)

PPP–see Pakistan People's Party (Pakistan)

PPP–see People's Progress Party (Papua New Guinea)

PPP–see People's Power Party (Philippines)

PPP–see People's Progressive Party (Saint Lucia)

PPP–see People's Political Party (Saint Vincent and the Grenadines)

PPR–see Progressive Republican Party (Brazil)

PPS–see Popular Socialist Party (Brazil)

PPS–see Popular Socialist Party (Mexico)

PPSC–see Popular Social Christian Party (Nicaragua)

PPT–see People's Party of Tajikistan

PPT–see Country for All (Venezuela)

PQ–see Parti Quebecois (Canada)

PQ–see Democratic Quisqueyan Party (Dominican Rep.)

PR–see Proportional Representation

PR–see Revolutionary Party (Guatemala)

PRB–see Party of the Rebirth of Benin

PRC–see Cuban Revolutionary Party

PRC–see Central African Republican Party

PRC–see Civic Renewal Party (Panama)

PRD–see Democratic Renewal Party (Angola)

PRD–see Democratic Renewal Party (Benin)

PRD–see Party of Democratic Renewal (Djibouti)

PRD–see Dominican Revolutionary Party (Dominican Rep.)

PRD–see Party of the Democratic Revolution (Mexico)

PRD–see Revolutionary Democratic Party (Panama)

PRD–see Democratic Renewal Party (Portugal)

PRD–see Democratic Reformist Party (Spain)

PRDS–see Social and Democratic Republican Party (Mauritania)

PRE–see Roldosista Party of Ecuador

Pref–see Reformist Party (Dominican Rep.)

PRF–see Revolutionary Febrerist Party (Paraguay)

PRI–see Italian Republican Party

PRI–see Independent Revolutionary Party (Dominican Rep.)

PRI–see Institutional Revolutionary Party (Mexico)

PRL–see Liberal Parties (Belgium)

PRLPN-Nakowa–see Republican Party for the Liberty and Progress of Niger-Nakowa

PRM–see Party of Greater Romania

PRN–see Party of National Reconstruction (Brazil)

PRN–see National Republican Party (Costa Rica)

PRP–see Popular Revolutionary Party (D. Rep. Congo)

PRP–see Party of Renovation and Progress (Guinea)

PRP–see Party of Renewal and Progress (Morocco)

PRP–see People's Reform Party (Philippines)

PRPB–see Popular Revolutionary Party of Benin

PRS–see Social Renewal Party (Angola)

PRS–see Radical Socialist Party (France)

PRS–see Social Renovation Party (Guinea-Bissau)

PRSC–see Reformist Social Christian Party (Dominican Rep.)

PRSD–see Social Democratic Radical Party (Chile)

PRT–see Revolutionary Party of the Workers (Mexico)

PS–see Portuguese Socialist Party

PS–see Socialist Parties (Belgium)

PS–see Socialist Party (Chile)

PS–see Socialist Party (France)

PS–see Solidarity Party (Panama)

PS–see Socialist Party (Senegal)

PSA–see Socialist Party of Andalucia (Spain)

PS–see Brazilian Socialist Party

PSB–see Burkina Socialist Party

PSC–see Christian Democratic Parties (Belgium)

PSC–see Social Christian Party (Ecuador)

PSC–see Social Christian Party (Guatemala)

PSCN–see Social Christian Party (Nicaragua)

PSD–see Social Democratic Party (Angola)

PSD–see Social Democratic Party (Benin)

PSD–see Social Democratic Party (Brazil)

PSD–see Democratic Socialist Party (Central African Rep.)

PSD–see Social Democratic Party (France)

PSD–see Social Democratic Party (Guatemala)

PSD–see Social Democratic Party (Guinea-Bissau)

PSD–see Social Democratic Party (Portugal)

PSD–see Social Democratic Party (Rwanda)

PSDA–see Angolan Social Democratic Party

PSDB–see Brazilian Social Democratic Party

PSDN-Alheri–see Niger Social-Democratic Party-Alheri

PSE–see Basque Socialist Party (Spain)

PSI–see Italian Socialist Party

PSL–see Polish Peasant Party

PSM–see Monegasque Socialist Party

PSN–see Nicaraguan Socialist Party

PSN–see National Solidarity Party (Portugal)

PSOC–see Social Conservatism Party (Nicaragua)

PSOE–see Spanish Socialist Workers' Party

PSP–see Popular Socialist Party (Cuba)

PSP–see Progressive Socialist Party (Lebanon)

PSP–see Pacifist Socialist Party (Netherlands)

PSs–see Regional Councils (Sri Lanka)

PSS–see San Marino Socialist Party

PSSH–see Socialist Party of Albania

PSUC–see Unified Socialist Party of Catalonia (Spain)

PSUM–see Unified Socialist Party of Mexico

PT–see Workers' Party (Brazil)

PTA–see Angolan Labor Party

PTB–see Brazilian Worker's Party

PTB–see Brazilian Labor Party

PTD–see Dominican Worker's Party

PTP–see Togolese Progressive Party

PUD–see Democratic Unification Party (Honduras)

PUDEMO–see People's United Democratic Movement (Swaziland)

PUND-Salama–see Party for National Unity and Development-Salama (Niger)

PUNR–see Romanian National Unity Party

PUNT–see National Workers' Party (Eq. Guinea)

PUP–see People's United Party (Belize)

PUP–see Popular Unity Party (Tunisia)

PUP–see Party of Unity and Progress (Guinea)

PUR–see Republican Union (Ecuador)

PUSC–see Social Christian Unity (Costa Rica)

PUU–see Party of Liberty and Progress (Belgium)

PvdA–see Labor Party (Netherlands)

PVE–see Spanish Green Party

PW–see Walloon Party (Belgium)

PWP–see Peasants and Workers Party (India)

PYO–see Progressive Youth Organization (Guyana)

RAAN–see Northern Atlantic Autonomous Region (Nicaragua)

RAAS–see Southern Atlantic Autonomous Region (Nicaragua)

RAKAH–see New Communist List (Israel)

RATZ–see Citizens Right Movement (Israel)

RC–see Communist Refoundation (Italy)

RCC–see Revolutionary Command Council (Ecuador)

RCC–see Revolutionary Command Council (Iran)

RCC–see Revolutionary Command Council (Libya)

RCD–see Rally for Culture and Democracy (Algeria)

RCD–see Congolese Rally for Democracy (D. Rep. Congo)

RCs–see Resistance Committees (Uganda)

RDA–see African Democratic Assembly (Burkina Faso)

RDA–see African Democratic Rally (Ivory Coast)

RDL–see Rally of Liberal Democrats (Benin)

RDP–see Rally for Democracy and Progress (Gabon)

RDP–see Reunification and Democracy Party (South Korea)

RDR–see Rally of Republicans (Ivory Coast)

Renamo–see Mozambique National Resistance

RF–see Republican Front (Ivory Coast)

RGB-MB–see Guinea-Bissau Resistance-Bah Fatah Movement

RMC–see Revolutionary Military Council (Grenada)

RN–see National Renovation (Chile)

RNB–see National Woodcutters Rally (Gabon)

RND–see National Democratic Rally (Algeria)

RND–see National Rally for Development (Comoros)

RND–see National Democratic Assembly (Senegal)

RNI–see National Assembly of Independents (Morocco)

ROAD–see Citizens' Movement for Democratic Action (Poland)

RP–see Republic Party (Trinidad and Tobago)

RPF–see Rwandan Patriotic Front

RPF–see Rally for the French People

RPF-SEE–see Reformational Political Federation (Netherlands)

RPG–see Assembly of the Guinean People

RPI–see Republican Party of India

RPP–see Popular Rally for Progress (Djibouti)

RPP–see Radical Political Party (Netherlands)

RP–see Republican People's Party (Turkey)

RPR–see Rally for the French Republic

RPSD–see Rally for Social Democracy (Madagascar)

RPT–see Rally of Togolese People

RSF–see Rhodesian Security Forces

RSFSR–see Russian Soviet Federated Socialist Republic

RSP–see Socialist Progressive Rally (Tunisia)

RSS–see Agrarian Party of Slovakia

RSS–see National Volunteer Organization (India)

RUC–see Royal Ulster Constabulary (Northern Ireland)

RUF–see Revolutionary Front (Sierra Leone)

RV–see Radical Liberals (Denmark)

RV–see Red Electoral Alliance (Norway)

S–see Janata Dal (India)

S or SAP–see Social Democratic Party (Sweden)

SAC–see Cabinet of the State Administration Council (North Korea)

SACP–see South Africa Communist Party

SAD–see Shiromani Akali Party (India)

SADC–see Southern African Development Council (Zimbabwe)

SADCC–see South African Development Coordination Conference (Malawi)

SADF–see South African Defense Force

SAP–see Structural Adjustment Program

SAP–see Social Action Party (Thailand)

SAPP–see Sabah Development Party (Malaysia)

SAR–see Special Administrative Region (China)

SBPF–see Sind-Baluch Pakhtoun Front (Pakistan)

SD–see Social Democrats (Denmark)

SDA–see Party of Democratic Action (Bosnia and Hercegovina)

SDF–see Social Democratic Front (Cameroon)

SDK–see Slovak Democratic Coalition

SDL–see Party of the Democratic Left (Slovakia)

SDLP–see Social Democratic and Labour Party (Northern Ireland)

SDP–see Social Democratic Party of Croatia

SDP–see Singapore Democratic Party

SDP–see Social Democratic Party (Bahamas)

SDP–see Social Democratic Party (Finland)

SDP–see Social Democratic Party (Iceland)

SDP–see Social Democratic Party (Japan)

SDP–see Social Democratic Party (Nigeria)

SDP–see Social Democratic Party (United Kingdom)

SdRP–see Social-Democratic Party of Poland

SDS–see Serb Democratic Party (Bosnia and Hercegovina)

SDS–see Union of Democratic Forces (Bulgaria)

SDSS–see Social Democratic Party of Slovenia

SDSS–see Social Democrat Party of Slovakia

SDUM–see Social Democratic Union of Macedonia

SEC–see Securities and Exchange Commission (U.S.A.)

SED–see Socialist Unity Party of Germany

SEPDF–see Southern Ethiopian Peoples' Democratic Front

SF–see Socialist People's Party (Denmark)

SF–see Sinn Fein (Northern Ireland)

SGP–see State Reform Party (Netherlands)

SHAS–see Sephardi Torah Guardians (Israel)

SIN–see Coalition of the Left and Progress (Greece)

SIP–see Industrial Union of Panama

SJKH–see National Council for New Politics (South Korea)

SJP–see Samajwadi Janata Party (India)

SKD–see Slovenian Christian Democrats

SKDL–see Finnish People's Democratic League

SKNLP–see St. Kitts & Nevis Labour Party

SKOI–see Standing Conference of the Civic Institute (Slovakia)

SKP–see Finnish Communist Party

SLD–see Democratic Left Alliance (Poland)

SLFP–see Sri Lanka Freedom Party

SLP–see St. Lucia Labour Party

SLP–see Socialist Labor Party (Egypt)

SLPP–see Sierra Leone People's Party

SLS–see Slovene People's Party

SMK–see Hungarian Coalition (Slovakia)

SMP–see Sipah-I-Muhamund (Pakistan)

SMS–see Great Council of Sinhalese (Sri Lanka)

SNAP–see Sarawak National Action Party (Malaysia)

SNC–see Supreme National Council (Cambodia)

SNE–see National Education Union (Morocco)

SNP–see Scottish National Party (UK of Great Britain)

SNS–see Slovak National Party

SNS–see Serb National Alliance (Bosnia and Hercegovina)

SNS–see Serbian People's Party (Croatia)

SNTVs–see Single Nontransferable Votes (Taiwan)

SODEP–see Social Democracy Party (Turkey)

SOP–see Party of Civic Understanding (Slovakia)

SP–see Socialist Parties (Belgium)

SP–see Samajwadi (Socialist) Party (India)

SP–see Samata Party (India)

SP–see Socialist Party (Netherlands)

SP–see Center Party (Norway)

SPA–see Supreme People's Assembly (North Korea)

SPD–see Social Democrats (Germany)

SPDC–see State Peace and Development Council (Myanmar)

SPK–see Socialist Party of Kazakhstan

SPLM–see Sudan People's Liberation Movement

SPO–see Social Democratic Party (Austria)

SPO–see Serbian Renewal Movement (Yugoslavia)

SPP–see Singapore People's Paarty

SPPF–see Seychelles People's Progressive Front

SPS–see Socialist Party of Serbia (Yugoslavia)

SPS–see Social-Democratic Party of Switzerland

SPU–see Socialist Party of Ukraine

SPZ–see Slovak Party of Entrepreneurs and Traders

SRA–see Argentine Rural Society

SRS–see Serbian Radical Party (Yugoslavia)

SRV–see Socialist Republic of Vietnam

SSIM–see Southern Sudan Independence Movement

SSP–see Sipah-i-Sahaba (Pakistan)

SSR–see Uzbek Soviet Socialist Republic

SSU–see Sudan Socialist Union

STV–see Single Transferable Vote (Ireland)

SUPP–see Sarawak United People's Party (Malaysia)

SV–see Socialist Left Party (Norway)

SVLP–see St. Vincent Labour Party

SVP–see Swiss People's Party/Democratic Center Union

SWAPO–see Southwest Africa People's Organization

SWAPO–see South West Africa People's Organization of Namibia

SWATF–see South West Africa Territorial Force (Namibia)

SZ–see Green Party (Czech Rep.)

SZS–see Green Party in Slovakia

TAIP–see Taiwan Independence Party

TAMI–see Movement for Jewish Tradition (Israel)

TANU–see Tanganyikan African National Union

TB–see Fatherland and Freedom (Latvia)

TC–see Tamil Congress (Sri Lanka)

TDP–see Telegu Desam Party (India)

TELO–see Tamil Eelam Liberation Organization (Sri Lanka)

TEU–see Maastricht Treaty of European Union

TGC–see Constitutional Tribunal (Ecuador)

THM–see Tapia House Movement (Trinidad and Tobago)

TI–see Struggle Movement (Pakistan)

TKP–see Communal Liberation Party (Cyprus)

TMC–see Tamil Maanila Congress (India)

TNP–see National Party (Grenada)

TPEs–see Provisional Electoral Tribunals (Ecuador)

TPLF–see Tigray People's Liberation Front (Ethiopia)

TPP–see True Path Party (Turkey)

TPSL–see Social Democratic League of Workers and Small Farmers (Finland)

TSE–see Supreme Electoral Tribunal (Ecuador)

TSE–see Supreme Electoral Tribunal (El Salvador)

TSP–see National Harmony Party (Latvia)

TTPI–see United Nations Trust Territory of the Pacific (Marshall I.)

TUC–see Trade Union Congress (Bahamas)

TUC–see Trade Union Congress (Zambia)

TULF–see Tamil United Liberation Front (Sri Lanka)

TUSIAD–see Turkish Industrialists and Businessmen's Association

TVS–see Tamil Nadu Agriculturalists' Association (India)

TWP–see True Whig Party (Liberia)

UBC–see Unified Buddhist Church (Vietnam)

UBP–see Party of National Unity (Cyprus)

UC–see Constitutional Union (Morocco)

UCC–see Center-Center Union (Chile)

UCD–see Union of the Democratic Center (Spain)

Ucede–see Union of the Democratic Center (Argentina)

UCN–see National Civic Union (Dominican Rep.)

UCN–see National Center Union (Guatemala)

UCP–see United Convention Party (Ghana)

UCR–see Radical Civic Union (Argentina)

UCRP–see Ukrainian Conservative Republican Party

UCs–see Urban Councils (Sri Lanka)

UCS–see Civic Solidarity Union (Bolivia)

UD–see Democratic Unity Party (Dominican Rep.)

UD–see Democratic Union (Guatemala)

UD–see Democratic Union (Poland)

UDA–see Ulster Defense Association (Northern Ireland)

UDC–see Cameroon Democratic Union

UDD–see Djibouti Democratic Union

Udemo–see Democratic Union of Mozambique

UDF–see Union for French Democracy

UDF–see United Democratic Front (Malawi)

UDI–see Independent Democratic Union (Chile)

UDI–see Independent Democratic Union (Panama)

UDI–see Unilateral Declaration of Independence (Zimbabwe)

UDJED–see Democratic Union for Justice and Equality in Djibouti

UDLP–see United Dominica Labor Party (Dominica)

UDM–see United Democratic Movement (South Africa)

UDN–see National Democratic Union (Brazil)

UDN–see National Democratic Union (El Salvador)

UDP–see United Democratic Party (Belize)

UDP–see Popular Unity Coalition (Bolivia)

UDP–see United Democratic Party (Gambia)

UDP–see United Democratic Party (Tanzania)

UDP–see Ulster Democratic Party (Northern Ireland)

UDP–see United Democratic Party (Zambia)

UDP-Amici–see Union for Democracy and Progress-Amici (Niger)

UDPE–see Union of the Spanish People

UDPM–see Democratic Union of Malian People

UDPS–see Democratic Republic of Congo

UDPS–see Union for Democracy and Social Progress (D. Rep. Congo)

UDPS-Amana–see Union for Democracy and Social Progress-Amana (Niger)

UDR–see Ulster Defense Regiment (Northern Ireland)

UDSG–see Gabonese Democratic and Social Union

UDS-R–see Senegalese Democratic Union

UDU–see Unionist Democratic Union (Tunisia)

UDV–see Volta Democratic Union (Burkina Faso)

UF–see United Force (Guyana)

UFA–see United Farmers of Alberta (Canada)

UFC–see Union of Forces of Change (Togo)

UFD–see Union of Democratic Forces (Mauritania)

UFM–see Uganda Freedom Movement

UFMD–see United Front for Multi-Party Democracy (Malawi)

UFPDP-Sawaba–see Union of Popular Forces for Democracy and Progress-Sawaba (Niger)

UFRI–see Union of Federalists and Independent Republicans (Democratic Republic of Congo)

UGEMA–see General Union of Algerian Muslim Students

UGT–see General Union of Workers (Spain)

UGTA–see General Union of Algerian Workers

UGTT–see General Union of Tunisian Workers

UIA–see Argentine Industrial Union

UIRP–see Uganda Islamic Revolutionary Party

UJD–see Union for Justice and Democracy (Togo)

UKUP–see United Kingdom Unionist Party (Northern Ireland)

ULCR–see Union of Reconstructed Communists (Burkina Faso)

ULD–see United Liberal Democrats (South Korea)

ULF–see United Labour Front (Trinidad and Tobago)

ULI–see Union of Independent Liberals (Togo)

ULIMO–see United Liberia Movement for Democracy

ULP–see United Labour Party (Saint Vincent and the Grenadines)

UM–see Union for Change Coalition (Guinea-Bissau)

UMA–see Union of the Arab Maghrib (North Africa)

UML–see Nepal-Unified Marxist Leninists

UMNO–see United Malays National Organization

UMOA–see West African Monetary Union

UMT–see Moroccan Union of Labor

UNA–see Ukrainian National Assembly

UNAG–see National Farmer's and Cattleman's Association (Nicaragua)

UNAMO–see Mozambican National Union

UNAVEM–see UN Angola Verification Mission

UNC–see United National Congress (Trinidad and Tobago

UNC–see Uganda National Congress

UND–see National Democratic Union (Monaco)

UNDC–see National Union for Democracy (Comoros)

UNDD–see National Union for the Defense of Democracy (Burkina Faso)

UNDD–see National Union for Development and Democracy (Madagascar)

UNDP–see United National Democratic Party (Antigua and Barbuda)

UNDP–see National Union for Democracy and Progress (Cameroon)

UNEC–see National Union of Education and Culture (Mali)

UNEEM–see National Union of Students and Pupils of Mali

UNFA–see National Union of Algerian Women

UNFP–see United National Federal Party (Zimbabwe)

UNFP–see National Union of Popular Forces (Morocco)

UNIDO–see United Democratic Opposition (Philippines)

UNIP–see United National Independence Party (Zambia)

UNITA–see National Union for the Total Independence of Angola

UNLDDA–see National Union for the Light of Democracy and Development in Angola

UNO–see Nicaraguan Opposition Union

UNOMOZ–see UN Operation Mozambique

UNP–see National Union for Prosperity (Guinea)

UNP–see United National Party (Sri Lanka)

UNPA–see National Union of Algerian Peasants

UNPP–see National People's Party (Sierra Leone)

UNR–see Union for the New Republic (Guinea)

UNS–see Sinarquista National Union (Mexico)

UNSO–see United Sabah National Organization (Malaysia)

UNTAC–see United Nations Transitional Authority in Cambodia

UNTM–see National Union of Malian Workers

UNZA–see University of Zambia

UP–see Patriotic Union (Colombia)

UP–see Unity Party (Liberia)

UP–see Union of Labor (Poland)

UPADS–see Pan-African Union for Social Democracy (Republic of Congo)

UPC–see Union of Cameroon Populations

UPC–see Ugandan People's Congress

UPDM–see Uganda People's Democratic Movement

UPDP–see Ukrainian Peasant Democratic Party

UPDP-Shamuwa–see Union of Democratic and Progressive Patriots-Shamuwa (Niger)

UPG–see Gabonese Peoples Union

UPG–see Union for the Progress of Guinea

UPM–see United Peoples Movement (Antigua and Barbuda)

UPM–see Ugandan Patriotic Movement

UPN–see Navarrese Peoples' Union (Spain)

UPO–see Union of the People of Ordino (Andorra)

UPP–see Union for the Progress of Chile

UPP–see Union for Peru

UPP–see United Progressive Party (Antigua and Barbuda)

UPP–see United Peoples Party (Liberia)

UPRONA–see Union for National Progress (Burundi)

UPV–see Volta Progressive Union (Burkina Faso)

URD–see Union for Democratic Renewal (Republic of Congo)

URNG–see Guatemalan National Revolutionary Unity

URP–see Ukrainian Republican Party

URS–see Social Reformist Union (Guatemala)

USC–see Cameroon Social Union

USC–see Ulster Special Constabulary (Northern Ireland)

USDA–see Union Solidarity Development Association (Myanmar)

USFP–see Socialist Union of Popular Forces (Monaco)

USG–see Union for Gabonese Socialism

US-RDA–see Marxist Sudanese Union (Mali)

UT–see United Togolese Committee

UTC–see Union of Colombian Workers

UTD–see Togolese Union for Democracy

UTJ–see United Torah Judaism (Israel)

UTM–see Mauritanian Workers' Union

UTO–see United Tajik Opposition

UUP–see Ulster Unionist Party (Northern Ireland)

UUUC–see United Ulster Unionist Council (Northern Ireland)

UV–see Valencian Union (Spain)

UVDB–see Union of Greens for the Development of Burkina

UW–see Freedom Union (Poland)

UWP–see United Workers Party (Dominica)

UWP–see United Workers' Party (Saint Lucia)

V–see Danish Liberal Party

V–see Left Party (Sweden)

VA–see Voter's Association (Finland)

VB–see Flemish Bloc (Belgium)

VBC–see Vietnam Buddhist Church

VCP–see Vietnam Communist Party

VGO–see United Green Party of Austria

VHP–see Progressive Reform Party (Suriname)

VLD–see Liberal Parties (Belgium)

VRD–see Democratic Republican Union (Venezuela)

VSI–see Federation of Employees (Iceland)

VU–see People's Union (Belgium)

VU–see Fatherland Union (Liechtenstein)

VVD–see People's Party for Freedom and Democracy (Netherlands)

WCPDM–see Women's Organization of Cameroon People's Democratic Movement

WDCs–see Worker's Defense Committees (Ghana)

WP–see Welfare Party (Turkey)

WP–see Worker's Party (Singapore)

WPA–see Working People's Alliance (Guyana)

WPO–see Women's Progressive Organization (Guyana)

WTP–see Progress of the Fatherland Party (Uzbekistan)

YAR–see Yemen Arab Republic

YATAMA–see Miskito Opposition Group (Nicaragua)

YCPDM–see Youth Organization of Cameroon People's Democratic Movement

YSP–see Yemeni Socialist Party

ZANC–see Zambian African National Congress

ZANLA–see Zimbabwe African National Liberation Army

ZANU–see Zimbabwe African Nationalist Union

ZANU-N–see Zimbabwe African National Union-Ndongo

ZANU-PF–see Zimbabwe African National Patriotic Front

ZAPU–see Zimbabwe African People's Union

ZCTU–see Zambia Congress of Trade Unions

ZDC–see Zambia Democratic Congress

ZDP–see Zambabwe Democratic Party

ZIPRA–see Zimbabwe People's Revolutionary Army

ZLA–see Zimbabwe Liberation Army

ZLSD–see United List of Social Democrats of Slovenia

ZNF–see Zimbabwe National Front

ZPA–see Zimbabwe People's Army

ZRC–see Zanzibar Revolutionary Council (Tanzania)

ZRS–see Worker's Association of Slovakia

ZS–see Agrarian Party (Czech Rep.)

ZUM–see Zimbabwe Unity Movement

ZUPO–see Zimbabwe United Peoples Organization